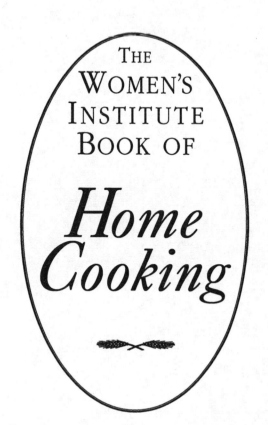

The Women's Institute Book of

Home Cooking

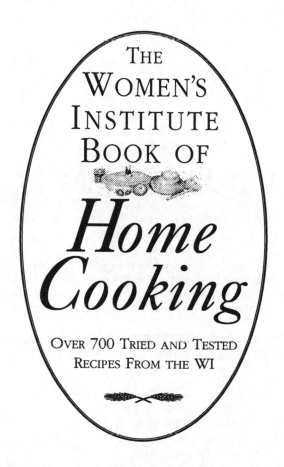

THE WOMEN'S INSTITUTE BOOK OF

Home Cooking

OVER 700 TRIED AND TESTED
RECIPES FROM THE WI

HarperCollins*Publishers*

First published in 1993 by
HarperCollins Publishers, London

The material in this book first appeared in the *WI Book of* series of
paperbacks published by WI Books Ltd

Text © WI Books Ltd, 1984, 1985, 1986, 1987, 1993
All rights reserved

Some of the recipes in this book might use raw eggs. Advice from the Department of Health states that everyone, especially vulnerable groups such as the elderly, the sick, babies, toddlers and pregnant women, should avoid eating raw eggs or uncooked dishes made from them. Readers are therefore advised to use their own judgement when selecting recipes.

Compiled and edited by Lewis Esson
Illustrations by Cooper-West Graphic Design, James Farrant and Vanessa Luff
Index by Susan Bosanko

For HarperCollins Publishers
Project Editor: Barbara Dixon
Designers: Rachel Smyth, Ray Barnett

A catalogue record for this book is available
from the British Library

ISBN 0 00 412934 2

Typset in Erhardt
Printed and bound by The Bath Press, Bath

Front cover photograph reproduced by kind permission of
Chris Beetles Ltd, London/Bridgeman Art Library: Miss Lydiard's Stall, Bath,
by Walter R. I. Tyndale (1856-1943)

About the WI

If you enjoy this book, the chances are you would enjoy belonging to the largest women's organization in the country – the WI.

We are women who receive enormous satisfaction from all the organisation has to offer; the list is long. You can make new friends, enjoy companionship, visit new places, develop new skills, take part in community services, fight local campaigns, become a WI Market producer, and play an active role in an organisation which has a national voice.

The WI is unique in owning a residential adult education establishment. At Denman College, you can take a course in anything from advanced motoring to paper sculpture, from book-binding to yoga, from cordon bleu cookery to fly fishing.

For more information about the WI, write to the **National Federation of Women's Institutes, 104 New Kings Road, London SW6 4LY** or telephone 071 371 9300. **The NFWI Wales Office is at 19 Cathedral Road, Cardiff CF1 9LJ,** telephone 0222 221712.

About the Authors

Maggie Black has been writing about cookery for many years. Her career in the field began when she joined Ward Lock Ltd to edit *Mrs Beeton's Cookery and Household Management*. Since then she has written about smoking foods, barbecuing and, in particular, the folklore of food and traditional dishes. Recently she has been working on cooking for health, especially for older people, concentrating on vegetable cookery and lighter meals.

Pat Hesketh was the WI's Home Economics and Specialized Crafts Adviser; she travelled extensively, lecturing and tutoring WI members in all aspects of home economics and crafts.

Angela Mottram, a trained Home Economics teacher, is a NFWI tutor and judge. She worked at the Meat Research Institute organizing their experimental kitchen and a taste panel, and, while her two children were young, was a freelance home economist. She has now returned to teaching and lectures in Food Science and Home Economics at South Bristol Technical College.

Mary Norwak has written over 70 books, including *The Farmhouse Kitchen, English Puddings* and more than a dozen titles on freezer cookery, and is the author of *The WI Book of Microwave Cookery*. She gives cookery demonstrations to many different groups. A member of the WI for over 25 years, belonging to Cley WI, she serves on the Executive Committee of the Norfolk Federation of Women's Institutes.

Janet Wier is a City & Guilds trained cookery teacher and taught the cake-icing and sweet-making courses at the WI's Denman College for several years. She is a WI National Cookery Judge, Demonstrator and Assessor. She belongs to Bramshaw WI, and is a past County Chairman and Voluntary County Market Organiser of Hampshire. Her other books include *Can She Cook? Cook – Yes She Can,* and *Cooking for the Family.*

CONTENTS

INTRODUCTION

If there is one thing with which the WI is associated in the minds of the general public it is 'good home cooking'. In this book, five of the most prominent food writers and home economists who teach for – or work with – the WI have contributed from considerable experience in their own particular areas of expertise to produce a bumper compendium of recipes and cookery knowledge – a virtual 'bible for the home cook'.

In keeping with the spirit of the WI, however, this is no mere compilation of endless variations on the pasty and the hot-pot. Today's home cooks like to try to recapture the good food they have experienced on holiday or in restaurants, so alongside traditional classics like Soused Herrings, Potted Meat and Spotted Dick you will find exotic specialities like Shrimp Bisque, Salmis of Duck, Coulibiac, Mexican Fish Salad, Osso Buco, Waldorf Salad and Gâteau Pithiviers, as well as wonderful, old, almost-forgotten regional dishes like Mendip Oggies, Poor Man's Goose and Wessex Turkey.

Arranged by courses and by ingredient, there are chapters on Soups, Snacks and Light Meals, Starters, Savouries and Finger Food, Fish and Seafood, Meat, Poultry and Game, Vegetable Dishes, Puddings, Desserts, Cakes and Pastries. So there are recipes for every occasion, and menu-making – be it for everyday family meals or special meals and entertaining – is simplicity itself.

In keeping with today's attitudes towards eating, there are shifts from recipes with lashings of wine and double cream, the emphasis being on good fresh food, simply prepared with a minimum of added fat. The extensive chapter on Vegetables also makes a special feature of sections on both vegetables and salads as light meals and main course dishes in their own right.

The book finishes with a very useful Basics chapter containing all those invaluable recipes for things like stocks, sauces, marinades, stuffings, pastries and various accompaniments – from Bacon Rolls to Home-made Mustard.

So help yourself to the combined wisdom of some of the best home-cooks in the country and enjoy a wide range of all that is best in British cooking. With this book on your shelf you need never look further for a recipe to suit any occasion.

WEIGHTS AND MEASURES

All the spoon measures in this book are level unless stated otherwise.

3 tsp = 1 tbsp
8 tbsp = 5 fl oz = 150 ml = ¼ pint

Eggs are taken to be size 2 unless stated otherwise.

When following these recipes please use either the metric measurements or the imperial; do not mix them and then all will be well.

When a recipe using one of the home-made pastries from the Basics section states '175 g (6 oz) pastry' it means pastry made using 175 g (6 oz) flour. It does not mean 175 g (6 oz) prepared pastry.

Measurements for can sizes are approximate.

American equivalents

	Metric	Imperial	American
Butter, margarine	225 g	8 oz	1 cup
Shredded suet	100 g	4 oz	1 cup
Flour	100 g	4 oz	1 cup
Currants	150 g	5 oz	1 cup
Sugar	200 g	7 oz	1 cup
Syrup	335 g	11 ½ oz	1 cup
Breadcrumbs, fresh	75 g	3 oz	1 ¾ cups
Cheese, grated	100 g	4 oz	1 ¼ cups
Rice (uncooked)	225 g	8 oz	1 cup

An American pint is 16 fl oz compared with the imperial pint of 20 fl oz.
A standard American cup measure is considered to hold 8 fl oz.

SOUPS, SNACKS AND LIGHT MEALS

ABOUT SOUPS

Soups vary from clear liquids to rich, stew-like mixtures and have many different uses. Concentrated stock sustains the Arctic explorer or gives a jogger a quick pick-me-up. A mild broth nourishes an invalid, while a hearty chowder makes a whole one-pot main course for vigorous youngsters. By contrast, a delicate consommé or velvety cream soup is the classic starter with which to begin an elegant meal.

The majority of classic soups are based on stock, the liquid made by simmering bones and meat, poultry, game or fish and/or vegetables with herbs and spices in water until their nutrients and flavour are extracted (see pages 333-37).

❦ Types of Soup ❦

A broth is the simplest type of soup, consisting of the liquid in which the soup ingredients have been cooked. It usually includes solid pieces of the ingredients themselves, as well as added ones.

A clear soup or consommé is a strong, clarified stock, flavoured and garnished to stimulate the appetite. It is therefore most often used as a starter. In hot weather, it may be served chilled and jellied.

A puréed soup is thickened to a creamy consistency by reducing the main soup ingredients to a pulp and returning them to the cooking liquid.

A thickened soup is made with a thickening agent, usually a cereal, as well as or instead of, a purée.

A cream soup is made by adding cream, and sometimes beaten egg yolk, to any puréed or thickened soup. A shellfish-based cream soup is called a bisque.

❦ Ingredients ❦

Besides a stock or other liquid base, flavouring ingredients are generally needed for the particular soup being made. The concentrated liquid from cooking can be used, but more often sliced, chopped or puréed solid ingredients are added, reserving a few choice pieces for garnishing.

A puréed soup made with potatoes or pulses does not, as a rule, need extra thickening. The most usual thickening agent added to other soups is a powdered or mealy grain such as plain flour, cornflour or ground rice, or a puréed, softened grain, potato or pulse. Other thickening agents used more rarely are soft breadcrumbs or (for hare soup) blood. Beaten egg and milk or cream may be used, which give a rich and velvety consistency, or in a few special soups, yoghurt.

Flour or a similar thickening agent may be added to a soup in various ways. It can be creamed with a little cold liquid, stirred into the hot soup, and brought to the boil for a few moments. Alternatively, it can be blended with fat as Beurre Manié (see page 367), stirred into the soup just below boiling point and allowed to dissolve before boiling. It can be cooked with fat, as in a white or brown roux, and blended with a little hot soup before stirring into the main soup. Pulses or breadcrumbs are generally added to the soup on their own, and are cooked with it for a while to blend in. Cream, egg, yoghurt or blood are added to the completed soup, off the boil; the soup must not be boiled again or these thickening agents will curdle.

Extra ingredients are sometimes added to a soup, to give it body or flavour, or to garnish it and improve the appearance. For instance, pasta is added to minestrone, a little port or sherry may be added to a game soup, or diced cooked vegetables to a clear consommé.

❦ Equipment ❦

A large stew-pan or preserving pan which can be tightly covered is a must for making a practical quantity of meat stock to store, although a small quantity can be made in a large pan. The only special equipment essential for classic soup-making is a jelly bag or muslin-lined round-bottomed strainer for clarifying stock for consommés. A food processor or blender, or a food mill which shreds, grates or sieves raw or cooked vegetables saves a great deal of time and work. If sieving is done by hand, a modern stainless metal or hard-meshed nylon sieve makes the task quicker and easier. The cooking time is also much shorter if soups are made in a pressure cooker or a microwave oven.

❦ Quantities to serve ❦

This will depend both on the type of soup and on the occasion. Only 150 ml (¼ pint) of a delicate consommé may be needed if used as a starter before a long or formal menu, while 275 ml (½ pint) or more may be needed of a hearty main–course broth or chowder (fish and potato soup). About 200 ml (⅓ pint) makes an average serving of most other soups when served as a first course.

❦ Serving ❦

Most hot soups are best served heated in deep plates or wide bowls, but consommés and all cold and jellied soups should be offered in small bowls or soup cups. Cold soups can be ladled into chilled cups ahead of time and refrigerated, but a hot soup is best brought to the table in a tureen or casserole. If there is any uncertainty about the starting time of the meal, it can be kept hot in a large vacuum flask.

GARNISHES AND ACCOMPANIMENTS

The finishing touches which will complement and enhance your soups.

They give them personality, providing contrasting textures, shapes, and often flavours. They may be added to the soup just before serving or be served with it for people to add themselves. Certain accompaniments are also commonly served with soups.

❦ Garnishes ❧

Chopped fresh herbs. Rinse and dry the herb sprigs. Remove the leaves and chop finely. Squeeze in soft kitchen paper to dry and sprinkle over soup (or other dishes) just before serving. Parsley and chives are the herbs most often used.

Use mint on green pea soup, tarragon or dill on chicken and fish soups, basil or marjoram on tomato soup, and chervil on any delicately flavoured cream soup.

Chiffonnade (shredded cooked green vegetables). Shred lettuce or sorrel leaves into fine ribbons. Simmer the chiffonnade for a few moments in butter, drain on soft paper and add to soups just before serving. A chiffonnade of sorrel is valued in French garnishing and cooking, but lettuce is more common in Britain.

Watercress, mint and other herb sprigs and leaves. Rinse and shake dry on the stem. Pick off small whole green leaves or pinch out the tiny top sprigs. Pat dry with soft kitchen paper. Scatter on any soup, especially chicken or vegetable cream soups, just before serving.

Sippets. Cut day-old bread into very small 1 cm (½ in) dice. Sauté in butter, tossing well, until crisp and golden all over. Sprinkle on thick soups, or serve in a separate bowl.

Pasta and rice. Boil tiny pasta shapes or 2.5 cm (1 in) lengths of vermicelli or other thin pasta in water for 3 to 4 minutes or less. Drain, rinse in a sieve or colander and shake dry. Sprinkle on consommés or broths just before serving. (Do not cook the pasta in consommé; it will make the soup cloudy.) Cooked long grain rice or pearl barley can be used as for pasta.

Rind strips and slices. Using a cannelle knife or a sharp kitchen knife, cut thin strips lengthwise, at equal intervals, out of the rind of a lemon, orange or cucumber. Blanch strips of rind for a moment or two in boiling water. Cut in half and scatter on soups just before serving. (Cucumber strips are a good alternative to chopped parsley, watercress leaves or chives.)

Alternatively, cut the prepared fruit into paper-thin slices and place 2 or 3 slices on each serving of soup. Lemon slices are attractive on clear soups and on fish or vegetable cream soups. Use orange slices on tomato soup.

Fried onion rings. Slice onions very thinly; dip in egg white or milk first, then in flour and sauté in a little butter until golden brown and crisp. Scatter on thick soups just before serving.

Grated hard cheese. Buy Parmesan or similar cheese in the piece if possible, as the taste is quite different from that of cheese bought ready-grated. Break into small pieces before grating; big pieces will break the blades on a small cheap appliance. Sprinkle the grated cheese over soups just before serving or hand round in a separate bowl.

Soured cream or yoghurt. Whisk yoghurt until liquid. Swirl either soured cream or yoghurt on the surface of a well-coloured soup in a 'Catherine wheel' ribbon. For a sophisticated flavour, mix 1 tablespoon of mayonnaise into 4 tablespoons soured cream before swirling on tomato soup.

❦ Accompaniments ❦

Serve these with soups or suitable starters.

Fairy toast. Bake very thin slices of day-old bread at 150C (300F) mark 2, until crisp and curled. Brown lightly under low grill heat.

Bread sticks. Cut the crusts off day-old square slices of bread. Brush the slices with melted butter, then cut into strips. Roll some in grated Parmesan cheese, sprinkle others with onion or celery salt. Dry on a baking sheet in the oven at 180C (350F) mark 4, until crisp (about 15 minutes). Turn over once while drying. Serve with puréed or cream soups.

Cheese Toast Fingers. Cut square slices of day-old bread without crusts into fingers about 6 cm (2 ½ in) long and 2.5 cm (1 in) wide. Toast lightly on one side under the grill. Spread the untoasted sides with softened butter and a little grated cheese, and toast until golden. Serve warm.

Rolled bread and butter. Cut the crusts off a day-old tin loaf. Butter one end thinly with softened butter all over. Slice the bread very thinly. Then roll up the slice like a baby Swiss roll. Repeat the process to make more rolls. Trim the ends. Serve with cold soups or with starters such as smoked salmon or other cold fish dishes.

CHIVE OR ONION DUMPLINGS

Makes 16 dumplings

100 g (4 oz) self-raising flour
50 g (2 oz) shredded suet
1 tbsp finely chopped parsley
1 tbsp finely chopped chives or grated onion
pinch of grated nutmeg
grinding of white pepper
1 egg
2 tbsp BasicVegetable Stock (see page 337)

❦ Mix all the ingredients, except the stock, thoroughly. Add about 2 tbsp stock if needed to make a firm dough.
❦ With floured hands, roll into 16 small 'marbles'. Drop into boiling water and simmer for 4–6 minutes or until tender and swollen. Remove with a slotted spoon.
❦ Add 1 or 2 to each helping of soup. (Other finely chopped herbs can be used instead of parsley.)

SALMON DUMPLINGS

Makes 16

80 g (3 ¼ oz) can salmon
1 tsp freshly chopped parsley
225 (8 oz) Suet Crust Pastry (see page 361)

❦ Put a pan of water to boil. Drain the salmon and remove all bones and skin. Break up the fish with a fork and stir in the parsley.

❦ Divide the pastry into 16 small pieces. Flatten each piece and put a little salmon mixture into the middle. Dampen the edges and gather up into balls. Flour well. Add to boiling water, and cook as for chive or onion dumplings (see above).

❦ This is an old recipe from the Severn and, no doubt, the dumplings were originally made from the odds and ends of fresh salmon. They are delicious cooked in a spring vegetable soup and then make a complete meal.

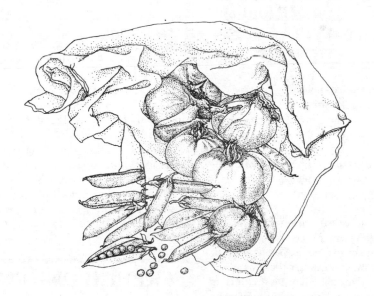

VEGETABLE AND PULSE SOUPS

A varied selection of appetising, nutritious and inexpensive recipes for hot and cold soups.

CREAM OF BARLEY SOUP

Serves 4

275 ml (½ pint) water
50 g (2 oz) pearl barley
1.2 litres (2 pints) Chicken Stock (see page 335)
1 small onion, halved
1 small carrot, quartered
25 g (1 oz) butter or margarine
1½ tbsp flour
150 ml (¼ pint) single cream
65 ml (2 ½ fl oz) milk
salt and pepper
1 small carrot, grated, to garnish

❦ Bring the water to the boil, pour over the barley and leave to soak for several hours.

❦ Mix the barley with the stock in a pan and add the onion and carrot. Cover, bring to the boil, reduce the heat and cook very gently for about 1 hour until the barley is very soft. Strain, reserving some of the barley.

❦ In a clean pan, melt the fat, add the flour and stir together for 3 minutes without colouring. Gradually stir in the stock. Bring to the boil and simmer for 5 minutes.

❦ Add the cream and milk and the reserved barley. Season and reheat very gently, without boiling. Serve the soup in bowls with a few shreds of carrot on top of each.

Variation
As an alternative garnish place a thin ring of fine dark rye breadcrumbs around the edge of each bowl of soup, or sprinkle some chopped chives on top of each bowl.

LEEK AND MUSHROOM BROTH

Serves 4

3 medium-sized leeks, washed
225 g (8 oz) button mushrooms
850 ml (1 ½ pints) Chicken Stock (see page 335)
2 tsp butter
2 tsp chopped parsley
1/8 tsp each ground black pepper, ground ginger and dry mustard powder
pinch of sugar

❦ Strip any coarse outer sheaths from the leeks and slice both the white and tender green parts into thin rings. Remove the mushroom stems (keep them for flavouring another dish) and quarter the caps.

❦ While preparing the vegetables, bring the stock to the boil and then simmer the sliced leeks in the stock with the butter and ½ tsp chopped parsley for 6–8 minutes, until soft and golden.

❦ Add the quartered mushrooms, ground pepper and ginger, mustard powder and sugar. Cook for 4–5 minutes longer until the mushrooms soften, stirring occasionally.

❦ Serve the broth in warmed bowls, sprinkling each helping with some of the remaining parsley.

TOMATO SOUP

Serves 4–6

1 onion
25 g (1 oz) butter or margarine
1.2 litres (2 pints) Chicken Stock (see page 335)
two 400 g (14 oz) cans of peeled plum tomatoes
2 fresh bay leaves or 1 dried
salt to taste
4 black peppercorns
strip of lemon rind
65 ml (1/8 pint) dry sherry
1 tbsp arrowroot
½–1 tsp lemon juice
4 tbsp single cream or whisked whole-milk yoghurt
chopped parsley to garnish

❦ Peel and finely chop the onion. Melt the fat in a pan, add the onion, and cook gently until it is soft but not coloured.

❦ Strain the stock, and add it with the tomatoes and their liquid, the bay, salt, peppercorns and lemon rind. Mix well with a wooden spoon, squashing the tomatoes. Cover and cook gently for 45 minutes.

❦ Pass the soup through a nylon sieve into a clean pan and add the sherry. Blend the arrowroot with 2–3 tbsp water, and stir into the soup.

❦ Reheat the soup to boiling point. Taste, add lemon juice and adjust the seasoning if necessary. Pour into warmed soup bowls.

❦ Swirl 1 tbsp cream or yoghurt on top of each helping just before serving and add a little chopped parsley (optional).

FRENCH ONION SOUP

Serves 4

225 g (8 oz) medium-sized onions
40 g (1 ½ oz) butter
1.5 litres (2 ½ pints) Basic Brown Stock (see page 335)
1 tbsp plain flour
salt and pepper
4 slices of bread from a French stick
125 g (4 oz) grated Gruyère cheese

❦ Peel and slice the onions into thin rings. Preheat the oven to 200C (400F) mark 6.

❦ Heat the butter in a pan and simmer the onions in it for 10 minutes, until golden and beginning to brown.

❦ While these are cooking, heat the stock to boiling point in another pan.

❦ Stir the flour into the onions and cook gently for 2–3 minutes, stirring constantly. Take off the heat and stir in the boiling stock gradually. Return to a low heat, and simmer, uncovered for 30 minutes. Season.

❦ While this is simmering, warm an ovenproof tureen or 4 ovenproof soup bowls. Place the slices of French bread in the bottom(s).

❦ Remove the bay leaf from the stock and pour the liquid into the tureen or bowls. Scatter grated cheese on each slice of floating bread. Place in the oven for 7–10 minutes, until the cheese has melted.

FRESH GREEN PEA SOUP WITH HERBS

Serves 4

1 small onion
1 tbsp margarine
900 g (2 lb) fresh shelled peas or 450 g (1 lb) frozen peas
425 ml (¾ pint) Chicken Stock (see page 335) or Classic White Stock (see variation, page 335)
3 sprigs fresh mint, or ½ tsp dried mint
1 fresh basil leaf or ¼ tsp dried basil,
3 sprigs fresh marjoram or 2 sprigs fresh thyme, or ½ tsp dried marjoram or ¼ tsp dried thyme
150-275 ml (¼-½ pint) milk
salt and pepper
cornflour or mashed potato (optional)
4 tbsp single cream (optional)
4 fresh mint sprigs to garnish

❦ Peel and chop the onion, and simmer in the margarine in a pan until soft but not coloured. Add the peas and stock.
❦ Tie the fresh herbs together with thread and add to the pan, or sprinkle the dried herbs over the vegetables.
❦ Bring the stock to the boil, cover, reduce the heat and cook gently for 35-45 minutes for fresh peas, as the packet directs if using frozen peas.
❦ When the peas are soft, remove the fresh herbs and purée the soup in batches in a food processor or blender. Measure the soup and return it to the pan.
❦ Add 150 ml (¼ pint) milk and season to taste. If you wish to thicken the soup, blend 2 tbsp cornflour or mashed potato for each 425 ml (¼ pint) soup with another 150 ml (¼ pint) milk and stir it in.
❦ Reheat the soup for about 5 minutes without boiling. Stir in the cream just before serving (optional). Garnish with fresh mint sprigs.

Variation
❦ Green pea and shrimp soup is an attractive alternative. Fry half a stalk of chopped celery with the onion, then cook and purée the peas as above without the herbs.
❦ While cooking, simmer the shredded heart of a small lettuce and a 200 g (7 oz) can of shrimps in 150 ml (¼ pint) milk for 3 minutes, reserving a few lettuce shreds and shrimp for garnishing.
❦ Instead of thickening the soup, add the lettuce and shrimps with the flavoured milk to the puréed soup when returning it to the pan. Reheat the soup for 1 minute only, then serve with the reserved lettuce and shrimps on top.

BORSCHT (RUSSIAN BEETROOT BROTH)

Serves 4

450 g (1 lb) raw beetroot
1 onion
1 carrot
1 turnip or ½ swede
salt and pepper
1.5 litres (2½ pints) Household Stock (see variation, page335)
small ham bone or strip of rind from bacon joint
400 g (14 oz) cabbage
½ garlic clove (optional)
2 tomatoes
mashed potato (optional)
sugar
tomato purée
chopped parsley
soured cream (optional)

❦ Peel the beetroot and cut the other root vegetables into match-sticks. Season the stock, bring to the boil with the ham bone or rind, and add the root vegetables. Cover and cook gently for 30 minutes.
❦ Meanwhile, shred the cabbage, chop the garlic (optional), and skin, de-seed and chop the tomatoes. Add the cabbage and garlic to the pan, and simmer, uncovered, for 20 minutes. Remove the ham bone or rind, add the tomatoes and cook for a further 5 minutes, adding a little mashed potato to thicken the soup slightly (optional).
❦ Flavour the soup to taste with sugar and tomato purée. Serve hot or cold sprinkled with parsley. Swirl a spoonful of soured cream on top of each individual serving, or serve a bowl of soured cream separately (optional).

POTAGE CRECY (CARROT SOUP)

Serves 4

450 g (1 lb) carrots
½ medium-sized onion
1 small stalk of celery
¼ small turnip
1 rasher of bacon, without rind
15 g (½ oz) butter or margarine
1 tbsp oil
850 ml (1 ½ pints) Brown Vegetable Stock (see page 336)
bouquet garni
salt and pepper
few drops of lemon or orange juice
3 tbsp flour
150 ml (¼ pint) milk
4 tbsp single cream or 2 tbsp cream and 1 egg yolk beaten together
chopped parsley to garnish

❦ Prepare and chop all the vegetables and the bacon (a food processor is the quickest tool to use).
❦ Heat the fat and oil in a pan and fry the vegetables and bacon for 5-6 minutes, stirring constantly, until softened. Add the stock, bouquet garni, a little seasoning and the fruit juice. Cover and simmer for 30-45 minutes until the vegetables are very soft.
❦ Remove the bouquet and sieve the soup or purée in a food processor or blender, in batches. Return the purée to the pan.
❦ Cream the flour with some of the milk, add the rest of the milk, and stir into the purée. Stir over a moderate heat, until the soup boils and thickens. Taste and season.
❦ Remove from the heat, and stir in the cream or cream and egg. Return to the lowest possible heat and stir to thicken the egg yolk (if using), but do not boil. Serve garnished with parsley.

CHILLED CELERY AND YOGHURT SOUP

Serves 4

3 spring onions, green and white parts
100 g (4 oz) small celery stalks and leaves
1 tbsp olive oil
425 ml (¾ pint) natural yoghurt
150 ml (¼ pint) Vegetable Stock (see page 336)
1 tsp ground almonds or hazelnuts
pinch of sugar
salt and pepper (optional)

❦ Chop the spring onions and celery finely in a food processor, or mince them, reserving the leaves.
❦ Stir in the oil over a low heat for about 5 minutes until they soften; do not let them colour. Turn out into a large bowl and allow to cool for 2-3 minutes. Then whisk in the yoghurt and remaining ingredients.
❦ Chill well before serving. Serve in chilled bowls and garnish with the celery leaves.
❦ If the yoghurt is sharp or you prefer a thinner soup, use 275 ml (½ pint) each of yoghurt and stock.

EASY GAZPACHO

Serves 4-6

450 g (1 lb) ripe tomatoes
1 medium-sized green pepper
100 g (4 oz) onion, peeled
1 large garlic clove, peeled
1 medium-sized cucumber
2 tbsp oil
2 tbsp red wine vinegar
425 ml (¾ pint) tomato juice
salt and ground black pepper

❦ Chop the tomatoes. De-seed and chop the pepper and the onion, garlic and cucumber.
❦ Purée the vegetables, oil, vinegar and 275 ml (½ pint) of the tomato juice in an electric blender, in batches if necessary.
❦ Turn the gazpacho into a large jug or bowl and add enough of the remaining juice to give the consistency you prefer. Season to taste.
❦ Serve in soup cups, well chilled and garnished with croutons.

MINESTRONE

Serves 4-6

2 tbsp olive oil
2 rashers of bacon without rind, cut into small
    squares, or finely diced cooked pickled pork
1 medium-sized onion, chopped
½ leek, finely sliced
1 garlic clove, peeled
1 celery stalk, thinly sliced
2 small potatoes, peeled and diced (about 100
    g/4 oz each)
1.2 litres (2 pints) Classic White stock (see vari-
    ation, page 335)
1 large carrot, thinly sliced
50 g (2 oz) cooked or canned white haricot
    beans or fresh or frozen sliced green beans
3 tbsp fresh or frozen garden peas
1 tbsp chopped fresh herbs (basil, thyme, mar-
    joram) or 2 tsp dried herbs
salt and pepper
¼ small cabbage, finely shredded
4 tbsp white or wholemeal shortcut elbow mac-
    aroni
3 tomatoes, skinned and cut into small pieces
grated Parmesan cheese

❦ Warm the oil in a pan. Add the bacon, onion and
leek, and squeeze the garlic over them. Stir over low
heat for 3 minutes. Add the celery and diced potatoes, and turn in the fat, stirring constantly, for 5
minutes.
❦ Add the stock, bring to the boil and add the carrot, beans, peas, herbs and seasoning. Cover, reduce
the heat and cook gently for 20 minutes. Add the
cabbage, pasta and tomatoes and simmer, covered,
for 20 minutes longer.
❦ Serve a bowl of grated Parmesan separately.

TOMATO SOUP WITH ORANGE

Serves 4-6

1 medium-sized onion, peeled
1 celery stalk
6 medium-sized tomatoes (garden-grown, if
    possible)
1 tbsp margarine or oil
1 dried bay leaf
850 ml (1 ½ pints) Chicken Stock (see page 335)
salt and pepper
1 tbsp cornflour
1 tbsp grated orange rind
juice of ¼-½ orange
pinch of sugar
4-6 tbsp single cream (optional)

Garnish
finely snipped celery leaves or 'match-stick'
    shreds of blanched orange rind

❦ Chop the onion and celery. Quarter the tomatoes
and squeeze out the seeds.
❦ Heat the margarine or oil in a pan and simmer the
onion and celery for 2 minutes, stirring. Add the
tomatoes, bay leaf and stock and season lightly.
Bring slowly to the boil, reduce the heat and simmer,
half-covered, for 30 minutes.
❦ Sieve, or purée in batches in a food processor or
blender. Return to the rinsed-out pan.
❦ Cream the cornflour with a little water. Add a little hot stock, then stir the mixture into the soup.
Bring to the boil, stirring all the time.
❦ Blanch the orange rind in a little boiling water for
1 minute. Stir into the soup with the orange juice,
then adjust the seasoning and add sugar to taste.
❦ Stir in the cream at serving point (optional),
before garnishing with celery leaves or orange rind.
Serve hot or cold.

RED LENTIL SOUP

Serves 4

2 medium-sized carrots
1 medium-sized onion
1 celery stalk
2 tbsp margarine
1 tbsp oil
7 tbsp split red lentils
575 ml (1 pint) water
275 ml (½ pint) milk
good pinch of ground coriander or cumin
few grains of cayenne pepper
salt and black pepper
chopped parsley to garnish

❧ Chop the carrots, onion and celery. Simmer with the margarine and oil for 2-3 minutes stirring constantly.

❧ Add the lentils, water, milk, spices and seasoning. Heat to simmering point, reduce the heat, cover and cook gently for 30-45 minutes, until the lentils are soft.

❧ Purée the soup in batches by sieving or in an electric blender. Return to the pan and reheat to simmering point. Taste and re-season if needed.

❧ Sprinkle with parsley just before serving.

LEEK AND POTATO SOUP

Serves 4

4 leeks, white parts only
1 medium-sized onion, peeled
25 g (1 oz) butter or margarine
2 tbsp oil
275 g (10 oz) potatoes
1 litre (1 ¾ pints) Chicken Stock (see page 335) or Classic White Stock (see, page 335)
salt and pepper
200 ml (7 fl oz) or 1 carton of long-life single cream

❧ Slice the leeks and onion. Heat the fat and oil and simmer the sliced vegetables gently in this for 8-10 minutes, without letting them brown.

❧ While these are simmering, peel and slice the potatoes thinly. Add them with the stock to the simmered vegetables. Season, cover, and cook until the vegetables are soft.

❧ Sieve or purée in batches in a blender. Return to the pan, and reheat if serving hot. Stir in the cream off the heat. If serving cold, turn into a bowl and blend in the cream and any extra seasoning you wish, then chill well, covered.

CREAM OF CAULIFLOWER SOUP

Serves 4

700 ml (1 ¼ pints) Vegetable Stock (see page 336)
40 g (1 ½ oz) long-grain rice
1 small onion, finely chopped or 2 tbsp dried sliced onions
bouquet garni
pinch of grated nutmeg
1 medium-sized cauliflower (350 g/12 oz prepared)
150 ml (¼ pint) milk
4 tbsp whipping cream
salt and pepper

❧ Bring the stock to the boil in a pan. Add the rice, onion, bouquet garni and nutmeg, and cook for 15-20 minutes until the rice is tender.

❧ Meanwhile, cut the cauliflower head into small florets and steam over boiling water for 10 minutes or until tender; do not overcook. Reserve a few sprigs for garnishing. Add the remainder to the stock with the milk. Simmer for 5 minutes then remove from the heat.

❧ Purée the soup in batches, in a food processor or blender. If very thick, add a little more milk. Return to the pan, stir in the cream and reheat without boiling. Taste and season. Serve garnished with the reserved cauliflower sprigs.

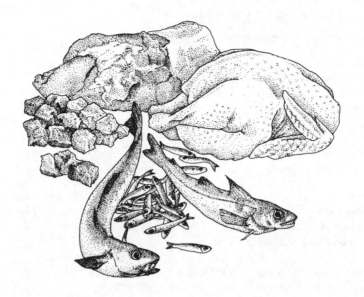

MEAT, POULTRY AND FISH SOUPS

*This section contains an interesting and varied selection of recipes
which make the most of meat, fish and poultry.*

PUREED CHICKEN SOUP

Serves 4-6

1 litre (1 ¼ pints) Chicken Stock (see page 335)
125 g (4 ½ oz) cooked white chicken meat
2 tsp lemon juice
25 g (1 oz) butter or margarine
25 g (1 oz) flour
pinch of ground allspice
salt and pepper
chopped parsley to garnish

❦ Skim the stock thoroughly. Cut the cooked white
chicken meat into small cubes. Put about 25 g (1 oz)
aside for garnishing. Purée the remainder, preferably in a food processor or blender, with the lemon

juice and enough stock to give the consistency of thin
cream.
❦ Melt the fat in a pan, add the flour and cook
together, stirring, for 1 minute. Slowly stir in the
remaining stock, and continue stirring until the mixture comes to the boil. Reduce the heat and simmer
for 2-3 minutes. Add the chicken purée, allspice and
seasoning. Reheat to simmering point, then stir in
the chicken.
❦ Sprinkle with parsley just before serving.

Variation
For cream of chicken soup, draw the pan off the heat
after adding the chicken. Stir a little of the hot soup
into 4 tbsp single cream, then stir the cream mixture
into the soup. Heat gently but do not re-boil as the
cream will curdle.

CLASSIC CONSOMME

Makes 1 litre (1 ¾ pints)

1.2 litres (2 pints) Basic Brown Stock (see page 335)
100 g (4 oz) shin of beef
150 ml (¼ pint) cold water
1 small onion, peeled and quartered
1 small carrot, scraped and quartered
1 small stalk of celery, sliced,
bouquet garni
¼ tsp salt
2-3 white peppercorns,
white and crushed shell of 1 egg
2 tsp dry sherry or Madeira (optional)

❦ Ensure that the pan, jelly bag or wire sieve lined with muslin, and any spoon or bowls are quite free from grease.

❦ Strain the brown stock into the clean pan to remove any fat droplets. Shred the meat, removing any fat, and soak in the water for 15 minutes. Prepare the vegetables while the meat is soaking.

❦ Place the meat, water, vegetables, bouquet garni and seasonings into the pan with the stock. Add the egg white and shell to clear the stock. Heat gently, whisking continuously, until a thick froth forms on the surface.

❦ Remove the whisk and bring to simmering point; reduce the heat at once, cover the pan, and simmer very gently for 1 ½-2 hours. Do not boil or the froth will break up and cloud the consommé.

❦ Scald a jelly bag or clean cloth. Tie it to the legs of an upturned stool to hold open. Filter the stock through gently, into a clean bowl, holding back the froth with a spoon at first, then letting it slide through on to the cloth. Pour the stock through the bag and egg white filter a second time into a second (white) bowl. The stock should be sparklingly clear; this is easy to see in the white bowl.

❦ Reheat, and season or flavour with alcohol if you wish; or cool, covered, then chill if wanted cold.

Variations

❦ To make jellied consommé, use Brown Stock (see page 335) made with veal bones. A cheaper, simpler alternative is to stir a little dissolved gelatine into the consommé before cooling; however the soup is then less clear and becomes cloudy when frozen.

❦ Consommés often take their name from their garnishes. To prevent the garnish from clouding the consommé, rinse it before adding to the soup.

Here are some classic garnishes for 1 litre (1 ¾ pints) of consommé:

Consommé jardinière
❦ Prepare about 6 tbsp of jardinière vegetables (carrot, turnip, cauliflower, small green peas or beans). Cut the carrot and the turnip into pea-sized ball shapes, with a very small vegetable baller, or cut into very small dice. Cut the cauliflower into tiny sprigs. Choose small peas or cut young thin green beans into diamond shapes by slicing diagonally.
❦ Cook the vegetables for a few minutes in unsalted boiling water, drain and season lightly.
❦ To serve, place in a warmed tureen or into soup bowls or cups. Pour the hot consommé over the vegetables.

Consommé julienne
❦ Prepare about 6 tbsp julienne vegetables. Using the largest holes on a grater, cut vegetables such as carrot and turnip into coarse shreds 2-3 cm (¾-1 ½ in) long. Finely slice the white of leek or celery.
❦ Boil the vegetables separately until just tender, season lightly, rinse and serve as for jardinière vegetables (see above).
❦ Julienne means thin match-stick shapes or very fine shreds of vegetables. Use as a garnish in many dishes or serve as a cold hors d'oeuvre or as a hot vegetable.

Consommé brunoise
❦ Prepare a mixture of 4-6 tbsp diced carrot and turnip and sliced leek and celery. Boil, season and rinse, serve as for jardinière vegetables (see above).

Consommé mimosa
❦ Press 3-4 hard-boiled egg yolks through a coarse sieve into the consommé (almost at boiling point) just before serving.

Consommé royale
❦ Make a steamed savoury egg custard as follows. Beat 1 egg yolk with 1 tbsp stock, milk or cream until fully blended. Season lightly. Strain into a small greased heatproof container, cover tightly with foil or greaseproof paper, and steam the custard until firm in a pan of gently simmering water. Cool the custard, turn it out, cut into thin slices, and then into rounds, lozenge or other fancy shapes. Add to the consommé Just before serving.
❦ Royale custard can be coloured with beet juice, tomato juice etc. Coloured royale shapes are part of the garnish of a number of consommés.

Consommé printanier

❧ Prepare a mixture of about 6 tbsp small carrot and turnip balls as for jardinière vegetables (see above), small young cooked green peas and finely shredded lettuce. Serve as for consommé jardinière.

Consommé Solange

❧ Add 2 tbsp rinsed, cooked pearl barley and 2 tbsp julienne of cooked chicken with a few small squares of lettuce to the consommé just before serving.

Clear mock turtle soup

❧ Clear mock turtle soup consists of White Stock (made with veal bones or knuckle, see page 335) cleared in the same way as consommé.

❧ Add 50 ml (2 fl oz) sherry and 2 tsp lemon juice to each litre (1 ¾ pints) of cleared soup before reheating. After reheating add diced cooked veal as a garnish.

OYSTER SOUP

Serves 6

1.2 litres (2 pints) Fish or Chicken Stock (see page 335)
24 oysters, shelled
50 g (2 oz) butter
25 g (1 oz) plain flour
150 ml (¼ pint) milk
1 blade of mace
½ tsp anchovy essence
salt and pepper
150 ml (¼ pint) single cream
1 tsp lemon juice
4 tbsp dry sherry

❧ Bring the stock to the boil. Drop in the shelled oysters and lift them out at once with a slotted spoon. Cut the oysters in half and keep to one side.

❧ In another pan over a low heat, melt the butter and work in the flour. Cook for 1 minute over a low heat and gradually add the stock, stirring well until boiling.

❧ Add the milk, mace, anchovy essence and seasoning, and bring slowly to the boil. Take off the heat and leave to stand for 10 minutes.

❧ Remove and discard the mace. Reheat the soup, stirring in the cream, lemon juice, sherry and oysters. Stir gently until hot, but not boiling.

OXTAIL SOUP

Serves 4-6

700 g (1 ½ lb) thick end of oxtail, jointed
1 medium-sized onion
1 large carrot
½ turnip
1 celery stalk
25 g (1 oz) dripping
2 litres (3 ½ pints) Basic Brown Stock (see page 335)
bouquet garni
1 rasher of streaky bacon, without rind (optional)
salt and pepper
3 tbsp plain flour
2 tbsp cream sherry (optional)

❧ Trim any excess fat off the oxtail. Prepare and slice the vegetables.

❧ Heat the dripping in a heavy-based pan and fry the joints, turning them over, for 2 minutes. Then add the vegetables and fry for 4-5 minutes, until the joints are browned all over.

❧ Add the stock and bouquet garni and bring slowly to the boil. Chop and add the bacon (optional). Cover the pan, lower the heat and simmer very gently for 3-4 hours, until the meat is very tender. Skim off excess fat occasionally while simmering.

❧ Strain the soup into a clean pan. Cut the meat off the bones, and mince into very small pieces. Return to the soup. Taste and season.

❧ Blend the flour with a little water and the sherry (optional), and stir in some of the soup. Stir the mixture back into the pan of soup, return to a moderate heat and reheat to the boil, stirring briskly all the time. Season again if necessary.

Variations

This soup can be used as a winter starter without the solid pieces of meat and with a thin half-slice of lemon floating on each serving, but its main use is as a family soup. It makes a good main-course soup for supper or an informal gathering if small Onion Dumplings are added (see page 15).

COCK-A-LEEKIE SOUP

Serves 4

1 boiling fowl
4 medium leeks
bunch of fresh mixed herbs or 1 bouquet garni
6 peppercorns
1 tsp salt
50 g (2 oz) long-grain rice

❦ Place the boiling fowl in a large saucepan. Prepare the leeks and cut into 5 cm (2 in) lengths. Add to the pan with the herbs, peppercorns and salt. Add sufficient water almost to cover the bird. Cover and bring to the boil. Remove any scum and simmer for approximately 2 hours, or until the bird is tender.
❦ Remove the bird from the pan and cut the flesh from the carcass. Cut the flesh into bite-size pieces and return to the pan with the rice. Bring to the boil, and simmer a further 20 minutes or until the rice is soft. Check the seasoning before serving.

CHICKEN AND VEGETABLE BROTH

Serves 4

1 small boiling fowl, complete with giblets (without liver or kidneys), if available
2 litres (3 ½ pints) water
1 onion
2 medium-sized carrots
1 celery stalk
1 tsp salt
¼ tsp pepper
2 fresh bay leaves or 1 dried
1 small courgette
2 tbsp long-grain rice
4 tbsp sweetcorn, cooked and drained, or canned
chopped parsley to garnish

❦ Joint the bird and wash the giblets (if used). Place in a large pan, cover with water and bring slowly to boiling point.
❦ Peel and halve the onion, dice the carrots and slice the celery thinly. Add to the pan at boiling point with the seasoning and bay leaves. Cover tightly and simmer slowly for 3 hours.

❦ Meanwhile, dice the courgette without peeling it.
❦ Strain the broth, reserving the meat. Let the broth stand for a few minutes, then skim off the fat, and blot off any remaining droplets with soft paper. Return the broth to the rinsed pan and sprinkle in the rice. Reheat and cook gently for 15 minutes or until the rice is cooked, adding the courgette and sweetcorn 5-6 minutes before the end with some of the chicken meat, diced.
❦ Sprinkle with parsley at serving point.

Variation
The broth can be made using a chicken carcass for economy. Simmer for 1 ½ hours only.

SHRIMP BISQUE

Serves 4-6

350 g (12 oz) cooked shelled shrimps
100 g (4 oz) softened butter
850 ml (1 ½ pints) Fish Stock (see page 336)
2 tbsp flour
65 ml (1/8 pint) dry white wine
65 ml (1/8 pint) water
1 egg yolk
150 ml (¼ pint) single cream
salt and pepper
few drops of lemon juice
grated nutmeg

❦ Put 8-12 shrimps aside for garnishing. Purée the remainder in a food processor with 65 g (2 ½ oz) of the butter and a few spoonfuls of stock.
❦ Melt the remaining butter in a pan, add the flour and stir over a low heat for 2 minutes without colouring. Slowly stir in the remaining fish stock, wine and water. Continue to stir until just boiling. Mix in the puréed shrimps, and take the pan off the heat.
❦ Beat the egg yolk into the cream and stir this mixture into the soup. Add extra cream if needed, to give the desired consistency. Season with salt and pepper, lemon juice and nutmeg to taste.
❦ Reheat if necessary, without boiling. Serve garnished with the reserved shrimps.

SIMPLE CHICKEN SOUP

Serves 3-4

1 chicken carcass, plus giblets, if available
1 medium onion, chopped
2 medium carrots, chopped
1 stick celery, sliced
1 matchbox-sized piece of swede, chopped
bunch of fresh mixed herbs or 1 bouquet garni
6 peppercorns
salt
Beurre Manié (see page 367)
double cream and chopped chives to garnish

❦ Place the chicken carcass, giblets, prepared vegetables, herbs and seasoning in a large saucepan. Cover with water and bring to the boil. Remove any scum, cover and simmer gently for approximately 1 ½ hours.
❦ Remove the carcass and the herbs. Sieve or liquidize the contents of the pan and thicken with beurre manié. Check the seasoning. Add any meat from the carcass, finely shredded, bring to the boil and simmer for 3-4 minutes.
❦ Serve in individual bowls with a swirl of cream and a few chopped chives.

LAMB BROTH

Serves 4-6

700 g (1 ½ lb) neck of lamb
1.5 litres (2 ½ pints) water
salt to taste
1 medium-sized carrot
1 medium-sized onion, peeled
1 small turnip
2 celery stalks
1 tbsp pearl barley
pepper
chopped parsley to garnish

❦ For easy handling, ask the butcher to leave the lamb bone in one piece. Cut the meat off the bone, discarding any fat, and cut into small dice.
❦ Place in a large pan with the water and salt to taste, and add the bone. Bring slowly to the boil, and skim. Reduce the heat and simmer for 30 minutes. Cool until the fat starts to solidify.

❦ While it is cooling, chop the carrot, onion and turnip, and slice the celery. Remove any fat from the broth and add the vegetables and pearl barley. Reheat to simmering point, cover and cook very gently for 1 hour, or until the vegetables and barley are soft. Remove the bone, adjust the seasoning and stir in the parsley just before serving.

Variations
This basic broth is one of a large family. Most recipes for Scotch broth, for instance, are similar and so are some recipes for hotch-potch. A good hotch-potch can be made by substituting 4-6 sliced spring onions for the onion, 100 g (4 oz) young broad beans or peas (shelled) for the celery, and by adding these and half a shredded small lettuce only 30 minutes before the end of the cooking time. A bouquet garni is an improvement.

GAME SOUP

Serves 4

1-2 carcasses of game, plus giblets if available
1 medium onion, chopped
1 medium carrot, chopped
1 celery stalk, sliced
bunch of fresh mixed herbs
6 peppercorns
salt
glass of red wine (optional)
1 litre (1 ¾ pints) water
Beurre Manié (see page 367)
2 tsp lemon juice
2 tsp redcurrant jelly

❦ Place the carcasses and giblets in a pan with the prepared vegetables, herbs and seasonings. Add the wine and sufficient water to cover. Cover the pan, bring to the boil and simmer for approximately 1 ½ hours.
❦ Remove the carcass, giblets and herbs. Sieve or liquidize the remaining contents of the pan. Thicken with beurre manié.
❦ Add the lemon juice and redcurrant jelly. Add any meat from the carcass, finely shredded. Simmer gently for 5 minutes. Serve.

CRAB AND TOMATO CREAM SOUP

Serves 4

40 g (1 ½ oz) butter
1 medium onion, finely chopped
1 garlic clove, crushed
1 green pepper
400 g (14 oz) can of tomatoes
150 ml (¼ pint) single cream
2 egg yolks
350 g (12 oz) crab meat
salt and pepper

❦ Melt the butter and fry the onion and garlic over a low heat for 5 minutes, stirring frequently.

❦ Remove the stem and seeds from the pepper and chop the flesh finely. Add to the pan and cook for 5 minutes, stirring well. Sieve the tomatoes and juice and add to the pan. Simmer for 20 minutes.

❦ Beat the cream and egg yolks together and add a little of the hot liquid. Stir together and add to the pan. Stir over a low heat until the mixture begins to thicken. Stir in the crab meat and season well.

❦ Heat gently and then serve hot, with plenty of crusty bread.

FISH AND BACON CHOWDER

Serves 4

450 g (1 lb) fresh cod fillets
salt
100 g (4 oz) piece of boiling bacon
450 g (1 lb) potatoes
225 ml (8 fl oz) water
1 small onion
275 ml (½ pint) milk
150 ml (¼ pint) single cream
pepper
pinch of grated nutmeg

❦ Skin the fish, discarding any bones. Cube the flesh and salt it lightly. Trim the rind off the bacon, and cut it into small dice. Peel the potatoes, and cut into 1 cm (½ in) cubes.

❦ Put the water in a pan, salt lightly and add the potatoes. Cover the pan and simmer over a low heat until the potatoes are almost tender. Draw off the heat when ready.

❦ While cooking the potatoes, fry the diced bacon in its own fat until crisp and golden. Transfer to a plate. Chop the onion and add to the bacon fat in the frying pan. Cook until soft and beginning to brown.

❦ Scoop the onion out with a slotted spoon and add to the potatoes. Pour half the milk into the frying pan and swill it round over a low heat for a moment or two. Transfer to the soup pan and add the remaining milk, the cream and the fish cubes. Also add 1 tbsp of the fried bacon.

❦ Return the chowder to a low heat and simmer until the fish cubes are tender. Season to taste with salt, pepper and nutmeg. Serve in warmed bowls, with the remaining bacon sprinkled on top.

JAPANESE CHICKEN SOUP

Serves 4

100 g (4 oz) long-grain rice
salt
2 raw chicken breasts
12 button mushrooms
4 spring onion bulbs
1 litre (1 ¾ pints) Chicken Stock (see page 335)
¼ tsp black pepper
small pinch of dry mustard
4 thin strips of lemon rind

❦ Cook the rice in salted boiling water for 15 minutes or until just tender.

❦ Skin and bone the chicken breasts and cut the meat into thin strips about 5 cm (2 in) long. Thinly slice the mushrooms and cut the spring onion bulbs diagonally into oval rings.

❦ Bring the stock to the boil, add the chicken meat, pepper, mustard and lemon rind. Cook for 5 minutes. Stir in the mushrooms and remove from the heat. Leave to stand while preparing 4 warm soup bowls.

❦ Drain the rice and divide between the bowls. Sprinkle the spring onions on the rice and place one strip of lemon rind in each bowl. Transfer the chicken and mushrooms to the bowls with a slotted spoon, then ladle in the stock.

SNACKS & LIGHT MEALS

All these dishes make good light lunches, suppers or snacks at any time of the day. Some are also good for special breakfasts or brunches, and many may easily be scaled down to make starters or served with vegetables as substantial meals.

PANCAKES WITH CHEESE FILLING

Serves 4

four 15 cm (6 in) pancakes, a little thicker than sweet Pancakes (see page 365)
1 tbsp grated Gruyère cheese

Filling
ground black pepper
pinch of grated nutmeg
75g (3 oz) grated Gruyère cheese
1 egg
150 ml (¼ pint) milk
1 ½ tbsp flour

❦ Prepare an oblong heatproof serving platter which will hold the folded pancakes side by side. Reheat the pancakes in a low oven if made ahead and keep them warm under greased foil.
❦ Make the filling: mix a grinding of pepper and the nutmeg into the cheese; set aside. Whisk together the egg, milk and flour in a pan. Place over low heat and whisk until the mixture comes to the boil; cook for 2-3 minutes until the sauce is thick. Take off the heat and whisk in the seasoned cheese.
❦ Lay the pancakes flat. Place a good 2 tbsp sauce in a strip along the centre of each pancake. Fold both sides of the pancake over it. Lay the pancakes side by side on the platter. If any sauce remains spoon it over, then sprinkle with the grated cheese.
❦ Place under the grill for a moment or two, to soften the cheese topping. Serve at once.

JACKET POTATOES WITH CHEESE

Serves 4

2 large baking potatoes
1 tbsp oil
120 ml (4 fl oz) natural yoghurt
tbsp finely snipped chives
1 tsp salt
few grains of cayenne pepper
4 tbsp grated Cheddar cheese
paprika

❦ Heat the oven to 200C (400F) mark 6.
❦ Scrub the potatoes well and pat dry. Brush with oil. Place on a baking sheet and bake for 45-75 minutes, until soft when pierced with a think skewer. Cool just enough to handle.
❦ Cut the potatoes in half lengthwise, and scoop out most of the flesh with a spoon, leaving a 5 mm (¼ in) shell.
❦ Mash the flesh in a bowl or beat with an electric beater, adding the yoghurt gradually. Blend well, then add the chives and seasoning to taste. Pile the mixture back in the shells. Sprinkle with the cheese mixed with a sprinkling of paprika.
❦ Reduce the oven to 180C (350F) mark 4 and bake for 10-15 minutes or until the cheese is melted and potatoes are hot.

WHITE FISH SOUFFLE

Serves 4-6

225 g (8 oz) cooked whiting or other delicate white fish
1 tbsp grated onion
2 tbsp butter or margarine
50 g (2 oz) grated cheese
2 tbsp cornflour
275 ml (½ pint) milk
2 eggs, separated, plus white of 1 egg
salt and pepper

❦ Heat the oven to 200C (400F) mark 6. Oil the inside of a 1.2 litre (2 pint) soufflé or similar dish.
❦ Flake the fish in a large bowl. Simmer the grated onion with 2 tsp of the fat until soft, and mix with the fish. Mix in the cheese.

❦ Put the cornflour in a heatproof jug, and blend with a little of the milk. Heat the remainder of the milk to boiling point with the remaining fat. Stir into the cornflour mixture. Return the mixture to the pan and heat, stirring constantly, until it boils and thickens. Remove from the heat, and stir into the fish mixture. Stir in the egg yolks and season well.
❦ Whisk all the egg whites stiffly and fold gently but thoroughly into the mixture. Turn into the dish, and bake for 25 minutes until well risen and coloured. Serve immediately.

QUICK PRAWN PIZZA

Serves 4-6

225 g (8 oz) self-raising flour
salt and pepper
pinch of cayenne pepper
50 g (2 oz) block margarine
100 g (4 oz) Cheddar cheese, grated
6 tbsp milk
4 large tomatoes
225 g (8 oz) peeled prawns
50 g (2 oz) black olives, halved
50 g (2 oz) Gruyère cheese
3 tbsp oil

❦ Heat the oven to 200C (400F) mark 6.
❦ Sieve the flour, salt, pepper and cayenne pepper into a bowl. Rub in the margarine until the mixture is like fine breadcrumbs. Stir in the grated cheese and mix to a dough with milk. Roll the dough out to a 23 cm (9 in) circle. Place on a lightly oiled baking sheet.
❦ Slice the tomatoes and arrange on top of the dough. Cover with 150 g (5 oz) of the prawns and the halved olives. Cut the cheese into very thin slices and arrange on top. Sprinkle with oil and season with salt and pepper.
❦ Bake for 30 minutes. Garnish with the remaining prawns and serve freshly baked.

SMOKED SALMON AND SCRAMBLED EGGS

Serves 4

4 large thin slices of smoked salmon
6-8 eggs, depending on size of salmon slice
25 g (1 oz) butter
4 tbsp milk
salt and pepper
soured cream, to serve

❦ Spread the salmon slices flat on a large tray.
❦ Scramble the eggs, with the butter, milk and seasoning, by your usual method; they should still be quite moist.
❦ Spread the scrambled egg over the salmon slices, then roll up the slices like Swiss rolls. Lay on a warmed platter and serve at once with a bowl of soured cream and a plate of Rolled Bread and Butter (see page 15).

Variation

For small pieces or trimmings of smoked salmon, make the dish as follows: use 175-225 g (6-8 oz) salmon, 8 eggs and 150 ml (¼ pint) fresh double cream instead of soured cream. Reserve a few small neat pieces of salmon for garnishing and shred the remainder. Make the scrambled eggs with 1 tbsp of the cream, adding the shredded salmon; the consistency should be soft. and creamy. Heat the remaining cream to simmering point. Garnish the eggs with the reserved salmon, and cover with hot cream. Serve immediately.

LEEK AND BACON FLAN

Serves 4-6

225 g (8 oz) quantity of Mixer Pastry (see page 358)
225 g (8 oz) leeks, cleaned and sliced
100 g (4 oz) lean rindless bacon
2 eggs
150 ml (¼ pint) single cream or milk
½ tsp mustard
2 tsp chopped olives
pinch of nutmeg or mace
25 g (1 oz) grated cheese (optional)

❦ Line a 20 cm (8 in) flan ring or dish with pastry. Prick the base and put a folded strip of foil around the edge to hold up the sides. Leave in a cool place to relax for 15 minutes. Heat the oven to 200C (400F) mark 6.
❦ Simmer the leeks in a little water for 5 minutes. Cool under a cold tap and drain well. Grill the bacon and cut into pieces.
❦ Beat the eggs with the cream and mix in the mustard and olives. Place the leeks and bacon in the flan dish, pour over the egg and cream mixture. Sprinkle with the nutmeg or mace and the cheese, if using.
❦ Bake for 30-40 minutes, until pastry is cooked and filling is set. If the filling cooks quickly, turn down the oven and cover the pie with greaseproof paper to finish cooking.
❦ Serve hot or cold. Excellent for picnics and packed lunches.

NOODLES WITH MUSHROOM SAUCE

Serves 4

225 g (8 oz) egg noodles (tagliatelle)
1 tbsp butter or margarine

Sauce
1 small onion, peeled
2 tsp butter or margarine
2 tsp oil
1 tsp chopped parsley
1 tsp flour
175 g (6 oz) button mushrooms, thinly sliced
about 8 tbsp Chicken Stock (see page 335) or as needed (use a stock cube if you have no home-made stock)

❦ Boil the pasta according to the packet directions. Drain, and keep warm.
❦ For the sauce: chop the onion finely. Heat the fat and oil in a pan, and fry the onion and parsley until the onion softens, stirring constantly. Sprinkle in the flour. Stir in the mushrooms and 6 tbsp of the stock. Simmer, stirring until the mushrooms soften. This should make enough liquid for a few spoonfuls of slightly thickened sauce. If not add a little more stock.
❦ Turn the pasta into a warmed dish, and toss with 1 tbsp fat. Spoon the sauce over it.

MENDIP OGGIES (SOMERSET PASTIES)

Serves 4-6

Simple Cheese Pastry made with 450 g (1 lb)
    wholemeal flour (see page 358)
450 g (1 lb) lean pork in 1 cm (½ in) cubes
225 g (8 oz) potato, scrubbed and diced
1 cooking apple, peeled, cored and chopped
1 tsp thyme
salt and pepper
egg to glaze

❦ Heat the oven to 220C (425F) mark 7. Make the
pastry and leave in the refrigerator to relax.
❦ Combine the meat, raw potato, apple, thyme and
seasoning. Divide the pastry into 4 or 6 and roll out
to circles about ½ cm (¼ in) thick. Divide the mixture between circles.
❦ Dampen the edges of circles and bring the pastry
up each side of the filling. Seal and crimp across the
top to give a frill effect. Glaze with egg and bake for
30 minutes.
❦ Lower the oven to 190C (375F) mark 5, cover the
oggies with greaseproof paper to prevent over-
browning and cook for 30 minutes more, or until
meat feels tender when tested with a fine skewer.
❦ Serve hot or cold.

BRANDADE OF SMOKED HADDOCK

Serves 6-8

675 g (1 ½ lb) smoked haddock
275 ml (½ pint) milk
275 ml (½ pint) olive oil
2 garlic cloves, crushed
150 ml (¼ pint) single cream
salt and pepper
pinch of ground nutmeg
1-2 tsp lemon juice
fried bread triangles to serve

❦ Poach the fish in the milk until just tender. Drain
well and discard the skin and bones. Flake the fish
finely into a bowl over a pan of hot water.
❦ Heat the oil and garlic together in another pan
until hot but not boiling. Put the cream into a small
pan and also heat gently to lukewarm.
❦ Pour a little oil in to the fish, beating with a wood-
en spoon. Add a little cream and beat well. Alternate
oil and cream, beating well, but do not over-beat the
mixture or it will separate.
❦ When all the oil and cream has been absorbed,
season to taste with salt, pepper, nutmeg and lemon
juice. Put the fish mixture into a warm serving bowl
and surround with fried bread triangles.

APPLE HERRINGS

Serves 4

4 herrings
salt and pepper
1 medium onion, thinly sliced
1 bay leaf
8 black peppercorns
4 cloves
blade of mace
150 ml (¼ pint) white wine vinegar
150 ml (¼ pint) apple juice

Sauce
450 g (1 lb) cooking apples
2 tbsp lemon juice
2 tbsp light soft brown sugar
pinch of ground ginger
pinch of ground nutmeg

❦ Heat the oven to 180C (350F) mark 4.
❦ Clean the herrings and divide each fish into two
fillets. Season with salt and pepper and roll up the
fish from the tail end, with the skin outwards. Place
in a single layer in a shallow ovenproof dish.
❦ Arrange the onion slices on top of the fish with
the bay leaf, peppercorns, cloves and mace. Mix the
vinegar and apple juice and pour over the fish. Cover
and bake for 45 minutes.
❦ While the fish are cooking, prepare the sauce.
Peel, core and slice the apples and put into a pan with
the remaining ingredients. Cover and simmer over a
low heat until the apples are soft.
❦ Sieve the sauce. Drain the fish and serve with the
sauce. The dish may be eaten hot or cold.

LEEK TART

Serves 4-6

225 g (8 oz) sliced white leek stems (from 3
   medium-sized leeks)
3 tbsp butter or margarine
2 large or 3 small eggs
150 ml (¼ pint) single cream or milk
pinch of grated nutmeg
salt and pepper
18-20 cm (7-8 in) pastry tart case, baked blind
   (see Rich Shortcrust Pastry, page359)
25 g (1 oz) grated Gruyère cheese

❦ Heat the oven to 190C (375F) mark 5.
❦ Cook the sliced leeks in the minimum of boiling
water for 5-7 minutes until soft. Drain, return to the
dry pan and toss in 2 tbsp of the fat until well coated. Take off the heat.
❦ Beat the eggs, cream or milk, and seasonings
together in a bowl. Stir in the leeks with any fat.
Turn the mixture gently into the pastry case, spreading the leeks evenly. Sprinkle with the cheese. Dot
with the remaining fat.
❦ Bake for 20-25 minutes until the custard is lightly set in the centre. Serve hot.

SMOKED HADDOCK FLAN

Serves 4-6

225 g (8 oz) Pâte Brisée or Rich Shortcrust
   Pastry (see page 359)
450 g (1 lb) smoked haddock
275 ml (½ pint) milk
2 hard-boiled eggs
25 g (1 oz) butter
25 g (1 oz) plain flour
2 tbsp chopped parsley

❦ Heat the oven to 200C (400F) mark 6. Roll out
the pastry and use to line a 20 cm (8 in) fluted oven-
proof china flan dish. Bake blind (see page 357).
Increase oven temperature to 220C (425F) mark 7.
❦ Simmer the haddock in the milk until tender.
Remove the fish and keep the milk. Carefully flake
the fish, discarding every scrap of bone and skin.
Chop the eggs and add to the fish.

❦ Make a parsley sauce: melt the butter in a pan,
add the flour and cook for 1 minute. Gradually add
the reserved milk and bring up to the boil, beating
all the time. Stir in the parsley and then fold in the
fish and egg mixture. Fill the flan case with the mixture. Stand the dish on a baking sheet and cook for
20 minutes, or until browned.

BURGERS (WITH TOMATO SAUCE)

Serves 4-6

Burger
450 g (1 lb) minced beef or pork
50 g (2 oz) bacon, finely chopped
2 tsp capers, chopped
2 tbsp wholemeal breadcrumbs
pinch of cayenne pepper
1 tsp marjoram
1 egg

Tomato sauce
450 g (1 lb) tomatoes, skinned and chopped, or
   large tin
1 onion, finely chopped
1 tsp sugar
1 tsp basil
1 tsp Worcestershire sauce

❦ Combine all the burger ingredients together and
form into a flat, circular shape. Fry in a little oil for
about 10 minutes a side, or until well browned and
cooked through. Keep hot until all the burgers are
cooked.
❦ Boil all the sauce ingredients together for 10-15
minutes, or until the onion is cooked and the sauce
is a suitable consistency.
❦ Serve with the burgers piled down the middle of
a serving dish, with the sauce poured over. Alternatively, serve each burger in a soft burger or picnic
roll, with salad, tomato and chutney inside or to
taste.
❦ Garnish with watercress and serve hot with salad
(mixed bean goes very well) or fresh vegetables and
jacket or chopped potatoes.
❦ The tomato sauce can be also used cold for picnics and packed lunches.

CRUMBED AVOCADOS

Serves 4

2 firm avocado pears
lemon juice or French Dressing (see page 347)
100 g (4 oz) cooked smoked cod or haddock
few drops of oil
3-4 tbsp soft breadcrumbs
2-3 tbsp butter, melted
lemon wedges

❦ Heat the oven to 180C (350F) mark 4.
❦ Cut the avocados in half lengthwise and remove the stones. If the stones are small or the surrounding flesh discoloured, scoop out a little of the flesh. Immediately brush the cut sides of the pears with lemon juice or French dressing.
❦ Flake the fish, removing any skin or bones, and mix with a few drops of oil, using just enough to hold the shreds of fish together. Pile the fish into the avocado halves, covering them. Sprinkle the whole surface with breadcrumbs and the melted butter.
❦ Place in a baking tin and bake for 20 minutes until well heated through. Serve at once with lemon wedges.

POTTED MEAT

Serves 4-6

225 g (8 oz) shin of beef in small cubes
1 knuckle end of veal (pork if veal unavailable)
½ tsp salt
6 allspice berries
6 peppercorns
1 onion, whole
1 bay leaf

❦ Put all ingredients in a lidded pan with enough water to cover, simmer slowly for 2-3 hours until meat falls away from the bones.
❦ Remove the meat from cooking liquor and take out the bones. Shred the meat using a knife and fork and place in an oiled mould. Reduce cooking liquor to about 275 ml (½ pint) and strain over meat. Leave to set.
❦ Turn out and cut in slices for serving with salads or in sandwiches.

HAKE BAKE

Serves 4

50 g (2 oz) butter
1 garlic clove, crushed
2 medium onions, sliced
175 g (6 oz) mushrooms, sliced
1 tsp fresh mixed herbs
4 hake (or cod) cutlets or steaks
salt and pepper
25 g (1 oz) fresh brown or white breadcrumbs

❦ Heat the oven to 190C (375F) mark 5.
❦ Melt the butter and reserve half of it. Use the rest to cook the garlic, onions, mushrooms and herbs over a low heat for 5 minutes, stirring well. Place in an ovenproof dish.
❦ Season the fish on both sides with salt and pepper and place it on top of the vegetables. Sprinkle with breadcrumbs and the remaining butter. Bake for 30 minutes.

FISH CORKS

Serves 4

225 g (8 oz) white fish, cooked
275 ml (½ pint) Parsley Sauce (see page 339)
25 g (1 oz) fresh white or brown breadcrumbs
2 eggs
salt and pepper
25 g (1 oz) plain flour
6 tbsp dry breadcrumbs
oil for frying

❦ Flake the fish into a bowl. Cook the parsley sauce until it is thick enough to hold a peak. Mix the fish, sauce and fresh breadcrumbs together.
❦ Beat the eggs and add just enough to bind the mixture. Season well. Leave until completely cold and then form into a long sausage on a floured board, making the cylinder about 2.5 cm (1 in) thick. Cut into 5 cm (2 in) lengths.
❦ Dip these in the flour, then beaten egg and finally the dry breadcrumbs. Fry in hot oil until golden brown and serve at once.
❦ These are a delicious home-made alternative to the fish finger. Some smoked fish may be included.

CREAM AND PRAWN FLAN

Serves 6-8

18-20 cm (7-8 in) pastry flan case, baked blind
  (see Rich Shortcrust Pastry, page 359)
175 g (6 oz) cooked, peeled prawns or 215 g (7 ½
  oz) can of prawns in brine
salt (optional)
150 g (5 oz) full-fat soft (cream) cheese
65 ml (2 ½ fl oz) white wine
4 tsp gelatine
120 ml (4 fl oz) whipping cream
chopped parsley

❦ Lightly salt the prawns if you wish, or drain the
can and pat dry. Spread evenly over the bottom of
the flan case.

❦ Then make the topping: cream the cheese with
the back of a spoon in a bowl. Pour the wine into a
heatproof jug, adding the gelatine to soften. Stand
the jug in hot water and stir until the gelatine dissolves. Remove the jug from the heat. Allow to cool
slightly while half-whipping the cream.

❦ Beat or stir the gelatine mixture into the cheese
thoroughly, then fold in the cream. Quickly, spread
the cream-wine mixture evenly over the prawn filling. Chill until needed, then sprinkle with chopped
parsley.

❦ Serve this rich flan in small wedges.

Filling Variations

(1) For salmon filling, spread 175 g (6 oz) of 'instant'
Salmon Pâté (see page 70) over the base of the flan
case.

(2) To make a mushroom filling, slice 225 g (8 oz)
button mushrooms thinly. Sauté in a little butter and
oil until lightly browned, then drain on soft paper.
Spread over the base of the flan case.

❦ If you want to serve this dish as a starter or as part
of a buffet meal, then out the filling and topping in
individual vol-au-vents. The cases can be home-
made or bought. Ready-baked ones are sold in packets. Frozen ones may be uncooked, ready for baking,
or fully baked; uncooked cases are sometimes haz-
ardous to use as they are designed to rise high, and
may topple over in the oven if not baked with care.

PRAWN AND MUSHROOM SALAD

Serves 4

450 g (1 lb) button mushrooms
150 ml (¼ pint) olive oil
4 tbsp lemon juice
1 garlic clove, crushed
salt and pepper
225 g (8 oz) prawns, peeled
3 tbsp fresh parsley, chopped

❦ Do not peel the mushrooms but wipe them and
slice them thinly. Put into a serving bowl. Mix the
oil, lemon juice, garlic and plenty of seasoning and
pour half the mixture over the mushrooms. Leave to
stand in a cool place for at least 2 hours.

❦ Pour the rest of the dressing over the prawns and
leave in a cool place.

❦ Just before serving, mix the prawns and their liquid with the mushrooms and toss lightly. Sprinkle
thickly with parsley.

❦ Serve with wholemeal or crusty white bread as a
light meal or first course.

BACON AND BEAN BAKE

Serves 4

225 g (8 oz) rindless bacon, chopped
1 onion, sliced
1 clove garlic, crushed
2 tbsp tomato purée
2 tbsp parsley, chopped
2 tbsp soft brown sugar
225 g (8 oz) haricot beans, soaked
black pepper
450 ml (¾ pint) chicken or vegetable stock

❦ Heat the oven to 150C (300F) mark 2. Layer all ingredients in a deep casserole and add enough stock to cover. Bake for 4–5 hours, until the beans are soft and the liquid has been absorbed. Check periodically and add a little more liquid if required.

❦ The bake can be cooked overnight in an oven at 120C (250F) mark ½ or in a slow cooker (read manufacturer's instructions for time).

❦ Serve with chunks of wholemeal, or granary bread and a side salad.

PLAICE ROLLS WITH SHRIMPS

Serves 4

4 fresh plaice fillets
200 g (7 oz) cooked peeled shrimp
25 g (1 oz) soft white breadcrumbs
pinch of ground mace
25 g (1 oz) softened butter
salt and pepper
3 tbsp dry white wine
120 ml (4 fl oz) Fish Stock (see page 336) or
    water
4–5 tbsp double cream
Rolled Bread and Butter (see page 15)
lemon wedges

❦ Heat the oven to 180C (350F) mark 4.
❦ Skin the plaice fillets. Reserve 16–20 shrimp for garnishing and chop the remainder. Mix with the breadcrumbs, mace and butter to make a stuffing. Season lightly. Spread the stuffing on the skinned sides of the fillets and roll up from the tail end.

❦ Place, seam side down, in a shallow, greased baking dish. Pour the wine and fish stock or water over the fish. Cover loosely and bake for about 20 minutes.

❦ Meanwhile, heat the cream. Place the stuffed rolls on 4 small warmed plates, spoon a little hot cream over each and garnish with the reserved shrimps. Serve hot, with rolled bread and butter and lemon wedges.

❦ If you prefer, use the liquid in which the fillets are cooked to make a white sauce to pour over instead of using cream.

CARIBBEAN TURKEY

Serves 4

450 g (1 lb) white turkey meat
2 tbsp plain flour
salt and pepper
1 tbsp cooking oil
25 g (1 oz) butter
450 g (1 lb) canned apricot halves
2 tbsp Worcestershire sauce
2 tbsp vinegar
2 tbsp Demerara sugar
2 tbsp lemon juice
150 ml (¼ pint) water
225 g (8 oz) long grain rice

❦ Cut the turkey meat into 2.5 cm (1 in) cubes. Place the flour, salt and pepper in a large polythene bag, add the turkey pieces and toss well.

❦ Place the oil and butter in a flameproof casserole and heat. Add the coated turkey pieces and fry until brown.

❦ Drain the apricot halves, reserve a few for the garnish and coarsely chop the remainder. Reserve the juice, and mix 150 ml (¼ pint) of it with the Worcestershire sauce, vinegar, Demerara sugar, lemon juice and water.

❦ Add any remaining flour to the turkey pieces and add the liquids to the pan. Stir gently and bring to the boil, add the chopped apricots, cover and simmer gently for 45 minutes, or until the meat is tender.

❦ Meanwhile cook the long grain rice. Dry the rice, and place in a ring around a large serving dish. Keep warm. When the turkey is tender, check the seasoning and pour the mixture into the centre of the rice. Garnish with the remaining apricots.

FISH CAKES

Serves 4-6

450 g (1 lb) cooked fish, flaked
450 g (1 lb) cooked potatoes
4 tbsp milk
50 g (2 oz) butter, melted
1 egg yolk
1 tbsp fresh parsley, chopped
1 tsp lemon juice
salt and pepper
flour
oil for frying

❧ The fish may be white fish, smoked haddock or kippers, or salmon, or a mixture of smoked fish and white fish may be used.
❧ Put the fish into a large bowl. Mash the potatoes with the milk and butter. Add to the fish and mix well and work in the egg yolk, parsley, lemon juice and plenty of salt and pepper.
❧ Shape the mixture into 12 round cakes and flatten them slightly. Dust lightly with flour and fry in shallow oil until golden on each side.
❧ If preferred, the fish cakes may be dipped in flour, egg and then breadcrumbs before frying.

TURKEY DIVAN

Serves 4

450 g (1 lb) frozen broccoli
700 g (1 ½ lb) potatoes, cooked and mashed
25 g (1 oz) butter
350 g (12 oz) cooked turkey, sliced
1 can condensed chicken soup
2 tbsp dry sherry or dry white wine,
50 g (2 oz) Cheddar cheese, finely grated

❧ Cook the broccoli in boiling salted water.
❧ Meanwhile pipe a bed of mashed potato into the centre of a warmed, flat, fireproof dish. Keep warm.
❧ Drain the broccoli and arrange around the potato; dot with butter. Place the turkey slices on top of the potato.
❧ Heat the soup undiluted in a saucepan, add the sherry or wine, and pour over the turkey, leaving most of the broccoli uncovered. Sprinkle the sauce with cheese, reheat and brown well under a hot grill.

HERRINGS WITH MUSTARD BUTTER

Serves 4

4 medium herrings
75 g (3 oz) butter
1 tsp mustard powder
salt and pepper
4 tomatoes

❧ Heat the oven to 190C (375F) mark 5.
❧ Clean and fillet the herrings and open them out flat. Cream the butter with the mustard powder, salt and pepper and spread on the flesh of each fish. Fold in half and wrap each fish in a piece of greased foil. Place on a baking sheet and bake for 15 minutes.
❧ Cut the tomatoes in half and place on the baking sheet. Season well and dot with a little butter. Continue baking for 10 minutes. Serve at once with brown bread and butter.

ROLL-MOP HERRING SALAD

Serves 4

8 roll-mop herrings
450 g (1 lb) potatoes
150 ml (¼ pint) Mayonnaise (see page 346)
1 tsp French mustard
2 red eating apples
lettuce or Chinese leaves
parsley sprigs for garnish

❧ Chop the roll-mop herrings into small pieces. Chop the onions with which they are pickled and mix with the herrings.
❧ Boil the potatoes until cooked, drain very well and leave until lukewarm. Mix the mayonnaise and mustard. Dice the potatoes and stir into the mayonnaise. Leave until just cold.
❧ Do not peel the apples, but core and dice them. Mix together the potato salad with the herring and onion pieces and apples.
❧ Arrange on a bed of lettuce or Chinese leaves and garnish with parsley sprigs. Serve freshly made.

KIPPER PUFFS

Serves 4-6

225 g (8 oz) kipper fillets
25 g (1 oz) butter
15 g (½ oz) plain flour
150 ml (¼ pint) milk
2 eggs
25 g (1 oz) Cheddar cheese, grated
salt and pepper
pinch of mustard powder

❦ Heat the oven to 220C (425F) mark 7.
❦ Poach the kippers in a little water until tender. Drain well, skin and mash the flesh.
❦ Melt the butter in a pan and work in the flour. Stir over a low heat for 1 minute and then stir in the milk. Stir over a low heat until the mixture thickens. Take off the heat.
❦ Separate the eggs and beat the yolks into the sauce with the cheese, salt, pepper and mustard. Stir in the pieces of kipper.
❦ Whisk the egg whites to stiff peaks and fold into the fish mixture. Spoon into 4-6 greased individual ramekins or soufflé dishes.
❦ Place on a hot baking sheet and bake for 15 minutes. Serve immediately.

QUICK KIPPER PIZZA

Serves 4-6

225 g (8 oz) self-raising flour
½ tsp salt
40 g (1 ½ oz) butter
150 ml (¼ pint) milk

Topping
100 g (4 oz) Cheddar cheese, grated
1 tsp mustard powder
½ tsp fresh mixed herbs
225 g (8 oz) tomatoes
8 kipper fillets
8 black olives, stoned
paprika

❦ Heat the oven to 200C (400F) mark 6. Sieve the flour and salt, and rub in the butter until the mixture is like fine breadcrumbs. Work in the milk to make a firm soft dough. Roll out lightly to make a 30 cm (12 in) circle. Place on a greased baking sheet.
❦ Mix the cheese, mustard and herbs in a basin and sprinkle this over the dough. Skin the tomatoes and slice them thinly. Arrange on top of the cheese. Arrange the kipper fillets on top in a wheel pattern. Place the olives between the fillets. Sprinkle with paprika. Bake for 30 minutes. Serve hot.

MIDDLE EASTERN EGG BAKE

Serves 4-6

175 g (6 oz) courgettes
salt
1 medium-sized onion
½ deseeded sweet red pepper
2 tbsp butter or margarine
1 tbsp oil
4 eggs
1 tbsp chopped parsley
black pepper

❦ Heat the oven to 160C (325F) mark 3.
❦ Cut the courgettes into 3 mm (⅛ in) slices. Sprinkle with salt and place on a tilted plate for 15 minutes. Drain and pat dry. Chop the onion and pepper finely.
❦ Heat 1 tbsp fat and the oil in a frying pan which will hold all the vegetables, and stir-fry the onion and pepper until soft. Add the remaining fat and sliced courgettes and stir until they are soft and golden. Drain the vegetables on soft paper.
❦ Butter generously the inside of an 18 cm (7 in) ovenproof pie plate or dish, about 4 cm (1 ½ in) deep and suitable for serving.
❦ Beat the eggs in a bowl and add the vegetables and parsley. Season to taste. Turn the mixture into the dish. Cover tightly with a lid or foil, and bake for 30 minutes. Uncover and bake for another 10 minutes or until the dish is firm in the centre.
❦ Serve from the dish in squares, slices or wedges. In the Middle East, beaten eggs are often mixed with meat or vegetables and baked or fried slowly, using low heat, until firmly set. The savoury egg 'cake' may be served in small wedges, squares or slices as a convenient first course.

BAKED COURGETTES

Serves 4

6 small courgettes, about 10 cm (4 in) long
salt
6 finely chopped shallots
2 tbsp soft fine breadcrumbs
pepper
2 tbsp butter
6 lean back bacon rashers
watercress sprigs, to garnish

❦ Heat the oven to 180C (350F) mark 4.
❦ Slice the courgettes in half lengthwise and simmer in lightly salted water for 5 minutes. Drain and
place cut side up on a baking sheet. Cover the cut
surfaces with the chopped shallots and sprinkle with
the breadcrumbs and salt and pepper. Dot with the
butter.
❦ Lay the bacon rashers flat, removing any rind and
fat, and cut 2 long, lengthwise strips of lean meat off
each rasher; they should cover the courgettes, and
overhang the ends. Lay one strip on each courgette
half.
❦ Place in the oven and bake for about 25 minutes
until the bacon is brown and crisp.
❦ Serve 3 courgette halves to each person, arrange
in a pattern on small plates with a garnish of watercress sprigs.

FISH CREAMS

Serves 4-6

225 g (8 oz) white fish
25 g (1 oz) melted butter
225 g (8 oz) peeled prawns
150 ml (¼ pint) White Sauce (see page 339)
1 egg white
salt and pepper
pinch of ground mace
pinch of cayenne pepper
150 ml (¼ pint) double cream

❦ Heat the oven to 180C (350F) mark 4.
❦ Poach the fish until just tender. Drain well and
remove the skin. Put into a food processor or liquidizer with the butter and 150 g (6 oz) of the
prawns. Blend until smooth. Add the white sauce

and egg white and blend until very smooth. Season
well with salt and pepper, mace and cayenne pepper.
❦ Whip the cream to soft peaks and fold into the
fish mixture. Place the remaining prawns in four to
six individual ovenproof dishes. Top with the fish
mixture. Place the dishes in a baking tin with hot
water to come halfway up the dishes. Cover with
greased greaseproof paper. Bake for 30 minutes.
❦ Serve with Hollandaise or Tomato Sauce (see
page 345 or 341).

SAVOURY PANCAKE GATEAU

Serves 6

six 15 cm (6 in) pancakes, a little thicker than
sweet Pancakes (see page 365)

Fillings
(1) 4 hard-boiled eggs, chopped, bound with 5-
6 tsp soured cream or thick yoghurt, salt and
pepper
(2) 3 large firm tomatoes, thinly sliced, sprinkled with chopped fresh or dried basil, salt
and pepper
(3) 5 tbsp low-fat soft curd cheese mixed with
¼ finely chopped green pepper, salt and
pepper

Topping
4 tbsp soured cream or whisked whole milk
yoghurt
chopped parsley

❦ Heat the oven to 160C (325F) mark 3. Mix the
three fillings in separate bowls.
❦ Lay one pancake flat on a heatproof serving plate.
Cover evenly with half of filling (1). Lay a second
pancake on top, and cover it with half filling (2). Add
a third pancake and spread with all filling (3).
❦ Repeat the layers, using fillings (2) and (1.) Top
with the last pancake. Cover with greased foil, and
reheat for about 15 minutes. Warm the soured cream
or yoghurt slightly, and spoon on top of the pancake
stack. Sprinkle with parsley.
❦ To serve, cut in wedges at the table.

HOT CRAB MOUSSE

Serves 4

175 g (6 oz) crab meat
50 g (2 oz) peeled prawns
1 tbsp lemon juice
85 g (3 oz) fresh brown breadcrumbs
2 tbsp tomato ketchup
2 eggs
3 tbsp single cream
salt
paprika
1 tbsp Parmesan cheese, grated

❦ Heat the oven to 180C (350F) mark 4. Grease 4 individual ramekins.
❦ Mix the crab meat, prawns, lemon juice, 50 g (2 oz) of the breadcrumbs and the tomato ketchup. Separate the eggs and work the yolks and cream into the crab mixture. Season well with salt and paprika.
❦ Whisk the egg whites to stiff peaks and fold into the mixture. Spoon into the ramekins. Mix the remaining breadcrumbs and the cheese and sprinkle on top of each ramekin. Bake for 20 minutes.
❦ Serve hot with buttered toast.

BUTTERED BLOATERS

Serves 4

4 bloaters
salt and pepper
50 g (2 oz) butter
2 tbsp lemon juice

❦ Heat the oven to 180C (350F) mark 4.
❦ Cut off the heads, tails and fins, and bone the bloaters. Sprinkle inside and out with salt and pepper. Place in a single layer in a greased ovenproof dish. Cover with flakes of butter and sprinkle with lemon juice.
❦ Cover and bake for 20 minutes. Serve with bread and butter, or with scrambled eggs.

TURKEY LOAF

Serves 4

350 g (12 oz) cooked turkey, minced
100 g (4 oz) fresh breadcrumbs
½ tsp dry mustard
1 medium onion, minced
75 g (3 oz) mushrooms, chopped
½ tsp celery salt
2 tbsp chopped fresh parsley
2 eggs, beaten
150 ml (¼ pint) milk
1 tsp Worcestershire sauce
salt and pepper

❦ Heat the oven to 180C (350F) mark 4.
❦ Into a large bowl place the turkey, breadcrumbs, mustard, onion, mushrooms, celery salt and parsley. Mix well together. Add the beaten eggs, milk and Worcestershire sauce. Mix again, ensuring all the ingredients are well blended. Season to taste.
❦ Place the mixture in a well-greased 900 g (2 lb) loaf tin. Bake in the oven, until firm, for about 1 hour. Leave in the tin for 5 minutes before turning out on a serving dish. Serve hot or cold.

KEDGEREE

Serves 4

175 g (6 oz) long grain rice
450 g (1 lb) smoked haddock or cod fillet
2 eggs, hard-boiled
2 tsp curry powder
2 tsp lemon juice
salt and pepper
100 g (4 oz) butter
1 tbsp fresh parsley, chopped

❦ Cook the rice in boiling salted water for 12–15 minutes until just tender. Drain well and keep warm.
❦ Meanwhile, poach the fish in water until cooked but unbroken. Drain well and remove the skin and any bones. Break into large flakes and mix with the rice.
❦ Chop the whites of the eggs roughly and mix into the rice with the curry powder, lemon juice, salt and pepper. Flake the butter and stir into the rice.
❦ Pile on a hot serving dish and sprinkle with the chopped egg yolks and parsley.

ARNOLD BENNETT OMELETTE

Serves 2

175 g (6 oz) smoked haddock fillet
4 large eggs
50 g (2 oz) Gruyère cheese, grated
salt and pepper
25 g (1 oz) butter
275 ml (½ pint) Cheese Sauce (see page 339)
25 g (1 oz) Parmesan cheese, grated

❦ Poach the haddock until tender. Drain well, cool and remove the skin and any bones. Flake the fish.
❦ Beat the eggs until light and frothy. Add the Gruyère cheese, haddock and seasoning to the eggs.
❦ Melt the butter in an 18 cm (7 in) omelette pan and pour in the egg mixture. Cook gently, lifting the egg and moving it with a fork until the omelette is almost set.
❦ Spoon on the warm cheese sauce and sprinkle on the Parmesan cheese. Do not fold the omelette but put under a hot grill to brown quickly. Serve immediately.

PETITE SALADE NICOISE

Serves 4-6

lettuce leaves
225 g (8 oz) cooled cooked new potatoes
2 medium-sized tomatoes, skinned and sliced
1 tsp chopped fresh basil
1 tsp chopped parsley
grated rind of 1 lemon
100 g (4 oz) cooled cooked French beans
50 g (2 oz) black olives
2 hard-boiled eggs, quartered
8 anchovy fillets, drained and split lengthwise
French Dressing (see page 347) with a squeeze
    of garlic

❦ Make a bed of lettuce leaves on a flat platter.
❦ Slice the potatoes and arrange on the lettuce with the tomato slices. Sprinkle with the herbs and lemon rind. Pile the French beans in the centre of the dish or scatter over it.
❦ Halve and stone the olives and chop into fairly large bits, sprinkle over the salad. Add the quartered eggs. Arrange the anchovy fillets in a lattice pattern on top. Sprinkle the salad well with the dressing, and leave to stand for 30 minutes before serving, to let the flavours blend.
❦ Serve with brown bread and butter. This is an attractive light version of this classic French salad dish, with its contrasting colours if well arranged.

HAM AND ASPARAGUS IN GRUYERE SAUCE

Serves 4

4 good slices of ham
225 g (8 oz) cooked asparagus
25 g (1 oz) wholemeal breadcrumbs to garnish

Sauce
25 g (1 oz) cornflour
25 g (1 oz) margarine or butter
275 ml (½ pint) milk
½ tsp powdered mustard
black pepper
¼ tsp paprika
2 tbsp cream (optional)
75 g (3 oz) Gruyère cheese, grated

❦ Heat the oven to 200C (400F) mark 6. Divide the asparagus between the ham slices and roll up. Place in a gratin dish or other shallow ovenproof dish. Cover with foil. Put the rolls in the oven to heat through while the sauce is being made.
❦ Make the sauce by heating the cornflour and margarine or butter until the consistency is like that of a honeycomb, take off the heat then gradually add the milk. Return to the heat and boil for about 3 minutes until thick.
❦ Add all the other ingredients and stir until the cheese is melted. Do not boil once the cheese has been added or the cheese will go stringy and become indigestible.
❦ Pour the sauce over the rolls and sprinkle with breadcrumbs. Return to the oven to brown.
❦ The dish can be assembled and left and then heated and browned at the same time. This will take about 30-40 minutes.
❦ This recipe can be made more economical by using cooked leeks and Edam cheese and still tastes delicious.

STARTERS, SAVOURIES & FINGER FOOD

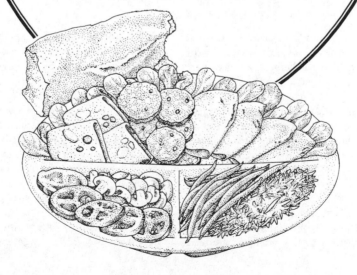

MIXED
HORS D'OEUVRE
OR ANTIPASTI

A colourful and decorative selection of easy-to-serve appetisers.

Both 'hors d'oeuvre' and 'antipasti' mean small portions of assorted cold savoury foods and preserves served 'outside', that is before, the main part of a meal. These mixed appetisers make an easy-to-serve, economical starter which can look very decorative if the items are colourful and well arranged. Kitchenware shops sell hors d'oeuvre trays holding six to nine small dishes, but it is easier to arrange a choice of five or six items on individual plates shortly ahead of the meal.

Cold cooked or salad vegetables, preserved fish such as sardines or smoked oysters, stuffed eggs, and firm savoury spreads are among the popular hors d'oeuvre foods to choose from. Select foods which differ in colour, texture and flavour from the next

course; omit, say, green beans if you serve them as your main hot vegetable. Always include one protein, conventionally it should be preserved fish or shellfish, but egg mayonnaise or a similar cold egg dish is attractive and often served instead. Sliced Continental sausage or cured meat is another choice, often mixed with a vegetable. Broad beans with shredded ham is a popular Italian appetiser.

When preparing hors d'oeuvre, place one item slightly bigger than the rest in the centre of each plate as a focus; a stuffed egg (see pages 54-5) or tomato cup (see page 49) is shapely. Surround with items which contrast with this and each other in flavour and colour. Place sliced salami between green peas and golden sweetcorn for instance, not next to spicy ratatouille (see page 50). Vary dressings, by using orange juice on grated carrot and a spoonful of white wine over chopped celery. Vivid garnishes, such as crumbled egg yolk on dark green spinach or chopped black olives on potato salad, add colour.

Hors d'oeuvre ingredients must look fresh and neatly trimmed, so although it is tempting, do not prepare them too far in advance. French dressing may run off salad leaves, leaving them wilted and soggy underneath. Mayonnaise may turn yellow and dull on standing. The later hors d'oeuvre are assembled, the crisper they will look.

The recipes which follow contain many items which can be used to make interesting mixed hors d'oeuvre. Use the recipes as a guide to making your own, using any home-made or bought ingredients which suit the rest of your menu.

MIXED HORS D'OEUVRE FOR SUMMER

Serves 4

4 large lettuce leaves
225 g (8 oz) cooked, peeled prawns
1 quantity Eggs in Jelly (see page 53)
½ unpeeled cucumber, sliced
salt
175 g (6 oz) cold cooked small green peas
chopped mint
8 small triangles of thin brown bread and butter
4 lemon wedges

❦ Shred the lettuce leaves, and spread on 4 small plates. Place a small pile of prawns in the centre of each plate.
❦ Unmould the eggs, and invert one on to each plate next to the prawns. Arrange slices of cucumber beside the egg on one side, and sprinkle lightly with salt. Mix the peas with a little chopped mint, and place a small pile opposite the cucumber.
❦ Fill the gap between the cucumber and peas with two bread and butter triangles and a lemon wedge for squeezing.

MIXED HORS D'OEUVRE FOR WINTER

Serves 4

4 anchovy fillets, drained
milk
4 round slices of smoked cod's roes, about 1 cm (½ in) thick
2 hard-boiled eggs
tomato purée (from tube)
Leeks à la Grecque, cold (see page 51)
Green Bean Salad (see page 49)
Russian Salad (see page 49)

❦ Soak the anchovy fillets in milk while preparing the hors d'oeuvre.
❦ Skin the slices of cod's roe if needed, and place one in the centre of each of 4 small plates.
❦ Shell the eggs, and cut each in half lengthwise. Place one half egg, cut side up, at the side of each plate beside the cod's roe. Squeeze a dab of tomato purée on each yolk.
❦ Using equal quantities of the three vegetables, make a complete ring around the cod's roe, placing the leeks and green bean salad next to the egg.
❦ Drain the anchovy fillets and curl one in the centre of each slice of roe.

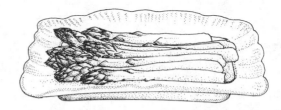

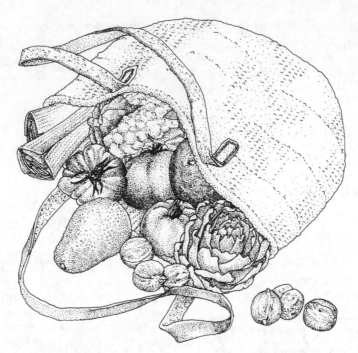

FRUIT AND VEGETABLE DISHES

*A selection of well-known and new recipes for
making the most of fresh fruit and vegetables.*

PEAR CUPS WITH WALNUTS

Serves 4

2 large firm eating pears
lemon juice
50 g (2 oz) walnut pieces, chopped
100 g (4 oz) dessert dates, pitted and chopped
1 small round lettuce
French Dressing (see page 347)

❦ Halve the pears lengthwise. Scoop out and discard the cores, then remove enough flesh to leave
spoon-shaped hollows. Reserve the flesh. Brush the
cut surfaces with lemon juice. Chop the reserved
flesh into small pieces and mix with the walnuts and
dates.
❦ Shred the lettuce finely and add a few shreds to
the walnut mixture. Spread the rest of the lettuce on
4 small plates and place a pear half, hollowed side up,
on each. Pare the rounded sides of the pears to make
them stand level.
❦ Toss the walnut mixture with just enough
dressing to make it moist and glistening. Pile the
mixture on the hollowed-out pear halves. Serve
cold but not chilled.

MELON AND GINGER

Serves 4

1 small honeydew melon
4 pieces of preserved stem ginger in syrup
4 tsp syrup from the ginger jar

❦ Cut the melon in half, scoop out and discard the seeds. With a potato or vegetable baller, cut the flesh into small balls. Place in individual stemmed dessert glasses, with any free juice.
❦ Chop the ginger very finely and scatter on the melon balls. Pour 1 tsp of the syrup over each helping.

MELON AND ORANGE COCKTAIL

Serves 4

1 honeydew melon
2 small oranges
10 cm (4 in) piece of cucumber
2 tbsp finely chopped mint
black pepper to serve

❦ Cut the melon flesh into small balls as for melon and ginger (above). Place in a bowl with any juice.
❦ Dip the oranges into boiling water, peel off the skins and any white pith. Cut the segments of flesh free from the membranes, cut in half and mix with the melon balls.
❦ Quarter the cucumber lengthwise, remove the seeds and dice the flesh. Mix the cucumber and mint with the fruit.
❦ Serve chilled, but not ice-cold, in dessert glasses. Offer a black pepper-mill.

❦ Suitable types of melon to offer as a starter are the small Charentais and Ogen melons, large Cantaloupe and Honeydew melons, or slices from a watermelon.
❦ Cut very small melons in half across and scoop out the seeds with a spoon; serve a half to each person, cut side up, on a small plate.
❦ Cut larger melons into segments, discarding the seeds. With a sharp knife, cut the flesh free from the skin; leave in place, and cut across into cubes. Offer a segment to each person, and hand round a bowl of ground ginger and containers of salt and cayenne.

❦ Cut slices of watermelon about 2 cm (¾ in) thick, and cut them in half. Serve a half slice or 'fan' of watermelon to each person, with lemon segments for squeezing instead of ginger.

SHERRIED GRAPEFRUIT

Serves 4

2 large grapefruit
warmed clear honey or brown sugar
4 tsp medium-dry sherry or mixed spice
4 fresh pitted cherries or maraschino cherries

❦ Cut the grapefruits in half across, and snip out the cores with scissors. Dig out the pips. Using a small serrated knife, cut round the fruit to separate the flesh and pith. With scissors, snip each side of the membrane separating the segments, but leave in place. Sprinkle the cut sides with the honey, or sugar, and sherry. Place a cherry in the centre.
❦ The grapefruit can be served hot. Sprinkle with mixed spice instead of sherry and place under the grill for about 3 minutes, or in a hot oven for 6–10 minutes. Add the fruit garnish just before serving.

AVOCADO PEAR VINAIGRETTE

Serves 4

2 large firm ripe avocado pears
2 tbsp lemon juice
Vinaigrette (see page 347)
watercress sprigs

❦ Halve the pears lengthwise and remove the stones. The flesh should not be discoloured or soft. Brush the cut surfaces with lemon juice at once.
❦ Place a half pear, cut side up, on each of four small plates. Fill the hollows with vinaigrette sauce, and garnish the plates with watercress.

Note
If the pears are discoloured or soft when cut open, take out the good-quality flesh in slivers, toss it with dressing and mix with cubed fresh or canned fruit (not bananas) or with salad vegetables. Serve in dessert glasses or bowls as a 'cocktail'.

AVOCADO AU FROMAGE BLEU

Serves 4

50 g (2 oz) Stilton or similar blue cheese with rind cut off
50 g (2 oz) low-fat smooth curd cheese
1-4 tbsp natural yoghurt
50 g (2 oz) salted cashew nuts
2 medium-sized ripe avocado pears
lemon juice

❦ Mash the blue cheese, then beat in the curd cheese until smooth. Add enough yoghurt to make the mixture like stiffly whipped cream. Chop the nuts into small bits and add to the mixture.
❦ Halve the pears lengthwise, remove the stones and brush the cut sides all over with lemon juice. Place a half pear, cut side up, in each of four small saucers or shallow bowls. Pile the cheese and nut mixture on top.
❦ Serve with Rolled Brown Bread and Butter (see page 15).

GLOBE ARTICHOKES

Serves 4

4 globe artichokes
salt
1 tbsp lemon juice
melted butter or Hollandaise Sauce (see page 345)

❦ Soak the artichokes upside down in cold salted water for 45 minutes to wash out any dust and insects. Lay each head in turn on the edge of a table with the stalk projecting over the edge. Bend and twist the stalk to remove it with the coarse hairs from the artichoke's base. Pare the base so that it will stand level, taking off the coarsest of the outside leaves. Square off the tips of all the remaining leaves with scissors, or slice off the top third of the whole artichoke with a sharp knife.
❦ Place the artichokes in one layer in a large pan, and pour in just enough water to cover them. Add a little salt and the lemon juice. Cover the pan and boil the artichokes for 15-45 minutes, depending on size, until a leaf pulls off easily. Turn the artichokes upside down to drain.
❦ Serve one to each person on a warmed plate. Equip each diner with paper napkins and a small spoon for removing the hairy 'choke' and eating the succulent artichoke base when the leaves have been nibbled. Supply a salad bowl for discarded leaves. Offer a warmed sauce boat of melted butter or Hollandaise sauce in which to dip the leaves.

Note
Globe artichokes can be served with Vinaigrette (see page 347). They can also be stuffed. In this case, they are partly cooled after cooking. The centre cone of tender leaves is then removed to expose the choke, which must be removed. The hollowed centre is filled with a thick savoury cream dip or spread such as creamed smoked salmon.

MOULDED BEETROOT RING

Serves 4-6

1 tbsp gelatine
4 tbsp dry white wine
¼ tsp salt
225 ml (8 fl oz) boiling water
1 tsp clear honey
3 tbsp lemon juice
8-10 thin slices of cucumber
175 g (6 oz) cooked skinned beetroot
Russian Salad (see page 49)

❦ Soften the gelatine in the wine in a large heat-proof jug. Add salt and boiling water, and stir until gelatine dissolves. Stir in the honey and lemon juice.
❦ Pour 4-5 tbsp of this liquid jelly into the bottom of a 700 ml (1 ¼ pint) ring mould. Cut the cucumber slices in half, and arrange in an overlapping ring at the bottom of the mould. Chill until the liquid jelly sets.
❦ Meanwhile, dice the beetroot. Chill the remaining jelly in the jug until it is like thick egg white. Fold in the beetroot. Spoon the mixture gently on top of the cucumber slices, making sure that all the beetroot is covered with jelly. Chill until fully set.
❦ Dip the mould quickly in hot water to the brim. Invert a serving plate over the mould and then turn both the plate and mould over together. Jerk sharply to free the jelly. Chill again, to firm the ring up. Fill the centre with Russian salad.

GREEN BEAN SALAD

Serves 4

350 g (12 oz) young French beans or bobby
    beans
1 medium-large onion
2 tbsp corn oil
1 tbsp lemon juice
salt and pepper

❧ Top and tail the beans and string if necessary.
Peel and slice the onion in very thin rings. Put the
beans and onion into boiling, unsalted water and
cook, covered, until the beans are just tender.
❧ Meanwhile, mix the oil, lemon juice and seasoning in a jug. Whisk well to blend. Drain the vegetables and toss in the dressing while still warm. Cool
and check the seasoning before use.

Note
This classic French starter can be served as part of a
mixed hors d'oeuvre, or by itself in small dishes.

RUSSIAN SALAD

Serves 4-6

2 medium-small boiled potatoes, peeled and
    diced
200-225 g (7-8 oz) cooked cauliflower florets
    with stems trimmed off (from 1 small head)
4 tbsp cooked peas
3 tbsp cooked diced carrot
2 tbsp cooked diced turnip
50 g (2 oz) celery, diced and blanched (1 stalk)
1 small eating apple, peeled, cored, diced and
    dipped in lemon juice (optional)
1 tbsp drained capers
salt and pepper
6-8 tbsp stiff Mayonnaise (see page 346)

Garnish
yolk from 1 hard-boiled egg
grated radish

❧ All vegetables should be quite cold. To use as part
of a mixed hors d'oeuvre or as a filling, season well
and toss all the ingredients with enough mayonnaise
to bind them. Keep in a covered bowl until needed.

❧ To serve the salad on its own as a first course,
layer some chopped egg, meat or shellfish between
two layers of mixed diced vegetables in a bowl, sprinkling each layer with seasoning, and spreading thinly with mayonnaise. Garnish the salad with sieved
hard-boiled egg yolk and a little finely grated radish.

Notes
Russian salad made with just cold cooked vegetables
bound with mayonnaise is useful in a mixed hors
d'oeuvre or for filling Tomato Cups (see page 49).
❧ It tastes fresher made with home-cooked vegetables, but a mixture of canned or frozen and fresh vegetables may be more practical.
❧ To make it a complete first course, add 2 coarsely chopped hard-boiled eggs or about 100 g (4 oz)
cold cooked diced chicken, meat or shellfish.

TOMATO CUPS

Serves 4

4 firm medium-sized tomatoes
soy sauce
4 tsp thick soured cream
shredded lettuce leaves

Filling
4 hard-boiled eggs
3 tbsp mayonnaise
finely chopped parsley or paprika
salt and pepper

❧ Cut the tomatoes in half across. With a teaspoon,
scoop out the seeds, pulp and cores. Sprinkle the
hollowed tomatoes with soy sauce and turn upside
down to drain.
❧ To make the filling, mash or blend the eggs with
the mayonnaise, add a little finely chopped parsley
and season to taste. Turn the cups right way up and
fill, mounding into a dome. Top each mound with a
dab of soured cream and sprinkle with parsley or
paprika.
❧ Serve 2 halves to each person on small plates covered with shredded lettuce.

Filling variations
Mix 3-4 tsp finely chopped fresh herbs into a 225 g
(8 oz) carton of any savoury-flavoured cottage
cheese.
❧ Fill the cups with Russian Salad (see page 49) or
spoonfuls of cold, creamy scrambled egg.

MUSHROOM AND TOMATO SALAD

Serves 4

350 g (12 oz) medium-sized button mushrooms
1 tbsp lemon juice or to taste
pinch of ground coriander
few grains of curry powder
salt and black pepper
2-3 tbsp thick double cream
lettuce leaves
3-4 medium-sized firm tomatoes

❦ Cut the mushrooms into thin slices lengthwise, trimming the stems if very long. Place the mushrooms in a bowl and toss with the lemon juice, spices and a little seasoning. Fold in 2 tbsp of cream. Taste, and add extra lemon juice or seasoning if you wish, or extra cream.
❦ Place in the centre of a bed of lettuce leaves. Slice the tomatoes thinly and lay in an overlapping ring around the mushrooms. Season the slices with pepper. Chill for a few moments before serving.
❦ Alternatively, lay the lettuce leaves on four small plates. Place three or four seasoned tomato slices in the centre of each leaf and put a small pile of mushroom salad on top.

TOMATO & MOZZARELLA SALAD

Serves 4

400 g (14 oz) firm tomatoes
100 g (4 oz) mozzarella cheese, thinly sliced
salt and freshly ground black pepper
1 tbsp finely snipped chives
½ tbsp walnut oil

❦ Discarding the ends, slice the tomatoes into thin rounds. Arrange them in overlapping rings on a flat plate. Cover with the cheese slices. Season lightly with salt and pepper and sprinkle with the chives and walnut oil. Serve at room temperature. This salad makes a good starter.

RATATOUILLE

Serves 4-6

2 medium-sized aubergines
salt
garlic
2 large onions
1 clove garlic
1 green pepper
2-3 courgettes
4-6 tomatoes
4 tbsp olive oil
ground black pepper
good pinch of ground coriander
2 bay leaves, chopped parsley

❦ Slice the aubergines thinly and cover with salt. Leave for 30 minutes.
❦ Meanwhile peel, halve and slice the onions, crush the garlic, slice and deseed the pepper, and slice the courgettes thinly. Skin and quarter the tomatoes.
❦ Heat the oil in a large frying pan. Add the onions, garlic and pepper. Cover and cook over a low heat for 5 minutes without allowing them to brown. Drain and add the aubergine slices. Reduce the heat and simmer for 10 minutes. Add all the other ingredients. Cover again, and cook gently for 30 minutes, stirring occasionally. Remove the bay leaves.
❦ Turn them into a serving dish, if using hot. Alternatively, cool in a covered bowl and serve cold.

LEEKS A LA GRECQUE

Serves 4-6

450 g (1 lb) young leeks

Stock
**6 parsley stalks
few coriander seeds
few fennel seeds
1 sprig fresh or dried thyme
8 black peppercorns
1 bay leaf
2 tbsp olive oil
2 tbsp lemon juice
425 ml (¾ pint) water
¼ tsp salt
½ medium-sized onion
½ celery stalk**

❦ Prepare and wash the leeks, and cut the white stems into 5 cm (2 in) lengths (keep the green leaves for soup). Tie the herbs loosely in a muslin bag. Place all the stock ingredients in a large pan. Bring to the boil, then reduce the heat. Simmer gently for 10 minutes, add the leeks and simmer for 10- 15 minutes longer. The stock should be well reduced and the leeks cooked through. Remove the onion, celery stalk and herb bundle.

❦ Turn out the leeks into a warmed serving dish, if serving hot. Boil down the stock rapidly until there is just enough to coat the vegetables well. Pour over the leeks. If serving cold, leave the leeks to cool in the stock.

Note
The style of cooking in a vegetable stock called 'à la Grecque' suits many vegetables. Any of them can be served hot or cold as part of a mixed hors d'oeuvre or as a first course on its own.

❦ Before cooking, slice courgettes, fennel hearts, celery or leeks; halve or quarter mushrooms or small onions unless tiny; quarter and deseed cucumbers or peppers and cut in pieces; cube aubergines.

❦ Some vegetables can be served raw; they are just heated in the sauce for 2-3 minutes and served hot, or put into the hot sauce and left to cool. Vegetables which need cooking are added to the sauce for the appropriate time while it simmers.

CELERIAC REMOULADE

Serves 4

**450 g (1 lb) celeriac
2 tsp salt
2 tsp lemon juice
4 tbsp Dijon mustard
3 tbsp boiling water
120 ml (4 fl oz) olive oil
2 tbsp white wine vinegar
chopped parsley to garnish**

❦ Peel the celeriac and shred it coarsely. Mix with the salt and lemon juice and leave to stand for about 30 minutes. Rinse well and dry with kitchen paper.

❦ Put the mustard in a warmed, dry mixing bowl. Whisk in the water gradually, with an electric beater if possible. Then whisk in the oil drop by drop at first as for mayonnaise; add enough to make a thick, creamy sauce. Whisk in the vinegar. Fold in the celeriac, cover and refrigerate overnight.

❦ Sprinkle with parsley just before serving.

Note
This classic salad is most often served alone as a starter, but it can also be used as a winter side salad, with cold turkey or game meat. The mustard dressing must not be confused with the mayonnaise-based rémoulade sauce served with grilled meats or fish.

CAULIFLOWER AND WALNUT SALAD

Serves 4-6

**1 small cauliflower broken into florets
75 g (3 oz) chopped walnut pieces
50 g (2 oz) sultanas
1 tbsp chopped fresh mint
150 ml (¼ pint) natural yoghurt
1 tbsp lemon juice
salt and pepper (optional)**

❦ Trim the ends of the cauliflower florets. Mix the florets with the walnuts, sultanas and mint in a bowl.

❦ Mix the yoghurt and lemon juice and use to bind the salad. Season to taste, adding a few more walnuts or sultanas if you wish. Serve in small chilled bowls.

ASPARAGUS

8-12 heads of asparagus per person, depending on thickness

melted butter or Hollandaise Sauce (see page 345)

❧ Scrape hard or coarse stems from the head end downwards. Trim the cut ends of the asparagus spears evenly to a length easy to cook and serve. A spear should stand upright in a jar placed inside the cooking pan with some head-space above it.

❧ Tie the spears in a bundle which will stand upright; place it, tips uppermost in a jar. Put the jar on a mat or cloth in a large pan. Pour in enough boiling water to cover all but the tips of the asparagus.

❧ Cover the pan, and cook at a medium boil for 15–20 minutes or until the spears are tender. Grasp the jar with a thick cloth and remove from the pan. Tip out the spears gently on to a cloth, untie and drain, then lay them gently on a white napkin in a warmed shallow dish. Fold the napkin over the spears until they are served.

❧ Offer with melted butter or Hollandaise sauce served separately in a warmed jug with a spoon or small ladle.

❧ Cook in the same way to serve cold. Cool on the cloth, then use as required.

Note
Asparagus as a starter by itself is best served hot, but is useful as a cold garnish or as a part of a mixed hors d'oeuvre.

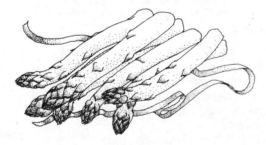

EGG AND CHEESE DISHES

A variety of easy-to-prepare dishes
which need little or no cooking.

EGGS IN JELLY

Serves 4

firmly jellied Consommé (see page 24)
4 round slices of pimento-stuffed olive
2 hard-boiled eggs, shelled
4 round slices of firm liver sausage, slightly
  larger than the moulds used
lettuce leaves

❦ Measure how much consommé is needed by filling 4 round, flat-bottomed moulds three-quarters full with water. The moulds should be deep enough to hold half an egg with about 1 cm (½ in) of head-space. Warm the consommé – just enough to melt it. Then let it cool until it is quite cold but not yet quite setting.
❦ Pour a thin layer into each mould, and place a slice of olive in the centre. Chill until set. Cut the eggs in half across, and place one in each mould, cut side down. Fill the moulds with enough consommé to come about half-way up the sides. Chill again until set. Then fill the moulds almost to the top, covering the eggs. Chill until almost set.
❦ Trim the slices of liver sausage to fit the moulds, and lay one on each mould. Chill until set, cover, and keep chilled until needed. Do not freeze. Unmould to serve, and garnish with lettuce.

EGGS WITH CHEESE & TOMATO SAUCE

Serves 4

4 tbsp Mayonnaise (see page 346)
4 tbsp full-fat soft (cream) cheese or Philadelphia
2 tsp tomato purée (from tube)
¼ tsp dried tarragon
2 tsp tomato juice
1-2 drops lemon juice (optional)
lettuce leaves
4 hard-boiled eggs
chopped parsley to garnish

❦ Beat together until smooth the mayonnaise, soft cheese, tomato purée, tarragon, tomato purée and lemon juice (optional). Shred a few lettuce leaves and spread them as a bed on 4 small plates. Cut the eggs in half across, and place 2 halves, cut side down, in the centre of each plate. Spoon the cheese and tomato mayonnaise on top and garnish with parsley.

Note
Chopped fresh tarragon and mayonnaise made with tarragon vinegar give an extra fresh flavour.

EGGS VAUDOISE

Serves 4-6

2 tbsp butter
50 g (2 oz) cooked, peeled shrimps
6 eggs
salt and pepper
3 tbsp dry white French vermouth
Browned Almonds (see page 367)

❦ Melt the butter and allow to cool slightly. Drain the shrimps.
❦ Beat or whisk the eggs in a bowl with seasoning to taste. While beating, trickle in the melted butter, then the vermouth. Turn the eggs into a frying pan, and scramble them over very low heat until almost set. Remove from the heat and stir in the shrimps.
❦ Turn into a warmed shallow dish, and sprinkle with a few browned almonds. Serve in small shallow dishes at the table and offer hot dry toast.

ANCHOVY-STUFFED EGGS

Serves 4

8 anchovy fillets, drained
milk
8 capers
6 hard-boiled eggs
1 tbsp softened butter
½ medium-sized cucumber, thinly sliced or thin rounds of buttered brown bread
salt
2 wide lemon wedges cut in half across, to garnish

❦ Soak the anchovy fillets in a little milk for 15 minutes. Drain. Chop the fillets finely with the capers.
❦ Shell the eggs, cut in half lengthwise and remove the yolks. Mash the yolks to a paste with the anchovies, capers and butter. Cut a sliver off the rounded bottom of each white so that it stands level. Fill the hollowed whites with the anchovy-yolk mixture.
❦ Arrange the cucumber or bread slices in a bed on 4 plates, sprinkle lightly with salt and arrange 3 egg halves, cut side up, on each bed in a tricorn-hat shape. Place a piece of lemon, skin side up, in the centre of each tricorn.

EGG MAYONNAISE

Serves 4

4 hard-boiled eggs
4 large flat lettuce leaves
150 ml (¼ pint) Mayonnaise (see page 346)
8 anchovy fillets
paprika

❦ Shell the eggs and cut them in half lengthwise. Place the lettuce leaves on 4 small plates. Arrange 2 egg halves, cut side down, on each plate. Spoon the mayonnaise over the eggs. Place an anchovy fillet on each egg half and sprinkle with paprika.

HERB-STUFFED EGGS

Serves 4

6 hard-boiled eggs
6 medium-sized tomatoes, thinly sliced
few drops of vinegar
black pepper
chopped parsley

Filling
1 tsp lemon juice
2 tbsp Mayonnaise (see page 346)
2 tbsp softened butter
1 tbsp finely snipped chives
1 tbsp finely chopped fresh herbs (thyme, marjoram, parsley or savory)
½ tsp dry mustard powder
½ tsp salt
few grains of chilli powder

❦ Shell the eggs and cut them in half across. Scoop out the yolks. Mash the yolks with all the filling ingredients.

❦ Cut a sliver off the rounded bottom of each white so that it stands level. Pile in the filling, mounding it high.

❦ Arrange the tomato slices in a bed on each of 4 small plates. Sprinkle with the vinegar, pepper and parsley. Arrange 3 egg halves, cut side up, on each bed and sprinkle with a little more pepper.

❦ If possible, use fresh, new-laid eggs for boiling hard. The raw whites are thick and viscous, and fill most of the shell. With age or in warm conditions, the whites become thin and watery, the air space at the rounded end enlarges, and the yolk no longer rests in the centre of the egg.

EGGS IN CREAM

Serves 4

4 eggs (new-laid if possible)
2 hard-boiled eggs
150 ml (¼ pint) double cream
pinch of paprika
salt and black pepper

❦ Warm 4 individual ramekins or small bowls. Hard-boil the new-laid eggs for the minimum time;

crack and place under running water immediately. Hold each egg in turn in a cloth, shell and quarter them.

❦ While the eggs are cooking, shell those that are already hard-boiled. Discard the whites (or keep them for a soup garnish). Crumble the yolks.

❦ Pour the cream into a small pan, and add the paprika and seasoning. Bring to the boil very slowly and simmer, stirring, until the cream thickens (within 2 minutes). Tip in the quartered eggs and turn in the cream to coat. Spoon 4 egg quarters into each ramekin or bowl with some cream sauce. Garnish with crumbled egg yolk.

TOMATOES WITH BLUE BRIE CREAM

Serves 4

1 leek, white stem only, salt
8 firm medium-sized tomatoes
2 small celery stalks from centre of head
pepper
100 g (4 oz) blue Brie-style cheese with rind scraped off
2 tbsp double cream
¼ tsp grated spring onion
4 tbsp French Dressing (see page 347)

❦ Slice the leek finely and blanch in lightly salted boiling water for 4 minutes until tender. Drain and cool. Cut off the smooth ends of the tomatoes and carefully take out the seeds and cores with a teaspoon. Drain upside down.

❦ Dice the celery finely and season lightly. Work the cheese with the back of a spoon until soft, then work in the cream. Chop and add 2 tbsp of the leek. Mix with the celery.

❦ Fill the hollowed tomatoes with the cheese-celery mixture. Replace the tops if you wish. Scatter the remaining leek on 4 small plates, and place the tomatoes on top, cut side up. Mix the grated onion into the French dressing, and spoon it over them.

MOCK CRAB

Serves 4

3 hard-boiled egg yolks
2 tbsp corn oil
1 tsp onion salt
1 tsp clear honey
1 tsp mixed English mustard
1 tbsp white wine vinegar
225 g (8 oz) Red Leicester cheese, shredded on
    the coarsest part of a grater
2 tbsp cooked white chicken meat, minced or
    shredded
lettuce leaves
tomato purée (from tube)

❦ Sieve the egg yolks. Keep 1 rounded tbsp of yolk
aside for garnishing. Work the rest to a smooth paste
with the oil, using the back of a spoon. Mix in the
onion salt, honey and mustard. Blend thoroughly.
Gradually add the vinegar to make a smooth, semi-
liquid sauce.
❦ Mix the cheese and chicken lightly with a fork,
keeping the cheese shreds separate. Mix in the sauce
lightly. Chill well.
❦ Lay the lettuce leaves in a bed on a shallow oval
dish. Spread the mixture in a slightly mounded layer
on top. Garnish with thin lines of sieved egg yolk and
tomato purée piped from the tube. Serve on small
plates at the table and offer hot dry toast.

TOMATO ASPIC MOULDS

Serves 4

2 tbsp gelatine
725 ml (1 ¼ pints) tomato juice
few drops of Worcestershire sauce or lemon
    juice (optional)
salt and pepper
75 g (3 oz) Mozzarella cheese
1 bunch of washed watercress to garnish

❦ Soften the gelatine in 150 ml (¼ pint) cold tomato juice. Heat the remaining 575 ml (1 pint) juice in
a pan. Take off the heat, and stir in the softened gelatine. Stir until the gelatine has dissolved. Flavour
with Worcestershire sauce or lemon juice (optional)
and season to taste. Pour about one-third of the aspic

into a 725 ml (1 ¼ pint) ring mould, or 4 individual
moulds. Chill until set. Keep the remaining mixture
at room temperature.
❦ Cut the cheese into 1 cm (½ in) dice. When the
chilled juice is firm, scatter with the cheese cubes.
Cover with the remaining juice which should be
cooled but still liquid. Chill again until firm.
Unmould on a serving plate or small plates, and garnish the centre of a ring mould with the watercress.
Use a few sprigs to scatter round individual moulds.
❦ Liver sausage rolled into marble-sized balls or
diced cooked vegetables can be used instead of
cheese.

PRINCESS COCKTAILS

Serves 4

1 quantity Curry Mayonnaise (see page 347)
2 tbsp seedless raisins
150 g (5 oz) Gruyère cheese in one piece
2 rings pineapple canned in natural juice
1 tbsp flaked almonds
4 maraschino cherries, drained

❦ Pour boiling water on the raisins and leave to
stand for 5 minutes. Cut the cheese into 1 cm (½ in)
dice. Drain the pineapple and cut each ring into 12
segments.
❦ Divide the mayonnaise between 4 stemmed
dessert glasses. Drain the raisins and mix all the salad
ingredients except the cherries. Pile on top of the
mayonnaise and top each 'cocktail' with a cherry.

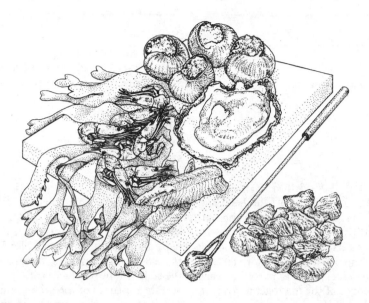

FISH & SHELLFISH DISHES

This selection of fish and shellfish dishes contains many old favourites with interesting variations.

GREENWICH WHITEBAIT

Serves 4

450 g (1 lb) whitebait
salt and pepper
pinch of curry powder or cayenne
   pepper
40 g (1 ½ oz) plain flour
oil for deep-frying

Garnish
parsley sprigs
lemon wedges

❦ Make sure that the whitebait are completely dry by patting them with kitchen paper. Mix the salt, pepper, curry or cayenne with the flour and coat the fish lightly.

❦ Heat the oil to 180C (350F). Put about one-third of the whitebait into frying basket and place in the oil. Shake them as they cook for 3 minutes until just coloured. Drain and place on a warm serving dish. Repeat the process with the other fish.

❦ Return all the fish to the frying basket. Let the oil reheat to the correct temperature and return the fish to the pan for about 1 ½ minutes, shaking the basket as they become golden and crisp.

❦ Drain quickly on kitchen paper and serve very hot with parsley and lemon wedges to garnish, and an accompaniment of thin brown bread and butter.

BAKED WHITING IN FOIL

Serves 4

4 small whiting
salt and pepper
50 g (2 oz) butter or margarine
lemon juice

Garnish
chopped parsley
lemon wedges

❦ Heat the oven to 180–190C (350–375F) mark 4–5.
❦ Clean the fish if required, cut off the head and
fins, and trim the tails square. Rinse inside and out,
and pat dry with soft paper.
❦ Lay each fish on a rectangle of foil large enough
to enclose it. Season the fish inside, dot with fat, and
sprinkle with lemon juice. Make a 'parcel' of each
fish by folding the edges of the foil together over it,
and twisting the foil at the head and tail ends.
❦ Lay the foil 'parcels' on a baking sheet. Bake for
20–25 minutes. To see if ready, run a poultry skewer through the foil into the fish which should be tender to the touch of the skewer.
❦ To serve, transfer from the foil to warmed plates,
pour any juices in the package over the fish and
sprinkle with chopped parsley. Offer lemon wedges
for squeezing.

Notes
Whole small fish such as trout, red mullet or whiting baked in foil make a good hot first course or light
meal because they are simple to prepare and serve,
and need no attention while cooking.
❦ If the oven is needed for the main course, they can
be baked in odd free corners or kept warm for a while
on the oven floor, without cross-flavouring other
foods or creating cooking odours. They can either be
presented as 'parcels' at the table, or be transferred
to warmed plates for serving.

SEAFOOD TOWERS

Serves 4

2 small hard-boiled eggs
Two 215 g (7 ½ oz) cans of red salmon
5 tbsp Mayonnaise (see page 346)
1 tsp tomato ketchup
1 large firm tomato
2 flat soft rolls
butter for spreading
salt and black pepper
paprika

❦ Shell the eggs, cut them in half across, and set
aside.
❦ Drain the salmon and mash it with the mayonnaise and ketchup until well blended. Cut the tomato across into four slices, discarding the ends. Split
the rolls and butter each half.
❦ Pile a quarter of the salmon mixture on the buttered side of each roll, and flatten it into a thick layer.
Place a tomato slice on top, and season it well. Cap
with half an egg, cut side down; sprinkle a little
paprika on top.
❦ Serve one 'tower' on each of four small plates.

SALMON COCKTAIL

Serves 4

175 g (6 oz) cooked, fresh or canned salmon
  without skin or bone
1 tbsp dry white vermouth
150 g (5 oz) unpeeled cucumber
100 g (4 oz) full-fat soft cheese
1 tsp lemon juice
salt and pepper

❦ Drain the salmon, if necessary, and flake roughly. Sprinkle with vermouth and divide between 4
dessert glasses.
❦ Cut 4 thin slices of cucumber for garnishing and
set aside. Cut the remaining cucumber into chunks.
Place the chunks with the cheese and lemon juice in
a food processor or blender and process until the
cheese is a pale green cream with tiny pieces of
cucumber. Season to taste.
❦ Spoon the cucumber cream over the salmon.
Chill. Just before serving, cut the reserved cucumber slices into butterflies or other decorative shapes,
and place one on each cocktail.

HERRING ROE SAVOURIES

Serves 4

4 very large tomatoes
225 g (8 oz) mixed hard and soft roes
25 g (1 oz) butter
salt and pepper
few drops of Worcestershire sauce
25 g (1 oz) grated Parmesan cheese
4 small slices buttered toast

❦ Heat the oven to 180C (350F) mark 4.
❦ Cut a thick slice from the top of each tomato.
Scoop out the insides, leaving a thick 'wall'. Discard
the seeds but reserve the pulp and liquid.
❦ Fry the roes in the butter until just firm. Mix with
the tomato pulp and liquid and season well with salt,
pepper and Worcestershire sauce.
❦ Pile into the tomato cases and sprinkle with
cheese. Put into a dish and bake for 20 minutes.
Serve each tomato on a piece of buttered toast.

CREAMED HERRING ROES

Serves 4

450 g (1 lb) soft herring roes
25 g (1 oz) plain flour
salt and pepper
50 g (2 oz) butter
275 ml (½ pint) single cream
2 tsp lemon juice
4 slices wholemeal toast
1 tbsp fresh parsley, chopped

❦ Rinse the roes under cold running water. Drain
well and pat dry with kitchen paper. Season the flour
well with salt and pepper and dust the flour lightly
over the roes.
❦ Melt the butter and fry the roes for 5 minutes
over a low heat, turning them often. Stir in the cream
and lemon juice and bring just to the boil.
❦ Pour over the toast and sprinkle with parsley.

ANCHOIADE

Serves 4

100 g (4 oz) can anchovy fillets
2 garlic cloves, crushed
3 tbsp olive oil
1 tbsp lemon juice
pepper
Four 5 cm (2 in) thick slices of French bread
1 tbsp fine breadcrumbs
1 tbsp fresh parsley, chopped

❦ Heat the oven to 190C (375F) mark 5.
❦ Chop the anchovy fillets and put into a bowl with
the oil from the can. Mash with a spoon and work in
the garlic, olive oil, lemon juice and pepper.
❦ Spread on the slices of French bread and put on
a lightly oiled baking sheet. Sprinkle with breadcrumbs and parsley. Bake for 15 minutes.
❦ Serve as a first course with a salad garnish, or as
a snack.

DEVILLED SPRATS

Serves 4

450 g (1 lb) sprats
50 g (2 oz) plain flour
2 tsp mustard powder
1 tsp cayenne pepper
salt and pepper
oil for deep frying
lemon wedges to serve

❦ Gut the fish through the gills, leaving the heads and bodies intact. Dry the fish with kitchen paper.
❦ Season the flour with the mustard, cayenne pepper, salt and pepper. Coat the fish evenly. Deep-fry in hot oil for 3-4 minutes until crisp and golden.
❦ Serve with lemon wedges.

SMOKED TROUT OR MACKEREL

Serves 4

4 whole fish or fillets
lemon wedges
watercress sprigs
horseradish sauce
shredded lettuce (for fillets)

❦ If you have whole fish, skin them. It is usual to leave the head and tail on, but these can be removed if you wish. Lay the fish on plates and garnish with the lemon wedges and watercress. Offer horseradish sauce and bread and butter separately.
❦ Skin fillets with care; if thin, they may break up. Lay them, flesh side up, on shredded lettuce, then garnish and treat like whole fish.

SMOKED SALMON

Serves 4

8 slices of smoked salmon
lemon wedges
watercress to garnish

❦ If possible, buy freshly sliced smoked salmon. For serving as it is, the salmon should be cut in paper-thin slices from the tail and towards the head. Serve the slices flat or folded, with lemon wedges, a mill of black pepper, and thin brown bread and butter. Garnish with watercress.
❦ Thicker scraps of smoked salmon from coarser parts of the side can be shredded and used to make patés, mousses, omelettes, etc. Smoked salmon and scrambled egg is another classic 'hot and cold' starter.

PRAWN COCKTAIL

Serves 4

225 g (8 oz) peeled prawns
1 crisp lettuce heart
150 ml (¼ pint) Mayonnaise (see page 346)
2 tsp concentrated tomato purée
few drops of Tabasco sauce
pinch of sugar
paprika
4 lemon slices
4 prawns in shell (optional)

❦ Use wide wine glasses for serving this popular first course.
❦ If the prawns are frozen, make sure that they are thawed and well drained. Shred the lettuce finely and divide between the glasses.
❦ Mix the mayonnaise with tomato purée, Tabasco sauce and sugar. Mix with the prawns and divide between the glasses.
❦ Sprinkle with paprika. Cut a slit in each lemon slice and suspend on the rim of each glass. If available, hang a prawn in a shell over each glass. Serve at once.
❦ For a cocktail base with a crunchy texture, use Chinese leaves or very finely shredded white cabbage instead of lettuce. Finely diced celery, eating apple or cucumber may be mixed into the base or used on their own.

KIPPER SALAD

Serves 4-6

8 kipper fillets
6 tbsp olive or nut oil
3 tbsp white wine vinegar
2 tsp French mustard
2 tsp dill seed (or dill weed)
pepper
lettuce or Chinese leaves

❧ Skin the raw kipper fillets by inserting a sharp pointed knife under the skin and stripping back the skin carefully. Cut the fillets into 1 cm (½ in) thin strips. Place in a bowl.
❧ Mix the oil, vinegar, mustard, dill and pepper and pour over the kippers. Cover and leave in a cool place for 12-24 hours, stirring the mixture occasionally.
❧ Arrange the lettuce or Chinese leaves on a serving dish and spoon on the kipper pieces and dressing.
❧ Serve as a first course with thin brown bread and butter.

TARAMASALATA

Serves 4

175 g (6 oz) smoked cod's roe, skinned
2 small garlic cloves, peeled
25 g (1 oz) soft white breadcrumbs
3 tbsp lemon juice
4-5 tsp olive oil
2 tsp cold water
black pepper

❧ Place the cod's roe in a bowl and squeeze the garlic over it. Mash with the breadcrumbs and lemon juice until free of lumps. Gradually whisk in alternating small amounts of the olive oil and water until the mixture has the consistency and flavour you prefer, and season with pepper. The mixture should be creamy but not too liquid, or it will separate on standing. Chill well. Serve in small bowls with warmed pitta bread and lemon wedges.
❧ Taramasalata can also be used as a spread or dip, depending on the consistency.

POTTED SHRIMPS

Serves 4-6

285 g (10 oz) unsalted butter
400 g (14 oz) peeled shrimps
4 tsp ground cloves
¼ tsp ground mace
¼ tsp white pepper

❧ Melt 225 g (8 oz) of the butter in a pan. Add all the other ingredients. Heat gently, stirring, until well blended. Turn into small ramekins and cool.
❧ When cold, melt the remaining butter until just liquid but not coloured. Strain over the ramekins without letting the milky liquid at the base of the pan go through the strainer. Chill until firm.
❧ Serve one to each person with lemon wedges and brown bread and butter.

OYSTERS ON THE HALF SHELL

Buy oysters from a reliable fish supplier and make sure they are tightly closed. If possible, ask an expert to open them just before serving.

If you prepare them at home, scrub them well, then open as follows. Hold each in turn in a cloth or gloved hand, with the deeper shell downwards; work the point of a sharp knife into the hinge between the shells, then cut the ligament which holds them together. (You can buy a special oyster knife for doing this.) Open the oyster carefully, remove its beard, and loosen it from the shell but leave it in place.

As a rule, serve 6 oysters in the deep shells to each person. Arrange them on plates, season lightly, and supply lemon wedges, Tabasco sauce or cayenne pepper, a mill of black pepper and thin brown bread and butter.

Small oysters, fresh or canned, can be used in cooked 'au gratin' and similar dishes, or can be mixed with a little cream sauce as a filling for vol-au-vents, patties etc.

Canned smoked oysters are drained, piled on small plates, then served with lemon wedges, black pepper and thin brown bread and butter.

Smoked sprats are arranged on plates and served in the same way.

ANGELS ON HORSEBACK

Serves 6

12 streaky bacon rashers
24 oysters, shelled
pinch of salt
pinch of pepper
pinch of paprika
1 tbsp fresh parsley, chopped
3 slices bread
butter

❦ De-rind the bacon and stretch with the back of a knife. Cut each rasher in half and place an oyster on each piece. Sprinkle with the seasonings and parsley. Roll the bacon round each oyster and secure with a cocktail stick or piece of stout cotton.

❦ Grill until the bacon is crisp, turning the oyster bundles once. Remove the cotton or sticks.

❦ Meanwhile toast the bread, butter well and cut each slice in half. Place 4 bacon-wrapped oysters on each piece of buttered toast and serve at once as a savoury course or as a light snack. Angels on Horseback may be served on cocktail sticks with drinks.

POTTED CRAB

Serves 4

100 g (4 oz) butter
1 tsp pepper
1 tsp ground mace
pinch of cayenne pepper
225 g (8 oz) crab meat
juice of ½ lemon

❦ Heat 25 g (1 oz) of the butter and add seasonings. Stir in the crab meat and lemon juice, and stir well until the crab is hot but not brown.

❦ Spoon into a serving dish or into 4 individual ramekins, and press down gently. Leave until cold.

❦ Melt the remaining butter until just liquid but not coloured. Strain over the crab without letting the milky liquid at the base of the pan go through the strainer. Leave until cold and set.

❦ Serve with hot toast and lemon wedges.

SMOKED MACKEREL POTS

Serves 4

2 fillets smoked mackerel
275 ml (½ pint) Cheese Sauce (see page 339)
1 tsp made mustard
25 g (1 oz) fresh brown or white breadcrumbs
25 g (1 oz) Parmesan cheese, grated

❦ Heat the oven to 200C (400F) mark 6.

❦ Skin the mackerel and remove any bones. Break the fish into large flakes and mix with the cheese sauce and mustard. Put into 4 greased individual oven-proof dishes. Mix the breadcrumbs and cheese and sprinkle on each dish.

❦ Bake for 15 minutes. If the cheese sauce is freshly made and hot, the pots will not need baking but may be placed under a hot grill for 5 minutes.

❦ Serve as a first course, or as a light meal with salad.

MARINATED HADDOCK

Serves 4

2 tbsp dried, sliced onions
350 g (12 oz) raw smoked haddock fillet, skinned
1 tsp chopped fresh mixed herbs as available (not mint)
black pepper
juice and grated rind of 1 large lemon
3 tbsp olive oil
lettuce leaves

❦ Soak the onions in scalding water for 5 minutes. Cut the haddock fillet into short thin strips and lay side by side in one or two flat (non-metal) dishes.
❦ Drain the onions and scatter them on top. Sprinkle with herbs and pepper. Mix the lemon juice, rind and oil in a jug and pour over the fish.
❦ Cover and marinate for 12-24 hours in a cool place, turning the strips over occasionally.
❦ Lay the fillet strips on lettuce leaves spread on small plates, and serve with wholemeal bread and butter.

MARYLAND CRAB CAKES

Serves 4

450 g (1 lb) crab meat
1 tbsp Mayonnaise (see page 346)
2 tsp Worcestershire sauce
1 egg yolk
1 tsp salt
1 tsp mustard powder
½ tsp pepper
1 tsp freshly chopped parsley
flour
beaten egg
dry breadcrumbs
oil for frying

❦ Place the crab meat in a bowl and mash lightly with a fork. Work in the mayonnaise and Worcestershire sauce with the egg yolk. Season with salt, mustard and pepper and add the parsley.
❦ Form the mixture into 8 flat cakes, pressing the mixture together firmly with the hands. Dip each in flour, then in beaten egg and finally in dry bread-crumbs. Fry quickly on both sides in shallow hot oil.
❦ Serve hot or cold with lemon wedges and a salad garnish. If liked, the crab cakes may be made small and bite-sized to serve as cocktail snacks.

SEAFOOD BUFFET ROLL

Serves 4-6

1 small carrot, finely chopped
1 small onion, finely chopped
25 g (1 oz) butter
2 tsp plain flour
225 g (8 oz) lobster, scampi or prawns
4 tbsp single cream
3 tbsp dry sherry
salt and pepper
225 g (8 oz) Puff Pastry (see page 360)
egg for glazing

❦ Heat the oven to 220C (425F) mark 7.
❦ Cook the carrot and onion in the butter over a low heat until the onion is soft and golden. Add the flour and cook for 30 seconds over a low heat. Remove from the heat and stir in the seafood, cream and sherry. Season to taste and leave to cool.
❦ Roll out the pastry thinly in a rectangle. Spread the seafood mixture over it, leaving about 2.5 cm (1 in) clear around the edges. Brush the edges with beaten egg and roll up like a Swiss Roll. Place on a baking tray and brush well with beaten egg. Bake for 30 minutes. Serve hot or cold in thick slices.
❦ This makes an excellent buffet dish with salads, but also makes an elegant lunch or supper dish with new potatoes and peas or French beans.

MEAT & POULTRY DISHES

*Most of the dishes in this section are fairly substantial
and thus are very suitable for buffet spreads or as
starters preceding light main course or salads.*

COLD PARSLEYED HAM

Serves 4

450 g (1 lb) piece of ham, cubed
275 ml (½ pint) well-flavoured stock
75 ml (3 fl oz) white wine
¼ tsp nutmeg
15 g (½ oz) packet powdered gelatine
2 tbsp tarragon vinegar
3-4 tbsp parsley
finely chopped cucumber and lettuce to garnish

❦ Simmer the ham in stock, wine and nutmeg for 5
minutes, and leave to cool.

❦ Dissolve the gelatine in a little water by heating
in a pan containing 2.5 cm (1 in) of water. Strain the
ham and add the stock to gelatine, followed by the
vinegar.
❦ Use some gelatine mixture to paint the sides and
bottom of a 1.2 litre (2 pint) mould or straight-sided
dish. Sprinkle parsley liberally around the mould
and leave to set. Leave the remainder of the gelatine
until on the point of setting.
❦ Mix the cubed ham with the remainder of the
parsley and tip the mixture into mould. Pour over
the gelatine. Do not stir as this will disturb the coating. Leave in a cool place to set firmly, preferably
overnight.
❦ When required, turn out and decorate with
cucumber slices and twirls, lettuce shreds or other
appropriate garnish.

MELON WITH PARMA HAM

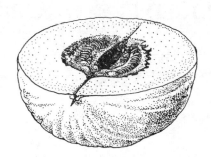

Serves 4

1 firm, ripe honeydew melon (or other green-
    fleshed melon)
12 slices Parma or Westphalian ham

❦ Cut sixteen 6 x 2 cm (2½ x ¾ in) sticks of melon.
Arrange four sticks diagonally on each individual
serving plate. Loosely roll-up the slices of ham.
Place a roll of ham between each of the melon sticks.
❦ Serve with brown bread and butter.

HAM, PEAR AND ALMOND ROLLS

Serves 4

1 large firm eating pear
juice of ½ lemon
100 g (4 oz) full-fat soft (cream) cheese
25 g (1 oz) Browned Almonds (see page 367)
salt and pepper
4 large thin slices cooked ham

Garnish
2 firm tomatoes, quartered
small lettuce leaves

❦ Peel, halve and core the pear. Cut into 1 cm (½
in) cubes. Toss in lemon juice, coating completely,
and drain. Set aside.
❦ Sieve the cheese into a bowl. Fold in the pear
cubes and browned almonds. Season.
❦ Lay the ham slices flat, and place a quarter of the
filling across the one end of each slice. Roll up the
slices around the filling. Trim the ends of the rolls
neatly.
❦ Lay on small plates garnished with tomato quarters and lettuce leaves. Serve with thin brown bread
and butter.

VEAL GALANTINE

Serves 8-12

1.5 kg (3 lb) breast of veal in one piece
450 g (1 lb) good quality sausage meat
225 g (8 oz) gammon or bacon in small cubes
3 hard-boiled eggs, whole or sliced
1 onion
¼ tsp thyme
¼ tsp parsley
1 bay leaf
1 level tbsp powdered gelatine

❦ Bone out the veal and keep the bones.
❦ Lay the breast out flat, skin side down. Spread the
sausage meat and chopped gammon or bacon evenly
over the veal. Add the eggs, either as a line down the
middle, or as a layer of sliced egg over the meats. Roll
up and sew together with cotton, leaving the end
hanging free. Wrap firmly in foil, or greaseproof
paper and pudding cloth.
❦ Place the bones in a large pan with the onion and
herbs. Place the galantine on top. Cover with water.
Bring to the boil and then simmer for 2-3 hours,
until tender. (Using a pressure cooker reduces this
time to 1 hour.)
❦ Remove the galantine and press it between two
plates until cold. Reduce the cooking liquor to 275
ml (½ pint) by boiling rapidly. Strain, discarding the
bones.
❦ Sprinkle the gelatine on to the reduced liquor and
stir to dissolve. Use on the point of setting, to glaze
galantine, which can be left whole, or carved into
overlapping slices.
❦ Serve as part of a buffet with various salads, or for
a picnic, or packed lunch.

SLICED BEEF IN ASPIC

Serves 4

8 slices of rare roast beef
cooked carrot, sliced
cooked button onions
fresh herb leaves

Aspic
425 ml (¾ pint) well-flavoured stock
150 ml (¼ pint) Madeira wine
1 packet or 4 tsp gelatine
1 tsp Worcestershire sauce
pinch cayenne pepper

❦ Place the meat in a shallow serving dish arranged in overlapping slices. Decorate by placing the carrot and onions between the slices. Arrange the herb leaves on top.
❦ Heat the stock and Madeira. Sprinkle on gelatine and leave to dissolve. Add Worcestershire sauce and cayenne pepper. Cool until aspic is syrupy. Glaze the beef and chill. Place the remaining aspic in another shallow dish and, when set, cut into cubes. Use chopped aspic to decorate the meat by forming two rows on either side of it.
❦ Serve with a salad or as part of a buffet table.

CHICKEN AND SHRIMP COCKTAILS

Serves 4

2 tsp dried sliced onions
4-6 lettuce leaves
150-175 g (5-6 oz) cooked white chicken meat
50 g (2 oz) cooked or canned peeled shrimps
2 tsp finely chopped parsley
1 tsp lemon juice
¼ tsp Worcestershire sauce
3 tbsp double cream
150 ml (¼ pint) Mayonnaise (see page 346)
salt and pepper

❦ Soak the dried sliced onions in boiling water for 5 minutes.
❦ Tear up the lettuce leaves and use to line 4 dessert bowls or stemmed dessert glasses.

❦ Dice or chop the chicken meat. Drain and add the onion. Set 12-16 shrimps aside for garnishing, and add the remainder to the chicken with the parsley.
❦ Stir the lemon juice, Worcestershire sauce and cream into the mayonnaise, and season to taste. Mix with the chicken and shrimps.
❦ Divide between the bowls or glasses, and garnish with the reserved shrimps.

CHAUD-FROID OF CHICKEN

Serves 4

4 small cooked chicken breasts, skinned and
    boned (about 65 g /2 ½ oz when prepared)
4 tbsp Aspic Jelly (see page 337)
4 tbsp thick Mayonnaise, chilled (see page 346)
4 pimento-stuffed olives
lettuce leaves

❦ Trim the chicken breasts neatly, and place on a wire cooling rack over a baking sheet.
❦ Place the aspic jelly in a heatproof jug. Stand the jug in hot water and stir until the jelly dissolves. Remove from the heat.
❦ Place the mayonnaise in a chilled bowl, and stir in the melted jelly little by little until evenly blended. Chill until the mixture reaches a thick coating consistency. Slice the olives into three rounds each, discarding the ends.
❦ Spoon the thick mayonnaise mixture over the chicken pieces. Leave in a cool place until almost set, then garnish each piece with three olive slices. Leave to set firmly. Arrange the chicken pieces on lettuce leaves laid on individual plates.
❦ The chaud-froid sauce is equally good on white fish fillets or cold, poached salmon cutlets or pieces. Garnish with capers.

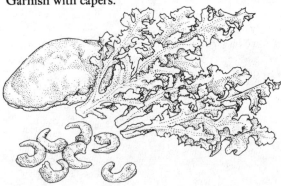

STUFFED CABBAGE OR VINE LEAVES

Serves 4-6

225 g (8 oz) cooked minced meat
225 g (8 oz) cooked rice (75 g/2 ½ oz uncooked)
2-3 spring onions, chopped
1 level tsp caraway seeds
25 g (1 oz) cashew or pine kernel nuts, chopped
1 tbsp tomato purée
1 egg
20-30 small cabbage or vine leaves
575 ml (1 pint) light stock or wine and stock
    mixture
4 tbsp oil

❦ Heat the oven to 150C (300F) mark 2. Make the stuffing by combining all the ingredients, except the leaves, stock and oil.
❦ Blanch the leaves in boiling water until pliable, about 2 minutes. It is sometimes easier to remove cabbage leaves without them tearing if the whole cabbage is boiled for a few minutes, then a few leaves removed and the process repeated.
❦ Divide the mixture between the leaves, ensuring there is not too much in each so that a good tight roll can be achieved. Roll up the leaves, tucking the sides in to form compact parcels.
❦ Pack closely together in an ovenproof dish, forming a second layer if necessary. Mix the stock and oil and pour over the stuffed leaves. Cover with a lid or foil and cook for 1 hour until the stock has been absorbed.
❦ Serve hot with a sauce such as tomato, or well chilled as a starter or buffet dish.

CHOPPED LIVER

Serves 4-6

450 g (1 lb) chicken livers
salt
175 g (6 oz) onions, peeled
2 tbsp chicken fat or oil
3-4 hard-boiled eggs
salt and pepper

Garnish
lettuce leaves
sliced tomatoes

❦ Rinse the chicken livers, cut into small pieces and salt well. Grill until they give off no more blood.
❦ Chop the onions, and fry in the chicken fat or oil until soft but not brown. Finely mince together the livers, onions and two or three of the hard-boiled eggs. Season well and mix to a paste with a little of the frying fat if needed.
❦ Shape into a mound or block. Chop the remaining egg finely and sprinkle on the liver in an attractive pattern. Garnish the base of the mound with lettuce and tomato.

SNAILS

Serves 4

coarse salt
215 g (7 ½ oz) can snails
24-30 Burgundy snail shells
1 quantity Garlic Butter (see page 344)

❦ Heat the oven to 200C (400F) mark 6.
❦ For each person, cover a large deep plate with a thick layer of coarse salt, and make hollows for 6-8 snail shells. In the same way, prepare with salt a large baking sheet which will hold all the snail shells.
❦ Drain the snails and put one (or two if tiny) in each shell. Tuck them well in. Cover thickly with the garlic butter. Place the shells, open side up, in the hollows on the baking tray. Place in the oven for 6 minutes or until the butter is melted and very hot.
❦ Using tongs or a cloth, transfer the snails to the plates and serve at once with hot dry toast.

PATES, TERRINES AND MOUSSES

*An interesting selection of pâtés and mousses,
ranging from Housekeeper's Pâté to Anchovy Mousse.*

It is seldom practical to make a pâté for just 4–5 people. Pâtés, terrines and mousses tend to be rich dishes, and the quantity needed for 4 first-course helpings would be too small to garnish and display attractively as a single dish. It is more usual therefore to make a larger quantity which will serve at least 6–8 people and to expect to serve it at a second meal. Most pâtés freeze perfectly if required.

SOFT ROE PATE

Serves 4-6

225 g (8 oz) soft roes
salt and pepper
150 g (5 oz) butter
1 tbsp lemon juice
1 tbsp fresh parsley, chopped

❦ Season the roes with salt and pepper. Melt 25 g (1 oz) of the butter in a frying pan and fry the roes lightly until cooked through, which will take about 10 minutes.
❦ Mash the cooked roes with a wooden spoon. Soften the remaining butter and work into the roes and mix well until smooth and evenly coloured. Mix with lemon juice and parsley and spoon into a serving dish.
❦ Serve with hot toast or brown bread and butter.

SUMMER FISH TERRINE

Serves 6-8

100 g (4 oz) courgettes
100 g (4 oz) French beans
100 g (4 oz) carrots
900 g (2 lb) cod or haddock
50 g (2 oz) fresh white breadcrumbs
4 tbsp double cream
2 tbsp French mustard
2 tbsp lemon juice
2 tbsp dry vermouth
salt and pepper

❦ Heat the oven to 180C (350F) mark 4.
❦ Wipe the courgettes but do not peel them. Trim the ends and cut into sticks the same size as the beans. Peel the carrots and cut into strips the same size as the beans. Blanch each vegetable in boiling water for 5 minutes. Drain and dry well and keep to one side.
❦ Skin the fish and mince (or use a food processor) with the breadcrumbs, cream, mustard, lemon juice and vermouth. Season well with salt and pepper.
❦ Butter a 1 litre (2 pint) terrine or loaf tin. Spread one-quarter of the fish mixture over the base. Arrange the beans lengthwise on top. Spread on a second quarter of fish mixture and top with the carrots arranged lengthwise. Put on the third quarter of the fish mixture, the courgettes lengthwise and the final layer of fish.
❦ Cover with a buttered piece of greaseproof paper and foil or a lid. Place the container in a roasting tin containing 2.5 cm (1 in) water. Bake for 50 minutes. Leave to stand for 30 minutes.
❦ Drain off any liquid and unmould on a serving dish. Slice carefully and serve warm or cold as a first course, or with salad.

SARDINE PATE

Serves 4

225 g (8 oz) canned sardines in oil
150 g (5 oz) cream cheese
2 hard-boiled eggs, finely chopped
2 tsp lemon juice
salt and pepper

❦ Put the sardines and oil into a bowl and add the cream cheese. Mash well with a fork. Work in the eggs but do not mash them. Season well with lemon juice, salt and pepper. Place in a serving dish and chill for 1 hour before using.
❦ Serve with toast or crusty bread, or as a spread for cocktail biscuits.

SMOKED HADDOCK MOUSSE

Serves 4

225 g (8 oz) smoked haddock fillets
275 ml (½ pint) natural yoghurt
2 hard-boiled eggs, finely chopped
1 tsp lemon rind, grated
2 tsp lemon juice
2 tsp gelatine
2 tbsp water
salt and white pepper
paprika

❦ Poach the haddock until just tender, cool and remove the skin and any bones. Flake the flesh finely and mix with the yoghurt. Add one of the eggs with the lemon rind and juice.
❦ Sprinkle the gelatine on the water in a cup and stand it in a pan of hot water. Heat gently until the gelatine is syrupy. Cool and stir into the fish mixture. Season well with salt and pepper.
❦ Spoon into 4 ramekins. Chill for 1 hour. Sprinkle with the remaining egg and dust with paprika.

BLOATER PASTE

Serves 4

4 bloaters
100 g (4 oz) butter, softened
squeeze of lemon juice
pepper

❦ Grill the bloaters until cooked through. Cool and remove the skin and bones. Flake the flesh and mix with the butter. Mash with a fork or spoon until smooth and well mixed. Season to taste with lemon juice and pepper, and press into a serving dish.
❦ Serve with hot toast or as a sandwich filling.

SALMON MOUSSE

Serves 4-6

225 g (8 oz) can red or pink salmon
½ lemon
salt and pepper
3 drops Tabasco sauce
150 ml (¼ pint) natural yoghurt
150 ml (¼ pint) Mayonnaise (see page 346)
4 tsp gelatine

Garnish
lemon slices
parsley, chopped

❦ Drain the salmon and remove the skin and bones. Mash with a fork. Add the grated rind and juice of the half lemon, the salt, pepper, Tabasco sauce, yoghurt and mayonnaise and mix thoroughly until evenly coloured.
❦ Put 1 tablespoon water into a cup and sprinkle on the gelatine. Put into a pan containing a little hot water and heat gently until the gelatine has dissolved and is syrupy.
❦ Stir into the salmon mixture. Cool and just before the mousse sets, spoon into a serving dish or into 4–6 individual dishes. Chill for 2 hours.
❦ Garnish with lemon slices and parsley just before serving.

SMOKED SALMON PATE

Serves 4

225 g (8 oz) smoked salmon trimmings
25 g (1 oz) unsalted butter, softened
1 tbsp dry sherry
1 tbsp lemon juice
pepper
6 tbsp double cream

❦ Cut the salmon into small pieces. Put into a liquidizer with the butter, sherry and lemon juice, and blend until smooth. Season with pepper and add the cream. Blend just long enough to mix the ingredients. Spoon into a serving dish and chill.
❦ Serve with hot toast and lemon wedges, or spread on small biscuits to serve with drinks.

INSTANT SALMON PATE

Serves 4

450 g (1 lb) cold cooked salmon without skin or bone, or one 440 g (15½ oz) can of red salmon
5 tbsp softened unsalted butter
1 tbsp sherry
½ tsp bottled anchovy sauce
pinch of ground mace
salt and pepper
4 thick slices of cucumber

❦ Drain the canned salmon and remove any bones. Flake fresh or canned salmon. Pound, or beat with an electric mixer to reduce to shreds (a food processor tends to reduce it to a grainy purée).
❦ Beat in 1-2 tbsp of the butter, then the sherry, anchovy sauce and mace; season very lightly. Beat in the remaining butter, then taste and adjust the seasoning. Turn into 4 individual pots or ramekins, level the tops and chill to firm up.
❦ Meanwhile, salt the cucumber slices well and place on a tilted plate for 30 minutes. Pat dry with soft paper. Chop the slices finely, and pat dry again. Sprinkle on the pâté just before serving.

SMOKED COD'S ROE PATE

Serves 4-6

175 g (6 oz) smoked cod's roe
2 garlic cloves, crushed,
1 lemon, rind and juice
salt and pepper
8 tbsp olive oil
6 tbsp double cream

❦ Mash the cod's roe with the garlic cloves. Add the grated lemon rind and juice and season well. Gradually work in the oil and finally stir in the cream.
❦ The mixture may be blended in a liquidizer or food processor. Chill for 1 hour before serving with warm buttered toast.

ANCHOVY MOUSSE

Serves 4

50 g (2 oz) can anchovy fillets, drained
milk
yolks of 3 hard-boiled eggs
6 tbsp Mayonnaise (see page 346)
3 tbsp double cream
good pinch of chilli powder
whites of 2 raw eggs
chopped parsley to garnish

❧ Cover the anchovy fillets in milk and soak for 15 minutes. Drain, and chop finely.
❧ Place all the ingredients except the egg whites in a food processor or blender, and blend until almost smooth. There will still be tiny flecks of anchovy.
❧ Turn the mixture into a bowl.
❧ Whisk the egg whites stiffly and stir 1 tbsp into the anchovy mixture. Fold in the remainder gently. Turn the mixture very carefully into 4 decorative small bowls and chill for at least 2 hours.
❧ Garnish with a little chopped parsley and serve with fingers of hot dry toast.

SMOKED MACKEREL PATE

Makes 600 g (1 ¼ lb)

50 g (2 oz) unsalted butter in small knobs
450 g (1 lb) smoked mackerel fillets
salt and black pepper
1 tbsp tomato purée
2 tbsp double cream
2 tbsp lemon juice
2 tbsp finely chopped fresh parsley
pinch of ground mace
few grains of cayenne pepper

❧ Soften the butter. Skin the fish fillets, discarding any bones. Mash the fish, and season lightly. Put the fish with half the butter and the tomato purée in a liquidizer or food processor. Blend until just mixed.
❧ Slowly add the remaining butter and the other ingredients in order, blending briefly after each addition. Purée the mixture to the consistency you prefer, then taste and adjust the seasoning if needed. Turn into a suitable container, taking care to knock

out any pockets of air. Cover the pâté and chill.
❧ Use within 36 hours, or freeze for up to 1 month.

KIPPER MOUSSE

Serves 4-6

350 g (12 oz) kipper fillets
275 ml (½ pint) single cream
25 g (1 oz) butter
25 g (1 oz) plain flour
275 ml (½ pint) milk
salt and pepper
2 eggs, separated
15 g (½ oz) gelatine
juice of ½ lemon
2 tbsp water

❧ Poach the kipper fillets until cooked through. Cool and remove the skin and bones. Break up the fish and put into a liquidizer with the cream. Blend until smooth. Melt the butter and stir in the flour.
❧ Cook over a low heat for 1 minute, stirring well. Remove from the heat and work in the milk. Cook over a low heat and bring to the boil, stirring well. Remove from the heat, season with salt and pepper and beat in the egg yolks.
❧ Sprinkle the gelatine on the lemon juice and water in a cup. Stand it in a pan of hot water and stir until syrupy. Stir into the white sauce. Cool to lukewarm and fold the sauce into the kipper mixture.
❧ Whisk the egg whites to soft peaks and fold into the fish. Spoon into a 750 ml (1 ½ pint) soufflé dish or into individual dishes. Leave in a cool place to set and chill for 1 hour before serving.
❧ The mousse may be garnished with thin slices of cucumber or lemon, or with sliced stuffed olives.

LIVER PATE

Makes 900 g (2 lb)

lard for greasing
350 g (12 oz) belly of pork without rind
450 g (1 lb) pigs' liver or pigs' liver and chicken
    livers, mixed
3 shallots, finely chopped
50 g (2 oz) soft white breadcrumbs
2 tbsp chopped parsley
½ tsp ground ginger
good pinch of grated nutmeg
2 tsp salt
¼ tsp ground black pepper
1 tbsp brandy
1 tbsp port or Madeira
2 tbsp double cream
3 fresh bay leaves

❦ Choose an oblong terrine, deep baking dish or loaf tin which has a capacity of 1.2 litres (2 pints). Grease well with lard. Place in a baking or roasting tin, and pour enough water into the tin to reach halfway up the sides of the dish. Remove the dish, and place the tin on the centre shelf of the oven. Heat the oven to 180C (350F) mark 4.
❦ Cut the meat and liver into small pieces, removing any gristle, tubes or membrane. Mince the meats together three times, using the finest cutter, or process in batches in an electric blender until smooth. Mix in thoroughly all the other ingredients except the bay leaves. Press the pâté firmly into the dish, leaving no air pockets. Level the top, and arrange the bay leaves diagonally in the centre. Cover the dish tightly with greased foil and place in the tin in the oven. Bake for 1 ½-1 ¾ hours. When done, the pâté will have shrunk slightly and its fat and juices will run clear yellow when the top is pressed. Cool the pâté under an even weight, then chill for 24-48 hours before cutting. Serve from the dish, garnished with chopped parsley, or turn out and place on a serving dish. Cut in slices for serving.

Variation
Pack a good half of the pâté evenly in the dish, then add a 3 mm (⅛ in) layer of seasoned cooked spinach, which has been well drained and pressed dry, before the adding the rest of the pâté.

HOUSEKEEPER'S PATE

Serves 4-6

175 g (6 oz) cooked game meat without skin and
    bone
175 g (6 oz) cooked dark chicken or turkey meat
100 g (4 oz) thick gammon or bacon rashers
    without rind
4 tbsp game or strong chicken stock
2 tbsp brandy
4 tbsp softened butter
salt and black pepper
few grains of cayenne pepper
75 g (3 oz) small mushrooms, coarsely chopped
2 spring onions (green parts only)

❦ Cut the game and poultry meat into small pieces, discarding any bone splinters and gristle. Cut the gammon or bacon into small pieces.
❦ Fry the gammon pieces in their own fat, until cooked through and lightly browned. Remove, leaving the fat in the pan.
❦ Place all the meat in a food processor or blender and process until finely shredded, in batches if necessary. Add the stock and brandy while processing. Stop the machine, add the butter and process again until well blended. Season to taste.
❦ If you do not have a processor or blender, mince the meats 2 or 3 times, then work in the liquids and butter to make a well blended mixture. Season.
❦ Put the chopped mushrooms and 1 chopped spring onion top in the frying pan, and simmer in the bacon fat until soft. Grease with butter a 18 x 9 x 6 cm (7 x 3 ½ x 2 ½ in) loaf tin.
❦ Turn half the meat mixture into this and press down evenly making sure that the corners are filled. Scatter the cooked mushrooms and spring onion on top. Cover with the remaining meat mixture in an even layer. Cover and chill until wanted.
❦ Turn out to serve, and garnish with the remaining finely chopped spring onion green. Serve this low-fat pâté with brown bread and butter or offer apricot chutney.

CHICKEN AND MUSHROOM PATE

Serves 4-6

450 g (1 lb) chicken meat (white or brown) without skin or bone
100 g (4 oz) lean pork
2 streaky bacon rashers without rind
100 g (4 oz) pork sausage meat
40 g (1 ½ oz) soft white breadcrumbs
175 g (6 oz) button mushroom caps, chopped
1 small onion, chopped
1 tomato, deseeded and chopped
2 tsp finely chopped fresh herbs (not mint) or 1 tsp dried mixed herbs
1 egg
salt and black pepper

❦ Grease an 18 x 9 x 6 cm (7 x 3 ½ x 2 ½ in) loaf tin, and heat the oven to 170C (325F) mark 3.
❦ Mince together the chicken meat, pork and bacon. Mix together the minced meat and sausage meat in a bowl. Work in the breadcrumbs, mushrooms, onion and tomato. Add the herbs. Beat the egg until liquid and use to bind the pâté mixture. Season to taste and turn into the tin, pressing well down into the corners. Cover tightly with greased foil.
❦ Stand the loaf tin in a baking tin, and pour in cold water to a depth of about 1 cm (½ in). Place in the oven and bake for 1-1 ½ hours, until the pâté begins to shrink and any free fat is translucent. Pour off the free fat, and leave the pâté in a cool place under a light weight for several hours until quite cold. Chill.
❦ Turn out and serve in slices or squares with hot toast and butter.

CHICKEN LIVER PATE

Serves 4-6

225 g (8 oz) chicken livers
100 g (4 oz) butter
1 shallot, finely chopped
1 garlic clove, finely chopped
salt and pepper
1 tbsp brandy
good pinch of mixed dried herbs
clarified butter

❦ Remove any sinews from the livers. Melt 25 g (1 oz) butter in a frying pan, and cook the shallot and garlic until soft. Add the livers and sauté briskly (about 10-12 minutes) until the liver is firm to the touch.
❦ Cool the liver, then rub through a fine sieve, mince, or liquidize. Cream the remaining butter and beat into the liver mixture. Season well, and add the brandy and herbs. Place in a china pot, or in small cocottes. Smooth over the top and cover with clarified butter. Store in the refrigerator, and use as required.
❦ Clarified butter is butter which has been 'cleared' by heating until it foams, and then by skimming and straining off the clear yellow oil, leaving the milk solids behind.

COLD EGG MOUSSE

Serves 6-8

4 tbsp Aspic Jelly (see page 337)
5 hard-boiled eggs
salt and pepper
pinch of paprika
few drops of Worcestershire or Harvey's sauce
2 tsp sherry
175 ml (6 fl oz) double or whipping cream
chopped parsley

Garnish
chopped aspic jelly

❦ Melt the jelly in a heatproof jug standing in hot water. Chill until cold but still liquid.
❦ Meanwhile, separate the eggs. Reserve the whites, and sieve the yolks into a bowl. Mix in a sprinkling of salt and pepper, a pinch of paprika and the Worcestershire or Harvey's sauce and sherry. Stir or beat in the liquid aspic to make a smooth liquid mixture; chill until gummy.
❦ Meanwhile, chop the egg whites into very small pieces and whip the cream until semi-stiff and about 275 ml (½ pint) in volume.
❦ Fold the whipped cream into the egg-yolk mixture so that no streaks remain; beat it briefly if necessary. Fold in the chopped whites. Turn the mixture into a 700 ml (1 ¼ pint) soufflé dish, and chill until set. Garnish with chopped aspic jelly. Serve from the dish, with hot dry toast.

TWO-CHEESE MOUSSE

Serves 4-6

2 ½ tsp gelatine
3 tbsp cold water
150 g (5 oz) Brie
4 tbsp double cream
5 tbsp milk
100 g (4 oz) cottage cheese, sieved
2 egg whites
4 thin slices of cucumber to garnish

❦ Soften the gelatine in the water in a heatproof container. Stand the container in scalding hot water and stir until the gelatine dissolves. Set aside.
❦ Cut the rind off the cheese as thinly as possible. Cut the cheese paste into small pieces if solid. Beat with an electric or hand mixer, gradually adding the cream, milk and cottage cheese, or put them all into a food processor, and process briefly until smooth. Beat in the gelatine mixture or add it to the processor and blend in. If made in a processor, turn into a bowl.
❦ Whisk the egg whites until they are fairly stiff. Stir 1-2 tbsp into the cheese mixture to loosen it, then fold in the rest as lightly as possible. Turn the mixture gently into a soufflé dish and chill until set.
❦ Shortly before serving, cut the cucumber slices in half and use to garnish the top of the mousse. Serve from the dish with Rolled Brown Bread and Butter (see page 15).

SAVOURY
PASTRIES

*Both hot and cold, savoury pastries make excellent
buffet food, snacks and starters.*

CURRY PUFFS

Makes 16

65 g (2 ½ oz) Choux Pastry (see page 364) with
 1 rounded tsp curry powder added with the
 flour
100 g (4 oz) cream cheese
1 rounded tsp finely chopped gherkins
paprika

❦ Heat the oven to 220C (425F) mark 7. Arrange
two shelves in the top half of the oven. Grease and
flour two baking sheets. Drop or pipe the pastry on
to the baking sheet, either with a teaspoon or in a
forcing bag with a 1 cm (½ in) plain pipe. Keep the
pieces of dough well apart.

❦ Cook for 10 minutes then reduce the temperature
to 160C (325F) mark 3 and continue for a further 20-
30 minutes until a warm honey brown and well risen.
Cool at once on a wire rack out of the draught. Make
a little slit in the sides of each puff to let out the
steam.

❦ Mix the cream cheese and gherkins together. Cut
each choux bun in half and fill with the mixture.
Replace the top half and dust it lightly with a little
paprika.

❦ If a teaspoon is used to drop the pieces of pastry
on to the baking tray, first dip it in water before each
bun is formed. The pieces of pastry will then slip off
the spoon more easily.

SAVOURY PROFITEROLES

Makes 18

65 g (2 ½ oz) Choux Pastry (see page 364) with salt and pepper added
25 g (1 oz) butter
25 g (1 oz) plain flour
275 ml (½ pint) milk
pinch of nutmeg
1 tsp chopped parsley
200 g (7 oz) can salmon

❦ Heat the oven to 220C (425F) mark 7. Prepare the shelves and baking sheets and cook the profiteroles exactly as for Curry Puffs (see page 75).
❦ Melt the butter in a pan. Stir in the flour and cook over a low heat for 1 minute. Remove from the heat and add the milk by degrees, beating continuously. Return to the heat, bring to the boil, and simmer for 2-3 minutes stirring all the time. Add nutmeg and seasoning. Put into a bowl and stir in the parsley.
❦ Remove all bones and skin from the salmon, flake it, and fold into the sauce. Enlarge the slit in the sides of the cooled profiteroles and fill with mixture.
❦ For alternative fillings see below.

HAM FILLING

100 g (4 oz) cooked ham
50 g (2 oz) apricot chutney
50 g (2 oz) butter
pepper

❦ Mince the ham. Stir in the chutney and butter and season to taste with pepper.

CHICKEN FILLING

100 g (4 oz) cooked chicken
50 g (2 oz) butter
salt and pepper
½ tsp Worcestershire sauce

❦ Mince the chicken finely. Beat in the butter, season generously and stir in the Worcestershire sauce.

SAVOURY ECLAIRS

Makes 18

65 g (2 ½ oz) Choux Pastry (see page 364) with salt and pepper added
100 g (4 oz) smoked salmon
3 tbsp Béchamel Sauce (see page 340)
lemon juice
black pepper

❦ Heat the oven to 220C (425F) mark 7. Grease and flour two baking sheets. Fill a forcing bag fitted with a 1 cm (½ inch) plain pipe with the choux. Pipe 6 cm (2 ½ inch) lengths on to the baking sheets, keeping well apart.
❦ Cook for 10 minutes then reduce the temperature to 160C (325F) mark 3 and continue for a further 20-30 minutes, until a warm honey brown and well risen. Slit the sides and cool on a wire rack out of the draught.
❦ Mash the salmon with a fork. Stir in the béchamel sauce and season well with lemon juice and black pepper. Split the éclairs in half. Fill the bottom halves with the mixture and replace the tops.

PRAWN AND ASPIC TARTLETS

Makes about 12

about 150 ml (¼ pint) aspic jelly (made from aspic jelly powder)
175 g (6 oz) Flaky Pastry (see page 361)
75-100 g (3-4 oz) frozen prawns
fennel or dill to garnish

❦ Make the aspic jelly according to the instructions.
❦ Heat the oven to 220C (425F) mark 7. Roll out the pastry as thinly as possible and cut into rounds with a 5 cm (2 inch) fluted cutter to fit patty tins. Position the pastry in the tins, pressing gently in with a little ball of pastry. Bake blind (see page 314). Cool on a wire rack.
❦ Defrost the prawns in warm water. Drain and pat dry. Put 1 or 2 prawns into each tartlet. Spoon the cold aspic, almost at setting point, over the prawns. Leave to set.
❦ Garnish each tartlet with the smallest feather of fennel or dill.

SEAFOOD PUFFS

Makes 15-18

450 g (1 lb) Shortcrust Pastry (see page 357)
40 g (1 ½ oz) butter
25 g (1 oz) plain flour
200 ml (1/3 pint) single cream
50 g (2 oz) Parmesan cheese, grated
225 g (8 oz) crab meat
50 g (2 oz) prawns, peeled
salt and pepper
1 egg yolk
1 ½ tbsp dry sherry

❧ Heat the oven to 200C (400F) mark 6. Roll out the pastry thinly and line individual tart tins. Bake blind (see page 314) for 10 minutes. Cool and remove from the tins and place on an ovenproof serving plate.
❧ Melt the butter and stir in the flour. Cook for 1 minute over a low heat. Remove from the heat and gradually stir in the cream. Cook very gently until the sauce thickens.
❧ Add half the cheese and stir until smooth. Remove from heat and stir in the crab meat and prawns. Season well and beat in the egg yolk and sherry.
❧ Spoon the mixture into the pastry cases and sprinkle with the remaining cheese. Put under a hot grill until the surface of the puffs is golden.
❧ Serve hot as a first course or with drinks.

CREAM CHEESE ECLAIRS

Makes 18

65 g (2 ½ oz) Choux Pastry (see page 364) with salt and pepper added
50 g (2 oz) shelled walnuts
100 g (4 oz) cream cheese
½ tsp Home-made Mustard (see page 366)

❧ Heat the oven to 220C (425F) mark 7. Prepare the shelves and baking sheets and cook the éclairs exactly as for Savoury Eclairs (see opposite).
❧ Chop the walnuts finely. Stir these into the cream cheese together with the mustard. Split the éclairs in half. Fill the bottom halves with the mixture and then replace the respective tops.

❧ Savoury éclairs, after being filled, are sometimes finished with a brushing of aspic jelly sprinkled with finely chopped salted almonds.

CHILLI WHIRLS

Makes about 30

350 g (12 oz) Puff Pastry (see page 360)
350 g (12 oz) minced beef
75 g (3 oz) red and green peppers, mixed
1 small onion, peeled
1 tsp mild chilli powder (not powdered chilli)
4 tbsp home-made Tomato Sauce (see page 341) or bought
salt
2 tsp cornflour
2 tbsp water
1 egg to glaze
75 g (3 oz) strong Cheddar cheese

❧ Heat the oven to 220C (425F) mark 7. Roll out the pastry to a 30 cm (12 inch) square. Cut in half and leave to relax.
❧ Fry the beef, finely chopped peppers and onion together in a pan until brown. Stir in the chilli powder, tomato sauce, salt and cornflour blended in the water. Cook for a few minutes, stirring well. Cool.
❧ Trim the edges of the pastry. Spread the mince over each piece to within 2.5 cm (1 inch) of the edge. Brush one edge of each with beaten egg. Roll up towards the egg-washed edges to form two rolls with the join underneath. Lift each roll on to a baking sheet lined with baking paper. Brush with beaten egg. Cut each roll into 15 slices, putting each piece flat on the baking paper as you cut it. (It does work out all right.)
❧ Sprinkle grated cheese on top of each whirl. Cook for about 20 minutes until golden and puffed up; watch them carefully.
❧ All the ingredients for these can be in your freezer or store cupboard and they are a change from the everlasting burger. They freeze perfectly. Re-heat to crisp up.
❧ When buying mince, think carefully. 'Minced beef' can be all sorts of beef minced and may be fatty and even have bits of gristle in it. Minced beef steak may be called 'minced chuck steak' and will be tender and lean, though more expensive. It is worth it every time to buy home-produced mince, of whatever quality, from a reputable source.

SMOKED COD'S ROE TARTLETS

Makes about 12

175 g (6 oz) Pâte Brisée or Rich Shortcrust
    Pastry (see page 359)
100 g (4 oz) smoked cod's roe
1 hard-boiled egg
few stuffed olives

❦ Heat the oven to 200C (400F) mark 6. Roll out the
pastry very lightly and cut into rounds about 9 cm (3
½ inches) across with a fluted cutter. Line patty tins
with the pastry. Cut out rounds of greaseproof paper
and line the tarts. Bake blind (see page 314) for 15
minutes. Remove the paper and beans and bake for
another 5 minutes or so. Cool on a wire rack.
❦ Skin the roe and mash with a fork. Chop the hard-
boiled egg as finely as possible and fold into the roe.
Fill the pastry cases very neatly with the mixture,
and top with a slice of stuffed olive.

INDIVIDUAL HAND-RAISED PORK PIES

Makes 6-8

350 g (12 oz) Hot Water Crust Pastry (see page
    362)
450 g (1 lb) lean pork
salt and pepper
½ tsp mixed herbs
3 tbsp stock
1 egg to glaze
Aspic or Savoury Jelly (see page 337)

❦ Keep the pastry warm. Heat the oven to 200C
(400F) mark 6.
❦ Mince the meat coarsely, season well and stir in
the herbs and stock.
❦ Raise the little pies with thumb and finger
straight on a baking sheet lined with baking paper.
Work the pastry as thin as will hold the filling. Fill
with the meat. Brush the edges with beaten egg.
Cover with the lids. Brush all over with beaten egg.
❦ Cook for 30-40 minutes. Cover lightly with
greaseproof paper and cook for another 30 minutes.
❦ When cool, fill with savoury jelly.

SMALL HAND-RAISED CHICKEN PIES

Makes 6

350 g (12 oz) Hot Water Crust Pastry (see page
    362)
350 g (12 oz) cooked chicken
salt and pepper
100 g (4 oz) mushrooms
2 rashers smoked bacon
1 egg to glaze
aspic jelly

❦ Keep the pastry warm. Heat the oven to 200C
(400F) mark 6.
❦ Cut the chicken into small pieces. Be sure there
are no tendons, skin or bone in it. Season well. Wipe
and slice the mushrooms. Trim the bacon carefully
and snip into small pieces.
❦ Sizzle the bacon in a frying pan, add the mushrooms and cook together for a minute or two. Spoon
on to the chicken and mix together.
❦ Divide the pastry into six portions and keep it
warm in a covered bowl. Take one piece. Cut off
one-third for the lid. Pat the larger piece into a scone
shape and place on baking paper on a baking sheet.
With the thumbs inside and the fingers outside gently shape the pastry into a hollow. Raise the little pie:
4 cm (1 ½ in) high and 5 cm (2 in) across is perfectly manageable.
❦ Fill it firmly with the chicken mixture. Neaten
the top. Brush the edge with beaten egg. Roll out the
lid and press it on. Flute the edge. Make the rest of
the pies. When all are on the baking tray, cut some
small leaves and roses from the trimmings. Make a
small hole in the top of each pie. Sit a rose in the hole
and put one or two leaves around it. Brush all the
pies with beaten egg – the sides as well as the top.
❦ Cook for 40 minutes or until the pies are brown
and shiny. Cool. Fill through the holes under the
roses with cool aspic jelly and leave to set.
❦ These pies should be made a day before they are
needed.

HARVEST SAUSAGE ROLLS

Makes 10-14, depending on size

225 g (8 oz) Wholemeal Shortcrust Pastry (see page 358)
wholemeal flour for dusting
1 egg (size 5 or 6)
½ tsp dried sage
225 g (8 oz) pork sausage meat
25 g (1 oz) bran

❦ Heat the oven to 200C (400F) mark 6. Roll out half the pastry in a strip about 20 x 10 cm (11 x 4 in). Do the same with the other half. Leave the strips to relax.

❦ Beat the egg and mix half of it into the sausage meat with the sage. Wash and dry your hands and dust in wholemeal flour. Mould the sausage meat into two rolls. Put one on each of the strips of pastry. Brush beaten egg along one edge of each and fold over. Press the edges firmly together. Brush each roll with beaten egg and sprinkle with bran.

❦ Cut diagonally to make individual sausage rolls. Put on a baking sheet and bake for 20-30 minutes. Cool on a wire rack.

❦ Eat hot or cold. Home-made Mustard (see page 366) makes these sausage rolls even more delicious.

FENNEL AND HAM SAVOURY PUFFS

Serves 2

175 g (6 oz) Puff Pastry (see page 360)
2 fennel bulbs
salt and pepper
25 g (1 oz) butter
25 g (1 oz) plain flour
275 ml (½ pint) chicken stock
4 tbsp milk
2 tbsp tomato purée
75 g (3 oz) cooked lean ham

❦ Roll out the pastry. Cut two circles to cover individual ovenproof bowls, about 12.5 cm (5 in) across. Leave the pastry to relax. Heat the oven to 220C (425F) mark 7.

❦ Wash the fennel. Trim the tops and slice off the base. (Use the trimmings for the stock pot.) Cut into thick slices and cook in boiling salted water for 15 minutes.

❦ Make a quick sauce by putting the butter, flour, stock and milk into a saucepan and whisking over a low heat until thick and creamy. Stir in the tomato purée and season well. Chop the ham finely and stir into the sauce.

❦ Divide the fennel between the dishes, pour the sauce over the fennel and leave to cool a little. Put the pastry circles lightly on top of the fennel in the dishes. Brush with milk.

❦ Cook for 20 minutes or until puffed and golden brown. The pastry circles sit, crisp and light, on top of the savoury fennel mixture.

CUCUMBER AND CHICKEN CUPS

Makes 14

175 g (6 oz) Shortcrust Pastry (see page 357)
about 350 g (12 oz) cooked white chicken meat
¼ cucumber
4 tbsp home-made Mayonnaise (see page 346)
salt and pepper
watercress to garnish

❦ Heat the oven to 200C (400F) mark 6. Roll out the pastry to a thickness of 5 mm (¼ inch). Cut out 14 rounds using a fluted cutter to suit the deepest patty pans you have. Line the tins and bake blind (see page 314). Cool on a wire rack.

❦ Cut the chicken meat into 1 cm (½ in) cubes. Dice the cucumber (do not peel it). Fold both into the mayonnaise. Season, and use to fill the tartlets.

❦ Serve very cold, topped with a small sprig of watercress.

FISH AND SEAFOOD

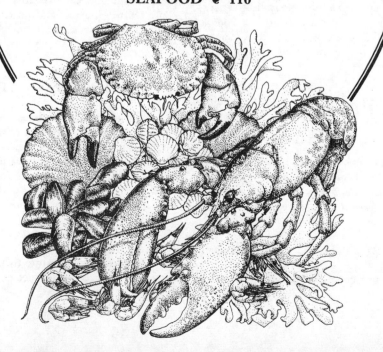

ABOUT FISH

Fish is an important source of food. It is nourishing and very quick to prepare. In these health-conscious days, it is important to remember that fish is an excellent source of protein, vitamins and minerals, and that fish oil is polyunsaturated, which helps to lower the body's cholesterol level. Calorific value varies, with 100 g (4 oz) of herring having 190 calories compared to 90 calories in the same amount of sole, but this compares to 350 calories for the same quantity of lamb chop.

There are so many different varieties of fish that menus can be endlessly changed, and a couple of fish meals a week can scarcely be a hardship. Even those who prefer meat will not scorn a fish cocktail or pâté to start a meal, while flans and sandwiches may incorporate fish in a way which appeals to the young.

There is a fishmonger in most towns, while villages are often served by a travelling van. Supermarkets now often have a fresh fish department or a special chilled cabinet. However, we need never be deprived of fish in even the most remote areas, for there is now a wide variety of frozen fish available as well as that traditional favourite – smoked fish. There is also canned fish, which is nutritious and tasty and can be turned into some splendid meals.

In this book you will find more than a hundred recipes for fish and their accompanying sauces, about enough for two meals a week to last a whole year. It is hoped that you will want to cook some of them even more often because they will quickly become family favourites.

❧ Choosing and Using ❧ Fish

Frozen and canned fish will have been prepared to exacting standards, so there is no problem in choosing the required quality. Fresh fish, however, needs to be chosen with care and there are one or two easy points to remember.

White fish fillets should be a white translucent colour and a neat shape.
Whole fish should have clear bright eyes, shiny colourful skin, firm flesh and a fresh sea smell.
Smoked fish should have a fresh smoky smell, and the fillets should be neat and firm.
Shellfish should be undamaged in shells and closed tightly without cracks. Ready-cooked shellfish should be moist with a fresh look and smell.

❧ Preparation ❧ and storage

A good fishmonger will clean, bone and fillet fish if required, and will also skin fillets or whole fish if necessary. He has the expertise and the sharp knife to do the job, and will always be happy to co-operate with special preparation if you have an unusual dish in mind (but don't expect too much attention on a busy weekend morning).

Fresh fish should be used as soon as possible, but may be stored in the refrigerator overnight if washed, patted dry and covered.

Frozen fish should be stored at - 18C (0F) or colder, as indicated on the packet. Usually frozen fish may be cooked immediately, but if it is to be defrosted, this is best done overnight in the refrigerator. It should not be thawed in water as it will quickly lose texture, flavour and nutritional value. Fish from the fishmonger should not be frozen, but fish straight from the sea or river may be frozen at home.

❧ Types of fish ❧

One of the advantages of choosing fish is that many species are interchangeable. Whole fish may be bought, as well as fillets and steaks. Fish are basically divided into white and oily varieties. Some white and oily fish are also sold smoked or salted. Shellfish is now often known as 'seafood' and for culinary purposes may be recognised as being of the crustacean or mollusc type.

White fish
There are two types of white fish, divided into flat and round. Large round species such as cod and

coley may be sold whole or prepared as fillets, steaks or cutlets. The smaller round fish such as whiting and haddock may be whole or filleted. All these round fish are interchangeable in recipes, varying slightly in flavour and texture.

Large flat fish like turbot and halibut are very special, and may be whole or in fillets and steaks, trimmed as required. Smaller flat fish include plaice, Dover sole and lemon sole, sold whole or in fillets.

Unusual flat fish include the monkfish (angler-fish) of which only the tail is eaten, tasting rather like scampi and with a similar texture. Skate is another delicious flat fish, of which the 'wings' are generally sold, ready-skinned. Odd round fish include the conger eel, the rather ugly John Dory, grey mullet, and red mullet which has a slightly 'gamy' flavour and is usually eaten uncleaned. If you do not recognise these fish, the fishmonger will be glad to tell you about them and to prepare them for cooking.

Oily fish
These tend to be smaller than other species, and are a particularly rich source of vitamins A and D. Herring, mackerel and sprat are the most commonly found, and they are sold whole, though often boned or filleted for cooking. Salmon also comes into this group.

Smoked and salted fish
Some white fish may be smoked, particularly cod, haddock and whiting, although smoked halibut is sometimes found, and is a delicacy. Smoked salmon and trout are often regarded as special occasion fish. The herring is one of the most adaptable fish, being salted or marinated, but also being smoked and appearing as the kipper or bloater. The small sprat may also be smoked and served on special occasions. Recently, mackerel has become a very popular smoked fish, and may be prepared in two ways. Cold smoked mackerel and kippers have a smoky flavour but are still raw and must be cooked. Hot smoked mackerel is prepared at a higher temperature so that the flesh cooks and the fish are ready to eat.

Seafood (shellfish)
Scallops, mussels, oysters, cockles, whelks and winkles are distinguished by their very hard shells. Oysters are generally eaten raw and can be opened by the fishmonger (if you have to do the job yourself, the shell is opened by inserting a knife through the hinge of the shell). Scallops and the smaller Queens may be sold in the shell or loose, and the deep shell is used for serving the cooked dish.

Mussels need to be scrubbed and the 'beards' removed before steaming open, but the fishmonger may have a supply of freshly cooked ones. The same applies to cockles and whelks. Winkles are sold ready-cooked but still in the shell.

Lobsters, crabs, prawns, shrimps and scampi (Dublin bay prawns) are recognised by their bright pinky-red shells when cooked. Prawns, shrimps and scampi may be sold in the shell or ready-peeled. Crabs and lobsters are generally sold boiled but not prepared, but some fishmongers sell dressed crabs.

Canned fish
A wide variety of fish is canned in oil, brine or sauce. Popular varieties include sardines, salmon, tuna, pilchard and mackerel, but it is also possible to find kipper fillets, herring roes, prawns, shrimps, clams and oysters. All are useful for the store cupboard.

❦ Cooking fish ❦

Whichever method is chosen, fish should never be overcooked. The flesh should be just set so that it remains moist and full of flavour.

Boiling
This is only recommended for large pieces of fish. The fish should be rubbed with lemon juice to keep it firm and white, then cooked in hot salted water or Court Bouillon (see page 337). Cook the fish in a large shallow pan or fish kettle, if possible in a piece of muslin or foil so that the fish can be lifted out without breaking. Bring the liquid to the boil and then simmer very gently until the fish is just cooked and ready to flake away from the bone. Timing depends on the thickness and shape of the fish, but usually 10-15 minutes per 450 g (1 lb) is enough. Drain the fish well before serving.

Poaching
Small pieces of fish or small whole fish may be cooked in this way. If poaching fillets, fold or roll them before cooking. Use milk, fish stock, or a mixture of milk and water in a saucepan or frying pan, and half-cover the fish with liquid. Simmer gently for 10 minutes per 450 g (1 lb). Drain and use the cooking liquid for an accompanying sauce.

Steaming
Thin pieces and fillets are best suited to steaming. Place the fish directly in a steamer over a pan of boiling water, and allow 15 minutes to 450 g (1 lb) plus

15 minutes for large fish (fillets will take 20 minutes). Small fillets or cutlets may be cooked on a greased deep plate with 1 tablespoon milk and seasoning over a pan of boiling water, covered with a second plate or lid – this method is particularly attractive for invalid dishes.

Shallow-frying

Allow just enough fat or oil to prevent the fish sticking, and use a shallow pan. When the fat or oil is just smoking, cook the fish quickly on both sides for a few minutes until golden brown, and finish cooking gently until the flesh loosens from the bone. For shallow-frying, the fish may first be lightly coated with flour; or with flour, then milk and flour again; or with flour, beaten egg and breadcrumbs. The fish should not be prepared in any of these ways until just before frying.

Butter-frying

A simple and delicious frying method suitable for fillets of flat fish and for small whole fish, if not more than 1 cm (½ in) thick. Dip the fish in seasoned flour, shake off the surplus, and then cook on both sides in hot butter. For 4 fillets, allow 50 g (2 oz) butter and cook for about 5 minutes each side. Place the fish on a serving dish without draining. Add a knob of extra butter to the pan and when hot and frothy, add the juice of half a lemon. Pour over the fish and sprinkle with chopped fresh parsley.

Deep-frying

The fish should be coated with egg and breadcrumbs (see Shallow-frying above) or coated with Coating Batter (see page 365). Use a deep pan and wire basket and enough fat to come three-quarters of the way up the pan. Use oil, clarified beef fat or lard, and make sure that the fat is pure and free from moisture. Heat the fat to 180-190C (350-375F). Put the fish into the wire basket and place in the hot fat. When the fish is golden, lift out the basket from the fat and drain the fried fish well on absorbent kitchen paper.

Stir-frying

A new and popular way of cooking fish quickly which uses only a small amount of oil. Use a wok or sauté pan and a tablespoon of oil (peanut oil is particularly good). Heat the pan and add finely chopped seasonal vegetables and small cubes of fish. Toss quickly over the heat and serve as soon as the fish has become opaque.

Grilling

Fillets and cutlets may be grilled after being seasoned and sprinkled with lemon juice and brushed well with melted butter or oil. The time taken under a medium grill is from 3-7 minutes on each side, depending on the thickness of the fish. Since fish tends to stick to the wire grill rack, it is best to line the grill pan with foil and to place the fish directly on this (which also makes the pan easier to clean). Whole fish should be scaled first and scored two or three times with a sharp knife on each side.

Barbecuing

Brush the fish well with oil, lemon juice and herbs, and baste it occasionally during cooking, so that the fish remains moist.

Baking

An excellent method for cooking whole fish in a greased dish, well seasoned with salt, pepper and lemon Juice. A little milk or water should be poured round the fish, which should be covered with a piece of greased paper. Allow 10-15 minutes per 450 g (1 lb) in a moderate oven, 180C (350F) mark 4, depending on the thickness of the fish and whether it is stuffed. As an alternative, the fish may be simply brushed with melted butter and sprinkled with breadcrumbs before baking; this is particularly suitable for cutlets.

Foil-baking is excellent for cutlets, tall-ends of fish, or small whole fish, such as salmon or trout. Wrap the fish in well buttered foil with plenty of seasoning, lemon juice and fresh herbs. Place the foil packet on a baking sheet and allow 20 minutes per 450 g (1 lb) in a moderate oven, 180C (350F) mark 4. The fish is exceptionally moist and full of juices when cooked by this method.

Microwaving

Fish cooked in the microwave is full of flavour – with an excellent texture and appearance. Add a little lemon juice and seasoning, slit the fish skin in two or three places to prevent bursting, and cover the fish with microwave-proof film. For timing, consult the manufacturer's booklet.

Cook, uncovered, unless otherwise stated. The use of cling film should be avoided in microwave cooking, use microwave-proof film. When a recipe requires you to cover the container, you should either cover with a lid or a plate, leaving a gap to let steam escape.

WHITE FISH

*An interesting collection of recipes for everyday
use and special occasions, from
Cornish Cod to Monkfish Kebabs.*

❧ Round Fish ❧

FISH FLORENTINE

Serves 4

675 g (1 ½ lb) white fish fillets
450 g (1 lb) frozen leaf spinach or 675 g (1 ½ lb)
   fresh spinach
salt and pepper
275 ml (½ pint) Cheese Sauce (see variation,
   page 339)
pinch of cayenne pepper
25 g (1 oz) Parmesan cheese, grated

❧ Skin the fish fillets and poach them until just tender. Drain and keep warm.
❧ Cook the frozen spinach according to packet instructions, or steam the fresh spinach until cooked. Drain very well and press out as much liquid as possible. Season the spinach and arrange in a buttered ovenproof dish. Place the white fish fillets on top of that.
❧ Season the cheese sauce well with salt, pepper and cayenne pepper. Spoon over the cheese sauce and sprinkle on the Parmesan cheese.
❧ Place under a hot grill until the surface is brown and bubbling. Serve at once.

SAVOURY BREAD AND BUTTER PUDDING

Serves 4

8 medium-thick bread slices
75 g (3 oz) butter
150 g (5 oz) Cheddar cheese, grated
350 g (12 oz) white fish
275 ml (½ pint) milk
150 ml (¼ pint) single cream
2 eggs
salt and pepper
few drops of Tabasco sauce

❦ Remove the crusts from the bread. Spread the bread generously with butter and sprinkle with grated cheese. Cut each slice in half. Remove the bones and skin from the fish and cut the flesh into small pieces.
❦ Arrange a layer of bread in an ovenproof dish. Add half the fish and spread it over the bread, then add another layer of bread. Top with the remaining fish and the remaining bread with the cheese uppermost.
❦ Beat together the milk, cream and eggs and season well with salt, pepper and Tabasco sauce. Pour over the bread. Leave to stand for 1 hour.
❦ Heat the oven to 180C (350F) mark 4. Bake the pudding for 45 minutes.
❦ Serve hot with vegetables or a salad.

FISH CRUMBLE

Serves 4

450 g (1 lb) white fish, cooked
75 g (3 oz) butter
1 small onion, finely chopped
4 tomatoes, skinned
1 garlic clove, crushed
1 tbsp fresh parsley, chopped
1 tbsp lemon juice
150 ml (¼ pint) water
1 tbsp cornflour
salt and pepper
75 g (3 oz) plain flour

❦ Heat the oven to 220C (425F) mark 7. Flake the fish into a bowl.
❦ Melt 25 g (1 oz) of the butter and cook the onion until soft and golden. Discard the seeds from the tomatoes and chop the flesh roughly. Add the tomatoes to the onion with the garlic, parsley, lemon juice and water and simmer for 5 minutes.
❦ Mix the cornflour with a little water and stir into the sauce. Simmer for 3 minutes and season well with salt and pepper.
❦ Stir in the flaked fish and put the mixture into a greased ovenproof dish. Rub the remaining butter into the flour and sprinkle over the fish. Bake for 20 minutes and serve hot.

Variations
A few button mushrooms may be added to the sauce, or some peeled prawns, chopped green pepper or cooked peas, or a mixture of these ingredients.

WINTER FISH CASSEROLE

Serves 4

675 g (1 ½ lb) white fish
50 g (2 oz) streaky bacon
40 g (1 ½ oz) butter
225 g (8 oz) potatoes
225 g (8 oz) carrots
100 g (4 oz) turnips
1 medium onion
1 bay leaf
salt and pepper
275 ml (½ pint) dry cider
25 g (1 oz) plain flour
150 ml (¼ pint) milk

❦ Heat the oven to 190C (375F) mark 5.
❦ Skin the fish and cut into cubes. Chop the bacon roughly. Melt the butter and stir in the fish and bacon. Cook over a low heat until the fish is golden brown on all sides.
❦ Peel the vegetables. Cut the potatoes into cubes and dice the carrots and turnips. Slice the onion thinly. Add the vegetables to the pan and stir well.
❦ Put the mixture into a casserole and place the bay leaf on top. Season well with salt and pepper. Pour in the cider, cover and bake for 30 minutes.
❦ Mix the flour with a little of the milk to make a smooth paste and then add the remaining milk. Stir into the casserole, return to oven and continue baking for 10 minutes.
❦ Serve hot with potatoes or rice.

FRENCH FISH CASSEROLE

Serves 4

450 g (1 lb) leeks
50 g (2 oz) butter
1 green pepper, deseeded and sliced
225 g (8 oz) tomatoes, quartered
salt and pepper
675 g (1 ½ lb) white fish fillets
1 tbsp lemon juice
1 tbsp fresh parsley, chopped

❦ Heat the oven to 180C (350F) mark 4. Clean the leeks well and chop into 2.5 cm (1 in) chunks.
❦ Melt 40 g (1 ½ oz) of the butter and cook the leeks and pepper until soft and golden. Stir in the tomatoes and season well with salt and pepper. Spoon into a greased ovenproof dish.
❦ Cut the fish into 4 portions and place on top of the mixture. Sprinkle with lemon juice and parsley and dot with the remaining butter. Cover and bake for 25 minutes.
❦ Remove the cover and continue baking for 5 minutes. Serve at once with boiled potatoes.

FRUITED FISH CURRY

Serves 4

675 g (1 ½ lb) white fish
1 medium onion, finely chopped
40 g (1 ½ oz) butter
1 tbsp curry paste
1 tbsp fruit chutney
1 tbsp sultanas
1 eating apple
40 g (1 ½ oz) plain flour
275 g (10 oz) long grain rice
1 egg, hard-boiled
100 g (4 oz) prawns, shelled (optional)

❦ Skin the fish, remove the bones and cut into serving portions. Cover with water and simmer for 10 minutes. Drain the fish and keep warm, and reserve the cooking liquid for stock.
❦ Fry the onion in the butter until soft and golden. Stir in the curry paste and cook for 1 minute. Add the chutney and sultanas. Do not peel the apple, but core and cut the flesh into dice. Stir into the pan and add the flour. Cook until the flour is golden, mixing all the time.
❦ Measure the fish stock and make up to 425 ml (¾ pint) of liquid with water, add to the pan. Bring to the boil and then simmer and stir until the sauce is smooth.
❦ Put the fish pieces into the pan and reheat. While the sauce is cooking, boil the rice in salted water for 12-15 minutes and drain well.
❦ Arrange the rice in a border on a hot dish and spoon in the fish. Garnish with chopped egg, and prawns if liked.

SPANISH FISH SALAD

Serves 4

450 g (1 lb) white fish or smoked haddock fillets
225 g (8 oz) long-grain rice
salt and pepper
4 tbsp olive oil
1 ½ tbsp white wine vinegar
1 garlic clove, crushed
½ tsp French mustard
2 large tomatoes, skinned
4 spring onions
7.5 cm (3 in) piece of cucumber, peeled
1 green pepper, deseeded and finely chopped
1 red pepper, deseeded and finely chopped

❦ Poach the fish until tender. Cool and break into flakes.
❦ Meanwhile boil the rice in salted water until tender. Drain well, rinse in cold water, drain and leave in a bowl until cool but not cold.
❦ Mix together the oil, vinegar, garlic, mustard, salt and pepper. Discard the pips from tomatoes and chop the flesh roughly. Chop the spring onions finely. Discard the seeds from cucumber and dice the flesh finely. Mix the fish, peppers, tomatoes, onions and cucumber into the rice and add the dressing. Toss lightly so that the fish does not break into very small pieces.
❦ Chill before serving.

Variation
Peeled prawns or shrimps may be added on top of the dish before serving.

SUMMER FISH SALAD

Serves 4

450 g (1 lb) white fish fillets
2 hard-boiled eggs, chopped
4 anchovy fillets, finely chopped
2 gherkins, finely chopped
2 tsp capers
2 tbsp olive oil
2 tsp lemon juice
1 tbsp chopped fresh chives
pepper
150 ml (¼ pint) mayonnaise

❦ Poach the fish until just tender. Cool and break into flakes. Mix with the eggs, anchovies, gherkins and capers.
❦ Stir together the oil and lemon juice with the chives and plenty of pepper. Pour over the fish and toss lightly. Press lightly into a shallow serving dish and spoon over the mayonnaise.
❦ Chill and serve with a green salad and thin brown bread and butter.

WHITE FISH SUPPER BAKE

Serves 4

450 g (1 lb) white fish
1 medium onion, chopped
2 eggs, beaten
275 ml (½ pint) milk
75 g (3 oz) butter, softened
75 g (3 oz) fresh white or brown breadcrumbs
1 tbsp lemon juice
salt and pepper
50 g (2 oz) Cheddar cheese, grated

❦ Heat the oven to 190C (375F) mark 5.
❦ Poach the fish until just tender and cool. Flake the fish into a bowl. Add the onion, beaten eggs, milk, butter, breadcrumbs, lemon juice and salt and pepper.
❦ Put into a greased ovenproof dish and sprinkle with cheese. Bake for 40 minutes.
❦ Serve hot with a mushroom or tomato sauce and crusty bread.

BAKED FISH CHARLOTTE

Serves 4

350 g (12 oz) white fish fillets
275 ml (½ pint) White Sauce (see page 339)
1 garlic clove, crushed
225 g (8 oz) tomatoes
75 g (3 oz) fresh white or brown breadcrumbs
salt and pepper
50 g (2 oz) butter

❦ Heat the oven to 220C (425F) mark 7.
❦ Poach the fish, cool and remove the skin and any bones. Flake the fish and mix with the white sauce and garlic. Skin the tomatoes and slice them thickly.
❦ Put half the fish mixture into a greased pie dish and top with a layer of tomatoes and breadcrumbs, seasoning the layers with salt and pepper. Repeat the layers and dot with butter. Bake for 20 minutes.
❦ Serve hot with a vegetable or salad.

GRANNY'S FISH SUPPER

Serves 4

675 g (1 ½ lb) white fish fillets
4 medium onions, thinly sliced
oil or fat for frying
4 medium potatoes, boiled
salt and pepper
25 g (1 oz) Cheddar cheese, grated
1 tbsp fresh parsley, chopped

❦ The fish may be cod, haddock, coley or any other white fish. Poach the fish, cool slightly and remove the skin and any bones. Break into flakes.
❦ Fry the onions in a little hot oil or fat until soft and golden, and drain well. Slice the potatoes thinly. Grease an ovenproof dish and put in a layer of potatoes, then onion and fish, seasoning lightly. Continue in layers, finishing with a layer of potatoes. Sprinkle with cheese.
❦ Either bake at 180C (350F) mark 4 for 25 minutes or put under a hot grill to brown if the ingredients are freshly cooked and still hot. Sprinkle with parsley and serve. This is a useful supper dish as it may be assembled early in the day and then refrigerated until it is needed.

GRAPEFRUIT GRILLED FISH

Serves 4

butter
4 haddock or cod steaks
few drops of Tabasco sauce
salt and pepper
paprika
1 grapefruit

❦ Line a grill pan with foil and grease the foil lightly with a little butter. Put fish in pan and sprinkle
with Tabasco sauce, salt, pepper and paprika. Grill
for 4 minutes on each side.
❦ Meanwhile peel the grapefruit and cut off all the
white pith. Remove the grapefruit segments with a
sharp knife so that they are unskinned. Arrange the
segments on top of the fish and continue grilling for
4 minutes.
❦ Serve with vegetables or a salad.

RUSSIAN FISH PASTRY

Serves 4

225 g (8 oz) Shortcrust Pastry (see page 357)
225 g (8 oz) cod, smoked haddock or salmon,
    cooked
2 large mushrooms, thinly sliced
1 medium onion, finely chopped
100 g (4 oz) long-grain rice, boiled
1 tbsp fresh parsley, chopped
salt and pepper,
2 hard-boiled eggs, sliced
beaten egg for glazing

❦ Heat the oven to 200C (400F) mark 6. Roll out
the pastry into a 25 cm (10 in) square.
❦ Flake the fish and mix with the mushrooms,
onion, cooked and drained rice, the parsley, salt and
pepper. Place half the mixture in the centre of the
pastry. Place the sliced eggs on top and cover with
remaining mixture. Fold over the two sides of the
pastry, overlapping them and sealing with a little
beaten egg. Seal the ends firmly with beaten egg.
❦ Place on a lightly greased baking sheet with the
join downwards. Brush well with egg and make two
or three diagonal slashes in the top of the pastry.

Bake for 25-30 minutes until golden-brown.
❦ Serve hot with Tomato Sauce (see page 341).

PAELLA

Serves 8-10

675 g (1 ½ lb) long grain rice
1 chicken, cut into 8-10 pieces
450 g (1 lb) lean pork, diced
3 tbsp oil
1 large onion, finely chopped
3 ripe tomatoes
225 g (8 oz) peas
3 red peppers, chopped
350 g (12 oz) white fish, such as cod, haddock or
    hake
16 mussels in shells
225 g (8 oz) prawns in shells
1 tsp salt
½ tsp pepper
pinch of saffron

❦ A large deep frying pan is best for the preparation
of this dish. Ingredients may be varied – runner
beans are often substituted for peas. Pieces of eel,
crab or lobster may be added to the dish.
❦ Rinse the rice in cold water and drain well. Put
the chicken pieces and pork into a pan with the hot
oil and cook until brown, add the onion and over a
low heat, stirring well, cook until the onion is soft
and golden.
❦ Peel and deseed the tomatoes. Chop the flesh
roughly and add to the pan. Stir and cook for 3 minutes and then add the rice. Cook and stir over a low
heat for 10 minutes. Add the peas and peppers; cook
for 5 minutes. Add the pieces of fish, and mussels in
their shells. Peel half the prawns and add to the pan.
Season with salt and pepper and simmer for 10 minutes.
❦ Add the saffron and stir in 1.8 litres (3 pints) boiling water. Bring to the boil and then simmer until
the rice is cooked and all the water has been
absorbed, stirring occasionally. Stir in the prawns in
their shells.
❦ To give the paella a rich golden colour, put the
pan into a low oven, 170C (325F) mark 3, for 5 minutes. Remove it from the oven and leave it to stand
for 2 minutes so that the mixture has a chance to
blend and settle before serving.

PORTUGUESE COD

Serves 4

4 cod steaks
salt and pepper
275 ml (½ pint) water
juice of 2 lemons
1 medium onion, chopped
1 garlic clove, crushed
4 tomatoes, peeled and chopped
25 g (1 oz) butter
1 tbsp fresh parsley, chopped
pinch of thyme
100 g (4 oz) button mushrooms

❧ Heat the oven to 180C (350F) mark 4.
❧ Arrange the cod steaks in a greased ovenproof dish and sprinkle with salt and pepper. Cover with a piece of foil and bake for 10 minutes.
❧ While the fish is cooking, put the water, lemon juice, onion, garlic, tomatoes and butter into a pan and simmer together for 10 minutes. Add the parsley, thyme and small whole mushrooms.
❧ Remove the foil from the fish and pour over the sauce. Continue baking for 15 minutes.
❧ Serve with potatoes or rice and a green salad.

CORNISH COD

Serves 4

675 g (1 ½ lb) cod fillets
salt and pepper
milk
plain flour
75g (3 oz) butter
24 mussels, cooked
100 g (4 oz) prawns or shrimps, peeled
2 tsp lemon juice
1 tbsp fresh parsley, chopped
lemon wedges to garnish

❧ Divide the fish into 4 fillets and season with salt and pepper. Dip in the milk and then flour. Melt 50 g (2 oz) of the butter and fry the fish on both sides until golden. Place it on a warm serving dish and keep it hot.
❧ In a clean pan, melt the remaining butter and toss the mussels and prawns or shrimps over a low heat.

Add the lemon juice and pour the mixture over the fish. Sprinkle with parsley and serve at once with lemon wedges to garnish.
❧ The mussel and prawn or shrimp garnish may be used for other white fish, including plaice or sole. For a less rich dish, the fish may be grilled if preferred.

FISH PUDDING

Serves 4

450 g (1 lb) cod fillets
1 small onion
575 ml (1 pint) White Sauce (see page 339)
50 g (2 oz) fresh white breadcrumbs
2 eggs
salt and pepper

❧ Skin the fish and cut the flesh into pieces. Mince the fish and onion, or blend together in a food processor. Mix with the white sauce, breadcrumbs and beaten eggs. Season well with salt and pepper.
❧ Spoon into a well-greased 750 ml (1 ½ pint) pudding basin. Cover with greaseproof paper and foil and steam for 1 hour.
❧ Turn out and serve with Parsley Sauce (see page 339). Garnish with a few prawns or some button mushrooms tossed in a little butter.

Variation
If preferred, the mixture may be placed in a pie dish and baked at 180C (350F) mark 4 for 1 hour, when it will puff up and be golden-brown on the surface.

GRILLED WHITING WITH ORANGE BUTTER

Serves 4

4 small whiting
25 g (1 oz) plain flour
salt and pepper
50 g (2 oz) butter
1 orange
4 streaky bacon rashers

❦ Remove the heads and tails from the whiting. Wash and dry the fish and toss in the flour seasoned with salt and pepper. Score the skin diagonally two or three times on each side of the fish.
❦ Line a grill pan with foil and place the fish in the pan. Spread with half the butter. Grill under a medium heat for 7 minutes on each side.
❦ While the fish are cooking, grate the orange rind and mix with the remaining butter. Remove the white pith from the orange and cut out the segments so that they have no skin. De-rind the bacon and stretch the rashers with the back of a knife. Cut each rasher in half and roll up.
❦ Grill the bacon rashers with the fish. When the fish is nearly cooked, spread over the orange butter and arrange the orange segments in the pan.
❦ When the orange pieces are hot, lift the fish on to a warm serving dish and garnish with orange segments and bacon rolls.
❦ Spoon over the pan juices and serve with mashed potatoes or rice and a green salad.

HAKE WITH CAPER SAUCE

Serves 4

4 hake cutlets
1 small onion, finely chopped
225 g (8 oz) canned tomatoes
salt and pepper
25 g (1 oz) butter
4 tsp capers

Garnish
parsley sprigs
lemon wedges

❦ Heat the oven to 190C (375F) mark 5.
❦ Place the fish in a greased, shallow ovenproof dish. Mix the onion with the chopped tomatoes and their juice. Season well and pour over the fish. Cut the butter into flakes and dot over the fish. Cover and bake for 25 minutes. Remove the fish and place on a serving dish.
❦ Sieve the tomato mixture from the dish. Reheat and stir in the capers. Pour over the fish and garnish with parsley and lemon wedges.

HUNGARIAN FISH CASSEROLE

Serves 4-6

6 cod cutlets
40 g (1 ½ oz) butter
2 medium onions, thinly sliced
1 tbsp paprika
25 g (1 oz) plain flour
275 ml (½ pint) milk
225 g (8 oz) canned tomatoes
salt and pepper
150 ml (¼ pint) soured cream

❦ Heat the oven to 180C (350F) mark 4. Place the fish in an ovenproof dish in a single layer.
❦ Melt the butter in a pan and add the onions. Cook over a low heat for 5 minutes, stirring well, until the onions are soft and golden. Stir in the paprika and cook for 1 minute. Stir in the flour and cook for 1 minute.
❦ Gradually add the milk and the tomatoes with their juice. Break up the tomatoes with a fork. Bring to the boil and then simmer for 20 minutes. Season well with salt and pepper and pour over the fish.
❦ Cover and cook for 45 minutes. Remove the lid and spoon the soured cream on top of the fish. Serve at once with rice or noodles and a green salad.

HADDOCK WITH GRAPE SAUCE

Serves 4

6 75 g (1 ½ lb) haddock fillets
25 g (1 oz) butter
25 g (1 oz) plain flour
3 tbsp double cream
100 g (4 oz) white grapes, peeled and halved
salt and white pepper

❦ Skin the fish and cut into 4 even-sized portions. Poach in water until tender but unbroken, reserve the liquid. Lift carefully on to a serving dish and keep warm.
❦ Melt the butter and work in the flour, and stir over a low heat for 1 minute. Add 275 ml (½ pint) of the cooking liquid and stir over a low heat until smooth and creamy. Stir in 2 tablespoons cream and take off the heat. Add the peeled and halved grapes, and season to taste.
❦ Pour over the fish. Drizzle the remaining cream on top and put under a hot grill to glaze.

BAKED STUFFED HADDOCK

Serves 6

900 g (2 lb) whole haddock
2 tbsp oatmeal
2 tbsp dripping, melted
1 small onion, finely chopped
2 tsp fresh parsley, chopped
2 tsp fresh thyme
salt and pepper
25 g (1 oz) butter, melted
25 g (1 oz) fresh white or brown breadcrumbs

❦ Heat the oven to 190C (375F) mark 5. Clean the fish and leave whole.
❦ Mix together the oatmeal, dripping, onion, herbs and plenty of seasoning. Stuff the fish with this and close the opening with cocktail sticks.
❦ Put the fish into a well-greased ovenproof dish and brush the surface of the fish with a little of the butter. Bake for 30 minutes, basting once or twice.
❦ Sprinkle the surface of the fish with the breadcrumbs and sprinkle on the remaining butter. Cover with greaseproof paper and bake at 200C (400F) mark 6 for 20 minutes.
❦ Remove the cocktail sticks before serving.

COD IN TOMATO SAUCE

Serves 4

4 cod steaks
1 large onion, finely chopped
100 g (4 oz) streaky bacon rashers, chopped
½ green pepper
1 tbsp oil
450 g (1 lb) canned tomatoes
½ tsp fresh mixed herbs
salt and pepper

❦ Grill or fry the cod steaks until golden on both sides.
❦ While the fish is cooking, fry the onion, bacon and pepper in oil for 5 minutes over a low heat, stirring well. Add the tomatoes and their juice with the herbs, salt and pepper. Bring to the boil and simmer for 10 minutes. Place the cod steaks on a warm serving dish and pour over the sauce. Serve at once with boiled potatoes or crusty bread.
❦ The sauce is very quickly made and may be served with any white fish or with seafood, such as scallops or scampi, which can be prepared while the sauce is cooking.

❦ Flat Fish ❦

MEXICAN FISH SALAD

Serves 4

450 g (1 lb) halibut or haddock fillets
4 limes
1 crisp lettuce
4 tomatoes, skinned
1 green pepper, deseeded and finely chopped
4 tbsp olive oil
1 tbsp wine vinegar
2 tbsp fresh parsley, chopped
2 tbsp fresh marjoram, chopped
salt and pepper

❦ Skin the fish and remove any bones. Cut into small cubes and put into a shallow dish. Grate the rind from 1 lime and squeeze out all the juice from all the limes. Sprinkle the rind and juice over the fish, cover and leave in the refrigerator for at least 3 hours.
❦ Arrange the lettuce leaves in a serving bowl. Discard the seeds from the tomatoes and chop the flesh roughly. Mix the tomato and pepper pieces and arrange in the bowl.
❦ Mix the oil, vinegar, parsley, marjoram, salt and pepper together and sprinkle over the tomatoes. Arrange the fish on top.
❦ The fresh lime juice has the effect of cooking the fish, which retains a beautifully fresh flavour. Bottled lime juice cordial should not be used for the dish.

HALIBUT AND HORSERADISH

Serves 4

675 g (1 ½ lb) halibut steaks, boned
150 ml (¼ pint) White Sauce (see page 339)
150 ml (¼ pint) single cream
3 egg yolks
1 tbsp horseradish cream
1 tbsp wine vinegar
salt and pepper
1 hard-boiled egg, finely chopped

❦ Heat the oven to 180C (350F) mark 4.
❦ Place the halibut steaks in a greased ovenproof dish. Add 3 tablespoons of water, cover and bake for 20 minutes.
❦ Drain off the liquid and place the fish on a serving dish to keep warm. Warm the white sauce and remove from the heat. Beat in the cream and egg yolks and heat just enough to warm through, but do not boil. Stir in the horseradish cream, vinegar and seasoning. Coat the fish with the sauce and sprinkle with chopped egg.
❦ Serve at once with boiled or sauté potatoes and peas.

BRITTANY HALIBUT

Serves 4

50 g (2 oz) butter
1 medium onion, finely chopped
25 g (1 oz) plain flour
150 ml (¼ pint) dry cider or dry white wine
2 garlic cloves, crushed
2 tbsp fresh parsley, chopped
2 tbsp lemon juice
salt and pepper
pinch of cayenne pepper
675 g (1 ½ lb) halibut fillets
flour
oil for frying

❦ Melt the butter and cook the onion over a low heat until soft and golden. Stir in the flour and cook for 1 minute. Stir in the cider or wine, with the garlic and parsley. Simmer for 5 minutes. Add the lemon juice and season well with salt, pepper and cayenne pepper.
❦ While the sauce is cooking, divide the fish into 4 pieces. Flour these lightly and cook in a little hot oil for 3 minutes each side until just golden.
❦ Put the fish in a single layer in a shallow ovenproof dish and cover with the sauce. Place under a hot grill for 2–3 minutes until golden and bubbling, and serve at once with boiled potatoes.

Variations
Cod or haddock may be used instead of halibut.

NORFOLK FISH PIE

Serves 6

450 g (1 lb) halibut, haddock or cod
225 g (8 oz) shelled lobster or scampi
4 scallops, shelled
butter
100 g (4 oz) shrimps, peeled
100 g (4 oz) button mushrooms
4 eggs
275 ml (½ pint) White Sauce (see page 339)
salt and pepper
450 g (1 lb) mashed potatoes

❧ Heat the oven to 180C (350F) mark 4.
❧ Poach the fish and flake the flesh into large pieces. Mix with the lobster or scampi.
❧ Remove the corals from the scallops and cut the white part into two circles. Cook for 2 minutes in a little butter and mix the white parts and corals with the white fish. Stir in the shrimps. Wipe the mushrooms but do not peel and cook In the butter for 2 minutes. Stir into the fish.
❧ Beat the eggs into the white sauce and add all the fish mixture. Season well and put into a pie dish. Cover with the mashed potatoes and mark lightly with a fork. Bake for 30 minutes.

Variations
This is a rich and delicious fish pie, but the ingredients may be varied according to season and budget. Some smoked haddock may be included, mussels may be added and prawns may be used, but the important thing is to get a variety of texture, colour and flavour. The fish may be fresh, canned or frozen, so it is always possible to get an interesting mixture, and while the result is a little expensive, the pie is good enough for a really special meal with guests.

SUMMER PLAICE WITH COURGETTES

Serves 4

450 g (1 lb) courgettes
50 g (2 oz) butter
1 tbsp fresh parsley, chopped
1 tsp rosemary
salt and pepper
8 plaice fillets
25 g (1 oz) fresh breadcrumbs
25 g (1 oz) butter, melted
1 tbsp Parmesan cheese, grated

❧ Heat the oven to 190C (375F) mark 5.
❧ Wipe the courgettes and slice them thinly without peeling. Melt the butter and fry the courgettes with the parsley and rosemary for 3 minutes.
❧ Remove from the heat, season well and place in the bottom of a shallow ovenproof dish. Fold the plaice fillets in half, skin side inwards and arrange on top of the courgettes. Sprinkle with breadcrumbs, drizzle with butter and sprinkle with Parmesan cheese. Bake for 20 minutes.
❧ Serve at once with new potatoes and a salad.

PLAICE ROLLS IN LEMON SAUCE

Serves 4

8 plaice fillets
100 g (4 oz) shrimps or prawns
15 g (½ oz) butter
15 g (½ oz) plain flour
275 ml (½ pint) milk
juice of 1 lemon
salt and pepper

❧ Heat the oven to 180C (350F) mark 4.
❧ Place the fish on a flat surface and divide the shrimps or prawns between the fillets. Roll the plaice round them and stand the fish upright and close together in a greased ovenproof dish.
❧ Melt the butter and work in the flour. Stir in the milk over a low heat and cook gently until the sauce thickens. Remove from heat and stir in lemon juice. Season well and pour over fish. Bake for 25 minutes.
❧ Serve with potatoes and vegetables.

PLAICE IN LEMON BUTTER

Serves 4

8 small plaice fillets
25 g (1 oz) plain flour
salt and pepper
75 g (3 oz) butter
1 tbsp oil
1 tbsp lemon juice
1 tbsp fresh parsley, chopped
lemon wedges to garnish

❦ Dry the fish on kitchen paper. Season the flour with salt and pepper and coat the fish lightly on both sides.

❦ Put 50 g (2 oz) of the butter into a frying pan with the oil, and heat until the butter has melted. Fry the fish for 4 minutes on each side until cooked through and golden. Lift on to a warm serving dish.

❦ Add the remaining butter, lemon juice and parsley to the pan and heat until golden brown. Pour over the fish, garnish with lemon wedges and serve at once.

BURNHAM PLAICE

Serves 2

2 small whole plaice
25 g (1 oz) brown breadcrumbs
1 celery stick, finely chopped
4 tbsp tomato juice
3 tbsp lemon juice
100 g (4 oz) peeled prawns

Garnish
parsley sprigs
lemon wedges

❦ Heat the oven to 200C (400F) mark 6.

❦ Clean and trim the fish but leave them whole. Place the fish on a flat surface with the white skin uppermost. Use a sharp knife to make a long slit down the backbone, and with the point of the knife, ease the flesh away from the backbone along both sides to make a pocket.

❦ Mix the breadcrumbs with the celery, tomato juice, lemon juice and half the prawns. Pack the mix-ture into the pockets in the fish, allowing it to spill loosely. Place the fish in a shallow ovenproof dish. Cover with greased greaseproof paper and bake for 20 minutes.

❦ Lift the fish on to individual plates and garnish with remaining prawns, parsley and lemon wedges.

SOLE WITH PRAWN AND MUSHROOM SAUCE

Serves 4

4 large fillets lemon sole
1 small onion, thinly sliced
1 bay leaf
8 peppercorns
150 ml (¼ pint) dry white wine
150 ml (¼ pint) water
squeeze of lemon juice
25 g (1 oz) butter
25 g (1 oz) plain flour
salt
50 g (2 oz) mushrooms, sliced
100 g (4 oz) prawns, shelled
8 tbsp double cream

❦ Heat the oven to 180C (350F) mark 4.

❦ Fold the fillets in three and put in a buttered ovenproof dish in a single layer. Add the onion slices, bay leaf and peppercorns. Pour over the wine and water and add a squeeze of lemon juice. Cover and bake for 15 minutes.

❦ Strain off and reserve the liquid and keep the fish warm. Melt the butter and work in the flour. Cook for 1 minute over a low heat. Gradually blend in the cooking liquid and stir over a low heat until the sauce has thickened. Season lightly with salt.

❦ While the sauce is cooking, simmer the mush-rooms in 1 tablespoon water with a squeeze of lemon juice until just cooked. Drain the mushrooms and add to the sauce with the prawns. Stir in the cream and adjust seasoning to taste. Pour over the fish and serve at once.

❧ Freshwater Fish ❧

TROUT WITH BACON STUFFING

Serves 4

4 trout
40 g (1 ½ oz) butter
4 streaky bacon rashers, finely chopped
1 small onion, finely chopped
100 g (4 oz) mushrooms, finely chopped
50 g (2 oz) fresh brown breadcrumbs
2 tbsp fresh parsley, chopped
2 tsp lemon rind, grated
salt and pepper
1 egg

❧ Heat the oven to 190C (375F) mark 5. Clean and gut the fish.
❧ Melt the butter and cook the bacon, onion and mushrooms over a low heat until soft and golden. Remove from the heat and mix with the breadcrumbs, parsley, lemon rind, salt, pepper and egg.
❧ Stuff the fish and secure with cocktail sticks. Arrange in a well-buttered ovenproof dish in a single layer. Bake for 25 minutes.
❧ Serve with boiled or sauté potatoes and a vegetable.

HERBED TROUT IN CREAM SAUCE

Serves 4

4 trout
50 g (2 oz) butter
50 g (2 oz) dry breadcrumbs
1 small onion, finely chopped
2 tsp fresh sage, finely chopped
salt and pepper
225 g (8 oz) button mushrooms
150 ml (¼ pint) single cream

❧ Heat the oven to 180C (350F) mark 4. Gut the trout, removing heads, although this is not necessary.
❧ Place in a buttered ovenproof dish and cover with buttered greaseproof paper. Bake for 20 minutes.

❧ Melt the butter and stir in the breadcrumbs, onion and sage. Cook over a low heat, stirring well, until the breadcrumbs are lightly golden. Season well with salt and pepper. Slice the mushrooms and put into a pan with the cream. Cover and simmer for 3 minutes.
❧ Pour the mushrooms over the cooked trout and sprinkle the breadcrumb mixture on top. Continue baking for 5 minutes.
❧ Serve hot with potatoes and a vegetable.

TROUT WITH ALMONDS

Serves 2

2 rainbow trout
25 g (1 oz) plain flour
salt and pepper
100 g (4 oz) butter
50 g (2 oz) flaked almonds
1 tsp lemon juice

❧ Clean and gut the trout, but leave the heads and tails intact. Season the flour well with salt and pepper and lightly coat the trout with the flour. Melt half the butter and fry the trout over a low heat for 5 minutes each side.
❧ Lift the fish on to a warm serving dish. Add the remaining butter to the pan and toss the almonds over a medium heat until golden. Add lemon juice to the pan and pour the almonds and pan juices over the trout.
❧ Serve immediately with plainly boiled potatoes and vegetables or a salad.

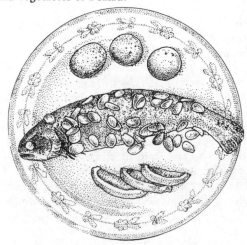

PIKE QUENELLES

Serves 1

450 g (1 lb) pike
salt and pepper
pinch of ground nutmeg
2 tbsp fresh parsley, chopped
2 egg whites
150 ml (¼ pint) double cream
275 ml (½ pint) Fish Stock (see page 337)
275 ml (½ pint) dry white wine

❦ Remove the skin and bones from the fish and mince the flesh finely (or make into a purée in a liquidizer or food processor). Mash the flesh with salt, pepper, nutmeg and chopped parsley, and put through a sieve. Beat in the egg whites until completely blended and chill for about 1 ½ hours. Then gradually work in the cream to make a light but firm mixture.
❦ Grease a shallow pan. Using two tablespoons dipped in hot water, shape the fish mixture into egg-shapes and place in the pan, leaving space between them as they swell during cooking.
❦ Bring the stock and wine to the boil in a separate pan and pour over the fish shapes. Poach gently until the shapes puff up and feel firm. Lift from the pan, draining well and place on a warm serving dish.

❦ Serve at once with Hollandaise Sauce (see page 345)

CRISP BROWN TROUT

Serves 4-6

6 brown trout
2 medium onions, chopped
I tbsp oil
1 garlic clove, crushed
salt and pepper
25 g (1 oz) fresh white or brown breadcrumbs
50 g (2 oz) butter, melted
2 streaky bacon rashers
1 tbsp fresh parsley, chopped

❦ Heat the oven to 180C (350F) mark 4. Clean and fillet the fish.
❦ Fry the onions gently in the oil until soft and golden. Stir in the garlic and season well. Place the trout in an oiled ovenproof dish. Cover with the onion mixture. Mix the breadcrumbs with butter and season with salt and pepper. Sprinkle on top of the onions. Bake for 25 minutes.
❦ While the fish are cooking, grill the bacon crisply and crumble into small pieces. Sprinkle the bacon and parsley on the fish and serve with boiled potatoes.

❦ Assorted Less Common Fish ❦

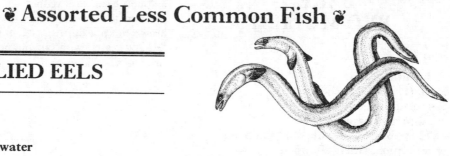

JELLIED EELS

Serves 4

900 g (2 lb) eels
850 ml (1 ½ pints) water
4 tbsp vinegar
2 tsp salt
1 tsp crushed peppercorns
1 medium carrot, sliced
1 medium onion, sliced
6 sprigs parsley
2 tbsp fresh parsley, chopped

❦ The eels can be skinned, but if the skin is very tough, it may be left on and removed after cooking. Cut the fish into 2.5 cm (1 in) slices.

❦ Put the water, vinegar, salt, peppercorns, carrot, onion and parsley sprigs into a pan. Bring to the boil and then simmer for 30 minutes. Strain the liquid into a clean pan.
❦ Add the pieces of eel and simmer for 15 minutes. Lift the eel from the pan and remove and discard bones. Put the pieces of eel into a bowl.
❦ Boil the liquid hard until it is reduced by one-third. Stir in the chopped parsley and pour over the eel. Cool and then chill until the liquid forms a soft jelly.
❦ Serve with brown bread and butter.

STUFFED JOHN DORY

Serves 4

900 g (2 lb) John Dory
1 small onion, finely chopped
50 g (2 oz) butter
50 g (2 oz) fresh white breadcrumbs
150 g (5 oz) Cheddar cheese, grated
1 egg
salt and pepper
1 tbsp grated Parmesan cheese

❦ Heat the oven to 190C (375F) mark 5. Prepare the fish as fillets.
❦ Put the onion and butter into a pan and cook gently for 5 minutes until the onion is soft and golden. Add the onion and butter to the breadcrumbs and Cheddar cheese and then add the beaten egg. Season well.
❦ Place half the fillets in a greased ovenproof dish and top with half the breadcrumb mixture. Cover with remaining fillets and then the remaining breadcrumb mixture. Sprinkle with Parmesan cheese. Bake for 35 minutes.
❦ Serve with vegetables or salad.

BAKED RED MULLET

Serves 4

4 red mullet
150 ml (¼ pint) dry sherry
2 tsp tomato ketchup
2 tsp anchovy essence
50 g (2 oz) button mushrooms, chopped
1 small onion, finely chopped
grated rind of 1 lemon
2 tsp fresh parsley, chopped
salt and pepper
2 tbsp brown breadcrumbs
50 g (2 oz) butter

❦ Heat the oven to 180C (350F) mark 4.
❦ Clean the mullet, removing the heads and tails. Score the fish with two diagonal cuts on each side and place in a shallow ovenproof dish.
❦ Mix together the sherry, ketchup, anchovy essence, mushrooms, onion, lemon rind, parsley, salt and pepper. Pour over the fish. Cover with the breadcrumbs and with flakes of butter. Bake for 25 minutes.
❦ Serve with vegetables or a green salad.

SKATE IN BLACK BUTTER

Serves 4

900 g (2 lb) skate wing pieces
850 ml (1 ½ pints) water
5 tbsp white wine vinegar
salt
6 parsley stalks
blade of mace
100 g (4 oz) butter
2 tbsp capers
2 tbsp fresh parsley, chopped
pepper

❦ Put the skate into a large shallow pan and cover with the water. Add 1 tbsp of the vinegar, 1 tsp salt, the parsley stalks and mace. Bring to the boil and then simmer gently for 12 minutes until the fish is tender. Drain the fish very thoroughly, and take off the skin. Place the fish on a warm serving dish.
❦ Put the remaining vinegar into a small thick pan and boil hard until reduced to half. Cut the butter into small pieces and add to the pan. Heat until brown but not burned. Stir in the capers and parsley, and season with salt and pepper. Pour over the fish and serve at once.

MONKFISH KEBABS

Serves 4

100 g (4 oz) button onions, peeled
100 g (4 oz) courgettes
450 g (1 lb) monkish, skinned
225 g (8 oz) streaky bacon
225 g (8 oz) mussels, cooked
100 g (4 oz) button mushrooms
8 bay leaves
salt and pepper
50 g (2 oz) butter, melted

❦ Use four long kebab skewers, not short meat skewers.

❦ Blanch the onions in boiling salted water for 2 minutes. Wipe the courgettes but do not peel them, and cut into 4 cm (1 ½ in) thick slices. Blanch the courgettes for 2 minutes. Drain the onions and courgettes very thoroughly.

❦ Cut the monkish into cubes. De-rind the bacon and stretch the rashers with the back of a knife. Cut each rasher in half and wrap a piece round each mussel. Wipe the mushrooms but do not peel.

❦ Thread a bay leaf on each skewer and then add the various ingredients, alternating vegetables and fish, and placing a bay leaf half-way. Season well with salt and pepper, and brush with the melted butter.

❦ Preheat the grill to a medium heat, and grill for 6 minutes. Turn the skewers, brush with butter, and continue grilling for 6-8 minutes.

❦ Serve with rice or warm pitta bread and fresh Tomato Sauce (see page 341).

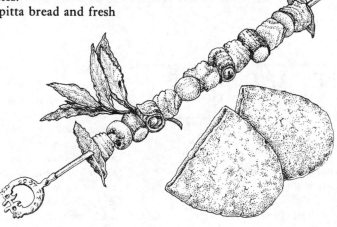

OILY FISH

*These fish are very nutritious and particularly
rich in vitamins A and D as well as mineral salts.*

SWEET AND SHARP HERRINGS

Serves 4

4 medium herrings
150 ml (¼ pint) malt vinegar
150 ml (¼ pint) water
1 tbsp tomato ketchup
1 tsp fresh parsley, chopped
3 bay leaves
6 peppercorns
50 g (2 oz) Demerara sugar
1 tsp mustard powder

❦ Heat the oven to 180C (350F) mark 4.
❦ Clean and fillet the herrings. Arrange in a single
layer in an ovenproof dish. Mix the vinegar, water,
tomato ketchup, parsley, bay leaves and peppercorns. Pour over the fish and cover with a lid or foil.
Bake for 1 hour.
❦ Remove from the oven and uncover. Mix together the sugar and mustard and sprinkle over the fish.
Do not cover but return to the oven for 15 minutes.
❦ Leave the herrings to cool in the liquid. When
cold, drain the fish and serve with salad.

SOUSED HERRINGS

Serves 4-6

6 herrings
salt and pepper
150 ml (¼ pint) wine or cider vinegar
150 ml (¼ pint) water
1 tbsp mixed pickling spice
4 bay leaves
2 small onions, thinly sliced

❧ Heat the oven to 150C (300F) mark 2.
❧ Clean and fillet the herrings. Season each fillet well with salt and pepper and roll up each fillet, skin inwards, from the tail end. Place close together in a single layer in an ovenproof dish.
❧ Mix the vinegar and water and pour over the fish. Sprinkle on the pickling spice and arrange the bay leaves and onion rings on top. Cover with a lid or foil and bake for 1 ½ hours.
❧ Leave to cool in the liquid, then drain the herrings and place on a serving dish garnished with onion rings. Serve with salad.

CROFTER'S CASSEROLE

Serves 4

4 large herrings
salt and pepper
1 large onion, thinly sliced
4 large potatoes, thinly sliced
50 g (2 oz) butter, melted

❧ Heat the oven to 200C (400F) mark 6.
❧ Clean and fillet the herrings and open them out flat. Arrange in a greased shallow ovenproof dish and sprinkle with plenty of salt and pepper. Arrange the onions on top and then the potatoes. Season well and brush with butter.
❧ Cover with a lid or foil and bake for 50 minutes. Remove the lid or foil and continue baking for 15 minutes. Serve with vegetables or a salad.

CRISPY HERRING FRIES

Serves 4-6

4 large herrings
25 g (1 oz) plain flour
2 eggs
salt and pepper
100 g (4 oz) porridge oats
½ tsp mustard powder
oil for deep frying

Garnish
lemon or orange wedges
parsley sprigs

❧ Fillet the herrings to yield 8 pieces of fish. Cut into 5 cm (2 in) strips and coat with flour. Beat the eggs in a shallow bowl and season well with salt and pepper. Dip the pieces of herring in the egg and then coat them in the oats mixed with mustard.
❧ Heat the oil to 180C (350F). Fry the herring pieces in batches for about 5 minutes until crisp and golden. Serve very hot, garnished with lemon or orange wedges and parsley sprigs.

SPICED SALT HERRINGS

Serves 4

2 salt herrings
1 small onion, thinly sliced
1 small lemon, thinly sliced
1 bay leaf
pinch of pepper
pinch of ground nutmeg
5 tbsp dry cider
3 tbsp salad oil

❧ Clean and bone the herrings and leave to soak in cold water for 12 hours.
❧ Skin the fish and cut the fillets into narrow strips. Arrange the strips in a shallow serving dish with the onion and lemon slices on top. Break the bay leaf into pieces and sprinkle over the top. Sprinkle with some pepper and nutmeg. Mix the cider and the oil and pour this over the herrings. Cover the dish and leave in a cool place for at least 3 hours.
❧ Serve with salad or with bread and butter or with small new potatoes.

SHETLAND TURNOVERS

Serves 4

350 g (12 oz) Shortcrust Pastry (see page 357)
3 medium herrings
100 g (4 oz) streaky bacon rashers
1 large potato, grated
grated rind of ½ lemon
salt and pepper
milk for glazing

❦ Heat the oven to 220C (425F) mark 7. Roll out the pastry and cut to make four 15 cm (6 in) squares.
❦ Clean and fillet the herrings and grill them flat, skin-side down, for about 8 minutes until cooked through. Remove the skin and flake the fish coarsely.
❦ Grill the bacon for 2 minutes. Chop into small pieces and mix with the fish. Add the potato, lemon rind and plenty of salt and pepper.
❦ Place the filling in the centre of the pastry squares. Fold over and seal the edges firmly with a fork. Place on a baking sheet and brush with milk.
❦ Bake for 10 minutes then reduce the heat to 190C (375F) mark 5 and continue baking for 25 minutes. Serve hot or cold.

HERRINGS WITH CREAM SAUCE

Serves 4

4 medium herrings
25g (1 oz) butter, melted
salt and pepper
150 ml (¼ pint) double cream
2 tsp made mustard
2 tsp lemon juice
1 small onion, grated
lemon wedges to garnish

❦ Clean the herrings and remove heads and tails. Brush all over with the butter and sprinkle well with salt and pepper.
❦ Grill under a medium heat for about 7 minutes on each side until cooked through and slightly crisp.
❦ Whip the cream to soft peaks and fold in the mustard, lemon juice and onion.
❦ Place the herrings on a warm serving dish with a garnish of lemon wedges. Serve the sauce separately.

MARGARETTA HERRINGS

Serves 4

4 large herrings
50 g (2 oz) butter
salt and pepper
4 tbsp single cream
3 tsp tomato purée
3 tsp made mustard

❦ Heat the oven to 180C (350F) mark 4.
❦ Fillet the herrings to yield 8 pieces of fish. Divide the butter into 8 pieces and put a piece on the surface of each fillet. Roll up the fish, skin side outwards, and pack into an ovenproof dish, in a single layer.
❦ Sprinkle with salt and pepper. Mix together the cream, tomato purée and mustard and pour over the fish. Bake for 30 minutes.
❦ Serve at once with plain boiled potatoes and peas or a green salad.

MACKEREL KEBABS

Serves 4

4 small mackerel
8 lean bacon rashers
20 button mushrooms
8 bay leaves
salt and pepper
1 tbsp lemon juice
½ teaspoon fresh mixed herbs
6 tbsp oil

❦ Prepare the mackerel to yield 8 fillets. Cut each fillet into 6 pieces. De-rind the bacon and spread out each rasher thinly with a broad-bladed knife. Divide each into 3 pieces, and roll up each piece of bacon.
❦ Take 4 long kebab skewers and thread on the mackerel, alternating with bacon rolls, mushrooms and bay leaves. Season well with salt and pepper and sprinkle with lemon juice and herbs. Place on a dish and sprinkle with oil. Cover and chill in the refrigerator for 2 hours.
❦ Grill under a medium heat for 15 minutes, turning the skewers frequently.
❦ Serve with Hot Mustard Sauce (see page 339), brown bread and a green salad.

MACKEREL WITH GREEN PEPPER SAUCE

Serves 4

4 mackerel
75 g (3 oz) butter
grated rind and juice of 1 lemon
salt and pepper
225 g (8 oz) tomatoes, skinned and chopped
1 garlic clove, crushed
2 green peppers, deseeded and chopped

Garnish
lemon wedges

❦ Heat the oven to 190C (375F) mark 5.
❦ Clean the mackerel and place on a piece of foil greased with 50 g (2 oz) of the butter. Add the grated rind and juice of the lemon and season well with salt and pepper. Fold over the foil to form a sealed packet. Bake for 45 minutes.
❦ While the mackerel are cooking, prepare the sauce. Melt the remaining butter and add the tomatoes, garlic and peppers. Simmer over a low heat until the peppers are soft.
❦ Place the mackerel on a serving dish and spoon over the sauce. Serve with lemon wedges.

STUFFED BAKED MACKEREL

Serves 4

4 mackerel
salt and pepper
lemon juice
225 g (8 oz) mushrooms, finely chopped
2 medium onions, finely chopped
1 tbsp fresh parsley, chopped
4 sprigs fennel

❦ Heat the oven to 180C (350F) mark 4.
❦ Fillet the fish, keeping each mackerel in one piece. Sprinkle inside with salt, pepper and lemon juice. Take a large piece of foil and place on a baking sheet.
❦ Mix the mushrooms, onions and parsley and season well with salt and pepper. Fill each fish with this mixture and arrange on the foil which has been well buttered. Put a sprig of fennel on each fish. Fold over the foil to make a flat parcel.
❦ Bake for 30 minutes. Open the foil carefully. Remove and discard the fennel. Slash the top of each fish diagonally three times at equal intervals.
❦ Do not cover again but return to the oven for 10 minutes. Lift the fish carefully on to a serving dish and spoon over any cooking juices.
❦ Serve at once with boiled potatoes and a vegetable.

ESSEX PICKLED MACKEREL

Serves 4-6

6 small mackerel
25 g (1 oz) butter
4 bay leaves
4 cloves
1 tsp peppercorns
575 ml (1 pint) vinegar
1 tbsp thyme
1 tbsp fresh parsley, chopped
1 tbsp fresh fennel, chopped
salt and pepper

❦ Heat the oven to 180C (350F) mark 4.
❦ Fillet the fish, wash and dry them. Arrange in a single layer in a greased ovenproof dish and dot with pieces of butter. Bake for 20 minutes.
❦ Put the bay leaves, cloves, peppercorns and vinegar into a pan and bring to the boil. Simmer for 10 minutes. Leave until cold and strain over fish. Leave in a cold place for 6 hours.
❦ Lift out the fish and drain well. Arrange on a serving dish and sprinkle with the herbs and plenty of salt and pepper.

MEDITERRANEAN MACKEREL

Serves 4

4 medium mackerel
8 tbsp oil
5 tbsp dry white wine
few drops of Tabasco sauce
salt and pepper
2 oranges
50 g (2 oz) black olives
4 bay leaves

❦ Clean and gut the mackerel and remove the heads. Make two or three diagonal slashes across both sides of each fish.

❦ Line a grill pan with foil and place the fish in the pan. Mix the oil, wine, Tabasco sauce and plenty of salt and pepper and pour over the fish. Leave to stand for 2 hours, turning the fish occasionally.

❦ Preheat the grill and grill the fish for 8 minutes on each side. Lift the fish on to a serving dish and pour over the pan juices. Leave until cold.

❦ Peel the oranges and cut them across thinly. Garnish the fish with olives, orange slices and bay leaves, and serve with brown bread and butter and a green salad.

MACKEREL WITH MUSTARD CREAM

Serves 4

8 mackerel fillets
2 tbsp lemon juice
25 g (1 oz) butter
salt and pepper
6 tomatoes, skinned
2 tbsp oil
1 garlic clove, crushed

Sauce
4 tbsp Mayonnaise (see page 346)
4 tbsp double cream
juice of 1 lemon
2 tsp French mustard

❦ Heat the oven to 200C (400F) mark 6.
❦ Place the fillets in a shallow ovenproof dish.

Sprinkle with lemon juice and top with flakes of butter. Season well, cover and bake for 20 minutes.

❦ Slice the tomatoes thickly. Heat the oil and add the tomato slices and garlic. Cook over a high heat for 2 minutes.

❦ Place the tomato slices and garlic on a hot serving dish. Arrange the mackerel fillets on top. Mix together the sauce ingredients and spoon over the top.

BAKED SPRATS

Serves 4

900 g (2 lb) sprats
salt and pepper
pinch of ground nutmeg
1 medium onion, sliced
4 bay leaves
275 ml (½ pint) white wine vinegar
25g (1 oz) butter
sprig of fennel
1 tsp fresh parsley, chopped
½ tsp fresh thyme

❦ Heat the oven to 180C (350F) mark 4.

❦ Remove the heads and tails from sprats. Wash and pat dry with kitchen paper. Arrange the fish head to tail in a shallow ovenproof dish. Season with salt, pepper and nutmeg.

❦ Break the onion slices into rings and arrange on top of the fish with the bay leaves. Pour over the vinegar and a little water, if necessary, to cover. Dot with flakes of butter and put on the fennel sprig. Cover with foil and bake for 1 hour.

❦ Cool the dish and then chill in the refrigerator. Just before serving, drain the sprats and arrange them on a serving dish. Sprinkle with parsley and thyme and serve with Tartare Sauce or Green Mayonnaise (see pages 346).

BAKED MACKEREL IN CIDER SAUCE

Serves 4

4 mackerel
salt and pepper
½ lemon
1 medium onion, thinly sliced
sprig of thyme
sprig of rosemary
2 bay leaves
425 ml (¾ pint) dry cider
150 ml (¾ pint) water
2 tsp arrowroot

❦ Heat the oven to 180C (350F) mark 4. Slit each fish along the belly and remove the guts. Use kitchen scissors to cut off the heads and fins. Wash the fish well, drain, and season well inside each fish with salt and pepper.

❦ Arrange the fish head to tail in a single layer in an ovenproof dish. Peel the rind thinly from the lemon and arrange on top of the fish with the sliced onions and herbs. Pour over the cider and water, and cover with foil. Bake for 30 minutes.

❦ Arrange the fish and onions on a warm serving dish and keep hot. Strain the cooking liquid until it measures 425 ml (¾ pint). Mix the arrowroot with a little cold water and stir into the cooking liquid. Bring to the boil, stirring all the time. Simmer gently, stirring often, until the sauce is clear.

❦ Pour over the fish and serve at once with jacket or boiled potatoes and a vegetable or green salad.

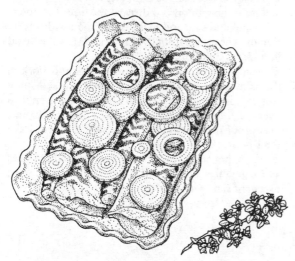

CURRIED TUNA PUFF

Serves 4-6

350 g (12 oz) Puff Pastry (see page 360)
1 small onion, finely chopped
1 eating apple, peeled and finely chopped
15 g (½ oz) butter
2 tsp curry powder
2 tsp plain flour
150 ml (¼ pint) stock or water
1 tbsp mango chutney
salt
50 g (2 oz) long grain rice
225 g (8 oz) canned tuna fish, drained
egg for glazing

❦ Heat the oven to 220C (425F) mark 7. Divide the pastry in half. Roll out into two rounds, one measuring 23 cm (9 in) and the other slightly larger. Place the smaller round on a baking tray.

❦ To make the filling, cook the onion and apple in the butter over a low heat until soft and golden. Stir in the curry powder and flour and cook for 1 minute. Blend in the stock or water and chutney and simmer for 5 minutes, stirring well. Season to taste with salt.

❦ Meanwhile cook the rice in boiling salted water for 12 minutes until tender. Drain well and add to the curry mixture. Flake the fish, add to the mixture, and leave until cold.

❦ Place the curry mixture in the centre of the pastry round, spreading it to within 1 cm (½ in) of the edge. Brush the edge of the pastry circle with beaten egg. Put the other piece of pastry on top and seal the edges well.

❦ Roll out any trimmings and cut out leaves to decorate the top of the pastry. Brush leaves with beaten egg and cut two slits in the top of the pastry. Bake for 30 minutes.

❦ Serve hot with vegetables or a salad.

SALMON AND MUSHROOM SLICE

Serves 4-6

225 g (8 oz) Puff Pastry (see page 360)
50 g (2 oz) butter
1 onion, peeled
25 g (1 oz) plain flour
150 ml (¼ pint) milk
salt and pepper
nutmeg
200 g (7 oz) cooked fresh salmon, flaked or
    200 g (7 oz) can salmon, drained
75 g (3 oz) mushrooms
1 egg to glaze
fennel or dill to garnish

❦ Heat the oven to 220C (425F) mark 7.
❦ Roll out the pastry to an oblong about 45 x 15 cm (18 x 6 in) – this will be thin. Trim the edges and cut in half. Put one half on baking paper on a baking sheet. Leave pastry to relax.
❦ Melt the butter and fry the finely chopped onion until tender but not brown. Stir in the flour. Mix well. Add the milk by degrees, stirring all the time. Bring to the boil and cook for a minute. Season with salt, freshly ground black pepper and the merest scrap of nutmeg. Mix in the flaked fish, being very careful about removing all bones.
❦ Put half of the salmon mixture on to the pastry on the baking sheet leaving a 2.5 cm (1 in) gap around the edges. Wipe the mushrooms, slice them thinly and lay over the salmon. Then cover with the other half of the salmon mix. Brush the pastry edges with beaten egg.
❦ Give the second piece of pastry a light roll to make it a little larger than the bottom piece. Fold it in half lengthwise. With a sharp knife, make four slanting cuts through the fold. Still folded, Put it on one half of the slice. Open it out to cover the other half. Press the edges together. Knock them up and brush the top with beaten egg. Cook for 20-30 minutes.
❦ Garnish with the smallest feather or two of dill or fennel. Both can be easily grown in the garden.

SALMON STEAKS IN CREAM SAUCE

Serves 4

Four 2.5 cm (1 in) thick salmon steaks
2 tbsp fresh parsley, chopped
2 tsp lemon rind, grated
salt and pepper
1 bay leaf
275 ml (½ pint) single cream

❦ Heat the oven to 190C (375F) mark 5.
❦ Grease a shallow ovenproof dish and put in the salmon steaks in a single layer. Sprinkle with parsley, lemon rind, salt and pepper. Put the bay leaf on top and pour over the cream. Bake for 25 minutes, basting occasionally during cooking.
❦ Serve at once with new potatoes and peas.

SALMON BAKE

Serves 4

225 g (8 oz) can pink or red salmon
One 4 cm (1 ½ in) thick slice of white bread
150 ml (¼ pint) milk
1 egg
25 g (1 oz) butter, melted
½ tsp lemon juice
salt and pepper

❦ Heat the oven to 180C (350F) mark 4.
❦ Drain the salmon and discard the liquid. Remove the bones and skin and mash the salmon with a fork. Remove the crusts from the bread and soak the bread in milk for 20 minutes.
❦ Beat the bread and milk with a fork and work in the salmon, egg, butter, lemon juice and seasoning (the fish is usually rather salty, so be careful not to over-salt). Mix well and put into a 500 ml (1 pint) ovenproof dish which has been well greased. Bake for 1 hour.
❦ Serve hot with new potatoes or mashed potatoes and vegetables, or cold with salad. Leftovers make an excellent sandwich filling.

SMOKED
FISH

A range of recipes both economical and expensive,
from Smoked Fish Soufflé to Fisherman's Pie.

SMOKED MACKEREL
PASTIES

Serves 4

350 g (12 oz) Shortcrust Pastry (see page 357)
275 g (10 oz) smoked mackerel
225 g (8 oz) potatoes, diced
1 medium onion, diced
2 tomatoes
4 tbsp tomato ketchup
1 tsp lemon juice
salt and pepper
milk for glazing

❦ Heat the oven to 200C (400F) mark 6. Roll out the pastry and cut into four 15 cm (6 in) circles.
❦ Skin the fish and remove any bones. Cut into small pieces, and mix with the potatoes and onion. Skin the tomatoes and discard the pips. Chop the flesh roughly and mix with the fish and with the tomato ketchup, lemon juice and plenty of salt and pepper.
❦ Divide the mixture between the pastry circles, placing it in the centre of each one. Dampen the edges with water and seal the pastry in the centre to give a pasty shape.
❦ Place on a lightly greased baking sheet and brush well with milk. Prick each pasty two or three times with a fork. Bake for 10 minutes, then reduce the heat to 150C (300F) mark 2 and bake for a further 25 minutes.
❦ Serve hot or cold, with vegetables or a salad.

PEPPERED SMOKED MACKEREL SALAD

Serves 4

2 peppered smoked mackerel
450 g (1 lb) potatoes
1 eating apple, peeled and diced
1 green pepper, deseeded and chopped
5 tbsp oil
2 tbsp lemon juice
1 tbsp fresh chives, chopped
salt and pepper
pinch of turmeric

❦ Remove the skin and any bones from the mackerel and break the fish into large flakes. Boil the potatoes, cool and dice. Mix together the fish, potatoes, apple and green pepper.
❦ Mix the oil, lemon juice, chives, salt, pepper and turmeric and pour over the fish. Toss lightly and serve on a bed of lettuce or other salad greens.

Variations
Plain smoked mackerel may be used for this recipe, but the variety which is coated in cracked black peppercorns is particularly delicious. The fish is also available with a thick coating of herbs.

SMOKED HADDOCK SALAD

Serves 4

450 g (1 lb) haricot or red kidney beans, cooked
450 g (1 lb) smoked haddock
milk and water
150 ml (¼ pint) natural yoghurt
2 tbsp lemon juice
1 tbsp fresh parsley, chopped
2 tsp curry powder
salt and pepper
crisp lettuce or Chinese leaves
1 hard-boiled egg, sliced

❦ For speed, well drained canned beans may be used.
❦ Poach the fish in a mixture of milk and water for 10 minutes and drain well. Let cool and remove skin and bones. Flake the fish and mix with the beans.

❦ Mix the yoghurt, lemon juice, parsley, curry powder and seasoning together. Pour over the fish and mix well.
❦ Shred the lettuce or Chinese leaves and arrange in a bowl or on a flat platter. Spoon on the fish mixture and garnish with sliced egg.

SMOKED FISH SOUFFLE

Serves 4

75 g (3 oz) butter
50 g (2 oz) plain flour
275 ml (½ pint) milk
3 eggs
175 g (6 oz) smoked haddock or kipper, cooked
salt and pepper
25 g (1 oz) Parmesan cheese, grated

❦ Heat the oven to 190C (375F) mark 5. Oil a 575 ml (1 pint) soufflé dish.
❦ Melt the butter and stir in the flour. Cook over a low heat for 1 minute, stirring well. Add the milk gradually, and stir over a low heat until the sauce is thick.
❦ Separate the eggs and beat the yolks into the sauce. Remove from the heat. Fold in the flaked fish and season well with salt and pepper.
❦ Whisk the egg whites until standing in stiff peaks. Mix a spoonful of these into the fish mixture to loosen it and then gently fold in the remaining beaten egg white.
❦ Fill the dish with the mixture, and run a palette knife in a line 2.5 cm (1 in) deep all round the mixture about 1 cm (½ in) from the edge of the dish (this gives the soufflé a puffy 'cauliflower' top when baked). Sprinkle with Parmesan cheese. Bake for exactly 45 minutes and serve immediately.

FISHERMAN'S PIE

Serves 4

450 g (1 lb) smoked haddock or cod fillet
275 ml (½ pint) dry cider
150 ml (¼ pint) milk
40 g (1 ½ oz) butter
40 g (1 ½ oz) plain flour
3 hard-boiled eggs, chopped
100 g (4 oz) peas, cooked
salt and pepper
350 g (12 oz) Puff Pastry (see page 360)
egg for glazing

❦ Heat the oven to 220C (425F) mark 7.
❦ Poach the fish in the cider and milk until just cooked. Drain the fish, reserving the cooking liquid. Remove the skin and bones, and break the fish into chunks.
❦ Melt the butter and stir in the flour. Cook for 1 minute over a low heat and gradually add the strained fish cooking liquid. Bring to the boil, stirring well, and then simmer until smooth and creamy. Remove from the heat and stir in the fish, chopped eggs and peas. Season well with salt and pepper. Turn into a pie dish.
❦ Roll out the pastry and cover the pie dish, using any trimmings to make decorative leaves. Brush well with beaten egg to glaze. Bake for 30 minutes.
❦ Serve with mashed potatoes and vegetables.

SEAFOOD

MEDITERRANEAN SCAMPI

Serves 4

450 g (1 lb) shelled scampi
3 tbsp olive oil
1 small onion, finely chopped
1 garlic clove, crushed
4 tomatoes
1 tbsp fresh parsley, chopped
2 tsp lemon juice
salt and pepper

❦ If the scampi is frozen, thaw and then drain well.
❦ Heat the oil in a thick pan and fry the onion and
garlic until the onion is soft and golden. Skin the
tomatoes and discard the pips. Chop the flesh roughly and add to the pan with the scampi. Cook over a
low heat, stirring well, for 6 minutes until the scampi
are tender. Remove from heat and stir in the parsley,
lemon juice, salt and pepper.
❦ Serve hot with buttered rice or with crusty bread.

SCAMPI NEWBURG

Serves 4

24 shelled scampi
50 g (2 oz) butter
1 small onion, finely chopped
1 garlic clove, crushed
1 tbsp concentrated tomato purée
salt and pepper
275 ml (½ pint) single cream
2 egg yolks
3 tbsp brandy

❦ The scampi may be frozen but should be thawed
and well drained before use.
❦ Melt the butter and stir in the onion and garlic.
Cook gently over a low heat for 5 minutes. Add the
scampi and stir over a low heat for 2 minutes. Stir in
the tomato purée and season with salt and pepper.
❦ Mix the cream, egg yolks and brandy. Stir into
the scampi and heat through but do not boil.
❦ Serve with boiled rice.

SWEET AND SOUR PRAWNS

Serves 3-4

225 g (8 oz) prawns, shelled
1 tbsp dry sherry
salt and pepper
2 tbsp oil
1 large onion, thinly sliced
½ green pepper, deseeded and chopped
½ red pepper, deseeded and chopped
5 tbsp Chicken Stock (see page 335)
4 rings canned pineapple
1 tbsp cornflour
2 tsp soya sauce
5 tbsp wine vinegar
50 g (2 oz) sugar

❦ Put the prawns into a bowl and add the sherry, salt and pepper.

❦ Heat the oil and soften the onion and peppers over a low heat for 5 minutes. Add the stock. Cut the pineapple into small pieces and stir into the pan. Cover and cook gently for 5 minutes.

❦ Mix together the cornflour, soya sauce, vinegar and sugar. Stir into the pan and stir over a low heat until the sauce thickens. Stir in the prawns, cover and turn off the heat.

❦ Leave to stand for 2 minutes and serve with boiled rice.

SEAFOOD FLAN

Serves 6

225 g (8 oz) white fish, cooked
350 g (12 oz) Shortcrust Pastry (see page 357)
1 small onion, finely chopped
25 g (1 oz) butter
175 g (6 oz) prawns, peeled
3 eggs
150 ml (¼ pint) single cream
6 tbsp milk
40 g (1 ½ oz) Gruyère cheese, grated
salt
few drops of Tabasco sauce

❦ The white fish may be of any variety, or even good-quality smoked haddock can be used.

❦ Heat the oven to 200C (400F) mark 6. Line a 23 cm (9 in) flan ring with the pastry. Bake blind (see page 314) for 15 minutes.

❦ Soften the onion in the butter and stir in the prawns. Remove from heat and place in base of the baked pastry case. Beat together the eggs, cream, milk and cheese. Break the white fish into flakes and arrange on top of the prawns. Season the egg mixture with salt and Tabasco sauce and pour into the pastry case.

❦ Turn the oven down to 180C (350F) mark 4 and bake for 45 minutes. The flan is best when eaten warm rather than very hot or very cold.

SEAFOOD SPAGHETTI

Serves 4

225 g (8 oz) spaghetti
6 rashers bacon, chopped
25 g (1 oz) butter
1 medium onion, chopped
1 garlic clove, crushed
100 g (4 oz) mushrooms, sliced
225 g (8 oz) canned tomatoes
salt and pepper
100 g (4 oz) peeled prawns
100g (4 oz) cooked mussels or cockles
25 g (1 oz) grated Parmesan cheese

❦ Cook the spaghetti in a large pan of boiling salted water for 10 minutes. Drain well and sprinkle with a little oil to prevent sticking. Pile into a serving dish or on four individual plates.

❦ While the spaghetti is cooking, prepare the sauce. Put the bacon and butter into a pan and heat gently until the fat oozes from the bacon. Add the onion and garlic and fry over a low heat for 5 minutes. Add the mushrooms and continue cooking for 2 minutes. Stir in the tomatoes and their juice and season well with salt and pepper. Simmer for 10 minutes, stirring often. Add the prawns and mussels or cockles and heat through.

❦ Pour over the spaghetti and sprinkle with cheese.

CURRIED SHRIMPS

Serves 4

1 large onion, finely chopped
25 g (1 oz) butter
1 tbsp curry powder
1 cooking apple, peeled and chopped
275 ml (½ pint) chicken stock
1 tbsp concentrated tomato purée
2 tbsp fruit chutney, finely chopped
350 g (12 oz) peeled shrimps
1 tbsp lemon juice

❦ Cook the onion in the butter for 5 minutes until soft and golden. Stir in the curry powder and continue cooking for 3 minutes. Add the apple and stir over a low heat for 3 minutes. Add the stock, tomato purée and chutney, stir well and bring to the boil. Cover and simmer for 20 minutes. Stir in the shrimps and lemon juice and heat thoroughly.
❦ Serve with boiled rice or as the filling for scooped-out baked jacket potatoes.

SAILORS' MUSSELS

Serves 4

60-70 mussels in shells
1 small onion, finely chopped
1 garlic clove, crushed
275 ml (½ pint) dry cider or dry white wine
150 ml (¼ pint) water
pepper
25 g (1 oz) butter
15 g (½ oz) plain flour
1 tbsp fresh parsley, chopped

❦ Put the mussels in cold water and discard any that float. Scrub the mussels very thoroughly, removing any 'beards' by tugging with a sharp knife. Discard any mussels that are broken and any which remain open.
❦ Place in a large pan with the onion, garlic, cider or wine, water and pepper. Cover and cook very gently until the shells open, about 5-7 minutes. Always check mussels after cooking and this time discard any whose shells have not opened. Drain the mussels, retaining the liquid. Remove the top shells from mussels and discard. Divide the mussels in half shells between 4 individual bowls.
❦ Put the cooking liquid into a clean pan and bring to the boil. Soften the butter and mix well with the flour. Add tiny pieces of this mixture to the hot liquid and simmer until the liquid has thickened slightly. Season with salt and pepper to taste and stir in parsley. Pour over the mussels and serve at once.

SCALLOPS IN CHEESE SAUCE

Serves 4

8 scallops
425 ml (¾ pint) milk
25 g (1 oz) butter
25 g (1 oz) plain flour
50 g (2 oz) Cheddar cheese, grated
pinch of mustard powder
salt and pepper
50 g (2 oz) prawns, shelled
25 g (1 oz) fresh breadcrumbs
25 g (1 oz) butter, melted
25 g (1 oz) Parmesan cheese, grated

❦ Heat the oven to 180C (350F) mark 4.
❦ Put the scallops into a shallow pan and cover with the milk. Simmer over a low heat for 5 minutes. Drain the scallops, reserving the milk, and slice each one in two horizontally, to make 16 pieces and the 8 corals.
❦ Arrange in a shallow ovenproof dish. Melt the butter and work in the flour. Cook over a low heat for 1 minute and gradually add the reserved warm milk. Stir over low heat until the sauce thickens. Remove from the heat and stir in the Cheddar cheese, and season with mustard, salt and pepper.
❦ Sprinkle the prawns over the scallops and pour on the cheese sauce. Sprinkle the breadcrumbs on top of the dish. Drizzle on the melted butter and sprinkle with the Parmesan cheese. Bake for 15 minutes.
❦ Serve at once with rice or potatoes and a green salad.

SCALLOPS IN WINE SAUCE

Serves 4

8 scallops
275 ml (½ pint) dry white wine
1 small onion, finely chopped
sprig of parsley
sprig of thyme
1 bay leaf
75 g (3 oz) butter
2 tbsp lemon juice
100 g (4 oz) button mushrooms
25 g (1 oz) plain flour
salt and pepper
25 g (1 oz) Cheddar cheese, grated
25 g (1 oz) fresh white or brown breadcrumbs
1 tbsp Parmesan cheese, grated

❦ If possible, keep four deep scallop shells for the presentation of this dish, but otherwise use individual ovenproof dishes.
❦ Put the scallops into a pan with the wine, onion and herbs. Simmer for 5 minutes and drain the scallops, reserving the liquid. Chop the scallops into three white pieces and the coral.
❦ Melt 50 g (2 oz) of the butter and add the lemon juice. Add the mushrooms and cook over a low heat for 5 minutes. Add the remaining butter to the pan and stir in the flour. Cook for 1 minute and then strain in the cooking liquid from the scallops. Simmer for 3 minutes.
❦ Take off the heat, season and stir in the Cheddar cheese. Add the scallops. Spoon into scallop shells or individual dishes. Mix the breadcrumbs and Parmesan cheese and sprinkle on top.
❦ Put under a hot grill to brown the breadcrumbs.

COCKLE PIE

Serves 4

575 ml (1 pint) cooked cockles
225 g (8 oz) Shortcrust Pastry (see page 357)
6 spring onions or 1 small onion, finely chopped
100 g (4 oz) streaky bacon rashers, finely chopped
pepper

❦ Freshly cooked cockles will produce their own liquor, but if they have been bought from a fishmonger or frozen, chicken stock may be used in finishing the pie.
❦ Heat the oven to 200C (400F) mark 6. Line a 20 cm (8 in) flan ring with pastry. Bake blind (see page 314) for 15 minutes.
❦ Put a layer of cockles in the base and sprinkle with onion and bacon. Season with pepper and repeat the layers and top with a few cockles. Sprinkle on 150 ml (¼ pint) cockle liquor or chicken stock. Make a lattice from any remaining pastry and place over the filling.
❦ Turn the oven down to 180C (350F) mark 4 and bake for 30 minutes. Serve hot or cold.

SUMMER SEAFOOD SALAD

Serves 4

1 crisp lettuce
225 g (8 oz) button mushrooms
3 tbsp lemon juice
450 g (1 lb) tomatoes, skinned
3 eggs, hard-boiled
225 g (8 oz) canned tuna in brine
225 g (8 oz) prawns, peeled
4 tbsp olive oil
2 tbsp wine vinegar
salt and pepper

❦ Shred the lettuce and place in a large serving bowl. Do not peel the mushrooms but wipe and then trim the stems and slice the mushrooms thinly. Put them into a separate bowl and sprinkle with lemon juice. Leave to stand while preparing the rest of the salad.

❦ Quarter the tomatoes. Quarter the eggs lengthwise. Place on the lettuce. Drain the tuna and break into chunks. Add to a bowl with the prawns. Stir in the mushrooms.

❦ Mix together the oil, vinegar, salt and pepper. Pour over the salad and toss lightly so that the eggs do not break.

❦ Serve with a bowl of Mayonnaise (see page 346) flavoured with lemon juice.

SAVOURY FLAN

Serves 4-5

175 g (6 oz) Shortcrust Pastry (see page 357)
25 g (1 oz) butter
25 g (1 oz) plain flour
275 ml (½ pint) milk
100 g (4 oz) grated cheese
3 hard-boiled eggs, sliced
50 g (2 oz) shelled prawns
1 tsp chopped parsley
salt and pepper
parsley sprig to garnish

❦ Heat the oven to 200C (400F) mark 6. Roll out the pastry to a thickness of 5 mm (¼ inch) and use to line a 20 or 23 cm (8 or 9 inch) fireproof dish or flan ring. Bake blind (see page 314).

❦ Make the parsley sauce: melt the butter in a pan, add the flour and heat well over a low heat. Remove from the heat. Add the milk little by little, beating all the time. Return to the heat and bring slowly to the boil, stirring continuously. Cook for a minute or two.

❦ Add the cheese, eggs, prawns and 1 teaspoon parsley. Bring back almost to boiling point and season to taste. Pour into the hot pastry case and serve at once, garnished with a small sprig of parsley.

MEAT

ABOUT MEAT

For centuries meat has been the centre of culinary art in many different cultures, and is closely linked with many customs and traditions. 'Roast beef of old England' is famed abroad, and research shows that over 90 per cent of the population still feel that a 'proper meal' should contain meat, and for a great number that meal will be 'meat and two veg'. In Britain the average family spends 30 per cent of its total food bill on meat. With such a financial investment, it obviously makes sense to use meat to its best advantage. Knowing more about meat and its potential may be of assistance in economizing while still providing interesting and nutritionally balanced meals for the family, or in creating a culinary masterpiece for a special occasion. This book should help to achieve both.

Today there is probably a greater awareness of nutritional values and product quality than ever before. More and more people are concerned with the importance of maintaining a healthy diet and are eager for information and advice. Unfortunately there is a great deal of conflicting material published and the consumer is often very confused about the issues. The recent nutritional guidelines, which have emerged in several reports from various medical and scientific committees, are that, as a nation, we would be much healthier if we modified our diet. The recommendations are that we should eat less fat overall and reduce the percentage of saturated fat (from animal sources), using unsaturated fats and oils (vegetable sources) instead; reduce our sugar and salt intake and increase the dietary fibre in our diet. A further recommendation is that we should increase the percentage of vegetable protein we eat; this would automatically increase the fibre intake as the main sources of vegetable protein (nuts, pulse vegetables, beans and whole grain cereals) are all high in fibre and low in vegetable oil content. How do these recommendations fit in with meat eating?

Meat does not contain sugar or salt, so providing we do not add a great deal during cooking this is not a problem. Salt is not required in cooking, except for flavour (other than in bread-making, where it is necessary for a good texture). Increasingly people are finding that they can cut down slowly on the amount of salt in their food, eventually leaving it out altogether. It is amazing what a delicious flavour some foods have when not masked by salt.

The recipes in this chapter do not require salt, unless stated, although all can be seasoned to taste, which may include salt, pepper or your favourite flavourings. Other flavouring is often required to compensate for the lack of salt: herbs, spices, tomato ketchup and many others can be used.

When cutting down on fat, especially animal fat, meat consumption must be considered, although it accounts for only a quarter of the saturated fat in our diets. Over the last few years the meat industry has appreciated the consumer's requirement for leaner meat, and the breeding of quickly maturing animals, slaughtering at a younger age, better butchery techniques with pre-sale trimming, have all contributed to much leaner meat being available. It is up to the consumer to look around and choose the meat required. With greater demand the meat industry will continue to respond and produce a product that will sell.

The farmers, producers and butchers are playing their part, but there is plenty the consumer can do. If the meat is not already trimmed, this should be done before cooking. Add little or no fat during cooking; this may mean adapting your usual methods to prevent drying out, but foil or covered containers can help. Pre-frying is not necessary before making stews etc, and can be left out, or a minimum of vegetable oil used. The recipes in this book tend to do the latter; readers can opt for leaving that stage out if they wish. Mince and bacon can be cooked in their own fat, provided they are heated slowly at the beginning. Leaving out the browning stage may require added flavouring to compensate. Wherever possible, grill rather than fry and drain food well if fried or roasted.

❦ What is meat? ❦

Meat is the flesh or muscle of animals, with its associated fat, and in its wider meaning includes any part of an animal normally consumed. In Britain this usually means the produce from cattle, giving veal and beef, from sheep, giving lamb and mutton, and from pigs, giving pork and bacon, along with offal such as liver, kidney etc from these animals.

Meat is also used to mean the flesh from poultry and game, but that is fully dealt with in the next chapter on Poultry and Game.

❦ Methods of cooking ❦ meat

Meat is cooked to add distinctive flavour, to make it more tender and to make it look more appetising. The choice of cooking method depends largely on the amount of fine gristle contained in the muscles of the cut of meat. In order to get tender meat from muscles with a high proportion of gristle, it is necessary to use long, moist cooking such as stewing, braising or pot roasting. Cuts with little gristle do not need long, moist cooking and are cooked by the dry methods of roasting, frying and grilling.

Oven roasting

This is in fact baking. The food is cooked in an enclosed space, the oven, and is heated mainly by the convection of hot air. If the joint is very lean, extra fat can be added before roasting, alternatively a roasting bag or foil will prevent drying. An average oven temperature is 180C (350F) mark 4, which is hot enough to give good browning, but not too much shrinkage. Some people roast at a higher temperature for a shorter time. If potatoes and Yorkshire pudding are to be cooked at the same time, raise the temperature, but cook the meat low in the oven.

Weigh the joint, including stuffing, to calculate the cooking time. The size, shape and percentage of fat all affect cooking time and if using foil or film, will require a little longer.

Beef, rare: allow 20 minutes per ½ kg, plus 20 minutes over (15 minutes per 1 lb, plus 15 minutes over).

Beef, medium: allow 25 minutes per ½ kg, plus 25 minutes over (20 minutes per 1 lb, plus 20 minutes over).

Pork: allow 35 minutes per ½ kg, plus 30 minutes over (25 minutes per 1 lb, plus 30 minutes over).

Lamb: allow 30 minutes per ½ kg, plus 30 minutes over (25 minutes per 1 lb, plus 25 minutes over).

The only accurate way to roast meat is to use a meat thermometer, ensuring that the tip is in the centre of the joint and not touching a bone. When the thermometer registers the following temperatures, the meat is cooked.

60C (140F) for rare meat
65C (150F) for underdone
70C (160F) for medium
80C (180F) for well done (pork should always be at least medium or well done.)

Meat, particularly if lean, can be basted during cooking. This is unnecessary with foil or roasting film, which gives a result more like pot roasting, but is very succulent and juicy.

Spit roasting

In olden times the meat was roasted by being impaled on a rotating spit in front of a glowing fire. This was true roasting, cooking by radiant heat. Nowadays many grills have a rotisserie attachment where the meat is placed on a mechanically operated spit and cooked over or under a direct source of heat.

Allow 20 minutes per ½ kg, plus 20 minutes over (15 minutes per 1 lb, plus 15 minutes over). Pork may require a little longer.

Grilling

This is a quick method of cooking by radiant heat from a preheated gas, electric or charcoal fire or grill. As the heat is fierce, the meat needs to be brushed with oil or butter to prevent drying.

Grilling times vary according to the thickness of the meat and the desired degree of cooking. Grilling is only suitable for small tender cuts. As a general guide, for a 2.5 cm (1 in) thick steak or chop, allow 5 minutes per side for rare, 7 minutes per side for medium and 12 minutes per side for well done.

Frying

As with grilling, frying is only suitable for small tender cuts. Shallow- or dry-frying, rather than deep-fat frying is used for meat. The fat should be preheated, to avoid greasy results. Turn the meat from time to time and drain well on absorbent paper before serving.

Cooking time varies according to the thickness of the meat and the desired degree of cooking. Allow 7-10 minutes for 2.5 cm (1 in) thick steaks, and 4-5 minutes for 1 cm (½ in) thick steaks.

Stewing

This is the cooking of pieces of meat in liquid, such as water, stock, wine or cider, with added flavourings and/or vegetables, herbs or spices, with or without a thickening agent.

The meat is cooked in 275-575 ml (½-1 pint) of liquid and should only simmer. Stewing can be done in a covered pan, or in a casserole dish in a slow oven, 170C (325F) mark 3, when it is usually called casseroling. Joints and large pieces of meat, when covered with liquid and simmered are cooked by boiling; this is, in fact, stewing.

Stews should be stirred from time to time and not allowed to boil dry. Ensure the lid fits well and top up with stock or water, if necessary. Time the cooking from when the stew or cooking liquor comes to the boil, and allow a minimum of 1 ½ hours. For larger joints, allow 30 minutes per ½ kg (25 minutes per 1 lb), plus an extra 30 minutes. Cuts with a lot of gristle may require longer.

If the meat is covered with water and brought to the boil, it produces a white stew. If the meat and vegetables are fried first, a brown stew is the result.

❦ Cuts suitable for different cooking methods ❦

Cooking method	Beef	Pork	Lamb
Frying & Grilling	Rump Fillet Steaks Sirloin	Fillet (tenderloin) Loin chops Spare rib chops Belly - sliced	Best end of neck cutlets Loin Chops Chump
Roasting	Topside Sirloin Fore rib Silverside Thick flank	Neck end (spare rib & blade bone) Loin Leg Hand & spring Belly	Loin Best end of neck Leg Shoulder Breast
Braising	Chuck & blade Brisket Thin flank Thick flank Topside Silverside Thick rib	Spare rib chops Belly	Middle neck Breast Shoulder Scrag
Pot Roasting	Silverside Thick flank Topside Thick rib Thin rib Brisket		
Boiling	Brisket (salted) Silverside (salted)	Belly (can be salted) Hand & spring (can be salted)	
Stewing	Thin flank Shin Leg Neck & clod Chuck & blade Skirt	Hand & spring Shoulder	Scrag Breast Middle neck

NB: All cuts of pork and most lamb cuts can be roasted.

Braising

After initial browning in hot fat, the meat is placed on a bed of fried vegetables (called a mirepoix) with just enough water, stock or wine to cover the vegetables. Braising can be done on top of the cooker or in the oven, but the pan must have a tightly fitting lid to prevent loss of moisture. Meat should be braised in a slow oven, 180C (350F) mark 4, or over a low heat on top of the cooker, for 50 minutes per ½ kg (45 minutes per 1 lb). With a minimum of 2 hours for joints, 1½-2 hours for steaks and ¾-1 hour for chops.

After cooking, the meat is removed and the cooking liquor reduced by boiling, and used to glaze the meat. The vegetables can be served with the meat, but as they are very well cooked it is usually more satisfactory to liquidize them, and use them as a basis for a sauce or gravy. If the braise is chilled overnight, any fat can be skimmed off before reheating.

Pot roasting

This is really a combination of frying and steaming. The meat is browned all over, then covered and cooked slowly with a minimum amount of liquid either in the oven or on top of the cooker.

The joint should be turned every 30 minutes, but do not remove the lid at other times, or the steam will be released. Allow 50 minutes per ½ kg (45 minutes per 1 lb) in an oven at 180C (350F) mark 4.

Using a pressure cooker for the moist cooking methods will reduce the cooking time to a third, in most cases. Consult the manufacturer's instructions for details. The amount of liquid required is usually a third less

❦ Carving and serving ❦

Carving is no problem given a few simple rules. The essential tools are a two pronged fork with a finger guard, a large sharp carving or cook's knife and an effective means of sharpening the knife at regular intervals. Boned and rolled joints are simply cut through. The butcher will usually bone a joint if asked, however with a good sharp knife and practice, it is easy to do yourself. Start from where the bone can be seen, work along it, cutting the meat away and follow the bone through. Any slips of the knife can be sewn up with cotton before cooking, provided it is removed before serving. Carving bone-in joints varies according to the position and shape of the bone. As a general rule, meat is carved down on to the bone, and the slice then cut off the bone.

Where a joint contains a backbone, chining by the butcher will aid carving. Ensure that the meat is stable, on a wooden board or spiked meat dish, which should be on a non-slip surface.

Wherever possible cut across the grain to shorten the muscle fibre length. When carving a leg or shoulder, it is often easier to hold the shank bone with one hand, using a tissue or paper towel. When doing this, the cutting edge of the knife must be angled away from the hand. With legs and shoulders, cut the meat down to the bone on one side and remove, then turn the joint over and repeat, or cut slices horizontally from the other side.

Inexperienced cooks may prefer to carve in the kitchen and reheat the meat to serve. Learning to carve can be a slow business, and the meat and vegetables can be cold by the time everything is ready. New cutting techniques and boneless joints, which are becoming more popular, will make carving and serving very much easier. Cold meat cuts up more economically than hot, and overcooked meat far less economically.

If meat is carved cold for reheating, it is imperative that the reheating must be quick and thorough, the meat must be served immediately and any not consumed discarded. All meat once cooked must be kept protected from contamination by dirt and pests, and refrigerated as quickly as possible. Warm meat is an ideal breeding ground for the bacteria that are responsible for food poisoning.

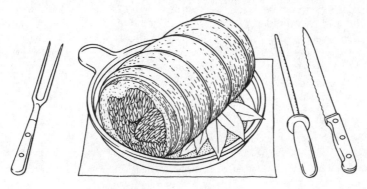

❦ Accompaniments when serving meat ❦

Meat	Sauces	Stuffing	Accompaniments
Beef	Horseradish cream Horseradish in white 　sauce Mustard sauce Brown onion sauce Red wine sauce	Sausage meat Cooked rice and bacon Mashed chestnuts Chopped cooked celery Mushroom and herbs	Yorkshire pudding Batter popovers Roast parsnips Suet or oatmeal 　dumplings
Veal	Thick gravy, 　sherry-flavoured Tomato Sauce Cumberland sauce Sherry or Marsala sauce	Lemon and thyme Cooked rice and ham Chopped parsley and 　bacon (cooked) Walnut, orange and 　coriander	Bacon Rolls Baked Ham or bacon Risotto, noodles or 　spaghetti
Lamb & Mutton	Mint sauce Onion sauce Caper sauce Madeira sauce	Garlic, cooked rice 　and capers Rosemary and/or onions Mint or watercress Lentils	Suet or oatmeal 　dumplings Braised onions Potato and onion 　casserole Redcurrant or mint 　jelly
Pork	Thin gravy, 　cider-flavoured Apple sauce Gooseberry 　purée Cranberry 　sauce or jelly	Sage and onion Chopped apples and 　raisins Chopped cooked 　celery and onions Prunes and walnuts Apricot and walnut	Pease pudding Sauerkraut Baked apples Cucumber salad Baked beans Red cabbage Apple cake
Bacon & Gammon	Parsley sauce Cumberland sauce Mustard sauce Gravy with cider Clove and brown 　sugar coating Raisin Sauce	Prunes Sage and onion Chopped apples and 　walnuts Almond and raisin Apricot	Apple or 　pineapple rings Half peaches Butter beans in 　parsley sauce Pease pudding

The table above gives some traditional accompaniments and new ideas.
Some of the recipes appear in Sauces, Marinades and Dressings and Stuffings and Accompaniments (see pages 338-55).

BEEF AND VEAL

*An interesting selection of beef and veal recipes ranging from
Pot Roast Beef with Whisky to Veal Orloff – to suit every taste and budget.*

❧ Beef ❧

When buying beef, it will be bright red when it is first cut, but goes darker on exposure to air. Look for fine even graining and firm fat. The colour of the fat depends on the breed and its feed, but is usually creamy white. Avoid meat which is dried or discoloured, and if it has too much marbling fat within the lean.

Cuts of beef
Shin (foreleg) and leg (hind-leg)
This is lean meat with a high proportion of gristle. It requires long slow moist cooking and can be used for stews, casseroles, stocks, soup and brawn.

Neck and clod
Normally cut up as stewing steak or minced.

Chuck and blade steak
A large, fairly lean cut of meat, removed from the bone and generally sold as chuck steak for braising, stewing and putting into pies.

Brisket
Brisket is sold in pieces, on the bone, or boned and rolled, and is suitable for braising or boiling. It can be salted and is excellent boiled and served cold. It is recognised by its layers of fat and lean.

Thin and thick ribs
These are usually sold boned and rolled, for braising or pot roasting.

Fore ribs
A good roasting joint on the bone or boned and rolled.

Sirloin
A tender and delicious cut of meat from the loin. It is sold either on or off the bone as a joint for roasting, or as steaks for grilling or frying. Sirloin steaks are slices of the main back muscle, sometimes called the eye muscle, removed from the backbone, but still with its layer of back fat. T-bone steaks are the same cut, but cut through the T-shaped backbone, and include a piece of the fillet muscle as well. Porterhouse steaks are cut from the fore rib end.

Fillet steak

The fillet is a long muscle running along the inside of the backbone, in the sirloin area. It is very tender as the muscle is hardly used in the live animal, consequently it is much sought after and therefore very expensive. Although tender, it often does not have as much flavour as other cuts of beef. It is sold whole, or in large pieces for such classic dishes as Beef Wellington (fillet steak in a puff pastry case) or in slices as fillet steak. It can be tied to keep it round, and steaks cut from this are called tournedos. Cut into strips, it is the basis for Beef Stroganoff, and minced, for Steak Tartare. The Châteaubriand steak is cut from the place where the fillet divides to join the muscles of the rump.

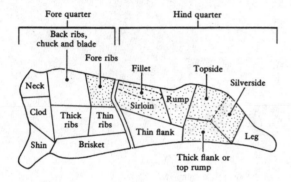

Rump steak

This is an excellent lean and tender cut, usually sold in slices for grilling and frying. Steaks are cut down, through the back fat to the hip bone, and have a characteristic oblong shape, with the fat at one end. One slice of rump steak, depending on the area from which it comes, is often quite enough to serve two.

Thin flank

Ideal for braising or stewing, it is often salted or pickled, and frequently sold as mince.

Thick flank

A lean cut suitable for roasting, pot roasting and braising, or when sliced for braising or frying.

Topside

A lean cut, with little or no natural fat, it is usually sold in rolled joints, which have had a layer of fat tied round them. It roasts and pot roasts well.

Silverside

A very lean joint, often treated like topside. If roasting, baste while cooking to prevent drying out. Silverside is traditionally salted and sold for boiling,

and is used for boiled beef and carrots. Uncooked salted beef is grey, but turns its characteristic pink during cooking.

❦ Veal ❦

The cuts of veal correspond in name and position with those of lamb (see page 135). However, the shank end of the leg is more usually called the knuckle end and the fillet end is often cut in thin slices, which are beaten out to produce escalopes. The animal is larger than the lamb, so joints, chops etc are correspondingly bigger. Cuts can be cooked in the same way, the lower part of the legs and necks are best stewed, the remainder can be roasted, grilled or fried according to cut. Take care if the veal is very thin that it does not dry out during cooking. Cover with a sauce, foil or a lid if necessary. Veal cooks very quickly, and spoils if overcooked. Marinating will often add flavour, and help to keep the meat moist..

BOILED SALT BEEF

Serves 6-8

900 g (2 lb) salt brisket
cold Basic Brown Stock (see page 335) to cover
2 onions, quartered
4 carrots, sliced
1 small turnip, chopped
1 tsp black peppercorns
2 tsp mixed herbs

❦ Soak the brisket overnight, then drain and discard the soaking water.
❦ Place the meat in a large pan and cover with stock. Add the vegetables, pepper and herbs (do not add salt). Cover and bring to the boil. Simmer, very slowly for about 1 ½ hours.
❦ Served sliced with unthickened cooking liquor and vegetables, and boiled potatoes. If serving cold, allow to cool in cooking liquor. Slice and serve with salads or in sandwiches, with horseradish sauce.

POT ROAST BEEF WITH WHISKY

Serves 4-6

900 g (2 lb) joint (flank, top rib or chuck)
4 tbsp oil
2 carrots, sliced
2 small parsnips, sliced
1 stick of celery, chopped
75 ml (3 fl oz) whisky

❧ Heat the oven to 180C (350F) mark 4. If possible, use a casserole in which the meat can be fried and roasted, or use a frying pan and then transfer the meat and fat to an earthenware casserole to pot roast.
❧ Brown the joint well in oil. Add the vegetables around the joint and pour in the whisky. Cover with a well-fitting lid. Cook for about 2 hours, turning the joint once, until the meat is tender. Transfer the meat to a warmed serving dish. Use the cooking liquor, liquidized if preferred, diluted with water and suitably thickened, for a sauce or gravy.

BRAISED MARINATED BEEF

Serves 4-8

Marinade for Red Meats (see page 345)
1-2 kg (2-4 lb) joint of beef (brisket, chuck, top ribs)
4 tbsp oil
50 g (2 oz) streaky bacon pieces
225 g (8 oz) onions, quartered
225 g (8 oz) carrots in strips
salt and freshly ground black pepper
stock or water

❧ Marinate the meat for several hours, but preferably overnight. If using the oven, heat to 180C (350F) mark 4.
❧ Use a deep pan or enamelled casserole and brown the joint of meat well in the oil. Remove the meat. Add the bacon, vegetables, and salt and pepper. Fry to brown. Leave in pan or transfer to casserole dish if necessary. Place the meat on top.
❧ Make the marinade up to 275 ml (½ pint) with stock or water and pour it over the meat. Cover and simmer or cook in the oven for 2 ½-3 hours until the

meat is cooked to the required degree. Turn the joint over once during cooking.
❧ Serve on a bed of boiled noodles with the vegetables around, or liquidized and used as a basis for a gravy or sauce.

BEEF CARBONNADE

Serves 4

450-700 g (1-1 ½ lb) chuck steak in large cubes
1 tbsp flour
2 tbsp oil
salt and freshly ground black pepper
1 large onion, sliced
4 celery stalks, chopped
2 carrots, sliced
275 ml (½ pint) beer or stout
1 tbsp vinegar
1 bouquet garni
1 tbsp chopped parsley to garnish

❧ Heat the oven to 170C (325F) mark 3 or simmer the carbonnade on top of the stove.
❧ Toss the meat in the flour and then fry in oil to brown. Season to taste and add the onion, celery and carrots and fry for a few minutes. Add the beer, vinegar and bouquet garni. Stir well and transfer to a warm casserole with lid, or cook on a very low heat in a covered pan.
❧ Cook for 2-2 ½ hours or until the meat is tender. Add a little water to the casserole if it becomes dry during cooking. Discard bouquet garni and adjust the seasoning.
❧ Garnish with chopped parsley. Serve with creamed or jacket potatoes.

STEAK AND KIDNEY PIE

Serves 4

700 g (1 ½ lb) braising steak
175 g (6 oz) ox kidney
25 g (1 oz) plain flour
salt and pepper
25 g (1 oz) dripping
1 onion, peeled and chopped
275 ml (½ pint) Basic Brown Stock (see page
   335) or water
1 ½ tsp Home-made Mustard (see page 366)
225 g (8 oz) Puff Pastry (see page 360)
1 egg to glaze

❦ Cut the steak and kidney into cubes, trimming excess fat, gristle and tubes away. Season the flour and toss the meat in it. Heat the dripping and fry the onion until brown. Add the meat and brown. Stir in the stock and mustard. Cover the pan and simmer slowly for 1 ½ hours then leave to cool.
❦ Heat the oven to 230C (450F) mark 8. Roll out the pastry to fit the top of a I litre (1 ¾ pint) oval or rectangular pie dish. Leave to relax.
❦ Spoon the meat into the dish. From the pastry trimmings roll out a 2.5 cm (1 inch) strip. Damp the edges of the dish, put on the strip; moisten it and carefully position the lid over the meat. Press the edges firmly together. Decorate the edge with the prongs of a fork and knock up (see page 357). Cut out a few leaves and a rose and put around the slit cut in the top to let out the steam. Brush with beaten egg.
❦ Cook for 30 minutes, covering with greaseproof paper if it starts getting too brown.

STEAK AND KIDNEY PUDDING

Serves 4

225 g (8 oz) Suet Crust Pastry (see page 361)
350 g (12 oz) chuck steak
100 g (4 oz) ox kidney
1 onion
50 g (2 oz) mushrooms
2 tbsp plain flour
salt and pepper
150 ml (¼ pint) Basic Brown Stock (see page
   335)

❦ Put a pan of water on to boil. Cut the meat into strips, trim the kidney and dice. Peel and slice the onion. Wipe and slice the mushrooms including the stalks. Season the flour and toss the meat in it.
❦ Grease a 750 ml (1 ½ pint) pudding basin. Roll out the pastry and use to line the basin (see page 362). Put the meat, kidney, onion and mushrooms into the lined basin. Do not pack it too tightly. Season the stock and pour into the basin. Damp the edges of the pastry. Roll the lid out to fit the top of the basin, position and seal well. Cover the basin.
❦ Stand the basin in the boiling water and cover the pan. Boil steadily, not too fast, for 3-3 ½ hours. Keep an eye on the water level and top up as necessary.
❦ This traditional pudding is served in the basin, with a linen napkin wrapped around the outside. A small jug of boiling water is served beside it. When the first piece of pastry is lifted out a tablespoon or two of boiling water is poured in, to make a little more gravy.
❦ Cheaper cuts of meat can be used, but will need pre-cooking. Let the meat get cold before putting into the pudding. It will then need 1 ½-2 hours' cooking.

BEEF STROGANOFF

Serves 4

450-700 g (1-1 ½ lb) fillet steak, cut in thin strips
ground black pepper
½ tsp basil
25 g (1 oz) butter
1 tbsp oil
50 g (2 oz) streaky bacon, cut in strips
1 onion, finely chopped
225 g (8 oz) mushrooms, sliced
½ tsp ground mace
1 tbsp parsley, chopped
150-275 ml (¼-½ pint) soured cream or natural
   yoghurt
chopped parsley to garnish

❦ Season the steak with the pepper and basil. Heat the butter and oil and stir-fry the steak and bacon for about 5 minutes until the meat is browned all over. Remove the meat from the pan and keep warm.
❦ Add the onion to the pan and fry gently until transparent; add the mushrooms and fry for 3 minutes. Return the meat to pan and add the mace, parsley and cream. Heat through but do not boil.
❦ Serve garnished with parsley on a bed of boiled or steamed rice or buttered noodles.

STEAK, KIDNEY AND MUSHROOM PIE

Serves 4-6

225 g (8 oz) Flaky or Mixer Pastry, using plain
  flour (see pages 361 or 358)
450 g (1 lb) stewing steak in 2.5 cm (1 in) cubes
100-225 g (4-8 oz) young ox kidney
1 tbsp flour, seasoned
½ tsp mixed herbs
1 onion, finely chopped or left whole and
  spiked with cloves
100 g (4 oz) mushrooms, sliced
water or stock
egg for glazing

❦ If time is short, the filling can be cooked in a pressure cooker, as for a stew. For the best flavour and
most delicious pie, however, the meat should be
cooked from raw, under the pastry crust.
❦ Heat the oven to 220C (425F) mark 7 for flaky
and 200C (400F) mark 6 for mixer pastry.
❦ Make the pastry and leave in a cool place to relax.
Toss the steak and kidney in seasoned flour. Mix in
the herbs, onion and mushrooms. Place in a 1 litre (2
pint) pie dish (with a flat rim). Ensure the dish is full,
if necessary pad out with raw potato. Add sufficient
stock or water to come half-way up the meat.
❦ Roll out the pastry to the shape of dish, plus about
1 cm (½ in) extra all round. Cut out the shape of the
pie dish. Use the trimmings to cover the rim of pie
dish. Use water to stick the pastry to the dish. Cover
with pastry, pressing down the edges to seal. Knock
up the edges, making horizontal cuts with the back
of a small knife, then flute around rim of pie by
bringing up the back of a knife, every 5 cm (2 in).
Decorate with pastry leaves, and cut a hole in the
middle to release the steam. Glaze with beaten egg.
❦ Bake for 30 minutes, then reduce heat to 180C
(350F) mark 4 for a further 1 ½-2 hours until the
meat feels tender when tried with a skewer through
the hole in the top. If necessary, cover the pastry
with greaseproof paper to prevent it burning. Top
up with stock if required.
❦ Serve with extra gravy.

PEPPERED BEEF

Serves 4

25 g (1 oz) flour
1 tsp ground ginger
salt and freshly ground black pepper
450-700 g (1-1 ½ lb) braising steak
3 tbsp oil
225 g (8 oz) tomatoes, skinned
1-2 tsp chilli or Tabasco sauce
1 tbsp Worcestershire sauce
2 tbsp wine vinegar
2 garlic cloves, crushed
150 ml (¼ pint) tomato juice or stock
1 small red pepper, deseeded and sliced in
  rings
1 small green pepper, deseeded and sliced in
  rings
1 yellow pepper, deseeded and sliced in rings (if
  available)
100 g (4 oz) mushrooms

❦ Heat the oven to 170C (325F) mark 3. Mix the
flour, ginger and seasoning and rub into the steak.
Fry in the oil to brown both sides. Transfer to a
casserole dish.
❦ In a liquidizer, combine the tomatoes, chilli
sauce, Worcestershire sauce, vinegar, garlic and
tomato juice. Pour over meat, cover and cook for
about 1 ½ hours. Add the peppers and mushrooms
and cook for a further 30 minutes or until meat is
tender and pepper cooked but not too soft.
❦ Serve with rice, pasta or jacket potatoes.

Variation
A can of red kidney beans can be added with the peppers if desired. This will stretch the meal to serve 6,
and provide vegetable protein and fibre.

GOULASH WITH NATURAL YOGHURT

Serves 4

450-700 g (1-1 ½ lb) stewing beef (or veal), cut in
  2.5 cm (1 in) cubes
3 tbsp oil
1 large onion, chopped
1 garlic clove, finely chopped
2 tbsp paprika
½ tsp caraway seeds
400 g (14 oz) can of tomatoes
425 ml (¾ pint) Brown Stock (see page 335)
1 red pepper, deseeded and cut in strips
450 g (1 lb) potatoes, scrubbed and sliced
100 g (4 oz) button mushrooms
black pepper to taste
150 ml (¼ pint) natural yoghurt (or soured
  cream)

❦ Heat the oven to 150C (300F) mark 2 or simmer
on top of the stove in a pan.
❦ Brown meat in hot oil. Add onion, garlic, paprika and caraway and fry for a few minutes, stirring
continuously. Add the tomatoes and stock. Cook
with a lid on, for 2-3 hours until meat is tender.
❦ Add the pepper and potatoes for the last 45 minutes, and the mushrooms for the last 10 minutes.
Adjust the seasoning, serve in a warmed dish, with
yoghurt poured on top and swirled in.
❦ Serve with a green or mixed salad. The potatoes
can be omitted and the goulash served with dumplings, pasta or rice.

BEEF AND PRUNE RAGOUT

Serves 4

575 ml (1 pint) Basic Brown Stock (see page
  335), beer or wine
225 g (8 oz) prunes
450-700 g (1-1 ½ lb) chuck steak, cut in cubes or
  pieces
25 g (1 oz) seasoned flour
3 tbsp oil
1 tbsp tomato purée
2 bay leaves
225 g (8 oz) small tomatoes, skinned

❦ Heat the stock and pour over the prunes. Leave
to soak, if possible overnight.
❦ Coat the meat in flour and fry in oil to brown.
Add the tomato purée, bay leaves and about 6 finely
chopped prunes, with the drained stock.
❦ Simmer for 1 ¼ hours until the meat is tender.
Add the remaining prunes and tomatoes, whole, and
cook for approximately 20 minutes until the prunes
are soft but the prunes and tomatoes have not collapsed in shape.
❦ Serve with potatoes, pasta or rice.

Variations
Prunes can be replaced with dried apricots, peaches
or large raisins.

BEEF AND HARICOT BEANS

Serves 4

100 g (4 oz) haricot beans, soaked overnight
450 g (1 lb) chuck or braising steak, cut in 2.5
  cm (1 in) cubes
100 g (4 oz) lean streaky bacon pieces
1 large onion, sliced
2 carrots, sliced
2 garlic cloves, crushed
225 g (8 oz) tomatoes, skinned
bouquet garni or 1 tsp herbs
275 ml (½ pint) Basic Brown Stock (see page
  335)
275 ml (½ pint) red wine or further stock
salt and freshly ground black pepper
chopped parsley to garnish

❦ Put all ingredients in a large pan and bring to the
boil. Stir well and cover with a well-fitting lid.
Simmer for 2-2 ½ hours, until the meat is tender.
❦ The casserole should not need thickening as the
haricot beans will absorb excess liquid, but adjust
consistency if necessary. Serve sprinkled with
chopped parsley.
❦ This dish re-heats well next day, and is delicious
served with a chunk of granary bread.

BRAISED BEEF AND CHESTNUTS

Serves 4

marinade (optional, see page 345) or 275 ml (½ pint) Basic Brown Stock (see page 335), if not using marinade
450-700 g (1-1 ½ lb) lean braising steak, cut 2.5 cm (1 in) thick
450 g (1 lb) mixed vegetables in season, cut in 1 cm (½ in) cubes
100 g (4 oz) dried or 225 g (8 oz) fresh, cooked chestnuts
1 red pepper, deseeded and sliced

❦ If using a marinade, steep meat in it for several hours, but preferably overnight.
❦ Heat the oven to 170C (325F) mark 3. Place vegetables in casserole dish with dried chestnuts, if using. Place the meat on top. Pour over the stock or marinade.
❦ Cover and cook slowly for 1 ½-2 hours. Add the pepper 30 minutes before the end of cooking, with fresh chestnuts if using. If the lid is not tight-fitting, more stock may be required.
❦ Serve with jacket potatoes cooked at the same time.

STIR-FRY BEEF

Serves 4-6

1 tbsp cornflour
450 g (1 lb) rump steak in paper-thin slices
3 tbsp oil
4 spring onions, finely chopped
100-175 g (4-6 oz) Chinese leaves or white cabbage, finely shredded
75 g (3 oz) bean sprouts
2 sticks celery, finely chopped
1 tbsp soy sauce or more to taste

❦ Mix the cornflour to a paste with 3 tbsp water and mix with steak. Heat the oil and stir-fry the meat for about 3 minutes over a high heat in a frying pan or wok. Remove from the pan, drain and keep hot.
❦ Adding a little more oil if necessary, stir-fry the vegetables, also over a high heat, for about 5 minutes or until cooked to taste. The vegetables should still be crisp. Pour over the soy sauce, return the meat to the pan and stir well.
❦ Serve immediately with boiled or fried rice, or as part of a Chinese meal.

BEEF SLICES IN RED WINE

Serves 4

4 slices of topside or similar, about 1 cm (½ in) thick
150 ml (¼ pint) red wine
1 onion, finely chopped
1 bay leaf
1 tsp parsley
¼ tsp marjoram
¼ tsp thyme
25 g (1 oz) flour
3 tbsp oil
275 ml (½ pint) Basic Brown Stock (see page 335)
salt and freshly ground black pepper
225 g (8 oz) button onions
225 g (8 oz) baby carrots
2 tbsp chopped parsley to garnish

❦ Lay the meat in shallow dish, or in sealable polythene container. Pour over the wine, add the onion and herbs and marinate for several hours, but preferably overnight.
❦ Heat the oven to 150C (300F) mark 2. Drain the meat well, reserving the marinade. Coat with flour and fry in oil to brown. Place meat in a casserole dish. Add any remaining flour to the fat, and cook to brown, but do not burn.
❦ Slowly add the stock and marinade. Season to taste, and pour over meat. Cover and cook slowly for 1-1 ½ hours. Add the onions and carrots and cook for a further hour until the meat is tender.
❦ Serve sprinkled with chopped parsley.

Variation
Other meats can be cooked in this way, using white wine with lighter meats.

SWISS STEAKS

Serves 4

1 tbsp seasoned flour
four 1 cm (½ in) thick slices of topside or
    similar
25 g (1 oz) butter or margarine
1 large onion, finely chopped
2 sticks celery, finely chopped
400 g (14 oz) can tomatoes, broken up
2 tsp tomato purée
½ tsp Worcestershire sauce
150 ml (¼ pint) Basic Brown Stock (see page
    335) or water
4 tbsp single cream or yoghurt (optional)

❦ Press flour well into the slices of meat. Fry in butter to brown both sides. Add the onion and cook for a few minutes. Stir in the celery, tomatoes, purée, Worcestershire sauce and stock, cover and simmer, or put into a casserole dish, and cook covered at 170C (325F) mark 3 for 2-2 ½ hours, until the meat is tender.
❦ Serve topped with cream or yoghurt, with boiled or creamed potatoes and fresh green vegetables.

STEAK DIANE

Serves 4

450 g (1 lb) grilling or frying steak beaten out to
    ½ cm (¼ in) thick
25 g (1 oz) butter
3 tbsp oil
1 onion, very finely chopped
1 garlic clove, crushed
50 g (2 oz) bacon, finely chopped
100 g (4 oz) mushrooms, finely chopped
1 tbsp fresh chives, chopped
freshly ground black pepper
3 tbsp brandy, warmed
150 ml (¼ pint) single cream

❦ Cut the beaten steak into a square with sides about 7.5 cm (3 in). Heat some of the butter and oil and when hot, fry the steak for 1 ½ minutes on either side. Drain and keep warm.
❦ Adding more fat if required, fry the onion for 2 minutes. Add the garlic, bacon, mushrooms, chives

and seasoning and stir-fry to cook, approximately 3 minutes. Return the meat to the pan.
❦ Warm the brandy, pour over meat and ignite. Let the brandy burn until it extinguishes. Pour in the cream and warm but do not boil.
❦ Serve on a warm platter with potato piped around as a border. This dish can be garnished with Bacon Rolls (see page 355), sliced mushrooms or chopped parsley.

CARPET BAG STEAKS

Serves 4

4 thick pieces of fillet or rump steak
24 prepared mussels (or 12 oysters), fresh,
    canned, frozen or smoked
50 g (2 oz) butter
2 tbsp parsley, chopped
1 garlic clove, crushed
2 tbsp lemon juice
salt and freshly ground black pepper
melted butter

❦ Split the steaks like flat purses to make pockets. Mix the mussels or oysters with butter, parsley, garlic, lemon juice and seasoning, and divide between the pockets in the steaks. Skewer or sew up. Brush with melted butter and sprinkle with ground black pepper.
❦ Grill or fry until cooked to personal taste. The cooking time will depend on thickness of the steak and the heat of the grill or pan.
❦ Turn once during cooking, and serve immediately with tomatoes, mushrooms and potatoes.

BEEF STEAK EN CROUTE

Serves 4-6

Red Meat Marinade (optional, see page 345)
4 fillet steaks or a piece 1-1 ½ kg (2-3 lb)
225 g (8 oz) Flaky or Mixer Pastry, using plain
    flour (see pages 361 or 358)
1 onion, finely chopped oil for frying, with
    some butter if preferred
100 g (4 oz) mushrooms, finely chopped
100 g (4 oz) liver pâté
2 tbsp brandy
3 tbsp cream
freshly ground black pepper
egg to glaze

❦ If using the marinade, steep the meat in it for a
few hours, or overnight. Drain. The marinade can be
used as a basis for a sauce.
❦ Make the pastry and leave in the refrigerator to
relax. Fry the onion in oil until soft, add the mushrooms and cook for a few minutes. Mix the onions,
mushrooms, pâté, brandy and cream together.
❦ Heat the oil and butter and fry the steaks for 1
minute each side. If using a large piece of meat, fry
turning regularly to brown, for about 5 minutes.
Longer or shorter cooking at this stage will make the
finished steak more well done or rarer.
❦ If using a large piece of meat, slit it down but not
through, into portions. Spread the pâté mixture on
each steak, or in the slits of the larger piece. Sprinkle
well with freshly ground black pepper. Heat the
oven to 230C (450F) mark 8.
❦ Roll the pastry out into 4 circles, or an oblong
approximately 20 x 25 cm (8 x 10 in), trim the edges.
Place the fillets pâté side down on the pastry, damp-
en the edges with water, and make into a parcel; wrap
the pastry around the large piece. Place on a baking
tray, join side down. Decorate with pastry leaves
made from trimmings, and glaze with beaten egg.
❦ Bake in the hot oven for 20-25 minutes for individual, and 40-45 minutes for a large croûte. The
pastry should be well risen and golden brown.
❦ Serve immediately.

Variations
Use ham or bacon, or chopped anchovies in place of
the pâté.
❦ The piece of steak can be prepared as above, and
then roasted for 45-60 minutes and served without
being cooked en croûte.

OSSO BUCO

Serves 4

4 thick slices of shin of veal with plenty of meat
    on them
1 tbsp flour
salt and freshly ground black pepper
2 tbsp olive oil
2 garlic cloves, finely chopped
1 Spanish onion, sliced
150 ml (¼ pint) White Stock (see page 335)
150 mi(¼ pint) white wine or more stock
3 tbsp tomato purée
4 anchovy fillets, finely chopped

Garnish
4 tbsp chopped parsley
grated rind ½ lemon

To serve
225 g (8 oz) long grain rice
pinch of saffron or ¼ tsp turmeric

❦ Dredge the meat with seasoned flour and fry in
oil to brown on both sides. Add the garlic, onion,
stock, wine and tomato purée and bring to the boil.
Cover and simmer for 1 ½-2 hours, until the meat is
tender. Add the anchovy fillets and cook for 5 minutes.
❦ Boil the rice with saffron or turmeric until cooked
but not soft, about 12 minutes for white rice and 20
for brown. Drain, rinse and dry for 15 minutes.
❦ Serve the Osso Buco sprinkled with parsley and
lemon rind, on a bed of – or with – the saffron rice.

VEAL OLIVES OR BIRDS

Serves 4

1 quantity stuffing or forcemeat (see pages 350-55)
4 veal (or pork or beef) escalopes, well beaten out
1 tbsp flour
15 g (½ oz) butter or 2 tbsp oil
150 ml (¼ pint) Chicken Stock (see page 335)
150 ml (¼ pint) dry white wine (red if using beef)
bouquet garni
salt and freshly ground black pepper
beurre manié (see page 367) or cornflour
75-150 ml (5 tbsp-¼ pint) single cream or natural yoghurt
chopped parsley to garnish

❦ Spread the stuffing evenly on the escalopes. Roll up and skewer or tie. Roll in the flour to coat and fry in butter or oil to brown.
❦ Add the stock and wine and bring to the boil, stirring continuously. Lower heat to simmer, add the bouquet garni and seasoning and cook slowly for 45-60 minutes or until meat is tender when pierced with a skewer.
❦ Remove the skewers or string and the bouquet garni. Place veal olives in serving dish and keep warm.
❦ Thicken the sauce to coating consistency using beurre manié or cornflour. Stir in the cream or yoghurt and heat but do not boil. Coat the meat with the sauce, and serve garnished with chopped parsley. Potato can be piped around the dish, or served as Duchesse Potatoes (see page 249).

VEAL CORDON BLEU

Serves 4

4 veal (or pork) escalopes beaten very thin
4 slices of Gruyère (or Edam) cheese
4 slices of ham
salt and freshly ground black pepper
beaten egg to coat
breadcrumbs to coat
oil for shallow- or deep-frying
lemon wedges and parsley to garnish

❦ This dish can be assembled in three ways. For thicker escalopes lay a cheese slice on a veal slice, top with a ham slice and season. Press well together and coat with egg and breadcrumbs. Shallow-fry for 3-5 minutes a side, depending on thickness of the meat.
❦ For thin escalopes, lay a cheese slice and then a ham slice on an escalope and season, roll up and skewer. Coat with egg and breadcrumbs and deep-fry for about 10 minutes, until cooked through and golden brown.
❦ For very thin escalopes, lay a cheese and ham slice on half of a veal slice and season. Fold over and sew round with cotton to enclose ham and cheese. Coat with egg and breadcrumbs. Shallow-fry on medium heat for 5-7 minutes a side. Remove the cotton and serve.
❦ For all methods, drain well and serve piled on a warm serving dish, garnished with lemon wedges and sprigs of parsley.

VEAL AND BEAN RAGOUT

Serves 4

450-700 g (1-1 ½ lb) stewing veal (allow extra for bone)
2 tbsp oil
1 large onion, chopped
1 tbsp wholemeal flour, seasoned
½ tsp oregano
½ tsp grated nutmeg
225 g (8 oz) tomatoes, skinned and quartered
275 ml (½ pint) White Stock (see page 335) or wine and stock
225 g (8 oz) haricot or other beans, soaked overnight
chopped parsley to garnish

❦ Brown the meat in the oil. Stir in the onion and cook for a few minutes. Stir in the flour, oregano, nutmeg and tomatoes. Blend in the stock or wine and stock. Add the beans. Cover and simmer for 1 ½-2 hours, until the meat is tender.
❦ Garnish with chopped parsley and serve with boiled or baked potatoes in their jackets and fresh green vegetables.

VEAL ORLOFF

Serves 4-6

1-1 ½ kg (2-3 lb) boned, rolled and tied joint of
    veal or lamb
3 tbsp oil
2 onions, 1 quartered and 1 chopped
2 carrots, sliced
1 stick celery, chopped
bouquet garni
150 ml (¼ pint) White Stock (see page 335) or
    water
175 g (6 oz) mushrooms, chopped
15 g (½ oz) butter
salt and freshly ground black pepper
1 tbsp breadcrumbs

Cheese Sauce
25 g (1 oz) butter or margarine
25 g (1 oz) cornflour
275 ml (½ pint) milk
¼ tsp mustard
75 g (3 oz) grated cheese

❦ Heat the oven to 200C (400F) mark 6. Fry the
veal in oil to brown it and transfer to a casserole dish.
Add the quartered onion, carrot and celery with the
bouquet garni and stock or water. Cover and braise
for 30 minutes.
❦ Lower the heat to 180C (350F) mark 4 and continue cooking for 1-1 ½ hours, until the meat juice
runs clear when meat is pierced with a skewer.
❦ Meanwhile fry the chopped onion and mushrooms in the butter until soft and golden brown.
Season as required.
❦ Make the cheese sauce by heating the butter or
margarine and cornflour together and cooking for 2-
3 minutes. Slowly blend in the milk and boil to thick-
en. Add the mustard, 50 g (2 oz) of the cheese and
seasoning to taste. Stir to dissolve the cheese.
❦ Remove the meat from the braise and cut into 4
or 6 thick slices. Arrange on a serving dish with the
mushroom and onion mix between slices. Coat with
cheese sauce, sprinkle with the remaining grated
cheese and the breadcrumbs, and return to the oven
for 10-15 minutes to heat through and brown the
cheese.
❦ This dish is fairly rich, so is best served with
boiled rice or creamed potatoes and fresh boiled vegetables. The vegetables and liquor from the braise
can be used as a basis for a gravy.

VEAL MILANESE

Serves 4

4 escalopes, well beaten, or veal steaks
seasoned flour to coat
1 beaten egg
breadcrumbs
oil for frying

Sauce
1 onion, grated
2 tbsp oil
3-4 tbsp tomato purée
1 tsp sugar
15 g (½ oz) flour
275 ml (½ pint) White Stock (see page 335)

To serve
225 g (8 oz) pasta shapes
15 g (½ oz) butter
25 g (1 oz) grated Parmesan cheese

❦ Dredge the meat in seasoned flour, pat well in,
then coat with the egg and breadcrumbs.
❦ Make the sauce by tossing grated onion in hot oil
and cooking for 1 minute. Stir in the tomato purée,
sugar and flour and cook for a few minutes. Slowly
add stock and boil for 5 minutes to thicken and cook
flour.
❦ Boil the pasta in plenty of slightly salted water,
until it is tender but still firm, about 12 minutes for
white pasta, and 15-17 minutes for wholemeal.
While the pasta is cooking, fry the prepared meat in
oil until cooked and golden brown, about 3 minutes
a side for very thin escalopes up to 10 minutes a side
for thick steaks. When cooked, drain well and keep
hot. Drain the pasta and stir in melted butter.
❦ Serve cooked meat, overlapping, on a bed of buttered pasta, with the tomato sauce poured over, and
Parmesan cheese sprinkled on top.

VEAL AND HAM PIE

Serves 4-6

225 g (8 oz) Flaky or Mixer Pastry (see pages 361
  or 358)
450 g (1 lb) boneless veal in small cubes
175 g (6 oz) bacon, diced or pieces
2 hard-boiled eggs, sliced
1 tbsp parsley, chopped
1 tsp grated lemon rind
salt and freshly ground black pepper
150 ml (¼ pint) White Stock (see page 335),
  water or white wine
egg to glaze

❦ Heat the oven to 230C (450F) mark 8. Roll out
the pastry to the shape of a 1 litre (2 pint) pie dish
plus 1 cm (½ in) all round. Layer the veal, bacon,
egg, parsley and lemon rind in pie dish and season.
Add enough stock, water or wine to come half-way
up the mixture.

❦ To cover the pie, cut the pastry to the shape of
the pie dish, and use 1 cm (½ in) trimming to make
a ledge of pastry round the rim of the pie dish.
Moisten this edge, and place on the cut pastry shape.
Press two layers together, knock up the edges with a
small knife, and use the back of knife to flute round
the rim of pie, bringing it up every 4 cm (1½ in).
Make a hole in the centre to allow the steam to
escape. Use any trimmings to make leaves and a rose
for centre.

❦ Glaze with beaten egg. Place on a baking tray and
bake for 15 minutes, then turn down the heat to
190C (375F) mark 5 for a further 1 ½ hours, or until
the meat is tender when tested with a skewer through
the hole in the top of the pie. If the pastry is getting
too brown, cover with greaseproof paper.

❦ Serve hot with fresh vegetables, or cold with
salad. If serving cold, stock can be topped up
through the hole in the top, using veal bone stock,
which will give a good set. For a picnic, use pastry
both beneath and above the meat, in order to cut out
a good slice (you will, of course, need double the
quantity of pastry).

BLANQUETTE OF VEAL

Serves 4

450-700 g (1-1 ½ lb) shoulder or knuckle veal,
  cubed
225 g (8 oz) small onions
2 carrots, sliced
2 bay leaves
1 lemon, rind and juice
salt and freshly ground black pepper
100 g (4 oz) button mushrooms
40 g (1 ½ oz) butter or margarine
40 g (1 ½ oz) flour or cornflour
1 egg yolk
150 ml (¼ pint) single cream or natural yoghurt
grated nutmeg

❦ Put the veal in a pan, cover with water and bring
to the boil. Strain and rinse any scum off the veal.

❦ Replace the veal in the pan with onions, carrots,
bay leaves, lemon rind and juice and seasonings. Add
850 ml (1 ½ pints) water (or very light stock could be
used), bring to the boil, cover and simmer for 1 ½
hours, adding the mushrooms for the last 30 minutes.

❦ Strain the meat and vegetables and place on a
warm serving dish, cover with foil and keep warm.
Reduce the cooking liquor to 575 ml (1 pint) by boiling rapidly.

❦ Heat the butter or margarine and flour or cornflour together to make a white roux. Cook for a few
minutes, but do not allow to brown. Slowly blend the
cooking liquor into the roux and heat and then boil
for 5 minutes. Adjust the seasoning if necessary. (If
the sauce is not smooth, strain or liquidize).

❦ Beat in the egg yolk and cream or yoghurt and
heat but do not boil. Pour the sauce over the meat
and sprinkle with grated nutmeg.

CHINESE VEAL

Serves 4-8

1 tbsp cornflour
1 tsp ground ginger
salt and freshly ground black pepper
450 g (1 lb) veal (or beef), well beaten and cut in strips
4 tbsp oil
1 onion, sliced
150 ml (¼ pint) White Stock (see page 335) or water
1 tbsp soy sauce
1 tbsp sherry
½ red pepper, deseeded and cut into strips
50 g (2 oz) mushrooms, sliced
1 tbsp crystallized ginger, chopped
15 g (½ oz) cornflour

❧ Mix the cornflour and ginger with seasonings and coat the meat strips well with this. Shallow-fry in the oil (or deep-fry if preferred), stirring to prevent burning, until meat is cooked, about 7-10 minutes. Drain and keep warm.
❧ Place the onion in a pan with the stock, soy sauce and sherry, and boil for 3-5 minutes. Add the pepper and cook for a further 2-3 minutes. Add the mushrooms and cook for 1-2 more minutes. Stir in ginger. Vegetables should still be crisp. Blend the cornflour with a little water and use to thicken the vegetable mixture.
❧ Serve in a hot bowl, with the fried meat added on top at the last minute. Vegetables can be cooked at the same time as the meat, but do not let vegetables stand or they will get soft.
❧ Serve with plain boiled rice, or as part of a Chinese-style meal.

ORANGE TARRAGON VEAL

Serves 4

4 veal chops or shoulder steaks
1 tbsp flour, seasoned
15 g (½ oz) butter
2 tbsp oil
1 large onion, sliced
175 g (6 oz) concentrated orange juice (usually frozen)
150 ml (¼ pint) Chicken Stock (see page 335)
1 tbsp dried tarragon leaves
15 g (½ oz) cornflour
150 ml (¼ pint) soured cream or natural yoghurt

❧ Heat the oven to 180C (350F) mark 4 or simmer on top of the stove in a pan.
❧ Coat the meat in seasoned flour. Heat the butter and oil together and fry the meat to brown on both sides. Stir in the onion and fry for a few minutes. Add the orange juice and stock (if concentrated juice cannot be obtained, use 325 ml (12 fl oz) normal strength, and dissolve a stock cube in it instead of using stock).
❧ Stir in the tarragon and simmer or cook in oven for 1-1 ½ hours, until the meat is tender.
❧ Place the meat in a hot serving dish and keep warm. Thicken the cooking liquor with cornflour to give a coating consistency. Stir in the soured cream or yoghurt and heat but do not boil. Pour over the meat.
❧ The dish can be garnished with fresh tarragon, orange slices or orange rind julienne strips.

VEAL VERONIQUE

Serves 4

4 veal (or pork) escalopes or chops, boned
1 small onion, finely chopped
50 g (2 oz) mushrooms, finely chopped
40 g (1 ½ oz) butter
½ tsp herbs to taste
salt and freshly ground black pepper
75 ml (1/8 pint) white wine
75 ml (1/8 pint) White Stock (see page 335)
150 ml (¼ pint) milk
25 g (1 oz) cornflour
100 g (4 oz) white grapes, skinned and
    deseeded

❦ Heat the oven to 190C (375F) mark 5 or cook on top of stove.

❦ Beat the escalopes to 1 cm (½ in) thick or trim the chops and make a pocket slit with a sharp knife. Fry the onion and mushrooms in 15 g (½ oz) of butter until cooked. Either spread the onion and mushroom mixture on the escalopes, roll up and secure with a cocktail stick, or push the mixture into the slits in the chops.

❦ Place in a casserole or pan with herbs, salt and freshly ground black pepper, wine and stock and cook slowly either in the oven or in a saucepan for 1–1 ½ hours, until the meat is tender. Transfer the meat to a hot serving dish and keep warm.

❦ Strain the cooking liquor and make up to 275 ml (½ pint) with milk. Heat the remaining butter and cornflour together and cook for 2–3 minutes. Gradually blend in the milk and cooking liquor and bring to the boil. Boil for 3–5 minutes until sauce is thick and glossy.

❦ Pour the sauce over the meat and sprinkle grapes over the top. Return to the oven for a few minutes if necessary, to heat through.

❦ The dish can be garnished with boiled, sieved, or piped potatoes.

LAMB

*A collection of recipes for every occasion from
Crown Roast of Lamb to delicious everyday dishes
such as Minted Lamb Parcels.*

British lamb is available fresh very nearly all the year round. It is cheapest and most plentiful from August until December. Britain imports frozen lamb from New Zealand. It is available all the year round, but has its 'new' season when British lamb is least available, from Christmas to Easter, at which time the imported meat can be a very economic buy.

When buying fresh lamb, look for firm, white fat, fine-grained, firm, pinky-brown lean, with very little gristle and a good proportion of lean to fat. Freshly cut surfaces should look slightly moist and the bones should be pinkish-blue.

Cuts of lamb

Scrag and middle neck

These are usually sold chopped into pieces and are used for stewing and braising. They are traditionally used for Irish stew and Lancashire hot-pot. Increasingly the meat is being cut off the bone and sold as neck fillet, it is sweet and easy to cook, and

very reasonably priced with no wastage. On small animals and frozen carcasses (such as New Zealand lamb), these cuts are left on the shoulder and more often sold in two halves.

Shoulder

A succulent, sweet, tender roasting joint, whether on the bone, or boned and rolled, with or without stuffing. Shoulders are sold whole or halved into blade and knuckle ends, both ideal for roasting or braising. Frozen carcasses are often cut into slices with a band-saw, giving shoulder steaks, weighing about 150 g (5 oz) each. These can be grilled, braised, baked or casseroled.

Best end of neck

This can be purchased as a roasting joint with 6-7 rib bones. If chined by the butcher, it is easier to carve. It can be roasted on the bone, or boned and rolled, with or without stuffing. It is frequently cut into cutlets with one rib bone to each. Two best ends of neck (preferably a pair from a left and right side) joined together and curved, bones outwards, makes a Crown Roast, and facing each other, fat side outwards, they make a Guard of Honour. Allow 2 cutlets per person. When boned and rolled and then cut into slices, the slices are known as noisettes.

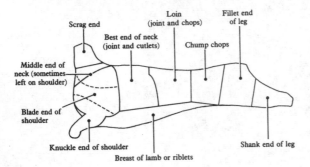

Loin

This is either roasted in a piece, on the bone, or boned and rolled, with or without stuffing, or cut into chops for grilling, frying or braising. A loin will cut into 6-7 chops. Allow 1 or 2 chops per person according to appetite and money available. Occasionally, valentine chops or steaks can be found. These come from a boned loin, cut into 2.5 cm (1 in) slices, and each one is cut nearly through, from the fatty side, and opened out to give a heart shape. Occasionally double loin chops are found, these are cut across the animal before the two sides are separated down the backbone. If a whole double loin is cut out it is known as a saddle, which traditionally includes the kidneys at one end and has a plait and bow or rose made from strips of fat down the centre back. It is an excellent roast when serving 8-10 people. To carve a saddle, cut down either side of the back bone, flatten the knife to loosen meat from bone, then cut slices as if carving a single loin.

Chump

This can be sold as a piece, but is normally cut into chump chops. They are larger than loin chops and vary according to where along the chump they are from. Chump chops are distinguished by a small round bone in the centre. Some also have a large piece of backbone.

Leg

The prime joint, excellent for roasting or for cutting up into cubes of succulent tender meat. It can be cooked on the bone, or boned and rolled, with or

without stuffing. It is frequently cut in two and sold as fillet and shank end. Slices off the fillet end are ideal for frying or grilling.

Breast

A long thin cut of lean, streaked with fat. Choose one with plenty of lean. This can be boned and rolled, which, with a tasty stuffing, provides an economical roast or braise. Cut into strips it can be roast or barbecued, this cut is known as riblets. If casseroling or stewing, it is sometimes worth roasting for 15 minutes to remove some of the fat, or boiling and discarding the water.

Boneless cutting methods

Many traditional roasting cuts, sold on the bone are impractical for small families, and those wanting a quick meal with no leftovers for the next day. New techniques have been developed whereby the carcass can be boned, the resulting meat butchered and cut into small boneless joints, steaks and slices which are suitable for quick cooking methods such as frying and grilling. Excess fat can be removed and the meat cut into suitably sized joints for the customer's needs. These are not likely to replace the traditional joints for those who still want them, but do make the animal more versatile.

CROWN ROAST OF LAMB

Serves 4-6

1 crown roast of lamb (2 best ends of neck with 6 chops each)
1 quantity stuffing of choice (see pages 350-55

❦ This is an impressive looking dish suitable for entertaining, which need not be very expensive. Stuffing may be in the middle, or in balls around the 'crown' in which case the centre is usually filled with vegetables.
❦ Unless you have the correct equipment, ask the butcher to prepare the meat for a Crown Roast, by cutting through the chops at the spine end only and by chining the joint. The rib bones should be scraped clean for 2.5 cm (1 in).
❦ Bend the two joints round a jar or similar, so that cuts between chops open out. Use a trussing needle and string to tie together at the ends. Weigh the joint, place in a roasting tin, remove the jar and fill with stuffing in the centre.

❦ Heat the oven to 180C (350F) mark 4. Cover the ends of the bones and the stuffing with foil. When the oven is properly hot, put in meat and cook it for 25 minutes for every ½ kg (1 lb) of meat, plus an extra 25 minutes.

❦ Remove the foil. Place the joint on a warmed serving platter and decorate with cutlet frills, glacé cherries or stuffing balls for the ends of the rib bones. Surround with colourful vegetables (small carrots, new potatoes, courgettes etc).

❦ Serve immediately with a thin gravy or suitable sauce (see page 338).

BRAISED, ROLLED SHOULDER OF LAMB

Serves 6-8

1 shoulder of lamb, boned, rolled and tied (can be stuffed if preferred)
1 tbsp flour
1 tsp paprika
salt and freshly ground black pepper
25 g (1 oz) butter or margarine
100 g (4 oz) dried apricots, soaked
50 g (2 oz) walnuts, broken in pieces
2 onions, sliced
2 large carrots, sliced
2 stalks celery, sliced
1 stock cube
275 ml (½ pint) water
3 tbsp tomato purée

❦ Heat the oven to 180C (350F) mark 4.

❦ Dust the joint with a mixture of flour, paprika and salt and pepper. Melt the butter and fry the joint to brown all round, remove and place in a casserole dish. Add the apricots and walnuts.

❦ Fry the onions, carrots and celery to lightly brown and then stir in the remaining flour mix. Blend the stock cube and water, add the tomato purée and mix. Add to the casserole dish. Cover and cook in the oven until the meat is tender, approximately 20 minutes per ½ kg (or 1 lb) weight of prepared joint.

❦ Place the meat on a warmed serving platter and keep hot. Either strain the vegetables and use the liquor as the basis of a sauce by adding water and thickening with cornflour or beurre manié (see page 367), or liquidize the vegetables with the cooking liquor and serve, reheated, as a sauce.

LAMB EN CROUTE

Serves 6

350 g (1 2 oz) Puff Pastry (see page 360)
1.4 kg (3 lb) leg of lamb
4 lambs' kidneys
50 g (2 oz) butter
100 g (4 oz) button mushrooms
100 9 (4 oz) fresh brown breadcrumbs
¼ tsp powdered rosemary
salt and freshly ground black pepper
1 egg to glaze

❦ Roll out the pastry to a rectangle about 35 x 40 cm (14 x 16 in). Trim, release from the board and leave to relax in a cool place. Heat the oven to 190C (375F) mark 5.

❦ Cut away most of the fat from the lamb, leaving just a thin layer. Bone the lamb using a sharp knife, or ask your butcher to do so. Feel with your fingers to make sure no little bits of bone have been left behind.

❦ Remove the skins and cores from the kidneys. Dice them and sauté in the butter. Slice the mushrooms and add them to the pan with the breadcrumbs and rosemary. Season well and cook for a few minutes longer. Cool.

❦ Stuff the lamb with the kidney mixture. Press the joint back into a reasonable shape. Tie firmly with string. Put the lamb, open end down, on crumpled foil in the roasting tin. Cook for 1 hour then take out of the oven and cool. Remove the string. Increase the oven temperature to 230C (450F) mark 8.

❦ Put the cold lamb on the pastry. Brush the pastry edges with beaten egg and fold up over the lamb to enclose it. Put this parcel on baking paper on a baking sheet, joins downwards. Cut a hole in the top to let out the steam. Brush the pastry all over with beaten egg to which a little water has been added. Make pastry leaves from the pastry trimmings and arrange around the hole. Glaze with egg.

❦ Cook for 30 minutes, or until well risen and dark golden brown. Cover the leaves lightly with foil if the pastry starts to get too brown. Serve hot with Cumberland Sauce (see page 343).

NOISETTES WITH REDCURRANT JELLY

Serves 4

marinade (optional, see page 345)
4-8 noisettes, chops or cutlets
about 2 tbsp redcurrant jelly
slices of wholemeal bread for croûtes
150 ml (¼ pint) stock
watercress to garnish

❦ Marinate the meat overnight if required.
❦ Heat the grill on high. Place the meat on the grid of the grill pan, ensuring pan is clean. Place 1 tsp redcurrant jelly on each noisette or chop. Place under the grill, lower the heat to medium. Grill for about 5-10 minutes depending on thickness. Turn over, add more redcurrant jelly and grill for further 5-10 minutes.
❦ Cut out four 7.5 cm (3 in) circles of bread and fry or toast to make croûtes. Place the croûtes on a serving dish, top with a noisette or chop on each, and keep warm.
❦ Add the stock to grill pan, mix well with any sediment and pour over chops.
❦ Serve garnished with watercress and Duchesse Potatoes (see page 249).

LAMB AND ORANGE RIBLETS

Serves 4

1 tbsp soy sauce
1 tbsp dry sherry
½ tsp ground ginger
25 g (1 oz) crystallized root ginger, finely chopped
2 oranges, rind and juice
450 g (1 lb) lean riblets or breast of lamb strips
1 onion, finely chopped
1 tbsp vegetable oil

❦ Mix the soy sauce, sherry, gingers and the rind and juice of the oranges, and marinate the meat overnight. Heat the oven to 180C (350F) mark 4.
❦ Fry the onion in oil until translucent. Add the onion to the meat. Turn the meat into a greased roasting tin and spread out. Bake for 1-1 ½ hours until the meat is tender. Turn and baste meat frequently with the marinade.
❦ Serve the meat on a bed of rice or pasta.

Variations
If more sauce is required, add a little stock to the meat at the last basting, and this will form a gravy. This dish may be eaten with the fingers like barbecued spare ribs in a Chinese meal and cooks well on a barbecue.

LAMB CHOPS WITH APRICOTS

Serves 4

400 g (14 oz) can of apricots in juice
1 tbsp red wine vinegar
2 spring onions, finely chopped
15 g (½ oz) cornflour or beurre manié (see page 367)
4 loin or chump chops, or leg or shoulder steaks of lamb
1 tbsp oil

❦ Heat the grill. Strain the apricots and mix the juice with the vinegar, onions and cornflour. Heat and boil just before serving, for an accompanying sauce.
❦ Brush the chops with oil and grill until tender, but still pink in the middle, about 7-10 minutes a side depending on thickness of chops. After the chops have been turned, arrange the apricots around the meat so that they heat through.
❦ Serve the chops with apricots around, and with the sauce to hand.

CITRUS LAMB CUTLETS

Serves 4

2 limes, rind and juice
1 lemon, rind and juice
2 tsp clear honey
4-8 lamb cutlets
15 g (½ oz) cornflour or beurre manié (see page 367)
slices of lemon and lime to garnish

❧ Mix the rind and juices with the honey and use to marinade the cutlets for a few hours or overnight if possible.
❧ Heat the grill and then grill cutlets until cooked, but still pink in the middle, about 5-7 minutes a side. Place on a warmed serving dish and keep warm.
❧ Make the remaining marinade up to 275 ml (½ pint) with stock or water and thicken with cornflour.
❧ Serve the sauce over cutlets, or separately. Garnish the meat with lemon and lime slices and serve with chipped, jacket or Duchesse Potatoes (see page 249).

MINTED LAMB PARCELS

Serves 4

225 g (8 oz) Mixer or Flaky Pastry (see pages 358 or 361)
4 lamb cutlets
4 mint leaves
small onion, finely chopped
15 g (½ oz) butter or margarine
4 tsp mint jelly
beaten egg to glaze

❧ Make the pastry and leave in cool place to relax. Heat the oven to 220C (425F) mark 7.
❧ Make slits along the cutlets and lay in the mint leaves. Heat the grill and when hot, grill the cutlets for 5 minutes a side.
❧ Fry the onion in butter or margarine until cooked and put a spoonful on each cutlet. Add a spoonful of mint jelly on top of the onion.
❧ Roll out the pastry and cut into 2.5 cm (1 in) strips. Dampen one edge with water. Wrap strips of pastry round cutlets, tucking the end underneath to seal. Decorate with pastry leaves and glaze with egg.

❧ Place on a greased baking tray and cook for 20 minutes, or until golden brown.
❧ Serve garnished with grilled tomatoes and watercress.

LAMB PILAU (PILAFF)

Serves 4

450-700 g (1-1 ½ lb) cubed leg or shoulder of lamb
575 ml (1 pint) stock or water
1 cm (½ in) fresh root ginger, thinly sliced
5 cm (2 in) cinnamon stick
¼ tsp grated nutmeg
1 green chilli pepper, chopped
6 black peppercorns
150 ml (¼ pint) natural yoghurt
1 lemon, rind and juice
½ tsp cayenne pepper or tandoori spice mix
225 g (8 oz) long grain rice
50 g (2 oz) butter or margarine
2 tbsp oil
1 onion, finely chopped
4 cloves
4 cardamom seeds
1 onion, sliced and fried to golden
2 tbsp raisins
2 tbsp slivered almonds, toasted
2 hard-boiled eggs, quartered

❧ Simmer the meat in stock containing the ginger, cinnamon, nutmeg, chilli, and peppercorns for 40 minutes.
❧ Transfer the meat to a bowl. Discard the cinnamon but reserve the liquor. Add the yoghurt, lemon rind and juice and cayenne or spice mix to the meat, stir and leave to marinade for 2 hours.
❧ Approximately half an hour before required, fry the rice in butter or margarine and oil for 3 minutes. Remove from the fat and put in a pan with the reserved cooking liquor, the chopped onion, cloves and cardamom seeds. Cover and simmer for about 12 minutes for white and 20 minutes for brown rice. All the liquid should be absorbed, if not drain.
❧ While the rice is cooking, drain and fry the marinated meat in the remains of the butter and oil until browned, and cooked through. Mix the cooked meat and rice and pile into a warmed serving bowl, top with fried onions, raisins and almonds, with the egg around the edge of the bowl.

LAMB AND COURGETTE SAUTÉ

Serves 4

450 g (1 lb) boneless neck fillet of lamb
1 tbsp soy sauce
2 tbsp dry sherry
½ tsp caraway seeds
25 g (1 oz) butter
2 tbsp oil
4-6 spring onions, cut in 2.5 cm (1 in) pieces
50 g (2 oz) button mushrooms
225 g (8 oz) small courgettes, cut in 2 cm (¼ in) pieces

❦ Mix the lamb with the soy sauce, sherry and caraway seeds. Heat the butter and oil and fry the meat until browned.
❦ Add the remaining ingredients and fry, turning periodically until meat is cooked and courgettes browned.
❦ Serve immediately.

FRENCH LAMB CASSEROLE

Serves 4

700 g (1 ½ lb) stewing lamb, allow more if a lot of bone included
2 onions, quartered
1 tbsp oil
25 g (1 oz) wholemeal flour
2 garlic cloves, crushed
575 ml (1 pint) stock
1 bouquet garni
2 tbsp brandy (optional)
225 g (8 oz) pickling onions
25 g (1 oz) butter or margarine
100 g (4 oz) peas
1 tbsp chopped parsley to garnish

❦ Heat the oven to 190C (375F) mark 5.
❦ Trim as much fat off the meat as possible. Put it in a large casserole. Cook the quartered onions in oil until well browned. Stir in flour and garlic and blend in stock, and pour over the meat. Add the bouquet garni and brandy (optional). Cover and cook in oven for 1-2 hours, or until meat is tender.

❦ Fry the pickling onions whole in the butter or margarine until golden brown. Drain well and add to the casserole with the peas about 15 minutes before the end of cooking time.
❦ Serve with boiled potatoes and garnish with chopped parsley.

LAMB AND BEAN HOT POT

Serves 4

450 g (1 lb) boned, or 700 g (1 ½ lb) with bone, stewing lamb or mutton
2 onions, sliced
3 carrots, sliced
1 small turnip or swede, cubed
100 g (4 oz) haricot or any other beans, soaked
1 tsp mixed herbs
salt and freshly ground black pepper
2 tbsp Worcestershire sauce
575 ml (1 pint) stock
450-700 g (1-1 ½ lb) potatoes, scrubbed and sliced
15 g (½ oz) butter, melted

❦ Heat the oven to 150C (300F) mark 2.
❦ Trim the fat from the meat where possible. If very fatty, just cover the meat with water, bring to the boil and simmer for 10 minutes, then drain, discarding the water with the melted fat.
❦ Layer all the ingredients except the potatoes and butter in a deep casserole. Top with sliced potato and melted butter. Cook uncovered for 2-2 ½ hours or until meat is tender. The oven can be turned up for the last 20 minutes, if necessary, to brown the potatoes.

Variations
This dish can be cooked in a slow cooker, follow manufacturer's instructions for time, and brown under a grill to colour the potato at the end. Stewing beef, veal and poultry can be cooked in the same way.

LAMB AND YOGHURT CASSEROLE

Serves 4

450-700 g (1-1 ½ lb) boneless lamb, cubed
1 tbsp flour
1 tsp chopped mint
freshly ground black pepper
15 g (½ oz) margarine or butter
1 tbsp oil
1 onion, chopped
275 ml (½ pint) stock
1 tbsp capers
1 -2 pickled dill cucumbers, sliced
1 lemon, rind and juice
1 tbsp chopped parsley or coriander leaves
275 ml (½ pint) natural yoghurt

❦ Heat the oven to 170C (325F) mark 3.
❦ Toss the meat in flour, seasoned with the mint and pepper. Melt the margarine or butter together with the oil and fry meat to brown. Transfer the meat to a casserole.
❦ Fry the onion until translucent and add to meat. Mix in the stock, capers, pickled cucumbers, lemon rind and juice and herbs. Cover and cook until meat is tender, 1-2 hours, depending on the cut used.
❦ Remove from the oven and stir in the yoghurt, adjust the consistency if required, and heat through but do not boil.
❦ The dish can be garnished with cucumber and lemon slices. Serve with rice, pasta or potatoes.

RAGOUT OF LAMB AND BUTTER BEANS

Serves 4

2 tbsp oil
1 tbsp wholemeal flour
1 tsp herbs, chopped
salt and freshly ground black pepper
½ tsp paprika
450 g (1 lb) boneless, or 700 g (1 ½ lb) with bone, stewing lamb
100 g (4 oz) butter beans, soaked
225 g (8 oz) shallots or small onions
400 g (14 oz) can of tomatoes
150 ml (¼ pint) natural yoghurt

❦ Heat the oil in a pan. Mix the flour, herbs, salt and pepper and paprika together and put in a polythene bag with the meat. Toss together thoroughly.
❦ Fry the meat in oil until browned. Add all the ingredients except the yoghurt to the pan and simmer, covered, for 1-1 ½ hours, or until meat and beans are tender. If very old or tough meat is being used, cook for ½ hour before adding the beans.
❦ Just before serving, stir in the yoghurt, and heat but do not boil. Serve garnished with chopped parsley and boiled potatoes or pasta.
❦ If the meat is very fatty, cook the day before, but refrigerate before adding the yoghurt. The next day, remove the layer of fat, reheat and finish as above.

DEVILLED KIDNEY PASTIES

Makes 4-5

225 g (8 oz) Pâte Brisée or Rich Shortcrust Pastry (see page 359)
4 lambs' kidneys
2 shallots
1 carrot
about 150 ml (¼ pint) Basic Brown Stock (see page 335)
1 bay leaf
pepper and salt
½ tsp Home-made Mustard (see page 366)
25 g (1 oz) fresh brown breadcrumbs
1 tsp tomato purée
milk to glaze

❦ Heat the oven to 200C (400F) mark 6. Roll out the pastry and cut 4 circles using a saucer about 15 cm (6 inches) in diameter as a guide. Leave to relax.
❦ Skin, core and quarter the kidneys. Peel and dice the shallots and carrot. Put in a pan with the stock and the bay leaf. Season well. Simmer until the kidneys are tender. Stir in the mustard, breadcrumbs and purée. Simmer until thick, then cool.
❦ Spoon the mixture into the middle of each pastry circle. Brush half the edges with water. Bring the sides up to the top and press firmly together. Flute with finger and thumb (see page 357).
❦ Brush with milk to glaze. Stand on a baking sheet and cook for about 20 minutes until golden brown.

LAMB AND CHICKPEA CURRY

Serves 4-6

100 g (4 oz) chickpeas
1 tbsp curry powder
½ tsp each of ginger, turmeric, paprika and
    cayenne pepper
1 tbsp flour
450 g (1 lb) lean lamb cubed (any cut is suitable)
25 g (1 oz) butter or margarine
2 tbsp oil
1 large Spanish onion, sliced
2 stalks celery
1 green pepper, deseeded and diced
25 g (1 oz) desiccated coconut
150 ml (¼ pint) milk
575 ml (1 pint) stock or water
50 g (2 oz) raisins
150 ml (¼ pint) natural yoghurt

❦ This dish should be started the day before
required for eating.
❦ Put the chickpeas to soak. Mix the curry powder,
spices and flour with the cubed meat and leave to
stand in the refrigerator, for a few hours, or
overnight.
❦ Melt the butter with the oil and fry the spiced
meat until browned all over. Remove the meat and
fry the onion, celery and pepper for a few minutes.
Return the meat to the pan.
❦ Boil the coconut with the milk and leave to cool,
then strain and add coconut milk to the meat and
chickpeas along with the stock. Cover and simmer
until the meat is cooked, 1-2 hours depending on cut
of meat, and age of animal.
❦ Stir in the raisins and yoghurt. Adjust the consistency, if necessary, with water or stock. Heat
through, but do not boil once the yoghurt has been
added.
❦ Serve with boiled rice and traditional curry
accompaniments, such as poppadoms, nan bread,
mango and apple chutney, preserved kumquats etc.

Variation
If an overnight soak and spicing is not possible, the
chickpeas can be brought to the boil and left to stand
for an hour instead of soaking. The flavour will not
have permeated the meat as well, but the result will
still be delicious.

SHISH KEBABS

Serves 4

450-700 g (1-1 ½ lb) cubed lamb, from the leg
8 baby onions
1 green pepper, deseeded
1 red pepper, deseeded
4 medium or 8 small tomatoes
100 g (4 oz) button mushrooms

Marinade
6 tbsp olive oil
4 tbsp dry sherry or vermouth
2 garlic cloves, finely chopped
¼ tsp cayenne pepper
¼ Spanish onion, finely chopped
2 tbsp fresh (1 tbsp dried) herbs (preferably
    marjoram, basil, oregano and parsley
    mixed)
freshly ground black pepper

❦ Combine the marinade ingredients and mix with
meat overnight. If marinating is done in a watertight,
sealed polythene container, it can be turned periodically to mix.
❦ Parboil or fry the onions. Cut the peppers into
pieces, and the tomatoes in half unless small.
❦ After marinating, assemble the ingredients on
skewers to give an attractive variety, evenly divide
between skewers.
❦ Brush the skewers with marinade and grill or barbecue until cooked, about 15 minutes. Turn frequently and re-brush with marinade during cooking.
❦ Serve with boiled rice or rice salad, chunks of granary bread, jacket potatoes or fresh vegetables and
salad.

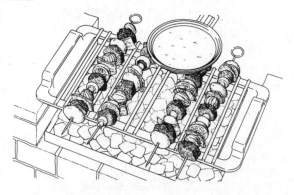

MUTTON PIES

Makes 6-8

350 g (12 oz) Hot Water Crust Pastry (see page 362)
450 g (1 lb) lean mutton or lamb
bouquet garni
salt and pepper
2 tbsp diced carrot
1 tbsp diced onion
1 tbsp diced potato
capers
1 egg or milk to glaze
1 ½ tsp powdered gelatine

❦ These pies should be made the day before they are needed.
❦ Keep the pastry warm. Heat the oven to 200C (400F) mark 6.
❦ Dice the meat. Put it into a pan with the bouquet garni, salt and pepper and barely cover with water. Simmer until just tender. Add the diced vegetables and simmer for another minute or two. Strain, reserving the stock.
❦ Put the meat and vegetables into a bowl ready for filling the pies, with just enough of the stock to moisten the mixture.
❦ Cut the pastry into six or eight pieces. Keep one-third of each piece for the lids. Roll out the larger pieces and use to line 10 cm (4 in) patty tins. Fill the pastry cases with the cold meat mixture, adding one or two capers to each little pie.
❦ Brush the edges with beaten egg, position the lids and press well together. Decorate and finish as for Individual Sausage and Egg Pies (see page 153). Cook for 20 minutes then reduce the temperature to 180C (350F) mark 4. Cover the pies with greaseproof paper and cook for a further 40 minutes. Cool before turning out.
❦ Remove the bouquet garni from the stock and make the stock up to 275 ml (½ pint) with water or cider. Dissolve the gelatine in the stock. As it cools, pour into the pies through the hole in the top. Cool and chill.

LAMB AND KIDNEY PASTIES

Makes 6

350 g (12 oz) Shortcrust Pastry (see page 357)
175 g (6 oz) lean boneless lamb
3 lambs' kidneys
75 g (3 oz) mushrooms
2 tbsp water
salt and pepper
smallest pinch of powdered rosemary
1 egg to glaze

❦ Heat the oven to 200C (400F) mark 6.
❦ Roll out the pastry and, using a large plain cutter or saucer, cut out 6 circles. Release from the board and leave to relax.
❦ Cut the meat into small dice. Skin, split and core the kidneys and cut into quarters. Wipe and slice the mushrooms. Put all these ingredients into a bowl with the water, salt and pepper to taste and the rosemary. Mix well.
❦ Divide the filling between the pastry rounds. Brush one half of the circle with beaten egg and bring up the edges to meet each other at the top. Press well together and flute (see page 357).
❦ Brush the pasties with beaten egg, place on a baking sheet and cook for 30 minutes. Reduce the temperature to 180C (350F) mark 4 and continue cooking for 20-25 minutes. Serve hot or cold.

SWEETBREAD FLAN

Serves 4

225 g (8 oz) Pâte Brisée or Rich Shortcrust
   Pastry (see page 359)
450 g (1 lb) lambs' sweetbreads
4 tbsp mixed diced vegetables
sprig of thyme
15 g (½ oz) butter
15 g (½ oz) plain flour
salt and black pepper
4 medium mushrooms to garnish
parsley sprigs to garnish

❦ Heat the oven to 200C (400F) mark 6. Line an 18
cm (7 in) flan case with the pastry and bake blind (see
page 357).
❦ Wash the sweetbreads. Put into boiling water for
a minute or two. Drain. Trim and cut off the gristly
bits. Put the sweetbreads into a pan with the mixed
diced vegetables and thyme. Barely cover with water
and simmer for 40 minutes. Drain the sweetbreads
and vegetables and discard the thyme, reserving the
cooking liquor.
❦ Make a sauce: heat the butter in a pan. Add the
flour and stir well for a minute or so. Gradually add
150 ml (¼ pint) cooking liquor, beating all the time;
bring to the boil. Taste and season.
❦ Add the sweetbreads and vegetables to the sauce.
Reheat and fill the warm flan case with the mixture.
Garnish with very finely sliced raw mushrooms (use
a mandoline grater) and a small sprig or two of parsley. Serve the flan hot.

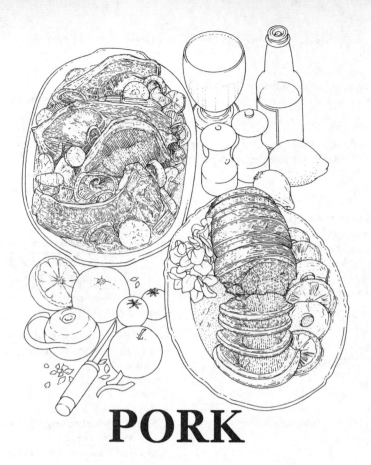

PORK

*This section includes a wide variety of
recipes from Sweet and Sour Pork to
Cheshire Pork Pie.*

When buying, choose pork which is pale pink, firm, smooth and lean. Avoid pale watery looking meat. The fat should be firm and white. There is usually very little gristle, and increasingly the fat will have been trimmed away to give a lean product.

Although British pork is available all the year round, it becomes a particularly economical buy in the summer, when demand is traditionally at its lowest.

Cooking pork

All joints can be roasted, grilled or fried. The forequarter cuts are reasonably priced and ideal for casseroles, stews and pies. Very little of a pig's carcass is not used for some edible item. No attempt has been made in this book to cover the full range of pork products.

For good crackling, ask the butcher to score the rind deeply and evenly. Brush the cut surface with oil and rub salt into the scores. Roast with the rind uppermost, in a dry roasting tin, and do not baste during cooking. The rind can be removed prior to cooking and roasted separately in a hot oven. This allows the joint to be cooked more slowly, or by a moist method, but still producing the crackling to serve with the meat.

Moist methods require the rind to be removed prior to cooking. Marinated and frozen meat frequently does not produce crisp crackling.

Cuts of pork

Neck end (spare ribs and blade bone)
Sometimes called shoulder of pork, this large economical joint is particularly good when boned, stuffed and rolled. Often divided into blade and spare rib (not the cut used for barbecued spare ribs which is usually rib bones with a reasonable amount of meat left on). These small cuts can be roasted, braised or stewed. Spare rib is excellent for pies and

spare rib chops are suitable for braising, grilling or frying.

Hand and spring
A large joint, often divided into hand and shank and thick end of belly. Suitable for roasting, casseroles and stews.

Belly
This is a long thin cut with streaks of fat and lean. Often thickly sliced as belly strips when it is ideally grilled or barbecued to remove some of the fat. Leaner belly can be used in casseroles and minced for pâtés and sausages. The thicker end can be stuffed and rolled for a very economical roast.

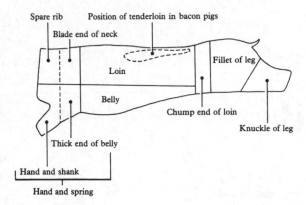

Chump end of loin
Usually sold in large, meaty chops, suitable for grilling, frying or roasting. It is sometimes sold as a roasting joint.

Leg
This is usually divided into fillet end and knuckle end, both of which can be cut into smaller joints. The fillet end is the prime joint of pork and is usually roasted, on the bone, or boned and stuffed, or sliced into steaks for grilling or frying. The knuckle is usually roasted. The feet are usually removed and treated as offal.

Loin
This is a popular roast on the bone, or boned and stuffed, and it produces good crackling. It is frequently divided into chops for grilling, frying or roasting. Those from the hindquarters often contain kidney.

Tenderloin
A tender lean cut found underneath the back bone of the hind loin of bacon-weight pigs, in the same position as beef fillet. In pork-weight pigs the tenderloin is left in the chops, but removed in bacon pigs prior to curing. It is usually served sliced or cubed for frying, or coating with a sauce. It needs little cooking. Although quite expensive per pound it has no wastage and no fat layer.

BRAISED PORK AND ORANGE

Serves 4-6

1-1 ½ kg (2-3 lb) joint of pork, boned and rolled
25 g (1 oz) butter or margarine
1 onion, sliced
2 carrots, diced
2 parsnips, diced
1 chicken stock cube
275 ml (½ pint) orange juice
½ tsp mixed spice
¼ tsp Tabasco or Worcestershire sauce

Garnish
1 apple, cored and sliced in rings
1 orange, peeled and sliced in rings
watercress

❦ Heat the oven to 170C (325F) mark 3. Fry the joint in butter or margarine, to brown. Remove and brown the onion, carrots and parsnips. Place the vegetables in a large casserole dish and place the meat on top.

❦ Dissolve the stock cube in orange juice, add the spice and sauce. Pour over meat. Cover and cook slowly for 2-2 ½ hours, until the meat is tender. Check periodically that the liquor has not boiled away, topping up with a little water if necessary.

❦ Poach the apple and orange rings for a few minutes in orange juice or water. Serve the joint with the rings of fruit around it, and with watercress to garnish. The vegetables and stock can be liquidized and used as a basis for a sauce or gravy, diluting and thickening with cornflour as required.

HONEY ROAST PORK

Serves 4-8

joint of pork which can be on the bone, or
    boned and rolled, with or without stuffing
1 tbsp oil
1 tsp salt
1 tsp ground allspice or cinnamon
4 tbsp clear honey
4 tbsp lemon juice
stuffing (see pages 350-55) to taste
½ fresh pear per person, peeled and cored

❦ Heat the oven to 180C (350F) mark 4. Cut the
rind off the pork and rub oil and salt into the
removed rind. Place in an ovenproof dish and roast
at the top of the oven.
❦ Weigh the joint and calculate the roasting time
(see page 117). Sprinkle spice on the fat of the joint,
which can be criss-crossed with a sharp knife to make
the fat crisp better. Mix the honey and lemon juice
and spread over joint.
❦ Roast the meat for the calculated time, basting
periodically, and adding more honey if desired.
Form the stuffing into balls, and bake for 40 minutes
on a baking tray. For the last 30 minutes add pear
halves around meat.
❦ Serve surrounded with pears topped with stuffing balls and broken up crackling.

PORK ENVELOPES

Makes 4-5

225 g (8 oz) Pâte Brisée or Rich Shortcrust
    Pastry (see page 359)
100 g (4 oz) pork fillet
25 g (1 oz) dried apricots
50 g (2 oz) mushrooms
50 g (2 oz) dripping
½ tsp dried sage
salt and pepper
150 ml (¼ pint) Béchamel Sauce (see page 340)
milk to glaze

❦ Heat the oven to 200C (400F) mark 6. Roll out
the pastry and cut into four 12.5 cm (5 in) squares.
Leave to relax.
❦ Dice the pork fillet. Wash the apricots and snip

them into small pieces. Wipe and dice the mushrooms. Sauté the pork in the dripping until tender.
Add the apricots and mushrooms and cook for a further 1-2 minutes. Stir in the sage, season well and
remove from the heat. Bind together with the
Béchamel Sauce. Spoon on to the middle of the
squares.
❦ Brush two sides of each square with water. Bring
the corners up to meet in the middle. Press together
firmly and flute. Make a leaf or two from the pastry
trimmings. Brush with milk and cook until well
browned for about 20-30 minutes.

SOMERSET PORK TENDERLOINS

Serves 4

450-700 g (1-1 ½ lb) pork tenderloin
1 egg
2 tbsp breadcrumbs or flour
50 g (2 oz) butter or margarine
1 large onion, finely chopped
175 g (6 oz) mushrooms, sliced
275 ml (½ pint) dry cider
salt and freshly ground black pepper
4 tbsp double cream
parsley to garnish

❦ Cut the tenderloin into 8 pieces. Place each piece
between greaseproof paper and beat with a mallet or
rolling pin until ½ cm (¼ in) thick.
❦ Coat the meat with egg and breadcrumbs or flour.
Melt the butter or margarine and fry the meat for
about 4 minutes a side. Remove from the pan, drain
well, and arrange on a serving dish and keep warm.
❦ Add the onion and mushrooms to the pan and fry
until soft. Stir in the remaining flour or breadcrumbs
and cook for 1 minute. Gradually blend in the cider
and bring to the boil, season and adjust consistency
if necessary.
❦ Stir in the cream, warm through but do not boil.
Pour over the meat and garnish with chopped parsley.
❦ Serve with boiled or jacket potatoes.

PORK WITH RED CABBAGE

Serves 4

4 trimmed pork chops or shoulder steaks
450 g (1 lb) red cabbage, finely chopped
450 g (1 lb) cooking apples, peeled cored and
    sliced
225 g (8 oz) onions, sliced
2 garlic cloves, finely chopped
¼ tsp each nutmeg, allspice, cinnamon and
    thyme
black pepper
1 tsp orange rind, grated
juice of orange
2 tbsp wine vinegar
1 tbsp Demerara sugar

❦ Heat the oven to 180C (350F) mark 4.
❦ Grill the chops for a few minutes on each side to
brown. Layer the cabbage with apple, onions, garlic,
spices and herbs, in a deep casserole. Add the pork
chops on top.
❦ Sprinkle over the rind, and pour over the juice
and vinegar. Sprinkle sugar on top. Cover with a lid
or foil and cook for 1 hour, or until meat and cabbage
are cooked.
❦ For a crisper top, remove the cover for the last 20
minutes of cooking time.

PORK CHOPS IN FOIL

Serves 4

butter or oil for greasing
450 g (1 lb) potatoes, thinly sliced
1 onion, finely sliced
4 pork chops or shoulder steaks
1 apple, cored and sliced
4 sage leaves, chopped
salt and freshly ground black pepper
4 tbsp lemon juice

❦ Heat oven to 190C (375F) mark 5. Butter or
grease with oil 4 pieces of foil approximately 25 cm
(10 in) square.
❦ Divide the ingredients between the 4 pieces of
foil, starting with a layer of potato, then onion, then
the chop with apple on top. Add the sage, salt and
freshly ground black pepper and lemon juice.
❦ Close up foil to form a parcel, and bake for 1 hour,
or until the meat is tender. For crisper, browner
meat, the foil parcel can be opened up for last part of
cooking.
❦ Cooking can be speeded up by browning the meat
first, parboiling the potatoes and frying the onion.
With this pre-cooking, the parcels can be cooked on
a barbecue in about 25-30 minutes, depending on its
heat.

PORK CHOPS WITH APPLE

Serves 4

4 trimmed pork chops or shoulder steaks
1 small onion, chopped
1-2 tbsp oil
1 small red pepper, deseeded and sliced in
    rings
200 ml (7 fl oz) apple juice
2 tbsp Calvados or brandy
2 medium-sized cooking apples

❦ Heat the oven to 190C (375F) mark 5. Grill or fry
the chops or steaks to brown the outside and partially cook. Place in a casserole.
❦ Fry the onion in oil until translucent, add to the
casserole, with the pepper, apple juice and Calvados
or brandy.
❦ Peel, core and slice the apples into 1 cm (½ in)
rings and place over the chops. Bake uncovered for
40 minutes, or until the meat is tender. If preferred,
the cooking liquor may be thickened with a little
blended cornflour or beurre manié (see page 367).
❦ This dish goes well with crisply cooked cabbage
and boiled or jacket potatoes.

PORK CHOPS OR STEAKS WITH MUSTARD

Serves 4

1 tbsp dry mustard
1 tbsp Demerara sugar
4 shoulder steaks, spare ribs or loin chops
25 g (1 oz) shredded almonds, toasted
salt and freshly ground black pepper
grilled halved tomatoes and mushrooms to
    garnish

❦ Mix the mustard and sugar together and rub into
chops, or blend with a little water, and spread over
both sides of chops.
❦ Grill under a preheated grill until cooked, about
8 minutes a side.
❦ Season and serve with almonds scattered on top,
and grilled halved tomatoes and mushrooms around.

STUFFED PORK CHOPS

Serves 4

4 pork chops with bone removed
stuffing (see pages 350-55, apricot or apple go
    particularly well)
450 g (1 lb) potatoes, scrubbed and sliced
1 small onion, finely chopped
¼ tsp ground mace
salt and freshly ground black pepper
150 ml (¼ pint) single cream
100 g (4 oz) grated cheese (optional) or 15 g (½
    oz) melted butter

❦ Heat the oven to 190C (375F) mark 5.
❦ With a sharp knife, slit the chops almost through,
making a pocket. Divide the stuffing between the 4
pockets. Part grill or fry to brown the chops.
❦ Parboil the potato slices for 2-3 minutes. Arrange
the potato slices in a wide ovenproof dish, sprinkling
onion and mace between layers. Season to taste. Pour
over the cream. Lay the chops on top, pushing them
down into the potatoes. Sprinkle with cheese (if
cheese is not used, brush chops with melted butter).
❦ Bake for 1-1 ½ hours, until the meat is cooked and
the potato soft. If the meat gets too brown, cover
with foil.

NORMANDY PORK

Serves 4

4 thick slices of pork (shoulder steaks, chops)
1 tbsp flour
½ tsp sage leaves, chopped
3 tbsp oil or 25 g (1 oz) butter
3 onions, sliced
275 ml (½ pint) dry white wine, cider or stock
1 tbsp Calvados or brandy
3 dessert apples, peeled, cored and sliced
salt and freshly ground black pepper

❦ Heat the oven to 180C (350F) mark 4.
❦ Coat the meat in flour mixed with sage. Fry to
brown in oil or butter and place in a casserole dish.
❦ Fry the onions until translucent. Add any
remaining flour and fry for a few minutes. Blend in
the wine, cider or stock and Calvados or brandy.
Pour over the meat. Add the apples and salt and
freshly ground black pepper.
❦ Cover and cook for 45 minutes or until meat is
tender.
❦ Serve with rice or boiled potatoes.

PORK STIR-FRY

Serves 4

450 g (1 lb) pork tenderloin or leg fillet, in thin
    strips
1 tbsp seasoned cornflour
1 garlic clove, finely chopped
4 tbsp oil
1 red pepper, deseeded and cut in strips
50 g (2 oz) mushrooms, sliced
100 g (4 oz) sweetcorn kernels, cooked
2 tbsp soy sauce

❦ Toss the meat in the cornflour. Heat the garlic in
oil in a frying pan or work, and when hot, stir-fry the
meat until brown.
❦ Add the pepper and mushrooms, and continue
stir-frying until the meat is cooked, about 10 minutes cooking in total. Add the corn and fry to heat
through.
❦ Pour over the soy sauce and serve immediately
with boiled brown rice or pasta.

SWEET AND SOUR PORK

Serves 4

450 g (1 lb) lean cubed pork
2 tbsp cornflour
4 tbsp oil
1 onion, sliced
1 tbsp tomato purée
1 garlic clove, crushed
1 tbsp soy sauce
2 tbsp wine vinegar
2 tsp clear honey
1 tbsp dry sherry
275 ml (½ pint) light stock
25 g (1 oz) crystallized ginger, chopped
½ tsp allspice, ground
½ star anise (optional)
50 g (2 oz) dried apricots, soaked
50 g (2 oz) mushrooms, sliced
½ red pepper, cored and sliced

❦ Coat the meat in cornflour. Heat the oil and fry the meat until browned. Remove and fry the onion until translucent.
❦ Return the meat to the pan and add all ingredients except the apricots, mushrooms and red pepper. Cover and simmer for 40 minutes.
❦ Add the remaining ingredients and simmer for a further 10–15 minutes until the meat is cooked.
❦ Serve with rice, or as one of the dishes of a Chinese meal.

PIG IN THE MIDDLE

Serves 4

4 lean, rindless belly strips, chops or steaks
1 or 2 pigs' kidneys, cored and quartered

Batter
1 egg
275 ml (½ pint) milk or milk/water mixture
¼ tsp salt
½ tsp mixed herbs
100 g (4 oz) plain flour

❦ Heat the oven to 220C (425F) mark 7. Lay the meat in a roasting dish large enough in which to cook a Yorkshire pudding. Roast for 10 minutes.

❦ Beat the egg, milk, salt and herbs into the flour to make a batter.
❦ Remove the meat from the roasting tin and swirl fat from meat around tin. Return the meat, add the kidneys and pour in the batter. Return immediately to the oven, and bake for 30–40 minutes until the batter is risen and golden brown.
❦ Serve immediately with green vegetables and gravy if desired.

CASSOULET WITH PORK

Serves 4

225 g (8 oz) cubed pork
2 tbsp oil
2 garlic cloves, finely chopped
100 g (4 oz) streaky bacon, cut in strips
175 g (6 oz) haricot beans, soaked overnight
400 g (14 oz) can of tomatoes
275 ml (½ pint) stock
4 tbsp tomato purée
bouquet garni
1 onion, chopped
3 carrots, finely sliced
100 g (4 oz) mushrooms, sliced

Topping
4 tbsp wholemeal breadcrumbs
2 tbsp finely grated cheese

❦ This dish can be cooked in an oven, slow cooker, pressure cooker, or simmered in a pan. If using an oven, heat to 180C (350F) mark 4.
❦ Fry the meat in oil to brown. Add the garlic and bacon and fry for a few minutes. Add all ingredients except the topping and cook slowly until beans and meat are tender, about 2 hours in the oven, 2–2 ½ hours in a pan, 30–40 minutes in a pressure cooker, and for a slow cooker according to manufacturer's instructions for a similar dish.
❦ Transfer to an ovenproof dish, add the topping and grill or bake in a hot oven for 15–20 minutes to brown.
❦ Serve with chunks of granary bread and a green salad.

BARBECUED SPARE RIBS OF PORK

Serves 4-8

450-700 g (1-1 ½ lb) spare ribs or belly strips of
   pork
2 tbsp each of soy sauce, Worcestershire sauce,
   tomato purée, vinegar, lemon juice, dry
   sherry and honey or soft brown sugar
4 tbsp water
1 tsp garlic purée or 1 clove, crushed
1 tbsp French mustard

❧ Heat the oven to 220C (425F) mark 7. Fry the
meat with a minimum of fat to brown well, or roast
for 20 minutes. Drain off and discard any fat.
❧ Combine all the remaining ingredients, pour this
over meat and roast (or cook in a multi-cooker/elec-
tric frying pan), turning and basting frequently until
the sauce is reduced and the meat is tender, about 40
minutes.
❧ Serve as a starter, for a main meal, or as part of a
Chinese meal.

PORK AND PRUNE COBBLER

Serves 4-6

450 g (1 lb) lean cubed pork
1 tbsp wholemeal flour
2 tbsp oil
1 onion, sliced
½ tsp ground allspice
½ tsp basil
275 ml (½ pint) dry cider
275 ml (½ pint) stock
225 g (8 oz) mixed root vegetables, diced
   (optional)
100 g (4 oz) prunes, soaked

Scone topping
225 g (8 oz) self-raising wholemeal flour (or add
   1 ½ tsp baking powder to plain)
salt to taste
25 g (1 oz) margarine
bare 150 ml (¼ pint) milk or water

❧ The stew can be made in the oven or simmered
in a pan and transferred to a casserole dish to cook
the 'cobbler' or scone topping. The same stew can be
served with dumplings or in a pie.
❧ Heat the oven, if using, to 180C (350F) mark 4.
Toss the meat in flour and fry in oil until browned.
Add the onion and fry a little longer. Stir in any
remaining flour and blend in all other ingredients
except the prunes and those for the topping. Either
cover and simmer for 1 ½ hours or until meat is
cooked, or turn into a casserole dish, cover and cook
in the oven for a similar time. Add the prunes 20
minutes before the end of cooking.
❧ Before making the topping, stir the meat well and
ensure there is 5 cm (2 in) headroom in the casserole
dish above the stew. Increase oven heat to 220C
(425F) mark 7.
❧ To make the scone mix, sieve the flour and baking powder (if used) with the salt, rub in the margarine and mix to a soft dough with the milk.
❧ Knead lightly and, using a floured board, roll out
to 2 cm (¾ in) thick. Cut out 5 cm (2 in) rounds, and
overlap these on top of the meat. Glaze with a little
milk or beaten egg.
❧ Bake for 30 minutes, or until scone mixture is
risen and golden brown. If the meat was cold, cook
for a little longer to heat the meat thoroughly. Cover
scone topping with greaseproof paper to prevent
over-cooking.

PORK AND LIMES

Serves 4

450 g (1 lb) cubed pork or 4 chops or steaks
3 limes, rind and juice
1 chicken stock cube
1 tbsp soy sauce
bunch of spring onions, cleaned
100 g (4 oz) button mushrooms
50-100 g (2-4 oz) bean sprouts
25-50 g (1-2 oz) cornflour to thicken
1 lime, sliced, to garnish

❦ Marinate the pork in lime juice and rind for several hours.
❦ Drain and measure the lime juice. Make up to 575 ml (1 pint) with boiling water. Stir a stock cube into the boiling water and lime juice. Add this stock and the soy sauce to the meat, and simmer slowly for 1-1 ½ hours until meat is tender.
❦ Fan the spring onions by cutting down the green part. Add the mushrooms, onions and bean sprouts, and simmer for a further 10-15 minutes so that the vegetables are just cooked, but still crisp. Thicken as necessary with cornflour, blended with a little water.
❦ Serve garnished with sliced limes and accompanied with boiled rice.

POACHER'S PIES

Makes about 6

350 g (12 oz) Flaky Pastry (see page 361)
Home-made Mustard (see page 366)
175 g (6 oz) smoked streaky bacon
100 g (4 oz) mushrooms
100 g (4 oz) pork sausage meat
100 g (4 oz) cooked chicken or pheasant
1 tsp fresh thyme leaves
salt and black pepper
1 egg to glaze

❦ Heat the oven to 220C (425F) mark 7. Roll out the pastry thinly and cut into 10 cm (4 in) diameter circles; leave to relax. Spread a little mustard on half the circles, the rest being 'lids'.
❦ Rind and trim the bacon, being careful to remove any little bits of white bone. Wipe the mushrooms. Put the bacon, mushrooms, sausage meat, chicken or pheasant and thyme through the coarse plate of the mincer. Mix well together and season with a little salt and season generously with black pepper.
❦ Put a little of this mixture on half the pastry circles on top of the mustard. Brush the edges with water. Put on the lids, pressing the edges together firmly. Make a small cut in the top of each and brush with beaten egg.
❦ Stand the pies on a baking sheet and cook for 15 minutes, then reduce the temperature to 180C (350F) mark 4 and continue for 30 minutes. Cover with greaseproof paper if getting too brown.

PORK EN CROUTE

Serves 4-5

350 g (12 oz) Flaky Pastry (see page 361)
450 g (1 lb) pork pie meat
½ tsp dried sage
50 g (2 oz) raisins
salt and black pepper
1 egg, beaten

❦ Heat the oven to 220C (425F) mark 7. Roll out the pastry to an oblong and trim the edges. Check the pork over, removing any gristly bits, then mince it coarsely. Add the sage, raisins, salt and freshly ground black pepper. Bind the mixture together with most of the egg. Keep the remaining egg for glazing.
❦ Shape the meat into a roll down the centre of the pastry. Brush one edge with water. Fold lightly over and press the edges and ends together. Place on baking paper on a baking sheet, joined side downwards. Make a pattern with a fork on the ends. Decorate with a few pastry leaves made from the trimmings around a small slit on the top.
❦ Brush with the remaining beaten egg. Cook for 30-40 minutes until golden brown.

INDIVIDUAL SAUSAGE AND EGG PIES

Makes 6-8

350 g (12 oz) Hot Water Crust Pastry (see page 362)
350 g (12 oz) pork sausage meat
1 egg, beaten
salt and pepper
½ tsp mixed herbs
½ tsp Home-made Mustard (see page 366)
3-4 hard-boiled eggs
1 egg or milk to glaze
Savoury Jelly (see page 337)

❦ These pies should be made the day before they are needed.

❦ Keep the pastry warm. Heat the oven to 200C (400F) mark 6. Cut the pastry into 6 pieces. From each piece keep back one-third for the lid. Roll out the pastry and use to line six to eight 10 cm (4 in) patty tins; roll out the lids.

❦ Mix the sausage meat, beaten egg, salt and freshly ground black pepper, mixed herbs and mustard together. Cut the hard-boiled eggs in half. Fill the pastry cases with the mixture, putting half an egg in each.

❦ Brush the edges of the pies with milk or beaten egg, position the lids and press well together. Cut into the edges with a sharp knife to decorate. Make a small hole in the centre of each pie. From the trimmings, make one or two leaves and a little pastry rose for each pie to go round the hole in the middle. Brush with beaten egg or milk to glaze. A pinch of salt in the beaten egg makes a very glossy glaze.

❦ Cook for 30 minutes then reduce the temperature to 180C (350F) mark 4. Cover the pies with greaseproof paper and cook for a further 30 minutes.

❦ Cool in the tins. Lift the roses off the pies and fill each with cooling jelly. Chill.

❦ To practise the handling of hot water crust pastry, try these small picnic pies. I bake mine in nonstick patty tins 10 cm (4 in) across. Four of these fit in a 23 cm (9 in) square baking tray.

HARVEST PIE

Serves 6

350 g (12 oz) wholemeal Hot Water Crust Pastry (see page 362), using plain wholemeal flour instead of white
175 g (6 oz) lean smoked gammon
1 onion
450 g (1 lb) pork sausage meat
1 egg, beaten
75 g (3 oz) mushrooms
salt and pepper
1 egg to glaze
Savoury Jelly (see page 337)

❦ Keep the pastry warm. Heat the oven to 200C (400F) mark 6. Mince the gammon and onion together. Mix with the sausage meat and the beaten egg. Wipe and slice the mushrooms (peel and slice if you are lucky enough to have field mushrooms). Mix them in with the sausage meat and season to taste.

❦ Roll out half the pastry and use to line an 18 or 20 cm (7 or 8 in) enamel plate. Spread the filling on the pastry. Brush the edges with beaten egg. Roll out the remaining pastry for the lid. Press the edges firmly together. Cut with a knife round the edge. Make a hole in the top and brush with beaten egg.

❦ Cook for 40 minutes. Reduce the temperature to 180C (350F) mark 4, cover lightly with greaseproof paper and continue for a further 30-40 minutes.

❦ This pie is good hot or cold. If to be eaten cold, fill as usual with Savoury Jelly. Then it is best if the pie is made the day before.

CHESHIRE PORK PIE

Serves 6

350 g (12 oz) Hot Water Crust Pastry (see page 362)
2 eating apples
3 tbsp white wine
450 g (1 lb) lean pork
1 onion
salt and pepper
pinch of dried sage
1 egg to glaze
Savoury Jelly (see page 337)

❦ Keep the pastry warm. Heat the oven to 200C (400F) mark 6.
❦ Peel, core and chop the apples and cover them with the wine. Mince together the pork and onion. Season and add the sage and stir the apples and wine into the mixture.
❦ Raise the pie (see page 362). Fill the case with the mixture and cover with the lid. Make some pastry leaves and a rose from the trimmings for a hole in the top. Brush with beaten egg. Cook for 30 minutes. Reduce the temperature to 180C (350F) mark 4, cover the top of the pie with greaseproof paper and cook for a further 1 ½ hours.
❦ Remove the paper cuff. Brush the sides with beaten egg and return to the oven for the sides to brown – about 20 minutes. When the pie is cold, fill with cooling Savoury Jelly.

PORK IN GINGER BEER

Serves 4

4 trimmed pork chops or steaks or 450 g (1 lb) cubed pork
2 tbsp oil
1 onion, sliced
4 sticks celery, chopped
2 carrots, thinly sliced
25 g (1 oz) wholemeal flour
1 stock cube
425 ml (¾ pint) ginger beer
1 lemon, rind and juice
225 g (8 oz) tomatoes, skinned and quartered
salt and freshly ground black pepper
2 tsp chopped crystallized ginger (optional)

❦ Heat the oven to 180C (350F) mark 4.
❦ Fry the meat in the oil, to brown. Remove and place in a casserole dish. Fry the onion until translucent, stir in the celery, carrots and flour. Add to the casserole.
❦ Mix the stock cube with 4 tbsp of water. Blend in ginger beer, stock and lemon rind and juice. Pour the mixture over the meat. Add the tomatoes, a little salt (the stock cube will have a high salt content) and freshly ground black pepper and ginger (optional). Cover and cook for 45-60 minutes until the meat is tender.
❦ Serve with boiled long-grain rice or potatoes, or some lightly buttered noodles.

BACON AND HAM

*A selection of bacon and ham recipes from
Bacon and Bean Casserole to Boiled Ham and Raisin Sauce.*

Bacon is pork which has been treated with curing salts, a mixture of common salt (sodium chloride) and other permitted preservatives (saltpetre and other related substances), which give bacon its characteristic colour and flavour, and is essential for preserving the meat effectively.

Store loose bacon in the refrigerator, in 'cling-film', a polythene bag or rigid polythene container. Bacon can be kept like this for 10–14 days. Without a refrigerator, bacon will keep in a cool place for 4 days. Vacuum packs usually include a sell-by or best-before date and these should be adhered to. Once opened, treat these like loose bacon. Cooked ham, unless refrigerated, should be consumed within a day. With refrigeration and suitable packing, it can be kept for 2–3 days. Bacon can be frozen, although the salt in the meat accelerates the development of rancidity in the fat.

Cuts of bacon
(weights where given are only approximate)

Prime back
This lean cut is normally sold as rashers, or boneless chops, which are usually grilled or fried. The chops can be baked or used in casseroles. A thick piece can be used for boiling or braising.

Middle or through cut
This is the back and streaky cut together, although in some localities it is cut into the two parts and sold separately. The through cut gives a long rasher of bacon with a mixture of lean and less lean meat and is an economical buy. It is generally used for grilling, or a piece can be rolled and tied and used for boiling or baking, and is particularly good if stuffed before it is rolled.

Long back

Normally sold as fairly thin cut rashers, it is ideal for grilling or frying, but can be cubed for casseroles, pies and flans.

Corner gammon

This is a small, economical, triangular cut off the gammon, which is excellent boiled and served hot with a traditional sauce such as parsley. It is cheaper because of its rather awkward shape. It weighs about 1.8 kg (4 lb).

Middle gammon

A prime, lean and meaty cut for boiling, baking or braising whole, weighing about 2.25 kg (5 lb) but often sold as smaller joints. It can be cut into 1 cm (½ in) thick rashers for grilling or frying.

Slipper gammon is sometimes cut from this joint and weighs about 700 g (1 ½ lb).

Gammon hock

Quite a high percentage of bone, especially at the lower end, but the meat is succulent and ideal for casseroles, soups and pies. Sometimes cut in half to give a reasonable boiling joint, ideal for a family meal. The hock is bought mainly for soup and stock. It weighs about 2 kg (4 ½ lb).

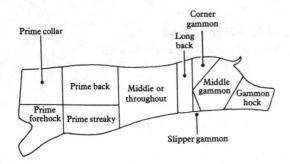

Prime streaky

These rashers combine lean with a percentage of fat. Look for a good proportion of lean. Excellent for grilling. Traditionally used to line pâté dishes and good for using in casseroles, pies, soups and rice dishes where carbohydrate helps to absorb the fat. A joint can be boiled and pressed. Streaky can be excellent value as it is the cheapest cut and with careful choosing can provide a filling meal, without necessarily having excess fat. Streaky usually contains little bits of cartilaginous bone, which should be cut out along with the rind before cooking.

Prime forehock

This provides an economical meat to be cubed or minced for casseroles meat loaves etc. It can be boiled, but is difficult to carve because of the position of the bones. Economical and weighing about 3.5 kg (8 lb) it is usually sold in smaller joints.

Prime collar. This makes an excellent joint, boiled or braised, as the bones are easily removed. It usually needs soaking as it can be rather salty. Collar is also sliced into rashers which are very lean. An inexpensive cut weighing about 2.5 kg (6 lb).

Cooking with bacon

Most joints are very versatile. When frying or grilling always remove the rind first. When boiling, some joints, notably the collar and hocks, may need soaking for a couple of hours to remove some of the salt. This is not always necessary with the larger, thicker joints, which today are usually less salty than was the case a few years ago. The quick and mild cures definitely need no soaking. Where instructions are given, these should be followed. Boiled joints are cooked with the rind on, this strips off easily when the meat is cooling. Baked joints usually benefit from a short period of boiling, so that the rind can be removed prior to baking. Slow baking with the meat wrapped in foil can produce a moist and succulent end result.

Cooking times

When baking, allow 20 minutes per 450 g (1 lb) and 20 minutes over for joints up to about 4.5 kg (10 lb). For larger joints only, allow 15 minutes per 450 g (1 lb).

When boiling, braising, casseroling or stewing, allow 20 minutes per 450 g (1 lb). Calculate the time from when the water comes to the boil. If using the oven, cover and cook at 180C (350F) mark 4.

When a combination of methods is used, the total time should be approximately 20 minutes per 450 g (1 lb). If meat has cooled down in between, allow a little for this.

CIDER BAKED GAMMON WITH ORANGES

Serving depends on joint size

joint of gammon
2.5 litres (4 pints) water
575 ml (1 pint) dry cider
1 onion, chopped
6 allspice berries
4 cloves
2 bay leaves

For basting
dry cider
2 tbsp Demerara sugar
1 tsp dry mustard
1 tsp mixed spice or ground allspice

Garnish
2 oranges, sliced with rind on
glacé cherries

❦ If the meat is a smoked or a salty joint, such as collar, soak overnight.
❦ Place the joint in a large pan, sufficient to allow liquid to cover and not boil over when cooking. Cover the joint with the water and cider. Add the onion, allspice, cloves and bay leaves. Bring to the boil and then simmer for 10 minutes per ½ kg (or 1 lb).
❦ Drain the joint and allow to cool a little, and cut off the rind. Score the fat in a criss-cross pattern.
❦ Heat the oven to 200C (400F) mark 6. Place the joint in a roasting tin and press the basting ingredients (other than the cider) into the fat. Pour over some of the cider and bake for 10 minutes per ½ kg (or 1 lb). Baste frequently with more mixture and more cider. When it is all used up, baste from around the joint.
❦ Remove when nearly cooked and cover with orange slices. These can be held on with cocktail sticks, but they should be removed prior to serving. Return to the oven and finish cooking. Before serving, garnish with cherries in the middle of each orange slice.
❦ Serve hot or cold. Ideal to serve hot at one meal, and to cut cold later (useful at Christmas time).

Note
For smaller joints, such as slipper and hock, reduce the ingredients to about half.

PEAR, PRUNE AND HAM RISOTTO

Serves 4

225 g (8 oz) wholemeal rice
1 onion, chopped
2 tbsp oil
575 ml (1 pint) light stock
150 ml (¼ pint) white wine or more stock
½ tsp basil
1 eating pear
2 tbsp lemon juice
½ red or green pepper, deseeded and diced
225 g (8 oz) cooked ham, cubed
50 g (2 oz) prunes, soaked, stoned and halved
pepper rings to garnish

❦ In a heavy-based pan, fry the rice and onion in oil, until the rice begins to brown. Allow to cool slightly and add the stock, wine or more stock and basil. Bring to the boil and then lower the heat, cover with a lid and simmer for 20 minutes, or until rice is soft, but not collapsed.
❦ Cut up the pear and toss in the lemon juice. Mix with the diced pepper. When the rice is cooked, add the ham, pear and prunes and heat through stirring all the time. Pile into a warmed serving dish and garnish with rings of red or green pepper.
❦ Serve hot or cold, this goes well with a green or mixed salad.

BAKED HAM AND STUFFED PEACHES

Serves 4-6

1.5 kg (3 lb) bacon joint
few cloves
2 tbsp clear honey
½ quantity of stuffing (see pages 350-355)
425 g (15 oz) can peach halves in juice
15 g (½ oz) cornflour

❧ Weigh the joint and calculate cooking time (see page 156). Place the joint in a large pan, cover with water and bring to the boil. Simmer for 20 minutes. Strain and, when cool enough to handle, remove the rind from joint.

❧ Heat the oven to 200C (400F) mark 6. Place the meat in an ovenproof dish. Slash the fat on the joint in a criss-cross pattern, press in the cloves and spoon over honey. Bake for the cooking time less 20 minutes.

❧ Meanwhile, make the stuffing and shape into balls, one per peach half. Bake on a greased baking tray for 20 minutes.

❧ Make up the peach juice to 275 ml (½ pint) with water. Blend with cornflour and boil for 5 minutes until thickened. Add the peach halves and simmer to heat them through.

❧ Serve the joint of bacon on a dish, surrounded with peach halves, topped with a stuffing ball. Serve the sauce separately. The dish should be garnished with watercress and served with fresh, coloured vegetables for best effect. It can be eaten cold and makes an excellent centre for a buffet.

HAM IN YOGHURT SAUCE WITH PASTA

Serves 4

350 g (12 oz) wholemeal pasta
25 g (1 oz) cornflour
25 g (1 oz) margarine or butter
150 ml (¼ pint) milk or light stock
150 ml (¼ pint) natural yoghurt
¼ tsp ground mace
175 g (6 oz) cooked ham, in strips
½ green pepper in thin strips
50 g (2 oz) sweetcorn kernels, cooked

❧ Cook the pasta in slightly salted boiling water until soft, about 15 minutes. Drain well.

❧ While the pasta is cooking, heat the cornflour and margarine together and cook for a few minutes until the mixture resembles a honeycomb. Slowly add the milk or stock, yoghurt and mace. Add the ham, pepper and sweetcorn and heat through.

❧ Spread the pasta around edge of a hot serving dish and heap the ham mixture in the middle. Garnish with grated cheese, breadcrumbs or a colourful salad vegetable. Serve immediately.

BOILED HAM AND RAISIN SAUCE

Serving depends on joint size

1 bacon joint for boiling, soaked if necessary
1 onion, chopped
peppercorns
cloves

Sauce
25 g (1 oz) cornflour
425 ml (¼ pint) stock (water in which bacon was boiled may be too salty)
25 g (1 oz) seedless raisins
1 tsp Worcestershire sauce

❧ Cover the joint with water and add the onion and spices. Bring to the boil and simmer for 20 minutes per ½ kg (or 1 lb) of bacon.

❧ Just before the meat is cooked, make the sauce by blending the cornflour with the stock, adding the raisins and Worcestershire sauce and boiling until thickened.

❧ Remove the bacon when cooked, and remove the rind. Serve separately as a joint with sauce, or carved in slices with the sauce poured over. One quantity of sauce serves up to 6 people.

❧ This dish is traditionally served with broad beans and carrots.

BACON CHOPS WITH PINEAPPLE RINGS

Serves 4

4 lean bacon chops (or gammon rashers)
1 small onion finely chopped
15 g (½ oz) margarine or butter
1 level tbsp cornflour
1 small can pineapple rings, with juice

❦ With scissors, cut into the fat around the chop or rasher (this prevents curling up during cooking). Grill or fry the chops until cooked, about 5-7 minutes per side.

❦ Make the sauce by frying the onion in the margarine or butter until soft, stirring in the cornflour and cooking for a few minutes, then gradually add the juice from the pineapple.

❦ Just before the chops are cooked, add the pineapple rings to the pan and fry or grill to heat them through.

❦ Serve the chops on a dish, garnished with the pineapple rings and with the sauce poured over.

❦ A watercress or grilled tomato garnish goes well with this dish. Serve with fresh vegetables and chipped or jacket potatoes.

BACON STUFFED COURGETTES

Serves 4

8 medium courgettes, topped and tailed
1 large onion, chopped
25 g (1 oz) margarine or butter
450 g (1 lb) collar or forehock bacon, soaked
350 g (12 oz) tomatoes, peeled and chopped (or a tin of tomatoes)
1 tsp marjoram or mixed herbs
salt and freshly ground black pepper

❦ Heat the oven to 180C (350F) mark 4. Cut or scoop out the flesh about halfway down into each courgette and use for soup or stew.

❦ Fry the onion in the margarine or butter until soft. Mince or finely chop the bacon, add to the pan and stir-fry for about 10 minutes. Add the remaining ingredients and mix well. Divide the mixture equally and stuff the courgettes. If there is too much

filling this can be put under the courgettes while baking.

❦ Place in an ovenproof dish and cover with a lid or foil. Bake for about 45 minutes until the courgette is cooked, but still crisp.

❦ Serve with a tomato, pepper or cheese sauce and wholemeal bread or rolls.

Variation
A marrow or squash can be used in the same way, but allow about 1 hour for cooking.

BACON AND BEAN CASSEROLE

Serves 4

225 g (8 oz) mixed beans, soaked overnight
3 tbsp oil
1 tsp cumin seeds
½ tsp cinnamon
bunch of spring onions, chopped
2 garlic cloves, crushed
225 g (8 oz) lean bacon, cubed
400 g (14 oz) tin tomatoes
100 g (4 oz) mushrooms, sliced
½ tsp each of ground coriander, turmeric and cayenne pepper
3 tbsp chopped parsley

❦ Drain the beans and boil in plenty of water for 10 minutes then drain again.

❦ Heat the oil in a large pan and fry the cumin and cinnamon for a few minutes. Add the onions and garlic and cook for 3 minutes. Add the bacon and stir-fry until the bacon starts to brown. Add all the remaining ingredients, reserving 1 tbsp parsley for garnish.

❦ Return the beans to the pan and simmer gently, stirring occasionally, until beans are cooked (30-60 minutes, depending on type and age of beans).

❦ The flavour is improved if the dish stands for several hours before serving. It is excellent hot or cold. Serve with fresh vegetables, salad, pitta bread or chunks of granary bread, garnished with the reserved parsley.

BACON, APPLE AND POTATO HOT POT

Serves 4

450 g (1 lb) bacon pieces or small joint, cubed
1 onion
450 g (1 lb) potatoes, scrubbed and quartered or
    sliced
225 g (8 oz) mixed root vegetables peeled and
    diced
2 eating apples, cored and thickly sliced
1 tsp sage leaves, chopped
275 ml (½ pint) stock
275 ml (½ pint) cider or more stock
chopped parsley to garnish

❧ Heat the oven to 180C (350F) mark 4.
❧ Put all ingredients in a large casserole dish with a
well-fitting lid and cook slowly until the meat is
cooked, about 1 ½ hours.
❧ This recipe is ideal for a slow cooker (see manufacturer's instructions for times). Serve garnished
with the parsley.

Variations
An alternative way to assemble the dish is to mix all
the ingredients together except the potatoes, and
arrange these in a layer on the top. Remove the lid
for last 30 minutes of cooking to brown the potatoes.
❧ Soaked butter or haricot beans can be substituted for the potatoes. No thickening is required with
the potatoes or beans.

MINCE

Mince is versatile and easy-to-use; make the most of it using these recipes which include old favourites and some that are more unusual

Always look for bright-coloured, moist-looking mince, avoiding that which is brown and dried with a lot of fat showing. The most usual type of mince to find is beef, but increasingly pork and, occasionally, lamb may be found. It is not necessary to buy meat ready minced. The increasing ownership of electric mixers with mincer attachments and food processors which chop the meat to mince in a few seconds, has encouraged many to buy the meat of their choice, and mince it at home. This appeals particularly to those who want very lean meat, or when less easily obtained meat such as veal or lamb are required. Purchased this way, mince is usually more expensive. The reason mince is normally so reasonably priced is that it utilizes the trimmings from the carcass and the cheaper less popular cuts. This of course does not apply when you buy to mince yourself.

Most recipes in this section can be made with any type of meat and experimentation is recommended. When a particular type of meat is more suitable for a recipe, it is mentioned.

CRANBERRY MINCE

Serves 4

1 onion, chopped
1 tbsp vegetable oil
450 g (1 lb) lean mince
25 g (1 oz) wholemeal flour
275 ml (½ pint) stock
1 tsp oregano
1 orange, grated rind and juice
75 g (3 oz) cranberries, fresh or frozen

❦ Fry the onion in oil over a low heat, until it is translucent. Stir in the meat, turn up the heat and brown. Stir in the flour, gradually add the stock and remaining ingredients, except the cranberries. Cover and simmer for 20 minutes.
❦ Add the cranberries and cook for a further 15 minutes or until the meat is tender. The cranberries should remain whole, but soft.

LASAGNE

Serves 4

½ quantity Bolognese Sauce (see page 344) with bacon and carrots
175 g (6 oz) lasagne or lasagne verde
1 tbsp finely grated Parmesan cheese
1 tbsp wholemeal breadcrumbs

Sauce
575 ml (1 pint) milk
50 g (2 oz) cornflour
50 g (2 oz) grated cheese, preferably Edam, Gruyère or cottage
¼ tsp nutmeg
salt and freshly ground black pepper

❦ To make the cheese sauce, heat the milk and blend the cornflour in a bowl with a little water. When the milk is nearly boiling, pour it on the cornflour, stir well and return to the pan and boil for about 3 minutes, or until the sauce is thickened. The sauce should be of a thin coating consistency. Add the cheese and nutmeg and season to taste.

❦ Heat the oven to 190C (375F) mark 5.

❦ Ensure the Bolognese mixture is fairly runny in consistency, adding a little water if necessary. The lasagne does not require previous cooking provided that the mixture has sufficient excess liquid for it to absorb.

❦ Arrange the Bolognese, lasagne and cheese sauce in layers in an ovenproof dish, starting with a layer of Bolognese, and finishing with sauce. The dish should be fairly wide so that the mixture is not more than about 6 cm (2½ in) deep, but leave 1 cm (½ in) space at the top, or the mixture will boil over.

❦ Sprinkle on the grated Parmesan and breadcrumbs and bake for 30 minutes or until brown and bubbling. Garnish with sliced tomato and serve with fresh vegetables or salad.

MINCE AND TOMATO PIE

Serves 4

225 g (8 oz) wholemeal Mixer Pastry (see page 358)
225 g (8 oz) mince
1 onion, chopped
25 g (1 oz) wholemeal flour
1 tsp basil
225 g (8 oz) tomatoes, skinned and chopped
black pepper
150 ml (¼ pint) stock
1 beaten egg

❦ The pastry is best made well in advance and chilled.

❦ Mix the mince and chopped onion and heat gently in a pan to melt the fat in the meat. When the fat runs, turn up the heat and brown the meat. Stir in the flour and cook for a few minutes.

❦ Add the other ingredients apart from the egg and simmer for 45 minutes, taking care not to boil dry, adding more water if necessary (this dish cooks well in a microwave oven in 10-15 minutes). Cool well. This dish can be made the day before if required.

❦ Heat the oven to 200C (400F) mark 6. Divide the pastry in two and use half to line the bottom of a 20 cm (8 in) greased flan ring or foil dish. Pack in the cold meat mixture and cover with the remaining pastry, using water to seal.

❦ Knock up the edges by making horizontal cuts with the back of a knife, then scallop by bringing up the back of the knife every 4 cm (1 ½ in). Pierce the top, decorate with pastry leaves and glaze with beaten egg. Bake for 40 minutes or until pastry is golden brown and firm.

❦ Serve hot or cold. Ideal for picnics and packed lunches.

STUFFED PANCAKES WITH CHEESE SAUCE

Serves 4-6

Batter
100 g (4 oz) wholemeal flour
¼ tsp salt
1 egg
275 ml (½ pint) milk or milk and water
vegetable oil for frying

Filling
1 small onion, finely chopped
1 tbsp oil
225 g (8 oz) lean mince
3 rashers bacon, chopped
3 tomatoes, skinned and chopped
100 g (4 oz) mushrooms, chopped
1 tsp marjoram
pinch cayenne pepper
ground black pepper
½ red pepper, chopped

Cheese sauce
25 g (1 oz) wholemeal flour
25 g (1 oz) butter or margarine
275 ml (½ pint) milk
¼ tsp mustard
pinch of grated nutmeg
50 g (2 oz) grated cheese, preferably Edam,
    Gruyère or cottage
wholemeal breadcrumbs

❦ First make the pancakes: Sieve the flour and salt into a bowl and break the egg into a well in the centre. Gradually add half the milk, beating it into the flour with a wooden spoon. Beat for about 3 minutes then beat in the remaining milk. Leave to stand for 1 hour if possible.

❦ Cook the pancakes in a 20 cm (8 in) frying pan. Ensure the pan is well seasoned by heating it with a little oil, then rubbing well with salt and wiping out with a damp cloth. Run a little oil around the pan; when hot run a little batter around the pan, to cover the bottom. The pancake should be thin and lacy. The mixture may need a few tablespoons of water added to thin it down. Cook over a high heat until the pancake comes away slightly from the edge.

Carefully turn over using a palette knife, or by tossing. The second side needs only about 15 seconds. Remove the pancake from the pan, and keep warm in a pile if using immediately, or spread out until cold if using later. These pancakes freeze very well.

❦ Make the filling: Fry the onion in the oil until translucent. Add the mince and bacon, and fry to brown. Add the remaining ingredients and stir-fry for about 7 minutes or until all the ingredients are cooked.

❦ Divide the mixture evenly between the pancakes and roll up, placing full rolls in an ovenproof dish.

❦ Make the sauce: Cook the flour and fat for a few minutes. Gradually add the milk and cook until thick. Add the mustard, nutmeg and cheese, reserving a little for finishing and stir until melted.

❦ Coat the pancakes with sauce, sprinkle with a mixture of the reserved cheese and the breadcrumbs and grill until golden brown. If the pancakes and filling are cold, reheat and brown at the same time in an oven at 190C (375F) mark 5 for 30 minutes.

BEEF AND SPINACH MEAT LOAF

Serves 4-6

225 g (8 oz) fresh spinach leaves, de-stalked
350 g (12 oz) mince (pork is excellent)
50 g (2 oz) mushrooms, finely chopped
50 g (2 oz) wholemeal breadcrumbs
1 onion, grated
1 garlic clove, crushed
1 tsp oregano
3 eggs, soft-boiled and shelled, or poached

❦ Heat the oven to 190C (375F) mark 5. Grease a 1 kg (2 lb) loaf tin.

❦ Blanch the spinach leaves in boiling water for 1 minute. Drain well. Line the sides and base of the prepared tin with the leaves, allowing them to hang over the edges to be wrapped over when the filling is added.

❦ Combine all ingredients except the eggs. Place half carefully in the tin, without disturbing the spinach. Make wells in the meat and place in the eggs. Cover with the remaining meat, flatten the top, and fold over the spinach leaves to cover the meat.

❦ Cover with foil or greaseproof paper. Bake for 1 hour until the meat is cooked.

❦ Turn out on to a serving dish and serve sliced. This is delicious hot or cold and goes well with a tomato, spicy or curry sauce.

MOUSSAKA

Serves 4-6

2 medium aubergines, sliced
2 tbsp vegetable oil
15 g (½ oz) butter
1 large onion, sliced
1 garlic clove, crushed
450 g (1 lb) minced meat (usually lamb)
1 tsp ground allspice or cinnamon
2 tbsp parsley, chopped
3 tbsp tomato purée
450 g (1 lb) potatoes, sliced and parboiled
150 ml (¼ pint) water or stock

Sauce
25 g (1 oz) butter or margarine
40 g (1 ½ oz) cornflour
425 ml (¾ pint) milk
salt and freshly ground black pepper
1 egg

❦ Fry the aubergine slices in oil and butter until browned on both sides. Fry in batches, adding a little more fat as necessary. Remove when browned and drain on absorbent paper.

❦ Add the onion and garlic to the pan and fry for a few minutes. Add the meat and brown, then add the spice, parsley and purée.

❦ Make the sauce by cooking the fat and cornflour together for a few minutes, gradually adding the milk and reheating and then boiling for 3-5 minutes, until the sauce has thickened. Season and, when cool, beat in the egg.

❦ Heat the oven to 190C (375F) mark 5. Assemble the moussaka in a deep ovenproof dish with alternating layers of aubergine, meat and potato. Add the water or stock. Pour over the sauce, and bake for 30 minutes until golden brown.

❦ Serve the moussaka hot or cold with fresh vegetables or a salad. This dish is particularly good with a sliced tomato and chive salad.

RISOTTO MILANESE

Serves 4-6

1 onion, chopped
2 garlic cloves, crushed
3 tbsp oil
225 g (8 oz) whole grain brown rice
225 g (8 oz) beef mince
100 g (4 oz) bacon, chopped
400 g (14 oz) tin tomatoes, chopped
2 tbsp tomato purée
½ tsp oregano
½ tsp tarragon
100 g (4 oz) sweetcorn kernels
salt and freshly ground black pepper
425 ml (¾ pint) stock or stock and white wine mixed
chopped parsley to garnish

❦ Fry the onion and garlic in oil for 3-5 minutes until translucent. Add the rice and stir-fry until brown, add the beef and fry for 5 minutes. Add all the remaining ingredients and simmer until the rice is cooked, about 15 minutes.

❦ Alternatively the mixture can be cooked in an oven heated to 190C (375F) mark 5 for 40-50 minutes, depending on the thickness of the dish.

❦ Serve hot or cold garnished with parsley.

Variation
Instead of mince, any type of cooked meat can be used. Cut it up in cubes, and stir in just before the rice is cooked, for 5 minutes cooking.

MEATBALLS WITH SOURED CREAM

Serves 4-6

75 g (3 oz) wholemeal bread
150 ml (¼ pint) milk or tomato juice
350 g (12 oz) mince
2 garlic cloves, crushed
2 tbsp parsley, chopped
2 tbsp curry powder or 1 tbsp anchovy essence
   or 2 tbsp tomato purée
150 ml (¼ pint) soured cream
flour for dusting
oil (if fried)

❧ Soak the bread in the milk or juice.
❧ Mash with all other ingredients except the soured cream. Form into balls approximately 2.5 cm (1 in) in diameter using flour to prevent sticking.
❧ Fry for 6-8 minutes or bake in an oven 180C (350F) mark 4 for 40 minutes. Pile on to a serving dish and top with soured cream.
❧ Serve with chunks of wholemeal or granary bread and salad or fresh vegetables, or on a bed of buttered noodles.

BOBOTIE

Serves 4

2 onions, sliced
2 tbsp oil
450 g (1 lb) minced meat, beef or pork
1 tbsp curry powder
1 tsp mixed herbs
2 tsp soft brown sugar
½ tsp salt
1 tbsp vinegar
1 tbsp lemon juice
2 eggs
100 g (4 oz) wholemeal bread
275 ml (½ pint) milk
25 g (1 oz) flaked almonds, toasted

Heat the oven to 200C (400F) mark 6.
❧ Fry the onions in oil until soft. Stir in the meat and fry until brown. Add the curry powder, herbs, sugar, salt, vinegar and lemon juice. Beat in one egg.
❧ Soak the bread in milk. Drain off excess milk and

beat this together with other egg. Beat the soaked bread with the meat mixture. Pour into a deep oven-proof dish. Pour the egg and milk mixture over the meat and sprinkle with almonds.
❧ Bake for 30 minutes, reduce oven to 180C (350F) mark 4 for a further 30 minutes.
❧ Serve with fresh vegetables or a salad, with potatoes, rice or pasta.

Note
This dish can be made with cooked meat, in which case only cook for 30 minutes.

BAKED MEAT ROLL

Serves 4-6

1 onion, peeled
dripping
350 g (12 oz) cooked meat, minced
1 tbsp mixed herbs
2-3 tbsp home-made Tomato Sauce (see page 341) or bought
225 g (8 oz) Suet Crust Pastry (see page 361)

❧ Heat the oven to 220C (425F) mark 7.
❧ Chop the onion and fry in the dripping until brown. Add the meat with the herbs and the tomato sauce. Season well and simmer for 10 minutes. Cool.
❧ Roll out the pastry to an oblong. Spread with the cooled mixture, leaving a narrow margin. Turn in the edges to keep the filling in. Brush with water and roll up firmly. Place on baking paper on a baking sheet, join side downwards.
❧ Bake for 1 hour until golden brown and crisp. If the pastry is getting too brown, cover it loosely with a sheet of greaseproof paper and turn the oven down to 200C (400F) mark 6.
❧ This is a very good way of using up meat which is left over from a joint.

CHILLI CON CARNE

Serves 4-6

100-175 g (4-6 oz) red kidney beans, soaked
    overnight
1 onion, chopped
1 tbsp vegetable oil
350-450 g (12-16 oz) minced beef or lamb
2 garlic cloves, crushed
1-2 tsp chilli powder (to taste)
400 g (14 oz) tin tomatoes, chopped
150 ml (¼ pint) Basic Brown Stock (see page335)
2 tbsp tomato purée
freshly ground black pepper

❧ Boil the soaked beans in plenty of water for 20
minutes. Discard the water.
❧ Fry the onion in oil until translucent. Add the
meat and fry to brown. Add the remaining ingredients and stir well. Add the cooked beans and simmer
with the lid on for 30 minutes until the meat is
cooked and the beans are soft but not collapsed.
Adjust the seasoning and serve on or with cooked
wholemeal rice and a salad.
❧ The flavour of this dish improves if it is made the
day before and kept in the refrigerator. Tinned beans
can be used and stirred in 5 minutes before the end
of cooking.
❧ Red kidney beans must be boiled for at least 10
minutes before eating, to ensure any mould that
might be present is destroyed. Once this has been
done, they are perfectly safe to eat, without further
cooking, in salads. Tinned beans have already been
cooked during the canning process.

POULTRY
AND
GAME

ABOUT POULTRY AND GAME

Poultry and game have been of great interest to the breeder, sportsman, hunter and cook for many hundreds of years.

Country people have always kept domestic poultry, particularly chickens and often geese and ducks. Rabbits and hares were regularly made into tasty dishes, though they would be considered luxury food by some families. Quite often they may have been poached from the local landowner's fields. More exotic game such as pheasant, partridge and venison regularly graced the tables of the gentry.

Nowadays, poultry is readily available and specialist shops display a good range of game birds and animals which can provide something different for a dinner party or that special celebration meal.

This chapter deals with the choice and preparation of poultry and game – both feather and fur. It gives many interesting and exciting, as well as traditional, ways of cooking and serving.

❧ Choosing poultry ❧ and game

Chicken

There are various types available.

Poussin: 6-10 weeks old; 700 g (1 ½ lb). Usually split down the backbone and best roasted, spit-roasted or grilled. One bird serves 2.

Broiler: Spring chicken; 3 months old; 900 g-1.2 kg (2-2 ½ lb). May be roasted, pot-roasted or sautéed. One bird serve 3-4.

Roaster: 6 months old; 1.5-1.8 kg (3-4 lb); the most popular size. Usually roasted or pot-roasted. One bird will serve 4-6.

Large roaster: 9 months old; up to 3.6 kg (8 lb). Cockerel which has been specially fattened. Can be roasted; is a good size for boning . One will serve up to 10.

Boiler: 12-18 months old; 1.8-2.5 kg (4-6 lb). Good for making broths and for cold dish es served with sauces. There is a tendency for them to become fatty, so gentle boiling is required, then cooling, thus enabling the fat to be skimmed off.

Turkey

A hen turkey has a small frame and more meat in ratio to bone than a stag (male turkey), though the latter is often preferred for flavour. Whole turkeys are available as follows:

Clean-plucked: Head, legs and intestines intact. Should be dressed as for chicken (see overleaf).

Oven-ready: Giblets packed separately; ready for the oven.

Frozen: Giblets not usually included. Frozen turkey should be defrosted slowly in a cool place (not in the fridge) for 36-48 hours.

Turkey is also widely available (fresh and frozen) as leg joints and roasts and breast roasts.

A 4.5-6 kg (10-13 lb) bird will serve 10-12 people, or 8 people with enough left over for a cold dish. A 4 kg (9 lb) frozen turkey is equivalent to a 5.4 kg (12 lb) clean-plucked turkey.

A 7.2-9 kg (16-20 lb) turkey should provide several meals for a family party of 6-8 people.

A 9.0-11.5 kg (20-25 lb) bird or larger will be required for a large household, and when lots of cold turkey is needed. When buying an extra-large turkey, first check your oven measurements.

Duck

Young ducks up to 8 months old may be roasted or spit-roasted. Birds over 12 months should be casseroled. They are at their best in early summer. They have a shallow breast and feed fewer people than a chicken of corresponding weight. A 1.8 kg (4 lb) bird will serve 3-4 people.

Goose

Available throughout the year but at its best at Christmas-time. A mature goose will weigh 4.5-6.3 kg (10-14 lb) and, like duck, is wasteful. Allow 450-550 g (1-1 ¼ lb) per person.

Guinea-fowl

A tasty bird with a flavour between chicken and pheasant. A young guinea-fowl is tender and good roasted. Older birds should be casseroled. Any recipe for chicken and pheasant may be used. One bird will serve 4-5 people.

Pheasants

Pheasants are sold by the brace – comprising a cock and a hen. A young cock will have short, rounded spurs which become longer and pointed with age. A young hen has soft pliable feet which harden with age. Young birds have pointed feathers – rounded feathers indicate age. Young birds are excellent roasted, but older birds should be potroasted or casseroled. One pheasant will serve 2-4 people, depending on its size.

Partridge

There are two varieties – the English, or grey, partridge, which is considered to be better flavoured than the larger French, or red-legged, partridge. The latter, although of Continental origin, tends to be more common. A young bird will have a soft beak and pointed feathers. Young birds are excellent plain-roasted. One bird serves 1-2 people, depending on its size.

Grouse

Young birds have bright eyes, soft pliable feet and smooth legs and a soft pliable tip to the breastbone. In older birds the bones become hard and the feet scaly with sharp claws. Young birds are good oven- or spit-roasted; older birds require moist cooking by casseroling or can be used in pies and terrines. One plump bird serves 2 people.

Black game or black grouse

A member of the grouse family and about twice the size of a grouse. With the exception of very young birds, the meat is rather dry and a moist cooking method is recommended. Any recipes suitable for older grouse may be used, but longer cooking time must be allowed. One bird serves 3-4 people, depending on its size.

Ptarmigan or white grouse

The smallest grouse, ptarmigan has not such a good flavour as grouse, but young birds have a delicate taste when roasted. Older birds may be bitter and should be casseroled, with well-flavoured ingredients. Any recipe for grouse may be used. One bird serves 1-2 people.

Capercaillie

The largest member of the grouse family. Young birds have supple feet and smooth pliable legs, they may be roasted. Older birds have rough scaly legs and should be casseroled. The gizzard has an unpleasant taste and should not be used for stock. A cock bird will serve 6-8; a hen will serve 3-4.

Wild duck

A collective name for a wide variety of duck species; the most usual ones being mallard, widgeon and teal. Although the mallard is the largest and the best known, it is the little teal which has most flavour. Unlike the domestic duck, the flesh is dry and needs plenty of fat for roasting. A mallard should serve 2-3 people, but teal will serve only one person. A duck shot on the fore-shore may have a 'fishy' flavour. This can be overcome by placing an onion or potato inside the cavity, and poaching the bird in salted water for 20 minutes. Rinse and dry thoroughly before roasting in the usual way.

Woodcock

Difficult to obtain in the shops and considered by many to be the best-flavoured of all game birds. Once a breakfast delicacy, it is now served for dinner either as a starter or main course. A minimum of one bird per person should be allowed.

Snipe

A small bird and a great delicacy. One bird per person will do for a starter, but two for a main course.

Quail

Rare in the wild but now reared on farms, this little bird is available from poulterers and delicatessens and can be bought frozen. One bird per person is needed for a starter and two for a main course.

Pigeon

All pigeons can be eaten but it is the wood pigeon which can have a gamy flavour. It is readily available, cheap and nutritious. Young birds can be roasted, but for best results, long, slow cooking is advisable. For a pie, they are best pre-cooked.

Rabbit

Rabbits are at their best between 3 and 4 months old. They should be plump with bright eyes, flexible feet and smooth claws. The ears of young rabbits will tear easily. Native wild rabbits have much more flavour than those bred for the table or frozen imported rabbit. One large rabbit will serve 3-4 people.

Hare

There are two types of hare: English (brown) and Scotch (blue). The brown is larger and has more flavour. A young hare (leveret) has a smooth coat, small white teeth, soft ears and well-hidden claws. Older hares have a wavy coat, large yellow teeth, an evident cleft in the jaw and protruding blunt claws. Only leverets can be roasted without being marinated to tenderize the meat.

Venison

There are several species of deer in Great Britain, but generally it is only the meat of the Red, Roe and Fallow deer that is eaten. Deer farms are now being developed all over the country and venison is becoming easier to obtain through country butchers and game shops. The quality of 'farmed' deer is normally good, as the age of the animal is known and facilities ensure good preparation of the carcass. Venison joints are available and also sausages and pâtés. Being lean, venison freezes well. The best joints for roasting are the haunch and saddle; cutlets and steaks make good frying and the shoulder can be stewed. Game venison generally requires marinating before roasting, but with good quality 'farmed' venison, marinating is a matter of taste, not necessity.

❦ Plucking, trussing ❦ and drawing poultry and game birds

Methods vary little from one type to another.

Plucking

Either hold the bird by its legs, or suspend it by its legs. Start plucking the feathers from the breast. Work with the legs towards you, and pull the feathers away from you. From the breast, work down the neck and then towards the tail and down the legs. Turn the bird over and remove the feathers from the back and the wings. It may be necessary to use pliers on the strong wing-pinion feathers. Keep pheasant tail feathers of a for garnish if the bird is to be roasted.

Drawing

Remove the legs – cut through the skin approximately 2.5 cm (1 in) below the knee joint, place the cut over the sharp edge of the table or a board, and with a sharp downward movement of the hand, break the leg. It should now be possible to remove the leg sinews by pulling the feet.

Remove the head – place the bird, breast-side down, and cut through the neck skin lengthwise from between the shoulders up to the head. Pull the skin away from the neck and sever the neck and skin just below the head. Cut through the neck by the shoulders, and retain the neck for stock.

Place the bird on its back, loosen the windpipe and food pipe from the neck skin, and remove the crop. If poultry has been starved before killing, the crop should be empty; in game it will usually be full of grain. Place the forefinger inside the neck cavity and loosen the lungs away from the ribs, by working the forefinger backwards and forwards around the rib cage.

Turn to the tail end, and with a sharp knife make a cut between the anus and the parson's nose. Insert the little finger and hook it around the back passage; insert the knife under the loop of the intestine and cut away from the parson's nose – this should cut out the anus completely.

Insert the forefinger into the cavity and loosen the intestines from the walls of the body cavity. Take hold of the gizzard (feels large and firm) and gently pull; the whole of the intestines should be removed, and also the lungs.

Carefully cut the heart away, and the liver. Cut the gall-bladder from the liver, taking care not to break it, otherwise it will impart a bitter flavour. Cut the gizzard away, cut through the muscular casing and remove the sack containing the partially digested food. Retain the heart, liver and gizzard casing with the neck for stock. Wrap the rest in newspaper and dispose of it.

Singe the bird over a clean flame to remove the fine down, then wipe with a clean damp cloth.

Trussing

Place the bird on its back, fold the wings to tuck behind the shoulders, and push the legs forward. With a trussing needle threaded with fine string, pass the needle from one hip joint through the body cavity to the other hip joint. Pass it up the length of one wing, across the back, just below the neck, and down the length of the other wing. Pull both ends of the string up tightly and tie the two ends together.

Take another length of string in the needle and pass the needle through the tail-end of the breast bone. Remove the needle, take the two ends of the string over the legs, cross them over the cavity and tie them behind the parson's nose.

Take the flap of neck skin and tuck it under the wings and string across the back.

Trussing variations for game birds

It is usual with game birds to leave the legs and feet on, although the toes are cut off. Often with pheasant and other larger birds, the feet and part of the leg may be removed. The scaly part of the legs should be dipped in boiling water and the scales scraped off.

Traditionally, small game birds such as quail, woodcock and snipe are not drawn. The head should be skinned and the eyes removed. (A woodcock should also have the gizzard removed.) The beak should be twisted around and used like a skewer to truss the bird. During cooking the trail (alimentary canal) turns to liquid and soaks into the toast on which the bird is cooked.

Today, many people prefer to draw and truss these birds as for other game birds.

❦ Jointing poultry and ❦ game birds

Place the bird, breast uppermost, tail towards you. With a sharp knife, cut through the skin between the leg and the breast; press the leg outwards and downwards, insert the knife in the hip joint, cut around and remove the leg. With a small chicken, the leg may be left as one portion; with a larger bird, it may be divided into two.

Cut down through the breast approximately 2.5 cm (1 in) in from the wing, and cut the wing off – this ensures a reasonable amount of breast meat on the wing joint. Fillet the breast meat off the carcass. Repeat on the second side. The carcass may be used for making stock

Pigeons

If acquired in large numbers, it is best to use only the breasts. With a sharp knife, cut along the breastbone, skin the breast area and fillet each breast 'steak' away from the carcass or, from the tail end lift the breast bone and, with scissors, cut through the skin and shoulder joints and lift the breast off completely.

❦ Boning out poultry ❦ and game birds

Place the bird breast down, and with a sharp knife, cut the skin down the backbone; keeping the knife close to the carcass, carefully fillet the meat away until you reach the leg joint. Ease the knife through the hip joint, and break the leg away from the carcass. Fillet the meat from the leg. Pull the leg completely inside out to remove the bone (for some recipes you can leave the bones in the legs to give a better shape to the finished item).

Continue cutting away the flesh and skin towards the breastbone. Allow the knife to follow the carcass, removing the meat. Take care down the centre of the breastbone that the skin is not cut. Cut the wing off at the joint furthest from the body. Remove the meat from one side first, then work on the other side.

Read the recipe on page 175 for finishing. The carcass may be used for making stock.

Turkey, goose and pheasant are also ideal for boning out and can be finished in a variety of ways.

❦ Carving poultry ❦ and game birds

Carving instructions are given with the recipes for the different types of bird. in each section, the basic recipe for each bird (usually a roasting recipe) contains the information you will need.

❦ Paunching and ❦ skinning rabbits and hares

Paunching

Rabbits should be paunched (gutted) as soon as they are killed, by making a slit along the length of the belly and removing the intestine and stomach. They may then be hung.

Hares should be hung head down before gutting. A bowl or polythene bag should be placed or hung under the head to catch any blood. This can be used as a liaison to thicken the sauce of, for example, Jugged Hare (see page 212). A teaspoonful of vinegar added to the blood will prevent it from clotting.

Skinning

Start by removing the lower part of the legs. From the slit along the belly, loosen the skin around the back and peel it off towards the hind legs. Turn the skin of the legs and peel it off like a stocking.

Pull the skin down over the body and forelegs similarly. The head of the rabbit is removed, but that of a hare is usually left on. Cut the skin away from the head, and remove the eyes with a sharp knife.

From the liver, remove the gall bladder, taking care not to break it. Reserve the liver, heart and kidney, also the blood which has collected under the membrane of the ribs of the hare. From the hare, remove the blue membrane which covers the meat. Rinse the meat well in cold water and dry well.

of skin attached to the rib cage. The carcass may be divided in two lengthwise by cutting down the backbone, each half again being cut into 2 or 3 pieces depending on the size of the rabbit or hare. In a hare, the saddle (backbone) is often left whole for roasting. Joint as above, but leave the backbone complete.

❧ Jointing rabbits ❧ and hares

Remove the hind legs by cutting through the hip joint with a sharp knife. Remove the forelegs by cutting through the shoulder joint. Trim away the flaps

❧ Hanging ❧

Hanging times will depend on personal taste and the weather. In warm humid weather, hanging time will be shorter than in cold dry weather. Game birds are hung by the neck, mammals by the hind legs.

❧ Game – availability and hanging times ❧

	Season	Best	Hanging times (in days)
Pheasant	1 Oct to 1 Feb	Nov & Dec	7-10
Partridge	1 Sept to 1 Feb	Oct & Nov	3-5 (young birds) 8 (older birds)
Grouse	12 Aug to 10 Dec	Aug to Oct	7-10
Black game	20 Aug to 10 Dec	Aug to Oct	3-10
Ptarmigan	12 Aug to 10 Dec	Aug to Oct	2-4
Capercaillie	1 Oct to 31 Jan	Nov & Dec	10-14
Wild duck	1 Sept to 31 Jan	Nov & Dec	up to 3
Woodcock	1 Oct to 31 Jan	Nov & Dec	3-5
Snipe	12 Aug to 31 Jan	Nov	3-4
Quail	(Farmed) all year		Little or none
Pigeon	All year		Little or none
Rabbit	All year		3-5
Hare	1 Aug to 28 Feb	Oct onwards	7-10
Venison	1 Aug to 30 Apr	Depends on species & sex	8-10 (red deer) 7 (fallow & roe)
	(Farmed) all year		2-5

POULTRY

Poultry can be cooked in hundreds of different and delicious ways. In this section chicken, turkey, duck and goose are roasted, casseroled, used in salads and made into pies.

CHICKEN WITH ASPARAGUS

Serves 4-6

25 g (1 oz) butter
1 tsp oil
1 chicken, 1.6-1.8 kg (3 ½-4lb), jointed (see page 171)
150 ml (¼ pint) Chicken Stock (see page 335)
150 ml (¼ pint) dry white wine
salt and freshly ground black pepper

Sauce
25 g (1 oz) butter
100 g (4 oz) button mushrooms, sliced
425 g (15 oz) canned asparagus spears
1 tsp plain flour
150 ml (¼ pint) single cream
1 tsp Parmesan cheese

❦ Heat the butter and oil in a flameproof casserole, and fry the chicken joints until golden brown. Add the stock, wine and salt and freshly ground black pepper. Bring to the boil and cover. Simmer gently for 45 minutes, or until the meat is tender.

❦ Meanwhile, make the sauce: melt the butter and gently sauté the sliced mushrooms. Drain the asparagus spears, reserving the liquid. Blend the flour with a little liquid, then add the cream to the flour, and stir well to blend.

❦ When the chicken is cooked, transfer the joints to a serving dish and keep warm. Measure the liquid, and make up to 425 ml (¾ pint) with the asparagus liquid, add the cream mixture and return to the casserole. Bring to the boil and stir until it thickens slightly.

❦ Add the mushrooms. Spoon over the chicken pieces and place the asparagus spears at each end of the dish. Sprinkle the sauce with the Parmesan cheese and put the dish under a hot grill to brown before serving.

ROAST CHICKEN (1)

Serves 4-6

1 chicken, 1.6-1.8 kg (3 ½-4 lb)
stuffing of own choice – traditionally parsley
    and thyme (see page 354)
100 g (4 oz) dripping
streaky bacon rashers (optional)
1 tbsp plain flour
275 ml (½ pint) Chicken Stock (see page 335)

❧ Heat the oven to 220C (425F) mark 7.
Place the stuffing in the cavity of the bird and, if
desired, place the bacon rashers over the breast – this
will prevent drying out.
❧ Heat the dripping in a roasting tin, and place the
bird in it, baste well and place in the oven. Reduce
the temperature after 15 minutes to 190C (375F)
mark 5, and roast for a further 1 hour, or until tender, basting regularly. 15 minutes before the end of
cooking, remove the bacon rashers (if used) and
sprinkle the breast with a little flour, baste well, and
continue cooking.
❧ To test to see if cooked, take a fine skewer, or a
cooking knife with a fine point and insert it into the
flesh of the thigh. If the juice that comes out is clear,
the bird is cooked; if there is any pinkness, continue
cooking.
❧ Transfer the bird to a serving dish and keep
warm. Remove most of the fat from the roasting tin,
place the tin over the heat and stir in the flour; cook
for 2-3 minutes, then gradually stir in the stock,
bring to the boil and simmer for 3-5 minutes. Strain
into a sauce boat.
❧ Serve the chicken with Bacon Rolls (see page 355)
and Bread Sauce (see page 342).

Note
If time allows, the bird will be much easier to carve
if, when cooked, it is placed on the serving dish, covered with foil and several layers of cloth, and allowed
to stand for at least 15 minutes. This resting period
allows the meat to set.
❧ To carve, hold the bird firmly with a carving fork,
insert the carving knife between the leg and the
breast, and cut through the skin. Gently press the leg
outwards and cut through the joint. Divide the leg
into 2 portions. Slice down the breast about 2.5 cm
(1 in) in from the wing joint, and cut through the
wing joint – this ensures that a reasonable amount of
breast is served with the wing. Carve the rest of the
breast into slices. Repeat the process for the second
side of the bird.

ROAST CHICKEN (2)

Serves 4-6

2-3 sprigs fresh thyme or rosemary
50 g (2 oz) butter
salt and pepper
1 chicken, 1.6-1.8 kg (3½-4 lb)
275 ml (½ pint) Chicken Stock (see page 335)
1 tsp arrowroot or cornflour

❧ Heat the oven to 200C (400F) mark 6.
❧ Place the herb with a good nut of butter and seasoning inside the bird, and rub the outside of the bird
with the rest of the butter. Place the bird breast side
up in a roasting tin with half the stock, cover with
buttered paper or foil and place in the oven.
❧ Roast for about 1 hour. After the first 15-20 minutes, baste the bird and turn it on one side. Baste and
turn again after another 15-20 minutes; finish off the
cooking with the breast side up, removing the paper
for the last few minutes to allow the breast to brown.
Test to see if the chicken is cooked (see above).
❧ Place the bird on a serving dish and keep warm.
Add the remaining stock to the roasting tin, and stir
well to ensure that all the pan juices are incorporated. Thicken with 1 teaspoonful arrowroot or cornflour mixed with 1 tablespoonful water. Strain into
a sauce boat.

Variation
Roasting in a chicken brick: soak the brick in cold
water as directed in the instructions. Season the
chicken well inside and out, and place in the cavity
either butter and herbs (as in the recipe above), or
for a delicate flavour, place 2 small onions and 1
lemon in the cavity. Place the bird in the brick and
cook according to the manufacturer's instructions.

ROAST BONED CHICKEN

Serves about 10 as a buffet dish

1 large chicken, 2.7-3.6 kg (6-8 lb), boned out
    (see page 171)
700 g (1 ½ lb) pork sausage meat
double recipe quantity Parsley and Thyme
    Stuffing (see page 354)
4-6 lambs' tongues, boiled, skinned and boned

❦ Heat the oven to 200C (400F) mark 6. Place the
boned-out chicken, skin side down, and cover with
the sausage meat. Lay half the stuffing down the centre and place the lambs' tongues on the stuffing;
cover with the remaining stuffing.
❦ Bring the sides to the centre and over-sew with
fine string. Turn the bird over and re-shape. Weigh
the bird. Roast as for method 2 (see above).
❦ This is ideal for serving as part of a buffet; it may
be eaten hot or cold, but will slice more easily when
cold.

ROAST CHICKEN
WITH HONEY

Serves 4-6

1 chicken, 1.6 kg (3 ½ lb)
salt and pepper
2 oranges
2 cloves
150 ml (¼ pint) dry white wine
150 ml (¼ pint) Chicken Stock (see page 335)
1 tbsp honey
1 tbsp cornflour
orange slices and watercress to garnish

❦ Heat the oven to 190C (375F) mark 5. Season the
chicken well inside, and place one orange, stuck with
the cloves, in the cavity. Place in a roasting tin.
❦ Mix the juice of the second orange with the wine,
chicken stock and honey and pour the mixture over
the chicken. Place in the oven and cover with buttered foil, and roast for approximately 1 hour.
❦ After the first 15-20 minutes, baste the bird and
turn it on one side. Baste and turn again after another 15-20 minutes. Finish off the cooking with the
breast uppermost, and remove the foil for the last
few minutes to allow the breast to brown. Test to see

if the chicken is cooked (see opposite). Transfer the
bird to a serving dish and keep warm.
❦ Measure the pan juices and make up to 275 ml (½
pint) with chicken stock. Mix the cornflour with a
little water, and add to the pan juices. Stir until it
boils and thickens, strain into a sauce boat and serve
separately.
❦ Serve the chicken garnished with orange slices
and watercress.

SPICY CHICKEN WITH
ALMONDS

Serves 6

1 large chicken, 2 kg (4 ½ lb)
1 tbsp ground coriander
1 tsp freshly ground black pepper
1 tsp ground ginger
½ tsp ground cardamom
½ tsp ground cloves
1 tsp salt
50 g (2 oz) butter, melted

Sauce
50 g (2 oz) butter
350 g (12 oz) onions, finely chopped or minced
1 tsp turmeric
150 ml (¼ pint) plain yoghurt
150 ml (¼ pint) single cream
150 ml (¼ pint) double cream
100 g (4 oz) blanched almonds, sliced
50 g (2 oz) raisins, chopped

❦ Heat the oven to 200C (400F) mark 6.
❦ Skin the chicken and prick well all over. Mix
together the spices with the salt, and rub into the
chicken. Pour the melted butter over. Roast for 1 ½-
1 ¾ hours (or spit-roast) until the meat is tender,
basting occasionally.
❦ Meanwhile, make the sauce. Melt the butter in a
pan and fry the onions until beginning to soften,
then stir in the rest of the ingredients.
❦ When the chicken is half cooked, pour the sauce
over, and baste every 15 minutes, for the rest of the
cooking time. Transfer the chicken to a serving dish
and pour the sauce over.
❦ Serve with plain rice and a green salad.

CHICKEN MARENGO

Serves 4-6

3 tbsp oil
1 chicken, 1.6 kg (3 ½ lb), jointed (see page 171)
12 small onions
1 tbsp plain flour
225 g (8 oz) fresh tomatoes, skinned and
    chopped, or canned tomatoes, chopped
3 tbsp tomato purée
150 ml (¼ pint) dry white wine
150 ml (¼ pint) Chicken Stock (see page 335)
100 g (4 oz) button mushrooms
salt and pepper

❦ Heat the oil in a deep frying pan and gently fry
the chicken joints until golden brown. Remove the
chicken pieces from the pan and keep warm.
❦ Add the onions, and lightly brown them.
Sprinkle in the flour, and cook for 3 minutes. Add
the tomatoes and the tomato purée, together with the
wine and the stock. Bring to the boil.
❦ Replace the joints in the pan, season well and add
the mushrooms. Cover tightly and simmer very
slowly for 1-1 ½ hours or until the chicken is tender.
❦ Check the seasoning and serve with sautéed potatoes and a green vegetable.

Note
This recipe is also excellent using pheasant, rabbit,
venison, etc., instead of chicken.

COQ AU VIN

Serves 4-6

1 chicken, 1.6 kg (3 ½ lb), jointed (see page 171)
2 tbsp plain flour
salt and freshly ground black pepper
75 g (3 oz) butter
1 tbsp oil
100 -175 g (4-6 oz) piece of fat bacon, diced
3-4 tbsp brandy (optional)
bunch of fresh mixed herbs or a bouquet garni
575 ml (1 pint) red wine
12 small onions
12 button mushrooms
Croûtes to garnish (see page 355)

❦ Coat the chicken joints in seasoned flour.
❦ Heat 25 g (1 oz) of the butter and the oil in a
flameproof casserole and fry the diced bacon until
crisp; transfer the bacon to a plate. Fry the chicken
joints until golden brown.
❦ Pour the brandy (if used) into a heated ladle. Set
the brandy alight and pour it whilst flaming over the
chicken. Allow the flame to die out.
❦ Add the herbs and the red wine. Cover and simmer for approximately 45 minutes, or until the
chicken is tender.
❦ Meanwhile, in another pan, melt the remaining
butter, add the onions and fry them lightly. Cover
the pan and allow the onions to cook until quite soft.
Add the button mushrooms and cook for 5 minutes
more.
❦ About 15 minutes before the chicken is cooked,
add the bacon, onions and mushrooms to the casserole. Serve garnished with croûtes.

CHICKEN WITH TOMATOES

Serves 4

1 chicken, 1.5 kg (3 lb), jointed (see page 171)
salt and pepper
50 g (2 oz) butter
2 tbsp oil
175 g (6 oz) onion, chopped
100 g (4 oz) ham, in a thick slice, cubed
450 g (1 lb) fresh tomatoes, skinned and
    chopped or canned tomatoes, chopped
2 cloves garlic, crushed
6 peppercorns, bruised
1 tsp sugar

❦ Heat the oven to 180C (350F) mark 4.
❦ Season the chicken joints. Heat the butter and oil
in a flameproof casserole and gently fry the chicken
joints until evenly browned. Transfer the chicken
portions to a plate.
❦ Place the onion and ham in the casserole and fry
gently until the onion starts to soften. Add all the
other ingredients, with salt to taste. Cook and stir
until a thick sauce is obtained.
❦ Replace the chicken joints in the casserole and
spoon the sauce over. Cover the dish tightly and cook
in the oven for ¾-1 hour, or until the meat is tender.

CHICKEN WITH ORANGE AND TARRAGON

Serves 4-6

25 g (1 oz) butter
2 tbsp oil
1 chicken, 1.6 kg (3 ½ lb), jointed (see page 171)
175 g (6 oz) onion, finely chopped
4 sprigs fresh tarragon or 1 tsp dried tarragon
275 ml (½ pint) fresh orange juice
275 ml (½ pint) Chicken Stock (see page 335)
salt and freshly ground black pepper
1 tbsp cornflour or arrowroot
150 ml (¼ pint) sour cream or yoghurt
chopped fresh tarragon or parsley and orange
   slices to garnish

❦ Heat the oven to 180C (350F) mark 4.
❦ Heat the butter and oil in a flameproof casserole,
and gently fry the chicken joints until golden brown.
Transfer them to a plate. Add the onion to the casserole and fry gently until soft. Add the tarragon and
stir in the orange juice, chicken stock and salt and
pepper. Bring to the boil.
❦ Replace the chicken joints in the casserole. Cover
and place in the oven to cook for about 1 ½ hours, or
until tender.
❦ Place the chicken on a serving dish and keep
warm. Blend the cornflour or arrowroot with a little
cold water, and add to the casserole. Bring to the
boil, stirring constantly. Check the seasoning, cool
slightly and stir in the sour cream or yoghurt.
❦ To serve, coat the chicken pieces with sauce and
garnish with orange slices and some chopped fresh
tarragon or parsley.

CHICKEN CACCIATORA

Serves 4-6

1 chicken, 1.6 kg (3 ½ lb), jointed (see page 171)
1 tbsp plain flour, seasoned
3 tbsp oil
1 large onion, chopped
2 garlic cloves (optional), crushed with a little
   salt
1 small green pepper, deseeded and thinly
   sliced
150 ml (¼ pint) red wine or Chicken Stock (see
   page 335)
450 g (1 lb) fresh tomatoes, skinned and
   chopped, or 425 g (15 oz) canned tomatoes,
   chopped
1 bouquet garni
50 g (2 oz) button mushrooms, sliced
chopped fresh parsley to garnish

❦ Toss the chicken joints in the seasoned flour.
Heat 2 tablespoonfuls of the oil in a flameproof
casserole, and fry the joints to a golden brown; transfer them to a plate.
❦ Add the remaining oil to the casserole and fry the
onion and garlic (if used) until soft. Add the green
pepper and fry for 5 minutes. Stir in any remaining
flour, add the wine or stock, the tomatoes and the
bouquet garni.
❦ Replace the chicken joints in the pan. Cover and
simmer gently for 1 hour or until tender. About 20
minutes before the end of cooking, stir in the mushrooms. Check the seasoning.
❦ Serve with generously buttered spaghetti, garnished with chopped parsley.

CELEBRATION CHICKEN

Serves about 8 as a buffet dish

25 g (1 oz) butter
175 g (6 oz) onion, chopped
1 tbsp curry powder
150 ml (¼ pint) well-flavoured Chicken Stock
  (see page 335)
2 tsp tomato purée
2 tbsp lemon juice
2 tbsp sieved apricot jam
1 recipe quantity Mayonnaise (see page 346)
3-4 tbsp single cream
1 chicken, 1.6 kg (3½ lb), cooked and cut into
  pieces when cold
lettuce leaves to garnish

❦ Melt the butter in a saucepan, and gently fry the onion until soft. Stir in the curry powder and cook for 2-3 minutes. Add the chicken stock, tomato purée, lemon juice and apricot jam. Bring to the boil and ensure they are well mixed. Allow to go cold.
❦ Mix with the mayonnaise and cream, and combine with the chicken. Line a large serving bowl with lettuce leaves and pile the chicken in the bowl.

JAMAICAN CHICKEN CASSEROLE

Serves 4

25 g (1 oz) plain flour
1 tsp salt
1 tsp curry powder
1 tsp dry mustard
¼ tsp ground mace
¼ tsp ground marjoram
4 chicken joints
2 tsp oil
225 g (8 oz) onion, chopped
1 celery stalk, chopped
100 g (4 oz) mushrooms, chopped
150 ml (¼ pint) sweetened orange juice
150 ml (¼ pint) Chicken Stock (see page 335)
3 tbsp rum

❦ Heat the oven to 180C (350F) mark 4. Mix together the flour, salt and spices, and coat the chicken joints with the mixture.

❦ Heat the oil in a flameproof casserole, and fry the chicken until a golden brown; transfer to a plate. Fry the onion and celery in the casserole until beginning to soften, add the mushrooms and cook for 3-4 minutes. Stir in any remaining flour/spice mixture. Blend in the orange juice and stock and bring to the boil.
❦ Add the rum and replace the chicken joints. Cover tightly and cook in the oven for about 1 hour or until tender.
❦ Serve with rice, or creamed potatoes with buttered spinach. Sliced bananas, sprinkled with lemon juice and topped with sour cream also make a good accompaniment.

CURRIED CHICKEN PIE

Serves 4-6

350 g (12 oz) Rough Puff Pastry (see page 360)
275 ml (½ pint) Béchamel sauce (see page 340)
1 tsp curry paste, or more to taste
225 g (8 oz) cold cooked chicken, diced
225 g (8 oz) cold cooked ham diced
salt and pepper
½ tsp lemon juice
milk to glaze

❦ Heat the oven to 220C (425F) mark 7. Roll the pastry out to a circle to fit a 23 cm (9 in) ovenproof plate. Cut a 2.5 cm (1 in) strip from around the edge. Leave to relax.
❦ Make a béchamel sauce and add the curry paste according to your taste. Stir in the diced meats. It is important to have no skin or tendon, no gristly bits and not too much ham fat. Season well. Stir in the lemon juice. Spoon the mixture on to the plate.
❦ Dampen the rim of the plate. Fit on the pastry strip and damp the strip. Lift the pastry over a rolling pin, and use to cover the meat. Press the edges together. Scallop the edges with a spoon and knock them up with the back of a knife (see the instructions on page 357).
❦ Brush the pie with milk to glaze and cook for about 30-40 minutes until well risen and golden brown.

Note
This is a good dish for after Christmas, using turkey and ham or tongue. A well flavoured béchamel is the secret of the dish.

CHICKEN COULIBIAC

Serves 6

225 g (8 oz) Flaky Pastry (see page 361)
25 g (1 oz) butter
1 small onion, peeled
50 g (2 oz) mushrooms
225 g (8 oz) cold cooked chicken, finely chopped
100 ml (4 fl oz) Chicken Stock (see page 335)
salt and pepper
1 hard-boiled egg
2 tsp chopped parsley
1 egg to glaze

❦ Heat the oven to 220C (425F) mark 7. Roll the pastry to an oblong on a lightly-floured cloth. Trim the edges. Cool and rest.

❦ Heat the butter in a frying pan. Finely chop the onion and mushrooms and sauté until tender. Add the chicken and moisten with the stock. Season well and simmer, stirring from time to time, until the ingredients are well combined. Cool a little.

❦ Put half the chicken mixture down the middle of the pastry, leaving a 2.5 cm (1 in) margin of pastry at each end. Chop the egg, mix with the parsley and put down the middle of the chicken. Cover with the rest of the chicken.

❦ Brush the edge of the pastry with beaten egg. Bring the edges up over the chicken. Press together and then press the ends together. Using the cloth, roll the coulibiac on to a baking sheet lined with non-stick baking paper. Brush off the surplus flour.

❦ Roll out the pastry trimmings, and cut into thin strips. Brush the roll with beaten egg and decorate with slanting strips of pastry. Glaze again with beaten egg. Cook for 20-30 minutes.

❦ This is a simplified version of a Russian dish which is good in a buffet, served hot or cold.

CHICKEN IN A CREAM SAUCE

Serves 4-6

1 boiling fowl
1 litre (1 ¼ pints) water
1 onion
1 bay leaf
salt and pepper
100 g (4 oz) mushrooms, sliced
50 g (2 oz) butter
25 g (1 oz) plain flour
275 ml (½ pint) Chicken Stock (see page 335)
150 ml (¼ pint) single cream
2 egg yolks
½ tsp ground nutmeg
1 tsp lemon juice

❦ Place the boiling fowl in a pan with the water, onion, bay leaf and salt and freshly ground black pepper. Cover and cook until tender (2-3 hours). Allow to cool slightly.

❦ While the chicken is cooling, sauté the mushrooms in half the butter. Remove the bones and skin from the cooled chicken, and cut the meat into medium-sized pieces. Place in a serving dish and sprinkle the sautéed mushrooms over.

❦ For the sauce: melt the remaining butter in a pan, add the flour and cook for 1 minute. Gradually add the chicken stock, and bring to the boil, stirring constantly. Season to taste. Boil for 3-4 minutes, and allow to cool slightly.

❦ Mix the cream and egg yolks together in a basin and add to the sauce with the nutmeg and lemon juice. Reheat without boiling and pour over the chicken pieces.

❦ Serve hot or cold.

Note
The liquid that the bird was cooked in may be boiled to reduce in volume and concentrate the flavour. It must be well skimmed. This may be used for the stock required in the dish, and the remainder used as the basis of a soup.

FRIED CHICKEN PROVENCALE

Serves 4-6

1 chicken, 1.6 kg (3½ lb)
8 sprigs fresh thyme
8 rashers bacon
50 g (2 oz) butter
2 tbsp oil
175 g (6 oz) onion, finely chopped
450 g (1 lb) fresh tomatoes, skinned and
    chopped, or canned tomatoes, chopped
1 tbsp tomato purée
1 tbsp plain flour
1 garlic clove, crushed with salt
275 ml (½ pint) white wine
salt and pepper

Garnish
slices of French bread, fried
chopped fresh parsley

❧ Joint the chicken into 8 portions (see page 171). Lay a sprig of thyme on each, and wrap in bacon. Tie with string.

❧ Heat the butter and oil in a large deep frying pan, and fry the chicken parcels to a golden brown. Remove from the pan to a plate.

❧ Add the onion to the fats in the pan and fry gently until soft. Stir in the tomatoes and tomato purée, and cook for a few minutes. Stir in the flour and garlic and cook for a further 2-3 minutes. Add the wine and some salt and freshly ground black pepper. Bring to the boil, and replace the chicken joints.

❧ Cover and cook gently for 30-40 minutes, or until the chicken is tender. Remove the string.

❧ Arrange the joints on a dish, skim the sauce, adjust the seasoning and spoon over the joints. Garnish with slices of fried French bread and some chopped fresh parsley.

SUFFOLK CHICKEN CASSEROLE

Serves 4-6

1 boiling fowl
1 onion
1 carrot
1 bay leaf
salt and pepper
1 litre (1 ¾ pints) water
25 g (1 oz) butter
1 tbsp oil
2 medium onions, thinly sliced
175 g (6 oz) mushrooms, sliced
425 ml (¾ pint) dry cider
2 tbsp Worcestershire sauce
1 tbsp cornflour
150 g (5 oz) natural yoghurt
2 medium apples to garnish

❧ Place the boiling fowl in a pan with the onion, carrot, bay leaf, salt and freshly ground black pepper and water. Cover and simmer gently until the meat is cooked (2-3 hours). Allow to cool slightly. Skin the bird, and remove the meat from the bones. Cut the meat into pieces and place them in a flameproof casserole.

❧ Heat the oil and butter in a pan and gently fry the onions until soft; add the mushrooms and cook for 4-5 minutes. Place the onions and mushrooms on top of the chicken pieces. Add the cider, Worcestershire sauce and salt and pepper. Cover tightly and simmer gently for ¾-1 hour.

❧ Blend the cornflour with a little water in a basin, mix in 2-3 tablespoonfuls of the cooking liquid, pour back into the casserole and bring to the boil. Remove from the heat and stir in the yoghurt. Check the seasoning.

❧ Meanwhile, core the apples and cut into 5 mm (¼ in) thick rings. Fry these gently in a little butter and use to garnish the casserole.

COLD CHICKEN SALAD

Serves about 8 as a buffet dish

1 chicken, 1.6 kg (3 ½ lb), cooked and cut into
    small pieces when cold
100 g (4 oz) mushrooms, sliced
25 g (1 oz) butter
4 eggs, hard-boiled and chopped
4 rashers bacon, crisply fried and chopped
425 g (15 oz) canned sweetcorn, drained
1 small packet frozen peas, cooked
1 red pepper, chopped
50 g (2 oz) walnuts, chopped
salt and pepper
150-275 ml (¼-½ pint) Mayonnaise (see page
    346), or Vinaigrette (see page 347)
1 tbsp lemon juice
asparagus spears, sliced cucumber and
    paprika pepper to garnish

❧ Prepare all the ingredients, sautéing the mushrooms in the butter.
❧ When they are cold, combine all the ingredients
in a large bowl, with the lemon juice and mayonnaise
(or vinaigrette). Pile on a large serving dish and garnish with the asparagus spears and cucumber slices;
a light sprinkling of paprika pepper will give extra
colour.
❧ Serve with a rice salad and a green salad.

ROAST TURKEY
(Slow Method)

See page 168 for servings

1 turkey
double quantity stuffing(s) of own choice (see
    pages 350-55)
50 g (2 oz) butter or dripping, or 225 g (8 oz)
    streaky bacon
plain flour
Giblet Gravy (see page 343)
Bread Sauce (see page 342)
Cranberry Sauce (see page 342)
sausages
Bacon Rolls (see page 355)

❧ Heat the oven to 170C (325F) mark 3. Prepare the
stuffings. A double quantity of the recipe will be

required for the cavity. The neck and cavity may
both be stuffed. Weigh the bird after stuffing to calculate the cooking time.
❧ Either smear the breast with fat, and completely
wrap in foil, or cover the breast with streaky bacon.
Place the bird in a roasting tin and cook.
❧ Under 6.3 kg (14 lb), allow 45 minutes per kg (20
minutes per lb) and 30 minutes over (say 3 hours 50
minutes for a 4.5 kg/10 lb bird).
❧ Over 6.3 kg (14 lb), allow 35-40 minutes per kg
(15-18 minutes per lb) and 15 minutes over (approximately 5 ½ hours for a 9 kg/20 lb bird).
❧ 45 minutes before the end of cooking, open up the
foil or remove the bacon rashers. Sprinkle lightly
with flour, continue the cooking and allow the breast
to brown.
❧ To test if cooking is finished, place a skewer into
the thickest part of the drumstick: if it goes in easily
and juices run clear, cooking is complete.
❧ Allow 20-30 minutes for dishing up. During this
time the bird may be placed on a serving dish, covered with foil, and then covered with several clean
tea-towels or a heavy cloth. This keeps the bird hot,
and allows the meat to 'relax' thus making carving
much easier. The bird can stand like this for up to 1
hour, meaning therefore that the oven is at liberty for
roasting potatoes, and preparing other accompaniments for dinner. Use the pan juices for the giblet
gravy.
❧ The traditional accompaniments to turkey are
Giblet Gravy, Bread Sauce, Cranberry Sauce, and
sometimes sausages or Bacon Rolls. Chestnuts are
often used either in a stuffing, or served with
Brussels sprouts; they may also be puréed and added
to the gravy to make it richer.
❧ To carve, cut through the skin between the body
and a leg, then gently ease the leg away from the
body, pressing the leg down towards the plate. This
enables the knife to be put through the joint at the
top of the thigh, thereby removing the leg completely. Carve the breast by slicing from the breast
bone towards the wing. In the case of a small bird, it
is usual to serve either a drumstick or a thigh from
the leg together with slices of breast meat for one
portion. With a larger bird, the leg meat is sliced off
and served without the bone.

ROAST TURKEY
(Quick Method)

See page 168 for servings

1 turkey
stuffing(s) of choice (see pages 350-55)
350 g (12 oz) streaky bacon rashers
100 g (4 oz) butter or dripping
plain flour
Giblet Gravy (see page 343)
Bread Sauce (see page 342)
Cranberry Sauce (see page 342)
sausages
Bacon Rolls (see page 355)

❦ Heat the oven to 220C (425F) mark 7. Prepare the stuffings (see note on page 181). Weigh the bird after stuffing to calculate the cooking time.
❦ Cover the breast with the streaky bacon. Heat the fat in a roasting tin, place the bird in the tin, baste well, and place in the oven. After 20 minutes, reduce the heat to 190C (375F) mark 5. The bird should be regularly basted throughout cooking.
❦ Under 6.3 kg (14 lb), allow 35 minutes per kg (15 minutes per lb) and 15 minutes over (approximately 2 ¾ hours for a 4.5 kg/10 lb bird).
❦ Over 6.4 kg (14 lb), allow 23 minutes per kg (10 minutes per lb) and 10 minutes over (approximately 3 ½ hours for a 9 kg/20 lb bird). Finish the bird as on page 181.

MOIST ROAST TURKEY

See page 168 for servings

1 turkey (not exceeding 6.3 kg/14 lb)
75-100 g (3-4 oz) butter
575 ml (1 pint) turkey or Chicken Stock (see page 335)
stuffing(s) of choice (see pages 350-55)

❦ Heat the oven to 220C (425F) mark 7. Stuff the turkey. Weigh the bird after stuffing to calculate the cooking time. Allow 35 minutes per kg (15 minutes per lb) and 15 minutes over (approximately 2 ¾ hours for a 4.5 kg/10 lb bird).
❦ Melt the butter in the hot stock. Place the turkey in a roasting tin with one side of the breast down. Pour the hot liquid over it and place in the oven.

❦ After 15-20 minutes cooking time, reduce the heat to 190C (375F) mark 5. Baste regularly with the liquid during cooking.
❦ After about one-third of the cooking time, remove the tin from the oven, turn the bird on its other side and continue cooking.
❦ After two-thirds of the cooking time, turn the bird on its back, so that the breast can brown. Test to see if cooking is complete (see page 181).
❦ The basting liquid can be used for gravy.

WESSEX TURKEY

Serves 4

1 turkey leg (thigh and drumstick)
2 medium onions
salt
275 ml (½ pint) water
100 g (4 oz) cooked ham or bacon
50 g (2 oz) butter
1 tbsp plain flour
150 ml (¼ pint) dry cider
pepper
Croûtes (see page 355)
chopped parsley to garnish

❦ Place the turkey joints in a pan with one of the onions, quartered, ½ teaspoon salt, and the water. Bring to the boil, cover and simmer for ¾-1 hour, or until tender. Lift out the pieces on to a plate, remove the skin and bone, and cut the meat into large pieces.
❦ Strain the stock, and reserve it. Chop the cooked onion. Cut the ham or bacon into 1 cm (½ in) strips. Slice the second onion, and fry until softened in the butter. Add the flour and cook for 2 minutes. Gradually stir in the cider and reserved stock. Bring to the boil, add the meats and the other onion, season to taste, and simmer for 7 minutes.
❦ Pour into a serving dish and garnish with croûtes and chopped parsley.

TURKEY SAUTE ANNETTE

Serves 4

1 tbsp oil
25 g (1 oz) butter
2 small turkey legs (thigh and drumstick)
1 medium onion, chopped
1 tbsp plain flour
575 ml (1 pint) stock (see page 335) or stock cube
    and water
275 ml (½ pint) white wine
salt and pepper
2 tsp chopped fresh chervil
2 tsp chopped fresh tarragon
1 tbsp chopped fresh parsley
1 tbsp lemon juice
chopped fresh parsley and strips of pimento to
    garnish

❦ Melt the oil and butter in a sauté pan, add the turkey joints and fry until golden brown. Remove the joints. Lightly fry the onion, add the flour and cook for 2 minutes. Gradually stir in the stock and wine, bring to the boil, and add salt and pepper.

❦ Replace the turkey joints in the pan and add the chervil, tarragon, parsley and lemon juice. Bring to the boil, cover and simmer gently for approximately 1 hour or until the meat is tender.

❦ Place the turkey joints in an oval dish, check the seasoning of the sauce, then pour it over the joints. Garnish with strips of pimento and chopped parsley.

SHERRIED TURKEY

Serves 4

25 g (1 oz) butter
1 tbsp cooking oil
450 g (1 lb) turkey joints (leg or wing)
1 small onion, chopped
50 g (2 oz) lean bacon, chopped
50 g (2 oz) mushrooms, chopped
1 tbsp plain flour
salt and pepper
275 ml (½ pint) turkey or Chicken Stock (see
    page 335)
3 tbsp dry sherry
chopped fresh parsley to garnish

❦ Heat the butter and oil in a heavy pan, add the turkey pieces and gently fry until golden brown. Remove the turkey from the pan.

❦ Add the onion and bacon and fry until the onion is soft, add the mushrooms and cook for 3 minutes. Stir in the flour and salt and pepper. Gradually add the stock, stirring continuously.

❦ Bring to the boil, add the sherry, replace the turkey pieces, cover and cook for approximately 45 minutes or until the meat is cooked.

❦ Check the seasoning; bring the sauce back to the boil. Pour into a shallow oval dish and garnish with chopped parsley.

TURKEY WITH BABY DUMPLINGS

Serves 4

575 ml (1 pint) Béchamel Sauce (see page 340)
450 g (1 lb) cold turkey
1 hard-boiled egg, chopped
1-2 tsp chopped capers
chopped fresh parsley to garnish

Dumplings
75 g (3 oz) self-raising flour
pinch of salt
35 g (1 ½ oz) shredded suet
1 tsp chopped fresh parsley and ½ tsp chopped
    fresh thyme or 1 tsp mixed dried herbs
3 tbsp water

❦ Make the sauce, cut the turkey into bite-sized pieces and place in the saucepan with the sauce. Heat gently. Stir in the egg and capers.

❦ Make the dumplings by sieving together the flour and salt into a bowl; add the suet and herbs. Mix with water to make a soft, but mouldable, consistency. Divide into 8 pieces and shape each into a dumpling.

❦ Drop carefully into fast boiling water and cook for 7-10 minutes. Lift out carefully, place in the sauce and cook for 2-3 minutes. Serve sprinkled with some chopped parsley.

MARINATED TURKEY

Serves 6–8

1 turkey about 4 kg (9 lb), jointed (see page 171)
3 tbsp cooking oil
2 large onions, sliced
2–6 garlic cloves, according to taste
2 tomatoes, skinned and chopped
4 peppercorns
2 cloves
½ tsp ground cinnamon
salt

Marinade
3 bay leaves
3 garlic cloves
4 peppercorns
1 medium onion, sliced
¼ tsp salt
575 ml (1 pint) white wine or white wine and
    water, or white wine and white wine vinegar

❦ Mix together the ingredients for the marinade.
Place the turkey in a deep dish, and pour the marinade over; leave at least 4 hours, or overnight if possible. Turn the joints occasionally.

❦ Remove the joints from the marinade and dry
well. Heat the oil in a heavy saucepan or casserole,
fry the turkey pieces until lightly browned, and
remove from the pan. Add the sliced onion and fry
gently until soft. Crush the garlic cloves and add to
the onion. Add the remaining ingredients.

❦ Replace the turkey pieces in the pan, and pour
over the strained marinade. Cover the pan tightly
and cook over a low heat for approximately 2½
hours. Alternatively, if in a casserole, it may be
cooked in the oven at 150C (300F) mark 2.

❦ When cooked, test the seasoning. If desired, the
sauce may be thickened with a little slaked cornflour.

TURKEY TETRAZZINI

Serves 4

225 g (8 oz) spaghetti
1 tbsp cooking oil
1 large onion, sliced
3 tbsp strips of streaky bacon
25 g (1 oz) plain flour
275 ml (½ pint) turkey or Chicken Stock (see
    page 335)
1 tsp concentrated tomato purée
1 green pepper and 1 red pepper, seeded, cut
    into strips and blanched
100 g (4 oz) small mushrooms, quartered
350 g (12 oz) cooked turkey, cut into strips
Parmesan cheese to sprinkle

❦ Cook the spaghetti in a large pan in fast boiling
salted water, until tender (approximately 15 minutes). Drain, and arrange around the edge of a
warmed flat serving dish.

❦ While the spaghetti is cooking, heat the oil and
gently fry the onion and bacon, until the onion is
soft. Add the flour and cook for 2 minutes. Stir in
the stock and tomato purée. Continue stirring and
bring to the boil. Add the peppers, mushrooms, and
turkey. Season to taste. Bring slowly to the boil,
cover and simmer for 10 minutes.

❦ Spoon the sauce into the centre of the spaghetti
and sprinkle with Parmesan cheese.

DEVILLED TURKEY JOINTS

Serves 4

4 turkey leg or wing joints
1 tsp curry powder
2 tbsp mustard powder
2 tsp Worcestershire sauce
salt and pepper
few drops of Tabasco sauce (optional)

❦ Remove the skin from turkey joints, and score the
flesh. Mix a sauce with the rest of the ingredients, and
cover each joint thoroughly. Either grill the joints
slowly until cooked, or bake in the oven at 180C
(350F) mark 4, until brown and the meat is tender.

❦ Serve with creamed potatoes and Brussels sprouts.

ROAST DUCK WITH ORANGE SAUCE

Serves 4

1 oven-ready duckling, about 2 kg (4 ½ lb)
salt and pepper
4 navel oranges
1 medium carrot, sliced
1 medium onion, sliced
150 ml (¼ pint) port or Madeira
2-3 tbsp Cointreau or Grand Marnier
few drops of lemon juice (if necessary)
25 g (1 oz) butter, softened

Sauce
3 tbsp red wine vinegar
3 tbsp granulated sugar
450 ml (¾ pint) duck stock, using the giblets
    (see page 336)
1 tbsp arrowroot
2 tbsp port or Madeira

❧ Heat the oven to 220C (425F) mark 7. Season the cavity of the duck. Remove the zest from the oranges with a zester (or with a potato peeler, then cut it into julienne strips) and simmer in 575 ml (1 pint) water for 15 minutes. Drain. Place one-third of the zest in the bird's cavity.

❧ Prick the skin around the thighs, back and lower breast. Place in a roasting tin with the vegetables. Roast in the oven for 15 minutes, reduce the heat to 180C (350F) mark 4, and turn the duck on its side. After 30 minutes, turn the duck onto its other side. Remove any accumulated fat occasionally. 15 minutes before the end of roasting time, turn the duck on its back, and sprinkle with salt. (Total cooking time 1 ¼ to 1 ½ hours).

❧ While the bird is roasting, prepare the sauce. Place the vinegar and sugar in a pan and heat to form a caramel. Remove from the heat and stir in 150 ml (¼ pint) of the stock. Simmer gently to dissolve the caramel. Add the remaining stock. Blend the arrowroot with the port or Madeira, and add to the stock, with the remaining orange zest. Stir, bring to the boil, and simmer for 3-4 minutes until the sauce clears. Adjust the seasoning.

❧ Remove the remaining skin from the oranges, and divide into segments.

❧ When the duck is cooked, remove it from the roasting tin, place on a serving dish and keep warm. Remove surplus fat from the roasting tin, add the port or Madeira and boil, incorporating the pan juices; reduce the liquid to 2-3 tablespoonfuls. Strain into the prepared sauce; bring to the simmer. Add Cointreau or Grand Marnier to taste (correcting over-sweetness with lemon juice). Just before serving, and away from the heat, stir in the butter.

❧ Garnish the duck with the orange segments and spoon a little sauce over; serve the rest separately.

❧ Ducks are awkward to carve, so it is best carried out in the kitchen. Cut straight through the breastbone and back, using scissors or game shears to cut through the bone. Lay each half cut side down, and make a slanting cut through the breast, separating the wing and the leg, ensuring each has some breast.

ROAST DUCK WITH BAKED APPLES

Serves 6

1 duck, 2.25-2.7 kg (5-6 lb)
salt
6 medium-sized cooking apples

Stuffing
4 large onions
10 fresh sage leaves, chopped
100 g (4 oz) fresh breadcrumbs
25 g (1 oz) butter or margarine
salt and pepper
1 egg, beaten

❧ Heat the oven to 200C (400F) mark 6.

❧ Prepare the stuffing: boil the onions for 10 minutes, then chop finely. Add the sage, breadcrumbs, butter and salt and freshly ground black pepper. Bind together with the beaten egg.

❧ Stuff the duck and truss it (see page 170). Sprinkle the duck with salt and prick the skin around the legs and the back. Place in a roasting tin in the oven, and when the fat starts running, baste well every 20 minutes. Roast for 35 minutes per kg (15 minutes per lb) and 15 minutes over.

❧ Peel and core the apples and place in the roasting tin with the duck, 45 minutes before the end of cooking. Serve the duck on a shallow plate, surrounded by the apples.

Variation
Stuff each apple with well-seasoned sausage meat, and cook as before.

DUCKLING PROVENCAL STYLE

Serves 4

1.8 kg (4 lb) duckling, cut into 4 joints
2 tbsp plain flour
salt and pepper
1 tbsp oil
25 g (1 oz) butter
225 g (8 oz) onion, chopped
2 garlic cloves, crushed
1 green pepper, deseeded and chopped
2 tomatoes, skinned, deseeded and chopped
1 tbsp tomato purée
2 tsp sugar
200 ml (7 fl oz) stock (see page 335)
200 ml (7 fl oz) white wine
2-3 stuffed olives, sliced
225 g (8 oz) long grain rice
lemon slices to garnish

❧ Heat the oven to 150C (300F) mark 2.
❧ Mix the flour and salt and pepper in a polythene bag, add the duckling joints and shake well to ensure the joints are well coated. Heat the oil and butter in a flameproof casserole, and fry the joints until evenly browned, then transfer them to a plate.
❧ Add the onion to the pan and fry gently to soften. Add the crushed garlic, the pepper and the tomatoes, and fry for 5-6 minutes. Add the tomato purée and sugar. Stir in the stock and wine, bring to the boil, replace the duckling joints and add the sliced olives. Cover tightly and place in the oven. Cook for 1 ½-1 ¾ hours or until the meat is tender.
❧ Cook the rice. Remove the duckling from the oven and check the seasoning. Skim off excess fat. Serve with the rice garnished with lemon slices.

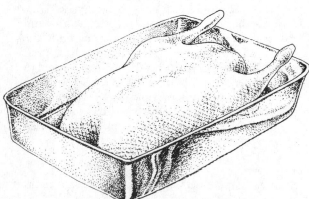

DUCK WITH SPICY ORANGE SALAD

Serves 4

1.8 kg (4 lb) duck
salt

Stuffing
450 g (1 lb) onions, chopped
150 ml (¼ pint) water
salt and pepper
75 g (3 oz) fresh breadcrumbs
2 tsp chopped fresh sage
50 g (2 oz) margarine

Spicy Orange Salad
2 tbsp oil
1 large onion, sliced and separated into rings
4 oranges
¼ tsp cayenne pepper
2 tbsp stuffed green olives, sliced
1 tbsp finely chopped fresh parsley

❧ Heat the oven to 230C (450F) mark 8.
❧ To make the stuffing, place the onions in a saucepan with the water and cook for 10 minutes. Season well. Strain, reserving the liquid, and mix with the breadcrumbs, sage and margarine, adding sufficient of the onion stock to moisten. Cool, then stuff the cavity of the duck, sprinkle the bird with salt, and prick around the legs and back.
❧ Place in a roasting tin, and roast for 30 minutes. Reduce the oven temperature to 190C (375F) mark 5, and cook for another hour, or until tender. Transfer to a serving dish.
❧ While the duck is cooking, make the salad. Heat the oil in a frying pan and fry the onion rings for approximately 10 minutes, but do not brown, Lift out of the pan and drain on absorbent paper.
❧ Cut the peel from the oranges, ensuring that all the pith is removed, and slice them into rings. Place the orange slices in a shallow dish, arrange the onion rings on top, and sprinkle with the cayenne pepper and the sliced olives. Chill for at least 30 minutes before serving. Serve sprinkled with the parsley.

CRUSTY DUCK PIE

Serves 8

350 g (12 oz) wholemeal Hot Water Crust
    Pastry (see page 362), using plain whole-
    meal flour instead of white
1 duck about 1.8 kg (4 lb), plucked
175 g (6 oz) raw gammon
175g (6 oz) lean pork
½ tsp dried sage
100 g (4 oz) liver pâté
salt and pepper
1 egg to glaze
2 tsp powdered gelatine

❦ Make a day ahead.
❦ Prepare the filling before making the pastry. Skin
the duck. Crisp the skin in the oven: there will be
nearly 275 ml (½ pint) dripping from it which can be
used in another recipe. Take the meat off the duck.
Keep the breast whole. Mince all the other pieces of
duck with the gammon and pork.
❦ Stir in the sage and season well. Put the bones on
to simmer to make a stock. Cut the duck breast into
strips and dice the pâté.
❦ Make the pastry. Heat the oven to 200C (400F)
mark 6. Raise the pie (see page 362). A 15 cm (6 in)
cake tin is perfect for this recipe. Lard the tin well.
Line with baking paper and lard that too. Take one-
third of the pastry for the lid. Line the tin with the
remainder of the pastry.
❦ Fill with a layer of minced meat, then a layer of
duck and pâté, until the filling is used up. Finish
with a layer of minced meat. Brush the edge with
beaten egg. Roll out the lid. Position and pinch the
edges well together. Make a hole in the middle and
cut the edges all round with a sharp knife to finish.
Brush with beaten egg.
❦ Cook for 30 minutes. Reduce oven to 180C
(350F) mark 4, cover with greaseproof paper and
cook for a further hour. Remove from the oven.
Leave for 15 minutes then turn out on a folded towel.
Quickly turn it back over on a board. Leave to cool.
❦ Reduce the duck stock. Put 275 ml (½ pint) of it
into a saucepan, season well and add the gelatine.
Heat and stir until it is dissolved. Cool. Fill the pie
with the jelly. Chill overnight

Notes
This amount of pastry is just enough to line and
cover the pie, using a 15 cm (6 in) cake tin. There is

none left over for leaves, but the finished pie is very
handsome and looks 'right'. There was just over 365
g (12 ½ oz) meat on the duck. (Which is why it is
always served on the bone in restaurants). However,
using all the ingredients, the finished pie weighed
over 1.4 kg (3 lb), which is enough for 8 people.
❦ In the 17th century, England imported large
quantities of 'crusty duck pies' from Picardy. The
crust must have been made from brown flour – there
was no other.

BRAISED DUCK

Serves 4

1 duck, cut into 4 joints
salt and freshly ground black pepper
1 tbsp oil
25 g (1 oz) butter
1 large onion, chopped
2 medium carrots, chopped
1 rasher bacon, chopped
1 tbsp plain flour
150 ml (¼ pint) red wine
275 ml (½ pint) stock (see page 335)
1 orange
bunch of fresh herbs – bay leaf, savoury, sage,
    parsley
50 g (2 oz) mushrooms
sliced orange slices and watercress to garnish

❦ Heat the oven to 170C (325F) mark 3.
❦ Season the duck joints well. Heat the oil and butter in a flameproof casserole, and lightly brown the
duck joints. Transfer them to a plate. Add the onion,
carrot and bacon to the casserole and fry gently until
the vegetables begin to soften. Add the flour and
cook for 1-2 minutes. Stir in the wine and stock and
bring to boil. Grate the orange rind and add it to the
stock with the herbs.
❦ Replace the duck in the casserole. Cover tightly
and cook in the oven for about 1 ¼ hours. Add the
juice of the orange and the mushrooms. Continue
cooking for a further 30 minutes or until tender.
Remove the joints to a serving dish and keep warm.
Strain the sauce, skimming off any excess fat. Adjust
the seasoning, and pour the sauce over the joints.
Garnish with orange slices and watercress.

Note
This recipe is a good way of using an older duck.

DUCKLING WITH BLACK CHERRIES

Serves 4

1.8-2 kg (4-4 ½ lb) duckling
salt

Stuffing
25 g (1 oz) butter
1 medium onion, chopped
100 g (4 oz) walnuts or cashews, chopped
100 g (4 oz) fresh breadcrumbs
1 tbsp chopped fresh parsley
1 tsp chopped fresh sage
1 tsp chopped fresh thyme
pinch of ground cinnamon
salt and freshly ground black pepper
grated rind of 1 lemon
juice of ½ lemon
beaten egg

Sauce
450 g (1 lb) canned black cherries (stoned) with
   their juice
3 tbsp red wine vinegar
2 tsp arrowroot or cornflour

❦ Heat the oven to 200C (400F) mark 6.
❦ To make the stuffing, heat the butter and gently fry the onion until it is soft; lightly fry the nuts to a golden brown. Place all the ingredients in a bowl and mix well, adding sufficient egg to bind. Place the stuffing in the cavity of the duck, and truss the duck.
❦ Sprinkle the duck well with salt and prick around the legs and back. Weigh the duck and cook (see page 185).
❦ When the duck is cooked, place it on a serving dish and keep warm. Remove the excess fat from the roasting tin, add a little hot water to the tin to deglaze.
❦ Place this in a measure, add the red wine vinegar and strained cherry juice, and make up to 275 ml (½ pint) with water. Blend the arrowroot or cornflour with a little cold water, add the juice mixture, place in a pan, and bring to the boil stirring constantly. Add the cherries, and cook gently for 2-3 minutes. Pour into a sauce-boat.
❦ Garnish the duck with watercress and serve with Duchesse Potatoes (see page 249).

SALMIS OF DUCK

Serves 4

1 duckling
salt

Sauce
25 g (1 oz) butter
duck giblets
1 small onion, diced
1 small carrot, diced
50 g (2 oz) bacon, cut in strips
1 tbsp plain flour
275 ml (½ pint) water
bunch of fresh mixed herbs or bouquet garni
salt and freshly ground black pepper
150 ml (¼ pint) red wine

Garnish
12 small onions, parboiled, and then cooked
   gently in butter
3-4 stuffed olives
Croûtes (see page 355)

❦ Heat the oven to 220C (425F) mark 7.
❦ Rub salt into the skin of the duckling and prick all over especially around the legs and back. Place in a roasting tin and roast for 45 minutes.
❦ While the duck is cooking, prepare the sauce. Melt the butter in a saucepan and lightly brown the giblets. Add the vegetables and bacon and cook for 5-7 minutes to soften the vegetables. Add the flour and cook gently until golden brown. Add the water, herbs and salt and freshly ground black pepper. Cover and simmer for 30 minutes. Add the wine, and allow to reduce in volume by one-third, removing any scum as it rises.
❦ Remove the duck from the roasting tin, and cut it into pieces. Place the pieces in a shallow ovenproof dish, and strain the sauce over. Cover the dish and cook in the oven at 180C (350F) mark 4 for 30 minutes, or until the duck is tender.
❦ Garnish with the onions, stuffed olives and croûtes, and serve with new potatoes and peas.

Note
Salmis is the term given to a rich brown stew of duck (or game). It is usual for the duck to be roasted for about three-quarters of the cooking time. It is then finished in a rich brown sauce made from the giblets, with red or white wine added.

ROAST DUCK WITH APRICOTS

Serves 6-8

2 plump ducks, each 1.8-2 kg (4-4 ½ lb)
salt
giblets
1 small carrot, diced
1 small onion, diced
small bunch of herbs
salt and freshly ground black pepper
575 ml (1 pint) water
1 large can apricot halves
juice of 1 lemon
1 tbsp cornflour
2 tbsp redcurrant jelly
2 tbsp apricot brandy

❦ Heat the oven to 200C (400F) mark 6. Prepare and roast the ducks (see page 185).

❦ Place the giblets in a pan with the carrot, onion, herbs, salt and freshly ground black pepper and water. Bring to the boil, cover and simmer gently for about 1 hour. Strain.

❦ Drain the juice from the apricot halves, and make the juice up to 575 ml (1 pint) with the strained giblet stock and lemon juice. Blend the cornflour with a little cold water in a basin, add a little of the juice and mix well.

❦ Pour into a saucepan, and bring to the boil, stirring continuously. Add the redcurrant jelly and stir to dissolve. Add the apricot brandy. Check the seasoning.

❦ Approximately 10 minutes before the ducks are cooked, place the apricot halves in the roasting tin to heat.

❦ To serve, place the ducks, jointed, on a serving dish, arrange the apricot halves around, and glaze the ducks with a little of the sauce. Serve the rest of the sauce separately.

ROAST DUCKLING WITH PEACHES

Serves 4

1 plump duckling, 1.8-2 kg (4-4 ½ lb)
salt
575 ml (1 pint) Espagnole Sauce, using the duck giblets (see page 340)
1 large can peach halves
120 ml (4 fl oz) dry sherry
2 tbsp peach brandy

Stuffing
50 g (2 oz) butter
100 g (4 oz) onion, finely chopped
25 g (1 oz) walnuts, chopped
50 g (2 oz) seedless raisins, chopped
rind and juice of ½ lemon
225 g (8 oz) pork sausage meat

❦ Heat the oven to 200C (400F) mark 6.

❦ Prepare the stuffing: melt the butter in a pan, add the onion and cook gently until softened. Place all the ingredients in a bowl and mix well. Stuff the cavity of the bird. Salt the outside of the bird, and prick the legs and back. Weigh the bird and cook (see page 185).

❦ Drain the peach halves. 10 minutes before the end of cooking time, place one peach half per person in the roasting tin to heat through. Chop the remaining peach halves. When the duck is ready, place it on a serving dish with the peach halves and keep warm.

❦ Remove the surplus fat from the roasting tin, and add a little hot water to the tin to deglaze it. Strain the liquid into the previously prepared Espagnole sauce, add the sherry, peach brandy, chopped peaches and 3 tablespoonfuls peach juice. Heat gently, adjust the seasoning and pour into a sauce boat.

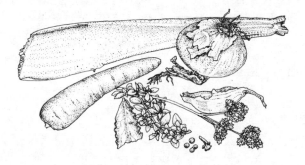

CASSEROLED DUCK WITH PORT

Serves 4

3 medium onions
5-6 sage leaves
1 duck
salt and freshly ground black pepper
duck giblets
bunch of fresh herbs or bouquet garni
1 tbsp each diced carrot and diced celery
425 ml (¾ pint) water or water and wine
1 tbsp plain flour
150 ml (¼ pint) port
lemon slices and croutons (see page 355) to
    garnish

❦ Heat the oven to 150C (300F) mark 2. Leave 1 onion whole and chop the others. Place the whole onion and the sage leaves in the cavity of the duck and season well.
❦ Place the giblets in a saucepan with the chopped onions, herbs, carrot, celery and salt and pepper with the water or water and wine mixture. Bring to the boil, cover and simmer for ¾-1 hour. Strain.
❦ Place the duck in a casserole and pour the giblet stock around. Cover, bring to the boil and cook in the oven for 1½-2 hours, or until the meat is tender.
❦ Joint the duck, place on a serving dish, and keep warm. Remove the excess fat from the cooking juices. Mix the flour with a little cold water, add a few tablespoonfuls cooking juices, mix well, and pour into the casserole with the port. Bring to the boil; adjust the seasoning as necessary. Pour the sauce over the duck and garnish with lemon slices and fried bread croutons.
❦ This recipe is a good way of using an older duck.

ROAST GOOSE

Serves 8

4.5 kg (10 lb) goose
double quantity Sage and Onion Stuffing (see
    page 353)
salt
25 g (1 oz) butter or dripping
watercress to garnish
Apple Sauce (see page 342)

❦ Heat the oven to 220C (425F) mark 7. Prepare the stuffing. Prepare the goose as for chicken (see page 170), but cut the wings off at the first joint before trussing. Place the stuffing in the cavity from the tall end. Prick the skin of the goose all over to allow the excess fat to run out during cooking. Sprinkle the breast with salt.
❦ Melt the fat in a roasting tin, place the goose in the tin, and put it in the oven. Cook for 30 minutes. Reduce the oven temperature to 180C (350F) mark 4; continue cooking, basting regularly with the fat which comes from the goose. Allow 35 minutes per kg (15 minutes per lb), but if the goose is old, and perhaps a little tough, allow 45 minutes per kg (20 minutes per lb) and reduce the oven temperature to 170C (325F) mark 3.
❦ When the goose is cooked, place it on a serving dish and keep warm. Pour off most of the fat from the roasting dish, and use the residue to make gravy.
❦ Garnish the goose with watercress and serve gravy and apple sauce separately.
❦ To carve, cut off the legs. Remove the wings by slicing a piece of breast meat with each wing. Cut the breast in slices parallel to the breast bone.

Variations
(1) Use Prune and Apple Stuffing (see page 353).
(2) Use Potato Stuffing (see page 353).
(3) For garnish, serve fried apple rings or fried pineapple rings.
(4) The gravy is improved if a sour apple is cooked in the roasting tin with the goose.

Using up leftover goose
(1) Slice and eat cold with jacket potatoes, Waldorf salad, or a green salad, accompanied by a damson or quince cheese.
(2) Curried: mince the leftover meat and mix with any stuffing left, plus 1 teaspoonful curry powder, 2 teaspoonfuls plain flour and sufficient gravy to moisten. Season to taste. Place in a greased shallow dish and cook in the oven at 200C (400F) mark 6 for 20-25 minutes. Serve with Croûtes (see page 355) and any green vegetable.
(3) Remember that goose fat is a very useful item to have in the kitchen, for example potatoes sautéed in goose fat have an incomparable flavour.

GAME BIRDS

Game birds, once food for kings, are now available to all from specialist shops and are a tasty alternative to poultry for that special-occasion dinner. In this section recipes for different varieties of game bird are given, from pheasant to the tiny snipe.

ROAST PHEASANT

See page 169 for servings

1 pheasant, trussed (see page 170-71)
50 g (2 oz) butter
½ apple or ½ small lemon
salt and pepper
3-4 rashers streaky bacon
150 ml (¼ pint) red wine (optional)
1 medium onion or carrot
Bread Sauce (see page 342)
Game Chips (see page 355)

❦ Heat the oven to 220C (425F) mark 7. Place 25 g (1 oz) of the butter in the cavity of the bird, with the apple or lemon. Rub the remaining butter over the surface of the bird, and sprinkle with salt and pepper. Cover the breast with the bacon. Place the bird in a roasting tin and put in the oven.

❦ Cook for ¾-1 ¼ hours, depending on size, basting regularly. The red wine may be poured into the roasting tin half-way through cooking and although most of it may disappear during cooking, it will give flavour when stock is added to the pan for making gravy.

❦ The giblets should be placed in a pan with water, salt and pepper and the onion or carrot and cooked gently. The resulting stock should be used with the pan juices from the roasting tin to make a thin gravy.

❦ Garnish the pheasant with watercress, with two tall feathers placed vertically between the legs. Serve with bread sauce, game chips and a green vegetable. Carve as for chicken (see page 174).

PHEASANT IN MADEIRA

Serves 4

25 g (1 oz) butter
1 pheasant
4 slices fat bacon, cut small
2 slices ham, cut small
1 medium onion, finely chopped
1 stick celery, finely chopped
1 carrot, finely diced
1 tsp chopped fresh parsley
pinch of nutmeg
salt and pepper
150 ml (¼ pint) Madeira
150 ml (¼ pint) stock (see page 335)
Croûtes (see page 355) to garnish

❦ Melt the butter in a flameproof casserole and fry the pheasant, bacon and ham until lightly browned. Transfer to a plate.
❦ Fry the onion, celery and carrot until soft. Replace the meats in the casserole. Add the parsley, nutmeg and seasonings. Pour in the Madeira and stock. Cover tightly and cook gently for approximately 1 hour, or until the meat is tender.
❦ Place the bird on a serving dish. Liquidize or sieve the sauce, adjust the salt and freshly ground black pepper and pour over the bird. Garnish with croûtes.

GYPSY PHEASANT

Serves 3-4

25 g (1 oz) butter
1 garlic clove, crushed
1 pheasant, jointed (see page 171)
350 g (12 oz) piece of bacon, cubed
2 large onions, sliced
4 ripe tomatoes, peeled and sliced
150 ml (¼ pint) sherry
salt and pepper
¼-½ tsp cayenne pepper

❦ Melt the butter in a flameproof casserole. Add the garlic. Fry the pheasant joints and the bacon until lightly browned. Transfer to a plate. Place the onions in the casserole, and fry gently until soft. Add the tomatoes and cook for 2-3 minutes. Replace the

pheasant joints, and pour the sherry over. Season lightly. Cover tightly and simmer gently for about 1 hour, or until the meat is tender.
❦ Just before serving, add the cayenne pepper to the sauce.

PHEASANT IN RED WINE

Serves 3-4

1 tbsp oil
50 g (2 oz) butter
1 large pheasant, jointed (see page 171)
2 shallots, finely chopped
275 ml (½ pint) red wine
12 button mushrooms
salt and pepper
1 tbsp plain flour

Glazed onions
12 small onions
25 g (1 oz) butter
1 tbsp granulated sugar
150-275 ml (¼-½ pint) stock (see page 335)

❦ Heat the oven to 170C (325F) mark 3.
❦ Heat the oil and 25 g (1 oz) of the butter in a flameproof casserole, add the pheasant joints and sauté gently until golden brown. Remove the joints to a plate.
❦ Add the shallots to the casserole and cook gently until soft. Pour in the red wine and combine with the pan juices. Replace the joints in the casserole and add the mushrooms and salt and pepper. Cover, and cook in the oven for approximately ¾-1 hour, or until the meat is tender.
❦ Meanwhile knead together the remaining butter with the flour. When the bird is tender, use the kneaded flour to thicken the sauce as required. Remove any fat from the surface.
❦ While the bird is cooking, prepare the onions. Place them in a pan with the butter and sugar and sufficient stock to barely cover. Cook gently in an open pan until the onions are tender and the stock is reduced to a glaze.
❦ Garnish the pheasant with the glazed onions. Serve with creamed potatoes or rice.

PEPPERED PHEASANT WITH ALMONDS

Serves 2-3

1 pheasant
50 g (2 oz) butter
1 tsp freshly ground black pepper
1 small onion, chopped
75-100 g (3-4 oz) piece of fat bacon
50 g (2 oz) flaked almonds

❦ Heat the oven to 170C (325F) mark 3.
❦ Mix together the butter and black pepper, and spread over the bird. Place the onion and bacon inside the bird. Place the bird on a piece of foil, and cover the breast with the almond flakes. Seal the foil, place the bird in a roasting tin and cook for 1 ½-2 hours.
❦ About 15 minutes before the end of cooking time, open the foil to allow the breast and almonds to brown.
❦ Serve with an orange and watercress salad.

NORMANDY PHEASANT

Serves 2-3

1 tbsp cooking oil
25 g (1 oz) butter
1 pheasant
1 small onion, finely chopped
2 tbsp Calvados or brandy
150 ml (¼ pint) stock (see page 335)
2 medium dessert apples, peeled, cored and
    sliced
salt and pepper
150 ml (¼ pint) double cream

Garnish
2 dessert apples, cored and sliced into rings
icing sugar
1 tbsp cooking oil
25 g (1 oz) butter

❦ Heat the oil and butter in a flameproof casserole. Gently brown the pheasant, then transfer it to a plate. Add the chopped onion to the casserole and fry it until softened. Drain off surplus fat. Replace the browned pheasant in the casserole.

❦ Pour the Calvados or brandy into a heated ladle, set alight and pour over the pheasant. Allow the flame to die, then add the stock and the apples.
❦ Cover the casserole tightly, and simmer gently for 45 minutes, or until the pheasant is tender.
❦ Remove the pheasant, carve as for chicken (see page 174) and arrange on a serving dish. Keep warm. Strain the sauce, stir in the cream, reheat, check the seasoning and pour over the pheasant.
❦ Garnish with the apple rings that have first been liberally sprinkled with icing sugar and then lightly fried in the oil and butter.

PHEASANT CASSEROLE WITH ORANGE

Serves 3-4

1 tbsp cooking oil
25 g (1 oz) butter
1 pheasant, jointed (see page 171)
225 g (8 oz) mushrooms, sliced
2 tbsp plain flour
275 ml (½ pint) stock (see page 335)
150 ml (¼ pint) orange juice
150 ml (¼ pint) dry white wine
salt and pepper
orange

❦ Heat the oven to 180C (350F) mark 4.
❦ Heat the oil and butter in a frying pan, and add the pheasant joints; fry until browned all over. Transfer the joints to a flameproof casserole. Add the mushrooms to the frying pan and fry for 4-5 minutes, then transfer to the casserole. Sprinkle the flour into the remaining fat, and cook for 2-3 minutes. Mix together the stock, orange juice and wine, and gradually add to the fat and flour. Bring to the boil, stirring all the time, season to taste, and pour into the casserole. Cover tightly, and cook in the oven for approximately 1 hour, or until tender.
❦ Meanwhile peel the zest from the orange and cut into fine strips. Place these in a pan with a little water and simmer gently until soft. Strain. Remove the peel from the orange and divide it into segments.
❦ When the pheasant is cooked, adjust the seasoning. Sprinkle the orange strips over the top of the joints, and garnish with the orange segments.

Note
This dish is a good way of using an older bird.

ROAST GUINEA-FOWL

Serves 4-5

1 guinea-fowl
4-6 streaky bacon rashers
1 tbsp plain flour
salt and freshly ground black pepper
275 ml (½ pint) stock using the giblets (see page 336)
150 ml (¼ pint) sour cream or yoghurt

Stuffing
6-8 olives, stoned and chopped
4 tbsp fresh breadcrumbs
freshly ground black pepper
25 g (1 oz) melted butter
beaten egg

❦ Heat the oven to 190C (375F) mark 5.
❦ Make the stuffing by mixing the ingredients together, and adding sufficient beaten egg to bind. Place the stuffing in the cavity of the bird. Cover the breast with the bacon rashers and roast for approximately 1 hour, or until the meat is tender, basting frequently.
❦ When cooked, place the bird on a serving dish and keep warm. Sprinkle the flour in the roasting tin and stir into the pan juices. Cook for 2-3 minutes. Gradually stir in the stock, bring to the boil, simmer for 3-4 minutes and add salt and pepper to taste. Stir in the cream or yoghurt, reheat carefully, and strain into a sauce-boat.
❦ Garnish the guinea-fowl with watercress and serve with Game Chips (see page 355) and a green vegetable. Carve as for chicken (see page 174).

ROAST PARTRIDGE

Allow 1 partridge for 1-2 persons

For each bird
knob of butter
salt and freshly ground black pepper
1 tsp lemon juice
1 rasher streaky bacon
1 vine leaf (optional)

Garnish
Croûtes (see page 355)
lemon wedges
watercress

❦ Heat the oven to 220C (425F) mark 7.
❦ Clean and truss the bird, and place the butter, salt and pepper and lemon juice in the cavity of the bird. If available, tie a vine leaf next to the skin of the bird with a rasher of bacon over it.
❦ Place in a well-buttered tin and roast in the oven for 20-25 minutes. (Alternatively, the bird may be spit-roasted.)
❦ Serve on a croûte with the pan juices poured over, garnished with lemon wedges and sprigs of watercress. As accompaniments, serve fried breadcrumbs, or Bread Sauce (see page 342), clear gravy and Game Chips (see page 355).
❦ To carve, cut the bird in half.

PARTRIDGE CASSEROLE

Serves 4

1 tbsp oil
25 g (1 oz) butter
2 partridges, cut in half
4 shallots, chopped
2 carrots, finely diced
small wedge of turnip, finely diced
2 rashers of streaky bacon, chopped
150 ml (¼ pint) red wine
275 ml (½ pint) stock (see page 336)
salt and freshly ground black pepper
beurre manié (see page 367)
❦ Heat the oven to 150C (300F) mark 2.
❦ Heat the oil and butter in a flameproof casserole and lightly brown the partridges. Transfer to a plate. Gently fry the shallots, carrot and turnip with the bacon. Return the partridges to the casserole, and add the red wine and stock. Season.
❦ Cover and cook in the oven for ¾-1 hour, or until the birds are tender. Thicken the sauce with a little beurre manié.
❦ Serve with some creamed potatoes and braised or pickled red cabbage.

PARTRIDGE WITH CABBAGE

Serves 3-4

1 hard green cabbage, about 900 g (2 lb)
salt and pepper
175 g (6 oz) streaky bacon in one piece
25 g (1 oz) butter
2-3 partridges (according to size)
8 small onions
2 medium carrots, sliced
225 g (8 oz) pork sausages
bunch of fresh herbs, including parsley, thyme
    and a bay leaf
275-575 ml (½-1 pint) stock (see page 336)
2 tsp arrowroot, mixed with 2 tbsp cold water

❦ Heat the oven to 170C (325F) mark 3.
❦ Cut the cabbage into quarters, and cook it in a pan
of boiling salted water for 6 minutes. Drain, and
refresh in cold water. Divide each quarter into 2-3
pieces. Season lightly.
❦ Place the bacon in cold water, bring to the boil,
drain and refresh. Melt the butter in a flameproof
casserole and gently brown the partridges, then
remove them to a plate. Place half the cabbage in the
casserole, and place on top of it the bacon, onions,
carrots, sausages and the partridges, with the bunch
of fresh herbs. Add some salt and pepper. Cover
with the remaining cabbage, and moisten with stock.
Cover tightly, using foil under the lid.
❦ Place in the oven, and cook for 1 ½-2 hours. If the
partridges are young, take them out after 35 minutes;
also remove the sausage. Keep covered, whilst the
cabbage continues cooking. Check occasionally to
make sure it does not become too dry.
❦ Replace the sausages (and partridges if removed)
approximately 10 minutes before the end of cooking
time to ensure that they are hot.
❦ To serve, cut each partridge in half, the bacon
into strips and the sausages into slices. Drain the
cabbage, having removed the herbs, and thicken the
strained juice with a little slaked arrowroot.
❦ Place the cabbage in a serving dish, arrange the
partridges on top, and decorate with the bacon,
sausage and onions. Spoon a little of the sauce
around the cabbage and serve the rest separately.

Note
This is a famous French recipe – *perdrix aux choux* –
for cooking older birds.

COLD PARTRIDGE IN VINE LEAVES

Serves 4

4 young partridges, dressed and trussed (see
    page 170)
salt and pepper
4 rashers of streaky bacon
8-12 vine leaves (fresh or tinned) or cabbage
    leaves

❦ Season the partridges with salt and pepper. Wrap
a rasher of bacon around each. Rinse any brine off
the vine leaves and simmer in a little boiling water
for 5 minutes. Wrap each bird tightly in 2-3 vine
leaves and tie securely. (Cabbage leaves may be used
if vine leaves are not available – these need blanch-
ing in boiling water, then refreshing in cold water.)
❦ Place the wrapped partridges in a pan, cover with
water, bring to the boil, then simmer for 35 minutes.
Plunge immediately into ice-cold water and leave to
cool for approximately 10 minutes. Remove the vine
leaves and bacon.
❦ Serve with a plain green salad, or Apple Sauce
(see page 342), Game Chips (see page 355) and sprigs
of fresh green watercress.

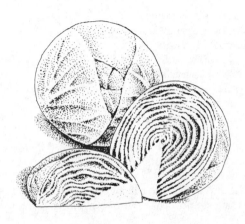

PARTRIDGE WITH MUSHROOMS

Serves 4-6

50 g (2 oz) butter
225 g (8 oz) mushrooms, sliced
salt and pepper
4 partridges, dressed (see page 171)
1 tbsp oil
1 small onion, finely chopped
1 tbsp plain flour
150 ml (¼ pint) dry sherry
425 ml (¾ pint) stock (see page 336)
100 g (4 oz) button mushrooms
chopped fresh parsley to garnish

❧ Melt 25 g (1 oz) butter in a saucepan and cook the sliced mushrooms slowly. Add salt and pepper. Divide the mushrooms into 4 and stuff the partridge cavities.

❧ Melt the oil and the remaining butter in a flame-proof casserole and gently brown the partridge. Add the chopped onion and cook for a further 3-4 minutes. Sprinkle in the flour; cook for 2 minutes. Gradually add the sherry and stock and bring to the boil. Season to taste.

❧ Cover and simmer gently for ¾-1 hour, or until the meat is tender. About 15 minutes before the end of cooking time, add the button mushrooms.

❧ Serve garnished with chopped parsley.

PARTRIDGES IN CREAM

Serves 4-6

4 young partridges
salt and pepper
juice of 2 lemons
25 g (1 oz) butter
4 slices of streaky bacon, chopped
1 small onion, chopped
½ tsp dried sage
275 ml (½ pint) single cream

❧ Heat the oven to 170C (325F) mark 3. Season the birds inside and outside, and sprinkle with some of the lemon juice.

❧ Melt the butter in a flameproof casserole. Add the partridges and brown all over. Add the bacon and onion and cook for 5 minutes. Add the herbs and the remaining lemon juice and sufficient water to prevent burning. Cover with a lid and cook in the oven for 30 minutes.

❧ Remove from the oven, stir in the cream, heat gently but do not allow to boil. Serve with Game Chips (see page 335).

POT ROASTED PARTRIDGES IN MILK

Serves 4-6

1 tbsp oil
4 partridges (reserve the livers)
2 large onions, quartered
8 small tomatoes
150 ml (¼ pint) sherry
275 ml (½ pint) water
275 ml (½ pint) milk
salt and pepper
2 tbsp capers
2 tbsp parsley
2 tbsp stoned olives

❧ Heat the oven to 150C (300F) mark 2.

❧ Heat the oil in a flameproof casserole and carefully brown the birds. Add the onions and the whole tomatoes. Cook gently for a further 5 minutes. Pour in the sherry, water and milk. Season with salt and pepper. Bring to the boil and simmer gently.

❧ Pound the livers with the capers, parsley and olives in a mortar, and add to the casserole. Cover tightly with foil under the lid, and cook in the oven for approximately 2 hours, or until the birds are tender.

❧ Serve straight from the casserole, accompanied by plain boiled potatoes and Brussels sprouts.

Note
This recipe is suitable for older birds.

ROAST GROUSE

Serves 4

50 g (2 oz) butter
juice of ½ lemon
salt and black pepper
2 young grouse
2 rashers of streaky bacon
4 Croûtes (see page 355)
1 tbsp oil

❦ Heat the oven to 220C (425F) mark 7.
❦ Combine the butter and lemon juice and season well with salt and pepper. Place the mixture inside the birds, and cover the breast of each with streaky bacon.
❦ Stand the birds on the croûtes and place on a roasting tin in the oven. Roast for 25–30 minutes, basting occasionally with oil. Serve on the croûtes, garnished with watercress and slices of lemon.
❦ To carve, cut into joints.

CASSEROLED GROUSE

Serves 4

2 grouse
2 rashers streaky bacon
25 g (1 oz) butter
1 tbsp oil
4 shallots, chopped
2 carrots, chopped
2 tbsp brandy
1 bouquet garni
275 ml (½ pint) red wine
275 ml (½ pint) stock (see page 336)
beurre manié (see page 367)
salt and black pepper
chopped fresh parsley to garnish
lemon slices to garnish

❦ Heat the oven to 150C (300F) mark 2.
❦ Tie a rasher of bacon around each bird. Heat the oil and butter in a flameproof casserole and lightly brown the birds. Transfer to a plate. Fry the shallots and carrots until soft.
❦ Return the birds to the casserole. Heat the brandy and ignite it; while it is flaming, pour over the birds. Add the bouquet garni, wine and stock. Season well.

Cover and cook slowly for 1½–2 hours, until the birds are tender.
❦ Thicken the sauce with beurre manié, adjust the seasoning and garnish with chopped parsley and lemon slices.

TEAL WITH ANCHOVIES

Serves 4

4 teal
butter
salt and pepper
75 g (3 oz) cheese, finely grated
8 anchovy fillets
150 ml (¼ pint) stock (see page 336)
lemon slices to garnish

Sauce
1 tsp mustard
1 tsp Worcestershire sauce
1 tsp anchovy essence
1 tbsp brown sugar
1 tsp mushroom ketchup
1 tbsp stock (see page 336)
2 tbsp port

❦ Heat the oven to 220C (425F) mark 7.
❦ Season the teal well, and smear with the butter. Place in a roasting tin in the oven for 20 minutes.
❦ Cut each teal in half and place in a casserole. Sprinkle with cheese and place an anchovy fillet on each piece. Moisten with stock, cover and cook at 170C (325F) mark 3 for 45 minutes. Meanwhile mix together the sauce ingredients in a bowl.
❦ When the birds are cooked, transfer them to a serving plate. Pour the sauce ingredients into the casserole and mix with the liquid. Bring to the boil and pour over the birds. Garnish with lemon slices.

ROAST WILD DUCK

Serves 2-4

2 wild duck (any variety)
piece of apple, onion or orange
butter
salt and black pepper
little red wine, port or orange juice
watercress to garnish

❦ Heat the oven to 220C (425F) mark 7.
❦ Place a piece of apple, onion or orange in the cavity of each bird, with a knob of butter and salt and pepper. Season the outside of the bird and smear the breasts with softened butter.
❦ Place in a roasting tin and cook for 30-50 minutes for mallard, 30-40 minutes for widgeon, 20-30 minutes for teal. Baste frequently with butter and red wine, port or orange juice. Wild duck is usually served underdone, although this is a matter of taste.
❦ Place on a warmed serving dish and garnish with watercress. Serve with a thin gravy made from the pan juices, having removed the excess fat, or with Orange Sauce (see page 185). Depending on size, either cut in half or into joints.

POT ROASTED WILD DUCK

Serves 4

2 wild duck (any variety)
salt and pepper
50 g (2 oz) butter
2 shallots, chopped
1 garlic clove, crushed
1 bouquet garni
1 wine glass of port
juice of 1 orange

Garnish
8 small dessert apples, peeled and cored
50 g (2 oz) butter
3-4 tbsp redcurrant jelly
2 tbsp wine vinegar

❦ Heat the oven to 180C (350F) mark 4.
❦ Season the ducks. Melt the butter in a flameproof casserole and brown the birds. Add shallots, garlic and bouquet garni. Cover tightly and place in the oven. Cook for 50-60 minutes, basting occasionally.
❦ Meanwhile, make the apple garnish: bake the apples in the oven with the butter until golden brown. Melt the redcurrant jelly in the vinegar and coat the apples with this.
❦ When the ducks are tender, cut in half and arrange on a warmed serving dish. Keep warm. Skim the fat from the casserole, add the port and orange juice to the juices in the casserole. Bring to the boil and adjust the seasoning. Pour a little sauce over the ducks to glaze, and serve the rest separately.

PLAIN ROAST WOODCOCK OR SNIPE

See page 169 for servings

1 woodcock or snipe
butter
salt and pepper
fat bacon (one piece per bird)
pieces of bread (one piece per bird)
lemon juice
watercress to garnish

❦ Press the legs and wings together, draw the head around and run the beak through the point where the legs and wings cross. Brush the bird with melted butter, season well and tie a piece of fat bacon around each bird.
❦ Spit or oven roast at 220C (425F) mark 7. Toast pieces of bread on one side only, and place one under each bird, untoasted side upwards, to catch the juices as they run out from the bird.
❦ Woodcock require cooking for 25-30 minutes, whereas the snipe, being a very small bird, should, as the saying goes, 'fly through the kitchen' and be cooked for 12-15 minutes.
❦ Serve with clear gravy flavoured with lemon juice, garnished with watercress and with Game Chips (see page 355).

SNIPE WITH MADEIRA

Serves 4

8 snipe
Croûtes (see page 355)

Sauce
15 g (½ oz) butter
50 g (2 oz) bacon, finely chopped
3 shallots, finely chopped
2 tsp plain flour
1 tsp tomato purée
50 g (2 oz) mushrooms, chopped
275 ml (½ pint) stock (see page 336)
salt and pepper
small bunch of fresh herbs
75 ml (2 fl oz) Madeira

❦ Cook the snipe as in the recipe for Plain Roast Woodcock or Snipe.

❦ While it is cooking, make the sauce. Melt the butter in a pan, add the bacon and shallot and fry until golden. Stir in the flour, and cook over a low heat until it turns a golden brown colour – stir during this time otherwise the flour will burn.

❦ Add the tomato purée, mushrooms and stock. Carefully bring to the boil, stirring; add salt and pepper and the herbs. Cover and simmer for 15-20 minutes. Strain, add the Madeira and simmer for another 3 minutes.

❦ Serve the snipe on croûtes with a little sauce poured over each, and the remainder of the sauce served separately.

WOODCOCK WITH ORANGE

Serves 4

4 woodcock
melted butter
salt and pepper
4 rashers of fat bacon
4 Croûtes (see page 355)
150 ml (¼ pint) white wine
3-4 tbsp concentrated stock (see page 336)
rind and juice of 1 orange
1 tsp melted butter
orange segments to garnish

❦ Prepare and cook the birds as in the previous recipe. Arrange on the croûtes, on a serving dish. Keep warm.

❦ Add the wine and game stock to the pan juices and simmer for 5 minutes. Add the rind and juice of the orange and stir in the melted butter and salt and pepper. Pour the sauce over the woodcock and garnish with orange segments.

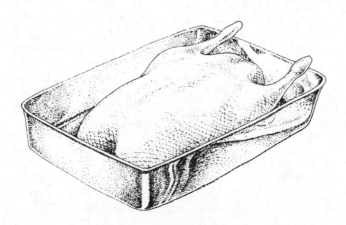

ROAST QUAIL

1 quail per person for a starter, 2 for a main course

quail
butter
fat bacon (one rasher per bird)
watercress to garnish

❦ Brush the birds with melted butter, and wrap a rasher of fat bacon around each. Place in a shallow casserole with butter and cook at 220C (425F) mark 7 for 20 minutes, basting frequently.
❦ Serve with a thin gravy made from the pan juices, and garnish with watercress.

Note
If available, vine leaves, wrapped around the birds, will improve the flavour.

QUAIL IN WHITE WINE WITH OLIVES

Serves 4

8 quail
salt and pepper
25 g (1 oz) butter
2-3 rashers streaky bacon, chopped
1 small onion, finely chopped
1 carrot, finely diced
2 tbsp brandy
425 ml (15 fl oz) stock (see page 336)
275 ml (½ pint) white wine
½ tsp dried sage
12 green olives, pitted

❦ Season the quail with salt and pepper. Heat the butter in a pan and brown the quail. Transfer them to a plate. Add the bacon, onion and carrot to the pan and fry gently until the vegetables begin to soften. Replace the quail in the pan.
❦ Warm the brandy, ignite it and, while it is still flaming, pour it over the birds. Add the stock, wine, sage and some salt and pepper, bring to the boil and simmer gently for 15 minutes. Add the olives and simmer for a further 10 minutes.
❦ Remove the quail to a serving dish, return the pan to the heat and boil to reduce the liquid by half. Pour over the quail.
❦ Serve with plain boiled rice and a green salad.

QUAIL WITH HERBS

Serves 4

8 quail
100 g (4 oz) butter
1 tbsp chopped fresh parsley
1 tbsp chopped fresh summer savory
1 tsp chopped fresh mint
½ tsp chopped fresh thyme
salt and black pepper
8 rashers streaky bacon
150 ml (¼ pint) white wine
150 ml (¼ pint) Chicken Stock (see page 335)
1 tbsp plain flour
Croûtes (see page 355)

❦ Heat the oven to 180C (350F) mark 4.
❦ Place a knob of butter in each quail. Place the birds in a roasting tin, and brush with melted butter. Mix together the herbs and salt and pepper and sprinkle over the quail. Cover each bird with a rasher of bacon. Mix together the wine and stock and pour it around the birds.
❦ Cook in the oven for about 45 minutes, basting occasionally. Remove the bacon rashers. Raise the oven temperature to 200C (400F) mark 6 and continue to cook the quail until they are browned and tender.
❦ Place the quail on a serving dish and keep warm. Strain off any surplus fat from the roasting tin. Stir the flour into the pan juices. Cook on top of the stove, stirring continuously, until it thickens. Boil for 1 minute. Pour the sauce over the quail and serve with croûtes.

QUAIL WITH MUSHROOMS

Serves 2

4 quail
seasoned plain flour
25 g (1 oz) butter
1 tbsp oil
3 rashers of streaky bacon, chopped
1 shallot, finely chopped
2 tbsp brandy
100 g (4 oz) mushrooms, sliced
425 ml (15 fl oz) stock (see page 336)
1 bouquet garni or bunch of fresh mixed herbs
salt and black pepper
juice of 1 orange
beurre manié (see page 367)

❦ Cut the quail in half and toss in seasoned flour. Heat the butter and oil in a pan and gently brown the quail; transfer them to a plate. Place the bacon and shallot in the pan and fry for 5 minutes.
❦ Return the quail to the pan. Warm the brandy, ignite it and, while it is flaming, pour it over the quail.
❦ Add the mushrooms, stock, herbs and salt and pepper. Bring to the boil, cover tightly and simmer for 20-25 minutes, until the birds are tender. Add the orange juice.
❦ If necessary, thicken the sauce with a little beurre manié. Serve with Duchesse or Potatoes (see page 249) or creamed potatoes and glazed carrots.

BRAISED PIGEON WITH ORANGE

Serves 4

4 small oranges
4 pigeons
4 rashers streaky bacon
50 g (2 oz) dripping or butter
4 shallots, chopped
1 tbsp plain flour
150 ml (¼ pint) port or red wine
275 ml (½ pint) stock (see page 336)
salt and pepper
bunch of fresh herbs (parsley, thyme, bay leaf, etc) or 1 bouquet garni
½ tsp crushed coriander seeds
beurre manié (see page 367)
1-2 tbsp Cointreau or Grand Marnier (optional)

❦ Heat the oven to 170C (325F) mark 3.
❦ Remove some thin slices of zest from half the oranges with a potato peeler or zester and place on one side. Place an orange in the cavity of each bird, and wrap a rasher of bacon around each. Secure with string.
❦ Heat the dripping or butter in a flameproof casserole, and fry the birds until golden brown. Transfer to a plate. Fry the shallots until golden brown. Stir in the flour and cook for 3 minutes. Gradually stir in the port or wine and stock and bring to the boil. Season.
❦ Return the pigeons to the casserole and add the herbs and coriander seeds. Cover tightly and cook in the oven for 1 ½-2 hours, or until the pigeons are tender.
❦ Meanwhile, cut the orange zest into strips, place in a small pan with a little water and simmer gently for 15-20 minutes. Strain and reserve the strips.
❦ When the pigeons are cooked, transfer them to a warmed serving dish. Strain the sauce into a saucepan and thicken as necessary with a little beurre manié. Adjust the seasoning and add the orange liqueur.
❦ Pour a little sauce over the pigeons and serve the rest separately. Sprinkle the orange strips over the pigeons. Serve with creamed potatoes and broccoli.

RAISED PIGEON PIE

Serves 6-8

breasts from 2 pigeons
1 tbsp oil
2 medium carrots, diced
1 onion, diced
1 stick of celery, sliced
275 ml (½ pint) stock (see page 336)
1 bouquet garni
salt and freshly ground black pepper
350 g (12 oz) pork sausage meat
225 g (8 oz) veal or fillet steak, cut up finely
2 pickled walnuts, chopped
beaten egg
jelly (made from 275 ml/½ pint stock, heated
  with 1 heaped tsp powdered gelatine)

Hot water crust pastry
225 g (8 oz) plain flour
¼ tsp salt
75 g (3 oz) lard
scant 150 ml (¼ pint) boiling water

❦ Remove the breasts from the pigeons. Heat the oil in a flameproof casserole and sauté the prepared vegetables until soft. Place the pigeon breasts on top of the vegetables and add stock to come to the top of the vegetables. Add the bouquet garni and salt and freshly ground black pepper. Braise the breasts until tender. Allow to cool.

❦ Heat the oven to 220C (425F) mark 7. Grease a raised pie mould, or prepare a collar of doubled greaseproof paper 10 cm (4 in) deep and 15 cm (6 in) in diameter. Grease well. Place on a greased baking sheet.

❦ Make the hot water crust pastry by sieving together the flour and salt. Rub in the lard and add most of the boiling water to make a soft dough, mixing well with a knife. Knead gently until smooth. Line the mould or collar with three-quarters of the pastry.

❦ Using three-quarters of the sausage meat, line the inside of the pastry. Mix the veal (or steak) with the walnuts and season well. Place half the mixture in the base of the mould, and lay the pigeon breasts on top. Cover with the remaining veal or steak mixture, and moisten with 3-4 tablespoonfuls of stock. Cover with the remaining sausage meat.

❦ Roll out the last piece of pastry and cover the pie, sealing the edges well. Decorate with pastry leaves as desired. Bake for 15 minutes, reduce the heat to 170C (325F) mark 3 and cook for a further 1 ¼ hours.

❦ Approximately 20 minutes before the end of cooking time, carefully remove the mould or collar and brush the pastry with beaten egg. After removing the pie from the oven, fill with hot, well-seasoned jelly.

PAPRIKA PIGEON

Serves 2-3

2 pigeons
1 tbsp plain flour
2 tsp paprika
salt
50 g (2 oz) dripping
1 onion, sliced
1 garlic clove, crushed
275 ml (½ pint) stock (see page 336)
150 ml (¼ pint) wine
bunch of fresh herbs (parsley, thyme, bay leaf)
  or 1 bouquet garni
2-3 tbsp soured cream or yoghurt
chopped fresh parsley to garnish

❦ Heat the oven to 170C (325F) mark 3.

❦ Cut the pigeons in half and toss in the flour mixed with the paprika and salt. Heat the dripping in a flameproof casserole, and fry the pigeons until golden brown. Transfer them to a plate.

❦ Add the onion and garlic to the pan and fry for 5 minutes. Gradually stir in the stock and wine, add the herbs and replace the pigeons in the casserole. Bring to the boil, cover and cook in the oven for 1 ½-2 hours, or until the pigeons are tender.

❦ Just before serving, stir in the soured cream or yoghurt. Adjust the salt and freshly ground black pepper. Sprinkle with chopped parsley.

CIDER-BRAISED PIGEON

Serves 4-6

1 tbsp oil
25 g (1 oz) butter
4 pigeons
4 rashers of bacon
225 g (8 oz) small onions
2 carrots, sliced
1 tbsp plain flour
275 ml (½ pint) stock (see page 336)
150 ml (¼ pint) dry cider
salt and pepper
225 g (8 oz) mushrooms, sliced

Garnish
2 eating apples
icing sugar
50 g (2 oz) butter
watercress

❦ Heat the oven to 180C (350F) mark 4.
❦ Heat the oil and butter in a flameproof casserole and fry the pigeons. Transfer to a plate. Cut the bacon into 1 cm (½ in) strips. Add the bacon, onion and carrots, and fry until the vegetables begin to soften. Stir the flour into the pan and cook for 2-3 minutes. Gradually add the stock and cider, stirring until the mixture boils. Season well. Return the pigeons to the casserole, and cover and cook in the oven for 45 minutes.
❦ Add the sliced mushrooms and continue cooking for a further 45 minutes or until the pigeons are tender. Place the pigeons on a serving dish, drain the vegetables and place around the pigeons. Keep hot. Adjust the seasoning of the sauce and, if necessary, thicken with a little more flour. Pour the sauce over the pigeons.
❦ During the latter stage of cooking, prepare the garnish. Core the apples and slice them into 5 mm (¼ in) slices. Dust thickly with icing sugar. Melt the butter in a frying pan, and gently fry the apple slices. Garnish the pigeons with the fried apple slices and some sprigs of watercress.

PIGEON CASSEROLE WITH STEAK

Serves 4

2 pigeons
25 g (1 oz) butter
1 tbsp oil
225 g (8 oz) chuck steak, cubed
2 rashers streaky bacon, diced
275 ml (½ pint) stock (see page 336)
100 g (4 oz) mushrooms, sliced
salt and pepper
1 tbsp redcurrant jelly
1 tbsp lemon juice
1 tbsp plain flour, slaked with 1 tbsp water
chopped fresh parsley to garnish

❦ Cut the pigeons in half. Heat the butter and oil in a pan and fry the pigeons, steak and bacon until lightly browned. Add the stock, mushrooms and salt and pepper to taste. Cover the pan tightly and simmer slowly for approximately 2 hours or until the pigeons are tender.
❦ Stir in the redcurrant jelly and lemon juice. Thicken the sauce with the slaked flour. Bring to the boil, cook for 2 minutes, and adjust the seasoning. Sprinkle with chopped parsley to serve.

GAME ANIMALS

The meat of wild rabbit, hare and venison has less fat on it than that of domesticated animals and can be dry. This section shows how to make many delicious dishes which make the most of the succulent juices and distinctive flavour of these game animals.

TASTY RABBIT

Serves 4-5

1 rabbit, jointed (see page 172)
salt and pepper
1 small onion, finely chopped
2 tsp dried or fresh mixed herbs
2 bay leaves
4 cloves
575 ml (1 pint) water and vinegar mixed
25 g (1 oz) butter
1 tbsp oil
225 g (½ lb) onions, finely chopped
plain flour

❦ Place the rabbit joints in a deep dish and sprinkle with salt and pepper. Add the onion and the herbs, bay leaves and cloves. Cover with the water and vinegar mixture, and leave to soak overnight. Remove from the liquid, and dry the joints thoroughly. Reserve the liquid.

❦ Heat the butter and oil in a strong saucepan or a flameproof casserole, lightly brown the rabbit joints, add the remaining onions and gently fry. Pour over the marinade in which the rabbit was soaked. Cover tightly and simmer gently for 1 ½ hours.

❦ Just before serving, thicken the gravy with a little flour, and adjust the seasoning. If the flavour is a little sharp, a teaspoonful sugar will rectify this.

❦ This tasty dish is good served with some jacket potatoes and a fresh green vegetable.

ROAST RABBIT

Serves 3-4

1 young rabbit, paunched and skinned (see page 171)
6-8 rashers of streaky bacon
100 g (4 oz) dripping
25 g (1 oz) plain flour
275 ml (½ pint) stock (see page 336)
Bacon Rolls (see page 355) to garnish

Stuffing
4 heaped tbsp fresh breadcrumbs
50 g (2 oz) shredded suet
salt and pepper
1 tbsp chopped fresh parsley and fresh mixed herbs
little grated lemon rind
little grated nutmeg
2 tbsp milk

❦ Heat the oven to 200C (400F) mark 6.
❦ Make the stuffing: mix the dry ingredients together and bind with the milk. Place the stuffing in the rabbit and sew it up. Tie the streaky bacon rashers over the back. Heat the dripping in a roasting tin and place the rabbit in it. Cover with greased, greaseproof paper or foil. Roast for 1 hour, basting regularly with the fat.
❦ When cooked, remove the paper or foil, and sprinkle with flour. Return to the oven for about 10 minutes to brown. Transfer to a serving dish, remove the trussing strings and keep warm.
❦ Drain most of the fat from the roasting tin, leaving about 1 tablespoonful. Sprinkle in the remaining flour, and cook for a few minutes. Gradually stir in the stock, ensuring that all the pan juices have been incorporated. Boil for 4-5 minutes, then strain into a sauce-boat.
❦ Garnish the rabbit with some bacon rolls, and serve, accompanied by redcurrant or quince jelly, with roast potatoes and fresh green beans. To carve, cut the rabbit into joints.

RABBIT HOT-POT

Serves 4-6

1 rabbit, jointed (see page 172)
50 g (2 oz) dripping
350 g (12 oz) onions, sliced
225 g (8 oz) carrots, sliced
25 g (1 oz) plain flour
850 ml (1 ½ pints) stock (see page 336)
450 g (1 lb) potatoes, thickly sliced
bunch of fresh herbs
salt and pepper
melted butter
chopped fresh parsley to garnish
Bacon Rolls (see page 355) to garnish

❦ Heat the oven to 170C (325F) mark 3. Place the rabbit joints in cold salted water and leave for 30 minutes to remove the blood. Remove and dry well.
❦ Heat the dripping in a frying pan, and fry the joints until golden brown, then transfer to a casserole. Fry the onions and carrots gently until beginning to soften, and then place on top of the rabbit in the casserole. Add the flour to the remaining fat in the frying pan, and cook for 2-3 minutes. Gradually stir in the stock and bring to the boil.
❦ Place the sliced potatoes in the casserole and season well. Pour the sauce from the frying pan over, and add the herbs. Cover tightly and cook in the oven for approximately 2 hours or until the rabbit is tender.
❦ 30 minutes before serving, the lid may be removed and the potatoes brushed with melted butter. Return the casserole to the oven without the lid, to brown the potatoes. Check the seasoning. Serve garnished with chopped parsley and bacon rolls.

RABBIT TENERIFE-STYLE

Serves 4

1 medium-sized rabbit, jointed (see page 172)
salt
4 tbsp oil
white wine
2 large garlic cloves
2 tsp paprika
small piece of hot red chilli pepper or ½ tsp
    cayenne pepper

Marinade
275 ml (½ pint) dry white wine
100 ml (3 fl oz) vinegar
2 sprigs fresh thyme
2 tsp fresh oregano
1 bay leaf

❦ Place the rabbit joints in a dish and sprinkle with salt. Mix together the ingredients for the marinade and pour over the joints. Allow to stand for a few hours, preferably overnight.
❦ Remove the joints and dry thoroughly, reserving the marinade. Heat the oil in a pan, and gently cook the joints until golden brown all over. Pour the marinade over, adding more wine if necessary to cover the joints. Partially cover the pan and simmer gently.
❦ Meanwhile, crush the garlic in a mortar with the paprika, chilli (finely chopped) or cayenne, and a little salt. Add this to the pan and check the seasoning – it should be slightly hot but not over-hot.
❦ Continue the cooking for approximately 1 hour or until the meat is tender, adding more wine if necessary. Check the seasoning again before serving.
❦ This tasty dish is one found in any local restaurant in Tenerife. It is a well-flavoured, spicy dish which improves if it is cooked the day before it is required, and then reheated. It is sometimes served with fried potatoes, but more often with fresh crusty bread, and of course, red wine.

CASSEROLED RABBIT

Serves 4-5

175 g (6 oz) streaky bacon, cut into strips
1 rabbit, jointed (see page 172)
350 g (12 oz) onions, finely chopped
1 tbsp chopped fresh parsley
salt and pepper
stock (see page 336)
1 tbsp plain flour
Forcemeat Balls (see page 354) to serve

❦ Heat the oven to 150C (300F) mark 2.
❦ Layer the bacon, rabbit and onions in a deep casserole, sprinkling the parsley and salt and pepper between the layers. Add sufficient stock just to cover.
❦ Cover with a tightly fitting lid and cook in the oven for approximately 2 hours, or until the meat is tender.
❦ Mix the flour with a little water in a basin, add several tablespoonfuls gravy from the casserole. Pour it all into the casserole and bring to the boil.
❦ Adjust the seasoning and serve with forcemeat balls and redcurrant jelly, accompanied by jacket potatoes and carrots.

RABBIT IN BEER

Serves 4-5

1 rabbit, about 900 g (2 lb), jointed (see page 172)
1 tbsp seasoned plain flour
25 g (1 oz) dripping
100 g (4 oz) streaky bacon, chopped
1 medium onion, sliced
275 ml (½ pint) pale ale
275 ml (½ pint) stock (see page 336)
1 tsp sugar
1 tbsp vinegar
1 bay leaf
1-2 tsp French mustard
12 soaked prunes

❦ Toss the rabbit joints in the seasoned flour. Heat the fat in a heavy pan or flameproof casserole and fry the joints until golden brown. Remove from the pan.
❦ Add the bacon and onion to the pan and fry until the onion is soft. Pour off any excess fat. Replace the joints in the pan.
❦ Add the ale, stock, sugar, vinegar, bay leaf and mustard. Bring to the boil, cover tightly and simmer gently until almost cooked (1-1 ½ hours).
❦ Season to taste, add the prunes, and cook for a further 20 minutes. Serve with jacket potatoes and green beans.

RABBIT AND SAUSAGE CRUMBLE

Serves 4-5

375 g (12 oz) sausage meat
1 rabbit, jointed (see page 172)
225 g (8 oz) onions, chopped
1 tbsp chopped fresh herbs
salt and pepper
stock (see page 336)
75-100 g (3-4 oz) fresh breadcrumbs
25 g (1 oz) butter

❦ Heat the oven to 150C (300F) mark 2.
❦ Place half the sausage meat in a casserole and arrange the rabbit joints on top. Sprinkle with the chopped onion and herbs, and some salt and pepper. Place the remaining sausage meat on top of that.

Then add just enough stock to half fill the casserole.
❦ Cover with the breadcrumbs, pressing down well. Put small knobs of butter on top. Cover with foil and cook for 1½ hours, or until the rabbit is tender. About 15 minutes before the end of cooking, remove the foil to allow the top to brown.
❦ Serve with some creamed potatoes and a crisp green vegetable.

CURRIED RABBIT

Serves 4

25 g (1 oz) butter
1 tsp oil
1 rabbit, jointed (see page 172)
2 large onions, chopped
1 large apple, chopped
½-1 tbsp curry powder
1 ½ tbsp plain flour
575 ml (1 pint) stock (see page 336)
1 tbsp sultanas
1 tsp chutney
1 tsp redcurrant or gooseberry jelly
salt and freshly ground black pepper

❦ Heat the oven to 170C (325F) mark 3.
❦ Heat the butter and oil in a frying pan and fry the rabbit joints until golden brown, then transfer them to a casserole. Add the chopped onion to the pan and fry until soft, then sprinkle these over the rabbit, together with the chopped apple.
❦ Put the curry powder and flour in the frying pan and fry for 1-2 minutes. Add the stock gradually, and bring to the boil. Add the remaining ingredients and pour into the casserole. Season, cover tightly and cook for 1 ½-2 hours, or until the meat is tender.
❦ Adjust the seasoning and, if too sweet, a little lemon juice will rectify this. Serve this dish with boiled long grain rice.

VERY SPECIAL RABBIT PIE

Serves 6

1 rabbit, about 1 kg (2 ¼ lb)
450 g (1 lb) Flaky Pastry (see page 361)
100 g (4 oz) can of pâté de foie gras
225 g (8 oz) belly pork
225 g (8 oz) lean ham
salt and pepper
1 egg
150 ml (¼ pint) aspic jelly

Marinade
2 tbsp brandy
1 glass white wine
2 sprigs of thyme
2 bay leaves
pinch of ground mace
few green peppercorns
1 onion, peeled and finely chopped

❦ Cut the meat off the rabbit, leaving all tendons and bone for a stock pot. Cut the meat into large dice. Prepare the marinade. Add the pieces of rabbit, mix thoroughly and leave for an hour or two, turning from time to time.
❦ Heat the oven to 220C (425F) mark 7. Roll out the pastry and leave to relax.
❦ Dice the pâté de foie gras (which, of course, could be home-made). Mince the well trimmed pork and ham together and season with salt and pepper. Remove the sprig of thyme and the bay leaves from the rabbit marinade.
❦ Cut the pastry into two circles to fit a 25 cm (10 in) enamel plate (so much better than an ovenproof glass one). Line the plate with one pastry circle. Pour a little marinade on the mixed meats and spread half this mixture on to the pastry. Put the diced rabbit with the green peppercorns and onion on top. Put the diced pâté on top of the rabbit and cover with the rest of the minced mixture. Pour on any remaining marinade.
❦ Brush the edge of the pastry with water. Put the second pastry circle on top and press the edges well together. Decorate with a fork and knock up the edges. Cut a hole in the top. Garnish with pastry leaves made from the trimmings and brush with beaten egg.
❦ Cook for 20 minutes, then reduce oven temperature to 190C (375F) mark 5 for a further 50-60 min-

utes. Lay greaseproof paper over the pie if it is getting too brown.
❦ To serve cold, pour 150 ml (¼ pint) of aspic jelly into the pie when cold and allow to set for 2-3 hours in the refrigerator. Aspic jelly from a packet is excellent for this purpose.

LAPIN AUX PRUNEAUX

Serves 6

1 rabbit, about 1 kg (2 ¼ lb)
275 ml (½ pint) red wine
10 prunes
1 small onion
sprig of thyme
350 g (12 oz) Puff Pastry (see page 360)
50 g (2 oz) dripping
25 g (1 oz) plain flour
½ tsp green peppercorns
salt and pepper
1 egg to glaze
150 ml (¼ pint) stock (see page 336)

❦ Cut the flesh off the rabbit, discarding tendons and bones (or put these in the stock pot). Marinate the rabbit flesh in the wine overnight with the stoned prunes, finely chopped onion and thyme.
❦ Roll out the pastry to a circle to cover a 23 cm (9 in) fluted ovenproof dish. Leave to relax. Heat the oven to 230C (450F) mark 8.
❦ Lift the rabbit, prunes and onion out of the marinade. Drain and fry in the dripping until the rabbit is browned. Stir in the flour, add a little marinade, stir well and add further marinade to make a thick gravy. Stir in the green peppercorns. Season to taste. Spoon the rabbit mixture into the dish and leave to cool.
❦ Brush the fluted rim of the dish with beaten egg. Lift the pastry on a rolling pin and cover the dish. Cut neatly around the fluting with a very sharp little knife. Brush the pastry with beaten egg. Make a hole in the centre to the let the steam out.
❦ Cook until risen and golden brown for about 20-30 minutes. Cover the pastry with greaseproof paper if it starts getting too brown. Serve hot.
❦ Make a gravy with the remaining stock and the marinade, reduced to 150 ml (¼ pint) by boiling.

Note
This dish is originally from Picardy.

RABBIT IN A BLANKET

Serves 8 hungry people

1 kg (2 ½ lb) young rabbit
225 g (8 oz) streaky bacon
1 tsp mixed dried herbs
salt and ground black pepper
675 g (1 ½ lb) Shortcrust Pastry (see page 357)
350 g (12 oz) pork sausage meat
2 hard-boiled eggs
1 egg to glaze

❦ Heat the oven to 200C (400F) mark 6.
❦ Joint and bone the rabbit (very easy). Rind the bacon, cut out any white bone and cut into strips. Mix with the rabbit meat and sprinkle with the herbs, salt and pepper.
❦ Roll out the pastry to a circle approximately 44 cm (16 in) across and put it carefully on to a baking sheet. Cut the pastry into the form of a broad cross. Mark a 25 cm (10 in) square in the middle and extend the sides to the edge of the pastry. Cut away the 'triangles'.
❦ Spread half the sausage meat on the square piece in the middle. Arrange the rabbit mixture on top of it. Slice the hard-boiled eggs on top of that, and finish with the other half of the sausage meat. Spread flat.
❦ Brush alternate edges of the pastry with beaten egg, and draw the square flaps up to meet over the rabbit. Pinch edges firmly together and flute with finger and thumb (see page 357). Make a little hole in the top to let the steam out. Brush the 'blanket' all over with beaten egg. Make some pastry leaves from the trimmings and place around the hole. Glaze with egg.
❦ Bake for 40 minutes then reduce the temperature to 180C (350F) mark 4 and continue to cook for another hour. Cover with greaseproof paper when the pastry is sufficiently browned.

Notes
Do put the pastry on the baking sheet before you start rolling. This is a very easy dish to make. Take your time and enjoy it.
❦ Rabbit in a Blanket is good cold if a jelly filling is put in when the pie has cooled; allow to set overnight. Bought aspic jelly is delicious for this. It 'matches' well, and is a great time-saver.

RABBIT AND PRUNE RAISED PIE

Serves 4-6

450 g (1 lb) Hot Water Crust Pastry (see page 362)
6 prunes
2 young rabbits, each about 1 kg (2 ¼ lb)
salt and pepper
¼ tsp dried sage
1 onion
175 g (6 oz) raw gammon
1 tbsp chopped parsley
2 hard-boiled eggs
2 tbsp stock (see page 336)
1 egg to glaze
Savoury Jelly (see page 337)

❦ Keep the pastry warm. Soak the prunes. Bone the rabbits and put the pieces in cold water for 1 hour.
❦ Rinse in cold water and dry. Cut the saddles and larger pieces into cubes. Season well and sprinkle with sage. Mince the small pieces of rabbit with the onion and gammon. Mix with the larger pieces. Stir in the parsley. Stone the prunes and slice the eggs. Heat the oven to 200C (400F) mark 6.
❦ Raise the pie (see page 362) or prepare a cake tin or pie mould (see page 363). Fill the pie with the meat, layering it with the egg slices and adding a prune now and then. Add the stock. Cover, decorate and brush with beaten egg. Cook for 30 minutes.
❦ Reduce the temperature to 180C (350F) mark 4, cover with greaseproof paper, and return to the oven for a further hour.
❦ When the pie is cold, fill with savoury jelly.

Note
This is a dish from Normandy.

ROAST HARE

Serves 4-6

1 leveret (with its liver)
6 rashers of fat bacon
100 g (4 oz) dripping
1 tbsp plain flour
575 ml (1 pint) strong stock (see page 336)
1 wine glass of port
1 tbsp redcurrant jelly
salt and pepper
watercress and lemon slices to garnish

Stuffing
175 g (6 oz) fresh breadcrumbs
1 medium onion, finely chopped
50 g (2 oz) shredded suet
1 tbsp chopped fresh parsley
½ tbsp chopped fresh thyme, or marjoram
grated rind and juice of 1 lemon
grated nutmeg
salt and pepper
1 egg

❦ Heat the oven to 200C (400F) mark 6.
❦ Prepare the hare (see page 171). Parboil the liver and finely chop it. Mix it with the stuffing ingredients, adding sufficient beaten egg to bind. Place in the cavity of the hare. Sew up and truss. Tie the rashers of bacon around the hare.
❦ Place the hare in a roasting tin with the dripping. Cover and place in the oven. Roast for 1 ½–2 hours, basting regularly.
❦ When the hare is nearly cooked, remove the bacon rashers and sprinkle with the flour. Return to the oven, uncovered, and cook for a further 20 minutes, basting occasionally, until well browned. Transfer the hare to a hot serving dish, and remove the trussing strings.
❦ Strain off any fat from the roasting tin, add the stock, port and redcurrant jelly, and simmer for about 5 minutes. Adjust the seasoning. If the sauce is too sweet, a little lemon juice may be added. Strain the sauce into a sauce-boat.
❦ Garnish the hare with watercress and lemon slices. Serve with roast potatoes, fresh green vegetables and redcurrant jelly. To carve, cut into joints.

To roast hare of doubtful age
Prepare and truss the hare so that it will fit into a steamer. Steam until tender, leaving unstuffed.

Place the hare in a roasting tin and cook as in the recipe above. Serve with Forcemeat Balls (see page 354) which may be roasted with the hare for the last 15 minutes.

HARE IN BEER

Serves 5-6

1 small hare, jointed (see page 172), blood reserved
1 tbsp plain flour
1 tsp paprika
50 g (2 oz) dripping
1 garlic clove, crushed with salt
2 medium onions, each stuck with 2 cloves
575 ml (1 pint) brown ale
1 wine glass of port
salt

❦ Heat the oven to 150C (300F) mark 2.
❦ Toss the hare joints in the flour mixed with paprika. Heat the dripping in a flameproof casserole and fry the joints until evenly brown. Add the crushed garlic, onions and brown ale. Bring to the boil, cover tightly and place in the oven.
❦ Cook slowly for 3–4 hours or until the meat comes off the bone. Remove the onions. Add several spoonfuls of the gravy to the reserved blood in a basin, mix well and pour back into the casserole. Add the port, and heat gently without boiling. Adjust the seasoning.
❦ Serve with redcurrant jelly, boiled potatoes and broccoli.

SADDLE OF HARE WITH CREAM

Serves 4

1 good plump hare, paunched and skinned (see
    page 171)
French mustard
25 g (1 oz) butter
150 ml (¼ pint) strong stock (see page 336)
150 ml (¼ pint) cream

Marinade
3 tbsp oil
2 small onions, sliced
2 small carrots, sliced
275 ml (½ pint) red wine vinegar
150 ml (¼ pint) red wine
large sprig fresh thyme
2 bay leaves
small sprig fresh rosemary
6 peppercorns
salt

❧ To prepare the marinade, heat the oil in a pan,
add the vegetables and cook gently until soft. Add
the remaining marinade ingredients, bring to the
boil and simmer for 7 minutes. Pour into a large bowl
and leave to cool.

❧ Joint the hare (see page 172), leaving the back
(saddle) whole. Place all the hare in the marinade and
leave for 36 hours, basting and turning occasionally.
Remove the saddle – the rest of the hare should be
put on one side and dealt with separately. Spread the
saddle with mustard.

❧ Heat the oven to 170C (325F) mark 3. Melt the
butter in a flameproof casserole, and gently brown
the saddle. Strain the marinade and pour over the
saddle, then simmer until the marinade is reduced
by about one third.

❧ Pour on the stock – the saddle should be barely
covered. Bring to the boil, cover tightly and cook in
the oven until absolutely tender (about 1 ¾ hours).

❧ Remove the saddle to a serving dish. Add the
cream to the remaining contents of the casserole and
boil up well for a few minutes. Adjust the seasoning.

❧ Strain the sauce, pour a little over the hare, and
serve the rest separately in a sauce-boat. Serve with
Game Straws (see page 355) and green beans.

HARE AND GROUSE PIE

Serves 4-6

1 casserole grouse
225 g (8 oz) stewing beef
2-3 joints of hare (fore-legs)
1 lambs' kidney, halved and sliced
50 g (2 oz) mushrooms, chopped
1 small onion, finely chopped
100 g (4 oz) streaky bacon, diced
stock (see page 336)
salt and pepper
225 g (8 oz) Flaky Pastry (see page 361)
Forcemeat Balls (see page 354)

❧ Heat the oven to 220C (425F) mark 7. Make the
forcemeat balls.

❧ Divide the grouse into 4 portions, cut the beef
into strips, and cut the hare joints into smaller
pieces. Layer the meats, mushroom, onion and
bacon in a 1½ litre (2½ pint) pie dish. Season well
between the layers. Barely cover with stock. Place
the forcemeat balls on top.

❧ Roll out the pastry and cover the dish, decorate
the edges, and make 4-6 pastry leaves with the trimmings for the top. Brush with beaten egg.

❧ Bake in the oven for 15 minutes. Reduce the heat
to 170C (325F) mark 3, and bake for a further 1 ½
hours or until the meat feels tender. If the pastry
browns too quickly, cover the pie with a piece of
greased greaseproof paper.

❧ Serve hot or cold.

JUGGED HARE

Serves 8

1 hare, paunched, skinned and cut into neat
    pieces (see pages 171-2), blood reserved
2 tbsp bacon fat
2 large onions, each stuck with 1 clove
4–5 peppercorns
1 stick celery, sliced
1 carrot, quartered
1 tsp whole allspice
bouquet garni of fresh herbs
juice of 1 lemon and a strip of rind
salt
½–1 litre (1-2 pints) stock (see page 336)
beurre manié (see page 367)
1 large glass of port or of the marinade
2 tsp redcurrant jelly

Marinade
150 ml (¼ pint) red wine
1 tbsp oil
1 shallot, sliced
2 bay leaves
freshly ground black pepper
6 juniper berries, crushed
salt

❦ Prepare the marinade: place all the ingredients in
a pan, bring to the boil, remove from the heat and
allow to cool. Place the hare in a deep dish, and pour
over the cold marinade. Leave to stand several hours,
or preferably overnight.

❦ Remove the pieces of hare from the marinade and
dry well. Heat the oven to 130C (275F) mark 1.

❦ Heat the bacon fat in a frying pan and quickly
brown the pieces of hare. Pack into a deep casserole
with the vegetables, spices, bouquet garni, lemon
rind, juice and salt. Barely cover with stock. Either
cover tightly with foil before closing the lid of the
casserole, or seal the edges of the lid with a flour and
water paste.

❦ Place the casserole in a deep pan of hot water and
cook in the oven for 3 hours.

❦ Remove the lid, pour off the gravy into a pan, and
remove the vegetables and bouquet garni. Thicken
the gravy with sufficient beurre manié to produce a
thin creamy consistency, bring to the boil and
remove from the heat.

❦ Add several spoonfuls of gravy to the reserved
hare's blood then carefully pour it back into the
pan. Add the port or strained marinade, and the
redcurrant jelly. Adjust the seasoning. When the
jelly has melted, pour the gravy over the hare and
reheat gently.

❦ Serve hot with Forcemeat Balls (see page 354),
accompanied by braised red cabbage.

Note
This is a classic dish which was originally cooked
slowly in a deep earthenware jug, standing in a deep
pan of hot water in a slow oven.

ROAST HAUNCH OF VENISON

Serves 6-8

1 haunch of venison
olive oil
100 g (4 oz) butter
350 g (1 2 oz) fat bacon rashers
plain flour and water paste to cover the joint
1 tbsp plain flour

Marinade
275 ml (½ pint) red wine
275 ml (½ pint) water
1 garlic clove, crushed
1 tbsp onion, chopped
1 tbsp carrot, chopped
1 celery stalk, chopped
50 g (2 oz) mushrooms, sliced
6 peppercorns
bay leaf

Sauce
1 tbsp plain flour
salt and freshly ground black pepper
juice of ½ orange

❦ Make the marinade by placing all the ingredients in a saucepan, bring slowly to the boil, boil for 2 minutes and allow to cool.

❦ Place the venison haunch in a deep dish and pour the cold marinade over. Marinate for 1-3 days, basting and turning the joint 2-3 times a day. When ready, remove the joint from the marinade and dry well. Reserve the marinade.

❦ Heat the oven to 230C (450F) mark 8. Rub the joint with olive oil, and cover with pats of butter. Wrap the bacon around the joint. Cover with the flour and water paste, or wrap in cooking foil. Place the joint in a roasting tin, and put in the oven for 15 minutes.

❦ Reduce the temperature to 150C (300F) mark 2 and roast the joint, allowing 55 minutes per kg (25 minutes per lb) for red deer, and 35 minutes per kg (15 minutes per lb) for roe or fallow deer.

❦ 15 minutes before the end of cooking time, crack the paste open, or unwrap the foil. Remove the bacon rashers, sprinkle the joint with flour, and baste well. Raise the oven temperature to 200C (400F) mark 6 and return the haunch to the oven for 15 minutes to brown the outsides nicely.

❦ Place the haunch on a serving dish. Pour the cooking juices out of the paste case or foil into a pan and skim off some of the fat.

❦ Mix the flour with salt and pepper and a little of the strained reserved marinade. Add to the pan juices, with more marinade as required and the orange juice. Stirring, bring to boil and simmer for 3-4 minutes. Adjust the seasoning and serve in a sauce-boat.

❦ Serve the venison accompanied with the sauce, the redcurrant jelly, roast potatoes and a purée of celeriac. Carve as for a leg of lamb.

VENISON STEAKS WITH RED WINE SAUCE

Serves 4

4 slices (1-2 cm/½-¾ inches thick) from the loin
    or haunch
salt and freshly ground pepper
25 g (1 oz) butter
1 tbsp oil
4 juniper berries, crushed
1 good sprig of fresh rosemary
150 ml (¼ pint) soured cream or yoghurt
salt and pepper
lemon slices to garnish

Marinade
2 shallots, finely chopped
strip of lemon rind
pinch of celery salt
200 ml (7 fl oz) red wine

❦ Lay the venison slices in a dish and season well with salt and freshly ground pepper. Add the ingredients for the marinade. Cover and leave to marinate for up to 2 days. Remove the meat from the marinade and dry thoroughly. Reserve the marinade.

❦ Heat the oil and butter in a large frying pan and gently brown the steaks on each side. Add the juniper berries and rosemary, and cover the pan. Lower the heat and cook gently until the meat is tender (about 30-40 minutes).

❦ Remove the steaks from the pan, place on a serving dish and keep warm. Strain the marinade into the pan, and dissolve the pan juices. Boil up to reduce the liquid a little.

❦ Add the soured cream or yoghurt and simmer for 2-3 minutes. Check the seasoning. Pour the sauce over the meat and garnish with lemon slices.

VENISON STEAKS WITH CHERRIES

Serves 5-6

700 g (1 ½ lb) loin of venison (without bone) or
**   slices from the top of the haunch**
3 tbsp oil
120 ml (4 fl oz) red wine or port
freshly ground black pepper
225 g (8 oz) canned cherries, stoned

Sauce
75 g (3 oz) onion, diced
75 g (3 oz) carrot, diced
1 small stick celery
diced trimmings from the venison
2 tbsp oil
1 tbsp plain flour
575 ml (1 pint) stock (see page 336)
25 g (1 oz) mushrooms, chopped
½ tsp tomato paste
small bunch of fresh herbs
120 ml (4 fl oz) red wine
2 tbsp red wine vinegar
1 tbsp redcurrant jelly

❧ Slice the venison into 2 cm (¾ in) steaks, and place them in a shallow dish. Sprinkle over 1 tablespoonful oil and the port or wine, with a liberal grinding of pepper. Cover and leave for a minimum of 1 hour.

❧ To make the sauce, heat the oil in a saucepan, add the vegetables and venison trimmings and cook gently until the vegetables start to soften and brown lightly. Add the flour and continue to cook gently until the flour becomes a golden brown colour.

❧ Gradually stir in two-thirds of the stock, and add the mushrooms, tomato paste, herbs and wine, bring to the boil, partially cover and simmer for 25 minutes. Remove any scum as it rises.

❧ Add half the remaining stock and bring to the boil, skimming again. Add the rest of the stock, re-boil, and skim. Strain the sauce into a clean pan, add the vinegar and the redcurrant jelly, bring to the boil, and simmer for 5-6 minutes until the jelly is dissolved. Add the cherries.

❧ Meanwhile, remove the venison from the marinade, and dry thoroughly. Heat 2 tablespoonfuls oil in a frying pan, and fry the venison in it for about 4 minutes on each side.

❧ Re-boil the sauce. Arrange the venison steaks on a flat warmed serving dish, with cherries at each end, pour a little of the sauce over the steaks and serve the rest separately.

❧ Serve with some Game Chips (see page 355) and artichoke hearts.

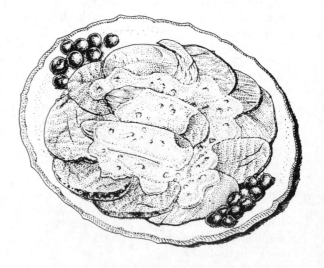

BRAISED VENISON

Serves 5-6

1.5-2 kg (3-4 lb) haunch or loin of venison
beurre manié (see page 367)
1 tsp redcurrant jelly
salt and freshly ground black pepper

Marinade
4 tbsp oil
100 g (4 oz) carrots, sliced
100 g (4 oz) onions, sliced
50 g (2 oz) celery, sliced
1 garlic clove, sliced
575 ml (1 pint) red wine or wine and water
6 juniper berries, crushed
sprig of fresh rosemary, sprig of fresh thyme
    and 3-4 fresh parsley stalks, tied together
1 bay leaf

Mirepoix
1 tbsp oil
225 g (8 oz) carrots, diced
225 g (8 oz) onions, diced
100 g (4 oz) celery, sliced
100 g (4 oz) turnip, diced

❦ To make the marinade, heat the oil in a pan, add the vegetables and cook gently to soften. Add the remaining ingredients, bring to the boil and simmer for 30 minutes. Leave until cold.

❦ Place the venison in a deep dish, pour the marinade over, leave up to 3 days, basting and turning the venison 2-3 times daily.

❦ Heat the oven to 190C (375F) mark 5. Remove the venison from the marinade, and dry well. Strain and reserve the marinade.

❦ Heat the oil for the mirepoix in a pan, add the vegetables, and gently sauté until softened. Place the vegetables in a deep casserole and moisten with some of the marinade. Place the venison joint on top and add sufficient stock to come a quarter of the way up the joint. Cover tightly and place in oven.

❦ Cook for 1 ½-2 hours, or until the meat is tender. Remove the meat, carve into slices, and place on a warmed serving dish. Keep warm.

❦ Strain the gravy from the casserole into a saucepan. Place it over the heat and reduce it a little, skimming off any fat. Thicken with beurre manié and add the redcurrant jelly. When the jelly is dissolved, check the seasoning. Pour some of the gravy over the sliced meat and serve the rest separately.

ROAST SADDLE OF VENISON

Serves 6-8

1 saddle of venison, 2-2.5 kg (4-6 lb)
8-12 rashers of streaky bacon
150 ml (¼ pint) port (optional)
beurre manié (see page 367)

Marinade
425 ml (¾ pint) red wine
150 ml (¼ pint) red wine vinegar
275 ml (½ pint) water
4 tbsp oil
2 sprigs fresh thyme
6 juniper berries, crushed
2 bay leaves
1 blade of mace
piece of orange rind (zest only), about 2.5 cm
    (1 in) square

❦ Trim the saddle, removing any hard skin. Place the saddle in a deep dish. Mix together the ingredients for the marinade, and pour it over the saddle. Allow to marinate for about 2 days, turning and basting 2-3 times daily.

❦ Heat the oven to 200C (400F) mark 6. Remove the saddle from the marinade and dry well. Strain and reserve the marinade.

❦ Place the bacon rashers over the top of the saddle and tie in place. Put the saddle in a roasting tin and cover tightly with foil. Place in the oven. After 30 minutes, reduce the temperature to 180C (350F) mark 4 and continue cooking.

❦ Allow a total cooking time of 55 minutes per kg (25 minutes per lb) for red deer, and 35 minutes per kg (15 minutes per lb) for fallow deer. During the cooking period, baste the saddle every 15 minutes with the marinade.

❦ About 15 minutes before the end of cooking time, remove the foil, and remove the bacon rashers, reserving them for garnish. Sprinkle the port over the saddle and raise the oven temperature to 200C (400F) mark 6 and allow the saddle to brown.

❦ Transfer the saddle to a serving dish. Add more marinade or water to the juices in the roasting tin, to make up to about 575 ml (1 pint). Stir over the heat to blend and thicken with beurre manié. Strain the sauce and serve separately.

❦ To carve, slice the meat across the ribs, parallel to the backbone, carving from the narrow end of the joint to the wide end (i.e. tail to head).

RAISED GAME PIE

Serves 6–8

350 g (12 oz) shoulder or neck venison
2 tbsp sherry
450 g (1 lb) Hot Water Crust Pastry (see page 362)
4 rashers streaky bacon
beaten egg to glaze

Filling
225 g (8 oz) pigs' liver, minced
1 medium onion, finely chopped
225 g (8 oz) pork sausage meat
1 hard-boiled egg
1 tsp chopped fresh parsley
½ tsp chopped fresh thyme
2-3 juniper berries, crushed
salt and freshly ground black pepper

❦ Prepare a collar of doubled greaseproof paper, 10 cm (4 in) deep and 18 cm (7 in) in diameter. Grease well. Place on a greased baking sheet.

❦ Cut the venison into fine strips and sprinkle with the sherry. Cover and leave to marinate for at least 1 hour.

❦ Heat the oven to 190C (375F) mark 5. Make the pastry. Use three-quarters of the pastry to line the base and sides of the collar, ensuring there are no thin places. Line this with the streaky bacon.

❦ Mix the ingredients for the filling together. Place one-third of the filling in the base of the mould and cover with half the venison. Continue filling the mould with alternate layers, finishing with a layer of the filling.

❦ Cover the pie with the remaining pastry, ensuring that the edges are well sealed. Use any pastry trimmings to make pastry leaves for decoration. Make a 1 cm (½ in) hole in the centre of the top to allow steam to escape.

❦ Bake the pie in the oven for 1½–2 hours. If the pastry appears to be browning quickly, then reduce the oven temperature after ¾–1 hour to 170C (325F) mark 3.

❦ About 20 minutes before the end of cooking, remove the paper collar and brush the pastry well with beaten egg to finish.

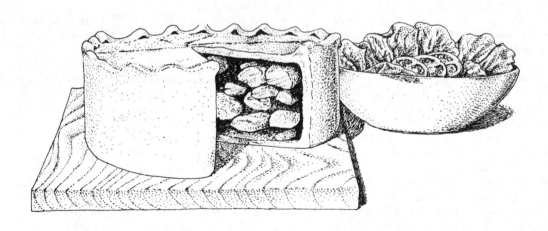

VEGETABLES AND SALADS

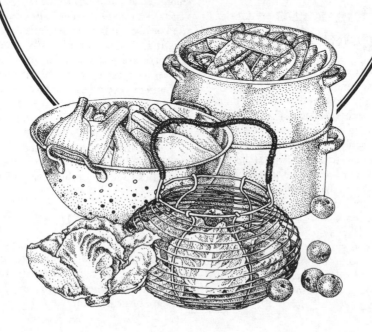

ABOUT VEGETABLES

Fresh vegetables are nourishing and full of vitamins, minerals and fibres that are essential to our diet. A huge range of home-grown and imported vegetables is available. Vegetables are delicious raw or cooked; they give a wonderful variety of colour, flavour and texture.

❧ Choosing fresh ❧ vegetables

Where possible use locally grown vegetables and buy them at their peak, just before they are fully mature. They will be both cheap and plentiful and at their freshest and best, full of nutrients and flavour. Vegetables begin to lose vital vitamin value as soon as they are harvested. Buy unwrapped vegetables if possible, to see just what you are being offered. Refuse any vegetables with discoloured or limp leaves or flesh, with wrinkled skins or with small blemishes which may hide rottenness within.

❧ Storing fresh ❧ vegetables

Use all except main-crop root vegetables as soon as possible. Onions and main-crop root vegetables store well for at least 2 months in a cool, dry dark place; potatoes and carrots, especially, must not be exposed to light. Young and early root vegetables, cabbages and fruits such as pumpkin, courgettes or marrow (if uncut) can be stored for several days in a cool, dry place or for up to 2 weeks in the case of large fruits with tough skins. Most other vegetables should be stored in a cool, dry place or the bottom of a refrigerator for not more than 2-3 days (1-2 days for fragile, tender and leafy vegetables). Greens such as Brussels sprouts and spinach and any vegetable which has been cut, should be wrapped in a plastic bag or cling film before storage. Do not store beansprouts, kohlrabi, mushrooms, young spinach or sweetcorn cobs.

❧ Preparing fresh ❧ vegetables

All vegetables lose vitamins rapidly from any cut surface which is exposed to air and light, so prepare them just before use. In general, leave root vegetables and fruits unpeeled unless the skins are coarse or blemished and cook them whole or in chunks. However heating, especially in salted cooking liquid, leaches out or destroys nutrients. Vegetables can therefore be cut up finely to shorten the cooking time. Salt should, when possible, only be added after cooking.

❧ Frozen, canned and ❧ dried vegetables

Frozen vegetables can be cooked in almost all the ways suggested for fresh vegetables, but will need less cooking time. They are best boiled or steamed without being thawed first. In the case of commercially frozen vegetables, follow the manufacturer's packet directions as to timing, but omit the fat and salt often suggested as additions to the cooking liquid. Frozen vegetables must be thawed and drained before being fried or used in fritters, and most are not suitable for roasting. A few commercially prepared vegetable mixtures are pre-seasoned, but like all vegetables benefit from being flavoured with herbs.

Canned vegetables, can be used instead of fresh if necessary and take less time. They are generally canned with salt, and often with sugar or other 'hidden' flavourings, or flavour and colour enhancers.

Freeze-dried and other dried vegetables ar useful standbys. Follow packet directions, but be wary of quantities suggested; they may be inadequate.

❧ Pulses ❧

Most pulses must be soaked before cooking, and they are then boiled and used as an alternative to potatoes, pasta or rice. A few recipes in this book include cooked, dried beans or lentils; in these cases, canned ones are quite suitable.

❦ Equipment for ❦ preparing and cooking vegetables

Hardly any special equipment is needed for preparing and cooking vegetables beyond a sturdy chopping board, a sharp knife and a pair of scissors. A short-bladed knife is easier to use for topping and tailing, scraping and similar tasks. A grapefruit spoon is helpful for removing the seeds from small fruits such as tomatoes. A food processor, blender or powerful food mill is almost essential for making smooth purées and for very fine chopping and grinding. A steamer or, if this is not available, a large, round-bottomed strainer or colander which fits over a saucepan is also useful.

For salad-making, a salad-shaker or basket produces crisp, attractive leaf salads instead of bruised limp ones; the salad can be drained and shaken in a nylon (not metal) round-bottomed strainer.

All salads should be prepared in a non-metal bowl. A wooden salad bowl is best for serving; it should be wiped dry after use, not washed, to give it the patina and aroma from the dressings used. Always make dressings in a non-metal jug or bowl, or for speed, in a jar or bottle with a firm stopper or screw-on top.

Additional tools such as a large and small vegetable baller, a cannelle knife for removing thin strips of peel, and an egg or tomato slicer are also useful. A garlic press saves kitchen smells and washing up.

❦ A healthy diet ❦

It is important to include all the essential nutrients in daily meals, and also dietary fibre and water. Vegetables play a large part in supplying all the components of a healthy diet.

Peas, beans and potatoes provide a good source of protein as well as the starchy carbohydrate which supplies energy. Beetroot contains the most sugar, but carrots, onions, parsnips and swedes all contain a higher than average content. Most vegetables contain little or no fat, but avocado pears are rich in saturated fat.

Carrots, tomatoes and leaf vegetables all contain carotene which the body can turn into vitamin A; and the darker their colour the more they have. Green leaf vegetables are good sources of B vitamins and vitamin C. Raw green salad leaves in spring and summer are especially valuable. Potatoes, green peppers, cabbage and broccoli supply vitamin C year-round. Calcium and iron are also found in green vegetables such as sprouting broccoli, watercress and parsley.

Trim vegetables as little as possible to keep their full fibre value and the nutrients just under the skins of root vegetables. Vitamins and minerals are destroyed by soaking and by over-cooking; cook them as soon as they are prepared, until just tender. Never add bicarbonate of soda to cooking water, as it destroys both B vitamins and vitamin C. Season after cooking and serve all vegetables as soon as possible.

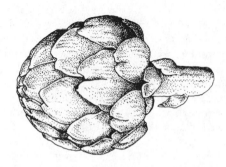

COOKING METHODS AND PREPARATION

A guide to cooking techniques, the preparation and basic ways of cooking individual vegetables.

To boil

Prepare the vegetables (see pages 222-30) and put them in a pan. Pour on just enough boiling liquid to cover the vegetables; use water, vegetable cooking water or barely seasoned stock. Sprigs of fresh herbs such as mint or parsley can be added. Cook for the time required, topping up with a little extra boiling water if needed. Boil only just long enough to cook, so that the vegetables are tender but retain a slight resistance when bitten. Drain the vegetables thoroughly, reserving any liquid for a gravy, sauce or vegetable soup, season and dress. Serve as soon as possible.

To blanch or parboil

Most vegetables are blanched before freezing, to prevent discoloration or to remove any 'raw' taste before they are used in salads. Sometimes, hard vegetables need parboiling, that is semi-cooking, before being processed by a quick cooking method such as grilling which will complete their cooking.

Prepare the vegetables. To blanch, tip the vegetables into boiling water for a few minutes only. Delicate vegetables should be put in a round-bottomed sieve, colander or frying basket, and just dipped in the water. This will prevent them being squashed when removed.

To parboil, cook the vegetables as for full boiling, but drain them when only partly cooked.

To seal and boil

This is sometimes called the conservation method of

boiling because it is designed to retain the nutrients. It is used mainly for root vegetables. The vegetables are cut into small pieces and tossed in a little oil or fat until the surfaces are sealed. They are then cooked in very little liquid – in fact half-steamed – in a covered pan until just tender. Chopped parsley and a dash of lemon juice are usually the only additions after cooking.

To steam
Delicate, young watery vegetables are better steamed than boiled to conserve their nutrients and prevent them becoming sodden. Prepare the vegetables as they will be served, place in the top of a steamer or in a colander and cook, covered, over just bubbling (not fast-boiling) water, until tender. Drain, shaking gently, toss with fresh herbs if used, season and serve.

To bake
Baking is suitable for large vegetables such as Spanish onions or a vegetable marrow, for individual portions of sliced root, bulb or fruit vegetables or for a whole dish of prepared small vegetables such as courgettes or stuffed peppers. Large vegetables are usually baked uncovered with their cut surfaces brushed with fat. Individual portions can be laid on pieces of foil large enough to enclose them with a light seasoning or a little flavouring liquid. The parcels are then closed; little or no nutrients are lost because any cooking liquid is served along with the vegetables.

To roast
Besides potatoes, onions, parsnips, swedes and pumpkin a few other vegetables can be roasted either round a joint in the oven or in a separate pan. They are generally better if lightly parboiled first, peeled if required, and cooked (topped with fat) at a fairly high temperature to crisp the outside and to cook them quickly. Only roast large chunks or segments of pumpkin; small ones shrivel.

To grill
This method is suitable for mushrooms and halved tomatoes or courgettes. Raw vegetables should be brushed with fat or oil before grilling.

To shallow-fry or sauté
Whole mushrooms, aubergines, courgettes, peppers and similar vegetables, sliced or cut into small cubes or balls, can be tossed in hot fat until just tender and lightly browned. Cooked potato slices can be heated and browned in the same way. Do not leave any vegetable to cook itself in shallow fat; it will absorb too much of the fat, get soggy and taste unpleasantly greasy. Shallow-fried vegetables should taste crisp.

Finely sliced or cut up vegetables cook in less fat if stir-fried in a wok or similar pan; it is an excellent and colourful way to cook mixed vegetables. Cut vegetables into small strips or thin rounds, place the hard ones, and soft ones on separate plates. Heat a few spoonfuls of oil in the pan until hot and toss the harder vegetables in it for a few moments before adding the rest. Stir quickly over a high heat for 2-4 minutes. Add a few spoonfuls of stock, wine or an unthickened spicy sauce. Season well and continue cooking, stirring quickly for a further few minutes, then serve immediately.

A few vegetables with a high water content can simply be cut up and then simmered gently in fat in a covered pan until soft. The pan is shaken often to prevent them sticking. They are tipped out into a serving dish when tender, are seasoned and served with their own liquid.

To deep-fry
The simplest deep-frying method is to slice the vegetables very thinly, dry them well, then immerse them in deep hot oil, 170C (325F). The vegetables are cooked until crisp and brown, they are then removed, drained on soft kitchen paper and seasoned with salt.

Alternatively, they can be fried in batter, or egg and breadcrumbs as fritters (for French Fries and Potato Crisps see page 228).

To braise
Vegetables such as celery, lettuce, fennel and chicory are sometimes braised on a mirepoix of vegetables simmered in fat (see page 367). The mirepoix is covered with stock and the prepared vegetable is laid on top. The pan is tightly covered and the vegetable is cooked very gently, with occasional basting, until tender. Seasoning is not generally necessary during this form of cooking.

To purée
All starchy vegetables and a good many others can be puréed for use in soups, as side dishes and as an ingredient of made-up dishes. Boil or steam the vegetables then mash, sieve, or process in a food processor or electric blender. Add a little butter, cream or a thick white sauce or panada (see page 339) and seasoning. Whip with a fork or whisk over a low heat until light and creamy.

❦ Artichokes, globe ❦

Globe artichokes are available all year round. Buy heads with tightly closed leaves, showing no signs of browned or dry edges. There should be no sign of swelling at the base of the artichoke. The bases of the leafy petals are edible and the artichoke bottom or heart is considered a delicacy.

Preparation Break off each stem by bending and twisting it. Remove tough leaves from the base and trim the leaves (optional). If using the bottoms only, remove all the leaves and trim the stem as close as possible to the base. If the artichoke or bottom is to be stuffed, carefully remove the hairy 'choke', pulling it away from the heart with your fingers or scrape it off gently with a knife or spoon. This is easier to do after the basic cooking. Plunge the prepared artichoke into cold water sharpened with 1 tablespoon of lemon juice per litre (1 ¾ pints), to prevent discoloration.

Basic cooking Place the heads in a large pan of boiling water containing a little lemon juice and oil. Cover and simmer for 25-35 minutes for small and medium-size heads, 40-55 minutes for large ones. Drain upside down on absorbent paper.

Serve hot with melted butter or Hollandaise Sauce (see page 345) or cold with a Vinaigrette (see page 347).

❦ Artichokes, Jerusalem ❦

These knobbly white tubers are available from November through to April.

Preparation Wash or scrub the tubers, or peel. If peeling prior to cooking, submerge in cold water with a little lemon juice or vinegar to prevent discoloration.

Basic cooking Boil with just enough water to cover, with a little lemon juice or vinegar added, for about 15-20 minutes until just tender, or steam for about 40 minutes. Drain well and rub or scrape off the skins if necessary. To roast, parboil for 5 minutes, drain, scrape then roast for about 1 hour. To deep-fry, parboil for 5 minutes, drain then scrape and cut into slices. Dip in batter and fry until golden brown. Drain on absorbent paper. Thinly sliced peeled raw artichokes can also be deep-fried as for Game Chips (see page 229). To purée, steam, drain, scrape and cut into pieces. Mash or sieve, season and add 1 tablespoon of butter and milk (optional) for each 450 g (1 lb) of raw artichoke used.

❦ Asparagus ❦

Asparagus is available all year round. Choose firm, fresh looking stalks.

Preparation Rinse each stalk and cut off any tough and woody ends. Scrape or shave each stalk, if thick, from just below the tip. Trim the stalks to roughly the same lengths and tie into even-sized bundles with the heads together. The spears in each bundle should be the same thickness.

Basic cooking Stand the bundles with the tips upright in a pan at least 5 cm (2 in) deeper than the height of the bundles with enough boiling water to come three-quarters of the way up the stalks. The stalks cook in the boiling water while the tips are steamed. Cover the pan tightly, bring the water back to the boil, and cook gently for 10-20 minutes, until the buds and upper parts of the stems are tender. Drain on absorbent paper and remove the string.

Serve hot with melted butter or Hollandaise Sauce (see page 345) or cold with a Vinaigrette (see page 347).

❦ Aubergines❦
(eggplants)

Aubergines are available all year round. Look for firm smooth aubergines with tight shiny skins. Size makes no difference to the flavour.

Preparation Slice off the stalk and any leaves and wipe or peel. If leaving whole or halved, score or prick the skin in several places. If halved or sliced, sprinkle with salt and leave for 30 minutes to remove any bitterness. Rinse thoroughly and pat dry.

Basic cooking Bake whole, or halved and stuffed, in a moderate oven, 180C (350F) mark 4, for 30-60 minutes depending on size. Coat slices with flour and shallow-fry with squeezed or minced garlic and chopped parsley; or deep-fry until golden brown in hot oil, after coating with egg and breadcrumbs.

❦ Avocado pears ❦

Avocados are available all year round. A ripe avocado should be soft and yielding all over.

Preparation Halve lengthwise, separate halves and remove stone. Brush cut surfaces with lemon juice immediately to prevent discoloration. Avocados are usually served raw, in the shell or sliced in salads.

❧ Beansprouts ❧

Available all year round. Good with oriental ingredients.
Preparation Rinse lightly. Serve raw in salads.
Basic cooking Steam or stir-fry for a few minutes.

❧ Beans, broad ❧

Broad beans are available during the summer. Choose smallish, full but not swollen pods as these are likely to be the youngest and most tender.
Preparation Tiny pods need topping and tailing only. Larger ones should be split and the beans removed.
Basic cooking Cook in boiling water until tender, 15-20 minutes according to age, or steam for 25-40 minutes. Drain well.

Toss with Maître d'Hôtel Butter (see page 344) or hot soured cream.

❧ Beans, French ❧

French beans are available all year, but are best between June and September when home-grown. Look for firm, strong beans with a bright green colour. They should break with a crisp snap and the inside should be fresh and juicy.
Preparation French beans are usually stringless and only need topping and tailing. Wash.
Basic cooking Boil 5-12 minutes or steam for about 15 minutes until tender but still crisp. Drain well.

Season with salt and pepper, toss with a little butter and a few savory or tarragon leaves.

❧ Beans, runner ❧

Available from July to October. Eat very young and fresh. To test a runner bean for freshness, snap it in two; it should break with a crisp snap and the inside should be fresh and juicy. Avoid large, dark green beans which are likely to be tough and stringy.
Preparation Wash in cold water. Top, tail and string sides of pod; slice if long and thick.
Basic cooking Cook in boiling water for 5-10 minutes or steam for 15-20 minutes until tender but still crisp. Drain well.

Toss with a little melted butter and a few savory or tarragon leaves.

❧ Beetroots ❧

Beetroots are available all year round. Look for firm smallish beetroots. The tops, if any, should be crisp and fresh looking. If buying ready-cooked, make sure the skins are not wrinkled or dry, and that any peeled, pre-packed beetroots are glossy.
Preparation Rinse carefully, taking care not to damage the skin or the colour and flavour will 'bleed' away during cooking. Twist off the roots about 2.5 cm (1 in) from the end and trim the tops.
Basic cooking Boil gently until soft, about 30 minutes for baby beetroots, up to 1 ¼ hours for large ones. To test if beetroots are cooked, remove one from the pan and rub the skin gently; it should slide off easily. To bake beetroots, clean and wrap in foil. If the beetroot is damaged, 'plaster' the broken skin with flour and water paste and then wrap in foil. Bake at 180C (350F) mark 4 for 1-2 hours, depending on size. The beetroots are cooked when the flesh yields when pressed with a finger. Remove the skin.

Slice or dice the beetroot and serve hot with a white sauce sharpened with a little lemon juice or vinegar, or chill thoroughly and serve in a salad or with French Dressing (see page 347).

❧ Broccoli ❧
calabrese and sprouting

Green calabrese is available all year round. Cape broccoli is available from February to March. Purple and white sprouting broccoli are available from February to March. Buy calabrese and Cape broccoli with a closely packed head and purple and white sprouting with strong stalks and heads. All varieties can be used as for cauliflower in salads (see overleaf).
Preparation For purple and white sprouting trim the stalk and leaves. Prepare calabrese and Cape broccoli as for cauliflower (see overleaf).
Basic cooking Cook purple and white sprouting in boiling water for 6-10 minutes or steam for 15 minutes; calabrese and Cape broccoli as for cauliflower.

Serve all varieties with melted butter or Hollandaise Sauce (see page 345).

❧ Brussels sprouts ❧

Available from August to March, choose small, even-sized sprouts that look closely packed and solid. Avoid any with wilted or discoloured leaves.

Preparation Wash thoroughly in cold water. Trim off tough outer leaves and the stem. Cut a small cross in the base to help the thick stem cook at the same speed as the leaves. Shred finely and use raw for salads.

Basic cooking Cook in boiling water or stock for 10-15 minutes or steam for 15-20 minutes. Sprouts can also be braised as for celery (see below). Drain thoroughly.

Toss in melted butter or mix with cooked mushrooms, chestnuts or almonds.

❦ Cabbages ❦

Green cabbage is available home grown all year round. Red cabbage is available home grown from October to February and imported from September to June. Spring greens are available home grown throughout the year. White cabbage is available from September to June. The most common types of cabbage are spring and summer open-hearted cabbage, spring greens, Savoy cabbage, hard white cabbage and red cabbage. The leaves of green cabbage should be fresh and crisp-looking; avoid any that show signs of yellowing. White and red cabbages should be round, closely packed and heavy for their size.

Preparation Discard any damaged leaves. Cut cabbage into wedges and rinse thoroughly. Cut away the tough stalk. Alternatively, shred cabbage with a sharp knife, discarding the stalk. Rinse well. Crisp varieties such as Dutch and Savoy make good salad vegetables. Shred finely for Coleslaw (see page 260).

Basic cooking Place shredded cabbage in boiling water and cook for 5-10 minutes or steam for 10-15 minutes, until tender but crisp. Cabbage wedges will cook in about 15 minutes. Add 1 tablespoon of vinegar, lemon juice or wine to the water before cooking red cabbage, then boil for 15-20 minutes. Drain well.

Season with salt, pepper and nutmeg and dress with a little melted butter or margarine.

❦ Carrots ❦

Carrots are available all year round. Choose brightly coloured, evenly sized carrots with smooth skins. Avoid soft or shrivelled carrots or hairy coarse ones.

Preparation For new carrots, top and tail, scrub thoroughly and leave whole. For older carrots, cut a slice from each end and scrape or peel thinly – slice, dice or cut lengthwise into quarters or match-sticks. Remove the core if it is at all woody. Grate young, raw carrots for use in mixed salads and garnishes.

Basic cooking Cook in boiling water for 8-10 minutes if sliced or diced, or 10-20 minutes if whole or quartered. Alternatively, steam for 20-25 minutes. Drain well.

Toss in melted butter and sprinkle with fresh herbs. Purée very large carrots or use for soup.

❦ Cauliflowers ❦

Available all year round, look for fresh green leaves surrounding a firm white head free of blemishes. The curd should be closely packed.

Preparation Cut away the green outside leaves. Cut the stalk level with the head and cut a cross in the end. Cut away any damaged parts of the head and wash thoroughly. Alternatively, cut the head into florets, discarding the centre stalk.

Basic cooking Cook a whole cauliflower, stalk down, in 2-5 cm (1-2 in) boiling water for about 15-20 minutes, until the stalk is tender but still firm. Cook florets for 5-15 minutes, and drain thoroughly.

Serve with butter, White Sauce or Cheese Sauce (see page 339).

❦ Celeriac ❦

Available from September to March, celeriac has a rich celery flavour and nutty texture.

Preparation Peel and toss in lemon juice or vinaigrette to prevent discoloration. Cut in dice or matchstick pieces or shred. For salads, grate, shred or dice and marinate in dressing to soften, or blanch; or serve grated with a mustard mayonnaise.

Basic cooking Cook in gently boiling water for up to 5 minutes if diced or 1 minute if shredded. Celeriac can also be steamed. Drain.

Serve hot with butter, White Sauce or Hollandaise Sauce (see pages 339 and 345), or make into a purée.

❦ Celery ❦

Celery is available all year round. Look for crisp whole heads with small inner stalks and 'heart'. Avoid over-large heads as they may be stringy. Winter celery has a sweet flavour and tender stalks.

Preparation Trim leaves and roots. Separate stalks and scrub well. String if required. Cut into 2.5 cm (1 in) lengths or leave whole. Use raw, chopped celery in salads.

Basic cooking Cook sliced celery in butter for 5 minutes, add a little stock, cover and simmer for 15-20 minutes until stalks are tender but still crisp. Alternatively, steam for 20-30 minutes until soft. Drain well.

Serve hot with herbs or Cheese Sauce (see page 347).

❦ Chicory ❦

Chicory is available all year round. Look for compact heads, with white leaves and yellow-green edges. Those with green tips will probably be too bitter for salads.
Preparation Wash in cold water if necessary and trim the root end and any damaged leaves. Remove the bitter centre core. Separate each leaf or leave the head whole and quarter or slice it lengthwise. Use the leaves raw in salads.
Basic cooking Blanch the whole heads in boiling water for 5 minutes and drain well. Cook in a very little fresh water with lemon juice and a little butter for 20-30 minutes until just tender. Season well.

Serve hot with chopped parsley or paprika or in a White or Cheese Sauce (see page 347).

❦ Chillies ❦

Available all year round. Green-skinned chillies are less hot than the red ones.
Preparation Trim off the stalk, wipe and use whole, or chop very finely. If cut, remove all the fiery hot seeds. Wash your hands after handling them.

Add chillies to pickles, curries, stews and hot or cold bean dishes.

❦ Chinese leaves ❦

Available from June to April. The head should be pale green, solid and heavy.
Preparation Wash and dry; shred finely for use raw in salads or halve, quarter or cut into wedges for cooking.
Basic cooking Cook shredded leaves in a little boiling water for 2-3 minutes until tender yet crisp, or steam for 4 minutes. Boil wedges for 7-10 minutes. Do not overcook. Drain well.

Serve hot sprinkled with herbs and lemon juice or French Dressing (see page 347). Chinese leaves can also be braised.

❦ Courgettes ❦
and small round squashes

Courgettes are available all year round, but are cheaper in summer when squashes can also be bought. Look for medium-sized courgettes with blemish-free skins as the larger ones tend to have tough skins. Courgettes are good raw, in salads.
Preparation Wash or wipe, top and tail. Cook whole, halve or quarter lengthwise or cut into rounds. Do not peel unless skins are tough. Young courgettes can be coarsely grated for use raw or stir-fried. Cook squashes whole or halved.
Basic cooking Steam whole courgettes for 10-20 minutes, or boil for the same time, until they are just tender. Cook slices in a little butter or oil in a covered pan for 5 minutes, and season well with salt, black pepper and a few drops of lemon juice. (Halved courgettes or squashes can be stuffed.)

Serve hot with Maître d'Hôtel Butter (see page 344), or cold with a yoghurt dressing.

❦ Cucumbers ❦

Available all year round, choose smallish, smooth-skinned cucumbers, as larger ones tend to be less tender, with bitter indigestible seeds and rather tough skins.
Preparation Wipe, cut off the ends, and cut into slices, dice or chunk. Peel if the skins are tough. Cucumber is usually eaten raw as a salad vegetable, but can also double for cooked courgettes.
Basic cooking Steam or boil for 3-10 minutes depending on sizes of pieces and drain, or sauté in butter.

Serve hot, tossed in butter with spring onion and herbs, or cold in a vinaigrette or yoghurt dressing.

❦ Fennel ❦

Imported Florence fennel bulbs are available year round. Select white or pale green, as dark green ones are likely to be rather bitter. Fennel has a crisp texture and a delicate aniseed flavour.
Preparation Trim off the root end and stalks, reserving any feathery leaves for garnish. Remove the coarse outer sheaths of a larger bulb. Either leave bulb whole, quarter it or slice thinly. Drop cut fennel in water with a little lemon juice to prevent discoloration. Use raw thinly sliced fennel in salads.

Basic cooking Blanch whole small fennel in boiling water for 5 minutes. Put whole or cut fennel into simmering water with lemon juice, or into chicken stock and cook gently for 10-15 minutes if sliced, 25-40 minutes if quartered or whole, depending on size. Alternatively, blanch whole heads of fennel briefly in boiling water, drain and sauté in butter until golden.

Serve hot tossed in melted butter. Serve raw as part of a crudité platter or green salad.

❧ Kale ❧

Kale is available from September to March. The leaves should be fresh and crisp-looking.
Preparation Wash and discard any damaged leaves. Use blanched in salads.
Basic cooking Cook in boiling water for about 8 minutes. Drain and season.

Serve hot tossed in butter.

❧ Kohlrabi ❧

Available from July to March. Look for young, small kohlrabi as old ones are tough and bitter.
Preparation Cut off the leaves and stalks. Peel thinly, cut into slices or cubes, or grate for serving raw.
Basic cooking Cook in boiling water for 10-15 minutes until tender.

Serve hot in a White or Cheese sauce (see page 339), or as a purée. Toss grated raw kohlrabi in French Dressing (see page 347).

❧ Leeks ❧

Leeks are available from August to April. Look for small tender leeks, well blanched at the root end and with crisp green tops. Finely sliced, leek stems are delicious raw in salads.
Preparation Cut off the root and any coarse leaves. Cut a lengthways slit nearly half way through the leeks or cut very large leeks lengthwise in half and wash thoroughly. Alternatively, slice and wash in a colander.
Basic cooking Steam sliced leeks for 5-7 minutes, or cook in boiling water for 20 minutes if whole or 5 minutes if sliced. Drain well.

Serve raw, thinly sliced and tossed in French Dressing (see page 347). Serve hot with White or Cheese Sauce (see page 339) or glazed with Maître d'Hôtel Butter (see page 344).

❧ Lettuce ❧
endive and other salad leaves

Cos lettuce is available from April to October, Iceberg and round or cabbage lettuce and endive and sorrel all year round. Crisp, firm-hearted varieties of lettuce have more flavour than the soft-leaved round lettuce. Look for fresh strong leaves without brown or damaged patches. The endive family includes curly endive, with a slightly bitter flavour, Batavia chicory and radicchio, Dandelion leaves, corn salad, purslane, mustard and cress, sorrel and watercress can also be used.
Preparation Wash the leaves and drain well, pat dry or shake well in a salad basket. Trim off any tough ribs or leaves. Keep covered in the refrigerator to retain crispness.
Basic cooking Lettuce wedges or small whole lettuce can be blanched and then braised until tender (see page 221). Crisp lettuce leaves are good sautéed in butter or oil for 2-3 minutes, stirring all the time, until they just begin to soften. Sorrel can be cooked as for spinach (see overleaf).

Toss raw whole or shredded leaves in a herb-flavoured dressing.

❧ Marrows ❧

Marrows are available from June to September. Look for marrows that weigh only about 1 kg (2 lb). Large marrows tend to be flavourless and fibrous.
Preparation Peel marrows thinly, scoop out the seeds and cut into chunks or slices.
Basic cooking Steam for 10-25 minutes according to age, drain thoroughly, or sauté in a little butter for 5-10 minutes.

Serve with melted butter and chopped parsley in a coating of White, Cream or Cheese Sauce (see page 339). Marrow is very good split in half and stuffed (see page 237).

❧ Mushrooms ❧

Cultivated mushrooms are available all year round, field mushrooms in September. Look for button mushrooms when appearance is important. For flavour, buy flat or field mushrooms. Eat as soon as possible after purchase.
Preparation Wipe with a damp cloth if necessary; do not peel unless the skin is damaged. Trim off any

earthy root. Fresh, raw mushrooms are an excellent source of texture and flavour for salads.

Basic cooking Poach in a little water and lemon juice for 3-5 minutes, drain well. Steam whole or sliced mushrooms for 5-10 minutes until tender. Grill flat mushrooms, brushed both sides with melted butter or margarine and seasoned with salt and pepper, for about 3 minutes on either side. Fry gill side up, in a little butter for 4-6 minutes until tender.

Serve in a Cream sauce (see page 339), or sprinkled with chopped parsley or fresh thyme.

❦ Mustard and cress ❦

Mustard and cress is available all year round.
Preparation Wash, cut and serve as part of a salad or as a garnish.

❦ Okra ❦

Imported okra is available all year round. The ribbed pods are best when no more than about 7.5-10 cm (3-4 in) long. A brown tinge indicates staleness so look for clean, dark green pods.

Preparation Rinse, top and tail the pods without cutting into the flesh if cooking whole. If the ridges look tough or damaged, scrape them. Slice or leave whole.

Basic cooking Cook in boiling water for 5 minutes or parboil and finish by tossing in butter, or sauté in oil for 5-10 minutes until tender.

❦ Onions ❦

Large onions and spring onions are available all year round. Pickling onions are available from September to December and shallots from June to July. Look for clean, firm onions with dry papery skins.

Preparation Cut a thin slice off the top of the onion. Remove the dry papery skin and peel off any soft outer layers. Hold the onion by the root and slice, or cut in half and chop. Discard the root. Spring onions are usually served raw in salads; the green leaves can be chopped and used for flavouring and garnishing. Use shallots raw or cooked like onions.

Basic cooking Cook large onions, with their skins on to preserve the nutrients, in boiling water for 20-50 minutes, depending on size. Drain well. Strip off the wet skin. Steam whole onions for 40 minutes and sliced onions for 15 minutes. Shallow-fry thinly sliced onion in enough fat to coat the bottom of the pan for 5-8 minutes until browned, turning occasionally. Drain well. Deep-fry thinly sliced floured onion rings until browned. To bake, parboil with the skin on for 20 minutes (optional) drain and dry. Wrap each onion in greased greaseproof paper, place in a greased baking tin and bake at 180C (350F) mark 4 until tender, about 45-70 minutes. Remove skin.

Serve boiled onions with White or Cheese Sauce (see page 339), and baked onions with melted butter.

❦ Parsnips ❦

Available from September to April. Young parsnips are the most tender and the flavour is best after several frosts. Look for firm clean roots without side shoots or soft brown blemishes.

Preparation Scrub well. Trim top and end root and peel thinly. Leave whole, slice or quarter as required. Cut out core from older coarser parsnips.

Basic cooking Steam sliced parsnips for 10 minutes. Parsnip quarters may be blanched in boiling water for 1-2 minutes, drained well and either sautéed or roasted around a joint. To sauté, cook in melted butter for 10-12 minutes until golden and tender. To roast, place in the roasting tin around the joint and cook at 200C (400F) mark 6 for about 40 minutes.

Serve with butter, or as a purée (see page 221).

❦ Peas ❦

Peas are available from March to November and mange-tout all year round. Peas should have crisp young, well-filled pods, with a little air space left between the individual peas. Over-full pods may give tough, hard peas. Home or locally grown ones are often the best because they are more likely to be freshly picked. Mange-tout should be eaten as soon as possible after picking. They are eaten whole before the peas start to swell in the pod.

Preparation Shell, discarding any that are blemished or discoloured and wash in running cold water. Use fresh peas as soon as they are shelled, or cover with washed pods if not used immediately; they lose their flavour if soaked. For mange-tout rinse pods and trim ends. Mange-tout can be eaten raw in salads.

Basic cooking Cook peas in boiling water, with a sprig of mint and 1 teaspoon of sugar, for 5-15 minutes or until just tender. Drain well. Either steam mange-tout for about 5 minutes, stir-fry or sauté in butter.

Season and toss in melted butter.

❧ Peppers ❧
green, red and yellow

Imported peppers are available all year round. Look for firm, shiny peppers. The flavour of green peppers is sharper than that of red and yellow peppers.
Preparation Rinse under cold running water, slice off the stem end and take out the core, seeds and inside ribs. Cut into slices or rings. Alternatively, grill until the skins blacken and blister, then rub the skins off. Slices of crisp-textured and strong-flavoured raw pepper make colourful additions to salads.
Basic cooking Steam whole peppers for 12 minutes, or stuff and bake whole or halved (see page 235).

❧ Potatoes ❧

Different varieties of potato are available all year round. New potatoes are in season in summer. Sweet potatoes are available from September to June. Look for smooth, evenly sized, firm potatoes, free of blemishes. New potatoes should have skins so soft they will rub off with your thumb.
Preparation Scrub new potatoes; scrub, then cut off any scabbed or discoloured parts of old or sweet potatoes, and gouge out any 'eyes'. Peel if to be cooked in slices or roasted. Cut large potatoes into even pieces, or scrub potatoes and cook them in their skins. Either eat the potatoes in their skins, which contain most of the goodness, or peel them after cooking. For deep-frying, cut peeled raw potatoes so that they are 7.5 x 1 cm (3 x ¼ in) square for chips, and 5 cm x 5 mm (2 x 1/8 in) for French fries. Soak the sticks in cold water for 30-45 minutes to remove excess starch. For baked potatoes, choose those of equal size and scrub. Prick with a fork and brush with oil. For game chips or potato crisps cut raw, peeled potatoes into very thin rounds. Rinse well and dry.
Basic cooking Cook new potatoes in boiling water for 15 minutes and old potatoes for 25-30 minutes. Drain well. New potatoes are delicious steamed for 20-25 minutes. For roast potatoes, parboil for 5-7 minutes and roast with the fat round the meat at 220C (425F) mark 7 for 40-50 minutes, turning halfway through. To shallow-fry or sauté, boil until just cooked, slice into 5 mm (1 ¼ in) rounds and cook gently in a little hot fat, until lightly browned on both sides. Drain on absorbent paper. To deep-fry, heat the oil to 190C (375F). Quarter-fill the basket with chips and lower into the oil. Cook until light

gold in colour. Drain on absorbent paper. Repeat with the remaining chips. Reheat the oil and fry all the chips until crisp and golden. Drain well and sprinkle with salt. Place baking potatoes in the oven at 200C (400F) mark 6 for 45-55 minutes. For game chips, fry thin slices until golden brown. Sweet potatoes can be baked, boiled or parboiled and then sautéed.

Serve boiled and steamed potatoes with melted butter. For creamed potatoes, mash with a fork or potato masher and beat in seasoning, butter and a little milk or single cream. Reheat gently, beating until fluffy. For baked potatoes, make a small cross-cut in the top of each potato and put a dab of butter, margarine or a little soured cream on top.

❧ Pumpkins ❧

Pumpkin is available from June to January.
Preparation Wash and peel. Cut into wedges or 5 cm (2 in) chunks.
Basic cooking Roast with a little butter and lemon juice for 1-2 hours, or steam for 35-40 minutes.

Serve with a little melted butter and chopped parsley if steamed.

❧ Radishes ❧

Radishes are available all year round. Look for firm, brightly coloured radishes, free from blemishes. Red is the most common colour, but yellow, white and black varieties are available.
Preparation Cut off any stalk or leaves and trim the roots. Wash in cold water. Radishes are usually eaten raw.
Basic cooking Cook in boiling water for 5-10 minutes, according to size. Drain.

Mix cooked radishes with other root vegetables in melted butter and parsley. Use raw radishes sliced, or grated in salads.

❧ Salsify ❧
and scorzonera

Available from October to March. These are long thin roots like parsnip; salsify is white and scorzonera black. Salsify is often known as the 'oyster plant' because of its distinctive flavour. Do not try to scrape or peel scorzonera as its distinctive flavour is mainly to be found in the thin layer of skin.

Preparation Scrub either root carefully and cut into 5 cm (2 in) lengths. Both shrivel and discolour when exposed to air so use immediately.

Basic cooking Put in boiling water sharpened with lemon juice and cook for about 30 minutes until tender. Drain.

Season and sprinkle lightly with melted Maître d'Hôtel butter (see page 344) or in a White Sauce (see page 339). Cooled cooked salsify can be served in French Dressing (see page 347) as a salad.

❦ Sea kale ❦

Available from December to May.

Preparation Wash and cut stems into short lengths.

Basic cooking Boil leaves and stems for 15 minutes until just tender, or steam for 10-20 minutes. Drain well.

Serve with Hollandaise Sauce (see page 347) or melted butter.

❦ Spinach ❦

Spinach is in season all year round. Look for bright green, tender leaves. Avoid spinach that is yellow or wilted. Buy plenty as spinach reduces greatly during cooking.

Preparation Wash well with several changes of water to remove all the grit. For winter or perpetual spinach, remove coarser stalks and centre ribs. For summer spinach, trim the base and stalks and keep the leaves whole. Raw young spinach leaves make a delicious salad.

Basic cooking Bring 1 cm (¼ in) water to simmering point. Put in the wet leaves and cook gently for 5-10 minutes until limp and tender. Drain, pressing out excess water. Steam for 5-10 minutes in the water that remains on the leaves after washing. Coarser spinach may take a little longer to cook. Drain cooked spinach well.

Season and dress hot spinach with melted butter or finely chop the leaves, dress with a little hot cream and season with salt, black pepper and a little pinch of nutmeg.

❦ Swedes ❦

Swedes are available from September to May. Select smaller swedes where possible, avoiding those that have been in any way damaged during the process of lifting.

Preparation Scrub and peel swedes to remove all the tough skin and roots. Cut into equal-sized pieces or slices and keep covered in water as swedes discolour quickly.

Basic cooking Cook in boiling water for 30 minutes until tender. Alternatively, steam for 35-40 minutes. Drain well. Swedes can also be mashed, roasted and puréed.

Season with black pepper.

❦ Sweetcorn ❦

Sweetcorn is available from July to October and from February to April. Choose medium-sized cobs with leaves wrapped tightly round them. When the leaves are parted the corn kernels should show plump and very pale yellow; they should exude a milky liquid when dented with a thumbnail.

Preparation Cut off the stalks and remove the outer leaves and 'silk'.

Basic cooking Place some of the husks in a large pan, with the cobs on top. Cover with boiling water and cook for 5-15 minutes depending on age, until a kernel lifts off the cob easily. Take care to drain the cobs well.

Serve at once with salt, black pepper and a generous amount of melted butter. If the cobs are very young, the kernels can be scraped off with a sharp knife, standing the cob on its stem end and slicing downwards towards the stem.

❦ Swiss chard ❦

A nutritious vegetable available from September to May. Choose fresh-looking crisp stalks and clean dark leaves.

Preparation Prepare and use the delicious fleshy stalks, raw or cooked, as for celery (see page 224). Wash and treat the leaves in the same ways as spinach (see left).

Basic cooking Cook the stalks in all the same ways as celery. Cook the leaves like spinach, but season less strongly.

Serve tossed in a little melted butter.

❧ Tomatoes ❧

Tomatoes are available all year round, but they are best from late spring to autumn. Look for firm, unblemished, light red tomatoes. Dark red tomatoes may be over-ripe.

Preparation Wash, wipe dry and remove the calyx and any stem. Halve, slice or cut into wedges as required. To skin, dip in boiling water for 1-2 minutes and then plunge into cold water. Strip off the skin from the stem end. Use raw or cooked.

Basic cooking Halve tomatoes and fry in hot oil for 3-5 minutes, turning once. Grill with a dab of fat on top of the cut side of each half for 5-10 minutes, depending on thickness. To bake tomatoes, cut a cross in one end, top with a little butter and seasoning and bake at 180C (350F) mark 4 for 10-20 minutes depending on size.

❧ Turnips ❧

Turnips are available all year round. Look for turnips with clean unblemished skins. Buy tender early turnips with pale green skins in spring and early summer. Main-crop turnips are less tender, with creamy coloured skins.

Preparation Trim early turnips and peel thinly for eating raw – leave the skins on for cooking. Peel main-crop turnips thickly and cut into pieces or slices before cooking. Cook immediately as they discolour rapidly.

Basic cooking Cook early turnips whole in boiling water for 20-30 minutes, drain and rub off the skins. Cook prepared main-crop turnips in boiling water for 15-25 minutes, depending on size. Drain well. Turnips may also be cut into large dice and steamed for 15 minutes.

Toss early turnips in melted butter or coat in Cheese Sauce (see page 339). Main-crop turnips can be mashed with milk and butter, or puréed (see page 221).

❧ Watercress ❧

Watercress is available all year round. It should be crisp, fresh and free from any discoloured or slimy leaves.

Preparation Trim and wash well and serve as part of a salad or as a garnish.

VEGETABLES AS LIGHT AND MAIN MEALS

A collection of filling and sustaining dishes from
Hot Stuffed Artichokes to Spinach Soufflé.

RATATOUILLE

Serves 4-6

3 medium-sized aubergines
salt
75 g (3 oz) margarine
2 large onions, skinned and sliced
1 garlic clove, crushed
1 green pepper, seeded and sliced
2-3 courgettes, sliced
4-6 tomatoes, skinned and quartered
pepper
2 bay leaves
chopped parsley to garnish

❧ Slice the aubergines and then sprinkle the slices with salt. Leave for 30 minutes while preparing the other vegetables.

❧ Melt the margarine in a pan, add the sliced onions, garlic and sliced pepper. Cover the pan and cook over a low heat for 5 minutes without browning. the onions.

❧ Drain and dry the aubergine slices and add them to the pan with all the other ingredients except the parsley. Cover and simmer for 30 minutes. Remove the bay leaves.

❧ Place the ratatouille in a warmed serving dish, and sprinkle with parsley; or leave, covered, in a cool place until cold.

❧ Serve hot or cold, as a starter, side dish or main dish with rice or pasta.

MIXED VEGETABLE STIR-FRY

Serves 4

225 g (8 oz) small cauliflower florets
1 yellow or red sweet pepper, deseeded and cut
  into small strips
3 tbsp oil
100 g (4 oz) onion, finely chopped
2 small carrots, coarsely grated
6 tbsp Basic Vegetable Stock (see page 336)
salt and freshly ground black pepper
2 small courgettes, coarsely grated
25 g (1 oz) flaked almonds
2 tbsp dry sherry
1 tbsp tomato juice
450 g (1 lb) freshly cooked or reheated brown
  rice

❦ Steam the cauliflower florets and strips of pepper over boiling water for 5 minutes.

❦ Heat half the oil in a wok or deep frying pan with a spatter-proof cover. Add the onion and fry until soft. Add the remaining oil, cauliflower florets, pepper strips and grated carrot. Stir over a fairly high heat for 3 minutes.

❦ Add the stock, reduce the heat and cover the pan. Cook gently for 4 minutes, stirring twice. Season and stir in the courgettes and all the remaining ingredients except the rice. Stir, uncovered, for 2 minutes, mixing the ingredients well.

❦ Serve with the brown rice.

SUMMER VEGETABLE FLAN

Serves 4

175 g (6 oz) Flaky Pastry (see page 361)
225 g (8 oz) or more, mixed young vegetables
1 tomato, peeled
1 spring onion
1 tsp chopped parsley
salt and freshly ground black pepper
275 ml (½ pint) Cheese Sauce (see page 339)
25 g (1 oz) cheese

❦ Heat the oven to 220C (425F) mark 7. Line an 18 cm (7 in) ovenproof plate or flan case with the pastry. Bake the pastry case blind (see page 357).

❦ Prepare a mixture of young summer vegetables: sliced carrots, small broad beans, peas and diced courgettes. Cut the flesh of the tomato into small squares. Finely chop the spring onion.

❦ Simmer the vegetables in salted water until just tender. Drain. Fold in the tomato and spring onion. Season well with salt and pepper. Add the parsley and fold it all into the sauce mornay. Fill the flan case and sprinkle with the finely grated cheese.

❦ Return to the oven for 15 minutes if serving hot, or serve cold.

GREEN VEGETABLE CURRY

Serves 4-6

100 g (4 oz) desiccated coconut
2 tsp ground coriander
1 ¼ tsp each ground cumin and ginger
pinch each of ground cinnamon and cloves
⅓ tsp chilli powder
⅓ tsp turmeric
75 g (3 oz) shredded cabbage
100 g (4 oz) green peas, shelled
100 g (4 oz) green beans sliced
225 g (8 oz) potatoes peeled and diced
3 tbsp corn oil
2 medium-sized onions, chopped
50 g (2 oz) green pepper, deseeded and chopped
¼-½ tsp salt
2 tsp lemon juice

❦ The coconut milk should be made and the spices mixed well ahead. Make the coconut milk by pouring 275 ml (½ pint) boiling water over the desiccated coconut. Leave for 2 hours. Process both the coconut and liquid in an electric blender for 30 seconds. Strain through a cloth-lined sieve and squeeze the residue in the cloth to extract all the milk. Mix all the spices together. Set to one side.

❦ Put the cabbage, peas, beans and diced potatoes into another 275 ml (½ pint) boiling water in a pan. Reduce the heat, simmer for 5 minutes and drain.

❦ Heat the oil in a second pan add the onions and stir until beginning to brown. Add the pepper and spices and stir. Add the simmered vegetables, season with salt and cook for 4 minutes, stirring once twice. Add the coconut milk and lemon juice and cook gently until the vegetables are tender.

LANCASHIRE TURNOVER

Serves 4-6

225 g (8 oz) Flaky Pastry (see page 361)
4 shallots
50 g (2 oz) butter
2 Cox's apples
225 g (8 oz) Lancashire cheese
salt and pepper
1 egg to glaze

❦ Heat the oven to 220C (425F) mark 7.
❦ Roll out the pastry to an oblong and trim the edges. Simmer the shallots in the butter until transparent. Peel, core and slice the apples thinly. Turn over a time or two in the butter with the shallots. Season.
❦ Grate the cheese over the top half of the pastry oblong, to within 2.5 cm (1 in) of the edge. Spread the onion and apple mixture evenly over the cheese. Brush the top edges with water. Fold the bottom half up and press the edges together firmly. Decorate with a fork or knock up (see page 357).
❦ Cut two or three diagonal slits across the top of the pastry and brush with egg yolk. Cook for 20-30 minutes until well risen and golden brown.

ASPARAGUS FLAN

Serves 4

175 g (6 oz) Flaky Pastry (see page 361)
225-300 g (8-10 oz) asparagus or 300 g (10 oz) can asparagus tips
salt
275 ml (½ pint) Béchamel sauce (see page 340)

❦ Heat the oven to 220C (425F) mark 7. Line an 18 cm (7 in) ovenproof plate or flan ring with the pastry. Bake blind (see page 357). Keep hot.
❦ Wash the asparagus; tie loosely into a bundle. Simmer in salted water until tender. Drain and cut into 2.5 cm (1 in) lengths, discarding any hard stalks. Keep hot.
❦ Arrange the asparagus in the pastry case, reserving a few tips. Pour the hot béchamel sauce over the asparagus and garnish with the tips. Serve at once.

GARLIC SALE

Serves 4

175 g (6 oz) Simple Cheese Pastry (see page 358)
275 ml (½ pint) Béchamel Sauce (see page 340), cooled
3 eggs
150 g (5 oz) grated garlic cheese
grate or two of nutmeg

❦ Heat the oven to 200C (400F) mark 6.
❦ Roll out the pastry and use to line an 18 cm (7 in) ovenproof flan dish. Bake blind (see page 357).
❦ Beat the eggs into the cool sauce followed by the cheese. Pour into the pastry case, grate a little nutmeg over it and cook for about 30 minutes until well browned.

LEEK PIE

Serves 4-6

4 rashers bacon
6 young leeks, washed and thinly sliced
1 bay leaf
black pepper
water or stock
1 egg, beaten
2 tbsp top of the milk
175 g (6 oz) Flaky Pastry (see page 361)

❦ Heat the oven to 220C (425F) mark 7.
❦ Rind the bacon, and cut into small strips. Put leeks and bacon with the bay leaf and black pepper into a pan. Cover with water or stock. Simmer until the liquid has almost gone. Take off the heat and cool a little.
❦ Beat the egg with the top of the milk and stir most of it into the leek mixture, retaining a little for glazing. Spoon into a shallow pie plate.
❦ Roll the pastry out thinly, a little larger than the dish. Cut a strip for the edge of the dish. Dampen the edge and press the strip on to it. Dampen the strip, cover the pie with the pastry and press well down. Knock up the edges with the back of a knife.
❦ Brush the pastry with the remains of the egg and milk. Make a hole in the top to let the steam out. Cook for 30 minutes until golden brown.

CREAMED SPINACH FLAN

Serves 4

175 g (6 oz) Flaky Pastry (see page 361)
350 g (12 oz) frozen spinach
salt and pepper
2 eggs
100 ml (4 fl oz) double cream
2 tbsp grated cheese
milk to glaze

❦ Heat the oven to 220C (425F) mark 7.
❦ Line an 18 or 20 cm (7 or 8 in) ovenproof plate with the pastry. Neaten the edge and prick decoratively with a fork. Bake blind (see page 357). Reduce the oven temperature to 180C (350F) mark 4.
❦ Cook the spinach in the water it produces as it thaws. When tender, drain well. Season with salt and freshly ground black pepper. Beat the eggs and cream together and fold into the spinach. Fill the pastry case with the mixture. Sprinkle with grated cheese.
❦ Brush the pastry edge with milk to glaze it. Cook for about 30 minutes until golden brown on top.

COURGETTE QUICHE

Serves 4

225 g (8 oz) Pâte Brisée or Rich Shortcrust Pastry (see page 359)
oil
1 onion, finely chopped
450 g (1 lb) courgettes, thinly sliced
salt and pepper
3 eggs
150 ml (¼ pint) milk
100 g (4 oz) finely grated cheese

❦ Heat the oven to 200C (400F) mark 6. Line a 20 cm (8 in) fluted flan dish with the pastry and bake blind (see page 357).
❦ Heat the oil and sweat the onion in it until translucent. Add some courgettes to the pan. Cook for 10-15 minutes. Cook in batches and keep hot.
❦ Lift the courgettes and onion out of the oil with a slotted spoon and put neatly into the warm flan case. Season.

❦ Beat together the eggs and milk. Pour carefully into the flan case and sprinkle the cheese over the top. Cook for 20-30 minutes until set and browned.
❦ Serve hot or cold.

STUFFED AUBERGINES

Serves 4

2 medium sized aubergines
salt
3-4 tbsp oil
100 g (4 oz) button mushrooms, finely chopped
1 medium-sized onion, skinned and finely chopped
1 medium-to-large tomato, skinned and chopped
1 tsp dried basil or thyme
50 g (2 oz) soft white breadcrumbs
1 tbsp chopped parsley
50 g (2 oz) black olives, stoned and chopped
2 tbsp grated Cheddar cheese

❦ Halve the aubergines lengthwise, and make crisscross slits in the cut sides. Sprinkle with salt, and leave cut side down on a rack for 30 minutes.
❦ Brush the cut sides with oil and cook gently under a low grill until tender, turning once. Scoop out most of the flesh, leaving shells 5-10 mm (¼-½ in) thick. Reserve the pulp. Heat the oven to 200C (400F) mark 6.
❦ Heat 2 tbsp of the remaining oil, and fry the mushrooms and onion for 3-5 minutes until soft. Add the tomato and dried herbs. Reserve 2 tbsp of the breadcrumbs and add the rest to the pan with the aubergine pulp, parsley and olives; mix well. Fill the aubergine shells with the mixture.
❦ Mix the remaining breadcrumbs and cheese together and use to cover the stuffing. Sprinkle with oil. Place the aubergine halves, cut side up, in an oiled shallow baking tin. Bake for 15-20 minutes until well heated through and golden on top.

STUFFED GREEN PEPPERS

Serves 4

2 large green peppers
1 tbsp oil
40 g (1 ½ oz) onion, finely chopped
40 g (1 ½ oz) celery, finely chopped
75 g (3 oz) carrot, grated or finely chopped
175 g (6 oz) cooked haricot beans, finely
    chopped
75 g (3 oz) tomato, chopped coarsely
¼ tsp salt
black pepper
pinch of dried thyme
good pinch of dried basil
3 sprigs parsley, chopped
150 ml (¼ pint) tomato juice
4 tbsp coarsely grated cheese

❦ Rinse the peppers, cut off the stalks and halve the
fruit lengthwise. Take out the cores, seeds and inside
ribs. Put the halves in a pan of boiling water, bring
back to the boil and leave to stand off the heat while
making the stuffing. Heat the oven to 180C (350F)
mark 4.
❦ Heat the oil in a fairly large frying pan, add the
onion and celery, and stir over a low heat until gold-
en brown. Add the carrot and continue stirring until
just tender. Stir in the beans, tomato, seasoning and
dried herbs and simmer, stirring, for 5-6 minutes
until well blended. Take off the heat. Stir in the
parsley. Leave to stand while draining the peppers.
❦ Place the pepper halves, cut side up, in a shallow
baking dish. Season inside and fill with the stuffing.
Pour the tomato juice into the dish around (not over)
the peppers. Cover the dish with greased foil.
❦ Bake for 30 minutes or until pepper halves are
tender. Uncover, and top the pepper halves with
cheese. Return to the oven, uncovered, for 5 minutes
to brown the cheese.

SAVOURY TOMATO PIES

Makes 4

225 g (8 oz) Hot Water Crust Pastry made with
    225 g (8 oz) flour, 90 g (3 ½ oz) lard and 3 ½
    tbsp liquid (see page 362 for method)
6 tomatoes
100 g (4 oz) green and red peppers, mixed
1 onion
1 garlic clove
½ tsp chopped marjoram
1 tsp freshly chopped basil
salt and pepper
1 egg to glaze
little stock
1 tsp powdered gelatine

❦ Keep the pastry warm. Heat the oven to 200C
(400F) mark 6.
❦ Skin the tomatoes and chop. Slice and deseed the
peppers. Peel and dice the onion and garlic. Reserve
any juices from the vegetables. Add the herbs and
season well.
❦ Divide the pastry into four. Use to line patty tins
as in the recipe for Mutton Pies (see page 143), keeping one-third of each piece for the lid. Fill with the
mixture and brush the edges of the pastry with beat-
en egg. Roll out the lids, position and press well
together.
❦ Make a hole in the top of each, flute, and decorate with a few small leaves and roses made from the
trimmings. Brush with beaten egg. Cook for 30-40
minutes.
❦ Use the reserved juice mixed with stock to make
up to 150 ml (¼ pint) and dissolve the gelatine in it
for a jelly. Pour into the pies when cold.

Variation
These can be made with canned tomatoes and
pimentos and a pinch of dried herbs.

CAULIFLOWER FRITTERS

Serves 4

225 g (8 oz) flour
1 tsp salt
2 tbsp oil
225 ml (8 fl oz) milk and water mixed
oil for deep-frying
600 g (1 ¼ lb) small cauliflower florets
3 egg whites

❦ Make a coating batter by sifting together the flour and salt into a bowl and making a hollow in the centre. Put in the oil and a little of the liquid. Stir in the flour, little by little, while adding the remaining liquid gradually; then beat the batter mixture briskly until smooth. Chill until the florets are ready. Set a pan of oil to heat to 180C (350F).
❦ Parboil the florets for 4 minutes, then drain and dry them thoroughly. Whisk the egg whites until stiff. Give the batter mixture a last beat, thinning it with a little more water if necessary, and fold in the egg whites.
❦ Dip the florets one by one in the batter and fry them in small batches in the hot oil, turning them as needed. Remove them with a slotted spoon when golden-brown and drain on kitchen paper.
❦ Serve with Hollandaise Sauce (see page 345).

SPRING LOAF

Serves 4-6

2 small carrots
1 medium-sized onion
1 tbsp oil
350 g (12 oz) cooked spring greens or cabbage, chopped
½ tsp each fresh thyme and marjoram, chopped, or ¼ tsp dried herbs
6 eggs
½ tsp salt
flaked butter or margarine

❦ Heat the oven to 180C (350F) mark 4.
❦ Grate the carrot and onion coarsely. Heat the oil and stir the grated vegetables in it for 2 minutes. Turn them into a bowl and mix in the chopped greens and herbs. Beat the eggs lightly and fold them in with the salt.
❦ Grease or line and grease a 450 g (1 lb) loaf tin. Turn in the mixture, and dot with flaked butter or margarine. Bake for 40 minutes.
❦ Serve hot, or cool in the tin for slicing cold. The loaf shrinks as it cools.

STUFFED TOMATOES

Serves 4

1 aubergine (about 275 g/10 oz)
½ tsp salt
8 firm tomatoes (about 100 g/4 oz each)
1 tbsp butter or margarine, softened
1 large egg, beaten
25 g (1 oz) onion, finely chopped
1 tsp dried thyme
salt and black pepper
6 tbsp grated Cheshire cheese
8 tbsp soft white breadcrumbs

❦ Peel the aubergine and slice it into rounds. Immediately put them into a pan, add the salt and pour in 2.5 cm (1 in) depth of boiling water. Cover tightly, bring back to the boil and cook until soft. While cooking, cut the tops off the tomatoes, scoop out the seeds and juice and turn upside down to drain. Heat the oven to 190C (375F) mark 5.
❦ Drain the aubergine slices. Mash them or blend in a food processor with the butter or margarine, egg, onion, thyme, seasoning and 3 tablespoons of the cheese. Add enough breadcrumbs to make a stuffing which is soft but not sloppy.
❦ Season the tomato cases lightly inside and fill with the mixture. Place cut side up in a greased, shallow baking tin or dish. Cover loosely with greased foil and bake for 25 minutes. Uncover, sprinkle with the remaining cheese and bake for a further 5 minutes or until the cheese is melted and the tomatoes are soft.

POOR MAN'S GOOSE

Serves 4-6

1 medium-sized marrow (about 1 kg/2 ¼ lb)
100 g (4 oz) margarine, softened
1 large onion, peeled
1 celery stalk
100 g (4 oz) cracked wheat
150 ml (¼ pint) strong Basic Vegetable Stock
    (see page336)
150 ml (¼ pint) dry still cider or apple juice
salt and pepper
1 cooking apple (about 175 g/6 oz)
6-8 fresh sage leaves, chopped or ½ tsp dried
    sage
50 g (2 oz) seedless raisins

❦ Wash the marrow, split it lengthwise and remove the seeds and fibre. Prick the skin of both halves with a knife point in several places and brush the hollows with a little of the margarine. Chop the onion and celery finely.

❦ Melt 50 g (2 oz) of the margarine in a large deep frying pan and fry the onion and celery until soft. Add the cracked wheat, stock and cider or juice with a little seasoning. Bring slowly to simmering point, cover and simmer for 15 minutes.

❦ While simmering, peel, core and chop the apple. When the cracked wheat is cooked, add the apple, sage and raisins. Mix well and leave until cool enough to handle. Heat the oven to 190C (375F) mark 5.

❦ Fill both marrow halves with the mixture. Reshape the marrow or bake the two halves separately. Put the re-shaped marrow or both halves (cut side up) in a baking tin. Roll any remaining stuffing into forcemeat balls and add them to the tin. Dot the tops of the marrow halves or the top skin of a reshaped marrow with margarine and add any left over to the tin.

❦ Cover the dish loosely with greased foil. Bake for 1-1 ½ hours; the marrow should be tender but not mushy. Baste with the margarine two or three times while baking.

❦ Uncover the tin for the last 20 minutes to brown the marrow, baste well, then complete the cooking. Serve with apple sauce.

CABBAGE AND MUSHROOM CRUMBLE

Serves 4

450 g (1 lb) firm-hearted green cabbage
3 tbsp margarine
1 tbsp clear honey
1 tbsp lemon juice
salt and black pepper
175 g (6 oz) button mushrooms
pinch of grated nutmeg
soft breadcrumbs from 2 wholemeal bread
    slices
25 g (1 oz) salted peanuts, chopped
melted margarine

❦Shred the cabbage, removing the core and any hard ribs. Melt the margarine in a pan and toss the cabbage in it over a moderate heat for 1 minute.

❦ Add the honey, most of the lemon juice, a little seasoning and 4 tablespoons water. Reduce the heat, cover, and simmer gently for 10 minutes, stirring twice during cooking.

❦ Meanwhile, slice the mushrooms and cook in a little water sharpened with the remaining lemon juice for 3 minutes, then drain and sprinkle with nutmeg.

❦ Spread half the cabbage in a shallow 18 cm (7 in) baking dish. Spread the mushrooms over it then top them evenly with the rest of the cabbage. Mix the breadcrumbs and peanuts and scatter them over the top. Sprinkle with melted margarine and put under the grill to brown.

SPINACH ROULADE

Serves 4

450 g (1 lb) cooked spinach, chopped
1 tbsp butter or margarine, softened
4 eggs, separated
1 tbsp plain flour
3 tbsp grated Cheddar cheese
salt and pepper

Filling
15 g (½ oz) butter
175 g (6 oz) mushrooms
275 ml (½ pint) White Sauce (thick coating consistency, see page 339)

❦ Heat the oven to 190C (375F) mark 5. Prepare a 20 x 33 cm (8 x 13 in) Swiss roll tin by greasing and lining with baking parchment. Grease the parchment lightly.
❦ Drain the chopped spinach in a nylon strainer. Cream the butter or margarine in a bowl by beating with an electric or rotary beater. Beat in the egg yolks until well blended. Sprinkle with the flour, cheese and seasoning and beat them in, followed by the spinach. In a separate bowl, whisk the egg whites until stiff, then fold them into the mixture.
❦ Spread the spinach mixture gently and evenly over the prepared Swiss roll tin. Bake for 15 minutes or until the spinach mixture is firm.
❦ Meanwhile make the filling by melting the butter and gently cooking the mushrooms. Drain. Heat through the white sauce and add the mushrooms.
❦ Place a sheet of greased baking parchment, greased side down over the tin. Holding the parchment and tin together, turn them over, and lay on a flat surface. Lift off the tin, and carefully peel off the lining parchment.
❦ Spread the spinach mixture with the filling, then roll it up like a Swiss roll from one short end. An easy way to do this is to lift the parchment under one end so that the end curls over, then use a palette knife to ease it gently into a scroll.
❦ Serve at once if possible; the roll solidifies as it cools; although still good even when cooled and reheated, it is not quite as delicious.

Variations
The roulade can also be stuffed with fish in a thick cream sauce; any stuffing mix; asparagus tips with prawns and Cheese Sauce (see page 339).

SPINACH SOUFFLE

Serves 6

450 g (1 lb) fresh spinach
2 tbsp onion, grated
75 g (3 oz) butter, softened
pinch of grated nutmeg
3 tbsp flour
275 ml (½ pint) milk
100 g (4 oz) full-fat soft cheese
pinch of paprika
salt and pepper
4 eggs, separated

❦ Remove the stalks and any coarse ribs from the spinach. Cook it in very little, if any, water until tender. Drain, then squeeze as dry as possible. Chop it, then mash, pound or process it in a food processor until smooth.
❦ Cook the grated onion gently in 4 teaspoons of the butter until soft, and mix it into the spinach purée with the nutmeg.
❦ Heat the oven to 190C (375F) mark 5. Grease a 750 ml (1 ½ pint) soufflé dish with a little butter.
❦ Melt the remaining butter over a low heat. Stir in the flour and cook, stirring, for 2 minutes, without letting the flour colour. Pour in the milk gradually, stirring constantly, and continue stirring until the sauce thickens.
❦ Add the cheese by spoonfuls and stir until melted and blended. Then stir in the spinach purée, a small pinch of paprika and seasoning to taste. Take off the heat and cool for 5 minutes.
❦ Meanwhile beat the egg yolks until liquid. Beat them into the spinach mixture. Whisk the egg whites until stiff but not dry. Stir 1 tablespoon into the spinach panada. Fold in the rest lightly. Turn the mixture gently into the soufflé dish. Bake for 25 to 30 minutes. Serve immediately.

CHICORY ROLLS

Serves 4

8 medium-sized heads of chicory with yellow
    leaf-tips
juice of ½ lemon
pinch of salt
8 slices of cooked ham, large enough to enclose
    chicory heads
butter or margarine
275 ml (½ pint) coating White Sauce (see page
    339)
25 g (1 oz) grated cheese

❦ Choose chicory heads about the same size. Trim
the root ends, then gouge out the centre cores.
Remove any discoloured leaves. Rinse.
❦ Put the heads into a pan of boiling water, and
blanch for 5 minutes to reduce the bitter taste.
Drain. Bring the minimum of fresh water to the boil,
add the lemon juice and salt and the chicory. Cook
until tender, 12–20 minutes. Drain, and allow to cool
slightly on a board, then gently squeeze out excess
moisture. Heat the oven to 180C (350F) mark 4.
❦ Spread one side of each ham slice with butter.
Lay a chicory head on the spread side of each slice;
wrap the ham around the chicory. Arrange the rolls
in one layer in a greased, shallow baking dish suitable for serving. Cover with the white sauce, sprinkle with cheese and bake for 7–10 minutes.

HOT STUFFED ARTICHOKES

Serves 4

4 large French globe artichokes
lemon juice
oil
450 g (1 lb) cooked green peas, fresh or frozen
few leaves of fresh mint
salt and pepper
grated nutmeg
275 ml (½ pint) coating White Sauce (see page
    339)
1 egg yolk, beaten
1–2 tbsp cream

❦ Trim the tops off the artichokes and neaten the
leaf tips and twist off the stalks so that they stand flat.
Immerse the artichokes, stem ends down, in gently
boiling water adding a little lemon juice and oil to
prevent discoloration.
❦ While boiling the artichokes, purée the peas with
the mint leaves and seasonings (in a blender if possible). Make the sauce, or reheat it if made ahead,
and beat in the egg yolk and cream. Stir over a very
low heat, without boiling, to cook the egg yolk and
blend into the purée. Heat the oven to 180C (350F)
mark 4.
❦ When the artichokes are cooked (30–50 minutes),
an outer leaf should pull off easily; turn them upside
down and allow to drain. Spread out the tops of the
artichokes and scoop out the hairy 'choke' with a
spoon. Fill the centre with the purée. Wrap each
artichoke in foil and reheat in the oven for 12–15
minutes.

MAGGIE'S STUFFED ARTICHOKES

Serves 4

4 large French globe artichokes
shredded smoked salmon trimmings
lemon juice
ground black pepper
425 ml (¾ pint) soured cream

❦ Trim the tops off the artichokes and neaten the
leaf tips and twist off the stalks so that they stand
level. Immerse in gently boiling salted water, adding
a little lemon juice and oil to prevent discoloration.
When the artichokes are cooked (30–50 minutes), an
outer leaf should pull off easily. Turn them upside
down and leaver to drain; allow to cool completely.
Spread out the leaves, removing the small centre
cone, and scoop out the inedible hairy 'choke' with a
spoon.
❦ Season the smoked salmon with lemon juice and
ground black pepper to taste. Fill the artichokes with
the mixture. The quantity will depend on the size of
the artichokes and the shreds. Serve with soured
cream.

Variation
For a decorative and cheaper filling, use two 200 g
(8 oz) packets of frozen crab sticks. Thaw and chop,
then bind with some of the cream or with mayonnaise and use as above.

BEANSPROUT AND OLIVE STIR-FRY

Serves 2

100 g (4 oz) wholemeal pasta shells
2 tbsp corn oil
2 carrots (75 g/3 oz each), coarsely chopped
1 sweet red pepper, deseeded and coarsely chopped
2 large shallots, thinly sliced
100 g (4 oz) button mushrooms, sliced
100 g (4 oz) garden peas
175 g (6 oz) beansprouts
10 black or green olives, drained, stoned and chopped
50 ml (2 fl oz) Basic Vegetable Stock (see page 336)
1 tbsp soy sauce
1 tbsp dry sherry
chopped parsley to garnish

❦ Cook the pasta shells in rapidly boiling salted water for 5-6 minutes or until tender. Drain and set to one side.

❦ Heat the oil in a wok or large frying pan. Add the carrots, pepper and shallots and stir over a medium-high heat for 3 minutes or until the pepper and shallot soften. Add the sliced mushrooms and stir for 2 minutes. Stir in the peas and beansprouts, and stir for another 2 minutes to soften the beansprouts. Mix in the pasta and olives and stir.

❦ Mix the liquids together and pour into the pan. Simmer for 2 minutes, stirring, to moisten the dish. Serve sprinkled with chopped parsley.

BRAISED CHINESE LEAVES

Serves 4

Chinese leaves (900 g/2 lb head)
2 slices of cooked ham, shredded
mirepoix of vegetables (see page 367)
Chicken or Vegetable Stock (see page 335 or 336)

Garnish
1 egg yolk, hard-boiled (optional)
chopped parsley (optional)

❦ Trim the root end of the head of leaves and remove any discoloured leaves or leaf tips. Wash the head and dry it. Slit from the top and almost to the root, carefully take out the crinkly pale heart and fill the space with the ham. Reshape the head and tie it tightly in two or three places. Parboil it for 5 minutes, then drain.

❦ Spread the mirepoix in the bottom of a heavy flame-proof casserole. Lay the head on top and pour in enough stock to cover half of it. Cover it with greased foil or greaseproof paper, then with a lid. Cook gently for 50-60 minutes on top of the stove or in the oven at 180C (350F) mark 4.

❦ Place the head on a serving dish and remove the string. Either boil down 150 ml (¼ pint) of the stock until syrupy and pour it over the cabbage, or top with crumbled hard-boiled egg yolk and chopped parsley.

VEGETABLES AS ACCOMPANIMENTS

A range of dishes using both common and unusual vegetables.

POLISH BROAD BEANS

Serves 4

450-675 g(1-1 ½ lb) broad beans, shelled
water or Basic Vegetable Stock (see page 336)
salt and pepper
2 tsp clear honey
1 tsp French Dijon mustard
150 ml (¼ pint) soured cream or natural
   yoghurt

❦ Cook the beans in the minimum of boiling water
or stock until just tender (12-15 minutes for very
small beans, 20-30 minutes for large ones). Drain
well and season lightly.
❦ Mix the honey and mustard with the cream or
yoghurt and add to the beans. Stir over a very low
heat, without boiling, until heated through.

FRENCH BEANS SOUBISE

Serves 4

450 g (1 lb) French beans
3 tbsp butter or margarine
12 large or 16 small spring onion bulbs,
   trimmed and sliced
juice of ½ lemon
salt and pepper

❦ Top, tail and string the beans and boil or steam
until just tender.
❦ Meanwhile, melt half the butter or margarine in
a pan, add the sliced onions and simmer until soft.
❦ Drain the beans when ready, toss with the
remaining butter, lemon juice and seasoning to taste,
and sprinkle with the onions.

MACEDOINE OF VEGETABLES

Serves 4

1 turnip
100 g (4 oz) carrots
few runner beans
225 g (8 oz) shelled peas
few cauliflower florets
225 g (8 oz) potatoes
850 ml (1 ½ pints) water
½ tsp salt
2-3 tbsp butter or margarine, melted
chopped parsley to garnish

❦ Prepare all the vegetables, and string, scrape or peel if needed. (Peel potatoes for this dish.) Cut the turnip, carrot and potato into 1 cm (½ in) dice and cut the beans into short lengths.
❦ Bring the water to the boil in a pan and add the turnip and carrot. Boil for 3 minutes. Add the beans and boil for 2 minutes more. Add the peas and cauliflower and finally the potato. Cook until the vegetables are tender but not broken or mushy. Drain (keep the cooking liquid for soup).
❦ Season, toss in butter and sprinkle with parsley. These make a colourful border or garnish for meat or other vegetable dishes.

Variation
A macédoine can also be served cold in mayonnaise. Omit the tossing in butter.

PETITS POIS A LA FRANÇAISE

Serves 4

¼ lettuce, shredded
6-8 spring onions (bulbs and white stems), sliced
1 sprig each of fresh mint and parsley
675 g (1 ½ lb) small tender fresh peas or frozen petits pois
75 g (3 oz) butter or margarine, melted
pinch of sugar
120 ml (4 fl oz) boiling water
salt and pepper

❦ Put all the ingredients except the seasoning and 25 g (1 oz) of butter or margarine into a pan, in the order given. Cover, and cook gently until the peas are tender, 5-10 minutes (or even less for petits pois). Remove the herbs, season well and add the remaining butter or margarine.

HERBED GREEN BEANS

Serves 4

450-675 g (1-1 ½ lb) green beans (French or runner)
2-3 tsp chopped parsley
2-3 tsp finely chopped chives or 2-3 tbsp finely chopped onion
salt and pepper
lemon juice
50-75 g (2-3 oz) Herb Butter (see page 344)

❦ Top, tail and string the beans. Slice the runner beans diagonally.
❦ Cook the beans, parsley and chives or onion in the minimum of boiling water until tender but still slightly crisp (small thin beans, 5-10 minutes, larger beans about 15 minutes). Drain well.
❦ Add a light seasoning of salt and pepper, a few drops of lemon juice and the herb butter in small portions. Toss to coat the beans with some of the butter. Serve in a warmed dish.

Note
If available, use thyme, savory or hyssop leaves for the herb butter.

BRUSSELS SPROUTS AND CHESTNUTS

Serves 4

350 g (12 oz) chestnuts
Brown Vegetable Stock (see page 346)
1 celery stalk, chopped
1 tsp sugar
675 g (1 ½ lb) Brussels sprouts
salt and freshly ground black pepper
butter for dressing

❦ Prepare the chestnuts by slitting the rounded sides of the outer skins. Put the nuts into cold water and bring to the boil. Drain and remove both the outer and inside skins. Quarter any large nuts.
❦ Return the nuts to the pan, just cover with stock and add the celery. Simmer gently until the nuts are tender, about 20-35 minutes.
❦ Cook the sprouts in the minimum of boiling water for 8-10 minutes. Drain, and return to the dry pan with the chestnuts. Season well with salt and black pepper and toss with butter.

GLAZED BRUSSELS SPROUTS

Serves 4

450 g (1 lb) Brussels sprouts
100 g(4 oz) button mushrooms
40 g (1 ½ oz) butter or margarine
salt and pepper
grated nutmeg
2 small onions, sliced into thin rings

❦ Boil the Brussels sprouts in the minimum of water until tender (8-10 minutes). Meanwhile, halve the mushrooms, or quarter them if large. Drain the sprouts when ready and set to one side.
❦ Melt 25 g (1 oz) of the butter or margarine in a frying pan big enough to hold the sprouts in one layer. Add the mushrooms, and sauté them for 2 minutes. Add the sprouts, and fry turning them over, for 4-5 minutes or until the sprouts are glazed and shiny and the mushrooms are tender.
❦ Season well with salt, pepper and a little nutmeg and transfer to a warmed shallow serving dish. Keep the dish warm.

❦ Add the remaining butter and the onion rings to the pan, and fry quickly until lightly browned. Spread them over the sprouts and mushrooms.
❦ Serve with roast meats or boiled ham.

SCALLOPED WHITE CABBAGE

Serves 4

1 small white cabbage, finely shredded
1 small onion, grated
275 ml (½ pint) boiling water
20 g (¾ oz) butter or margarine
2 level tbsp flour
150 ml (¼ pint) milk
75 g (3 oz) grated cheese
salt and pepper
grated nutmeg

❦ Boil the cabbage and onion in about 275 ml (½ pint) water for 5-8 minutes until tender. Drain, reserving the liquid. Put the cabbage in a greased ovenproof dish.
❦ Make a white sauce (see page 339) with the butter or margarine, flour, milk and 150 ml (¼ pint) of the reserved liquid. Reserve 2 tablespoons of the cheese and stir the rest into the sauce with the seasonings over a gentle heat. When the cheese melts, mix the sauce with the cabbage.
❦ Sprinkle with the reserved cheese and place under the grill to brown.

CASSEROLED RED CABBAGE

Serves 6

2 medium-sized onions, skinned and sliced
25 g (1 oz) bacon fat, dripping or margarine
1 kg (2 ¼ lb) red cabbage, finely shredded
350 g (12 oz) cooking apples, peeled, cored and sliced
2 tbsp golden syrup
salt and freshly ground black pepper
2 tbsp red wine vinegar
2 tbsp water
juice of ½ lemon

❧ Fry the onions in the fat until lightly browned. Layer the cabbage in a large casserole with the onions and the frying fat, the apples, syrup and seasoning.
❧ Pour over the vinegar, water and lemon juice. Cover tightly, and cook on the stove over a low heat, or in the oven at 180C (350F) mark 4 for 1 ½ hours.
❧ The cabbage re-heats perfectly or can be used cold instead of pickled red cabbage.

VICHY CARROTS

Serves 4

450 g (1 lb) carrots
425 ml (¾ pint) water
pinch of salt
3 tbsp butter
1 tbsp sugar
freshly ground pepper
chopped parsley to garnish

❧ Slice old carrots but leave young 'baby' carrots whole. Blanch old carrots in boiling water for 2 minutes, then drain.
❧ Return the carrots to the pan with the measured water, salt, 1 tablespoon of the butter and the sugar. Bring to the boil, and cook, uncovered, over a low heat until all the liquid has evaporated (30-45 minutes).
❧ Add 1-2 extra tablespoons butter to the pan, and a grinding of pepper. Shake the carrots, to mix them with the melting butter. Turn into a warmed dish and sprinkle with parsley.

GLAZED CARROTS

Serves 4

150 ml (¼ pint) water salt
600 g (1 ¼ lb) young carrots, cut into 'match-sticks'
2 tbsp butter or margarine
2 tsp light brown sugar
1 tsp lemon juice

Garnish
1 tsp chopped chives
1 tsp chopped parsley

❧ Bring the water to the boil in a pan. Add all the ingredients except the herbs. Half-cover and cook over a medium heat, shaking the pan, until almost all the water has evaporated.
❧ Take the pan off the heat, and continue shaking it until the carrots are all coated with glaze.
❧ Turn into a warmed dish and sprinkle with the herbs.

WHOLE STEAMED CAULIFLOWER

Serves 4

1 medium-sized cauliflower
2 tbsp butter, melted
salt and pepper

Garnish
1 hard-boiled egg yolk, sieved or 1 tbsp finely snipped chives and 1 tbsp crisply cooked crumbled bacon

❧ Cook the cauliflower stalk side down, in 5 cm (2 in) boiling water for 15-25 minutes until tender when pierced with a skewer.
❧ Put the head, again stalk side down, in a warmed serving dish. Pour the melted butter over it, season, and sprinkle with sieved egg yolk or chives and crumbled bacon.

CAULIFLOWER AU GRATIN

Serves 4

1 medium-sized cauliflower
40 g (1 ½ oz) butter or margarine
3 tbsp flour
275 ml (½ pint) milk
100 g (4 oz) grated Cheddar or Gruyère cheese
salt and pepper

❧ Cook the cauliflower stalk side down, in 5 cm (2 in) boiling water for 15-25 minutes until tender. Place the cooked head, stalk side down, in a warmed ovenproof dish.

❧ Make a cheese sauce by melting the butter or margarine then stirring in the flour and cooking for 2 minutes. Off the heat, trickle in the milk slowly, stirring constantly. Return to a low heat, bring to the boil, still stirring, and continue stilling until thick. Stir in 75 g (3 oz) of the cheese with the seasoning.

❧ As soon as the cheese melts, pour the sauce over the cauliflower. Sprinkle with the remaining cheese, and place under the grill or in a hot oven to brown the top.

❧ Alternatively, steam cauliflower florets over gently boiling water for about 15 minutes, lay them in a shallow dish and coat them with the sauce. Complete the dish as above.

GLAZED BROCCOLI

Serves 4

4 large or 8 small broccoli spears
3 small onions about 50 g (2 oz) each
3-4 small inside celery stalks
275 ml (½ pint) Brown Vegetable Stock (see page 336)
gravy browning
12-16 small strips of sweet red pepper

❧ Cut the stems off the broccoli to within 2 cm (¾ in) of the head. Slice the onions and celery thinly.

❧ Bring the stock to the boil in a pan with a few drops of gravy browning if it is pale. Add the broccoli, onion and celery and cook gently for 10-15 minutes or until the broccoli and celery are tender. Add a little extra stock if the liquid begins to dry out. At the end of the cooking time, it should be reduced to a syrupy glaze. Add the strips of pepper about 5 minutes before the end of the cooking time.

❧ Lift out the broccoli and place in a well-warmed dish. Arrange the flowers close together and tip the onions, celery and glaze over them. Top the dish with the shreds of pepper.

CELERIAC PUREE

equal quantities of smooth mashed potato (see page 228) and puréed celeriac (see page 221)
salt and freshly ground black pepper
¼ tsp grated nutmeg per 450 g (1 lb) puréed vegetables
softened butter (up to 2 tbsp per 450 g/1 lb puréed vegetables)
milk or single cream (up to 2 tbsp per 450 g/1 lb puréed vegetables)

❧ Beat together the mashed potato and celeriac purée until fully blended. Taste the purée and mix in extra potato if needed; a large celeriac root can be strongly flavoured.

❧ Season the mixed vegetable purée with salt and pepper and weigh it. Beat in the nutmeg and softened butter to taste. Add milk or cream little by little (a sloppy purée is unattractive on the plate and difficult to eat).

❧ Taste and adjust the seasoning, then cover and reheat gently in a bain-marie or in the top of a double-boiler.

❧ Serve as a side dish, as a filling for hollowed tomatoes or as a 'bed' for poached eggs.

BRAISED CELERY

Serves 4

1 medium-sized head of celery
mirepoix of vegetables (see page 367)
Chicken or Basic Vegetable Stock (see page 336)
25 g (1 oz) butter or margarine
salt and pepper

❦ Heat the oven to 180C (350F) mark 4.
❦ Cut the leaf ends of the celery stalks off square and pare the root. String the outer stalks if required. Tie the head in two or three places to hold it in shape.
❦ Parboil it in water for 6–8 minutes. Spread the mirepoix in the base of a heavy casserole or oval pot-roaster. Lay the celery on top. Pour in enough stock to cover half the celery, dot the top with the butter or margarine and season. Cover tightly with greased greaseproof paper, then with a lid. Cook for 1–1 ½ hours.
❦ Transfer the celery to a warmed dish; remove the strings and serve with some of the cooking liquid poured over.

BOILED CELERY

Serves 4

4 small tender heads of celery or 2 large ones,
    halved lengthwise
1 tbsp lemon juice
salt and pepper
275 ml (½ pint) coating White Sauce or Parsley
    Sauce (see page 339)

❦ Cut off the leaf ends and leaves, and pare the root ends of the celery. Scrape and string the outside stalks if required. Cut the celery stalks across into 5 an (2 in) pieces, discarding any immature yellow leaf tips.
❦ Bring a pan of water to the boil, add the lemon juice and celery, and cook for 10–20 minutes, depending on the thickness of the pieces, until they are tender. Drain, and season well.
❦ Serve coated with the sauce.

COURGETTE MEDLEY

Serves 4

2 small onions or 6 spring onions
1 garlic clove
2 tbsp butter or margarine
1 tbsp oil
4 large or 6–8 small courgettes, sliced (5 mm/¼
    in thick)
2 tomatoes, skinned and sliced
1 tbsp tomato purée
1 tbsp dried basil
3 tbsp white wine or 1 tbsp lemon juice and 2
    tbsp water
salt and freshly ground black pepper

❦ Slice the onions thinly and squeeze the garlic over them. In a large frying pan, stir the onion in 1 tablespoon of the butter and the oil for 30 seconds over a low heat.
❦ Add the remaining butter and the courgettes, and sauté them for about 3 minutes until they begin to colour. Add all the other ingredients except the seasoning, stir and then cover the pan with a spatter-proof cover or plate. Reduce the heat and cook gently for 8–10 minutes, stirring occasionally, until the courgettes are tender but not mushy.
❦ Season to taste before serving.

Variation
Cucumber can be cooked in the same way.

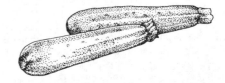

SIMMERED FENNEL

Serves 4

4 medium-sized bulbs of Florence fennel
2-3 parsley stalks
1 sprig fresh or dried thyme
1 garlic clove, peeled (optional)
2 fresh or 1 dried bay leaf
7-8 coriander seeds
6 black peppercorns
4 tbsp olive oil
juice of 1 lemon
275 ml (½ pint) water
salt and pepper

❧ Prepare the fennel by removing the root ends and coarse outer leaves. Cut off the stem ends and slice them to add to the bouquet garni. Reserve any feathery shoots. Make up the bouquet garni by tying the parsley, thyme, garlic (optional), bay leaf, coriander seeds and peppercorns together in a small square of muslin.

❧ Put the olive oil, lemon juice, water, bouquet garni and salt in a pan. Cover, bring slowly to the boil and simmer for 10 minutes. Meanwhile halve or quarter the fennel bulbs, depending on their size. Add them to the pan, and continue cooking until they are tender, about 10 minutes.

❧ Drain the bulbs, reserving the liquid and season to taste. Serve with a little of the liquid poured over to moisten (optional). Garnish with the shredded feathery leaves.

'FRIED' SPRING GREENS

Serves 4

450 g (1 lb) whole heads of young spring greens
boiling water
2 tbsp butter
1 tbsp olive oil
good pinch each of salt, pepper, grated nutmeg
    and brown sugar

❧ Bring 2.5 cm (1 in) depth of water to the boil in a pan which will hold the heads side by side. Add the heads and turn them over using two wooden spoons. Cook for 3 minutes or until the leaves soften.

❧ Cover the pan, reduce the heat, and simmer for 5 minutes. Drain, reserving the liquid. Lay the heads on a cloth, fold it over them, and squeeze out any free liquid.

❧ Cut the heads of spring greens in half lengthwise. Heat the butter and oil in the dry pan, then return 5 mm (¼ in) depth of reserved liquid and the greens. Add the seasonings. Cover, and simmer until the stem ends and ribs are tender, turning occasionally. Drain, or serve with the liquid.

BAKED LETTUCE

Serves 4

1 large firm Webb's lettuce
salt and pepper
2 tsp dried marjoram or oregano
4 spring onions, green and white parts, thinly
    sliced
6 cm (2 ½ in) piece of unpeeled cucumber, diced
4-6 tbsp strong Basic Vegetable Stock (see page
    336)

❧ Heat the oven to 170C (325F) mark 3.

❧ Remove any loose, damaged or wilted leaves or tips. Wash the lettuce well without breaking it apart. Cut off the root, and cut the lettuce in quarters, lengthwise.

❧ Lay each segment on a piece of foil large enough to enclose it. Sprinkle with salt and pepper, and the herbs, then with the sliced spring onion and cucumber. Turn up the edges of the foil so that the liquid cannot run off, and pour the stock over the segments. Enclose each segment completely in its foil sheath by folding and pinching the foil edges over it.

❧ Place in a shallow baking tin and bake for 20-25 minutes until the lettuce is tender when pierced with a skewer through the top of the foil parcel. Unwrap and serve with the liquid in each parcel.

Variations
Cos lettuce or Chinese leaves can be cooked the same way but will take slightly longer. Cut away any tough root end or core before cooking.

STEWED OKRA WITH TOMATOES

Serves 4-6

400 g (14 oz) fresh okra pods
150 ml (¼ pint) vinegar
85 ml (3 fl oz) olive oil
2 large onions, coarsely chopped
8 medium-sized tomatoes, skinned and
    chopped
2 tbsp chopped chives
1 tbsp chopped parsley
1 tsp fresh or dried thyme
salt and pepper

❦ Cut off the stems of the okra pods without cutting into the pods themselves. In a shallow bowl, marinate the pods in the vinegar for 40 minutes, then drain and rinse them well.

❦ Heat the oil in a pan, add the chopped onions and stir until browned. Add the tomatoes and simmer for 5 minutes. Now add the okra pods, herbs, seasoning to taste and just enough hot water to cover three-quarters of the vegetables. Cook gently, uncovered, for 40-50 minutes, stirring occasionally.

PARSNIP PUREE

Serves 4-6

450 g (1 lb) parsnips
2 small carrots
350 g (12 oz) boiled, peeled potatoes
50 g (2 oz) butter or margarine
2-4 tbsp milk
salt and freshly ground black pepper
pinch of grated nutmeg
1-2 tbsp cream (optional)
2 tbsp unsalted butter or chopped parsley to
    garnish

❦ Wash, peel or scrape and trim the parsnips and carrots. Quarter the parsnips and take out the hard cores. Slice both the parsnips and carrots thinly.

❦ Melt half the butter or margarine in a heavy pan, add the parsnips and carrots and cook gently for about 6 minutes, turning and tossing the slices. Add the minimum of boiling water and cook for about 20 minutes until soft. Drain thoroughly.

❦ Purée the parsnips, carrots and the potatoes together, using a sieve or a food processor. Mix thoroughly with the remaining butter and some or all of the milk; do not make the purée sloppy. Season well and stir in the cream (optional). Reheat (without boiling) if required.

❦ Serve each helping with a dab of butter on top or sprinkled with parsley.

SCALLOPED POTATOES

Serves 4

4 medium large raw potatoes peeled and
    thinly sliced
2 large onions, skinned and thinly sliced
2 tbsp chopped parsley
½ tsp salt
good grinding of black pepper
4 tbsp melted butter or margarine
175 ml (6 fl oz) milk or Basic Vegetable Stock
    (see page 336)

❦ Heat the oven to 190C (375F) mark 5.

❦ Spread half the potatoes in an even layer about 2.5 cm (1 in) deep in a well-greased shallow baking dish suitable for serving. Spread the onions and half the parsley over the potatoes and season. Cover evenly with the remaining potato slices. Season again and sprinkle with the melted butter or margarine. Pour in enough milk or stock to show through the top layer of potatoes.

❦ Bake for 1-1 ¼ hours or until the potatoes are crusty on top and soft underneath. Sprinkle with the remaining parsley.

POTATO RISSOLES

Makes 12-14

350 g (12 oz) smooth mashed Potato (see page 228)
1 tsp chopped parsley
50 g (2 oz) cooked minced ham (optional)
salt and pepper
beaten egg to coat
brown breadcrumbs or melba toast crumbs
fat for shallow-frying

❧ Cool the mashed potato if freshly made. Mix in the parsley and the ham (optional). Season well. Shape the mixture into balls, then flatten them slightly with your palm.
❧ Coat with egg, then with breadcrumbs or toast crumbs. Fry in fat, turning once, until golden brown on both sides.
❧ Drain on soft kitchen paper, and serve very hot.

Variation
For potato croquettes, use 450 g (1 lb) smooth mashed potato, 25 g (1 oz) butter, 1 tsp parsley and 2 egg yolks for the mixture. Form into cork shapes and coat with egg and breadcrumbs twice, then deep-fry in hot oil for 4–5 minutes.

DUCHESSE POTATOES

Serves 4

450 g (1 lb) hot peeled and boiled potatoes
50 g (2 oz) butter, softened
1 egg or 2 egg yolks, beaten
salt and pepper
grated nutmeg

❧ Heat the oven to 200C (400F) mark 6.
❧ Mash the potatoes until very smooth. Beat in the butter and beaten egg or egg yolks, and seasoning and nutmeg.
❧ Pipe into rosettes on a greased baking sheet. Bake for about 20 minutes until golden and tipped with brown.
❧ The potato rosettes can be made and refrigerated ahead of time.

POMMES DE TERRE DAUPHINE

Makes 10-12

450 g (1 lb) potatoes, boiled
salt and pepper
25 g (1 oz) butter
1 egg
fat for deep-frying
65 g (2 ½ oz) Choux Pastry (see page 364)

❧ Sieve the boiled potatoes, season, and beat in the butter and egg.
❧ Heat the fat. Mix the choux pastry and potato mixture together. Beat with a wooden spoon and season well. Put as much as you can handle comfortably into a forcing bag fitted with a 1 cm (½ in) plain pipe.
❧ Pipe 2.5 cm (1 in) lengths one by one on to a damp tablespoon. Slip gently into hot fat. Fry until the potato is honey-coloured. Remove with a slotted spoon on to absorbent kitchen paper.
❧ Keep hot while frying the remainder and serve at once.

Note
This is a culinary conjuring trick. The choux comes to the outside, leaving a soft centre of rich potato.

BAKED PUMPKIN ON THE SHELL

Serves 4

900 g (2 lb) segment of pumpkin, unpeeled
lemon juice
salt and pepper
sprinkling of ground ginger or paprika
2 tsp butter or margarine
chopped parsley to garnish

❦ Heat the oven to 200C (400F) mark 6.
❦ Cut the segment of pumpkin in half across into two 450 g (1 lb) pieces. These are more convenient to cook than a single long segment and hold any fat or liquid better than small serving portions. Scrape out the seeds and fibre and sprinkle with a little lemon juice.
❦ Place the pieces in a greased, shallow baking tin, flesh side up. Sprinkle well with salt and pepper and ginger or paprika. Dot with the butter or margarine. Cover with greased foil, tucking it well in around the pumpkin. Bake for 30–40 minutes or until the pumpkin is tender when pierced with a skewer.
❦ To serve, cut each piece in half to make 4 portions. Remove the rind and sprinkle with a little more lemon juice (optional) and with some chopped parsley.

SWEETCORN FRITTERS

Serves 4

oil for deep frying
200 g (7 oz) canned sweetcorn kernels, drained
1 large egg, separated
65 g (2 ½ oz) flour
½ tsp baking powder
½ tsp salt
pinch of paprika

❦ Set a pan of oil to heat to 185C (360F).
❦ Mash the sweetcorn kernels with a potato masher or in a food processor. Turn them into a bowl. Beat the egg yolk until thick and stir it into the mashed kernels.
❦ Sift together the flour, baking powder, salt and paprika, and stir this dry mixture into the corn in small quantities, blending each in thoroughly.
❦ Whisk the egg white until stiff. Stir in one spoonful to lighten the corn mixture, then fold in the rest.
❦ Drop small spoonfuls into the hot oil and fry until golden-brown, turning as required. Drain on soft kitchen paper.
❦ Serve at once with grilled ham, roast or fried chicken, or baked stuffed tomatoes.

CORN OYSTERS

Serves 4 (8-10 fritters)

200 g (7 oz) canned sweetcorn kernels, drained
2 eggs
6 tbsp sifted flour
½ tsp baking powder 1
⅛ tsp grated nutmeg
salt and pepper
2 tbsp butter or margarine
½ tbsp oil

❦ Mash the sweetcorn kernels with a potato masher or in a food processor. Beat the eggs in a bowl until frothy. Sift in the flour, baking powder, nutmeg and seasoning. Beat well, then fold in the mashed kernels.
❦ Heat the butter and oil in a large frying pan. Drop in separately 4 or 5 spoonfuls of the corn batter. Fry until browned underneath, then turn and brown the second sides. Drain on soft paper, then keep warm while frying the remaining batter.
❦ Serve as a side dish with grilled ham or fried chicken, or as a breakfast, brunch or supper dish with grilled bacon.

SALADS AS LIGHT AND MAIN COURSE DISHES

A collection of more elaborate salads containing vegetables,
fruit and also some form of protein.

MANGE-TOUT AND PASTA SALAD

Serves 4-6

225 g (8 oz) green noodles
120 ml (4 fl oz) Mayonnaise (see page 346)
1 garlic clove, squeezed
2 tbsp white wine vinegar
2 medium-sized courgettes
225 g (8 oz) mange-tout topped and tailed
100 g (4 oz) button mushrooms, sliced
175 g (6 oz) cherry tomatoes, cut in half
1 tbsp finely chopped parsley
1 tbsp finely chopped fresh mint

❧ Cook the noodles in boiling water until just tender. Drain and put in a bowl.
❧ Mix together the mayonnaise, garlic and vinegar, and toss the mixture with the noodles. Set to one side.
❧ Cut off the ends of the courgettes and split in half lengthwise, then slice across thinly into half-moons. Slice the mange-tout into strips diagonally if large. Put both vegetables in a round-bottomed sieve or strainer and dip in boiling water for a few seconds, then toss to dry them.
❧ Add to the noodles with the mushrooms and halved tomatoes. Sprinkle with the herbs, and chill until needed. Bring back to room temperature to serve.

Variation
Replace half the mayonnaise with soured cream.

CURRIED BEAN AND EGG SALAD

Serves 4

600 g (1 ¼ lb) drained cooked butter beans or
    two 450 g (16 fl oz) cans
salt and pepper
2 medium-sized onions
3 tbsp vegetable oil
2 tsp curry powder
120 ml (4 fl oz) hot water
50 ml (2 fl oz) soured cream
4 hard-boiled eggs, shelled
paprika for sprinkling

❦ Season the drained beans with salt and pepper.
Chop the onions.
❦ Heat the oil in a pan and fry the onions until
beginning to colour, stirring constantly. Mix in the
curry powder thoroughly, then stir in the beans.
Continue stirring for 1 minute. Add the water and
simmer for 3 minutes or until the water has almost
evaporated. Mix in the soured cream. Turn half the
beans into a bowl.
❦ Cut the eggs in half and place on top of the beans,
then cover with the rest of the beans. Cool completely. Sprinkle the salad lightly with paprika
before serving.

TOMATO, CELERY AND CHEESE SALAD

Serves 4

5 medium-sized tomatoes, skinned
4 medium-sized stalks celery
One 200 g (7 oz) can of sweetcorn kernels,
    drained
225 g (8 oz) Cheddar cheese, finely diced
4 tbsp Mayonnaise (see page 346)
lettuce leaves (from a round lettuce)
25 g (1 oz) chopped walnuts
1 tsp grated orange rind
walnut halves or watercress sprigs to garnish

❦ Quarter the tomatoes lengthwise. Put four quarters to one side. Scrape out the seeds and pulp of the
rest and cut the flesh into small pieces. Top and tail
the celery stalks, string if needed and slice finely.

❦ Mix the celery, sweetcorn and cheese with the
tomato pieces and toss lightly with the mayonnaise.
Make a 'bed' of lettuce leaves on a flat platter and
pile the salad on top. Sprinkle with chopped nuts
and orange rind.
❦ Garnish the centre of the salad with the four
reserved tomato quarters, skinned side up, arranged
like flower petals. Place the walnut halves or tiny
sprigs of watercress around the edge of the salad.

TOMATO AND MOZZARELLA SALAD

Serves 4

400 g (14 oz) firm tomatoes
100 g (4 oz) Mozzarella cheese, thinly sliced
salt and freshly ground black pepper
1 tbsp finely snipped chives
½ tbsp walnut oil

❦ Discarding the ends, slice the tomatoes into thin
rounds. Arrange them in overlapping rings on a flat
plate. Cover with the cheese slices.
❦ Season lightly with salt and pepper and sprinkle
with the chives and walnut oil.
❦ Serve at room temperature. This salad also makes
a good starter.

BROCCOLI AND PASTA SALAD

Serves 4

75 g (3 oz) fresh broccoli spears
75 g (3 oz) French beans
75 g (3 oz) cooked pasta spirals, drained and cooled
2 spring onion bulbs with white stems, sliced
50 g (2 oz) black olives, stoned and chopped
2 cocktail gherkins, chopped

Dressing
2 tsp dry whole grain mustard
1 tbsp lemon juice
3 tbsp oil

❦ Cut off the broccoli stems. Break the heads into small florets, and peel and slice the stems if tender. Top and tail the beans, and cut diagonally into small lengths.
❦ Cook the vegetables together until just tender, drain and cool. Mix with the pasta, spring onions, olives and gherkins in a salad bowl.
❦ Whisk together the dressing ingredients and sprinkle over the salad.

BEETROOT WITH YOGHURT DRESSING

Serves 4

6 medium-sized beetroot, cooked
225 ml (8 fl oz) French Dressing with Lemon (see page 347)
150 ml (¼ pint) natural yoghurt
green tops of 3 medium-sized spring onions, finely sliced

❦ Skin the beetroots and slice them. Put them in a bowl with the French dressing, and leave for several hours.
❦ When ready to serve, whisk the yoghurt until liquid and stir in the spring onion tops. Pour any free dressing off the beetroot and pour the yoghurt mixture over it.

MIXED BEAN AND CORN SALAD

Serves 4

175 g (6 oz) cooked runner or French beans, sliced into small pieces
200 g (7 oz) each drained cooked or canned cannellini beans, red kidney beans and sweetcorn kernels
2 small inside stalks of celery, finely chopped (optional)
½ medium-sized onion, finely chopped
2 tbsp Walnut Dressing (see page 348)

❦ Mix all the ingredients in a bowl, and toss with the dressing. Serve at room temperature.

CALABRESE SALAD

Serves 4-6

175 g (6 oz) small cauliflower florets
175 g (6 oz) calabrese heads cut into small florets
125 g (4 oz) young carrots, thinly sliced
125 g (4 oz) green beans, sliced
2 small courgettes, thinly sliced

Marinade
6 tbsp soya oil
6 tbsp cider vinegar
3 tbsp lemon juice
pinch of sugar
½ tbsp grated onion
½ tsp dry mustard
½ garlic clove, squeezed
½ tsp oregano

❦ Steam the cauliflower, calabrese, carrots and beans over simmering water for 9 minutes. Drain, mix at once with the courgette slices and cool.
❦ Mix all the marinade ingredients in a jar with a secure stopper. Shake the marinade vigorously to blend. Put the partly cooled vegetables in a bowl and pour the marinade over them. Toss lightly; cover and refrigerate for several hours, stirring occasionally.
❦ Drain off any free marinade before serving.

SALADE NIÇOISE

Serves 4

large flat green lettuce leaves
200 g (7 oz) can of tuna in oil, drained
2 hard-boiled eggs cut in segments
salt and freshly ground black pepper
4 medium-sized tomatoes, skinned and sliced
4 tbsp finely chopped onion
4 tbsp finely sliced cooked celery
1 green pepper, deseeded and cut into small
    thin strips
50 g (2 oz) can anchovy fillets, drained
8 black olives, stoned
French Dressing (see page 347)
pinch each of dried rosemary and basil

❦ Make a bed of lettuce leaves on a large flat platter. Chop the tuna roughly and place it with the egg
segments in a level layer in the centre of the bed.
❦ Season all the vegetables and arrange them in a
ring around the tuna and egg. Split the anchovy fillets lengthwise and lay in a lattice pattern on the
dish, with the olives in the spaces between the fillets.
❦ Serve with French dressing with the herbs mixed
into it.

SPAGHETTI SALAD WITH TUNA

Serves 6

225 g (8 oz) spaghetti
salt
Two 200 g (7 oz) cans tuna in oil
400 g (14 oz) green peppers (2 large peppers)
275 g (10 oz) firm tomatoes
150 g (5 oz) onions

Dressing
reserved oil from cans of tuna
120 ml (4 fl oz) Mayonnaise (see page 346)
3 tbsp milk
4–5 drops Tabasco
1 tbsp soy sauce
2 tsp tomato ketchup
salt and black pepper
pinch of white sugar
good pinch of paprika

❦ Break the spaghetti into 7.5 cm (3 in) lengths and
cook it in lightly salted water until just tender. Drain
and cool.
❦ Meanwhile, drain the tuna, reserving the oil.
Split the peppers, remove the cores, seeds and inside
ribs and cut the flesh into small thin strips. Skin and
quarter the tomatoes, remove the seeds, cores and
pulp and dice the flesh. Skin and shred the onions.
❦ Whisk the reserved oil with the other dressing
ingredients, seasoning well; the flavour should be
spicy. Flake the tuna coarsely, and mix it with the
spaghetti, most of the pepper strips and all the tomato and onion. Toss with the dressing. Chill, covered,
for 30 minutes.
❦ Turn the salad on to a shallow serving platter and
garnish with the reserved pepper strips.

WALDORF SALAD

Serves 4

4 red skinned eating apples
2–3 tbsp lemon juice
1 tsp caster sugar
150 ml (¼ pint) Mayonnaise (see page 346)
1 head of celery with outside stalks removed
50 g (2 oz) walnuts
lettuce leaves

❦ Wash the apples, quarter and core them; leave
them unpeeled. Dice them, and toss the dice at once
with the lemon juice, sugar and 1 tablespoon of the
mayonnaise. Set to one side.
❦ Trim the root and leaf ends of the celery stalks,
and slice finely. Set aside a few perfect nuts for garnishing and chop the remainder.
❦ Just before serving, combine the celery, chopped
nuts and remaining mayonnaise with the apples and
add to a salad bowl lined with lettuce leaves. Garnish
with the whole nuts.

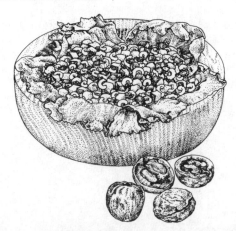

SMOKED MACKEREL SALAD

Serves 4

8 medium-sized new potatoes
225 g (8 oz) cooked, cooled French beans
4 small tomatoes
2 eggs, hard-boiled
225 g (8 oz) skinned smoked mackerel fillet
4 large lettuce leaves
2-3 tbsp French Dressing with Lemon (see page 347)

❦ Boil the potatoes in their skins and cool. While cooling, top and tail the French beans and cut diagonally into 2.5 cm (1 in) lengths. Quarter the tomatoes and eggs. Cut the fish into small pieces.
❦ Lay the lettuce leaves in a bed on a flat platter. Scrape the skins off the potatoes and cut them into small cubes. Arrange the potato cubes, beans, tomatoes, eggs and fish on the lettuce.
❦ Sprinkle the salad with dressing.

MOULDED PARTY SALAD

Serves 4

1 large open-hearted lettuce
4-6 large round slices pressed tongue
6-7 medium-sized tomatoes, skinned and sliced
150 g (5 oz) Edam cheese, thinly sliced without rind
3 hard-boiled eggs, quartered
sliced gherkins
Blue Cheese Dressing (see page 348) or soured cream

❦ Separate the lettuce leaves and rinse and dry them carefully.
❦ Lay one medium-sized leaf in the bottom of a 1 litre (2 pint) pudding basin. Cover it with a slice of tongue. Cover this with another lettuce leaf, then put in a layer of tomato slices, another lettuce leaf and a layer of sliced cheese. Repeat the layers until all the ingredients are used, separating them with lettuce. The top layer should also be lettuce.
❦ Cover the basin with a round of greaseproof paper, then put a small plate and a heavy weight on top of that. Chill the mould for at least 1 hour.
❦ Shortly before serving, shred any remaining lettuce. Drain off any free liquid on top of the pressed salad. Unmould it onto a serving platter. Arrange the lettuce round it, with the eggs and gherkins on top.
❦ Spoon the dressing over the salad.

Variation
The salad is also delicious made with 150 g (5 oz) thinly sliced smoked salmon instead of tongue.

CHEF'S SALAD

Serves 4

4 large cos lettuce leaves
1 tbsp French Dressing (see page 347)
75 g (3 oz) cold cooked turkey meat without skin
75 g (3 oz) cold cooked ham in one thick slice
75 g (3 oz) cold cooked tongue in one thick slice
75 g (3 oz) Gruyère cheese
chopped parsley to garnish

❦ Wash, dry and shred the lettuce, and toss with just enough dressing to moisten it. Place it in the bottom of a salad bowl.
❦ Cut all the meats and the cheese into small strips and jumble them on top of the lettuce. Sprinkle with any remaining dressing and garnish with parsley.

TURKEY SALAD

Serves 4

225 g (8 oz) cooked turkey, diced
225 g (8 oz) cooked long grain rice
½ red pepper and ½ green pepper, deseeded and finely sliced
2 tbsp cooked sweetcorn kernels
25 g (1 oz) walnuts, chopped
25 g (1 oz) sultanas
Vinaigrette Dressing (see page 347)
sliced cucumber to garnish

❦ Mix together the turkey, rice, peppers, sweetcorn, walnuts and sultanas. Add sufficient vinaigrette dressing to moisten.
❦ Pile on a plate and garnish with a ring of finely sliced cucumber.

ROYAL TURKEY SALAD

Serves 4

150 ml (¼ pint) soured cream
1 tbsp cress, chopped
salt and pepper
pinch of white sugar
½ tsp French mustard
350 g (12 oz) cold cooked brown turkey meat
    without skin
3 medium sized tomatoes, quartered
10 cm (4 in) piece cucumber, unpeeled
3 large or 4 small spring onions, green and
    white parts with roots and leaf tips removed
yolk of 1 hard-boiled egg

❦ Mix together the soured cream, cress, seasoning, sugar and mustard in a bowl which will hold all the turkey meat. Dice the turkey and mix it with the dressing.
❦ Pile the mixture in the centre of a flat salad plate. Remove the seeds and pulp of the tomatoes. Chop the tomato flesh and cucumber, not too finely, and slice the spring onions. Mix these three ingredients together and season well. Place them in a ring around the edge of the turkey salad.
❦ Sieve the hard-boiled egg yolk over the turkey.

TURKEY AND HAM SALAD

Serves 3-4

100 g (4 oz) cooked turkey, diced
100 g (4 oz) cooked ham, diced
150 g (6 oz) cooked long grain rice
3-4 tbsp fresh or canned pineapple, diced
3-4 tbsp melon, diced
2 eating apples, cored and sliced
4-6 tbsp Mayonnaise (see page 346)
lettuce, tomato and cucumber to garnish

❦ Mix together the turkey, ham, rice, pineapple, melon and apple. Fold in the mayonnaise.
❦ Arrange the lettuce on a serving dish, and pile the salad on top. Garnish with sliced or quartered tomatoes and sliced cucumber.

TURKEY WITH AVOCADO SALAD

Serves 4

2 avocados
fresh orange juice
½ small red pepper and ½ green pepper,
    deseeded
225 g (8 oz) cooked turkey, diced
1-2 tsp Worcestershire sauce
2-3 tbsp Mayonnaise (see page 346)
salt and pepper

❦ Peel and core the avocados, slice, and arrange in overlapping slices in a circle on a serving plate. Brush with orange juice.
❦ From each of the peppers, reserve a few fine slices for garnish, and finely chop the remainder.
❦ Mix the turkey with the chopped peppers, Worcestershire sauce and mayonnaise. Season to taste. Pile the mixture in the centre of the avocado slices. Garnish with the reserved slices of peppers.
❦ Chill well. Serve with a watercress salad.

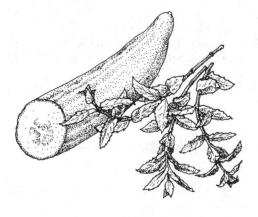

CHICKEN, HAM AND FRUIT SALAD

Serves 4

225 g (8 oz) cold cooked chicken meat without skin
100 g (4 oz) cold cooked ham in one thick slice
225 g (8 oz) cold cooked new potatoes
1 medium-sized sharp eating apple
3 tbsp cider vinegar
100 g (4 oz) fresh ripe red plums
salt and pepper
pinch of dry mustard
¼ tsp caster sugar
2 tbsp sunflower oil
½ small Webb's lettuce, shredded

❦ Dice both the meats. Scrape the skins off the new potatoes and dice. Mix all three in a bowl. Peel, core and dice the apple and toss in the vinegar. Halve, stone and chop the plums.
❦ Pour the vinegar off the apples into a bowl, and mix in the seasoning, mustard and sugar. Whisk in the oil slowly. Add the fruits and a little shredded lettuce to the meat and potato, and toss with the dressing.
❦ Spread the remaining lettuce on a flat platter, pile the salad on top and serve at once.

SAVOURY RICE SALAD

Serves 4

100 g (4 oz) shelled green peas
25 g (1 oz) Parma or Westphalian ham
36 cooked shelled prawns
275 g (10 oz) cooked brown rice
salt and white pepper
good pinch of grated nutmeg
2 tbsp olive oil
2-3 tsp lemon juice
2 tbsp chopped parsley

❦ Cook the peas in unsalted water until almost tender. Cut the ham into thin short strips and add it to the pan. Cook for 1 minute longer. Drain and cool. Mix in the prawns.
❦ Toss the rice to separate the grains. Mix together all the remaining ingredients to make a dressing, reserving some parsley for garnishing. Mix the dressing with the rice, then fold in the peas, ham and prawns. Garnish with the reserved parsley.

SPINACH SALAD WITH BACON

Serves 4

225 g (8 oz) young spinach leaves
1 tbsp chives, finely snipped
pinch of paprika
pinch of salt
1 thick slice of wholemeal bread without crusts
Garlic Oil for frying (see page 348)
4 rashers of rindless streaky bacon
French Dressing (see page 347)

❦ Wash and dry the spinach leaves, and tear them into bite-sized pieces. Mix with the chives, paprika and salt.
❦ Cut the bread into dice and fry in a little garlic oil until crisp and lightly scented. Drain on soft paper.
❦ Add the bacon to the pan and fry until crisp. Drain on soft paper, and crumble finely. Mix with the spinach.
❦ Put the bread cubes in the bottom of a salad bowl and pile the spinach salad on top. Just before serving, sprinkle or toss the salad with a few drops of French dressing.

SALADS AS SIDE DISHES

A selection of ways to provide interesting salad accompaniments to all sorts of meals – from a Simple Green Salad to a Watercress and Mushroom Salad.

SIMPLE GREEN SALAD

Serves 4

1 small round lettuce
1 small bunch watercress
mustard and cress
4 medium-sized spring onions, green and white parts
6 cm (2 ½ in) piece of cucumber, unpeeled
1-2 tbsp chopped fresh mixed herbs as available (e.g. parsley, tarragon, thyme, hyssop, marjoram, rue, sweet cicely, savory)
French Dressing with Lemon (see page 347)

❦ Remove the roots and any damaged or discoloured leaves from the lettuce and watercress. Separate the lettuce leaves and take the watercress leaves off the stems. Cut off the stems of the cress.

❦ Rinse the leaves under running water and shake or toss them in a salad basket or cloth to dry. Tear the lettuce into small pieces, chop any large watercress leaves and slice spring onions finely. Dice the cucumber.

❦ Mix all the leafy ingredients lightly in a bowl with the onions, cucumber and chopped herbs. Just before serving, toss with the dressing.

❦ If fresh herbs are not available, add one or two croutons (see page 355) to the salad bowl and remove just before serving.

CARROT AND ORANGE SALAD

Serves 4

350 g (12 oz) carrots
2 medium-sized oranges
50 g (2 oz) raisins
1 tbsp French Dressing (see page 347)
good grinding of black pepper

❦ Top, tail and scrape the carrots and grate them. Blanch and peel the oranges, and cut the flesh into segments removing the pith, membrane and pips. Cut the segments in half across and mix with the grated carrots. Add the raisins and mix.
❦ Moisten the salad with the French dressing and grind black pepper over it before serving.

Variations
Add 2 tablespoons of finely snipped chives to the salad. For a salad with a sharper flavour to accompany game birds or pork, substitute 2 tablespoons of drained capers for the raisins.

CAULIFLOWER SALAD

Serves 4

1 medium-sized cauliflower
salt and white pepper
Vinaigrette Dressing (see page 347)

❦ Divide the cauliflower head into small sprigs, and cook in boiling water for 5 minutes.
❦ Drain well, season lightly, and toss with the dressing in a bowl while still hot. Cool completely, turning the sprigs over occasionally. Pour off any free liquid before serving.

ITALIAN SALAD

Serves 4-6

1 head of curly endive
75 g (3 oz) radicchio
50 g (2 oz) button mushrooms, sliced
½ green pepper, cut across, deseeded and cut into thin rings
½ medium-sized courgette, thinly sliced
salt and black pepper
1 tbsp pine nut kernels
sprinkling of lemon juice

Dressing
350 g (12 oz) tomatoes
1 tbsp grated onion
salt and black pepper
½ tsp lemon juice (for very ripe tomatoes)
2 tbsp olive oil
chopped fresh basil

❦ Separate the endive stalks and rinse well, then pat dry. Use the outer leaves to line a salad bowl. Tear the small centre leaves into pieces.
❦ Shred the radicchio, removing any core. Mix the torn endive leaves, radicchio, mushrooms, pepper rings and courgette slices, season and turn into the lined bowl. Sprinkle with the pine nuts and lemon juice.
❦ For the dressing, scald and skin the tomatoes. Chop them roughly, then process for ½ minute in an electric blender with the onion, seasoning, lemon juice if used and oil. Stir well just before serving, and sprinkle with basil. Serve the dressing separately.

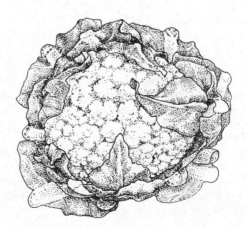

COLESLAW

Serves 4-6

450 g (1 lb) firm white cabbage
3 medium-sized carrots
1 sharp eating apple
1 tbsp lemon juice
25 g (1 oz) seedless raisins
salt and freshly ground black pepper
150 ml (¼ pint) Mayonnaise (see page 346), or
    mayonnaise and natural yoghurt mixed

❦ Remove any discoloured leaves and core the cabbage; shred it finely. Top, tail and scrape the carrots and grate them coarsely. Quarter, core and dice the apple, toss the dice at once with the lemon juice, and mix with the cabbage and carrot. Add the raisins. Season well, then bind with the mayonnaise or mayonnaise and yoghurt.

CELERY AND FENNEL SALAD

Serves 4

2 fennel bulbs with feathery shoots
6 medium-sized celery stalks
2 small courgettes

Dressing
4 tbsp lemon juice
1 tsp dry mustard
2 tsp clear honey
6 tbsp corn or sunflower oil

Garnish
3 tbsp sesame seeds
25 g (1 oz) walnut pieces

❦ First prepare the garnish, scatter the sesame seeds on a baking sheet, and toast in the oven at 180C (350F) mark 4 for 15 minutes, stirring twice while toasting; the seeds should be light gold. Chop the walnuts finely and mix with the seeds.
❦ To make the salad, snip off the feathery fennel shoots and set to one side. Take off any stubs of stem and coarse outside sheaths and pare the root ends. Quarter the bulbs lengthwise and blanch in boiling water for 2 minutes; drain and cool.

❦ Trim the tops and root ends of the celery stalks and string if necessary. Cut off the ends of the courgettes. Slice the celery thinly. Slice the fennel and courgettes lengthwise and cut into small strips. Mix the vegetables in a salad bowl.
❦ Make the dressing by whisking the lemon juice, mustard and honey in another bowl, and gradually whisking in the oil. Pour enough of the dressing over the salad to moisten it well. Scatter the sesame-walnut garnish over the salad. Snip the feathery fennel shoots, and sprinkle on top.

CELERY AND APPLE SALAD

Serves 4

2 red-skinned dessert apples
2 tbsp lemon juice
100 g (4 oz) inside celery stalks, trimmed and
    finely sliced
50 g (2 oz) sultanas
4 cocktail gherkins, thinly sliced
lettuce leaves (optional)

Yoghurt dressing
4 tbsp natural yoghurt
4 tbsp Mayonnaise (see page 346)
1 tsp clear honey

❦ Quarter, core and dice the apples. Coat at once with the lemon juice. Mix the apple dice, celery, sultanas and gherkins in a salad bowl.
❦ Whisk together the dressing yoghurt ingredients, then toss the salad in it. Make a bed of lettuce leaves on a platter and pile the salad on top or serve it in individual bowls.
❦ Serve as a side salad with curries or barbecued meats or as a starter.

Variation
French Dressing (see page 347) may be substituted for yoghurt dressing.

MELON AND CUCUMBER SALAD

Serves 4

1 large orange
½ medium-sized cucumber
½ small honeydew melon
1 tbsp fresh mint finely chopped
1 tsp white wine vinegar
pinch of salt
½ tsp clear honey
lemon juice

❧ Put the orange in boiling water for 1-2 minutes, turning it over once. Drain. Holding it in a cloth, peel it and cut the flesh into segments, remove the pith, membrane and pips. Cut the segments in half across and put in a salad bowl.
❧ Cut the unpeeled cucumber into 1 cm (½ in) dice, and jumble them with the orange. Quarter the melon, discarding any seeds, and cut the flesh free from the rind; then cut it into 1 cm (½ in) cubes. Mix the cubes into the salad with the mint.
❧ Stir the remaining ingredients together, using lemon juice and water to adjust the flavour of the dressing; it should be tangy. Sprinkle the dressing over the salad, and toss to coat it.
❧ Serve with chaud-froid of chicken, a cold fish mousse and similar dishes.

Variation
Mint vinegar can be used, either bought or home-made (see page 348) instead of wine vinegar.

CUCUMBER SALAD

Serves 4

1 large cucumber
salt and white pepper
3 tbsp French Dressing (see page 347)
2 tsp fresh mint leaves, finely chopped

❧ Slice the cucumber thinly into a shallow bowl. Season lightly. Mix the dressing with the mint leaves and pour over the cucumber. Chill, covered, for 30 minutes.
❧ Drain off any free liquid before serving.

MINTED CUCUMBER AND YOGHURT SALAD

Serves 4

1 small cucumber
salt
1 garlic clove
150 ml (¼ pint) natural yoghurt
1 tbsp olive oil
1 tbsp finely chopped fresh mint

❧ Cut off the ends of the cucumber, and shred the rest coarsely. Spread on a plate and sprinkle well with salt. Leave for 30 minutes.
❧ Meanwhile, squeeze the garlic into the yoghurt, add the oil and whisk to blend them. Add half the mint. Drain, rinse and dry the cucumber and mix with the dressing.
❧ Taste before serving and add a little extra salt if you wish. Serve the salad sprinkled with the remaining mint.

CHICORY SALAD

Serves 4

4 medium-sized heads of chicory
4 small inside celery stalks

Dressing
1 large egg yolk
1 ¼ tsp made English mustard
salt and pepper
1 tbsp corn oil
1 tbsp double cream
1 tbsp white wine vinegar
¼ tsp dried dill leaves

❧ Wash the chicory and celery stalks and dry in a cloth. Cut off the root ends of both. Gouge out the bitter cores of the chicory heads, and remove any celery leaves. Slice both vegetables and mix in a bowl.
❧ To make the dressing, whisk the egg yolk in a small bowl with the mustard and seasoning. Whisk in the oil drop by drop as for mayonnaise. When it thickens slightly, add the cream and whisk in the vinegar little by little with the dried dill.
❧ Pour the dressing over the salad ingredients.

PEPPER AND CUCUMBER SALAD

Serves 4

2 sweet red peppers
1 large mild onion
10 cm (4 in) piece of cucumber
few drops of soy sauce
lemon juice
6 tbsp natural yoghurt

❧ Cut off the tops of the peppers, and remove the cores and seeds. Peel the onion and chop it finely. Slice both the peppers and cucumber thinly, and arrange them in overlapping circles on a platter. Sprinkle with the onion.
❧ Mix enough soy sauce and lemon juice into the yoghurt to give it a spicy flavour. Pour it over the salad and serve at once.

POTATO SALAD WITH DILL

Serves 4-6

6 large new potatoes or waxy old potatoes
120 ml (4 fl oz) French Dressing (see page 347)
2-3 tbsp chopped parsley
2 tbsp finely snipped fresh dill leaves
salt and pepper

❧ Steam the potatoes in their skins until just tender. Cool just enough to handle and then scrape off the skins. Cut the potatoes into 1 cm (½ in) dice. Put in a bowl, add the French dressing and herbs, and toss together lightly. Season to taste. Cool thoroughly, turning over once or twice while cooling. Drain off any excess dressing before serving.

TOMATO SALAD

Serves 4

6-8 medium sized tomatoes
1 tbsp olive oil
½ tsp white wine vinegar or cider vinegar
2 large spring onion bulbs, thinly sliced
salt and freshly ground black pepper
fresh or dried basil or thyme leaves

❧ Slice the tomatoes thinly. Lay them in overlapping rings in a shallow bowl or on a serving plate. Sprinkle well with the oil and vinegar. Separate the spring onion slices into rings and scatter them over the dressed tomato slices. Season well, and sprinkle the herb leaves on top.

WATERCRESS AND MUSHROOM SALAD

Serves 4

225 g (8 oz) button mushrooms, thinly sliced
50 g (2 oz) watercress leaves
1-2 tsp chopped parsley
2 tsp finely snipped chives
French Dressing made with tarragon vinegar
   (see page 347)

❧ Mix together the mushrooms, watercress, parsley and chives. Sprinkle with the French dressing just before serving.

PUDDINGS AND DESSERTS

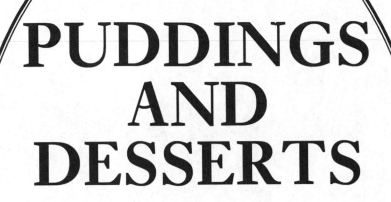

STEAMED AND BOILED PUDDINGS

These recipes are for 'family' puddings – traditionally cheap, nourishing and easy, and used by generations of countrywomen to fill a hungry gap.

❧ About steamed and ❧ boiled puddings

It will be useful to know what the terms 'steamed' and 'boiled' mean. Puddings such as the Spotted Dick and the Jam Roly-poly are literally cooked in boiling water.

The 'steamed' puddings are not, these days, cooked in a steamer over boiling water; they are put, in their basins, into a closely lidded pan of boiling water. The water should reach half-way up the basin and there should be at least 2.5 cm (1 in) between the basin and the edge of the pan so that the steam can circulate. The water should be kept steadily simmering and replenished with boiling water as it evap-

orates. The recipes state how long the pudding should cook for, but when it is done and out of the pan, let it stand for a minute or two. The pastry will shrink slightly and it will then turn out more easily.

Pudding cloths are handy things to have and easily made from an old sheet. They have a string to pull them in and a handle sewn to the top. They are meant for a conventional china pudding basin with a rim – still much the best sort.

The boiled puddings are wrapped in a floured oblong cloth like Tom Kitten and you can hook them out by the strings at the ends.

If the pudding cooked in a basin has sunk, or the roly-poly is soggy, it is because the water has gone off the boil. If a fruit pudding collapses when turned out, it is often because there is not enough filling.

❦ Sauces ❦

Custard powder, of course, makes an easy, economical sauce for family puddings. It is greatly improved by the use of soft brown sugar instead of white, and an egg yolk beaten into the milk and powder at the mixing stage. The whisked egg white can be folded in when the custard is cool.

Greaseproof paper cut to fit the bowl or jug, dampened and pressed smoothly over the custard, prevents that bane of childhood, the thick skin.

Sweetened condensed milk, fruit yoghurts, pure fruit juice from a can, and a bar of chocolate melted with the top of the milk, all make quick and easy sauces. All chocolate should be melted in a basin over hot water or in a microwave oven. Evaporated milk will whip if chilled for 24 hours beforehand.

SPONGE PUDDING

Serves 4-6

100 g (4 oz) butter
100 g (4 oz) caster sugar
2 eggs
225 g (8 oz) self-raising flour
50 ml (2 fl oz) milk
3 tbsp jam or golden syrup

❦ Grease a 750 ml (1 ½ pint) pudding basin with a little of the butter.
❦ Cream the remaining butter and sugar until pale and fluffy. Beat the eggs and add to the mixture. Beat again. Sieve the flour and fold in with a metal spoon. Add the milk, still folding gently, to make a soft dropping mixture.
❦ Add the jam or syrup to the basin, spreading it over the base, then add the sponge mixture. Cover with pleated greaseproof paper and a pudding cloth or foil, and steam for 1 ½ hours.
❦ When ready, turn out on a serving dish and serve with extra melted jam or syrup as a sauce.

Notes
The creaming and then the beating of the butter, sugar and eggs incorporates air which makes the pudding light. The gentle folding in of the flour with a metal spoon makes certain that the air is not knocked out again. Butter really is best for this one.
❦ This is the basic steamed sponge; it is quick to make and pretty well fool-proof.

GUARD'S PUDDING

Serves 4

200 g (7 oz) fresh brown breadcrumbs
175 g (6 oz) shredded suet
100 g (4 oz) dark soft brown sugar
¼ tsp salt
3 tbsp strawberry jam
1 egg (size 1 or 2)
½ tsp bicarbonate of soda

❦ Mix the breadcrumbs, suet, sugar and salt together. Beat the jam into the egg with the bicarbonate of soda. Mix well and add to the other mixture.
❦ Turn into a well-greased 750 ml (1 ½ pint) pudding basin. Cover with a pleated circle of greaseproof paper and a pudding cloth or foil. Steam for 2 ½ hours.
❦ Turn out and serve with custard sauce or Crème à la Vanille (see page 349).

FUDGE PUDDING

Serves 4-5

4 slices bread (brown or white)
25 g (1 oz) raisins
25 g (1 oz) glacé cherries, quartered
25 g (1 oz) soft brown sugar
1 tbsp ground almonds
50 g (2 oz) granulated sugar
2 tbsp water
2 eggs
275 ml (½ pint) milk
butter for greasing

❦ Butter a 750 ml (1 ½ pint) pudding basin. Cut the bread into cubes. Put into a bowl and mix with the raisins, cherries, sugar and ground almonds.
❦ Gently heat the granulated sugar in the water in a heavy-based pan until melted. Do not stir. Turn up the heat and darken to a honey brown. Take off the heat and cool.
❦ Beat the eggs. Add the milk and the caramel. Stir and pour the mixture around and over the bread.
❦ Leave to soak for 10 minutes. Turn into the basin. Cover with pleated greaseproof paper and a pudding cloth or foil and steam for 1 hour.
❦ Turn out and serve.

BELVOIR ORANGE PUDDING

Serves 4

100 g (4 oz) butter
200 g (7 oz) caster sugar
2 eggs, separated
100 g (4 oz) fresh white breadcrumbs
grated rind and juice of 2 oranges
scant ½ tsp baking powder
2 Cox's orange pippin apples

❦ Grease a 750 ml (1 ½ pint) basin with a little of the butter.
❦ Cream the remaining butter and 100 g (4 oz) sugar, add the egg yolks and beat well. Add the breadcrumbs, the orange rind and juice. Mix lightly and then add the baking powder. Spoon into the basin, cover with pleated greaseproof paper and a pudding cloth or foil and steam for 40 minutes.
❦ Heat the oven to 220C (425F) mark 7. Prepare the meringue base. Peel, core and dice the apples. Whisk the egg whites until stiff. Fold in nearly all the remaining sugar and then the diced apple. Spread on a glass ovenproof plate and dust with the remaining sugar.
❦ About 10 minutes before the pudding is due to be ready, set the meringue in the hot oven. Turn the pudding out into the middle of the soft meringue and serve.
❦ A spoonful or two of orange juice is a good and easy sauce for this fresh, light pudding – which really does call for butter.

CHOCOLATE PUDDING

Serves 4-5

225 g (8 oz) self-raising flour
½ tsp salt
1 tbsp cocoa
100 g (4 oz) shredded suet
2 tbsp caster sugar
150 ml (¼ pint) milk
butter for greasing

❦ Grease a 750 ml (1 ½ pint) basin with butter. Sift the flour, salt and cocoa into a bowl, add the suet and sugar and mix well together. Add the milk and mix

all the ingredients to a soft dropping consistency.
❦ Turn into a basin and cover with pleated grease-proof paper and a pudding cloth or foil. Steam for 2 hours. Turn out and serve with hazelnut yoghurt or with a hot chocolate sauce.

RAISIN PUDDING

Serves 4

100 g (4 oz) stoned raisins
100 g (4 oz) butter
100 g (4 oz) caster sugar
2 eggs
100 g (4 oz) self-raising flour

❦ Line a buttered 750 ml (1 ½ pint) pudding basin with the raisins (they do stick on). Cream the butter and sugar until light and fluffy. Beat the eggs. Sieve the flour and fold into the mixture with alternate spoonfuls of egg. Very gently spoon it into the basin, which should be no more than three-quarters full. All steamed puddings should expand.
❦ Cover as usual with pleated greaseproof paper and a pudding cloth or foil. Steam for 1 ¾ hours.

Notes
Without the raisins this is a 'canary pudding', or if cooked in individual moulds, it becomes 'castle puddings', and of course if you change your mind half-way through, it is a Victoria sandwich mixture.

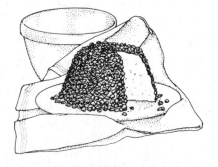

SPICED LAYER PUDDING

Serves 4

225 g (8 oz) self-raising flour
½ tsp salt
50 g (2 oz) caster sugar
100 g (4 oz) shredded suet
150 ml (¼ pint) cold water
50 g (2 oz) margarine
100 g (4 oz) cut mixed peel
1 tsp ground cinnamon or mixed spice

❦ Sieve the flour and salt together. Add the sugar and suet and mix well. Add the water to form a soft-ish dough. Divide into four graduated pieces. Soften the margarine and blend it with the mixed peel.
❦ Grease a 750 ml (1 ½ pint) pudding basin and roll out the smallest piece of dough to fit the base. Spread with the mixed peel and give a light sprinkling of spice. Roll out a slightly larger piece of dough and proceed as before. Add the third round with the mixture spread on it and the spice. Use the last round for the top.
❦ Cover with pleated greaseproof paper and a pudding cloth or foil. Steam for 2 hours. Turn out and serve with custard sauce.

SPOTTED DICK

Serves 4-6

225 g (8 oz) Suet Crust Pastry (see page361)
100 g (4 oz) seedless raisins

❦ Put a pan of water on to boil. Make the suet crust pastry as usual but add the raisins to the dry ingredients before adding any liquid.
❦ Grease a 500 ml (1 pint) pudding basin. Shape the pastry into a ball and put into the basin. Cover the basin (see page 362). Stand the basin in the boiling water and boil steadily for 2 hours.
❦ Remove the basin and let stand for a minute or two. Turn out and serve with custard.

Variation
If you like smaller spots, use currants with 50 g (2 oz) sugar in place of raisins.

SUSSEX POND PUDDING

Serves 4-6

225 g (8 oz) Suet Crust Pastry (see page 361)
50 g (2 oz) butter
50 g (2 oz) soft brown sugar
grated rind and juice of 1 lemon

❦ Put a pan of water on to boil. Grease a 750 ml (1 ½ pint) pudding basin. Roll out the pastry to a thick round and use to line the basin, letting the ends fall over the edge of the basin.
❦ Work the butter and sugar together, adding the rind and juice of the lemon. Put this mixture into the middle of the pudding. Fold the edges over the top and seal with water. Cover the basin (see page 362)
❦ Stand the basin in the boiling water and boil steadily for 2 ½-3 hours. Remove the basin and let stand for a minute or two.
❦ Turn out and serve plain.

JAM ROLY-POLY

Serves 4

225 g (8 oz) self-raising flour
½ tsp salt
100 g (4 oz) shredded suet
about 150 ml (¼ pint) cold water
4-6 tbsp jam

❦ Sieve the flour and salt into a bowl. Add the suet and mix with sufficient water to give a soft, springy dough.
❦ Roll out on a lightly floured board to an oblong 25 x 20 cm (10 x 8 inches). Trim the edges and spread generously up to 1 cm (½ in) from the edge with jam. Roll up tightly. Wrap loosely in greased greaseproof paper, then in a floured pudding cloth or foil – not too tight, for the roly-poly swells.
❦ Tie the ends with string and boil for 2 ½ to 3 hours.

Variation
For a version of Spotted Dick, spread the rolled-out suet pastry with some warmed golden syrup, sprinkle mixed dried fruit liberally over this and then proceed as for Jam Roly-Poly.

PLUM JAM LAYER PUDDING

Serves 4

225 g (8 oz) Suet Crust Pastry (see page 361) made with wholemeal self-raising flour
225 g (8 oz) home-made plum jam

❦ Put a pan of water on to boil. Grease a 500 ml (1 pint) pudding basin. Divide the pastry into four pieces (each one slightly larger than the last). Roll the smallest piece into a round to fit the base of the basin. Cover the pastry with jam. Add another slightly larger round and cover with jam.

❦ Add a third round and cover with jam. Finish with the largest piece rolled into a round.

❦ Cover the basin (see page 362). Stand the basin in the boiling water and boil steadily for 2 hours, topping up with boiling water as necessary.

❦ Remove the basin and let it stand for a minute or two. The pastry will shrink a little, making it easier to turn out. Serve at once with cream or custard.

Variation
A syrup pudding can be made in the same way, using 50 g (2 oz) golden syrup with 50 (2 oz) breadcrumbs mixed with it. Layer the pudding as for the jam one. This would be served with warm syrup.

DORSET APPLE PUDDINGS

Makes 4

50 g (2 oz) butter
50 g (2 oz) brown sugar
1 tbsp rum
4 medium eating apples
225 g (8 oz) Suet Crust Pastry (see page 361)

❦ Put a pan of water on to boil. Mix the butter, sugar and rum together; beat until soft. Peel and core the apples. Divide the pastry into four pieces. Roll out into rounds large enough to enclose the apples. Put an apple on each round and fill the hole with the butter mixture. Brush the edges of the rounds with water.

❦ With floured hands, enclose each apple in its pastry, by bringing the edges to the top. Press to seal.

Loosely wrap each dumpling in a square of good quality kitchen foil, twisting the top firmly to seal, but leaving room for the dumpling to expand.

❦ Put into boiling water and bring back to the boil. Cover and simmer for 30-40 minutes. Lift the parcels out with a slotted spoon and remove the foil. Put the dumplings on a hot dish, sprinkle with caster sugar and serve at once, with cream.

Note
Eating apples cook well. They do not collapse like Bramleys and are a good size for these dumplings.

APPLE HAT

Serves 4-6

225 g (8 oz) Suet Crust Pastry (see page 361)
450 g (1 lb) cooking apples
2 tbsp soft brown sugar
1 lemon, juice and grated rind
2 tbsp water

❦ Put a pan of water on to boil. Grease a 750 ml (1 ½ pint) pudding basin. Roll out the pastry and use to line the basin (see page 362).

❦ Peel, core and slice the apples, mix with the sugar, lemon juice, rind and water. Damp the edges of the pastry. Roll out the remaining pastry for a lid and position. Press well together. Cover the basin (see page 362).

❦ Stand the basin in the boiling water and boil steadily for 3 hours, topping up with boiling water as necessary.

❦ Remove the basin and let stand for 2-3 minutes. Turn out and serve with brown sugar and cream.

DUTCH APPLE PUDDING

Serves 4-6

225 g (8 oz) Suet Crust Pastry (see page 361)
450 g (1 lb) cooking apples
brown sugar
golden syrup

❧ Heat the oven to 200–220C (400–425F) mark 6–7.
Divide the pastry in half. Roll out one piece into a
round and use to line a well greased 20 cm (8 in) pie
plate (preferably enamel).
❧ Peel, core and slice the apples. Put the slices
thickly on the pastry round. Sprinkle well with sugar
and dampen the edge of the pastry.
❧ Roll out the remaining pastry for a lid and cover
the apple with it, pressing the edges firmly together.
Brush the top of the pie generously with warmed
golden syrup and sprinkle with some more brown
sugar. Cook for 30–40 minutes until the pie is brown
and the top crisp like toffee.

CUSTARDS, CREAMS AND JELLIES

Here is a selection of simple but delicious recipes fit to grace any table. Old favourites such as Old English Trifle and Crème Brûlée appear alongside jellies and custard-based recipes, together with plenty of new and interesting ideas.
Custards and creams should be smooth and creamy, and jellies well set but by no means firm, for flavour is linked to texture in these delicate dishes. Although milk is fine for the family there is absolutely nothing like cream and it is not really very extravagant. If you need to cook for more people than the recipe says, make two layers instead of one, and perhaps use a different flavour or colour.

OLD ENGLISH TRIFLE

Serves 4

175 g (6 oz) sponge cake
75 ml (3 fl oz) dry sherry
3 tbsp raspberry jam
3 egg yolks
1 tsp caster sugar
1 vanilla pod
425 ml (¾ pint) milk
150 ml (¼ pint) double cream
angelica, almonds, ratafia biscuits, glacé cherries

❦ Put the sponge cake in a glass dish. Soak with sherry and dot with the raspberry jam. Use the egg yolks, sugar, vanilla pod and milk to make a Crème à la Vanille (see page 349). Pour over the sponge cake and leave until set.
❦ Whip the cream and spoon on to the custard. Decorate with small diamonds of angelica, blanched split almonds, ratafia biscuits and a few cherries.
❦ This is a classic trifle which has no jelly and no fruit. It is easy to make, but take care not to let the custard curdle.

Variation
Add layers of soft fruit – raspberries or blackberries.

CREME BAVAROISE

Serves 4

2 eggs, separated
50 g (2 oz) caster sugar
275 ml (½ pint) milk
1 vanilla pod
15 g (½ oz) powdered gelatine
150 ml (¼ pint) double or whipping cream

❦ Whisk the egg yolks with the sugar until pale. Heat the milk with the vanilla pod. Leave to infuse while you dissolve the gelatine in a bowl with 2 tablespoons water, standing in a pan of hot water. Remove the vanilla pod.
❦ Pour the hot milk on to the yolks, beating all the time. Cook slowly over hot water until the yolks begin to thicken, beating all the time. Add the gelatine to this mixture, pouring it in a thin stream as you stir. Let the mixture cool.
❦ Whisk the egg whites stiffly and whip the cream. Fold the cream and egg whites together. Stir a little into the custard (this helps to give an even texture) then fold in the remainder, thoroughly but gently and carefully.
❦ Spoon into individual glasses and leave to set.

Variations
The crème may be flavoured with chocolate, coffee or fruit.

CREME BRULEE

Serves 4

4 egg yolks
25 g (1 oz) caster sugar
1 vanilla pod
575 ml (1 pint) double cream
extra caster sugar

❦ Beat the egg yolks with the sugar until light and fluffy. Put the vanilla pod into the cream in the top of a double saucepan, or a basin over a saucepan of hot water. Bring the cream almost to the boil (but it must not boil). Remove the vanilla pod.
❦ Pour the cream on to the egg yolks, stirring all the time. Return to the double saucepan and cook the mixture gently until it thickens, stirring all the time.

Pour it into a shallow dish and leave it to stand for several hours and then chill.
❦ Before serving, dust with an even layer of caster sugar and brown carefully under a moderate grill. Serve at once.

Note
This rich dessert is a speciality of Trinity College, Cambridge.

BANANA CUSTARD

Serves 4-6

575 ml (1 pint) Crème à la Vanille made with brown sugar (see page 349)
75 g (3 oz) soft brown sugar
75 g (3 oz) butter
3 bananas

❦ Make up the custard as usual, but using brown sugar instead of caster. Melt the sugar and the butter in a frying pan. Peel and slice the bananas. Gently poach them in the sugar until soft.
❦ Put a layer of bananas in the bottom of a glass bowl and cover with custard. Continue to layer until the fruit is used up. Finish with a layer of custard.
❦ A round of damp greaseproof paper pressed lightly on the top of the custard prevents a skin from forming, or cover the dish with cling film.

RICE CONDE

Serves 4-6

65 g (2 ½ oz) Carolina rice
575 ml (1 pint) milk
1 vanilla pod
50 g (2 oz) caster sugar
15 g (½ oz) powdered gelatine
2 tbsp top of the milk

Cook the rice slowly in the milk with the vanilla pod and sugar for about 40 minutes. Cool. Remove the pod (wash it, dry it and put back in the sugar jar).
Dissolve the gelatine in 2 tablespoons water in a bowl set over a pan of hot water. Fold the dissolved gelatine through the rice with the top of the milk. Set in an appropriate mould.

CREME CARAMEL

Serves 4

75 g (3 oz) caster sugar
4 eggs, plus 4 egg yolks
2 tbsp sugar
575 ml (1 pint) milk
1 vanilla pod

❦ Heat the oven to 180C (350F) mark 4.
❦ Put the sugar with 1 teaspoon water in a heavy-based saucepan and melt slowly without stirring. When it starts colouring, stir equally slowly and carefully until it is a dark honey colour. Pour this caramel into a warmed china soufflé dish. Turn it round and about to coat the sides and base.
❦ Break the eggs into a bowl, add the extra yolks and sugar and beat well. Boil the milk with the vanilla pod. Remove the pod and pour the milk on to the eggs, beating all the time. Pour carefully into the caramel-lined dish.
❦ Stand in a roasting tin containing 4 cm (1 ½ in) water and cook until the custard is set, about 40 minutes. Remove from the oven and leave until cold, then chill before turning out.

Note
This, as with all baked custards, does very well in a slow cooker.

LEMON SURPRISE

Serves 4

50 g (2 oz) butter
100 g (4 oz) caster sugar
grated rind and juice of 1 lemon
2 eggs, separated
25 g (1 oz) plain flour
275 ml (½ pint) milk

❦ Heat the oven to 180C (350F) mark 4. Butter a 1 litre (2 pint) pie dish.
❦ Cream the butter with the sugar until pale and fluffy. Beat the lemon rind into the butter and sugar. Beat in the egg yolks. Sieve the flour and add it by degrees with the milk followed by the lemon juice. (It will curdle now but do not worry.)
❦ Beat the egg whites stiffly and fold evenly into the

mixture. Turn into the pie dish and bake for about 40 minutes, until golden brown. You will find that the curdled mixture has separated into a lemon custard with a sponge top.

GOOSEBERRY WHIP

Serves 4-6

450 g (1 lb) gooseberries
100 ml (4 fl oz) white wine
100 ml (4 fl oz) water
thinly pared rind of 1 lemon
100 g (4 oz) sugar
2 eggs
walnut halves or almonds to decorate

❦ Top and tail the gooseberries and wash them. Simmer until tender with the wine, water and lemon rind. Sieve to remove the seeds. Return to the pan and cook over a gentle heat. Add the sugar and stir until dissolved. Remove from the heat and cool.
❦ Separate the eggs. Beat the yolks and fold into the mixture. Whisk the egg whites stiffly and fold into the gooseberry mixture.
❦ Pour into individual glasses and decorate with a walnut or a blanched almond.

ORANGE JELLY

Serves 4

75 g (3 oz) lump sugar
3 oranges
1 lemon
15 g (½ oz) powdered gelatine
275 ml (½ pint) cold water or fresh or canned
    orange juice

❦ Rub the sugar lumps over the rinds of the fruit. Squeeze the juice.
❦ Dissolve the gelatine in 2 tablespoons water over a pan of hot water. Add to the fruit juices in a pan, with the sugar. Make up to 425 ml (¾ pint) with water, or with fresh or canned orange juice. Heat the mixture gently to dissolve the sugar, then pour into a wetted mould and leave to set.
❦ Chill thoroughly before turning out. Serve with whipped cream.

CHRISTMAS JELLY

Serves 4

275 ml (½ pint) water
two 10 cm (4 in) cinnamon sticks
4 cloves
4 blades of mace
1 packet of blackcurrant jelly
150 ml (¼ pint) port

❧ Simmer the spices in the water for 10 minutes. Stand for 1 hour. Strain and warm again.
❧ Melt the jelly in the spicy water. Add the port and make up to 575 ml (1 pint) with cold water. Transfer to a jelly mould or into individual glasses and chill until set.
❧ Best served in tall, sparkling, individual glasses. Its lovely rich colour and warm taste need no further adornment.

APPLE JELLY

Serves 4-6

450 g (1 lb) cooking apples
2 cloves
25 g (1 oz) caster sugar
1 lemon
2 tbsp bramble jelly
15 g (½ oz) powdered gelatine

❧ Peel, core and slice the apples. Cook with the cloves and sugar in very little water (Bramleys will need none). Discard the cloves and beat the apples to a cream. Grate the rind and squeeze the juice from the lemon; stir into the apples with the bramble jelly.
❧ Dissolve the gelatine in 2 tablespoons water in a bowl over a pan of hot water. Fold evenly into the apples, stirring all the time. Turn into a wetted mould and leave to set.
❧ Turn out and serve with cream and home-made almond tuiles or other decorative biscuits. This is a particularly easy and delicious pudding.

PINEAPPLE CHARLOTTE

Serves 4-6

575 ml (1 pint) milk
4 egg yolks
1 tsp arrowroot or cornflour
50 g (2 oz) caster sugar
425 g (15 oz) can pineapple rings
275 ml (½ pint) double or whipping cream
15 g (½ oz) powdered gelatine
2 egg whites
1 packet of sponge fingers

❧ Heat the milk. Beat the egg yolks with the arrowroot and sugar. Pour the hot milk on to the eggs, beating all the time, then leave to cool. Drain the pineapple. Keep the juice. Chop half the rings to give about 4 tablespoons. Whip the cream fairly lightly.
❧ Soak the gelatine in 3–4 tablespoons of pineapple juice (it is fresh pineapple that stops gelatine setting). Dissolve over a pan of hot water. Pour into the custard in a thin stream, then fold in three-quarters of the cream.
❧ Leave until the custard starts to set, then whisk the egg whites stiffly and with a metal spoon fold them, with the chopped pineapple, into the charlotte. Turn into a greased charlotte mould, a china soufflé dish or a cake tin. Chill until set.
❧ Turn out carefully on to a serving dish. Spread the sides with the rest of the cream and stick the sponge fingers around the sides. Decorate the top with the remaining pineapple rings.
❧ Spring-release cake tins make this recipe much easier, and are worthwhile investing in if you do much entertaining.

ICE-COLD ZABAGLIONE

Serves 4

50 g (2 oz) sugar
1 tbsp water
1 egg, plus 2 egg yolks
1 tbsp Marsala

❦ Melt the sugar with the water in a strong saucepan. Bring to the boil until bubbling and syrupy. Take off the heat. Separate the egg. Beat the egg white until stiff. Pour the syrup on to it and beat until it is absorbed. This makes a meringue mixture.
❦ Put the 3 egg yolks with the Marsala into a bowl. Whisk over a saucepan of hot water until thick, then fold into the meringue mixture. Pour into glasses and refrigerate until ice-cold. Serve with sponge fingers and cream.

Variation
This can be served warm: beat 3 egg yolks with the sugar and Marsala over heat until thick. It is easier to make, but must be served at once, which could be a bore if you are cooking for a dinner party.

FRUIT FOR ALL SEASONS

The mouth-watering recipes in this section range from light summer dishes made with fresh fruit to substantial cooked puddings. A few delicious time-saving recipes using canned fruits have also been included.

❦ About Cooking Fruit ❦

'Stewing' fruit in water and sugar can all too often result in a sort of 'wash-day afters'. If the trouble is taken to make a syrup first, then adding the prepared fruit, poaching it and simmering carefully until the fruit is cooked, all the richness and texture of the fruit is retained. A cheap frying pan kept only for fruit and meringue poaching is a very handy item of equipment.

Canned fruit can often be substituted for fresh fruit, though it may need a little extra attention. Poaching canned peaches or pears in their own syrup, for example, improves their texture and flavour beyond belief.

PEAR CONDÉ

Serves 4-6

4 large pears
150 ml (¼ pint) Sugar Syrup (see page 367)
Rice Condé (see page 271)
glacé cherries
Apricot Glaze (see page 367)

❦ Peel, halve and core the pears. Poach in sugar syrup until tender. If using canned pears, poach them in their own syrup. Leave in the syrup to cool.
❦ Drain the fruit and arrange it on a bed of rice condé. Decorate this sparingly with some glacé cherries and then coat with apricot glaze.

Note
Almost any fruit is suitable for a condé.

JAMAICAN BANANAS

Serves 4-6

6 bananas
2 tbsp rum
4 tsp soft brown sugar
25 g (1 oz) flaked almonds
225 ml (8 fl oz) evaporated milk, chilled
4 tsp instant coffee powder

❦ Slice the bananas into a glass bowl. Cover them with the rum and brown sugar. Toast the almonds under the grill or in a pan. They burn easily so watch carefully.
❦ Chill the evaporated milk for 24 hours, then it will whip quite easily. Whip the evaporated milk, adding the coffee little by little. Cover the bananas with the coffee cream and sprinkle with toasted almonds.

Note
When cooking with instant coffee, always use a good quality one.

GOLDEN CHARTREUSE

Serves 4-6

300 g (11 oz) can Cape goldenberries
300 g (11 oz) can mandarin oranges
425 g (15 oz) can peaches
1 packet of lemon jelly
1 packet of orange jelly

❦ Drain the fruit as the juices will be too sweet to use. Make up the jellies together following the instructions on the packet. Cool almost to setting point.
❦ Using a 1 ½ litre (2 ½ pint) glass dish or jelly mould, put some jelly in the bottom, then a layer of goldenberries. Add a layer of jelly and chill until set. Cover with a layer of mandarins, pour jelly over them and leave to set. Then arrange a layer of thinly sliced peaches over the set jelly; cover with more jelly and leave to set. Continue until all the fruit and jelly is used up. Leave to set firmly in the refrigerator.
❦ To turn out, dip the mould briefly in hot water and invert on to a serving dish. If serving in the dish, a scattering of chopped jelly on the top is attractive.

Notes
For a buffet luncheon, melt the jellies separately and make up as above but in glasses, using the jellies alternately.

PINEAPPLE FLAMBE

Serves 4-6

440 g (15 ½ oz) can pineapple rings or a fresh pineapple
caster sugar
50 g (2 oz) butter
50 ml (2 fl oz) brandy or rum

❦ Strain the pineapple rings. There will be six or seven. Keep the juice for something else. If a fresh pineapple is used, peel, core and slice it. Dust the rings with caster sugar.
❦ Sizzle the butter in a frying pan. Put in as many rings as you can and brown them. The sugar will caramelize. Take out one or two to make room for the spares. Brown them too. Return them all to the pan, sprinkle again with sugar and get them really hot.
❦ Pour the brandy or rum over the pineapple rings. It will probably light at once. If not, set a match to it. Serve while flaming.

Notes
If you have a suitable frying pan you can prepare half of this in the kitchen and then put it over a burner in the dining room. The little methylated spirit lamp under a fondue dish is first class for this but a chafing dish is the proper job.
❦ Bananas are equally delicious when given this treatment.

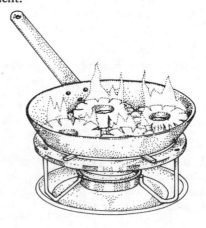

RHUBARB FOOL

Serves 4

450 g (1 lb) rhubarb
150 ml (¼ pint) Light Sugar Syrup (see page 367)
2 tsp custard powder
150 ml (¼ pint) milk
sugar
150 ml (¼ pint) double or whipping cream

❧ Prepare the rhubarb, trim and cut it into short lengths. Poach in the sugar syrup until tender. Strain the rhubarb and leave to cool. Make the custard with the milk according to instructions on the packet. Sweeten to taste and cool. If the rhubarb is very soft, mix it up with a wooden fork. If not, rub it through a sieve, then sweeten to taste.
❧ Fold the custard into the rhubarb. Whip the cream and fold through the mixture very lightly so that it all looks streaky.
❧ Chill thoroughly and serve in glasses with sponge fingers.

PLUM COMPOTE

Serves 4

450 g (1 lb) plums
1 glass of port
50 g (2 oz) redcurrant jelly
grated rind and juice of 1 orange
about 50 g (2 oz) sugar

❧ Wipe the plums, halve and remove the stones. Put the port, jelly, the grated rind and juice of the orange and the sugar into a frying pan. Heat gently to melt the jelly and sugar.
❧ Add the plums to this syrup, cut sides down, and poach – for that is what it is – for 10-15 minutes, spooning the syrup over the plums. Cool a little, then spoon carefully into a bowl. Pour the remaining syrup over the plums.
❧ Serve with either thin slices of sponge cake or with sponge fingers.

MELON SURPRISE

Serves 4-6

1 honeydew melon
225 g (8 oz) fresh strawberries or raspberries
1 fresh peach, peeled and stoned
1 dessert pear, peeled and cored
75 g (3 oz) caster sugar
2 tbsp dry sherry

❧ Cut the top off the melon and reserve as a lid. Cut a very small slice off the base of the melon so that it will stand. Scoop out the seeds. Take out the flesh in balls with a vegetable scoop or a strong teaspoon. Be careful not to go through the side. Put the melon balls in a bowl, and the melon shell and lid in a polythene bag. Put them all in the refrigerator to chill. (The bag is a must because otherwise the smell of melon will filter into everything else in the refrigerator.)
❧ Pick over and hull the strawberries or raspberries. Reserve a few and add the rest to the melon balls. Dice the peach and pear and add to the fruit in the bowl. Sprinkle the fruit with caster sugar and sherry and leave to stand for half an hour.
❧ Take out the melon shell and fill it carefully with fruit mixture, finishing with the melon balls. Add the reserved strawberries or raspberries and put the melon lid on top. To serve, sit the melon on two or three vine leaves, if available, on an attractive plate.

APPLE FLORENTINE

Serves 4-6

700 g (1 ½ lb) cooking apples
50 g (2 oz) butter
2 tsp cooking oil
75 g (3 oz) soft brown sugar
¼ tsp ground cinnamon
grated rind of 2 lemons
225 g (8 oz) Flaky Pastry (see page 361)
little milk
150 ml (¼ pint) cider
nutmeg
5 cm (2 in) cinnamon stick
icing sugar

❧ Heat the oven to 220C (425F) mark 7.
❧ Peel and core the apples and cut into quarters but
no smaller. Fry in the butter and oil until beginning
to colour. Sprinkle with the sugar, cinnamon and
grated rind of one lemon. Turn into a round ovenproof dish or shallow pie dish. Dampen the edge.
❧ Roll out the pastry 5 mm (¼ in) thick and use it
to cover the apples. Press the pastry down on the
edge and trim. Glaze lightly with milk and cook for
30 minutes.
❧ Spice the cider by heating it in a small saucepan
with a good grating of nutmeg, the cinnamon stick
and the grated rind of the second lemon. Let it stand
for 20 minutes, add sugar to taste, and then strain.
❧ When the pastry is done, lift it off the pie by running a knife between the edge and the dish. Cut it
into segments. Pour the hot spiced cider into the
dish. Put the pastry pieces back in place and dust
with icing sugar. Serve with thick cream.

APPLE SNOW

Serves 4-6

grated rind and juice of 1 lemon
575 ml (1 pint) apple purée
50 g (2 oz) caster sugar
15 g (½ oz) powdered gelatine
2 tbsp water
whites of 2 eggs

❧ Add the lemon rind and juice to the apple purée
with the sugar. Dissolve the gelatine in the water in

a bowl over a pan of hot water. Pour in a thin stream
into the purée, beating all the time.
❧ Whisk the egg whites stiffly. Fold into the purée
with a metal spoon. Serve in individual glasses with
sponge fingers.

Note
Traditionally 'snows' are not set with gelatine and
must be served soon after they are made. This one,
however, can be made the day before.

BAKED APPLES

Serves 4

4 large cooking apples
2 tbsp raisins
1 tbsp mixed peel
golden syrup

❧ Heat the oven to 180C (350F) mark 4.
❧ Peel the apples and remove the cores with a corer
or potato peeler. Put them in a buttered pie dish. Fill
the cavities with the raisins and mixed peel or any
other kind of filling if preferred.
❧ Pour melted golden syrup over the apples and
cover the dish with a lid or foil. Bake until tender –
45-60 minutes.

LIMOGES CLAFOUTIS

Serves 4-6

700 g (1 ½ lb) fresh ripe cherries
3 eggs
50 g (2 oz) plain flour
¼ tsp salt
50 g (2 oz) caster sugar
425 ml (¾ pint) milk
50 g (2 oz) butter

❧ Heat the oven to 220C (425F) mark 7.
❧ Stone the cherries. Beat the eggs, flour, salt and
sugar together. Warm the milk and pour on to the
egg mixture, beating all the time. Leave to stand for
20 minutes.
❧ Butter a pie dish and put the cherries into it. Pour
the egg mixture, which is a batter, over the cherries.
Cook for 25-30 minutes.

APPLE AND BLACKBERRY CRUMBLE

Serves 4-6

4 cooking apples
450 g (1 lb) blackberries
2 tbsp sugar
50 g (2 oz) bramble jelly
150 g (5 oz) wholemeal flour
50 g (2 oz) Demerara sugar
75 g (3 oz) butter
25 g (1 oz) chopped almonds

❦ Heat the oven to 220C (425F) mark 7.
❦ Prepare and slice the apples. Wash and dry the blackberries. Put half the apples in the base of a buttered pie dish. Add all the blackberries with the sugar and bramble jelly. Cover with the remaining apples.
❦ Mix the flour and sugar together and rub in the butter. Add the almonds and mix until they are thoroughly blended. Spread evenly over the fruit and cook for 20-30 minutes.

RANCIN

Serves 4-6

6 slices of white bread
75 g (3 oz) butter
450 g (1 lb) black cherries
75 g (3 oz) caster sugar

❦ Heat the oven to 200C (400F) mark 6.
❦ Spread the bread (home-made bread is best, and home-made brioche is superb) generously with butter. Stone the cherries – use a cherry pitter or hook them out with a large hairpin. Put a layer of bread and butter, butter side up, in the base of an ovenproof dish.
❦ Gently poach the cherries in as little water as possible with plenty of sugar. Spoon the cherries on to the bread, adding not too much juice. Cover with slices of buttered bread, butter side up, and dust with sugar. Bake until brown and crisp – about 25 minutes.

Note
This is a regional dish from Alsace.

PEASANT GIRL IN A VEIL

Serves 4-6

900 g (2 lb) ripe Victoria plums
100 g (4 oz) granulated sugar
175 g (6 oz) butter
about 25 g (1 oz) caster sugar
175 g (6 oz) fresh white breadcrumbs
1 egg white
150 ml (¼ pint) whipping cream

❦ Heat the oven to 180C (350F) mark 4.
❦ Wipe the plums, slit the sides and take out the stones. Fill each cavity with a teaspoon of granulated sugar and a tiny knob of butter. Arrange the fruit, cut side up, in an ovenproof dish. Cover with caster sugar according to taste and cook for 30 minutes. Leave to cool.
❦ Fry the crumbs lightly in the remaining butter and sprinkle over the plums. Whisk the egg white until stiff and lightly whisk the cream. Fold the two together and spoon over the plums.

SWEDISH RASPBERRY SHORTCAKE

Serves 6-8

100 g (4 oz) plain flour
75 g (3 oz) butter
25 g (1 oz) icing sugar
1 egg yolk
450 g (1 lb) raspberries
100 g (4 oz) redcurrant jelly
150 ml (¼ pint) whipping cream

❦ Heat the oven to 190C (375F) mark 5.
❦ Sieve the flour into a bowl. Make a dip in it and put in the butter, sugar and egg yolk. Work with the fingertips, drawing the flour down from the sides until you have a smooth mixture. Cover and chill.
❦ Use non-stick baking paper to line a baking sheet. Put the mixture on it and pat out into a round, about 5 mm (¼ in) thick. Cover with greaseproof paper and beans and bake blind for 20 minutes (see page 357). Remove paper and beans and leave to cool.
❦ When cold, arrange the raspberries, pointed end uppermost, over it. Melt the redcurrant jelly (home-made is best) and spoon over the raspberries.

APRICOT AND WALNUT GALETTE

Serves 4-6

100 g (4 oz) walnut pieces
150 g (5 oz) plain flour
½ tsp salt
100 g (4 oz) butter
25 g (2 oz) caster sugar
225 g (8 oz) fresh or canned apricots
150 ml (¼ pint) whipping cream
icing sugar

❦ Heat the oven to 180C (350F) mark 4.
❦ Run a rolling pin over the walnut pieces. Sieve the flour with the salt into a bowl. Sprinkle in the nuts. Make a dip in the flour and put the butter and caster sugar into it. Lightly draw the flour down from the sides and work until you have a smooth dough. The nuts will be incorporated as you work. Chill for 30 minutes.
❦ Divide the dough into three pieces. Roll each into a circle about 15 cm (6 in). Slip on to baking sheets lined with baking paper. Cook for 20-30 minutes. Cool.
❦ Cut the apricots into quarters. Whip the cream and fold the fruit through it. When the pastry is cold, sandwich together with the fruit and cream. Dust with icing sugar.

BLACKBERRY BETTY

Serves 4-6

4 cooking apples
175 g (6 oz) blackberries
50 g (2 oz) sugar
100 g (4 oz) fresh white breadcrumbs
50 g (2 oz) light soft brown sugar
50 g (2 oz) butter, melted

❦ Peel, core and slice the apples. Poach them in very little water with the blackberries and sugar until tender. Cool.
❦ Using individual glasses, layer the fruit, breadcrumbs, a little brown sugar and a spoonful of melted butter, continuing until you have used all the fruit. Finish with a layer of crumbs, sugar and butter. Top with a spoonful of cream if liked.

BAKED QUINCES

Serves 6

6 quinces
50 ml (2 fl oz) water
4 cloves
6 tbsp honey

❦ Heat the oven to 150C (300F) mark 2.
❦ Peel the fruit and leave whole, with the stalks on if you can manage it. Stand the fruit, stalk end upwards, in an ovenproof dish with a good lid, with the water and the cloves. Spoon the honey over each quince.
❦ Cover tightly and cook for 2, or even 3, hours until tender.
❦ Serve chilled with whipped cream. This fruit turns the most ravishing colour and keeps its unique fragrance.

AUTUMN CREAM

Serves 6

450 g (1 lb) blackberries
5 tbsp blackcurrant syrup
1 tbsp brandy
175 g (6 oz) caster sugar
200 ml (8 fl oz) whipping cream
2 tbsp red wine
2 tbsp icing sugar, sieved

❦ Pick the blackberries over. Put them in a bowl with the blackcurrant syrup (the sort you use for small children) and add the brandy. Sprinkle this with all the sugar and leave for several hours in the refrigerator.
❦ When ready, spoon it carefully into tall individual glasses, leaving room for the cream. Whip the cream thickly, blending in the wine and icing sugar by degrees. The cream will turn pink and looks lovely on top of the blackberries.

HUNGARIAN PEACHES

Serves 4

4 large peaches
50 g (2 oz) ground almonds
50 g (2 oz) icing sugar, sieved
2 small bought sponge cakes
½ glass of red wine
caster sugar

❦ Heat the oven to 180C (350F) mark 4.
❦ Skin the peaches (pour boiling water over them then the skins come off easily). Halve, and remove the stone. Remove a little of the flesh to make a larger hole.
❦ Mix the ground almonds and the sieved icing sugar with the sponge cakes and the spare peach flesh. Moisten this with a little wine and use the mixture to stuff each peach half. Put the halves together, one on top of the other, and put in an ovenproof dish. Pour the rest of the wine over them and dust with caster sugar.
❦ Cook until the sugar caramelizes; serve hot.

DAMSON SUEDOISE

Serves 4-6

450 g (1 lb) damsons
175 g (6 oz) caster sugar
150 ml (¼ pint) water
15 g (½ oz) powdered gelatine

❦ Stone the damsons. Put them with the sugar and water into a pan. Simmer slowly until the sugar is dissolved and the fruit tender.
❦ Blend the fruit or rub through a sieve. Make up to 575 ml (1 pint) with water. Dissolve the gelatine in 2 tablespoons water in a bowl over a pan of hot water, and pour into the purée in a thin stream (this prevents the gelatine from 'stringing'). Mix well and pour the purée into a glass dish or mould.
❦ Set for several hours in the refrigerator.

Notes
A suédoise is a fruit purée set with gelatine. Custard made from a packet, not too thickly, is surprisingly good with this.

MERINGUES, MOUSSES AND SOUFFLES

*This section contains an exciting range of simple and more
elaborate recipes for meringues, mousses combined with fruits
or other flavourings, and hot and cold soufflés.*

❧ About meringues, ❧ soufflés and mousses

Meringues are everyone's favourites and there are
several different ways of making them. Meringue
cuite is the very firm one used for making meringue
baskets and other shapes. 'Cuite' means cooked – it
isn't cooked, but is whisked over heat, which is probably how it acquired the name. Our everyday
meringue is known as meringue suisse, and is suitable for individual meringues as well as for piping or
spreading over various puddings or desserts which
call for a meringue topping. Pavlova is the Australian
meringue shell with the crisp outside and soft, gooey
centre, made with the addition of vinegar and cornflour. Don't forget too, that soft brown sugar makes
delicious meringues and does away with any prob-
lems of pale, coffee-coloured meringues – for they
are that colour even before they are baked.

A cold soufflé has whisked egg whites folded into
it just before it sets, regardless of the base, which
may be custard or fruit purée. It is turned into a soufflé dish which has a stiff paper or foil 'collar' tied
round it so when set, it may be removed to reveal the
soufflé standing about 2.5 cm (1 in) above the rim of
the dish.
With a hot soufflé, the base gives the flavour and the
egg white the raising power. Fill the prepared dish
not more than three-quarters full, and cook on a hot
baking sheet towards the bottom of the oven with
nothing else in the oven. Keep the family waiting, for
it sinks rapidly when removed from the oven. No
collar is necessary for a hot soufflé.

A mousse is creamier and denser than a soufflé,
usually containing more egg yolks and less, or even
sometimes no, whisked egg white. It is set into a bowl
and, unlike a soufflé, never comes above the dish.

MERINGUE CUITE

whites of 4 eggs
250 g (9 oz) icing sugar (flavoured with a
   vanilla pod)

❦ If you use an electric whisk, all well and good. If not, whisk with the basin over a pan of hot water on a low heat. Put the whites with the sieved icing sugar into a warmed, dry bowl. Whisk them until very firm indeed.
❦ Use a forcing bag fitted with a 1 cm (½ in) pipe to apply, or according to individual recipes.

MERINGUE SUISSE

whites of 2 eggs
100 g (4 oz) caster sugar

❦ Whisk the egg whites very stiffly. Whisk in half the sugar, a little at a time, and then fold in the rest with a metal spoon. The meringue should be a velvety dense mass, stiff enough to stay in the inverted bowl.

MERINGUE SHELLS

Makes 5-6 complete meringues

whites of 2 eggs
100 g (4 oz) caster sugar
whipping cream

❦ Heat the oven to 120C (250F) mark ½.
❦ Make the meringue suisse mixture as above and shape the shells by taking a dessertspoon of the mixture and spooning it out with another dessertspoon. Do this until you achieve a smooth oval shape, then spoon it on to a baking sheet lined with non-stick paper. As the second dessertspoon comes away, tip a little tail over the top of the meringue. This is the classic shape.
❦ Cook in a cool oven until firm, dry and set (about 2 hours), reversing the sheets in the oven after an hour.
❦ Sandwich the shells together with firmly whipped cream.

BROWN SUGAR MERINGUE

2 egg whites
100 g (4 oz) soft light brown sugar

❦ Heat the oven to 120C (250F) mark ½. Make a meringue suisse mixture (see left), but using soft light brown sugar instead of caster.
❦ Whisk the egg whites a little longer at both stages of whisking, and fold in the remaining sugar in small amounts. Shape or pipe on to baking sheets lined with non-stick paper and cook for 2-2 ½ hours. Use for any meringue suisse recipe. These take a little longer to dry out.

APPLE SPONGE MERINGUE

Serves 4-5

150 g (5 oz) butter
250 g (9 oz) caster sugar
3 eggs
200 g (7 oz) self-raising flour
3 or 4 cooking apples
50 g (2 oz) caster sugar
¼ tsp ground cinnamon
2 egg-white quantity of Meringue Suisse (see left)

❦ Heat the oven to 160C (325F) mark 3. Butter a 25 cm (10 in) fluted ovenproof china flan case or other ovenproof dish.
❦ Cream the butter and sugar together until light and fluffy. Add the eggs one at a time and beat well. Fold in the sieved flour. Turn into the flan case and cook for 40 minutes.
❦ Peel, core and slice the apples, simmer with the sugar and cinnamon in a very little water until tender, then rub through a sieve or mash.
❦ When the sponge base is cool, spread the apple over the surface. Fill a forcing bag fitted with a 2.5 cm (1 in) star pipe, and use to make circles of meringue over the apple, or put it on with a spoon and swirl with a fork.
❦ Cook for 1 hour until the meringue is crisp.

BAKED ALASKA

Serves 4-6

1 Victoria sandwich layer, 18 cm (7 in) across
1 family block ice-cream or 1 litre (1 quart) in
    a round tub (vanilla or any other flavour)
2 egg-white quantity of Meringue Suisse (see
    page 283)

❦ Heat the oven to 230C (450C) mark 8.
❦ Put the sponge cake on an ovenproof plate. Turn
the stiffly frozen ice-cream on to the cake, keeping it
in the centre. Use the meringue to completely mask
the ice-cream and cake, leaving no gaps. Cook in the
centre of the oven for 4 minutes and serve at once.

Variations
Place fruit under and around the ice-cream. Use a
flavoured ice-cream to go with the fruit.

PAVLOVA

Serves 6-8

whites of 4 eggs
225 g (8 oz) caster sugar
4 tsp cornflour
2 tsp white vinegar
275 ml (½ pint) whipping cream
4 fresh peaches

❦ Heat the oven to 120C (250F) mark ½.
❦ Whisk the egg whites until stiff. Add the sugar, 2
tablespoons at a time, beating between each addition.
When the sugar is used up, beat for 1-2 minutes until
the meringue is dense, velvety and very, very stiff.
Then beat in the cornflour, sprinkling it over the
meringue, and finally the vinegar.
❦ Butter an attractive shallow ovenproof dish. Put
the meringue into it, making a hollow dip in the centre. Bake for 1 ½ hours until really firm and set.
❦ Whip the cream. Peel and slice the peaches and
fold into the cream. When the meringue is cooked,
put the fruit into it. Serve without too much delay.

Notes
This is an Australian meringue. The addition of
cornflour and vinegar give it a soft texture inside and
a crisp outer crust. Fresh fruit really is best for this.

STRAWBERRY VACHERIN

Serves 4-6

4 egg-white quantity of Meringue Cuite (see
    page 283)
450 g (1 lb) strawberries
sugar
275 ml (½ pint) whipping cream

❦ Heat the oven to 160C (325F) mark 3.
❦ Line a baking sheet with non-stick baking paper
and draw a 15-18 cm (6-7 in) circle on it. Put a sheet
of rice paper over this. The pencil mark will show
through. Fill a forcing bag fitted with a 2.5 cm (1 in)
pipe with meringue. With a spoon, put the remaining meringue on the rice paper to cover the whole
circle about 1 cm (½ in) deep. Smooth it with the
spoon.
❦ Holding the tube upright, pipe the first ring of
your basket on to the meringue base around the edge,
but still on the meringue. Then pipe two more rings,
one on top of the other, taking care to keep the 'walls'
even.
❦ Cook for 1 ½ hours or until really firm. Have the
serving dish ready. Slip the vacherin case on to it –
the rice paper comes easily away from the baking
paper.
❦ When cold, trim the rice paper from the sides of
the meringue with your fingers. Cut the strawberries
in half. Dust them with sugar and reserve a few for
decoration. Whip the cream until stiff, fold the
strawberries into it and very gently pile into the case,
putting the reserved strawberries on the top.
❦ Serve reasonably soon after making.

Note
A vacherin is a meringue case or basket. It is made
with meringue cuite which is especially stiff and
holds its shape well.

RASPBERRY MERINGUE PIE

Serves 4

1 Swiss roll
425 g (15 oz) can raspberries
2 egg-white quantity of Meringue Suisse (see page 283)

❦ Heat the oven to 180C (350F) mark 4.
❦ Cut the Swiss roll into slices. Arrange over the base and sides of a glass ovenproof dish. Spoon the raspberries and their juice over the sponge cake. Pile the meringue on top, swirling it attractively with a fork.
❦ Cook until the meringue is crisp, about 30 minutes. It will be soft inside.

CHOCOLATE MERINGUE CASTLE

Serves 6-8

4 egg-white quantity of Meringue Suisse (see page 283)
275 ml (½ pint) whipping cream
100 g (4 oz) plain chocolate

❦ Heat the oven to 120C (250F) mark ½.
❦ Line 2 baking sheets with non-stick baking paper. Fill a forcing bag fitted with a large star pipe with the meringue and use to make 24 stars on the prepared baking sheets. Cook for about 1 ½ hours, until lightly coloured, reversing the sheets in the oven after an hour. Cool.
❦ Arrange a circle of stars closely together on a decorative plate. Whip the cream stiffly and pipe stars between and on top of the meringues. Continue to build the meringue with the cream into a pyramid shape, using the stars as decoration.
❦ Melt the chocolate in a bowl over hot water and spoon over the castle from the top. The chocolate sets hard and gives a wonderful variety of textures in this cake.

RASPBERRY MERINGUE BASKETS

Makes about 6

4 egg-white quantity of Meringue Cuite (see page 283)
225 g (½ lb) fresh raspberries
1 packet of raspberry jelly

❦ Heat the oven to 120C (250F) mark ½.
❦ Line two baking sheets with non-stick baking paper. Draw six circles about 7.5 cm (3 inches) across. Put rice paper over them. Fill a forcing bag fitted with a 1 cm (½ in) plain pipe with as much meringue as you can comfortably handle (refill when you need more). Pipe six little baskets using the same method as for the big vacherin case (see opposite). Pipe a circle to cover the base and then build up the 'walls'. Cook for about 1 ½ hours, or until firm and dry.
❦ Make up the packet of jelly with 210 ml (7 ½ fl oz) water, cool until nearly set. Turn the fresh raspberries in this, reserving six for decoration. Remove the baskets from the oven. Slip them off the baking paper and trim away the spare rice paper. Put the basket on a serving dish. When they are perfectly cold, fill with the jelly-covered raspberries. Top each with a reserved raspberry.
❦ The raspberries should only be lightly jellied.

Variation
Children like mandarin orange segments to be used in this pretty dessert. Pat the segments dry and use orange-flavoured jelly.

HAZELNUT COFFEE MERINGUES

Makes about 10

2 egg-white quantity of Meringue Suisse (see page 283)
50 g (2 oz) hazelnuts, very finely chopped
½ tsp instant coffee powder
150 ml (¼ pint) whipping cream

❦ Heat the oven to 120C (250F) mark ½. Line 2 baking sheets with non-stick baking paper.
❦ Make up the meringue suisse, then fold in the chopped hazelnuts and 1 teaspoon of instant coffee powder. Either pipe or make into 'shells' with dessertspoons (see page 283) on to the baking sheets, and cook for 2 hours at least, reversing the sheets after 1 hour.
❦ Whip the cream with the remaining instant coffee until stiff, then use to sandwich the meringues together.

RASPBERRY MOUSSE

Serves 6-8

900 g (2 lb) raspberries
175 g (6 oz) caster sugar
1 tbsp lemon juice
25 g (1 oz) powdered gelatine
4 tbsp water
275 ml (½ pint) whipping cream

❦ Pick over the raspberries and reserve 6 or 7 for decoration. Mash the remainder with the sugar and lemon juice. A wooden salad fork is good for this. Dissolve the gelatine in the water in a bowl over hot water. Pour into the raspberries in a thin stream, folding as you pour.
❦ Whip the cream until it is thick but not too stiff and fold it through the raspberries with a metal spoon. Pour into a dish and leave to set in the refrigerator.
❦ Take the mousse out of the refrigerator 1 hour before serving, as intense cold masks the flavour. Decorate with the reserved raspberries.

Note
There are no eggs in this mousse.

BRAMBLE MOUSSE

Serves 4-6

450 g (1 lb) blackberries
225 g (½ lb) cooking apples
75 g (3 oz) caster sugar
3 eggs
15 g (½ oz) powdered gelatine
grated rind and juice of 1 lemon
150 ml (¼ pint) whipping cream

❦ Pick the blackberries over. Peel, core and slice the apples. Put all the fruit into a pan with 25 g (1 oz) sugar and cook over a very gentle heat until the juice has run and the fruit is soft. Sieve and cool.
❦ Whisk the eggs with 50 g (2 oz) sugar over a pan of hot water until the mixture is thick and creamy. Cool a little.
❦ Dissolve the gelatine in the lemon juice in a bowl over hot water. Add the rind to the fruit purée and fold in the liquid gelatine. Whip the cream.
❦ Fold the egg mixture through the fruit purée followed by the cream. Pour into a dish and chill until set.

APRICOT MOUSSE

Serves 4

170 g (6 fl oz) can evaporated milk
15 g (½ oz) powdered gelatine
425 g (15 oz) can apricots
3 eggs
50 g (2 oz) caster sugar
25 g (1 oz) toasted flaked almonds

❦ Chill the unopened can of milk for 24 hours.
❦ Dissolve the gelatine in 2 tablespoons of water in a bowl over hot water. Purée the apricots in the blender or rub through a sieve. Beat the eggs with the sugar until light and fluffy, then fold into the purée. Fold in the gelatine, pouring in a thin stream. Whip the evaporated milk until thick and fold in. Pour into a dish and chill until set.
❦ Sprinkle the top with toasted flaked almonds before serving.

Variation
This simple recipe can be followed using 275 ml (½ pint) of any fruit purée, even apple.

CHOCOLATE AND ORANGE MOUSSE

Serves 4-5

175 g (6 oz) dark chocolate
3 tbsp black coffee
15 g (½ oz) butter
grated rind and juice of 2 oranges
3 eggs, separated

❦ Melt the chocolate with the coffee in a bowl over hot water. Stir in the butter and remove from the heat.

❦ Grate the rind and squeeze the juice from the oranges. Separate the eggs and beat the yolks into the warm chocolate mixture one at a time, together with the orange rind and juice.

❦ Whisk the egg whites stiffly and fold quickly into the mousse. Pour into a 15-17 cm (6-7 in) dish. Leave to set in the refrigerator.

Note
There is no gelatine in this mousse as the chocolate and eggs set it.

LEMON SOUFFLE

Serves 4-6

175 g (6 oz) caster sugar
3 eggs, separated
grated rind and juice of 2 lemons
15 g (½ oz) powdered gelatine
3 tbsp water
175 ml (6 fl oz) whipping cream

❦ Prepare a 575 ml (1 pint) soufflé dish, sometimes called a case, by tying a paper or foil cuff round it to come 2.5-5 cm (1-2 in) above the rim. The cuff should be lightly oiled to make it easy to remove before serving.

❦ Whisk the sugar with the egg yolks in a basin until light and fluffy. Add the rind and juice of the lemons to the eggs. Put the bowl over a pan of gently simmering water and whisk until the mixture is thick and creamy. (This is the most important part of making a cold soufflé.) Whisk, off the heat for a moment or two more. Cool.

❦ Dissolve the gelatine in the water in a basin over hot water. Add to the mixture, pouring it in a thin stream. This prevents the gelatine from 'stringing'. Whisk the egg whites until just stiff. Lightly whip the cream. Very lightly and with a metal spoon, fold the cream into the lemon mixture followed by the egg whites.

❦ Pour the mixture into the dish and chill until set. Remove collar just before serving.

ORANGE SOUFFLE

Serves 4-6

3 eggs, plus 2 extra egg yolks
25 g (1 oz) caster sugar
grated rind and juice of 2 oranges
15 g (½ oz) powdered gelatine
150 ml (¼ pint) whipping cream
2 glacé orange slices

❦ Prepare the soufflé dish as for lemon soufflé (see above). Break the eggs into a bowl and add the extra yolks with the sugar. Add the orange rind to the eggs. Whisk over a pan of hot water until thick. Take off the heat and whisk until cool.

❦ Dissolve the gelatine in the orange juice in a bowl over hot water. Make up to 175 ml (6 fl oz) with water or pure canned orange juice. Whisk into the mixture and leave until on the point of setting. Lightly whip the cream and fold in. Pour into a dish and chill until set.

❦ Remove the collar and decorate with quartered glacé orange slices.

Note
This soufflé is made by a different method, called Milanese.

GINGER SOUFFLE

Serves 4-6

425 ml (¾ pint) milk
3 eggs, separated
50 g (2 oz) caster sugar
2 tbsp ginger syrup
15 g (½ oz) powdered gelatine
50 g (2 oz) stem ginger, sliced
150 ml (¼ pint) whipping cream
extra whipped cream and stem ginger to decorate

❦ Prepare an 850 ml (1 ½ pint) soufflé dish as for lemon soufflé (see page 287).

❦ Boil the milk. Beat the egg yolks and sugar together until pale. Add the ginger syrup. Pour the milk on to the eggs, beating all the time. Return to the pan and heat gently, stirring all the time until the mixture thickens.

❦ Dissolve the gelatine in 2 tablespoons of water in a basin over hot water. Add to the mixture. Stir well and cool. Fold in the sliced stem ginger.

❦ When almost at setting point, whisk the egg whites firmly and whip the cream lightly. Fold the cream into the mixture followed by the egg whites, using a metal spoon. Pour into the dish and leave until it is set.

❦ Remove the collar and decorate with whipped cream and a few slices of stem ginger.

Variations
This soufflé can also be made with a good ginger wine and crystallised ginger.

HOT CHOCOLATE SOUFFLE

Serves 4-6

100 g (4 oz) good dark block chocolate
2 tbsp water
425 ml (¾ pint) milk
50 g (2 oz) vanilla sugar (keep a pod in the sugar jar)
40 g (1 ½ oz) arrowroot
15 g (½ oz) butter
3 eggs, plus white of 1 extra egg
icing sugar

❦ Butter a 1 litre (2 ¼ pint) soufflé dish. Heat the oven to 190C (375F) mark 5 with a baking sheet in it.

❦ Melt the chocolate with the water over a gentle heat. Heat the milk in a large pan, keeping back 50 ml (2 fl oz), and dissolve the sugar in it. Pour the melted chocolate into the milk and mix well. Blend the arrowroot with the remaining milk. Pour some of the hot chocolate mixture on to it. Stir well, return to the saucepan and bring to the boil, stirring continuously. Remove from the heat, dot with the butter, cover the pan and cool.

❦ Separate the eggs and beat the egg yolks into the cooled mixture, one at a time. Whisk all the whites stiffly and fold in with a metal spoon. Turn into the dish. Stand on the baking sheet and cook for 20-30 minutes. Serve immediately.

HOT BANANA SOUFFLE

Serves 4-6

4 bananas, not more than 450 g (1 lb) unpeeled weight
grated rind and juice of 1 orange
grated rind and juice of 1 lemon
75 g (3 oz) caster sugar
25 g (1 oz) walnut pieces, chopped
whites of 3 eggs
pinch of salt

❦ Prepare an 18-20 cm (7-8 in) soufflé dish by buttering it well. Heat the oven to 180C (350F) mark 4, with a baking sheet in it.

❦ Peel and mash the bananas. Add the lemon and orange juice and rind to the bananas with the sugar and nuts. Whisk the egg whites until stiff with a pinch of salt. Fold into the banana purée and turn into the dish.

❦ Stand the dish on the baking sheet in the lower half of the oven and cook at once for 30 minutes. The top of the dish should be at the middle line in the oven.

❦ Serve immediately.

HOT LEMON SOUFFLE

Serves 4-6

40 g (1 ½ oz) butter, plus more for greasing
40 g (1 ½ oz) plain flour
425 ml (¾ pint) milk
50 g (2 oz) caster sugar
grated rind and juice of 2 lemons
3 eggs, separated
icing sugar

❦ Prepare an 18-20 cm (7-8 in) soufflé dish by buttering it well. Heat the oven to 190C (375F) mark 5 with a baking sheet in it.
❦ Melt the butter in a large pan. Remove from the heat and stir in the flour. Put back on the heat and gradually add the milk, stirring all the time until boiling. Remove from the heat, add the sugar, grated rind and juice of the lemons and beat well.
❦ Beat in the egg yolks one at a time. Whisk the whites stiffly and fold into the mixture with a metal spoon. Pour into the dish and cook, standing the dish on the baking sheet, for 30 minutes. When cooked, dust the top very quickly with a little icing sugar and serve immediately.

HOT VANILLA SOUFFLE

Serves 4-6

275 ml (½ pint) milk
1 vanilla pod
50 g (2 oz) vanilla flavoured sugar
5 eggs
40 g (1 ½ oz) plain flour
little icing sugar

❦ Prepare a soufflé dish by buttering it well. Heat the oven to 190C (375F) mark 5 with a baking sheet in it.
❦ Simmer the milk and vanilla pod together. Cream the sugar with one egg and an egg yolk until pale and very fluffy. Sieve the flour and stir in. Remove the pod from the milk. Pour the hot milk on to the egg mixture, stirring all the time. Return to the heat and cook gently, stirring continuously, until thick and smooth. Cover and cool.
❦ Separate the remaining eggs. Beat the yolks into the cooled vanilla cream, one at a time. Whisk the egg whites firmly and fold into the mixture with a metal spoon. Turn into the dish, stand it on the baking sheet and cook for 30 minutes. When cooked, dust with a little icing sugar. Serve immediately.

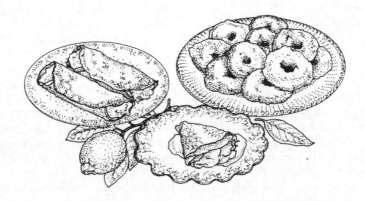

PANCAKES
AND FRITTERS

Pancakes are delicious and are now eaten all year round – not just on Shrove Tuesday, when all the rich ingredients would be used up in preparation for Lent. Nowadays there are as many savoury fillings as sweet, but it takes a lot to beat the traditional lemon and sugar pancakes.

APRICOT AND WALNUT PANCAKES

Makes 10-12

225 g (8 oz) can apricots
25 g (1 oz) walnut pieces
275 ml (½ pint) Pancake Batter
   (see page 365)
butter or oil for frying
little caster sugar

❦ Mash the apricots with a wooden salad fork. Stir in the walnut pieces.
❦ Heat the pan and make the pancakes as for Shrove Tuesday pancakes (see opposite). Spread them with the apricot mixture and roll up. Dust with sugar and serve at once.

Notes
Home-made apricot jam is as good as, if not better than, canned apricots for the filling. Bought jam is not. Home-made jam of any kind makes a delicious filling for pancakes, with the addition of a few nuts or a spoonful of sherry.

SHROVE TUESDAY PANCAKES

Makes 10-12 pancakes

butter or oil
275 ml (½ pint) Pancake Batter (see page 365)
lemons
caster sugar

❧ Heat the pan and add a little butter or oil. Pour in a tablespoon of batter and twist the pan so the base is evenly coated. Cook until beginning to bubble on top. Turn with a palette knife or toss over and cook the other side until lightly browned.
❧ Keep warm in a folded tea towel, or in the oven in a covered dish until all the pancakes are made.
❧ Squeeze lemon juice liberally over each pancake. Dust with sugar. Roll up and serve at once with lemon wedges.

CREPES BRETONNES

Serves 4

100 g (4 oz) wholemeal flour
¼ tsp salt
1 egg
1 tbsp olive oil
275 ml (½ pint) milk and water
butter or oil for frying
lemon juice
sugar

❧ Mix the flour and salt in a bowl. Make a well in the centre. Beat the egg and oil together and pour into the well. Draw down a little flour and stir. Pour the milk slowly into the egg mixture, continue to draw the flour down and beat well. Finally beat for 2 minutes. Leave to stand for 1 hour. Then add more milk if the mixture is too thick (it should be like thin cream).
❧ Heat the pan and add a little butter or oil. Make the pancakes as Shrove Tuesday pancakes above). Sprinkle with lemon juice and sugar and roll up. Serve side by side in a warm dish, with lemon wedges.

Notes
These are the buckwheat pancakes sold to everyone who holidays in Brittany. With the upsurge of whole-food shops, buckwheat flour can sometimes be found. If not, use wholemeal as stated in the recipe.

ALMOND AND PEAR CREPES

Makes 10-12

275 ml (½ pint) Pancake Batter (see page 365)
1 tbsp brandy
butter or oil for frying
100 g (4 oz) butter
50 g (2 oz) icing sugar, sifted
50 g (2 oz) ground almonds
¼ tsp almond essence
425 g (15 oz) can pears or 4 fresh pears
25 g (1 oz) butter, melted (optional)
extra icing sugar

❧ Stir the brandy into the butter. Heat the pan and make the pancakes as for Shrove Tuesday pancakes (see left).
❧ Cream the butter and icing sugar together until light and fluffy. Stir in the ground almonds and essence. Peel and core the pears if they are fresh, drain them if they are canned. Dice the pears and stir with the butter mixture. Spoon this mixture on to the pancakes, slightly to one side. Fold in half and then fold again to make triangles. Put in an ovenproof dish, dust with a little icing sugar and serve at once.
❧ If the pancakes are to be kept warm in the oven, brush first with melted butter and then dust with icing sugar.

RASPBERRY PANCAKES

Makes 10-12

275 ml (½ pint) Pancake Batter (see page 365)
100 g (4 oz) raspberry jam (preferably home-
    made)
50 g (2 oz) flaked almonds, toasted
150 ml (¼ pint) whipping cream

❦ Heat the pan and make the pancakes as for Shrove
Tuesday pancakes (see page 291). Spread with raspberry jam. Roll up and arrange side by side in an
ovenproof dish. Sprinkle with the almonds and serve
with lightly whipped cream.
❦ The pancakes can be kept warm in a covered dish
in a moderate oven for about 20 minutes.

CREPES BEURRE
AU CHOCOLAT

Makes 10-12

275 ml (½ pint) Pancake Batter (see page 365)
butter or oil for frying
175 g (6 oz) butter, softened
175 g (6 oz) dark plain chocolate

❦ Make up the pancake mixture as before, but a little thinner. Heat the pan and make the pancakes as
for Shrove Tuesday pancakes (see page 291). Keep
warm in a folded tea towel (the garçons of Paris of
course make them one at a time, on demand).
❦ Spread the softened butter on the crêpes. Grate
the chocolate and sprinkle it over the butter. Fold
into four, put in a hot dish and serve at once.

Notes
Those of you who know Paris envy the skill of the
garçons who so casually pour batter on to a hot-plate
and produce a perfect crêpe every time, then fold it
in four and hand it to you in a paper cornet.

CREPES PRALINEES

Makes 10-12

275 ml (½ pint) Pancake Batter (see page 365)
50 g (2 oz) butter
50 g (2 oz) caster sugar
3 tbsp Praline (see page 367)
1-2 tbsp rum (optional)

❦ Heat the pan and make the pancakes as for Shrove
Tuesday pancakes (see page 291). Keep warm.
❦ Cream the butter and sugar until light and fluffy.
Put a rolling pin over the praline to crush it. Fold the
powdery result into the butter and add the rum if
used. Spread on the crêpes, fold in four and serve.

CREPES SUZETTE

Makes 8-10 pancakes

3 tbsp brandy
275 ml (½ pint) Pancake Batter (see page 365)
butter or oil for frying
50 g (2 oz) caster sugar
25 g (1 oz) butter
grated rind and juice of 2 oranges
1 tbsp Grand Marnier

❦ Add 1 tablespoon of brandy to the batter. Heat
the pan and make the pancakes as for Shrove
Tuesday pancakes (see page 291). Keep hot.
❦ Melt the sugar slowly in a saucepan with 1 teaspoon of water (no more); heat until it caramelizes.
Add the butter and the grated rind and juice of the
oranges. Stir gently.
❦ Run the crêpes through this sauce and fold each
into four. Put in an ovenproof dish. Add the Grand
Marnier to the remaining sauce and pour over the
crêpes.
❦ Heat the remaining brandy in a ladle over a can-
dle flame at the table. Put a match to it and pour
whilst flaming over the crêpes. Serve immediately.

SAUCER PANCAKES

Makes 6

275 ml (½ pint) Pancake Batter (see page 365)
raspberry or other jam

❦ Heat the oven to 190C (375F) mark 5. Butter six saucers – large, comfortable, breakfast-sized ones.
❦ Divide the batter between them. Put a teaspoon of any jam into the middle of each and bake for 15-20 minutes.

SWEET YORKSHIRE PUDDING

Serves 4

100 g (4 oz) plain flour
¼ tsp salt
2 eggs (size 3 or 4)
200 ml (7 fl oz) milk and water, mixed
75 g (3 oz) butter
1 tbsp oil
golden syrup, warmed

❦ Heat the oven to 220C (425F) mark 7.
❦ Sieve the flour and salt into a bowl. Make a well in the centre. Break the eggs into this, or into a cup first if you are doubtful. Stir to break the yolks. Add a little of the milk and water and beat with a wooden spoon. Draw down the flour by degrees, then add all the liquid, beating to keep the batter smooth. Beat for 2 minutes, then leave to stand for 30 minutes.
❦ Put the butter and oil into a 20-23 cm (8-9 in) square baking tin and put this into the hot oven. When it is piping hot, pour the batter into the hot fat. Cook for 45 minutes. Pour melted syrup over it and serve at once.

BATTERED SANDWICHES

275 ml (½ pint) Pancake Batter (see page 365)
bread, butter and jam
margarine
caster sugar

❦ Make jam sandwiches. Cut each into three. Dip into the batter and fry in plenty of piping hot melted margarine. Dust with sugar and serve at once.

Notes
These were made, and no doubt invented, by a Hampshire countrywoman, and fed straight into the mouths of ten children who still remember them with love. They make a humble, homely but delicious contrast to their sophisticated equivalents from across the Channel, as does the following recipe.

COLLEGE PUDDING

Serves 4

100 g (4 oz) plain flour
¼ tsp salt
1-2 eggs
275 ml (½ pint) milk
50 g (2 oz) butter
2 tsp oil
450 g (1 lb) cooking apples
bramble jelly
75 g (3 oz) caster sugar

❦ Heat the oven to 220C (425F) mark 7.
❦ Make a batter by sifting the flour and salt together. Beat the eggs and milk gradually into it, until absolutely smooth. Leave to stand for 30 minutes.
❦ Heat the butter and oil in an ovenproof casserole (the oil prevents the butter from burning). Peel, core and slice the apples and add them to the hot butter. Dot with teaspoons of bramble jelly and sprinkle with sugar.
❦ Give the batter a stir before pouring it over the apples. Cook for about 1 hour or until brown and risen.
❦ Serve at once, as baked batters tend to sink if they are kept waiting.

APPLE FRITTERS

Serves 4

275 ml (½ pint) Sweet Fritter Batter (see page
    365)
3 or 4 apples
caster sugar
ground cinnamon
oil for frying

❧ Peel, core and cut the apples into rings 1 cm (½
in) thick. Place them on a plate and sprinkle with
caster sugar and cinnamon. Dip the rings in the batter " a skewer with the end turned up is a handy tool
for this.
❧ Heat about 5 cm (2 inches) of oil in a deep frying
pan to 190C (375F). Test the temperature by dropping a little of the batter into the oil: if the batter siz-
zles, the oil is hot enough.
❧ Cook the rings a few at a time until golden brown
on each side. Remove with a slotted spoon and drain
on absorbent kitchen paper. Keep piping hot in the
oven until all the fritters are ready.
❧ Arrange the fritters overlapping each other
slightly in a hot dish. Dust with caster sugar and
serve immediately.

PRUNE FRITTERS

Serves 4

15 prunes
½ glass of red wine
1 cup of strong tea (no milk)
15 unblanched almonds
25-40 g (1-1 ½ oz) mixed peel
275 ml (½ pint) Sweet Fritter Batter (see page
    365)
oil for frying

❧ Stone the prunes and simmer in the wine and tea
for 8-10 minutes. Stuff each prune with an
unblanched almond and a little mixed peel. Pat dry
with absorbent kitchen paper.
❧ Dip each prune in the batter and fry as for Apple
Fritters (see above). Serve immediately arranged in
a hot dish dredged with caster sugar and accompanied by whipped cream.

CORN FRITTERS

Serves 4

100 g (4 oz) sweetcorn, frozen or canned
100 g (4 oz) plain flour
¼ tsp salt
1 egg
275 ml (½ pint) milk
50 g (2 oz) butter
oil
golden syrup

❧ Thaw or drain the sweetcorn. Sieve the flour and
salt into a bowl. Make a well in the centre and break
the egg into it. Add a little milk. Beat again and gradually draw in the flour, beating in more milk until
the mixture is creamy and smooth. Leave to stand
for 1 hour.
❧ Stir the corn into the batter. Heat the butter with
a little oil in a frying pan. Drop teaspoonfuls of the
mixture into the hot fat. Cook until lightly browned
and cook the other side until golden.
❧ Drain on absorbent kitchen paper and serve very
hot with golden syrup.

APRICOT FRITTERS

Serves 4

6 fresh ripe apricots
275 ml (½ pint) Sweet Fritter Batter (see page
    365)

❧ Skin the apricots (dip them in boiling water), split
and remove the stones. Dip each in the batter and fry
as for apple fritters (see left) until honey brown.
❧ Drain on absorbent kitchen paper and serve in a
hot dish with whipped cream.

POOR KNIGHTS OF WINDSOR

Allow 2 for each person

bread – a sliced loaf does well
150 ml (¼ pint) milk
50 g (2 oz) caster sugar
1 egg
butter and sunflower or corn oil

❧ Cut the bread into 5 cm (2 in) wide fingers. Warm the milk, sweeten it to taste. Beat the egg. Soak the fingers in the sweet milk. Drain. Dip in the beaten egg. Fry in sizzling butter and oil (the oil stops the butter burning).
❧ Serve piping hot with melted golden syrup or warmed jam.

Variation
The Swedish go one better with rich knights – Rika Riddane. Prepare as poor knights, but after the egg dip, draw the slices through chopped almonds and sugar before frying. Serve these rich fellows, of course, with cream.

SUET DOUGHNUTS

Makes 8 round and 8 ring doughnuts

50 g (2 oz) caster sugar
1 tsp ground cinnamon
225 g (8 oz) Suet Crust pastry (see page 361)
100 g (4 oz) lard or white fat or vegetable oil

❧ Shake the sugar and cinnamon together in a paper bag. Roll out the pastry to a thickness of 1 cm (½ in). Cut into eight 7.5 cm (3 in) rounds. Remove the centre of the rounds using a 4 cm (1 ½ in) cutter.
❧ Heat the fat or oil in a frying pan. Gently fry the rings and the rounds for 8-10 minutes, until cooked and golden brown on both sides. Drain on absorbent kitchen paper and toss in the paper bag with the sugar.
❧ Serve the doughnuts at once on a hot dish.

GOLDEN TRIANGLES

Makes 4

100 g (4 oz) Suet Crust Pastry (see page 361)
100 g (4 oz) fat or oil to fry
golden syrup or honey

❧ Roll out the pastry into a round about 1 cm (½ in) thick. Cut into four triangles. Melt the fat and shallow-fry the triangles for 8-10 minutes, turning once, until golden brown on both sides. Serve at once with warm golden syrup or honey.
❧ Both these recipes are lovely for high tea on a cold winter's night and come from old farmhouse days.

ICE-CREAMS, SORBETS AND PARTY DESSERTS

This section contains spectacular desserts in a different vein. Cool and elegant concoctions served in pretty glasses, on delicate plates and even in their own shells, to bring a splendid ending to any dinner party.

❧ About ice-creams ❧ and sorbets

Ice-creams and sorbets are much easier to make than is generally thought, and they taste so good. They can form the base of many desserts, from Pêche Melba to the interesting Brown Bread Ice-cream. They also keep well in a freezer for several months.

Fruits feature here too, with the well-named Raspberry Flummery, ideal to make when there is a glut of soft fruit; or there is the famous Strawberry Romanoff and one of the most refreshing of all desserts – Oranges in Caramel.

Mostly simple to prepare and make, those desserts needing a little more time also require to be made in advance, so you can always provide something really splendid on those special occasions.

BROWN BREAD ICE-CREAM

Serves 4-6

3 tbsp fresh brown breadcrumbs
1 tbsp caster sugar
600 ml (1 pint) Vanilla Ice-cream (see right)

❧ Heat the oven to 180C (350F) mark 4.
❧ Put the breadcrumbs on a baking sheet and sprinkle them with caster sugar. Brown slowly in the oven for about 30 minutes or until really brown (but not burnt). Remove and cool. Beat into the still frozen ice-cream and return to the freezer until needed.
❧ The contrasts of the tastes and textures of the crumbs and creamy ice in this dish are delicious.

VANILLA ICE-CREAM

Serves 6-8

175 g (6 oz) caster sugar
150 ml (¼ pint) water
5 egg yolks
275 ml (½ pint) whipping cream

❦ Dissolve every grain of the sugar in the water over a gentle heat. Bring to the boil and boil fast for 5 minutes. Cool slightly.
❦ Beat the egg yolks. Pour the sugar syrup on to the yolks in a thin stream, beating all the time. Put the bowl over a saucepan of hot water and whisk until the mixture is thick. Leave until cold.
❦ Whip the cream until stiff and fold into the mixture. Turn into a container, cover and freeze. When just beginning to set, remove to a bowl and beat hard again. This breaks down tiny ice crystals. Put back to freeze until completely firm.
❦ Home-made ice-cream is usually harder than the bought variety, so bring it out of the freezer about 15 minutes before you need it.

PECHE MELBA

Serves 6

6 ripe medium peaches
Light Sugar Syrup (see page 367)
450 g (1 lb) raspberries, fresh or frozen
100 g (4 oz) icing sugar
575 ml (1 pint) Vanilla Ice-cream (see above)

❦ Skin the peaches by dipping them in boiling water. Lightly poach in a vanilla-flavoured light syrup. Drain, cool and chill. Rub the raspberries through a sieve and add the well-sieved icing sugar to this purée.
❦ Put the ice-cream into a chilled glass dish or six individual glasses and cover it with halved peaches. Pour the raspberry purée, known all over the world as 'sauce Melba', over the whole thing. Serve at once.

Note
This is the famous dish created by Escoffier 'The King of cooks and cook of Kings' for Dame Nellie Melba. It is probably only at home that this lovely confection is properly made.

COFFEE ICE-CREAM

Serves 6-8

175 g (6 oz) caster sugar
150 ml (¼ pint) water
5 egg yolks
150 ml (¼ pint) whipping cream
1 ½ tbsp instant coffee powder

❦ Make as for Vanilla Ice-cream (see left), but add the coffee with the cream.

GOOSEBERRY ICE-CREAM

Serves 6

450 g (1 lb) gooseberries
3 tbsp water
1 vanilla pod
3 tbsp caster sugar
1 tbsp packet custard powder
265 ml (½ pint) milk
1 egg
150 ml (¼ pint) whipping cream
green food colouring (optional)

❦ Top, tail and wash the gooseberries. Simmer in the water with the vanilla and 1 tablespoon of caster sugar, until tender. Remove pod and sieve the fruit.
❦ Make the custard using the custard powder, milk and the rest of the sugar according to the instructions. Leave to cool covering the top with a circle of damp greaseproof paper to stop a skin forming.
❦ Separate the egg and beat the yolk into the cooled custard, then fold in the gooseberry purée. Whisk the egg white stiffly. Whip the cream until thick and fold into the purée followed by the egg white. Add a few drops of green food colouring if liked.
❦ Pour into a container and freeze. When half frozen, whisk again until smooth. Return to the container, cover and freeze until firm. If frozen in a 500 ml (1 pint) pudding basin, the ice-cream can be turned out like a 'bombe'.

Notes
Without food colouring this ice-cream is fawn-coloured. If you wish to colour it, do be very careful to use your colouring literally one drop at a time.

ORANGE SORBET

Serves 6

6 good-looking oranges
water or pure unsweetened orange juice
lemon juice
350 g (12 oz) granulated sugar
white of 1 egg
small fresh bay leaves or mint leaves to deco-
    rate (optional)

❦ Wash the oranges. Take a small circle right out of
the top of each and a small slice off the base so they
will 'sit'. Spoon out the insides into a bowl. Brush
the raw edges with lemon juice. Put these cases into
the freezer.
❦ Sieve the orange flesh to extract all the juice.
Make up to 850 ml (1 ½ pints) with water, or better
still, pure unsweetened orange juice from a carton.
Put the liquid with the sugar into a pan. Heat to melt
the sugar completely then boil rapidly without stirring for 5 minutes. These measurements and timing
are crucial. Take the pan off the heat, strain into a
basin and leave to cool.
❦ Whisk the egg white stiffly and fold into the
cooled mixture. Persevere with this. Pour into a suitable container and put into the coldest part of the
freezer.
❦ When firm, after maybe 3 hours, turn into a bowl
and beat with an electric beater until smooth. This
will give it the characteristic look of a sorbet. Bring
out the oranges, and, working rapidly, spoon the sorbet into them, leaving a rough, piled top. Put the lids
on at an angle with a bay or mint leaf tucked in, if
using.
❦ Put each orange into a polythene bag and put back
into the freezer until wanted. They freeze very well,
with no loss of colour so can be made in advance, but
serve straight from the freezer to the table, without
giving them time to melt.

Variation
Lemon sorbet can be made in exactly the same way,
using lemons. A dish of lemon and orange sorbets
served in their respective fruit shells looks absolutely stunning.

ORANGES IN CARAMEL

Serves 4-6

8 small oranges
850 ml (1 ½ pints) water
200 g (7 oz) granulated sugar
150 ml (¼ pint) carton orange juice

❦ Peel the oranges and remove all traces of pith. Put
them to simmer in the water with 25 g (1 oz) sugar
for 10 minutes. Remove them, drain and put into a
decorative dish.
❦ Meanwhile, scrape or cut all the pith away from
the peel of 2 oranges. Cut the peel into fine shreds,
about 5 cm (2 inches) long. Dissolve 100 g (4 oz)
granulated sugar in the orange juice, add the shreds
and simmer steadily until the liquid becomes syrupy.
Pour the syrup over the oranges, arranging the
shreds on top.
❦ Melt the remaining 50 g (2 oz) sugar in 2 tablespoons water. Boil rapidly, without stirring, to a
warm honey colour. Pour over the oranges, re-
arranging a few of the shreds so they sit on top of the
oranges.
❦ Serve chilled.

TOM POUCE

Serves about 10

225 g (8 oz) **Pâte Sucrée** (see page 359)
100 g (4 oz) almonds, toasted
75 g (3 oz) butter, softened
75 g (3 oz) caster sugar
1 tsp instant coffee powder (good quality)
Coffee Glacé Icing (see page 304)

❦ Heat the oven to 190C (375F) mark 5. Line two baking sheets with non-stick paper.
❦ Make the pastry, cover and leave to relax in the refrigerator while you make the crème noisette.
❦ Put 75 g (3 oz) chopped nuts in a bowl and beat in the butter, sugar and the coffee powder.
❦ Roll out the pastry and cut it into 5 cm (2 in) squares. Put on the prepared baking sheets and cook for about 10 minutes or until honey-coloured. Cool on a wire rack.
❦ Sandwich very gently together in pairs with the crème noisette, allowing a little to show at the edges. Ice lightly with a coffee glacé icing and put a tiny sprinkling of the remaining chopped nuts in the middle. This is lovely with vanilla ice-cream.

APRICOT CHANTILLY

Serves 4-6

450 g (1 lb) fresh apricots or dried apricots
    soaked overnight
grated rind and juice of 2 oranges
100 g (4 oz) granulated sugar
2 tbsp Cointreau
150 ml (¼ pint) whipping cream
25 g (1 oz) flaked almonds, toasted

❦ Wash and stone the apricots. Drain if necessary. Simmer them together with the orange rind and juice gently adding a little water to cover. Stir in the sugar and melt over a low heat. Cool.
❦ Purée in the blender or rub through a sieve, then add the Cointreau. Whip the cream until stiff and fold through the apricot purée. Serve in individual glasses with a few toasted almonds on top.

CREAM POSSET

Serves 4-6

2 medium lemons
275 ml (½ pint) whipping cream
50 ml (2 fl oz) dry white wine
about 2 tbsp caster sugar
whites of 3 eggs

❦ Grate the rind and squeeze the juice of the lemons. Whip the cream until stiff and fold in the grated lemon rind. Stir in the lemon juice and the wine and about 2 tablespoons of sugar, or to taste.
❦ Whisk the egg whites stiffly and fold into the creamy mixture. Serve in glasses.

POTS DE CHOCOLAT

Serves 6

175 g (6 oz) good dark chocolate
50 g (2 oz) butter, not margarine
2 eggs, separated
2 tbsp rum, or milk if preferred

❦ Melt the chocolate in a basin over a pan of hot water. Remove from the heat. Cool a little then beat in the butter and the egg yolks followed by the rum or milk.
❦ Whisk the egg whites very stiffly and fold into the chocolate mixture using a metal spoon. This will take quite a time, so gently persevere.
❦ Spoon into six small ramekins (which is the classic way to serve this) or into glasses (old-fashioned custard glasses look charming), and leave to set.
❦ Serve with home-made macaroon or ratafia biscuits.

CHARLOTTE RUSSE

Serves 4

1 packet of lemon jelly
glacé cherries
angelica
about 12 bought sponge fingers
275 ml (½ pint) milk
1 vanilla pod
15 g (½ oz) packet gelatine
3 egg yolks
25 g (1 oz) caster sugar
150 ml (¼ pint) whipping cream

❦ Prepare a 750 ml (1 ½ pint) charlotte mould or soufflé dish. Make the jelly as directed on the packet. When cool, pour about 1 cm (½ in) into the dish and chill until set. Decorate on top of the set jelly with a few cherries and angelica diamonds (this is important). Set another 1 cm (½ in) of jelly. Leave the rest of the jelly to set.

❦ Trim the bottom of the sponge fingers. Fit closely around the sides of the dish. The number needed will depend on the size of the dish.

❦ Bring the milk to the boil with the vanilla pod. Dissolve the gelatine in 2 tablespoons of water in a bowl over hot water. Whisk the egg yolks and sugar until light and fluffy. Remove the vanilla pod and pour the hot milk over the eggs, beating all the time. Strain this custard into a bowl. Add the gelatine, pouring in a thin stream. Cool until just starting to set at the edges.

❦ Whisk the cream lightly and fold into the custard with a metal spoon. Spoon at once into the charlotte case. Cover with foil and put into the refrigerator to set. When ready to serve, dip the dish into very hot water for a second or two. Turn out on to an attractive plate.

❦ Chop the remaining jelly and spoon around the base of the charlotte.

Notes
This is a famous 19th-century French dish.
❦ Cover all milk and cream dishes in the refrigerator, otherwise they pick up the flavours of other foods around them.

LES CREMETS

Serves 4

whites of 2 eggs
275 ml (½ pint) whipping cream
100 ml (4 fl oz) double cream
225-350 g (8-12 oz) strawberries or raspberries
    or home-made redcurrant or raspberry jelly

❦ Whisk the egg whites and then whip the whipping cream until stiff. Fold the egg whites into the cream with a metal spoon.

❦ Have ready four squares of fresh muslin. Fit them into four little heart-shaped moulds which have holes in the bottom. Spoon the cream into the moulds. Fold the muslin over. Stand on a rack to drain overnight if wanted at midday, or all day if wanted in the evening.

❦ To serve, turn out on to individual pretty plates and cover completely with the unwhipped double cream. Serve with fresh strawberries or raspberries, or in the winter with a spoonful or so of home-made redcurrant or raspberry jelly.

Notes
The charming little dishes can be bought very reasonably at all good kitchen shops. Have all your equipment ready before starting. To save time, whisk egg whites before cream when using both, then you don't have to wash the beaters in between.

STRAWBERRY ROMANOFF

Serves 4-6

450 g (1 lb) strawberries
1 tbsp Grand Marnier
grated rind and juice of 1 orange
50 g (2 oz) caster sugar
150 ml (¼ pint) whipping cream

❦ Cut the strawberries in half. Soak the fruit in the liqueur with the orange rind and juice and the sugar, reserving a teaspoon of sugar. Leave for an hour, or longer as convenient, giving a gentle stir from time to time.
❦ When required, spoon the fruit carefully into a glass serving dish. Whip the cream with the remaining sugar, thus producing crème chantilly.
❦ Pile on top of the strawberries and serve within an hour.

Notes
Fresh fruit, not canned, is required for this classic dish. Fresh ripe peaches or nectarines are lovely used in this way. Do not use more than 1 tablespoon of liqueur for a Romanoff, otherwise you will spoil it.

RASPBERRY FLUMMERY

Serves 4-6

225 g (8 oz) raspberries
50 g (2 oz) caster sugar
275 ml (½ pint) whipping cream
150 ml (¼ pint) sweet white wine

❦ Look over and lightly bruise the raspberries. Leave a few whole. Sprinkle with 25 g (1 oz) sugar.
❦ Whip the cream stiffly. Fold in the remaining sugar and the wine. Fold the raspberries gently through and through the cream until it is striped with pink.
❦ Pile into sparkling glasses and decorate each with a whole raspberry or two. Serve chilled.

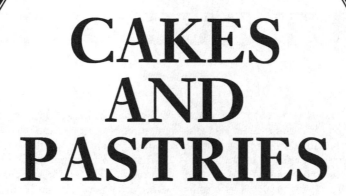

CAKES AND PASTRIES

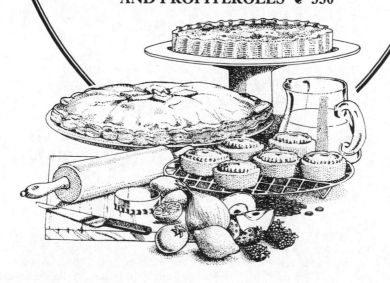

ABOUT CAKE-MAKING

There are three principal ways of making cakes: the melting method is used for items like gingerbread and involves heating the fat gently with the other ingredients (the raising agent is usually bicarbonate of soda); the creaming method is employed for heavier cakes like fruit cakes and involves creaming the fat and sugar to a mousse-like consistency without allowing it to melt (rising is usually achieved by using self-raising flour); and finally the whisking method, as for sponge cakes, where air is beaten into the mixture to provide the raising agent.

Whatever the method, there are several good rules to help you to successful cake-making every time: always measure your ingredients carefully ahead of time and do as much preparation, like grating, as possible before you actually start making the mixture; try to keep the ingredients at room temperature and your hands cool at all times, unless otherwise instructed; always sift dry ingredients, especially flour, to help add air and thus lightness to the mixture. Never open the oven door in the first half hour of cooking or it will sink, but do check in the later stages of cooking and, if it appears to be browning too quickly, you can cover the top with foil or greaseproof paper. If you are not sure whether or not the cake is done: press it lightly with the tip of a finger; it should be springy to the touch. A fine skewer inserted into the centre of the cake should also come out clean, dry and very hot.

For most cakes, only a thorough greasing and light dusting of the pan with flour is all that is required to prevent the cake sticking. However, if the cake is delicate, like a sponge, or is to be in the oven for quite a long time, as in the case of a fruit cake, one or two layers of greased greaseproof paper are required to insulate the base and/or the sides of the cake from the heat. In the case of sponges, the greased paper is also lightly dusted with flour.

❧ Fillings and Icings ❧

This section begins with a range of pastry creams and icings with which to fill, sandwich and assemble cakes and gâteaux and to top them decoratively.

CHOCOLATE ICING

100 g (4 oz) cooking chocolate
2 tbsp water
75 g (3 oz) sieved icing sugar

❧ Melt the chocolate with the water in a bowl over a pan of hot water. Stir in the icing sugar until smooth and pour over the cake.

GLACE ICING

175 g (6 oz) icing sugar
warm water

❧ Sieve the icing sugar and gradually add 1 tbsp warm water to start with. Add more water in very small quantities to give a thick coating consistency. Add flavouring or colouring very sparingly, if liked.

MOCK FONDANT ICING

2 tsp liquid glucose
2 tsp warm water
icing sugar

❦ Dissolve the glucose in the water. Add sufficient icing sugar to give a coating consistency. Beat well. Colour or flavour as desired. Use at once.

CHOCOLATE MARQUISE

175 g (6 oz) good dark chocolate
3 tbsp strong black coffee
25 g (1 oz) butter

❦ Melt the chocolate with the coffee in a bowl over hot water, then beat in the butter. Use at once to spread over the cake.

CREME AU BEURRE A LA MERINGUE

whites of 2 eggs
100 g (4 oz) sieved icing sugar
225 g (8 oz) butter, softened

❦ Put the egg whites and sieved icing sugar into a basin over hot water. Beat until stiffly standing up in peaks. Take off the heat and beat until absolutely cold. Add the butter, whisking it in a little at a time.

CREME AU BEURRE MOUSSELINE (CHOCOLAT)

75 g (3 oz) granulated sugar
75 ml (3 fl oz) water
2 egg yolks
100 g (4 oz) butter
2 tbsp dark chocolate, melted

❦ Put the sugar into the water. Melt completely and boil until syrupy (a short thread, to those of you who make sweets). Take off the heat at once. Whisk the yolks and pour the sugar on to them in a thin stream, whisking all the time. Whisk until thick and spongy.
❦ Beat the butter until it is very soft and creamy, then whisk into the spongy egg mixture by degrees.
❦ Melt the chocolate in a basin over hot water and gradually whisk into the crème. For a plain crème au beurre mousseline, omit the chocolate.

❧ Classic Cakes ❧

CELEBRATION FRUIT CAKE

Serves 16

175 g (6 oz) butter
175 g (6 oz) soft dark brown sugar
2 tbsp black treacle
225 g (8 oz) wholemeal self-raising flour
2 tsp ground mixed spice
3 eggs
2 tbsp milk
700 g (1 ½ lb) mixed dried fruit
100 g (4 oz) glacé cherries

❧ Heat the oven to 160C (325F) mark 3. Line a 20 cm (8 in) round cake tin with buttered greaseproof paper.
❧ Cream the butter, sugar and treacle until light and fluffy. Stir together the flour and spices. Beat the eggs and milk together lightly. Add the flour and eggs alternately to the creamed mixture, beating well between each addition. Fold in the dried fruit. Cut the cherries into quarters and fold into the mixture.
❧ Pour the mixture into the prepared tin and bake in the centre of the oven for about 1 ½ hours. Check after about 1 hour, if the cake seem to be browning too quickly, cover with a sheet of damp greaseproof paper and reduce the oven temperature to 150C (300F) mark 2 for the final half-hour.
❧ Remove the cake from the oven and leave to cool slightly in the tin. Turn out on a wire rack to cool completely.

NO-SUGAR FRUIT CAKE

Serves 8-12

350 g (12 oz) mixed fruit
210 ml (7 fl oz) water
100 g (4 oz) polyunsaturated margarine
225 g (8 oz) wholemeal self-raising flour
1 egg, beaten
rind and juice of 1 orange

❧ Heat the oven to 160C (325F) mark 3. Line a 15 cm (6 in) round cake tin.
❧ Place the fruit, water and margarine in a saucepan and simmer gently for 20 minutes. When cold, mix with the remaining ingredients.
❧ Transfer the mixture to the prepared cake tin and cook for about 1 ½ hours.
❧ Allow to cool slightly in the tin and then turn out on a wire rack to cool completely.

CHOCOLATE HAZELNUT CAKE

Serves 12-16

Base
100 g (4 oz) soft margarine
100 g (4 oz) caster sugar
2 eggs
100 g (4 oz) self-raising flour
50 g (2 oz) cocoa
50 g (2 oz) finely ground hazelnuts
150 ml (¼ pt) milk

Filling
50 g (2 oz) unsalted butter
50 g (2 oz) icing sugar
50 g (2 oz) finely ground hazelnuts

Icing
100g (4 oz) plain chocolate
25 g (1 oz) butter

❧ Heat the oven to 160C (325F) mark 3 and line a 20 cm (8 in) round cake tin.
❧ Cream the margarine and sugar until light and fluffy. Beat the eggs lightly together. Sieve the flour and cocoa together. Add the eggs and flour alternately to the creamed mixture, beating well between each addition. Fold in the hazelnuts. Stir in the milk and beat until the mixture is light and fluffy.
❧ Put into the prepared cake tin and bake for 40-45 minutes. Leave to cool slightly and then turn out on a wire rack to cool.
❧ When completely cold, split carefully and fill. Make the filling by creaming the butter until soft and then working in the icing sugar and hazelnuts.
❧ Make the icing. Put the chocolate and butter into a bowl and melt over a pan of hot water, stir well until smooth and pour over the cake.
❧ Leave until cold and place on a serving plate.

PINEAPPLE UPSIDE-DOWN CAKE

Serves 4-5

2 tbsp clear honey
4 pineapple slices
4 glacé cherries
100 g (4 oz) butter, plus more for greasing
100 g (4 oz) caster sugar
2 eggs
175 g (6 oz) self-raising flour
little milk, if needed

❦ Preheat the oven to 180C (350F) mark 4. Grease an 18 cm (7 in) round cake tin and line it with buttered greaseproof paper. Even if it is a non-stick tin, do line it.

❦ Coat the base of the prepared tin with honey. Arrange the pineapple slices, with the cherries in the holes, on the honey.

❦ Cream the butter and sugar together until pale and fluffy. Beat in the eggs. Sieve the flour and fold into the mixture. Add a little milk to make a dropping consistency. Spoon it into the tin, level the top and bake for about 40 minutes.

❦ Turn out the pudding and remove the paper carefully. Serve with warmed honey and lightly whipped cream.

Note

To test a baked sponge mixture, open the oven gently, press the top of the sponge lightly with the fingertips. If it feels springy to the touch and is just beginning to shrink away from the sides of the tin, it is done. Practice makes perfect with this test.

FRENCH CHOCOLATE CAKE

Serves 4

oil for greasing
50 g (2 oz) unsalted butter
100 g (4 oz) good dark chocolate
3 eggs, separated
50 g (2 oz) caster sugar
2 tsp plain flour
50 g (2 oz) ground almonds

❦ Heat the oven to 180C (350F) mark 4. Oil a 15-18 cm (6-7 in) round cake tin, line with baking paper and oil again.

❦ Soften the butter. Melt the chocolate in a basin over hot water and separate the eggs. Beat the butter and egg yolks into the chocolate. Fold in the sugar, flour and ground almonds. Whisk the egg whites very stiffly and fold into the chocolate mixture with a metal spoon.

❦ Turn into the prepared tin and cook for about 45 minutes. Turn on to a wire rack and leave to cool.

Notes

This is a small rich, utterly French cake which can be eaten plain or with a good chocolate icing poured over it. Alternatively it can be masked with whipped cream.

ANGEL CAKE WITH GRAPES

Serves 6-8

50 g (2 oz) plain flour
175 g (6 oz) caster sugar
whites of 6 eggs
pinch of salt
¾ tsp cream of tartar
2 drops (but no more) vanilla essence (not
  flavouring)
1 drop of almond essence
275 ml (½ pint) whipping cream
450 g (1 lb) green grapes

❦ Heat the oven to 190C (375F) mark 5. Have a ring mould, 20-23 cm (8-9 in) across ready; do not grease it. Sieve the flour and 75 g (3 oz) sugar at least twice.

❦ Put the egg whites, salt and cream of tartar into a large basin – dry and polished. Whisk until the mixture is foamy. Add the remaining sugar a little at a time and whisk until very stiff and dense. Add the essences and whisk again. Fold in the flour with a metal spoon. Spoon into the dry cake tin.

❦ Cook the cake for 30-35 minutes until no dent is made on its surface by a light finger prod. Turn the whole tin upside down on a wire rack. Cool. The cake will then drop out.

❦ Lightly whip the cream and use to mask the very delicate cake. Fill the centre with skinned and deseeded grapes.

GÂTEAUX
AND
TORTES

All gâteaux make impressive desserts and are usually prepared, or at least part-prepared well in advance, to leave the cook plenty of time to put the finishing touches to the dinner party.

❧ About Gâteaux ❧ and Tortes

Many gâteaux are sponge-based, created with layers of feather-light Génoise sponge (borrowed from the French) and filled with creamy mixtures, often containing chocolate or fruit. Some gâteaux are completely masked with whipped cream or some form of crème, and may then have the sides coated in chopped nuts or grated chocolate. Others are left plain or may be topped with glacé icing or jam glaze.

All sponge cakes freeze perfectly and are immensely useful to have at hand for cakes such as the ones in this chapter. Let them thaw before filling and decorating.

Not all gâteaux are sponge-based. Some have layers of puff pastry, others, like Sachertorte have their own special type of baked layers. Meringue and delicate sweet pastry layers are also featured.

Don't be put off by the thought of the various stages necessary in gâteaux-making. They are really quite simple, and before you know it, an elegant gâteau will be in front of you.

GENOISE SPONGE CAKE

oil for greasing
4 eggs
115 g (4 ½ oz) caster sugar
90 g (3 ½ oz) best fine white plain flour
90 g (3 ½ oz) butter (butter is a must)

❦ Heat the oven to 180C (350F) mark 4. Prepare a 20 cm (8 in) cake tin: oil it lightly, line it carefully with baking paper and oil that too.
❦ Break the eggs into a bowl, add the sugar and whisk over hot water until the mixture has almost doubled in bulk and the whisk leaves a heavy trail. Take off the heat and continue to whisk for a minute or two.
❦ Sift the flour twice to incorporate as much air as possible. Melt the butter and cool until just running. Fold the flour into the mixture with the melted butter. Mix swiftly but gently.
❦ Turn into the prepared tin and cook for 20-30 minutes until the cake is just shrinking from the sides of the tin. Turn out on to a cloth, invert on to a wire rack and leave to cool.

Note
This is a lighter French version of our English Victoria sponge, and is the perfect base for many gâteaux and petits fours.

GATEAU CARDINAL

Serves 6-8

Crème au Beurre à la Meringue (see page 305)
50 g (2 oz) glacé cherries
2 tbsp kirsch
20 cm (8 in) baked round Génoise Sponge Cake (see above)
3 tbsp finely chopped nuts
100 g (4 oz) redcurrant jelly

❦ Keep back 4 or 5 tablespoons of the crème for decoration. Chop the cherries and fold them with the kirsch into the rest of the crème. Split the cake in half and spread lavishly with the filling. Reassemble.
❦ Spread some of the reserved crème around the sides of the cake. Put the chopped nuts on grease-proof paper and roll the cake like a wheel across them to decorate the sides.

❦ Stand the cake on a serving plate. Melt the red-currant jelly and spoon it carefully on top of the cake and leave to set. Put the rest of the crème into a forcing bag fitted with a small star pipe and work a neat shell pattern around the edge of the jelly.

Note
You may have seen this delicious cake in Boulogne, where it is a speciality.

GATEAU ST GEORGES

Serves 4-6

oil for greasing
4 egg recipe quantity of Génoise Sponge (see left)
100 g (4 oz) dark chocolate
2 eggs, separated
50 g (2 oz) butter, softened
2 tsp rum
100 g (4 oz) caster sugar

❦ Heat the oven to 180C (350F) mark 4. Prepare a 20-23 cm (8-9 in) sponge flan tin: oil it well, put a round of baking paper on to the bottom and oil again.
❦ Pour the génoise mixture into the tin and cook for 20-30 minutes, until the cake starts to shrink away from the sides of the tin. Turn out and leave to cool.
❦ Melt the chocolate with 1 tablespoon of water in a basin over a pan of hot water. When completely melted, remove from the heat. Beat the egg yolks, one at a time, into the chocolate with the butter and the rum. When the butter is completely absorbed, pour into the sponge flan case. Leave to set.
❦ Heat the oven to 160C (325F) mark 3.
❦ Use the egg whites and caster sugar to make a stiff Meringue Suisse (see page 283). Swirl the meringue on to the set chocolate and cook until set on the outside, about 20 minutes. It need not dry out like meringue shells, but must be firmly set on top. Serve cold.

Note
A wooden spoon is too thick for any folding operation. The thin edge of a metal spoon cuts through mixtures without breaking down the airy texture.

STRAWBERRY CREAM CAKE

Serves 6-8

1 recipe quantity Génoise Sponge (see page 309)
plain Crème au Beurre Mousseline (see page 304)
175 g (6 oz) strawberries
Glacé Icing (see page 304)
crystallized violets

❦ Heat the oven to 180C (350F) mark 4. Oil and line a 20-23 cm (8-9 in) round cake tin with baking paper, then oil again.
❦ Cook the mixture in the prepared tin for about 20-25 minutes. Turn out and cool on a wire rack. When cold, split carefully into three layers.
❦ Make the crème au beurre mousseline, but without the chocolate. Crush the strawberries and fold into the crème. This makes a bulky filling. Spread over the layers of cake and reassemble.
❦ Pour white, or the very palest pink, glacé icing all over the cake. You may need a second coat. When the icing is cold and set, move the cake to its serving plate.
❦ Decorate with an informal group of real crystallized violets on the top. Wait until the icing has set or the colour will run.

GATEAU CITRON

Serves 6-8

1 recipe quantity of Génoise Sponge baked in an 18 cm (7 in) square tin (see page 309)
plain Crème au Beurre Mousseline (see page 304)
3 lemons
about 175 g (6 oz) icing sugar
yellow food colouring
40 g (1 ½ oz) granulated sugar

❦ Split the cake into three layers. Make the crème as on page 304, but without the chocolate. Grate the rind and squeeze the juice of 2 lemons. Beat the grated rind of 1 lemon into the crème.
❦ Spread the sponge layers with two-thirds of the crème and reassemble the cake. Reserve a little crème for piping and spread the sides of the cake with the remainder, using a small palette knife.
❦ Make a lemon glacé icing with the sieved icing sugar and lemon juice. Beat in the grated rind of the second lemon and tint the palest yellow with food colouring. Carefully spread over the top of the cake and leave to set. Pipe small rosettes of the crème, or a shell pattern if you prefer, around the edge to neaten its appearance.
❦ Cut six thin slices from the remaining lemon and remove the pips. Poach them gently in a little water until the rind is almost transparent. Remove carefully. Add the granulated sugar to the water – about 50-75 ml (2-3 fl oz) by now – and stir until completely dissolved. Put the slices back and simmer for 5 minutes over a very low heat. Lift the slices on to a wire rack over a basin. Reduce the syrup without darkening, pour over and leave to set.
❦ Complete the decoration of the gâteau with a diagonal row of these overlapping glazed lemon slices.

APRICOT GENOISE CAKE

Serves 6

Génoise Sponge Cake baked in a 20 cm (8 in) round tin (see page 309)
about 450 g (1 lb) apricot jam
Mock Fondant Icing (see page 305)
few drops of kirsch
50 g (2 oz) toasted chopped almonds

❦ Split the génoise cake horizontally into three layers. Rub the apricot jam through a sieve. Spread a layer of jam on one layer of cake, cover with the middle layer, spread this with jam too, and set the last layer on top. Adjust to fit neatly.
❦ Cover the top and sides of the cake with apricot jam. Ice it with a fondant icing to which you have added a few drops of kirsch and sprinkle with chopped, browned almonds if liked. Leave to set.

Note
Contrary to what most people think, gâteaux can be quite simple to make and this one is a good example.

GATEAU MARGOT

Serves 12

oil for greasing
100 g (4 oz) plain flour
¼ tsp salt
4 eggs
175 g (6 oz) caster sugar
450 g (1 lb) strawberries
1 tbsp caster sugar
100 g (4 oz) good dark chocolate
275 ml (½ pint) whipping cream

❧ Heat the oven to 190C (375F) mark 5. Oil a ring mould, approximately 1.75 litres (3 pints). Sieve the flour and salt together.

❧ Whisk the eggs and 175 g (6 oz) sugar in a bowl over a pan of hot water until thick. Take off the heat and whisk until cold. Fold in the flour with a metal spoon and turn into the prepared tin. Cook for 35-40 minutes, then turn out on to a wire rack to cool.

❧ For the filling, take 175 g (6 oz) strawberries, blend them with 1 tablespoon of sugar (or rub through a sieve or mash them). Melt the chocolate in a basin over hot water. Cut the cake across into three layers. Spread each layer with chocolate and leave to set.

❧ Whip the cream stiffly, fold one-third into the strawberry purée and use this to spread over the chocolate on each layer.

❧ Reassemble the cake and stand on a serving plate. Use the rest of the whipped cream to completely mask the cake, spreading with a palette knife. Fill the centre with the rest of the strawberries.

HAZELNUT GALETTE

Serves 4-6

100 g (4 oz) plain flour
pinch of salt
75 g (3 oz) butter
50 g (2 oz) sugar
75 g (3 oz) ground hazelnuts
6-8 apricot halves, fresh or canned
150 ml (¼ pint) whipping cream
icing sugar

❧ Heat the oven to 180C (350F) mark 4. Line three baking sheets with baking paper.

❧ Sieve the flour with the salt. Make a well for the butter and sugar and sprinkle in the nuts. Draw the flour gradually into the middle, mixing with the fingertips until you have a firm, smooth dough. Wrap and chill for 20 minutes.

❧ Divide the dough into three. Roll each piece into a circle about 15 cm (6 in) across. Put the circles on the baking paper. Cook for about 20 minutes until golden brown. Remove carefully and cool on wire racks.

❧ Chop the apricots. Whip the cream stiffly and fold into the apricots; use to sandwich the galette together. Dredge the top with icing sugar and serve fairly quickly.

Note

A galette is a French Twelfth Night Cake, usually made with flaky pastry and traditionally eaten on Twelfth Night in the provinces north of the Loire. It has come to be used in English cookery, as rounds of pastry of various types with a rich filling.

SACHERTORTE

Serves 4–6

75 g (3 oz) good dark chocolate
1 tbsp rum
90 g (3 ½ oz) butter, plus more for greasing
150 g (5 oz) caster sugar
5 eggs (size 1 or 2), separated
90 g (3 ½ oz) unblanched hazelnuts, ground
40 g (1 ½ oz) fresh white breadcrumbs, dried
½ tsp powdered cloves
Chocolate Icing (see page 305)

❦ Heat the oven to 200C (400F) mark 6. Melt the chocolate and rum in a bowl over hot water. Grease and line a 23 cm (9 in) straight-sided sandwich tin with non-stick baking parchment with the side band coming 5 cm (2 in) above the rim, and grease again.
❦ Cream the butter and sugar until light and fluffy. Separate the eggs. Beat in the egg yolks one at a time, then fold the chocolate and rum into the mixture with a metal spoon. Fold in the ground hazelnuts, the breadcrumbs and the cloves.
❦ Stiffly whisk the egg whites (which should never be kept waiting) and fold them into the mixture. Turn into the prepared tin and cook until firm to the touch – about 30 minutes.
❦ Turn on to a wire rack and leave to cool. When cold, cover with chocolate icing. Serve with whipped cream.

Note
There is no flour in this cake.

NUSSKUCHEN

Serves 6

oil for greasing
75 g (3 oz) butter
75 g (3 oz) caster sugar
1 egg
50 g (2 oz) unblanched hazelnuts, ground
75 g (3 oz) plain flour
1 tsp instant coffee powder
2 tbsp milk
1 tsp baking powder
1 egg white
150 ml (¼ pint) whipping cream
450 g (1 lb) cooking apples
grated rind and juice of 1 lemon
50 g (2 oz) apricot jam
Chocolate Marquise (see page 304)

❦ Heat the oven to 190C (375F) mark 5. Oil and line a 20 cm (8 in) deep sandwich tin and oil again.
❦ Cream the butter and sugar until light and fluffy. Beat in the egg, nuts and sieved flour followed by the coffee and milk. Beat again. Fold in the baking powder and the stiffly beaten egg white. Turn into the prepared tin and cook for 20 minutes. Turn out on a wire rack and leave to cool.
❦ Peel, core and slice the apples. Simmer with the grated rind and juice of the lemon and the apricot jam until soft, then cool.
❦ Whip the cream. Split the cake in half and sandwich together with a layer of cream and a layer of the apple mixture. Cover the whole cake with chocolate marquise and serve fairly soon after it has set.

DOBEZ TORTE

Serves 6-8

oil for greasing
4 eggs
175 g (6 oz) caster sugar
150 g (5 oz plain flour
175 g (6 oz) granulated sugar
2-recipe quantity Crème au Beurre Mousseline
     Chocolat (see page 304)
75 g (3 oz) good dark chocolate, grated

❦ Heat the oven to 180C (350F) mark 4. Mark five circles on the underside of non-stick baking paper about 20 cm (8 in) across. Lightly oil and put on to baking sheets.

❦ Whisk the eggs in a bowl over hot water adding the caster sugar by degrees until thick. Fold in the sieved flour with a metal spoon. Spoon and smooth on to the circles. Bake until golden brown, about 15-20 minutes.

❦ When cooked, carefully remove from the paper and cool on wire racks (you need lots of room and may have to bake in two batches). Trim the edges neatly – a saucepan lid may do the trick. Choose the best one for the top.

❦ Melt the granulated sugar with 4 tablespoons water in a heavy-based pan and cook until caramel coloured, and then pour over the top layer. When just about to set, mark into sections with the back of a knife.

❦ Spread the other four pieces liberally with the chocolate crème and sandwich lightly together placing the caramel layer on top.

❦ Spread the sides evenly with the crème and press grated chocolate on the sides. Pipe neat rosettes of crème to neaten off the caramelized edge.

GATEAU ALLEMAND

Serves 4-6

oil for greasing
4 eggs
175 g (6 oz) caster sugar
grated rind and juice of 1 lemon
75 g (3 oz) semolina
25 g (1 oz) ground almonds
100 g (4 oz) home-made raspberry jam
150 ml (¼ pint) whipping cream
little Glacé Icing (see page 304)
pink or green food colouring

❦ Heat the oven to 190C (375F) mark 5. Lightly oil a 20 cm (8 in) square cake tin. Line the base with baking paper and oil again.

❦ Separate the eggs. Beat the yolks and sugar together until thick. Add the rind and juice of the lemon, the semolina and the ground almonds. Mix well. Whisk the egg whites stiffly and fold into the mixture. Turn into the tin and cook for 20-30 minutes.

❦ Turn out on to a wire rack and leave to cool. Split the cake in half carefully. Spread one half with plenty of raspberry jam and whipped cream, and put the other half on top very lightly.

❦ Coat the top thinly with glacé icing, tinted pale pink or green with liquid food colouring. Leave the cake to set.

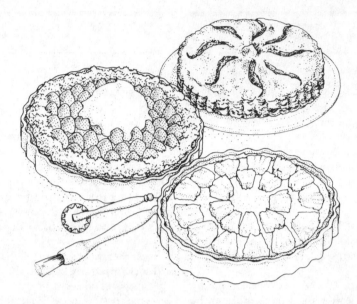

PIES, SLICES AND TURNOVERS

❦ About Pastry-making ❦

Pastry making is an art, but one quickly and easily mastered. The secret is to have everything cool – both ingredients and utensils – and to use only the fingertips when rubbing in to keep the pastry light and airy. It is the air incorporated into the dough which gives the characteristic texture to each type of pastry. Different pastries are made with varying proportions of fat to flour, and it is the method of rolling and folding or rubbing in which defines the type of pastry. For further information on pastry-making and the basic recipes for various types of pastry see pages 00-00.

Once made, pastry will freeze for up to 6 months if suitably wrapped in thick foil or polythene. This means it is possible to make up large quantities and freeze the surplus for future use.

Cornflour is good for dredging the pastry board. It is so light that it brushes off the pastry easily and does not unbalance the recipe.

The flans and tarts in this section are made and baked in various ways with a wide selection of fillings. Take care when making the pastry each time,

for it is a very important part of the recipe.

To 'bake blind', heat the oven to 200C (400F) mark 6 for shortcrust pastry or 220C (425F) mark 7 for flaky pastry. Line the pastry case with grease-proof paper, non-stick paper or foil and fill it with baking beans. Cook for 15 minutes standing on a hot baking sheet. Remove the beans and paper or foil and return to the oven for a further 5-10 minutes to dry out. Let the pastry cool before either lifting off the flan ring or removing from a tin or plate.

For baking beans to weight it, use any dried bean such as haricot, or dried lentils or rice. Retain and store for continual use. Pseudo 'beans' made of synthetic material are also available in some shops.

As an alternative to a fluted china flan dish, heavy flan tins can be bought at good kitchen shops. Tin is a superb conductor of heat, which means that the base of the flan is always cooked. Oblong tins are also available, about 28 x 20 cm (11 x 8 in), or individual ones, all with loose bottoms. Grease them well and bake blind in a hot oven to prove them before use. Line the base with non-stick parchment.

CHESTNUT TORTE

Serves 4-6

225 g (8 oz) Pâte Sucrée (see page 359)
225 g (8 oz) can chestnut purée
275 ml (½ pint) Crème Chantilly (see page 349)
50 g (2 oz) plain chocolate, grated
icing sugar

❦ Heat the oven to 190C (375F) mark 5. Make the pastry and divide into three portions. Roll each piece as thinly as possible into an 20 cm (8 in) circle. Trim using a plate and a sharp knife. Cook on a baking sheet for 20 minutes. Cool on a wire rack.

❦ Break up the chestnut purée with a fork, and very gently fold the crème chantilly into it. Spread the filling generously on two of the pastry circles and sandwich together. Carefully cut the third circle into six segments, pressing down with a sharp knife. Arrange the six segments on top of the crème chantilly. Cover with grated chocolate and dust with icing sugar.

DEVONSHIRE TURNOVERS

Makes 6

225 g (8 oz) Flaky pastry (see page 361)
white of 1 egg
100 g (4 oz) strawberry jam
caster sugar

❦ Heat the oven to 220C (425F) mark 7.

❦ Roll the pastry into an oblong. Trim the edges and cut into six 10 cm (4 in) squares. Brush half-way round the squares with beaten egg white. Put a spoonful of home-made strawberry jam on each. Fold over into a triangle. Press firmly just inside the edge to seal. Place on a baking sheet.

❦ Knock up the edges and put in a cool place to rest for 20 minutes. Brush the turnovers with beaten egg white and sprinkle with caster sugar. This gives a sparkly finish.

❦ Cook for 20 minutes, then cool on a wire rack. Serve with lots of clotted cream.

APRICOT TURNOVERS

Makes 10

225 g (8 oz) dried apricots
50 g (2 oz) apricot jam
1 tbsp ground almonds
grated rind and juice of 1 lemon
225 g (8 oz) Shortcrust Pastry (see page 357)
milk to glaze
few flaked almonds
caster sugar

❦ Soak the apricots overnight.

❦ Heat the oven to 200C (400F) mark 6. Strain the apricots, discarding the water. Cut them up and mix with the jam, ground almonds, lemon rind and juice.

❦ Roll out the pastry to a rectangle approximately 50 x 20 cm (20 x 8 in) and trim the edges. Cut in half lengthwise and again into pieces about 10 cm (4 in) square. Turn the squares over and brush two edges with water or milk.

❦ Put 2 teaspoons of the apricot mixture on each and fold the pastry over corner to corner. Press edges together, brush with milk, sprinkle a few flaked almonds on each and lightly dredge with caster sugar.

❦ Cook for 30 minutes. Cover with greaseproof paper if the almonds brown too quickly.

STRAWBERRY TARTLETS

Makes 16-20

225 g (8 oz) Shortcrust Pastry (see page 357)
450 g (1 lb) strawberries
225 g (8 oz) strawberry jam
1 tbsp water

❦ Heat the oven to 200C (400F) mark 6.
❦ Roll out the pastry to a thickness of 5 mm (¼ in). Release from the board with a palette knife and leave to relax for 10 minutes. Lightly grease the tartlet tins. Cut out 16-20 rounds of pastry with a fluted cutter a little larger than the tins. Flip over and line the tins with the pastry. Bake blind (see page 314). Cool before taking out of tins.
❦ Arrange the fruit in the tartlets, points uppermost. Put the jam and water into a pan and simmer, stirring gently. Rub through a sieve or whizz up in a blender. Spoon carefully over the fruit in the tartlets and leave to set.

Note
End-of-season jam strawberries are ideal.

PLATE APPLE PIE

Serves 4

225 g (8 oz) Shortcrust Pastry (see page 357)
450 g (1 lb) cooking apples
50 g (2 oz) brown sugar
2 tbsp apricot jam
25 g (1 oz) butter
white of 1 egg
caster sugar

❦ Heat the oven to 200C (400F) mark 6.
❦ Peel, core and slice the apples. Mix in a bowl with the sugar, apricot jam and butter.
❦ Cut the pastry in half. Roll out one half and use to line the base of an 18 or 20 cm (7 or 8 in) enamel plate. Put the prepared fruit on the lined plate. Brush the edge of the pastry with lightly beaten egg white. Roll out the other half of the pastry and use to cover the pie. Press the edges firmly together, knock-up and flute the edges (see page 357).
❦ Make three slashes across the top (to let the steam out). Brush with the rest of the egg white and sprinkle lightly with caster sugar. Bake for 40 minutes.

Notes
Apples shrink in cooking, so crowd them in. Apricot jam is a perfect match for apples.

MINCE PIES

Makes 12

225 g (8 oz) Shortcrust Pastry (see page 357)
350 g (12 oz) mincemeat
milk to glaze
caster sugar

❦ Heat the oven to 200C (400F) mark 6.
❦ Roll out the pastry and cut out rounds with a fluted cutter to fit the patty pans. Roll out the remaining pastry and trimmings, and with a plain cutter, cut 12 rounds a little larger than the patty tins (pastry shrinks as it is cooked). Flip these over and use to line the tins.
❦ Spoon mincemeat into each. Brush the plain edges with milk and cover with the fluted tops. Make a little hole in the top of each pie, brush with milk and dust with sugar. Cook on a baking sheet for 20-25 minutes.

Note
Fluted tops at least one size smaller than the little pans can be used. They sit on top of the mincemeat, look very attractive and do away with a mouthful or two of pastry for those to whom such things are of concern.

CHEESE AND APPLE PIE

Serves 4-6

175 g (6 oz) Shortcrust Pastry (see page 357)
100 g (4 oz) cheese
100 g (4 oz) sugar
¼ tsp salt
25 g (1 oz) flour
¼ tsp nutmeg
grated rind of 1 lemon
450 g (1 lb) cooking apples
milk to glaze
caster sugar

❦ Heat the oven to 200C (400F) mark 6.

❦ Dice the cheese into a basin, add the sugar, salt, flour, grated nutmeg and lemon rind. Mix them all well.

❦ Roll out the pastry to a thickness of 5 mm (¼ in). Line a 500 ml (1 pint) pie dish and trim the edge.

❦ Peel, core and slice the apples and use some to cover the bottom of the lined pie dish. Add half the cheese mixture and then another layer of apples and the remaining cheese. Finish with a layer of apples.

❦ Turn in the pastry edge to just overlap the fruit. Brush with milk. Roll out the pastry trimmings, cut into thin strips and use to lattice the top of the pie. Brush the pastry with milk and dust with caster sugar. Wipe the pie dish edge clean.

❦ Stand on a baking sheet and cook for 25 minutes. Cover with greaseproof paper and cook for a further 15 minutes.

Note

Lancashire cheese is the cheese for melting. It has a wonderfully subtle taste and melts into a thick cream. It is renowned for its splendid toasting qualities, and is perfect for this North-country tart.

ALLUMETTES

Makes 15-20

225 g (8 oz) Flaky Pastry (see page 361)
175 g (6 oz) icing sugar
white of 1 egg
50 g (2 oz) flaked almonds

❦ Heat the oven to 220C (425F) mark 7.

❦ Roll out the pastry to an oblong 25 x 15 cm (10 x 6 inches). Trim, cut in half lengthwise and leave to rest for 20 minutes.

❦ Make the royal icing: sieve the icing sugar into a basin. Put the egg white into another. Add the sieved icing sugar a spoonful at a time, beating well after each addition. Use all the sugar to obtain a firm smooth icing.

❦ Cut the pastry into strips approximately 7.5 x 2.5 cm (3 x 1 in). Put on baking paper on a baking sheet. Cover each strip with royal icing, starting from the middle so that it spreads slowly outwards. Sprinkle flaked almonds over the icing.

❦ Cook for 15-20 minutes then cool on a wire rack.

Note

Allumettes give a lift to ordinary bought ice-cream and can make a dinner party dessert more interesting and appealing.

CREAM SLICES

Makes 8

225 g (8 oz) Flaky Pastry (see page 361)
175 ml (6 fl oz) whipping cream
175 g (6 oz) raspberry jam
50-75 g (2-3 oz) icing sugar
little milk

❦ Heat the oven to 220C (425F) mark 7.

❦ Roll the pastry to a 30 cm (12 in) square; trim the edges. Cut into three 10 cm (4 in) strips. Put on baking paper on a baking sheet. Prick with a fork and leave to rest for 20 minutes. Cook for 10-12 minutes. Cool on a wire rack.

❦ Whip the cream until stiff. With a very sharp pointed knife, cut each strip of cooked pastry into 4 cm (1 ½ in) slices. Spread one slice with raspberry jam, cover with cream. Put the next slice on top, cover with jam and cream. Turn the third slice upside down and press gently on top of the slices. Make eight cream slices in this way.

❦ Cover the top of each slice with glacé icing made from icing sugar and a little milk, letting it spread from the middle to the edge.

❦ Ice some pastries with white and some with pink glacé icing to make a charming dish of pastries.

Variations

Some recipes suggest making the pastries up with the three larger strips, and then cutting into slices. This needs a great deal more care.

❦ Crème Pâtissière (see page 349) is also used for these slices. They are then called Vanilla Slices.

ECCLES CAKES

Makes 8

225 g (8 oz) Flaky Pastry (see page 361)
50 g (2 oz) butter
100 g (4 oz) currants
50 g (2 oz) chopped peel
50 g (2 oz) brown sugar
white of 1 egg
caster sugar

❦ Heat the oven to 220C (425F) mark 7.
❦ Roll out the pastry to a rectangle 30 x 15 cm (12 x 6 in). Trim the edges, cut into two pieces, 30 x 7.5 cm (12 x 3 in) then cut each half into four 7.5 cm (3 in) squares. Leave to relax.
❦ Melt the butter in a pan. Add the currants, peel and sugar. Put a little of the mixture into the centre of each pastry square. Damp the edges and draw up like a little purse. Turn over and roll gently into a round, about 7.5 cm (3 inches) across.
❦ Place on baking paper on a baking sheet. Slash the top with a knife to make a criss-cross pattern. Rest for 20 minutes.
❦ Cook for 15 minutes. Brush with egg white, sprinkle with caster sugar and return to the oven for a further 5 minutes. Cool on a wire rack.

Notes
Both Banbury and Eccles Cakes need the resting after rolling to their characteristic shapes. It helps to keep that particular shape whilst these cakes are being cooked.

BANBURY CAKES

Makes 6

225 g (8 oz) Flaky Pastry (see page 361)
25 g (1 oz) butter
1 tbsp plain flour
100 g (4 oz) currants
25 g (1 oz) mixed peel
50 g (2 oz) soft brown sugar
scrape or two of nutmeg
2 tbsp milk
white of 1 egg to glaze
caster sugar

❦ Heat the oven to 220C (425F) mark 7.
❦ Roll out the pastry to a rectangle 30 x 15 cm (12 x 6 in). Leave to relax.
❦ Melt the butter in a pan, stir in the flour and cook for a minute or two stirring all the time. Remove from the heat. Stir in the fruit, brown sugar, spice and milk. Leave to cool.
❦ Trim the edges of the pastry. Cut in half lengthwise. Cut each half into three equal pieces. Put a little of the mixture on to each piece. Damp the edges and draw them up into a little purse. Turn them over. Roll in one direction to an oval about 12.5 x 9 cm (5 x 3 ½ in). Put on to baking paper on a baking sheet and rest for 20 minutes.
❦ Make three cuts with a sharp knife across the top of each oval. Cook for 15 minutes then brush lightly with beaten egg white and dust with caster sugar. Bake a further 5 minutes. Cool on a wire rack.

GATEAU ST GEORGES

Serves 4-5

175 g (6 oz) Flaky Pastry (see page 361)
175 g (6 oz) good dark chocolate
100 g (4 oz) butter
2 eggs, separated
50 g (2 oz) caster sugar

❦ Heat the oven to 220C (425F) mark 7.
❦ Roll out the pastry and use to line an 18 cm (7 in) ovenproof flan dish. Bake the pastry case blind (see page 314). Reduce the oven temperature to 180C (350F) mark 4.
❦ Melt the chocolate in a basin over hot water or in a microwave. Remove from the heat and cool a little. Stir in the butter a little at a time. Beat the egg yolks and stir them into the chocolate. Mix well. Pour into the pastry case and leave until cold.
❦ Whisk the egg whites stiffly. Fold in the caster sugar. Spoon the meringue on to the chocolate and swirl with a fork. Cook the meringue for 15 minutes. It will be marshmallowy inside, not set like a meringue shell.

Notes
Butter, not margarine and a very good chocolate are essential for this dessert.

APPLE CHAUSSON

Serves 6

175 g (6 oz) Flaky Pastry (see page 361)
450 g (1 lb) cooking apples
50 g (2 oz) butter
75 g (3 oz) currants and sultanas mixed
grated rind of 1 lemon
brown sugar
caster sugar

❧ Heat the oven to 200C (400F) mark 6.
❧ Make the pastry and leave it to relax for about 20 minutes in the refrigerator.
❧ Peel, core and thickly slice the apples. Melt the butter in a pan. Add the apples in layers with the dried fruit (check for stalks), lemon rind, and brown sugar to taste. Keep on a low heat for 5-10 minutes, shaking the pan from time to time. Turn out to cool. The apples will be buttery but not cooked.
❧ Divide the pastry in half and roll out into two 20 cm (8 in) circles. Put one circle on to a baking sheet and spoon on the apples, leaving a 2.5 cm (1 in) margin of pastry round the edge. Brush the margin with water. Put the remaining circle of pastry on top and press the edges together. Trim.
❧ Make the classic pattern on the top with the point of a knife – six or eight curved lines from the middle to the edge, and two circles around the edge. Brush with water, sprinkle with caster sugar and cook for 40 minutes.

CONQUES

Makes about 30

175 g (6 oz) Puff Pastry (see page 360)
caster sugar

❧ Heat the oven to 220C (425F) mark 7.
❧ Roll out the pastry as thin as possible. Cut out small circles with a 4 cm (1 ½ in) cutter.
❧ Sprinkle the board with caster sugar. Elongate each little circle on the sugar with the rolling pin. Leave to relax. Place on a baking sheet lined with non-stick baking paper.
❧ Cook for 10 minutes (but watch them). Cool on wire racks. Store in an airtight tin. Serve with ices or fools. They may need crisping before use.

GATEAU PITHIVIERS

Serves 4-6

350 g (12 oz) Puff Pastry (see page 360)
50 g (2 oz) butter
50 g (2 oz) caster sugar
50 g (2 oz) ground almonds
white of 1 egg to glaze
sugar to glaze

❧ Heat the oven to 220-230C (425-450F) mark 7-8.
❧ Roll out the pastry and cut two 18 cm (7 in) circles from it. Roll one out a little larger. Leave to relax.
❧ Make the filling – a crème pithiviers: cream the butter and sugar together, add the ground almonds and egg yolk. Stir well.
❧ Line a baking sheet with baking paper. Lift the smaller circle of pastry on to it. Roll out the trimmings. Cut a 2.5 cm (1 in) strip from them. Brush the pastry circle edge with water and press the strip gently around it. This will stop the filling from leaking out.
❧ Spoon the filling on to the base. Brush the strip with water. Lift the second circle on to it. Press lightly with the fingertips to seal. Decorate the edges with the tip of a spoon. Knock up with the back of a knife. Cut a hole in the top to let out the steam and with the point of a sharp knife, lightly cut the traditional cartwheel whirls on the top. Brush with beaten egg white and dust with caster sugar.
❧ Cook until honey-coloured and well-risen, for about 30 minutes. Serve cold with cream.

CREAM HORNS

Makes 8

225 g (8 oz) Flaky Pastry (see page 361)
1 egg
milk
150 ml (¼ pint) whipping cream
50 g (2 oz) raspberry jam

❧ Prepare the cream horn tins: brush them with melted white fat, not necessarily lard, but butter and margarine are inclined to stick. Put in a cool place. Heat the oven to 220C (425F) mark 7.
❧ Roll out the pastry to a rectangle about 20 x 25 cm (8 x 10 in). Cut into strips 2.5 x 25 cm (1 x 10 in). Brush one edge of each strip with lightly beaten egg. Roll on to the outside surface of the horn tins, starting at the pointed end and ensure that the pastry does not come over the open end of the tin. Overlap each new turn of pastry.
❧ Press gently on to baking paper on a baking sheet, the tail of the pastry underneath. Brush with milk. Cook for 15-20 minutes.
❧ Take the cooked horns gently off the baking paper. Cool on a wire rack and, as they cool, remove the tins from the pastry.
❧ Whip the cream until stiff. Put a little raspberry jam into the tip of the pastry horn (a coffee spoon is handy.) Fill with cream.

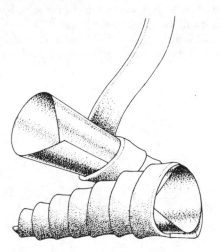

APRICOT JALOUSIE

Serves 6-8

350 g (12 oz) Puff Pastry (see page 360)
100 g (4 oz) apricot jam
450 g (1 lb) fresh apricots
100 g (4 oz) caster sugar
275 ml (½ pint) water
1 tbsp Benedictine
1 egg to glaze
sugar to glaze

❧ Heat the oven to 220-230C (425-450F) mark 7-8.
❧ Roll out the pastry to a 30 cm (12 in) square. Cut in half lengthwise. Roll one piece a little larger. Trim both. Put the smaller piece on to baking paper on a baking sheet.
❧ Sieve the jam and spread it on this piece of pastry to within 2.5 cm (1 in) of the edge. Cut the apricots in half, removing the stones. Dissolve the sugar in the water and boil for a few minutes. Gently poach the apricots in the syrup for a few minutes. Lift out with a slotted spoon. Drain and arrange attractively on the jam on the pastry. Sprinkle with Benedictine. Brush the edge with some beaten egg.
❧ Dust the second piece of the pastry with cornflour. Fold in half lengthwise, flour side inside. With a very sharp knife make slits right through the pastry 2.5 cm (1 in) apart. Unfold and put carefully over the apricots, pressing the edges together to seal. Decorate the edges by cutting with a knife, and knock up. Brush with beaten egg, being careful not to brush the slits together.
❧ Dust with caster sugar and cook for 30 minutes until golden brown.

Notes
Both these traditional French pastries – Gâteau Pithiviers and Apricot Jalousie – will freeze well. Like all pastry dishes they need crisping in the oven after defrosting.

BANANA TURNOVERS

Makes 4

175 g (6 oz) Puff Pastry (see page 360)
2 tbsp jam
4 bananas
1 lemon
50 g (2 oz) soft brown sugar
1 egg to glaze
25 g (1 oz) flaked almonds

❦ Heat the oven to 220-230C (425-450F) mark 7-8.
❦ Roll out the pastry and use to cut four circles about 15 cm (6 inches) across. Leave to relax for 20 minutes. Then brush each circle with jam to within 1 cm (½ in) of the edge.
❦ Mash the bananas with the grated rind and juice of the lemon and the sugar. Spoon into the centres of the pastry circles. Brush around half the edge of each circle with beaten egg. Fold over, press together and flute the edges, and knock them up. Stand on a baking sheet and brush the turnovers with beaten egg.
❦ Cook for 15-20 minutes until starting to brown. Sprinkle with flaked almonds and return to the oven for a further 5 minutes. Serve hot or cold.

Variation
Rum can be added to the mashed banana.

MILLE FEUILLES

Serves 4-6

350 g (12 oz) Puff Pastry (see page 360)
450 g (1 lb) raspberries
75 g (3 oz) caster sugar
275 ml (½ pint) whipping cream
100 g (4 oz) icing sugar
little milk

❦ Heat the oven to 220-230C (425-450F) mark 7-8.
❦ Roll out the pastry thinly. Cut five 20 cm (8 in) rounds from it, using a plate as a guide. Put the rounds on baking paper on baking sheets. Prick them to prevent them from rising too high. Cook until golden brown, about 20 minutes. Cool on wire racks.
❦ Dust the raspberries with caster sugar. Reserve a few of the best for decoration. Whip the cream and fold in the raspberries. Put a pastry circle on the serving plate. Cover with raspberries and cream. Put on the next circle; cover with the mixture. Continue in the same way until the last circle. Put this on top.
❦ Make a little firm glacé icing with the icing sugar and a tablespoon or less of milk. Spoon on the top round of pastry so that it forms a small pool. Set the reserved raspberries in it. Serve fairly soon after making.

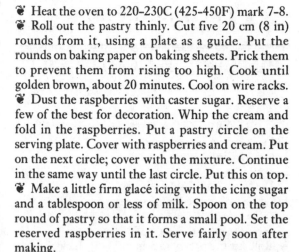

PALMIERS

Makes about 20

350 g (12 oz) Puff Pastry (see page 360)
caster sugar

❦ Heat the oven to 220C (425F) mark 7.
❦ Roll out the pastry to a rectangle about 35 x 25 cm (14 x 10 in). Trim the edges. Sprinkle the pastry amply with caster sugar. If you keep one or two vanilla pods in the sugar jar, so much the better.
❦ Fold the long sides of the pastry to meet in the middle. Fold one side on to the other so that you now have a strip about 35 x 6 cm (14 x 2 ½ in). Seal the strip firmly with the rolling pin.
❦ With a sharp knife, using a pressing rather than a sawing movement, cut slices 1-2 cm (¼-½ in) wide. Put these on baking paper on baking sheets, widely spaced, as they will expand. Leave to relax for 20 minutes.
❦ Cook until pale gold, for about 5 or 6 minutes. Cool on wire racks.

Note
These are sometimes sandwiched together with raspberry jam and whipped cream. This makes them rather difficult to eat and is rather gilding the lily.

❦ Tarts and Flans ❦

PINEAPPLE CURD TART

Serves 4-6

175 g (6 oz) Shortcrust Pastry (see page 357)
225 g (8 oz) cream cheese
2 tbsp granulated sugar
2 egg yolks
150 ml (¼ pint) single cream
425 g (15 oz) can pineapple rings

❦ Heat the oven to 180C (350F) mark 4.
❦ Roll out the pastry to 5 mm (¼ in) thick and use to line a 20 cm (8 in) fluted ovenproof flan case (or use a flan ring). Press the pastry down well and prick the base.
❦ Beat the cheese until smooth, add the sugar, egg yolks and cream. Turn the mixture into the pastry case and bake until it is firm to the fingertips, about 20-30 minutes.
❦ In the meantime, poach the pineapple slices in their own syrup until almost caramelized. This needs care.
❦ When the cake is cooked, leave until cold. Arrange the pineapple slices on the top and spoon any remaining syrup over them.

TREACLE TART

Serves 6

225 g (8 oz) Shortcrust Pastry (see page 357)
175 g (6 oz) golden syrup
50 g (2 oz) fresh white breadcrumbs
1 tsp lemon juice

❦ Heat the oven to 190C (375F) mark 5.
❦ Make the pastry. Cut off a quarter to lattice the top. Roll out the remainder and use to line a buttered 20 cm (8 in) ovenproof plate. Flute the edges.
❦ Warm the syrup in a saucepan, add the bread-crumbs and lemon juice and pour on to the pastry. Roll out the remaining pastry and cut it into narrow strips to twist. Criss-cross the strips over the treacle, sticking the ends to the edges of the tart with water.
❦ Bake for 30 minutes. Serve hot or cold.

FRESH RASPBERRY TARTLETS

Makes 16-20

225 g (8 oz) Shortcrust Pastry (see page 357)
450 g (1 lb) raspberries
225 g (8 oz) raspberry jam
1 tbsp water

❦ Heat the oven to 190C (375F) mark 5.
❦ Make the pastry and roll out to 5 mm (¼ in) thick. Cut 16-20 rounds using a fluted cutter. Turn the rounds over and use to line patty tins. Bake blind (see page 314) for 15 minutes. Remove the paper and beans and return to the oven for a further 10 minutes. Cool on a wire rack.
❦ Hull and pick over the fruit. Arrange in the tartlets, pointed end uppermost. Put the jam in a saucepan, add the water. Bring to the boil, stirring all the time, then cool. Rub through a sieve or the fine plate of a food mill.
❦ Carefully spoon the warm jam over the tartlets. Hand round whipped cream separately.

Note
These empty tartlets freeze perfectly.

GRAPE AND LIME TART

Serves 4

225 g (8 oz) Shortcrust Pastry (see page 357)
1 packet of lime jelly
450 g (1 lb) green grapes
1 lime

❦ Heat the oven to 200C (400F) mark 6.
❦ Make the jelly using 50 ml (2 fl oz) water less than the directions suggest. Peel and de-seed the grapes (a hair-pin makes a super gadget for this).
❦ Roll the pastry out to a thickness of 5 mm (¼ in) and use to line a 20 or 23 cm (8 or 9 in) fluted oven-proof dish. Bake blind (see page 314).
❦ When the pastry is cool, put the grapes in circles on it. Grate the zest from the lime, squeeze the juice and add both to the jelly. Stir, and spoon the jelly carefully over the grapes. Allow to set and serve with cream.

Note
A Swiss roll tin could be used for this. The tart should then be turned out.

RAISIN AND CIDER TART

Serves 6

1 tbsp cornflour
275 ml (½ pint) cider
350 g (12 oz) seedless raisins, washed and
    drained
25 g (1 oz) brown sugar
175 g (6 oz) Shortcrust Pastry (see page 357)
milk to glaze
Demerara sugar

❦ Heat the oven to 200C (400F) mark 6.
❦ Blend the cornflour with a little cider. Put it with the remaining cider, raisins and brown sugar into a saucepan. Bring slowly to the boil stirring all the time. Cook for 1 minute, then cool.
❦ Cut the pastry in half. Roll out one piece and use to line a 23 cm (9 in) ovenproof plate. Turn the mixture on to the pastry. Brush the edge of the pastry with milk.
❦ Roll out the second piece of pastry and use to cover the tart. Press the edges firmly together,

knock-up and flute the edges (see page 357). Make two slanting cuts in the top, brush with milk and sprinkle lightly with Demerara sugar.
❦ Bake for 30 minutes.

CUSTARD TART

Serves 4-6

175 g (6 oz) Pâte Sucrée (see page 359)
275 ml (½ pint) milk
1 egg, plus 2 extra egg yolks
15 g (½ oz) caster sugar
scrape of nutmeg

❦ Heat the oven to 200C (400F) mark 6. Butter a 20 cm (8 in) ovenproof fluted china flan case.
❦ Roll out the pastry as thinly as possible on a board lightly dusted with cornflour. Lift on to the rolling pin (flan pastry is more difficult to handle than ordinary shortcrust) and use to line the flan case. Using a little ball of pastry as a pusher, press out all the air which is trapped between the pastry and the case. Prick the pastry and press again.
❦ Cook on a baking sheet for about 15 minutes. Meanwhile make the custard.
❦ Boil the milk. Beat the egg and the yolks with the sugar. Pour the boiling milk over them, beating all the time. Beat for another few minutes, by which time the flan case should be cooked.
❦ Pull the oven rack with the flan case a little way out of the oven, and using a jug, gently pour the custard into the case. Sprinkle with a little grated nutmeg. Ease gently back into the oven and cook for about 30 minutes until set.

Notes
Egg yolks make a custard creamy and egg whites set it, which is why the recipes use the rather irritating proportion of yolks to whole eggs. It is worth doing just what is suggested for a creamy, well-set custard. If whole eggs are used, the custard will be too firm.

BLACKCURRANT TART

Serves 4

175 g (6 oz) Pâte Sucrée (see page 359)
225 g (8 oz) prepared blackcurrants
100 g (4 oz) caster sugar
1 tsp ground cinnamon
caster sugar for dredging

❦ Heat the oven to 200C (400F) mark 6.
❦ Roll out the pastry and use to line an 18 cm (7 in) fluted china flan dish Reserve the trimmings.
❦ Simmer the blackcurrants in their own juice with the sugar and cinnamon, stirring all the time until the mixture is thick and glossy. This is called a *marmelade*. Cool a little and turn into the flan case.
❦ Roll out the pastry trimmings, cut into narrow strips and make a twisted lattice top for the tart. Brush with water and sprinkle with caster sugar to glaze.
❦ Bake in the centre of the oven on a hot baking sheet for 30–35 minutes.

ORANGE AND APPLE FLAN

Serves 4

175 g (6 oz) Pâte Sucrée (see page 359)
700 g (1 ½ lb) cooking apples,
2 oranges
50 g (2 oz) granulated sugar
caster sugar
Apricot Glaze (see page 367)

❦ Heat the oven to 200C (400F) mark 6.
❦ Roll out the pastry and use to line an 18 cm (7 in) fluted china flan dish. Push well into the base with a little ball of pastry.
❦ Peel, core and slice the apples. Grate the rind and squeeze the juice of one orange. Put the apples with the sugar and the orange rind and juice into a pan and simmer until reduced to a thick pulp. Depending on the apples, you may need a tablespoon of water to prevent the fruit from catching.
❦ Fill the flan with the apple. Stand the flan on a baking sheet and dust with caster sugar. Bake in the centre of the oven for 30 minutes.
❦ With a sharp knife, cut away the peel and all the pith from the other orange. Slice very thinly and when the flan is cooked, put overlapping circles of orange on the apple. Brush with apricot glaze and serve warm.

FRESH STRAWBERRY FLAN

Serves 6

1 packet of strawberry jelly
225 g (8 oz) Pâte Sucrée (see page 359)
450 g (1 lb) strawberries
150 ml (¼ pint) double cream

❦ Make the jelly and leave it to cool almost to setting point. Heat the oven to 190C (375F) mark 5.
❦ Make the pastry and use it to line a 20 cm (8 in) ovenproof fluted china flan dish. Bake blind for 20 minutes (see page 314). Cool. If you are turning it out, now is the moment for that.
❦ Arrange the hulled strawberries in the flan case, pointed ends upwards. Spoon just enough of the setting (but not set) jelly over the strawberries barely to cover them.
❦ Leave the remaining jelly to set then chop it and use to decorate around the top edge of the flan. Whip the cream and pile very neatly into the centre of the flan to finish.

BUTTERSCOTCH FLAN

Serves 4-6

175 g (6 oz) Pâte Sucrée (see page 359)
100 g (4 oz) soft dark brown sugar
50 g (2 oz) cornflour
425 ml (¾ pint) milk
2 egg yolks
25 g (1 oz) butter
2 tsp honey
150 ml (¼ pint) whipping cream
25 g (1 oz) flaked almonds, browned

❦ Heat the oven to 200C (400F) mark 6.
❦ Line an 18 cm (7 in) fluted flan case with the pastry. Bake blind (see page 314).
❦ Put the sugar, cornflour (blended with a little of the milk) and the rest of the milk into a pan. Cook until the mixture thickens, stirring all the time. Remove from the heat. Beat the egg yolks and stir in, followed by the butter and honey. Cook for a further few minutes. Leave to cool.
❦ When cold pour into the cooked pastry case. Decorate with the firmly whipped cream, either piped or swirled on to the top of the filling. Scatter toasted almond flakes over the cream.

Notes
To brown the nuts put them into a non-stick frying pan and toss them over a gentle heat. They brown readily because of the oil in them. Alternatively toast under a moderate grill.

DEVONSHIRE FLAN

Serves 4-6

175 g (6 oz) Pâte Sucrée (see page 359)
450 g (1 lb) cooking apples
2 cloves
75 g (3 oz) caster sugar
1 or 2 eating apples
lemon juice
Apricot Glaze (see page 367)

❦ Heat the oven to 200C (400F) mark 6.
❦ Line a 20 cm (8 in) flan dish with the pastry. Bake blind (see page 314).
❦ Chop the cooking apples roughly. Simmer in very little water with the cloves until tender. Remove the cloves and rub the apples through a sieve. Sweeten to taste with the sugar. Spoon the purée into the cooked pastry case.
❦ Quarter, core, but do not peel, the eating apples. Cut into thin slices and dip in lemon juice to keep them white. Arrange decoratively on top of the puréed apple.
❦ Pour or brush warm apricot glaze over the fruit. Serve with lots of clotted cream.

FRUIT BORDER TART

Serves 6-8

225 g (8 oz) Flaky Pastry (see page 361)
1 egg
75 g (3 oz) strawberry jam
450 g (1 lb) or more of strawberries
100 g (4 oz) caster sugar

❦ Heat the oven to 220C (425F) mark 7.
❦ Roll the pastry out to a rectangle. Trim the edges. Cut a 2.5 cm (1 in) strip from each side. Put the rectangle of pastry on a damp baking sheet and prick all over with a fork. Brush the edges with beaten egg. Put the pastry strips, trimming to fit, on the edges of the rectangle, just inside so they don't slip off when cooking. Leave to relax for 20 minutes.
❦ Brush the top of the pastry strips with beaten egg. Cook for 20 minutes and then cool on a wire rack.
❦ Sieve the jam, warm it and brush the bottom of the tart with it. Hull the strawberries. Sit them on the jam, pointed end uppermost.
❦ Dissolve the sugar in 175 ml (6 fl oz) water. Boil without stirring until syrupy and just beginning to colour. Spoon over the strawberries. Serve cold with cream.

Notes
The empty case freezes perfectly. Any fruit can be used for this simple tart.

NORSKA LINSER

Makes 12-14

225 g (8 oz) Lemon Pastry, chilled (see page 359)
icing sugar

Custard
175 ml (6 fl oz) single cream
2 egg yolks
1 tbsp sugar
2 tsp cornflour
grated rind and juice of 1 lemon

❦ Heat the oven to 200C (400F) mark 6.
❦ Roll out the pastry on a board lightly dredged
with cornflour. Using a heart-shaped cutter approximately 7.5 x 5 cm (3 x 2 in), cut out 24 or so pastry
hearts. Turn them over and leave to relax.
❦ For the custard: mix together all the ingredients
except the lemon juice. Beat well and cook in the top
of a double saucepan until thick. The cornflour will
stop the cream from separating, but do not let it boil.
Cool.
❦ Put half the hearts on to a baking sheet lined with
non-stick baking paper. Spoon a little thick custard
on to the centre of each. Brush the edges with water
and carefully put on the other hearts to form the lids.
Press down gently. Cook for 20 minutes.
❦ Transfer to a wire rack. When cool, dust sparingly with sieved icing sugar or, if you prefer, use the
juice of the lemon with a little icing sugar for equally sparing lemon glacé icing.

Notes
These are attractive and delicious little Scandinavian
pastries, just right for engagement parties, wed-
dings, anniversaries and christenings. In very good
kitchen shops you can sometimes find trays of shallow heart-shaped tartlet tins. These obviously allow
a little more filling.

FRENCH APPLE TART

Serves 6-8

225 g (8 oz) Flaky Pastry (see page 361)
6 apples
100 g (4 oz) granulated sugar
225 ml (8 fl oz) water
1 or 2 cloves
bramble jelly
3 eggs, separated
50 g (2 oz) caster sugar
50 g (2 oz) ground almonds

❦ Heat the oven to 220C (425F) mark 7.
❦ Roll out the pastry and use to line a 23 cm (9 in)
fluted ovenproof flan dish. Bake blind (see page 314).
Reduce the oven temperature to 200C (400F) mark 6.
❦ Peel, core and slice the apples thinly. Poach these
gently in a syrup made from 100 g (4 oz) granulated
sugar dissolved in 225 ml (8 fl oz) water with one or
two cloves. Dissolve every grain of sugar before
bringing to the boil. Simmer until getting thick.
When just tender, remove the apple slices from the
syrup with a slotted spoon. Arrange in the pastry
case. Melt the bramble jelly and spoon it over the
apples.
❦ Whip the egg whites stiffly. Whip the yolks with
the caster sugar until really fluffy. Fold the whipped
whites with the ground almonds into the egg yolks.
Spoon on to the bramble jelly. Dust with a little caster sugar. Cook for 20-30 minutes, until honey-
coloured and sparkly on top.

Note
The spare syrup will keep, if put in a jam jar with a
tightly-fitting lid, until the next time you need it.

CHEESECAKE

Serves 6

50 g (2 oz) butter
100 g (4 oz) caster sugar
300 g (10 oz) cottage cheese
50 g (2 oz) ground almonds
50 g (2 oz) ground rice
50 g (2 oz) seedless raisins
1 lemon
2 eggs

❧ Heat the oven to 180C (350F) mark 4. Grease a 23-25 cm (9-10 in) loose-bottomed flan tin. Line the base with non-stick baking paper.
❧ Cream the butter, sugar and cheese until white. Beat in the ground almonds and the ground rice and fold in the raisins. Grate the rind and squeeze the juice from the lemon.
❧ Separate the eggs. Beat the yolks into the mixture with the lemon rind and juice. Whisk the egg whites stiffly and fold evenly through the mixture. Cook for one hour, then cool and chill.
❧ This is the classic cheesecake.

NORMANDY CHERRY AND APPLE TART

Serves 8

225 g (8 oz) Flaky Pastry, made with butter (see page 361)
175 g (6 oz) granulated sugar
350 ml (12 fl oz) water
700 g (1 ½ lb) apples
50 g (2 oz) caster sugar
450 g (1 lb) cherries
2 tsp Calvados
2 tsp kirsch

❧ Heat the oven to 220C (425F) mark 7.
❧ Roll out the pastry and use to line a 20 cm (8 in) fluted ovenproof pastry dish. Bake blind (see page 357).
❧ At the same time cook two 2.5 cm (1 in) strips of pastry which will fit across the pastry case. They will be used to mark the tart into quarters.
❧ Make a sugar syrup with the granulated sugar and the water over a gentle heat until dissolved. Then boil without stirring until syrupy but not coloured. Put aside.
❧ Peel, core and cut up half the apples. Simmer them in as little water as possible with the caster sugar, to make an apple purée.
❧ Pour half the sugar syrup into a clean pan (a cheap frying pan kept for this purpose is useful). Peel, core and slice the rest of the apples thinly. Poach them very gently in the sugar syrup until just tender. Lift them out to drain. Reserve the syrup.
❧ Wipe and stone the cherries. Poach them in the other half of the syrup for just a minute or two. Drain. Reserve this syrup.
❧ Put the pastry strips across the tart – tuck them in on to the bottom. Fill the two opposite quarters with puréed apple. Arrange apple slices decoratively on it, overlapping a little. Arrange the cherries in the other two quarters.
❧ Bring the apple syrup to the boil, reduce a little. Stir in the Calvados and spoon over the apples. Do the same with the cherry syrup, add the kirsch and spoon over the cherries. Leave to set. Serve with thick cream handed separately.

Notes
The syrups can be combined and used again. You can see these tarts in all the pâtisseries in Normandy. They won't taste nearly as good as your own home-made tart.

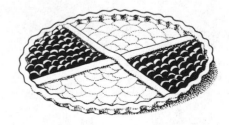

LEMON CHEESECAKE

Serves 4-6

175 g (6 oz) Lemon Pastry (see page 359)
2 eggs, separated
175 g (6 oz) cottage cheese, sieved
grated rind and juice of 1 lemon
25 g (1 oz) caster sugar
2 tsp plain flour
25 g (1 oz) raisins, soaked in rum overnight

❧ Heat the oven to 200C (400F) mark 6.
❧ Roll out the pastry on a board lightly dredged with cornflour. Lift the pastry on the rolling pin and use to line a greased ovenproof 18 or 20 cm (7 or 8 in) flan case. Push it down with a little ball of the pastry and trim the edges.
❧ Stir the rind and juice of the lemon into the cheese. Mix the egg yolks and cheese together. Beat the egg whites until stiff, folding in the sugar and flour as you beat. Fold into the cheese mixture.
❧ Spoon the filling in to the pastry case. Sprinkle the rum-soaked raisins over it: some will sink. Cook for 45 minutes until firm and lightly browned.

GREEK HONEY PIE

Serves 4-6

225 g (8 oz) Pâte Frolle (see page 359)
100 g (4 oz) cottage cheese
100 g (4 oz) honey
50 g (2 oz) ground almonds
2 eggs, beaten
milk
little caster sugar

❧ Heat the oven to 200C (400F) mark 6 with a baking sheet in the oven. Roll out the pastry and cut two circles to fit a 20 cm (8 in) ovenproof plate – enamel if possible. Line the plate with a circle of pastry.
❧ Mix together cheese, honey and almonds. Add the eggs and stir thoroughly. Put the mixture on the pastry on the plate. Brush the edge with milk and cover with the second circle. Press the edges firmly together. Decorate with fluting (see page 000).
❧ Brush with milk and dust lightly with caster sugar. Stand on the hot baking sheet to ensure the bottom is well cooked and bake for 30-40 minutes.

TARTE AU CITRON

Serves 6

1 recipe quantity Pâte Sucrée (see page 359)
50 g (2 oz) caster sugar
1 egg
50 g (2 oz) ground almonds
3 lemons
275 ml (½ pint) water
1 vanilla pod
300 g (10 oz) granulated sugar
few angelica leaves

❧ Heat the oven to 200C (400F) mark 6.
❧ Roll out the pastry and use it to line an 18-20 cm (7-8 in) plate. Decorate the edge with the tip of a teaspoon.
❧ Prepare the almond cream: add the caster sugar to the egg with the ground almonds and the grated rind of 1 lemon. Beat really well. Spread over the base of the pastry and cook for 25 minutes.
❧ For the glazed lemon slices, slice the other 2 lemons thinly and poach until quite soft in the water with the vanilla pod. Remove the pod with a slotted spoon. Make the water up to 275 ml (½ pint) again and add the granulated sugar. Heat to dissolve the sugar then replace the lemon slices. Poach gently for 20 minutes. Remove the slices and place on a baking sheet or flat plate.
❧ Reduce the syrup until thick, cool and use to brush over the top of the tart. Arrange the lemon slices as attractively as possible on the tart and spoon the syrup sparingly over them. Put a few little diamonds of angelica around the edge like leaves.

AUSTRIAN CHEESECAKE

Serves 6-8

175 g (6 oz) digestive biscuits
75 g (3 oz) butter, melted
1 tsp ground cinnamon
450 g (1 lb) cream cheese
2 eggs
150 g (5 oz) caster sugar
grated rind and juice of 1 lemon
150 ml (¼ pint) soured cream
hazelnuts and maraschino cherries

❦ Heat the oven to 190C (375F) mark 5.
❦ Crush the biscuits in a polythene bag with a rolling pin. Put the crumbs into a bowl with the butter and cinnamon and mix well. Press into the bottom and up the sides of a 20-23 cm (8-9 in) fluted china ovenproof flan dish. Neaten the top.
❦ Beat the cheese until smooth. Whisk the eggs with 75 g (3 oz) of the sugar until light and fluffy. Fold into the cheese with the grated rind and juice of the lemon. Pour on to the biscuit base and cook for 30 minutes.
❦ Remove from the oven, then increase the oven temperature to 240C (475F) mark 9.
❦ Mix the soured cream (you can sour fresh cream with 1 tablespoon of lemon juice) with the remaining 25 g (1 oz) of sugar. Spoon on the cake and return to the very hot oven for 10 minutes. Cool and chill.
❦ Take out of the refrigerator about an hour before you need it and decorate the top with two straight lines of hazelnuts, with a line of maraschino cherries between them.

CURD CHEESECAKE

Serves 6

175 g (6 oz) Shortcrust Pastry (see page 357)
25 g (1 oz) currants
25 g (1 oz) butter
1 egg, beaten
225 g (8 oz) curd cheese
50 g (2 oz) soft brown sugar
grated rind of 1 lemon

❦ Heat the oven to 190C (375F) mark 5 with a baking sheet in it.
❦ Roll out the pastry to a thickness of 5 mm (¼ in). Leave to relax while you wash the currants.
❦ Melt the butter in a saucepan, add the currants, beaten egg, cheese, sugar and grated lemon rind. Stir well and set aside.
❦ Line a 15 or 18 cm (6 or 7 in) fluted porcelain ovenproof dish with the pastry and trim off with the rolling pin. Pour the cheese mixture into the pastry case. Cook on the hot baking sheet for 40 minutes.

Note
The inexperienced cook will realize the enormous advantage of not having to turn out this cheese cake. These beautiful white dishes have saved many a kitchen panic.

❦ Choux Puffs ❦ Eclairs and Profiteroles

Light and airy choux pastry allows you to make delicious confections which are actually not nearly as calorie-laden as they appear. Choux buns may also be used as 'building blocks' in the assembly of elaborate and impressive centrepieces, like Paris-Brest and the Party Ring.

POLKAS

Makes 16

65 g (2 ½ oz) Choux Pastry (see page 364)
75 g (3 oz) apricot jam
1 small lemon
275 ml (½ pint) Crème Pâtissière (see page 349)
icing sugar

❦ Heat the oven to 200C (400F) mark 6. Grease two trays of deep tartlet tins with butter. Line the tins with choux pastry. A wet teaspoon does the trick.

❦ Bake in the top half of the oven for 5 minutes, reduce the temperature to 160C (325F) mark 3 and continue for a further 10 minutes, or until the little cases are a warm honey brown.

❦ Remove gently from the tins and place on a wire rack. Sieve the jam with the zest and juice of the lemon. Put a teaspoon of the jam into each polka, fill with crème pâtissière and dust with icing sugar.

❦ In days gone by the icing sugar was thickly powdered and was then 'touched by a red-hot flat iron'.

CHOCOLATE ECLAIRS

Makes 12

65 g (2 ½ oz) Choux Pastry (see page 364)
275 ml (½ pint) whipping cream
25 g (1 oz) caster sugar
75 g (3 oz) plain chocolate
225 g (8 oz) icing sugar
2 tbsp hot water

❦ Heat the oven to 200C (400F) mark 6. Arrange two shelves in the top half of the oven. Grease and flour two baking trays.

❦ Pipe 9 cm (3½ in) lengths of choux diagonally on the baking sheets, leaving plenty of room between them. Use a forcing bag fitted with a plain 1 cm (½ in) pipe.

❦ Cook for 20 minutes then reduce the temperature to 160C (325F) mark 3. Reverse the position of the trays in the oven and cook for a further 20 minutes. Make a small slit in the side of each éclair and cool on a wire rack.

❦ Extend the slit and fill with whipped cream sweetened with caster sugar.

❦ For the chocolate icing: break up the chocolate and put in a basin. Stand the basin in a pan of hot (not boiling) water. Sieve the icing sugar into a bowl, add the 2 tablespoons of hot water and stir until well mixed. Add the softened chocolate and beat until glossy.

❦ Cover the top of each éclair with chocolate icing from the tip of a spoon and leave to set.

Variation
Coffee icing can be used as an alternative to chocolate. Dissolve 4 tablespoons of instant coffee in 1 tablespoon hot water and gradually beat into 225 g (8 oz) icing sugar until smooth.

CHOCOLATE PROFITEROLES

Serves 6

65 g (2 ½ oz) **Choux Pastry** (see page 364)
275 ml (½ pint) **whipping cream**
1 tsp **caster sugar**

Chocolate Sauce
175 g (6 oz) **good dark chocolate**
1 tsp **cornflour**
salt
25 g (1 oz) **butter**
25 g (1 oz) **caster sugar**

❦ Heat the oven to 220C (425F) mark 7. Arrange two oven shelves in the top half of the oven. Grease and flour two baking sheets.
❦ Drop or pipe the pastry on to the baking sheets, either with a teaspoon or in a forcing bag with a 1 cm (½ in) plain pipe. Keep the pieces of dough well apart.
❦ Cook for 10 minutes then reduce the temperature to 160C (325F) mark 3 and continue for a further 20-30 minutes until a warm honey brown and well risen. Cool at once on a wire rack out of the draught. Make a little slit in the sides of each to let out the steam.
❦ Whip the cream stiffly with the caster sugar. Using a forcing bag with a 1 cm (½ in) plain pipe, fill the choux buns with the cream. Pile up into a dish.
❦ For the chocolate sauce: melt the chocolate in a bowl over hot water then stir 75 ml (3 fl oz) water into it. Mix the cornflour and salt with a little water in another bowl. Bring 50 ml (2 fl oz) water to the boil. Pour on to the blended cornflour, stirring all the time. Return to the pan, cook for a minute or two, then add the chocolate mixture to the cornflour sauce. Beat in the butter and sugar. It is important to keep stirring until the sauce is made.
❦ Just before serving, pour the warm chocolate sauce over the profiteroles.

PARIS-BREST

Makes about 10

65 g (2 ½ oz) **Choux Pastry** (see page 364)
2 tbsp **flaked almonds**
275 ml (½ pint) **Crème Pâtissière** (see page 349)
2 tbsp **Praline** (see page 367)
icing sugar

❦ Heat the oven to 200C (400F) mark 6. Arrange two shelves in the top half of the oven. Line two baking sheets with baking paper.
❦ Put the choux pastry into a forcing bag with a 2.5 cm (1 in) plain pipe. Pipe out circles about 7.5 cm (3 in) across. Sprinkle with flaked almonds and dust lightly with icing sugar.
❦ Cook for 15 minutes, reduce the temperature to 190C (375F) mark 5 and continue for a further 20 minutes.
❦ Put on to a wire rack and make a little slit in each to let out the steam. Cool. Split in half carefully and mix the crème pâtissière with the praline and use to fill each little circle. Replace the tops and dust a little icing sugar over the almonds on the tops.

Variations
This can be made in the form of one single larger ring, about 18 cm (7 in) in diameter. Use 65 g (2 ½ oz) choux pastry and a 4 cm (1 ½ in) plain pipe. About 275 ml (½ pint) crème pâtissière will be sufficient to fill it.

PARTY RING

Serves 6

65 g (2 ½ oz) Choux Pastry (see page 364)
275 ml (½ pint) whipping or double cream
4 ripe peaches
100 g (4 oz) icing sugar
peach food colouring
angelica

❦ Heat the oven to 200C (400F) mark 6. Put the oven shelf in the top half of the oven. Grease an 18 cm (7 in) sandwich tin with butter.

❦ Put the pastry into a forcing bag fitted with a 2.5 cm (1 in) pipe. Pipe a ring of pastry around the edges of the tin. (This is an easy way of making a choux ring.)

❦ Cook for 20 minutes. Reduce the temperature to 160C (325F) mark 3 and continue for 20–25 minutes until the ring is a warm honey brown. Cool on a wire rack. Make a small slit in the side to let out the steam.

❦ Whip the cream stiffly. If using double cream, take care not to end up with butter. Dip the peaches in boiling water. Skin them and cut into small pieces. Fold into the cream.

❦ Split the ring in half. Fill the bottom half with the peach mixture and replace the lid. Make the glacé icing with the icing sugar and about 2 tablespoons of water faintly tinged with peach liquid food colouring. Pour the icing over the ring and decorate sparingly with angelica diamonds.

Note
The pastry ring can be made in the morning or the day before. Put it into an absolutely airtight tin when cold. It can then be filled just before the party.

BASIC RECIPES

STOCKS,
JELLIES
AND ASPICS

*This section shows how to make a variety of stocks which are the basis of all good soups, deli-
cate consommés (clear soups) and aspic, as well as many classic sauces.*
*Most stocks need long slow cooking, so a wise cook makes large quantities at a time and
freezes what is not used immediately. Stock can be reduced by boiling to a small quantity of
concentrated nutrients and frozen in ice-cube trays. It can then be brought back to the original
strength and flavour by adding water.*

CHICKEN STOCK

Makes 2 litres (3 ½ pints)

2 dried bay leaves
3 sprigs of parsley
6 white peppercorns
4 litres (7 pints) water
½ large boiling chicken, skinned and jointed (1.1 kg/2 ½ lb)
chicken giblets (minus liver and kidneys)
4 medium carrots (optional)
4 celery stalks with leaves, cut into short lengths
4 medium onions, peeled and quartered
salt

❧ Loosely tie the herbs in muslin. Place all the ingredients in a large pan. Bring to the boil and skim off any fat or scum. Reduce the heat, cover, and simmer for about 3 hours. Stir occasionally, and skim frequently.
❧ Cool slightly, then strain into a clean bowl. Stand the bowl in chilled water until the stock is cold. Refrigerate, covered, until any fat on the surface is hard. Remove the fat and chill or freeze the stock until required.
❧ Chicken stock can also be made with the carcass of a whole roasted bird and any scraps and skin. Use only 1.2 litres (2 pints) water and half the flavouring vegetables, herbs and spices.

Variation
Classic (but expensive) White Stock is made with 900 g (2 lb) veal bones or knuckle, 2.3 litres (4 pints) water and half the flavouring vegetables, herbs and spices above. Add 1-2 tsp lemon juice and simmer as above for at least 4 hours. This stock makes a good base for aspic jelly.

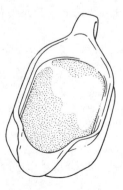

BASIC BROWN STOCK

Makes 2.8 litres (5 pints)

350 g (¾ lb) chicken carcass or bones
900 g (2 lb) beef bones, sawn into short pieces
700 g (1 ½ lb) stewing beef (flank or skirt), cut into small pieces
350 g (12 oz) onions, quartered
2 medium carrots, thickly sliced
1 outside celery stalk, cut into 2 cm (¾ in) lengths
5 sprigs of parsley
2 fresh or 1 dried bay leaf
2 sprigs of fresh thyme or rosemary if available
4 litres (7 pints) water
salt

❧ Heat the oven to 220C (425F) mark 7.
❧ Spread out the carcass, bones and meat in a large roasting tin, and roast for 30-40 minutes. Halfway through, turn the bones and meat over. Prepare the vegetables and add the onions and carrots to the pan with the herbs loosely tied in muslin.
❧ Transfer bones and meat to a large pan. Add 275 ml (½ pint) water to the tin, and place over a moderate heat. Stir with a metal spoon to loosen any sediment. Pour into the pan, add the rest of the water and the other ingredients. Bring to the boil, skim, then reduce the heat, cover and simmer for 4 hours.
❧ Remove the bones and strain the stock through a fine sieve into a heatproof bowl. Adjust the seasoning, if necessary. Stand the bowl in chilled water.
❧ Refrigerate when cool enough. Remove any fat from the surface when hardened, and chill or freeze the stock until wanted.

Variation
For a quick Household Stock for everyday use, collect the bones from any brown poultry or any game bird or animal, as well as trimmings from a chicken carcass and add to the beef bones. Freeze in a plastic bag until needed, then add root vegetables, herbs and flavourings (not green vegetables, potatoes or pulses). Use the same proportions of solids and water as for Basic Brown Stock (above). Simmer (without browning first), then strain, cool and store as for Basic Brown Stock.
❧ Household Stock is useful for family soups and stews, but for more luxurious soups, use Basic Brown Stock. For jellied stock or consommé include some veal bones when making the brown stock.

FISH STOCK

Makes 1.5 litres (2 ½ pints)

900 g (2 lb) heads, bones and trimmings of
    white fish
juice of 1 large lemon
2 large onions, peeled and quartered
3 celery stalks, cut in 5 cm (2 in) lengths
1 medium-sized carrot, quartered
1 fresh or ½ dried bay leaf
10 white peppercorns
6 parsley stalks
1 sprig of fresh thyme if available
1.5 litres (2 ½ pints) water
salt

❦ Place all the ingredients in a large pan, using
enough water to cover the solids. Bring to the boil,
then reduce the heat and simmer gently, uncovered,
for 30 minutes. Skim as needed while cooking.

❦ Soak a double layer of muslin in cold water and
wring it out. Use to line a colander placed over a
heatproof bowl. Strain the stock through the muslin
into the bowl. Stand the bowl in chilled water and
stir until the stock is tepid. Season lightly. Leave
until cold, then cover and refrigerate or freeze.

BASIC VEGETABLE STOCK

Makes 1.75 litres (3 pints)

5 small onions, peeled and halved
5 medium carrots, halved
4 medium tomatoes, quartered
½ garlic clove, squeezed over the tomatoes
3 small celery stalks, cut in 2 cm (¾ in) lengths
6-8 parsley stalks
2 litres (3 ½ pints) water

❦ Place all the ingredients in a large pan, making
sure that the water covers the solids. Bring to the
boil. Reduce the heat, cover, and simmer for 1 hour.

❦ Leave to stand off the heat for 30 minutes. Strain
through a colander lined with damp muslin into a
suitable container. Cool by standing the container in
chilled water until cold.

❦ Use the same day if not refrigerated. Chill, covered, for 2 days only, or freeze for up to 2 months.

BROWN VEGETABLE STOCK

Makes 2 litres (3 ½ pints)

25 g (1 oz) margarine
3 small onions, quartered
3 medium-sized carrots, sliced
2 outside stalks of celery, sliced
2 tomatoes, sliced
6 parsley stalks
1 fresh or ½ dried bay leaf
6 black peppercorns
1 whole blade of mace
lemon juice to taste
2 litres (3 ½ pints) boiling water
salt

❦ Heat the margarine in a pan. Add the onions, carrots and celery, and stir-fry until the vegetables are
lightly browned. Add all the remaining ingredients
except the salt. Bring to the boil. Reduce the heat,
cover and simmer for 1 hour.

❦ Leave off the heat for 20 minutes. Strain through
a colander lined with damp muslin into a bowl.
Season. Cool completely, then remove any fat from
the surface. It will keep in the refrigerator for 2 days
or freeze up to 2 months.

GAME STOCK

carcass of bird to suit recipe plus giblets if
    available, or carcass of game
1 medium onion, sliced
2 medium carrots, sliced
1 matchbox-sized piece of swede, diced
1 celery stalk, sliced
1 bouquet garni, or bunch of fresh herbs
seasoning

❦ Place the ingredients in a saucepan with water to
cover. Bring to the boil and remove any scum as it
rises. Simmer for 1 ½-2 hours. Strain into a bowl and
use as required. Should a strong stock be required
for a recipe, the stock should be placed in a saucepan
and boiled to reduce and concentrate the contents.

❦ Stock may be frozen or stored in a refrigerator. If
not required the day of making, cool quickly and
freeze or store. Re-boil the next day if not required.

COURT BOUILLON

1.2 litres (2 pints) water (or water and white
   wine)
75 g (3 oz) onions
1 medium carrot
1 garlic clove
1 celery stalk
1 parsley sprig
1 thyme sprig
½ bay leaf
1 clove
2 tsp salt
4 peppercorns

❦ Put all the ingredients into a pan, cover and simmer for 30 minutes. Strain, cover and refrigerate for
up to 3 days.
❦ Use for poaching or boiling fish.

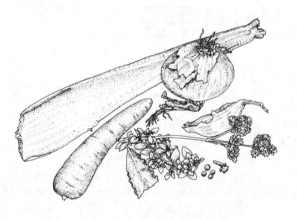

ASPIC JELLY

Makes 1 litre (1 ¾ pints) jelly

2 dried bay leaves
sprig of thyme
strip of lemon rind
6 black peppercorns
1 litre (1 ¾ pints) cold White or Basic Brown
   Stock (see page 335)
120 ml (4 fl oz) white wine or half white wine
   and half dry sherry (with brown stock)
2 tbsp white wine vinegar
40 g (1 ½ oz gelatine)
whites and crushed shells of 2 eggs

❦ Tie the bay leaves, thyme, lemon rind and peppercorns loosely in a muslin bag.
❦ Skim any fat from the stock. Place in a large scalded pan (not aluminium) with all the other ingredients. Stir with a scalded whisk until the gelatine softens. Heat, whisking constantly until simmering
point is reached. Remove the whisk. When the liquid boils up, remove the pan from the heat.
❦ Allow to stand for a few moments, taking care not
to break the crust formed by the egg white. The egg
white traps the sediment in the stock and clears the
aspic. Strain gently through a jelly bag as for consommé (see page 24), without breaking the egg white crust.
❦ If required strain through the crust a second time.
The jelly must be quite clear. Cool, then chill. Test
for firmness.

JELLIED STOCK

Makes 575 ml (1 pint)

ham bones
2 pigs' trotters
1.2 litres (2 pints) water
salt
1-2 sprigs of thyme

❦ Pigs' trotters with a few ham bones make a wonderful jelly. Put the ham bones with the pigs' trotters into the water. Add salt and a sprig or two of
thyme. Bring to the boil and simmer for several
hours, reducing the jelly to 575 m (1 pint) or less.
❦ Strain, cool and leave overnight in the refrigerator. Remove the fat when the jelly is set. Melt when
needed.

SAVOURY JELLY

Makes 275 ml (½ pint)

275 ml (½ pint) stock (meat extract is good for
   this)
1 heaped tsp powdered gelatine
salt and pepper

❦ This is a simpler recipe than the one for jellied
stock. Put the stock and gelatine into a saucepan. Stir
over a gentle heat until every grain of gelatine has
disappeared. Season well. Use when the jelly is cool.

SAUCES, MARINADES AND DRESSINGS

This section gives several savoury sauces and butters to serve with fish, meat, poultry and game as well as appropriate marinades and stuffings. There are also a wide range of light oil and vinegar dressings for tender-leafed green salads and creamy, spicy or mayonnaise-based dressings to go with crisp or more strongly flavoured vegetables. The section concludes with some classic and very useful sweet sauces.

BASIC BROWN SAUCE

1 onion, finely chopped
1 carrot, finely chopped or grated
40 g (1 ½ oz) cooking fat
40 g (1 ½ oz) flour
575 ml (1 pint) water
1 bay leaf
¼ tsp mixed herbs
seasoning to taste

❦ Fry the onion and carrot in the fat until well browned. Stir in flour and cook for 2-3 minutes. Slowly add the water and stir well.
❦ Add the herbs and seasoning and simmer gently for about 30 minutes. Strain and use as required, thinning if necessary for gravy, and boiling to reduce if a thicker sauce is required.

SAUCE MORNAY
(CHEESE SAUCE)

25 g (1 oz) butter
25 g (1 oz) plain flour
275 ml (½ pint) milk
salt and pepper
scrape of nutmeg
50 g (2 oz) grated cheese

❦ Melt the butter in a pan. Stir in the flour. Beat well and cook this roux for 2 or 3 minutes, stirring all the time.
❦ Gradually add the milk, beat well and simmer for 5 minutes, stirring continuously (this cooks the flour). Season with salt and pepper and the nutmeg.
❦ Remove from the heat and stir the grated cheese into the sauce.

BASIC WHITE SAUCE

25 g (1 oz) butter or margarine
25 g (1 oz) flour or cornflour
275 ml (½ pint) milk for a coating sauce or 425 ml (¾ pint) for a pouring sauce

❦ Melt the fat in a small pan. Stir in the flour and mix well. This mixture is called a roux. Cook gently for 2-3 minutes until the mixture appears to resemble a honeycomb.

❦ Remove from the heat and gradually add the milk, stirring well and heating between each addition. Boil gently for 3-4 minutes until the sauce is the required consistency and smooth and glossy.

❦ A roux can be stored in a refrigerator for a few weeks, and a little used as required to make sauces, or thicken soups and stews.

❦ Use as a basis for such sauces as caper, mushroom, cheese, mustard, as well as sweet sauces, by the addition of the appropriate ingredients. Cream, yoghurt, sherry, brandy etc can all be beaten in just before using. Heat, but do not boil after the addition of cream or yoghurt.

❦ The sauce can be made ahead: press dampened or greased greaseproof paper over it to prevent a skin forming. Reheat when required.

Variations
For a thick coating consistency, say for a vol-au-vent filling, use 40 g (1 ½ oz) butter and 4 tablespoons of flour.

❦ For a binding consistency or panada, use 50 g (2 oz) butter and 50 g (2 oz) of flour. This is used mainly for fritters and croquettes or as the basis of a vegetable soufflé.

❦ For a Cream Sauce: stir 1 beaten egg yolk and 1 tablespoon of single or double cream into the completed sauce (any consistency); reheat without boiling.

❦ For a Cheese Sauce: remove the sauce from the heat and stir in 75 g (3 oz) grated cheese, with a pinch of dry mustard, salt and cayenne pepper.

❦ For an Egg Sauce: add 2 finely-chopped hard-boiled eggs to the sauce.

❦ For a Parsley Sauce: add 2 tablespoons chopped fresh parsley to the sauce with a squeeze of lemon juice (optional).

❦ For a Hot Mustard Sauce: add 2 teaspoons mustard powder to the sauce.

❦ For a Shrimp Sauce: stir 75 g (3 oz) peeled shrimps into the sauce and season with a few drops of Tabasco or other similar hot pepper sauce.

❦ For Hot Tartare Sauce: add 1 teaspoon chopped fresh parsley, 1 teaspoon finely chopped onion, 3 finely chopped pickled gherkins and 12 chopped capers to the sauce.

❦ For a Mushroom Sauce: cook 50 g (2 oz) chopped mushrooms in 25 g (1 oz) butter until just tender and stir into the cooked sauce. Season with nutmeg, salt and pepper.

❦ For a White Onion Sauce: simmer 2 medium-sized onions, skinned and chopped, in lightly salted water until soft. Drain well, reserving the liquid. Make 275 ml (½ pint) white sauce, using half milk and half the onion cooking liquid. Fold the onions into the completed sauce with the grated rind of half a small lemon (optional). Season to taste.

❦ All these variations also apply to white sauce made by the all-in-one method (see below).

WHITE SAUCE
(ALL-IN-ONE METHOD)

20 g (¾ oz) softened butter or soft tub margarine
2 level tbsp plain flour
275 ml (½ pint) milk or milk and vegetable-flavoured liquid
small pinch of nutmeg (optional)
salt and pepper

❦ Put all the ingredients together in a pan and whisk over a medium heat until the sauce comes to the boil and thickens. Continue cooking for 2-3 minutes.

BECHAMEL SAUCE

275 ml (½ pint) milk
1 small onion, stuck with 4 cloves
1 piece of carrot
sprig of fresh parsley
blade of mace
6 peppercorns
25 g (1 oz) butter
25 g (1 oz) plain flour
salt

❦ Place the milk in a saucepan with the onion, carrot, parsley, mace and peppercorns and bring slowly to the boil. Remove from the heat, cover and allow to infuse for 20-30 minutes, then strain.
❦ In a clean pan, melt the butter, add the flour and cook for 2-3 minutes. Gradually add the milk, stirring constantly, bring to the boil, and simmer for 2 minutes. Check the seasoning. Use as required.

SIMPLE BECHAMEL SAUCE

1 blade of mace
1 bay leaf
6 peppercorns
2 slices of onion
275 ml (½ pint) milk
25 g (1 oz) butter
25 g (1 oz) plain flour
salt and pepper

❦ Infuse the mace, bay leaf, peppercorns and onion in the milk over a low heat with the lid on, for 10 minutes.
❦ Melt the butter in a pan. Add the flour and stir well over a low heat for a minute or so. Strain the milk and add slowly to the flour and butter mixture, beating all the time until boiling.
❦ Simmer slowly for 20 minutes, stirring now and then, to ensure a velvety, well-flavoured sauce. Season to taste.

ESPAGNOLE SAUCE

25 g (1 oz) butter
1 tbsp oil
1 rasher of bacon, chopped
100 g (4 oz) onion, chopped
100 g (4 oz) carrot, chopped
25 g (1 oz) plain flour
575 ml (1 pint) stock
50 g (2 oz) mushrooms, chopped
1 tbsp tomato purée
bunch of fresh mixed herbs or bouquet garni
salt and pepper
1 glass of sherry

❦ Heat the butter and oil in a pan and fry the bacon, add the onion and carrots and fry gently to soften. Sprinkle in the flour and cook gently to a golden brown colour.
❦ Gradually add the stock and bring to the boil, stirring constantly. Add the mushrooms, tomato purée and herbs. Cover and simmer for approximately 30 minutes.
❦ Strain into a clean pan, add the sherry and season.

POIVRADE SAUCE

❦ Make as for Espagnole Sauce (above), but use marinade and red wine vinegar for part or all of the stock.
❦ The zest and juice of 1 orange may be added together with 1 tablespoonful redcurrant jelly.

DEMI-GLACE SAUCE

❦ Make as for an Espagnole Sauce (see above), but add half the stock to start with, bring to the boil and simmer for 30 minutes, skimming as necessary. Add half the remaining stock, boil for 5 minutes, skim, add the remaining stock and repeat the process. Strain into a clean pan, add the sherry, and cook to a consistency which will coat the back of a spoon.

INSTANT PARSLEY SAUCE

275 ml (½ pint) soured cream
½ lemon
2 tsp tomato purée
3 tbsp fresh parsley, chopped
salt and pepper

❦ Put the soured cream into a bowl. Add the grated rind and juice of the lemon. Stir in the tomato purée and parsley. Beat well to combine ingredients and season with salt and pepper.
❦ Serve with white fish or smoked fish.

MUSTARD SAUCE

1 medium onion, finely chopped
2 sprigs of parsley
275 ml (½ pint) dry white wine
25 g (1 oz) butter
25 g (1 oz) plain flour
1 tsp French mustard
salt and pepper

❦ Put the onion and parsley into a pan with the wine. Simmer for 5 minutes and leave to stand while preparing the rest of the ingredients.
❦ In a small pan, melt the butter and stir in the flour. Cook over a low heat for 1 minute, stirring well. Remove from the heat and stir in the strained wine. Return to the heat and cook over low heat, stirring well for 5 minutes. Stir in the mustard, salt and pepper.
❦ Serve with oily fish.

GOOSEBERRY SAUCE

225 g (8 oz) gooseberries, fresh or frozen
4 tbsp water
2 tsp sugar
25 g (1 oz) butter
squeeze of lemon juice

❦ Put the gooseberries into a pan with the water and simmer gently until the fruit has broken and is soft. Put through a sieve into a clean pan. Stir in the sugar, butter and lemon juice. Heat gently and serve hot.
❦ Serve with oily fish.

TOMATO SAUCE

1 small onion, finely chopped
1 small carrot, finely chopped
15 g (½ oz) butter
1 tbsp oil
1 garlic clove, crushed
1 tsp fresh parsley, chopped
pinch of marjoram or basil
225 g (8 oz) fresh ripe tomatoes, skinned
salt and pepper

❦ Fry the onion and carrot in the butter and oil for 5 minutes over a low heat. Add the garlic and cook for 1 minute. Stir in the herbs and chopped tomatoes. Simmer over a low heat for 10 minutes.
❦ Sieve and reheat, adjusting seasoning to taste. If preferred, canned tomatoes may be used, but the sauce will be thinner, and it is better to strain the juice and keep it in reserve to adjust the consistency as required.
❦ Serve with white or oily fish.

RICH TOMATO SAUCE

1 small onion
25 g (1 oz) butter
25 g (1 oz) lean cooked ham
450 g (1 lb) fresh ripe tomatoes
1 garlic clove
salt and pepper
1 sherry glass of Marsala

❦ Peel the onion and slice it thinly. Fry in the butter. Add the ham cut into tiny pieces. Skin and quarter the tomatoes; peel and chop the garlic. Add to the pan and season well. Simmer for 5-10 minutes, stirring with a wooden fork. Pour in the Marsala and cook for a further minute or two.

Notes
This sauce will freeze well. You could make a good deal in a tomato glut and have it tasting just as fresh at Christmas-time. Cover it closely because of the garlic. Canned Italian tomatoes are useful too for this sauce if fresh ones are not readily available.

CRANBERRY SAUCE

450 g (1 lb) cranberries
100 g (4 oz) sugar
2 tbsp port (optional)

❦ Place the cranberries in a pan, add sufficient water to cover, bring to the boil and simmer gently, bruising the cranberries with a wooden spoon, until reduced to a pulp. Stir in the sugar and port, and cook until the sugar is dissolved.

BREAD SAUCE

275 ml (½ pint) milk
1 small onion, stuck with 3-4 cloves
blade of mace
1 bay leaf
75-100 g (3-4 oz) fresh breadcrumbs
salt and pepper
pinch of ground nutmeg
25 g (1 oz) butter

❦ Place the milk in a saucepan with the onion, mace and bay leaf and bring slowly to the boil. Remove from the heat, cover and leave to infuse for 15-20 minutes.
❦ Remove the onion, blade of mace and bay leaf. Stir in the breadcrumbs with the seasoning and butter, and beat well.

CIDER SAUCE

275 ml (½ pint) dry cider
40 g (1 ½ oz) butter
40 g (1 ½ oz) plain flour
425 ml (¾ pint) Fish or Chicken Stock (see pages 336 or 335)
salt and pepper

❦ Put the cider into a small pan and cook quickly until reduced by half.
❦ Melt the butter in another pan; add the flour and stir over a low heat for 1 minute. Gradually work in the stock and stir over a low heat until thick and smooth. Add the cider and season well.
❦ Stir over a low heat for 3 minutes and serve hot.

APPLE SAUCE

450 g (1 lb) cooking apples
25 g (1 oz) butter
2-3 tbsp water
strip of lemon rind
sugar to taste

❦ Peel, core and thickly slice the apples. Place in a pan with the butter, water and lemon rind. Cover and cook gently until soft (a good cooking apple should fluff up during cooking and it should not be necessary to sieve it).
❦ Remove the lemon rind, and beat well with a wooden spoon until smooth (or pass through a coarse sieve). Add sugar to taste.

CUMBERLAND SAUCE

4 tbsp redcurrant jelly
2 sugar lumps
1 orange
1 lemon
2 glasses of port
1 tsp arrowroot

❦ Put the jelly in a pan. Take the zest off the orange with the sugar lumps. Add to the pan with the orange juice, the finely grated rind and juice of the lemon. Simmer gently for a few minutes.

❦ Strain and return to the pan. Add the port, bring to the boil and stir in the arrowroot, slaked with a tablespoon of water. This is best made the day before it is needed.

GIBLET GRAVY

poultry or game bird giblets (heart, liver, gizzard and neck)
1 small onion
1 small carrot
small piece of celery
bunch of fresh herbs or bouquet garni
6 peppercorns
salt and pepper
575-850 ml (1-1 ½ pints) water
cooking juices from the roasting tin
1 tbsp plain flour

❦ Place the giblets in a pan with the onion, carrot, celery, herbs, peppercorns and salt and 575 ml (1 pint) of the water in a pan. Bring to the boil, cover and simmer for at least 1 hour, or for the duration of the bird's cooking time.

❦ Strain the stock and make up to 575 ml (1 pint) with water. Pour a little into the roasting tin in which the bird was cooked (excess fat having been removed) and stir around well to ensure that all the pan juices and sediment have been incorporated.

❦ Blend the flour with a little cold water in a basin, add some of the stock and pour into a saucepan. Add the remaining stock. Stir until it boils, adjust the seasoning and simmer for 2-3 minutes.

❦ This gravy is suitable for any bird.

CURRIED OR INDIAN MINCE FILLING

1 tart apple
lemon juice
1 onion, chopped
1 tbsp vegetable oil
450 g (1 lb) lean minced beef or lamb
25 g (1 oz) wholemeal flour
275 ml (½ pint) beef stock
1 tsp each turmeric, ground coriander and ground cumin
3-6 whole cardamom seeds
1 tbsp mustard pickle
25 g (1 oz) seedless raisins
1 tbsp redcurrant jelly
1 banana, sliced

❦ Core and chop the apple and coat in lemon juice. Fry the onion in the oil until translucent, add the meat and brown. Stir in the flour, and blend in stock. Add the spices, pickle, raisins and jelly and simmer with lid on for 45 minutes. If mixture gets too dry, add more water.

❦ Ten minutes before the end of cooking, add the cored and chopped apple. When cooked, stir in banana and warm through.

❦ Serve sprinkled with coconut in hot pitta bread; pancakes, optionally with a sauce to coat them; jacket potatoes; vol-au-vents; or as a pic filling; with side dishes such as sliced tomato, grated carrot and mango chutney.

BOLOGNESE SAUCE FOR PASTA

1 onion, chopped
1 tbsp vegetable oil
1-2 garlic cloves, crushed
450 g (1 lb) lean mince
2 tbsp tomato purée
400 g (14 oz) tin tomatoes, chopped
275 ml (½ pint) stock
1 tsp honey
1 tbsp wine vinegar
1 tsp basil
1 tsp oregano
black pepper
50-100 g (2-4 oz) streaky bacon, chopped
    (optional)
100 g (4 oz) carrots, finely diced (optional)
Parmesan cheese, grated to garnish

❧ Fry the onion slowly in oil to soften. Add the garlic and meat and fry to brown. Stir in the purée, tomatoes, stock and remaining ingredients. Simmer in a covered pan for about 30 minutes, adding more water if the mixture becomes too dry.
❧ Serve on freshly boiled spaghetti, with the cheese sprinkled over, or use as a stuffing for baked cabbage, tomatoes or courgettes.

FLAVOURED BUTTERS

100 g (4 oz) unsalted butter
flavouring
seasoning

❧ The butter should be at room temperature and may be prepared by hand or in a blender or food processor. When the butter has been creamed, flavouring and seasoning may be added.
❧ The butter should then be formed into a cylinder, wrapped in foil and chilled. It is unwrapped and sliced into pats for serving.

Variations
For Anchovy Butter, add 2 teaspoons of anchovy essence while creaming the butter, and season with salt and pepper to taste.
❧ For Parsley Butter, add 2 tablespoons of finely chopped parsley, a squeeze of lemon juice and some

seasoning to taste.
❧ For Watercress Butter, Add ½ bunch watercress to the machine while blending so that the watercress is finely chopped. Season with salt, pepper and 1 tablespoon lemon juice.
❧ For Curry Butter, beat 1 teaspoon of curry powder, ½ teaspoon of lemon juice, ground black pepper and salt to taste.
❧ For Garlic Butter, beat ½-1 clove of minced garlic with salt to taste into the softened butter.
❧ For Herb Butter, beat 2 teaspoons of finely chopped fresh herb leaves with salt to taste into the softened butter.
❧ For Maître d'Hôtel Butter, beat 6 finely chopped sprigs of blanched parsley with a few drops of lemon juice, white pepper and salt to taste into the softened butter with salt to taste.

GARLIC AND ONION BUTTER

2 garlic cloves, peeled
2 tbsp finely chopped spring onion bulb
3 tbsp white wine
2 tbsp finely chopped parsley
150 g (5 oz) unsalted butter, cut into knobs
1 tbsp lemon juice (or to taste)
salt and black pepper

❧ Squeeze the garlic over the onion in a small pan. Add the wine. Simmer over a very low heat until the wine has evaporated.
❧ Remove the pan from the heat, mix in the parsley, then beat the mixture into the butter. Continue beating while adding a little lemon juice and seasoning. Taste and adjust the flavour if needed.
❧ Press into a pot and cover or roll into a cylinder in a piece of foil, and refrigerate until needed.

HOT LEMON AND HONEY MARINADE

150 ml (¼ pint) lemon juice
2 tbsp white wine vinegar
1 heaped tbsp clear honey
1 onion, finely chopped
1 bay leaf
1 tbsp chopped verbena, if available, or mint
1 tbsp fresh parsley, chopped
freshly ground black pepper
2-4 tbsp oil

❦ Slowly heat all ingredients to boiling point. Use 4 tbsp of oil if using as a baste as well. Stir well to dissolve the honey. Pour over cubed meat and allow to cool.

Notes
This is an excellent marinade for pork or poultry which is to be barbecued. The hot marinade impregnates the meat with flavour quicker than does a cold marinade.

MARINADE FOR RED MEATS

150 ml (¼ pint) red wine
2-4 tbsp vegetable oil
1 onion, finely chopped
½ tsp marjoram
½ tsp basil
1 bay leaf
dash of cayenne
salt and pepper
1 garlic clove, crushed or chopped

❦ Combine all the ingredients, and steep the meat in the marinade for at least 2 hours, turning frequently.
❦ The remaining marinade can be used as a basis for the cooking liquor, or as an accompanying sauce. If this is to be the case, use the lesser amount of oil.

MARINADE FOR WHITE OR LIGHT MEATS

150 ml (¼ pint) white wine
2-4 tbsp vegetable oil
1 onion, finely chopped
1 carrot, thinly sliced
½ tsp thyme
1 tbsp freshly chopped parsley
1 bay leaf
½ tsp sugar
1 garlic clove, crushed or chopped

❦ Combine all the ingredients and steep the meat in the marinate for at least 2 hours, turning frequently.
❦ It can be used to baste during cooking, in which case use the greater amount of oil.

HOLLANDAISE SAUCE

2 tbsp white wine vinegar
1 tbsp water
2 egg yolks
75 g (3 oz) butter or as needed, cut into small bits
salt and pepper

Place the vinegar and water in a small pan, bring to the boil and reduce to about 1 tablespoon. Cool slightly then pour into a heatproof basin over a pan of very hot water.
❦ Whisk in the egg yolks and one at a time, continue whisking until the mixture thickens. Whisk in the butter, one bit at a time, blending thoroughly. Season to taste.
❦ If the sauce is too sharp, whisk in another 25 g (1 oz) of butter. The sauce, when ready, should just hold its shape. Serve while still warm (but not hot).

HOLLANDAISE SAUCE
(QUICK METHOD)

3 egg yolks
1 tbsp lemon juice
1 tbsp warm water
salt and white pepper
100 g (4 oz) unsalted butter

❧ Mix the egg yolks, lemon juice and water in a blender or food processor. Season lightly with salt and pepper. Melt the butter without browning and pour into the machine while it is running. Adjust the seasoning when the sauce is thick, and serve warm.

Variations
For Sauce Aurore, fold 3 tablespoons of mayonnaise and 150 ml (¼ pint) whipped cream into the sauce. Serve warm with cold fish.
❧ For Mousseline Sauce, fold 150 ml (¼ pint) whipped cream into the sauce. Serve warm with cold fish.
❧ For Orange Hollandaise, stir 1 teaspoon grated orange rind and 1 tablespoon orange juice into the sauce and serve warm with cold fish.

MAYONNAISE

275 ml (½ pint) corn or soya oil
3 egg yolks
1 tbsp white wine vinegar or juice
½ tsp salt
¼ tsp dry mustard

❧ Bring all the ingredients to room temperature.
❧ Warm the oil slightly until just tepid. Rinse a mixing bowl in hot water and dry it thoroughly. Put in the egg yolks and beat for 2 minutes or until the yolks thicken. Add the vinegar or lemon juice, salt and mustard, and beat for another half minute.
❧ Still beating, add the oil drop by drop until the liquid in the bowl thickens. Occasionally beat without adding extra oil to make sure that all the oil is being absorbed.
❧ When the mixture thickens, add the oil a little more quickly, but continue beating constantly until the mayonnaise thickens or all the oil has been added.
❧ To prevent the mayonnaise curdling, beat in 1 tablespoon boiling water at the end. Beat in extra seasoning to taste.

Notes
If the mayonnaise separates, beat 1 tablespoon of mayonnaise into 1 teaspoon of made mustard in a clean warmed bowl. Beat until the mayonnaise thickens. Repeat the process, adding the mayonnaise in small spoonfuls.
❧ Store completed mayonnaise in a tightly covered container in the refrigerator.

Variations
Olive oil can be used but it is heavy and slightly more difficult to mix in smoothly than a lighter oil. Use a flavoured oil such as garlic oil, or a herb-flavoured vinegar as a variation.
❧ For Curry Mayonnaise, add 1 tablespoon tomato purée, 1 tablespoon curry paste, 1 teaspoon lemon juice and 2 tablespoons double cream to the mayonnaise and process just enough to blend. Serve with crab or prawns.
❧ For Green Mayonnaise, add 1 chopped garlic clove with 1 tablespoon chopped parsley, 1 tablespoon chopped chives and 1 tablespoon chopped basil to the mayonnaise and process until well blended. Serve with white fish.
❧ For Tartare sauce. fold in 1 teaspoon chopped fresh parsley, 1 teaspoon finely chopped onion, 3 finely chopped pickled gherkins and 12 chopped capers with a little of their liquid. Serve with grilled or fried white fish.

BLENDER MAYONNAISE

1 egg
½ tsp salt
¼ tsp dry mustard powder
1 tbsp white wine vinegar or lemon juice
225 ml (8 fl oz) corn or soya oil, or as needed

❧ Break the egg into the blender goblet, add the seasonings and blend at top speed until foaming and thickening. Blend in the vinegar or juice.
❧ With the motor running, add the oil through the hole in the lid drop by drop until the mayonnaise thickens, then slightly faster. The mayonnaise will stiffen quickly, and will be thicker than if made with a whisk.
❧ Beat in 1 tablespoon of boiling water at the end, to prevent the mayonnaise curdling, and add extra seasoning to taste.

VINAIGRETTE

2-3 tbsp corn or groundnut oil
pinch of dry mustard powder
salt and black pepper
1 tbsp white wine vinegar
½ tsp finely chopped chives
½ tsp finely chopped parsley
½ tsp finely chopped fresh dill, tarragon or
   chervil
1 tsp finely chopped capers
1 tsp finely chopped pitted green olives or
   gherkin

❧ Mix the oil and seasonings and stir or beat in the vinegar drop by drop as for French dressing (above). Add the flavourings, mix well, and leave to stand for 1-2 hours before use.

FRENCH DRESSING

2-3 tbsp corn or other light oil
pinch of dry mustard powder
pinch of sugar
salt and pepper
1 tbsp wine vinegar or 2 tsp vinegar and 1 tsp
   lemon juice

❧ Mix the oil with the seasonings in a bowl. Stir or beat in the vinegar, or vinegar and juice, drop by drop until an emulsion forms. Stir or beat again just before use.
❧ Alternatively, shake the oil and seasonings in a securely stoppered jar, add the vinegar, stopper the jar and shake vigorously. Repeat just before use.
Use any pure light oil (not a blended one). Olive oil is too heavy for dressing delicate green salad leaves. Malt vinegar is also generally too strong. Both are best kept for dressing strongly flavoured vegetables and leaves such as chicory and endive. a dressing for fruits is best made partly with lemon juice.

FRENCH DRESSING WITH LEMON

5 tbsp corn or other light oil salt to taste
1 tbsp wine vinegar
2 tbsp strained fresh lemon juice
white pepper (freshly ground if possible)
pinch of sugar

❧ Try to make the dressing not more than ½ hour before use.
❧ Whisk the oil and salt together in a bowl (try just a sprinkling of salt at first). Add the vinegar and lemon juice, then grind in the pepper, add the sugar and whisk for a full 30 seconds.
❧ Pour the dressing into a jar with a secure stopper. Shake the jar quite hard for 10-20 seconds before sprinkling the dressing on the salad.

Variation
For French dressing with herbs, add 1 tablespoon mixed fresh herbs (e.g. finely snipped chervil, chives, tarragon) to the dressing when whisking, or for a Tomato-flavoured French dressing add ½ teaspoon of tomato purée when whisking.

CURRY MAYONNAISE

1 tsp lemon peel
2 tbsp lemon juice
1 tsp clear honey
½ tsp curry paste
6 tbsp Mayonnaise (see left)

❧ Grate the lemon; squeeze and strain the juice. Mix the peel and juice with the honey and curry paste in a small bowl. Stir in the mayonnaise by spoonfuls, blending thoroughly.

THOUSAND ISLAND DRESSING

120 ml (4 fl oz) Mayonnaise (see page 346)
1 tbsp chilli sauce
½ tbsp finely chopped chives
½ tbsp finely chopped green olives
1 tbsp finely chopped canned pimento
1 tbsp tomato ketchup
½ tsp white wine vinegar
½ tsp paprika

❦ Beat all the ingredients together until they are well blended
❦ There are many versions of this classic American dressing. This spicy mayonnaise would be good over hard-boiled eggs or diced cooked potatoes.

BLUE CHEESE DRESSING

40 g (1 ½ oz) blue cheese without rind
120 ml (4 fl oz) soured cream
1 tbsp lemon juice
1 large spring onion bulb, finely chopped

❦ Sieve the cheese into a bowl. Work in the soured cream and lemon juice little by little until the mixture is smooth. Add the onion. Pour into a jar with a screw-topped lid. Close and shake well. Chill for 2 hours.
❦ Shake again just before use. Pour over cucumber or tomato salad, or a plain white cabbage slaw.

WALNUT DRESSING

1 ½ tbsp white wine vinegar
½ tbsp French Dijon mustard
1 tsp clear honey
50 ml (2 fl oz) walnut oil

❦ Whisk together the vinegar and mustard until blended, then whisk in the honey and oil.
❦ Turn into a jar with a secure stopper and close. Shake vigorously just before use.
❦ Use on strongly flavoured leaf or herb salads.

GARLIC OIL

275 ml (½ pint) pure corn or groundnut oil
3-4 garlic cloves

❦ Put the oil and garlic cloves in a bottle or jar with a flat, screw-on top. Put in a cool place, standing on a saucer. Invert the bottle every day for 10 days; do not shake it.
❦ Use to make salad dressings or for frying bread dice to make garlic-flavoured croutons (see page 355).

Variation
For Tarragon or Thyme Oil, wash 2-4 sprigs of the herb, blot dry and place in the oil instead of garlic cloves.
❦ For Lemon Oil, put in a wide strip of thin yellow rind and omit the garlic.

TARRAGON VINEGAR

2 fresh tarragon sprigs
700 ml (1 ¼ pints) white wine vinegar

❦ Leave the tarragon in a dark place for 4 to 5 days. Put it in a wide-necked clear glass jar with a vinegar-proof seal with the vinegar for 2 to 3 weeks. Take out the sprigs and add a few sprigs of fresh herbs; stopper securely.

Variations
Use the same method for making other herb vinegars such as basil, mint or thyme vinegar.

CREME PATISSIERE

1 egg, plus 1 extra egg yolk
25 g (1 oz) cornflour
50 g (2 oz) caster sugar
275 ml (½ pint) milk
1 vanilla pod

❦ Put the egg and yolk into a basin and beat together with the sugar until light and pale. Add the sieved cornflour and beat again. Heat the milk with the vanilla pod.
❦ Remove the pod, add the milk to the egg mixture beating all the time. Pour into a clean pan and bring slowly to the boil, stirring all the time; turn down the heat and simmer for a couple of minutes. The cornflour will stop it from curdling, but care is still needed. It will set when cold and can then be used instead of cream for tarts and pastries.

Note
Remember the egg yolks make the creaminess and egg white does the setting, so the proportion, though fiddly, is essential.

CHOCOLATE SAUCE

100 g (4 oz) plain chocolate
150 ml (¼ pint) hot water
25 g (1 oz) sugar
50 g (2 oz) butter

❦ Break up the chocolate and put it with the water and sugar in a bowl over hot water. Heat until melted, stirring all the time. Raise the heat and cook for a minute or two. Remove from the heat, gradually beat in the butter and leave to cool.

CREME A LA VANILLE

575 ml (1 pint) milk
25 g (1 oz) caster sugar
1 vanilla pod
4 egg yolks

❦ Heat the milk to just below boiling with the sugar and the vanilla pod. Beat the egg yolks. Discard the vanilla pod and then pour the milk slowly on to the egg yolks, beating all the time.
❦ Return to a gentle heat and, stirring continuously, cook until the custard coats the back of a spoon.
❦ Turn into a bowl and cool, with a piece of damp greaseproof paper touching the surface of the custard to prevent a skin forming.

Notes
This is known as a 'boiled' custard, which it most certainly must not be, or it will curdle. It is the basic egg custard used for many of these recipes. The addition of a teaspoon of cornflour or custard powder at the mixing stage will help the inexperienced cook to prevent any risk of curdling the custard.

It is worth persevering with the genuine article, for it is beyond compare when properly made, and the basis for many superb desserts.

CREME CHANTILLY

white of 1 egg
275 ml (½ pint) double or whipping cream
2 tsp caster sugar

❦ Stiffly whisk the egg white. Whip the cream carefully with the sugar until very thick. Fold the egg white gently but thoroughly into the whipped cream.

Notes
Keep a vanilla pod in the jar of caster sugar instead of using vanilla essence (and never use vanilla flavouring). 'Whipping cream' is now available everywhere. Its use does seem to prevent the sudden and unwelcome drama of butter-making which can so easily overtake the unwary cook when whipping double cream.

STUFFINGS
AND
ACCOMPANIMENTS

This section shows how to make a variety of stuffings and accompaniments for all sorts of dishes, from meat and poultry to game and fish.

❧ About stuffings ❧

Stuffings, farces and forcemeats are usually based on either fresh breadcrumbs, which can be brown or white, cooked rice, oatmeal or rolled oats, or starchy vegetables and nuts, such as potatoes and chestnuts.

To this base can be added any ingredients to give flavour and/or succulence; these are frequently chopped onion, herbs and spices, savoury sauces and sometimes finely minced meat, such as sausage meat,

veal or pork, or some chopped rashers of bacon.

Any combination can be tried. As a general rule, pre-cook the ingredients which will not cook during the cooking time of the meat (this usually includes onion) or if by pre-cooking, flavour or colour is added (such as bacon).

The stuffing is generally bound together by a little added beaten egg, milk, fruit juice, vegetable juices etc. It can be used to stuff a bird or a joint, or it may be cooked separately.

BASIC STUFFING

100 g (4 oz) breadcrumbs, rice or oatmeal
50-100 g (2-4 oz) flavouring ingredients according to type of stuffing
1-2 tbsp herbs
seasoning to taste
binding ingredient

❦ From this basic recipe most stuffings can be made. Some specific recipes are given below.

BRAZIL AND DRIED PEACH STUFFING

100 g (4 oz) Brazil nuts
100 g (4 oz) dried peaches or prunes
1 onion, finely chopped
25 g (1 oz) butter or margarine
100 g (4 oz) wholemeal breadcrumbs
1 tsp allspice, ground
1 tbsp parsley, chopped
1 tsp orange rind, finely grated
2 tbsp sherry
1 egg

❦ Finely chop or mill the Brazil nuts. Soak the peaches and then chop them. Fry the onion in the butter until cooked. Combine all the ingredients.
❦ This stuffing is suitable for all meats and poultry.

APRICOT AND PINE KERNEL STUFFING

100 g (4 oz) apricots, soaked and chopped
1 onion, grated
25 g (1 oz) pine kernels or cashew nuts
25 g (1 oz) sunflower seeds
1 tbsp fresh herbs, chopped
1 egg
seasoning to taste
25 g (1 oz) melted butter (optional)

❦ Combine all the ingredients together.
❦ The pine kernels and sunflower seeds can be replaced by any other chopped unsalted nuts.

VEAL FORCEMEAT
(stuffing)

100 g (4 oz) fresh breadcrumbs
25 g (1 oz) butter, melted, or suet, shredded
1 tbsp parsley, chopped
½ tsp thyme
rind and juice of ½ lemon
¼ tsp ground nutmeg or mace
beaten egg to mix
100 g (4 oz) lean sausage meat
minced veal or pork (optional)
1 onion, finely chopped and fried (optional)

❦ Combine all the ingredients and use to stuff a joint, or escalopes of meat. The stuffing can be made into forcemeat balls and baked or fried to accompany meat.
❦ This stuffing is very suitable for lighter meats.

RICE STUFFING

100 g (4 oz) cooked rice
50 g (2 oz) sultanas
4 rashers of streaky bacon, grilled and chopped
1 lamb's kidney, grilled and chopped
½ tsp rosemary, chopped
1 tsp lemon rind
seasoning to taste
egg or egg yolk to mix

❦ Combine all the ingredients in a bowl with sufficient egg to bind them together.
❦ Use to stuff joints and escalopes, or cook in a separate dish to serve with meat.
❦ Stuffing balls coated in egg and breadcrumbs make an unusual starter when deep-fried and served with a tomato or piquant sauce.

TOMATO STUFFING
(for fish)

100 g (4 oz) fresh white or brown breadcrumbs
2 tbsp butter, melted
3 large tomatoes, skinned
½ red pepper, finely chopped
1 garlic clove, crushed
salt and pepper

❦ Put the breadcrumbs into a bowl and add the butter. Chop the tomatoes roughly and discard the seeds. Add to the breadcrumbs with the chopped pepper and the crushed garlic. Season well.
❦ Enough for 1 large fish or 4 smaller ones.

LEMON PARSLEY STUFFING
(for fish)

100 g (4 oz) fresh white breadcrumbs
2 tbsp melted butter
2 tbsp fresh parsley, chopped
1 lemon
salt and pepper
milk

❦ Put the breadcrumbs into a bowl. Add the butter and parsley with the grated rind and juice of the lemon. Season well with salt and pepper. Add a little milk just to bind the ingredients but to leave them slightly crumbly.
❦ Enough for 1 large fish or 4 smaller ones.

MUSHROOM STUFFING
(for fish)

100 g (4 oz) fresh white or brown breadcrumbs
2 tbsp butter, melted
50 g (2 oz) mushrooms, finely chopped
1 tbsp fresh parsley, chopped
squeeze of lemon juice
salt and pepper

❦ Put the breadcrumbs into a bowl and add the butter. Add the mushrooms, parsley, lemon juice and seasoning and mix.
❦ Enough to stuff 1 large fish or 4 smaller ones.

WATERCRESS OR MINT STUFFING

1 onion, chopped
25 g (1 oz) butter or margarine
50-100 g (2-4 oz) streaky bacon, chopped and fried (optional)
4 tbsp mint, chopped or 6 tbsp watercress, chopped
½ tsp ground allspice
100 g (4 oz) fresh breadcrumbs

❦ Fry the onion in butter until soft and golden. Fry the bacon (optional). Mix all the ingredients together in a bowl, using a little milk if the mixture will not bind together.
❦ Use to stuff joints, or escalopes of meat, especially lamb.

WALNUT AND ORANGE STUFFING

1 onion, chopped
25 g (1 oz) butter or margarine
2 tsp ground coriander
grated rind of 1 orange
50 g (2 oz) walnuts, chopped
75 g (3 oz) raisins, chopped
75 g (3 oz) fresh breadcrumbs
1 tbsp parsley, chopped
seasoning to taste
2 tbsp orange juice
beaten egg to mix

❦ Fry the onion in butter until soft and golden. Mix all ingredients in a bowl, with sufficient egg to bind together.
❦ Use to stuff pork, veal or lamb, or to make stuffing balls.

SAGE AND ONION STUFFING

75 g (3 oz) onion, chopped
175 g (6 oz) fresh breadcrumbs
2 tsp fresh chopped sage
3 tbsp melted butter (or margarine) or 50 (2 oz) grated suet
salt and pepper
beaten egg

❦ Place the onion in a pan with a little water and simmer gently until soft. Drain well and mix with the dry ingredients. Add sufficient beaten egg to bind.

❦ Both this stuffing and the parsley and thyme one (see overleaf) may be shaped into balls, rolled in seasoned flour and baked in the roasting tin around a bird, or in a separate tin for 40–45 minutes, basting and turning occasionally.

SAUSAGE AND CHESTNUT STUFFING

25 g (1 oz) butter
1 tbsp oil
1 turkey liver
100 g (4 oz) streaky bacon, chopped
100 g (4 oz) onion, chopped
225 g (8 oz) chestnuts, peeled and chopped
450 g (1 lb) pork sausage meat
1 tbsp fresh chopped parsley
salt and pepper

❦ This stuffing is suitable for turkey.

❦ Heat the oil and butter in a frying pan and fry the turkey liver until firm and the bacon until crisp. Remove from the pan. Chop the liver into small pieces. Fry the onion until soft.

❦ Place all the ingredients in a large bowl and mix well to thoroughly combine. Allow to get cold before using to stuff the neck end of a turkey.

❦ Any remaining stuffing may be formed into balls and cooked as in the recipe for sage and onion stuffing (above).

POTATO STUFFING

225 g (8 oz) onions, finely chopped
550 g (1 ¼ lb) potatoes
75 g (3 oz) butter or double cream
1 tbsp fresh chopped sage
salt and pepper

❦ This stuffing is good for goose.

❦ Place the onion in a pan with sufficient water to cover and simmer gently until soft. Drain well. Boil the potatoes, and drain well. Mash the potatoes and blend in the butter or cream. Stir in the sage and onions, mix well and season to taste.

ANCHOVY AND HERB STUFFING

175 g (6 oz) fresh breadcrumbs
1 rasher of streaky bacon, chopped
1 medium onion (or 4 shallots), finely chopped
2 tsp chopped chives
1 tsp fresh thyme
2 tsp fresh chopped parsley
4–6 anchovy fillets, chopped
grated rind and juice of ½ lemon
6 tbsp melted butter or 50 g (2 oz) shredded suet
beaten egg

❦ This stuffing is good for roast hare.

❦ Mix all the dry ingredients together, add the lemon juice and melted butter (if used) and bind with beaten egg.

PRUNE AND APPLE STUFFING

15–20 prunes (depending on size)
575 ml (1 pint) red wine, or water, or wine and water mixed
700 g (1 ½ lb) cooking apples

❦ This stuffing is good for goose.

❦ Soak the prunes in the wine or water overnight. Remove the stones. Peel, core and quarter the apples. Use to stuff the cavity of a goose after it has been seasoned.

PORK AND HERB STUFFING

1 medium onion (or 4 shallots), finely chopped
25 g (1 oz) butter
450 g (1 lb) shoulder pork, minced
100 g (4 oz) fresh breadcrumbs
1 tbsp fresh chopped parsley
1 tsp fresh thyme and 1 tsp fresh marjoram, or
    1 tsp mixed dried herbs
½ tsp ground nutmeg
beaten egg
salt and pepper

❦ Melt the butter in a pan and gently fry the onion until soft. Mix all the ingredients together, season well and bind with the beaten egg.
❦ This stuffing is suitable for turkey.

OATMEAL STUFFING

50 g (2 oz) butter
1 small onion, chopped finely
100 g (4 oz) medium oatmeal
1 tbsp fresh chopped parsley
salt and pepper
milk to mix

❦ Heat the butter in a pan and gently fry the onion until soft. Add the oatmeal, parsley and seasoning. Mix well. Add milk to moisten further if necessary, but do not make it too wet. Allow to cool before using.
❦ This stuffing is suitable for chicken.

CELERY STUFFING

25 g (1 oz) butter
1 tbsp oil
4 stalks of celery, finely chopped
1 small onion, chopped
175 g (6 oz) fresh breadcrumbs
salt and pepper

❦ Heat the butter and oil in a pan and gently cook the celery and onion for 5 minutes. Add the breadcrumbs and seasoning, mix well, adding a little more melted butter, if necessary, to bind.

FORCEMEAT BALLS

1 small onion, finely chopped
1 rasher of bacon, chopped
4 tbsp fresh breadcrumbs
1 tbsp suet
1 tbsp fresh chopped parsley
1 tbsp fresh lemon thyme or marjoram
beaten egg
breadcrumbs
butter for frying

❦ Cook the onion with the bacon until soft. Add the rest of the ingredients, mix well and bind together with beaten egg. Shape into balls, coat in egg and breadcrumbs and fry in butter until golden brown.

Variation
Omit the onion and bacon, and do not coat in egg and breadcrumbs or fry in butter.

PARSLEY AND THYME STUFFING

100 g (4 oz) fresh breadcrumbs
1 tbsp chopped fresh parsley or 2 tsp dried
    parsley
2 tsp fresh thyme or 1 tsp dried thyme
½ tsp grated lemon rind
salt and pepper
2 tbsp melted butter (or margarine) or 40 g (1 ½
    oz) grated suet
beaten egg

❦ Mix the ingredients together in a bowl, and add sufficient beaten egg to bind – take care not to add too much otherwise the stuffing will be hard.

APPLE STUFFING

700 g (1 ½ lb) cooking apples, peeled, cored and
   diced
50 g (2 oz) butter
salt and pepper
1 tsp grated lemon rind
2 tbsp sugar
225 g (8 oz) fresh breadcrumbs

❦ Prepare the apples and cook gently in the butter
until soft. Add the remaining ingredients, and
moisten with a little water if necessary.

GAME CHIPS

potatoes
deep fat/oil for frying
salt

❦ Peel the potatoes, and shape into cylinders. Slice
very finely into wafers (the use of a mandolin slicer
would be advantageous). Soak in cold water to
remove the surface starch. Heat the oil to 190C
(375F).
❦ Drain the potato wafers, and dry thoroughly.
Lower them gently into the hot oil, and keep them
moving to prevent them sticking. After 1-2 minutes,
the wafers will rise to the surface of the oil, indicat-
ing that they are nearly cooked. Watch carefully as
they change colour. They should be golden brown
and crisp.
❦ Drain the wafers and sprinkle with salt.

GAME STRAWS

potatoes
deep fat/oil for frying

❦ Peel the potatoes, and cut into 3 mm (⅛ in) slices.
Cut each slice into 3 mm (⅛ in) sticks. Soak in cold
water to remove the surface starch. Heat the oil to
190C (375F). Drain the straws and dry thoroughly.
❦ Lower the straws into the hot oil and keep shaking the basket gently to keep the straws separate. Fry
for 3-4 minutes, then remove from the oil.
❦ Reheat the fat, and again lower the straws into the
oil, and cook for approximately 1 minute until the
straws are golden brown and crisp. Drain well on
absorbent kitchen paper and serve immediately.

BACON ROLLS

Allow 1-2 rolls per person

rashers of streaky bacon

❦ Take rashers of streaky bacon, place on a board,
hold one end of a rasher with the left hand, and with
a firm palette knife, working from left to right, stroke
the bacon to stretch it.
❦ Cut into 7.5 cm (3 in) lengths, roll up each length
and secure with a skewer. Grill or cook in the oven
until crisp.

CROUTES
AND CROUTONS

slices of bread
butter for frying (optional)

❦ Croûtes are thick slices of bread, cut in squares or
circles, either fried in butter or toasted. Small game
may be served with and/or cooked on croûtes.
❦ Croutons are small dice or fancy shapes of bread,
usually fried, but may be toasted. The fancy shapes
are used to garnish savoury dishes. The small dice
are used to garnish soup and salads.

Variation
For Garlic Croutons, first rub the bread with
crushed garlic or use Garlic Oil (see page 348).

PASTRIES DOUGHS AND BATTERS

❦ About pastry-making ❦

There is a real art to making good pastry, but it is one that can easily be mastered if a few simple rules are followed. Patience is essential; so too is the all important 'light touch' necessary when making pastry. The 'feel' of the pastry is governed mainly by the amount of liquid added, but the lightness is achieved by incorporating air - either by rubbing the fat into the flour or by folding and rolling to catch air between the layers of dough or by beating it in as in the case of choux pastry.

Treat pastry gently and lightly; do not pull or stretch it or throw it around, and above all use the fingertips. Keep everything cool, both the ingredients and the implements, and do allow the pastry time to relax before rolling out.

It is often better to dust the pastry board with cornflour rather than flour; it is very light and silky and does not unbalance the recipe by adding more flour to it than is necessary.

Most pastries call for plain flour, the exception being suet crust. However, some people have their own versions of the basic pastries which may contain a proportion of self-raising flour and they will swear their pastry is the best around - it may be good, but it will not beat a well-made true basic pastry.

Many recipes in this book call for the pastry to be cooked on baking sheets lined with baking paper. This will prevent sticking and ensure ease of movement but is not strictly necessary. A damp or lightly greased baking sheet may also be used.

Pastry trimmings can be utilized by cutting them into pastry leaves, circles, diamonds etc., glazing them with beaten egg or milk and cooking them on a shelf under the main dish. They can then be frozen and used for garnishes to soups and stews and as party nibbles or hor d'oeurve.

To line a flan ring

Put the flan ring on baking paper on an oven tray. Roll the pastry out on a cornfloured board to a thickness of 5 mm (¼ in) and 5 cm (2 inches) larger than the ring. Lift it on the rolling pin. Slip it off over the ring and push into place, without stretching it, using a little ball of pastry. Roll across the top of the ring with the rolling pin to cut off overhanging pastry.

To bake blind

Preheat the oven to 200C (400F) mark 6 for shortcrust and most flan pastries, and 220C (425F) mark 7 for flaky pastry. Line the flan ring or ovenproof dish with pastry rolled out to a thickness of about 5 mm (¼ in). Poke down into the dish using a little ball of the pastry as a pusher.

Line with greaseproof paper and fill with baking beans or any other beans. Bake for 15 minutes, remove the beans and paper. Bake for a further 10 minutes to dry out (less for tartlets).

Baking a flan case 'blind' makes it easy to turn out of the case or ring.

To cover a pie

Roll out the pastry 5 cm (2 in) larger than the dish. Cut off a strip all around, 2.5 cm (1 in) wide. Brush the rim of the pie dish with water. Fit on the pastry strip. Brush with water. (One wet and one dry surface of pastry stick together better than two wet surfaces.) Lift the remaining piece of pastry on the rolling pin and transfer to the filled dish. Press the edges firmly together and trim. Knock up the edges and flute (see below).

Knocking up and fluting

'Knocking up' is making horizontal cuts with the back of a knife along the edge of the pastry. These cuts release it so it can rise. 'Fluting' is decorating the edge of pastry by pinching or by using a fork for savoury dishes (the tip of the spoon for sweet dishes).

Freezing

Pastry cases freeze very well but are fragile when frozen so need careful handling. Thaw before filling and cooking. If the filling is to be cold or uncooked, crisp the flan case in the oven before using it.

❧ Shortcrust Pastry ❧

Shortcrust pastry is very versatile, as the recipes in this book show. It can be used for meat pies as well as the fruit pies and tarts featured in the Desserts and Cakes and Pastries chapters. It may also be used for buffet treats like sausage rolls.

The most popular and useful of all pastries. It gets its name from the short fibres developed during the light cool 'rubbing in'.

Handle the pastry as little as possible and roll it with short light strokes. A dusting of cornflour on the pin and the board is better than flour (never dust the pastry). Half lard and half margarine with plain flour makes the crispest pastry.

Pastry made with wholemeal flour, or a proportion of wholemeal flour, can be used for all the shortcrust recipes in this book. Follow the basic recipe, though do not make the startling mistake of sieving wholemeal flour before using it. This is a real 'country' pastry. There is also now on the market some excellent brown self-raising flour which makes delicious scones, dumplings and suet puddings.

SHORTCRUST PASTRY

225 g (8 oz) plain flour
¼ tsp salt
50 g (2 oz) margarine
50 g (2 oz) lard
about 3 tbsp cold water

❧ Sieve the flour and salt into a bowl. Add the fats and rub in gently and lightly.
❧ Mix to a stiff dough with the water (if the dough is too wet the pastry will be tough).
❧ Knead very lightly and handle as little as possible. Roll out evenly and lightly.

WHOLEMEAL SHORTCRUST PASTRY

225 g (8 oz) wholemeal flour
50 g (2 oz) lard
50 g (2 oz) margarine
½ tsp salt
about 4 tbsp water

❦ Mix the salt into the flour with your fingertips. Rub in the fats until the mixture resembles bread-crumbs. This takes longer but try to do it lightly.
❦ Add the water, cut and stir with a knife until the mixture starts to bind.
❦ Gather into a ball with the fingertips and roll out on a board lightly dredged with cornflour.

Notes
This is naturally a rather crumbly pastry because of the large particles in the flour. You might prefer to make a start with 85% extraction flour, and see how it goes. Alternatively use half wholemeal flour and half plain white flour.

SIMPLE CHEESE PASTRY

175 g (6 oz) plain flour
salt
cayenne pepper
½ tsp mustard powder
75 g (3 oz) butter
100 g (4 oz) grated cheese
1 egg yolk
little water

❦ Mix the flour, mustard, and seasonings well together with the fingertips. Rub in the butter, then mix in the cheese. Add the egg yolk and a little water if necessary to mix to a firm but pliable dough. Cover and leave to relax. Use as required.
❦ Cook at 200C (400F) mark 6.

Notes
This is a classic cheese straw mixture.

MIXER PASTRY

75 g (3 oz) polyunsaturated margarine
100 g (4 oz) plain wholemeal flour
100 g (4 oz) self-raising white or wholemeal
    flour
3 tbsp cold water

❦ Using a small hand mixer, mix together the mar-garine with 2 tbsp of water and half of the flour. The mixture will resemble that of a cake rather than a usual pastry one. Cut and fold in the remaining flour with a little more water only if it is necessary to make a pliable consistency. Refrigerate well before using.
❦ Use and bake as shortcrust pastry at 200C (400F) mark 6.

Variation
For cheese pastry fold in 50–75 g (2–3 oz) finely grat-ed cheese, with ¼ tsp mustard and a dash of cayenne with the flour.

❧ Flan Pastries ❧

Flan pastries are richer than shortcrust pastry, having a higher proportion of fat and often beaten egg, egg yolks and milk as the binding agents. They are quite fragile to handle and benefit from chilling before rolling out to help ease the process. When cooked, the pastry should be thin and crisp.

All the basic recipes in this section (apart from the lemon pastry) are made in the French way. This involves sieving the flour and salt together and then making a well in the centre. The fat and eggs etc are put into the well and after mixing this the flour is gradually drawn in with the fingertips.

As with all pastry, success requires a light touch, use of fingertips only and keeping everything cool. Do not over-knead, as this only makes tough pastry.

PATE BRISEE

225 g (8 oz) plain flour
good pinch of salt
75 g (3 oz) butter
1 egg (size 3 or 4)
125 ml (scant ¼ pint) water

❧ Sieve the flour and salt together and make a well in the centre. Put the butter, egg and water into the well. Mix well together with the tips of the fingers, then gradually draw the flour down into the mixture, mixing as lightly as possible until all is incorporated.
❧ Knead the dough for a minute, then roll the pastry into a ball, cover and leave to relax for 1-2 hours.
❧ Cook at 200C (400F) mark 6.

RICH SHORTCRUST PASTRY

225 g (8 oz) plain flour
pinch of salt
150 g (5 oz) butter
2 egg yolks
little cold water if needed

❧ Sieve flour and salt into a bowl and rub in butter.
❧ Beat the egg yolks. Make a well in the flour, add the egg yolks and mix well. Gradually draw down the flour from the sides and work it all in with the tips of the fingers. It should be a firm yet soft dough, so

add a teaspoon or two of cold water if necessary.
❧ Cover and leave to cool and relax.
❧ Cook at 200C (400F) mark 6.

PATE SUCREE
(sweet flan pastry)

❧ Add 25 g (1 oz) sieved icing sugar or caster sugar to the dry ingredients in either of the Pâte Brisée or Rich Shortcrust pastry recipes.

PATE FROLLE
(almond pastry)

225 g (8 oz) plain flour
75 g (3 oz) ground almonds
1 egg
75 g (3 oz) caster sugar
100 g (4 oz) butter
1 drop of almond essence

❧ Sieve the flour into a bowl. Sprinkle the ground almonds over the flour. Make a well in the centre and break the egg into the well. Add the sugar, butter and essence. Mix with the fingertips, then start drawing the flour down gradually until all is incorporated.
❧ Roll into a ball, cover and leave to cool and relax in the refrigerator for an hour or two.
❧ Cook at 190C (375F) mark 5.

LEMON PASTRY

100 g (4 oz) butter
50 g (2 oz) caster sugar
1 egg yolk
grated rind and juice of 1 lemon
175 g (6 oz) plain flour

❧ Cream the butter and sugar until light and white. Break in the egg yolk. Add the lemon rind and juice to the mixture and beat well.
❧ Sieve the flour and fold lightly into the mixture. Form into a ball with the fingertips. Cover and put into the refrigerator for an hour or two before using.
❧ Cook at 200C (400F) mark 6.

❦ Puff and Rough ❦ Puff Pastry

Puff and Rough Puff Pastries take time to make because of the rolling and folding processes necessary to entrap the air between the layers of pastry; this gives the traditional flaked texture. However, the effort is well worthwhile and once the simple art has been mastered, it will encourage further use of these mouth-watering pastries. Puff is the richer of the two, while rough puff is the easier and quicker to make (hence the name).

Both pastries freeze extremely well, so it is possible to make up a double quantity and store the excess, wrapped in thick polythene or foil in the freezer, for up to 3 months. They will also keep in the refrigerator for 3–4 days if closely wrapped.

Keep everything as cool as possible, use the fingertips and roll out with short, sharp definite strokes (in one direction only); this which prevents overstretching or pulling out of shape, thus giving every reason for the pastry not to shrink during cooking.

It is better to dust the pastry board with cornflour rather than flour. It is very light and silky and does not unbalance the recipe by adding more flour to it.

Leftover scraps of pastry can also be frozen. Lay them one on top of the other; this keeps the fibres the right way and the pastry will roll out properly and cook better than if you roll the scraps up into a ball. Tiny snippets of leftover unsweetened pastry make delicious little mouthfuls if dropped into boiling soup or a stew for a few minutes.

It is useful to know just how much pastry you need when preparing your own recipes. The following is a rough guide: 350 g (12 oz) puff, rough puff or flaky pastry covers a 1 litre (2 pint) pie dish or a 23 cm (9 in) pie plate. It makes eighteen 6.5 cm (2 ½ in) tartlets, or 12 cream horns.

Although it is time-consuming to make and needs practice to overcome the hazards of inexperience, home-made puff pastry has an incomparable taste and texture. A lovely skill to master.

Frozen puff pastry can be bought everywhere and is good as well as useful. All the following recipes can be made with frozen or home-made puff or rough puff. They are interchangeable with flaky pastry too.

PUFF PASTRY

175 g (6 oz) plain flour
pinch of salt
175 g (6 oz) butter
about 150 ml (¼ pint) ice-cold water

❦ Sieve the flour and salt together in a bowl. Rub in a walnut of butter. Add sufficient water to mix to a firm dough. Roll out to an oblong about 1 cm (½ in) thick.

❦ The butter should be firm; not soft, not hard. Put the butter, shaped into an oblong pat, on to the lower half of the dough. Fold the top half down. Press the edges together. Leave to cool for 15–20 minutes.

❦ With the sealed ends towards you, roll lightly but firmly away from you into the original oblong. Do not 'push'. (Roll out on a surface lightly dredged with cornflour. It is smooth and light and does not clog up the works.)

❦ Fold the pastry into three; bottom third upwards and top third downwards. Turn the open end towards you. Roll out again to an oblong. Repeat folding and rolling process twice more. Fold in three again and leave to rest and relax before using.

❦ This pastry freezes well and can also be kept in the refrigerator wrapped in a dampish cloth for two or three days.

❦ Puff pastry is cooked at 220–230C (425–450F) mark 7–8.

ROUGH PUFF PASTRY

175 g (6 oz) plain flour
pinch of salt
150 g (5 oz) butter
about 150 ml (¼ pint) iced water

❧ Sieve the flour and salt into a bowl. Cut the butter into walnut-sized pieces. Mix these pieces into the flour " do not rub in. Add sufficient water to mix to a firm dough. Leave to rest in a cool place for 15 minutes.

❧ Turn on to a surface lightly dredged with cornflour. Press the dough lightly together. Roll lightly and evenly into a strip about ½-1 cm (¼-½ in) thick. Fold into three as for puff pastry and press the edges lightly together to entrap air.

❧ Give the pastry a half-turn. Roll out to an oblong again, fold in three and give a half-turn. Repeat the rolling and folding process three times.

❧ Leave to cool and relax before using. Cook as for puff pastry at 220-230C (425-450F) mark 7-8.

❧ Flaky Pastry ❧

Flaky pastry is made by a mixture of the methods for short and puff pastry. Some fat is rubbed in, the rest flaked on to the rolled-out dough. Flaking and rolling three times produces the light, airy pastry known as 'flaky'. It is essential to have everything as cool as possible and to understand that the object is to have thin layers of fat between very thin layers of dough, entrapping air as you work. The heat expands the air, which lifts the thin dough.

FLAKY PASTRY

175 g (6 oz) margarine and lard, mixed
225 g (8 oz) plain flour
¼ tsp salt
150 ml (¼ pint) cold water

❧ Mix the fats, divide into four and cool. Sieve the flour and salt into a basin. Rub in one part of the fat lightly with the fingertips. Add the water and mix to a soft dough. Turn out on to a board lightly dredged with cornflour and knead until smooth. This kneading is important for it distributes the ingredients evenly and strengthens the fibres of the dough. Cool for 20 minutes wrapped in greaseproof paper, foil or polythene to prevent a skin forming.

❧ Roll out the dough to an oblong, brushing off surplus flour. Flake one portion of fat over the upper two-thirds of the pastry to within 1 cm (½ in) of the edge. Fold the bottom one-third up and the top one-third down. Press the edges together with the rolling pin to seal the air. Cover and leave to cool for 20 minutes.

❧ Half turn the pastry so that the folded edge is on the right hand side. Repeat from the processes of rolling, flaking and folding twice more, resting and rolling in between and giving the pastry a further half turn each time.

❧ Brush off the surplus flour. Rest in a cool place until firm. The pastry can be made the day before and kept in the refrigerator.

❧ Cook at 220C (425F) mark 7.

❧ Suet Crust Pastry ❧

Suet crust is one of the easiest pastries to cook really well, but to achieve a light, feathery texture, care should be taken. The ingredients simply must be weighed and measured, whatever your grandmother did. The dough needs the lightest of handling and the pot must be watched to see that it does not go off the boil.

The basic recipe given below uses self-raising flour and shredded packet suet. These produce perfect results and obviously are quicker and easier than plain flour with baking powder and butcher's suet, which has to be grated.

For 'boiled' puddings (those where the basin stands in a pan of boiling water) there should be not less than 2.5 cm (1 in) between the pudding basin and the sides of the pan. This lets the steam circulate.

The water should reach half-way up the sides of the basin. Keep an eye on the water and top up with boiling water. If the water goes off the boil the pastry will be heavy and soggy.

Boiled puddings can be cooked in a slow cooker or a microwave oven, but read the appropriate instructions before you start.

To line a pudding basin with suet crust pastry

For a 750 ml (1 ½ pint) basin, you will need about 225 g (8 oz) pastry. Roll it out into a circle 5-7.5 cm (2-3 inches) larger than the top of the basin. Cut a third out in the shape of a triangle.

Grease the basin well and fit the larger piece into it on a dress-making principle. Dampen one of the edges and very slightly overlap the other. Press well together. Roll the small piece into a circle to form the lid and position it.

To cover a boiled pudding

Cover the basin with a pudding cloth, or buttered greaseproof paper, pleated and tied on, or strong kitchen foil twisted tightly under the rim. A pudding cloth can be very easily made with a stitched-on handle and string run through the hem to tie it on. It makes the putting in and getting out much easier.

Boilable plastic pudding basins with lids can be bought. Check that the lids really do clip on tightly before you buy a set. A sheet of greased greaseproof paper under the lid will make quite sure.

SUET CRUST PASTRY

225 g (8 oz) self-raising flour
½ tsp salt
100 g (4 oz) shredded suet
150 ml (¼ pint) water

❦ Sieve the flour and salt together into a bowl. Add the suet and mix well. Pour the water on to the flour. Cut with a round-bladed knife through the mixture until all the water has been absorbed.

❦ Turn the dough on to a floured board and knead very lightly for a minute or two.

Form into a ball, cover and leave to relax for 5 minutes.

❦ Hot Water ❦ Crust Pastry

Hot water crust pastry is quite different from any other pastry. It has to be strong enough to stand up on its own and to hold up the weight of a pie filling which is usually, but not always, meat or game. It has to withstand long cooking in order that the closely-packed filling will be properly cooked and when it finally comes to the table; cold, it must be velvety inside and richly crisp outside.

Boiling water and lard are added to the flour, so you start with a partly-cooked dough of considerable strength. The pastry must be moulded while it is still warm. If it gets cool it will crack and be difficult to handle. However, do not try to mould it too hot; you will burn your hands and the pastry will just flop about. To keep it warm, have it in a bowl in a warm place with a cloth over it.

As described below, pies can be raised by hand, or moulded round a jar, made in a loose-bottomed cake tin, or in a special hinged pie mould. Handy small individual pies can also be made..

Contrary to the general idea of raised pies being savoury, there are some traditional sweet fillings.

Raised pies are finished with pastry leaves and a rose or tassel fitted into a hole in the top. The filling shrinks away from the pastry as it cooks. When the pie is out of the oven and cooling, this gap is filled with a savoury jelly, poured in through the hole under the rose, which is lifted out and then put back.

Hot water crust pies are firm, crusty and the greatest fun to make. Skilfully handled they can be simply stunning centrepieces on a cold buffet table.

A pie can be raised in three different ways:

By hand

350 g (12 oz) hot water crust pastry (see over)

Put one-third of the pastry aside for the lid. Pat the larger piece into a scone shape and place on a baking sheet lined with baking paper. With the thumbs inside and the fingers outside, gently shape the pastry into a hollow, then begin to raise the walls of the pie. Tie with a stiff paper cuff, and put the filling into the pie bit by bit as the walls of the pie are raised higher and higher. The filling helps hold the shape of the case.

By using a mould

450 g (1 lb) hot water crust pastry (see below)

The mould can be a jar or cake tin, turned upside down, and measuring 15 cm (6 in) in diameter.

Keep the pastry warm. Cut off one-third for the lid. Roll out the rest to a circle about 30 cm (12 in) across. Upturn the mould and dredge it heavily with flour.

Lift the pastry on a rolling pin and transfer it to the mould. Shape the pastry by pressing it firmly to the mould. Cut a double piece of greaseproof paper to go right round the pastry and cover it completely. Tie round the mould in two places. Rest the pastry in a cool place until it is firm.

Turn the mould over, stand the pastry case on a baking sheet and gently ease the mould out of the case, giving it a little twist to loosen it. Leaving the greaseproof paper still tied in a cuff around the case, put in the filling, packing it well to hold the shape of the pie. Brush the edge of the pastry with beaten egg.

Roll out the remaining pastry for the lid and position it. Press the edges well together, trim and flute (see page 357) or make fine cuts with a sharp knife. When the maker is experienced, the pie can be raised using only 350 g (12 oz) pastry.

By using a cake tin

A pie can also be cooked quite easily in a conventional cake tin. Lard the tin, press non-stick baking paper around the sides and on the bottom, and lard that too.

Using two-thirds of the pastry, line the tin, pushing and moulding it to the sides and base. Use the remaining one-third for the lid.

Turn the pie out, once cooked, on to a folded cloth. It can then be turned up the right way before the jelly is put in.

A loose-bottomed cake tin is even better than an ordinary one, and a 450 g (1 lb) loaf tin makes a handsome pork pie.

HOT WATER CRUST PASTRY

350 g (12 oz) plain flour
1 tsp salt
150 g (5 oz) lard 1
50 ml (¼ pint) milk and water, mixed

❦ Sieve the flour and salt together in a bowl. Put the lard and liquid into a pan and heat gently until the lard is melted, then bring to the boil. Pour immediately on to the flour in one go and mix well with a wooden spoon.

❦ The moment you can handle it, turn the pastry out on to a floured board. Knead it quickly and lightly. Keep the pastry warm and covered with a clean cloth. As a rough guide you will use two-thirds of the pastry for the pie and one-third for the lid.

❦ Cook at 200C (400F) mark 6 unless the recipe says otherwise.

❦ Choux Pastry ❦

Pâte à choux (or choux pastry as it is known here) is as French as suet crust is English. It is a decorative party pastry, light, attractive and crisp. Surprisingly it is not difficult to make.

The ingredients must be carefully measured and the flour really dry. The chief ingredient of successful choux is air, so the mixture, after the addition of each egg, must be really well beaten to introduce air as the raising agent, for choux relies on this natural lift.

Choux needs more thorough cooking than people think. If the pastry is not cooked enough, the sides will be softer than the top and the whole thing will collapse when it comes out of the oven. If the cooking is well done a natural hole will form in the centre.

Although in this country we know eclairs and cream buns best, there are all sorts of exciting things that can be done with this fascinating pastry. A forcing bag and one or two plain pipes, 1 cm (½ in) and 2.5 cm (1 in) are useful items of equipment for this pastry, though not essential.

What went wrong
It is important to have the right proportions in choux pastry. Measure, don't guess. If the mixture does not rise when cooking, did you think self-raising flour would be best to use? It is not - do stick to plain flour.

If it sinks when it comes out of the oven it was not cooked long enough.

CHOUX PASTRY

150 ml (¼ pint) water
50 g (2 oz) butter
pinch of salt
65 g (2 ½ oz) plain flour
2 eggs

❦ Heat the oven to 220C (425F) mark 7.
❦ Put the water, butter and salt into a saucepan. Bring to the boil. Continue boiling until all the butter has melted. Sieve the flour on to a piece of paper.
❦ Remove the pan from the heat and tip the flour in all at once. Mix well and beat thoroughly with a wooden spoon. Return to very low heat, beating well until the mixture forms a ball and leaves the side of the pan. Remove from the heat at once.
❦ Cool a little and add by degrees the beaten eggs, beating all the time. A hand-held electric mixer is good to use. You may not need all the second egg. The mixture should look satiny and drop heavily from the spoon.
❦ Cook for 10 minutes then reduce the temperature to 190C (375F) mark 5 and continue for a further 30 minutes, or according to the recipe.
❦ Eclairs, profiteroles and so on should be put straight on a wire rack to cool, out of the draught. A slit should be made in the side of each, with a sharp pointed knife, to let out the steam so that the inside will dry.
❦ Sweet choux can have a little caster sugar put into the original recipe with the water. Savoury choux should be well seasoned with salt and pepper at the beating stage.

❧ Pancakes and Batters❧

PANCAKE BATTER

Makes 12-14 pancakes

4 tbsp butter or margarine
225 g (8 oz) plain flour
175 ml (6 fl oz) water
175 ml (6 fl oz) milk
4 eggs
½ tsp salt

❧ Melt the fat and set to one side. Sift the flour, then re-measure. If possible make the batter an hour before it is needed.

❧ For speed and smoothness, use a blender if possible. To make the batter using a blender, put the liquids, eggs, salt, flour and melted fat into the goblet in order, then cover and blend at top speed until quite smooth. Stop the machine, push down any bits of flour or batter sticking to the walls of the goblet, and blend again briefly. Leave to stand in a cool place.

❧ To make the batter with a hand beater, beat the eggs into the sifted flour, then beat in the liquid gradually, followed by the melted fat and salt. Strain the batter to remove any lumps and leave in a cool place for an hour or more.

❧ Spices, herbs or other flavourings, or even well-chopped solid ingredients can be added to a pancake batter if you wish.

❧ Just before use, test the consistency of the batter. If it is thicker than pouring cream, blend or beat in 1-2 tbsp water.

❧ To make the pancakes, brush a shallow 15 cm (6 in) frying pan or pancake pan with oil. Heat it to very hot, then reduce the heat. Lift the pan off the heat. Pour in and swirl round just enough batter to cover the whole pan thinly. (If you are quick, you can pour any excess batter back into the container.)

❧ Replace the pan on the heat and shake gently for about 1 minute. Loosen the pancake with a round-ended palette knife, and flip it over; the underside should be patched with brown. Brown the second side for about 15 seconds, then lift off the pan and transfer to a sheet of greaseproof paper. Oil the pan again and repeat the procedure to make more.

❧ You will probably not be able to make all the pancakes one after another because any heavy pancake pan gets too hot. If the batter sets before running all over the pan's surface, cool the pan for a moment or two and thin the batter slightly with water.

❧ Stack the pancakes as you make them in piles of 6 or 8, putting thick and thin pancakes in separate piles. Thicker pancakes are more suitable for savoury fillings, thin pancakes for sweet ones. Wrap securely and freeze. They thaw in moments in a low oven.

Variations
Basic pancake batter can be thinned down for crêpes, those wonderful French delicacies which are really very simple to make. The batter can be made using milk or a combination of milk and water. For really rich, thin pancakes, add an extra beaten egg.

COATING BATTER
(for frying fish)

100 g (4 oz) plain flour
2 tbsp oil or melted butter
2 eggs, separated
pinch of salt
150 ml (¼ pint) warm water

❧ Sift the flour into a bowl. Add the oil or butter with the egg yolks, salt and water. Beat well and leave to stand for 1 hour.
Whisk the egg whites to stiff peaks and fold into the batter just before using.

❧ To use the batter, dip the fish in a little plain flour to coat it lightly. Coat fish with batter and allow surplus batter to drain off. Fry at once in hot oil or fat.

SWEET FRITTER BATTER

150 g (5 oz) plain flour
25 g (1 oz) caster sugar
2 eggs
1 tbsp butter, softened
275 ml (½ pint) milk

❧ Put the flour and sugar into a bowl. Make a well and drop one whole egg and the yolk of the second egg into it. Stir the eggs. Add the milk and draw down the flour by degrees, beating continuously until smooth.

❧ Beat in the butter. Let stand for 1 hour.

❧ Just before using, whisk the egg white stiffly and fold it evenly through the batter.

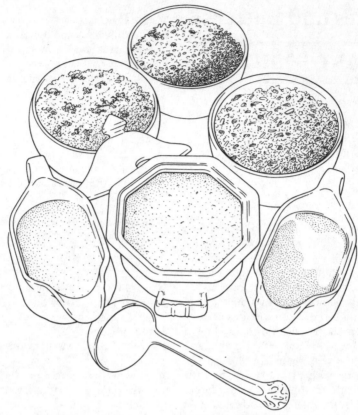

GARNISHES, RELISHES AND MISCELLANEOUS PREPARATIONS

HOME-MADE MUSTARD

50 g (2 oz) each, white and black mustard seeds
150 ml (¼ pint) herb vinegar
3 tbsp honey
1 tsp salt
½ tsp powdered mace

Put all the ingredients in a bowl. Leave overnight to soften the seeds. Mix in a blender until it has a thick

❦ If too thick, add a little more vinegar. Leave a proportion of the seeds whole - do not blend until there are no seeds to be seen.

❦ Store in small jars with plastic lids. Keep airtight, or the mustard will dry out.

❦ The flavour can be varied with different spices, different vinegars, more or less honey. The mustard is an attractive addition to the table and useful for 'devils' and as a flavouring ingredient in a wide range of dishes, especially beef and game stews, casseroles and pies.

BEURRE MANIE
(KNEADED BUTTER)

25 g (1 oz) butter or margarine
50 g (2 oz) plain flour

❦ Knead the fat and flour together, and add small knobs to the casserole or pan, off the heat. Stir well and boil for a few minutes to cook the flour.
❦ This is used as a liaison or thickener for soups, stews and sauces. It can be used instead of making a roux, or instead of using blended cornflour to adjust the consistency before serving.

MIREPOIX OF VEGETABLES

2 tsp butter or margarine
2 tsp frying oil
25 g (1 oz) rindless bacon, diced
1 onion, skinned and chopped
1 carrot, scraped and chopped
1 celery stick, thinly sliced
2 shallots, skinned and chopped (optional)
Basix Vegetable Stock (see page 336)

❦ Heat the butter and oil in a pan. Add the bacon and vegetables, cover and cook gently for 10 minutes, stirring occasionally. Add enough stock to cover the vegetables. Place the food to be braised on top. Cover the pan tightly and simmer until the braised meat or vegetable is cooked; baste occasionally with the liquid.
❦ A mirepoix of mixed chopped vegetables is used as a 'bed' when braising meat or other vegetables such as celery or cos lettuce. It can also be used as a side dish or garnishing vegetable in its own right, or as the basis of a puréed soup.

LIGHT SUGAR SYRUP

100 g (4 oz) granulated sugar
225-275 ml (8-10 fl oz) water

❦ Dissolve the sugar in the water, making sure every grain is disolved before bringing it to the boil, then boil for 2 minutes.

❦ Use for poaching fruit. If the fruit is very sour, do not make the syrup heavier, but simply add a little extra sugar while the fruit is still hot.

Notes
This syrup keeps well. If you keep a vanilla pod in your sugar jar, this greatly improves the flavour of the fruit, as well as many other dishes.

PRALINE

75 g (3 oz) unblanched almonds
75 g (3 oz) caster sugar

❦ Put the nuts and sugar in a heavy saucepan. Melt over a low heat. When turning pale brown, stir with a metal spoon until nut brown.
❦ Pour on to an oiled slab or baking sheet. When cold, pound or crush with a rolling pin. Store in an airtight jar. Use in cakes and pastries.

APRICOT GLAZE

100 g (4 oz) apricot jam
100 g (4 oz) sugar
150 ml (¼ pint) water

❦ Put the jam, sugar and water in a pan. Gently dissolve the sugar. Bring to the boil and boil to reduce to almost half the quantity. Sieve.
❦ Reheat to glaze fruit tarts etc. Always use a glaze boiling hot for glazing fruit.
❦ This glaze will keep for some weeks in a screw-top jar.

BROWNED ALMONDS

1 tsp butter
1 tsp oil
25 g (1 oz) flaked almonds

❦ Heat the butter and the oil in a small pan over a gentle heat. Add the flaked almonds and stir constantly until they start to brown.
❦ Take the pan off the heat at once, stir until the almonds are light gold. Transfer at once to absorbent paper and toss to drain, then cool.

INDEX